Read this first!

Here's how to find the incredible wedding and special event information in *Here Comes The Guide:*

- **Event Venues**

  Sites are organized by region and city, with illustrated descriptions and details about capacities, fees and services. To find a specific site, see the index starting on page 557.

- **Useful Questions to Ask Venues & Event Professionals**

  Not sure what to ask a potential event location, photographer, caterer, etc.? Our lists of questions on pages 21–42 will make it easier for you to interview them and help you decide who to hire.

Don't forget to check out HereComesTheGuide.com!

HereComesTheGuide.com has the most up-to-date information on event venues, services and bridal fairs—as well as lots of photos and virtual tours. And if you have a certain type of location or event professional in mind, you'll really appreciate our amazingly useful search engine. We make it easy to find exactly what you're looking for.

Our Cover Photographer

Ashley Kelemen Photography

Our cover photo was shot by Ashley Kelemen. The first thing that drew us to it was the contrast between the couple's upscale look and the urban background. Then there's the pair's amazing fashion sense—the dapper groom seems completely at ease in his suit, which is formal and yet not your typical groomiform. However, it's his bride that steals the show: Her feminine, flowing gown is utterly unique, from the skirt festooned with bold floral appliqués to her Deco-inspired bodice and accessorizing. This is a wedding couple that's clearly confident expressing their personal style!

To find out more about Ashley and her work, *Here Come's The Guide's* editor had a conversation with her:

Q *How did you get into wedding photography?*

A I was living in New York, working in the fashion industry, with no intention of becoming a wedding photographer. But I began second shooting at weddings for friends and just fell in love with it. Although I worked with some great photographers in NY before my husband and I moved to California, I'm basically self-trained.

Q *What is it that keeps you hooked on shooting weddings?*

A I'm a big lover of people, and getting married is one of the most personal things a couple can do. A wedding is a huge event in their life, and I really enjoy being a part of that experience.

Q *Why do you think your clients like working with you?*

A Well, they tell me I make them feel comfortable. Most people don't like being in front of a camera, but I get them laughing and relaxed. I'm able to build relationships easily and quickly ... and I seem to attract people I love to be around and who trust me! Plus, I only take on a limited number of weddings every year so I'm able to spend time with the couples I have.

Q *How would you characterize your photographic style?*

A I like to create "frameable" artistic images (my editorial approach), but on the flip side I love capturing candid, authentic moments. Whatever style of photo I'm shooting, I try to make every situation comfortable so that the couple just behaves naturally.

Q *You seem to have a way with shooting in natural light. Is that something you're known for?*

A Yes, it is. I do tend to shoot a lot of outdoor weddings and really love working in natural light. I'm a big fan of film and use it 90% of the time, because for me it handles light better. And when I'm shooting with film I feel that I "see" better: I'm aware of everything in my frame, and my photographic vision comes to life.

Q *What do you hope to accomplish through your photography?*

A It's really important to me to relate to the couples I work with, and to have a body of work that conveys a consistent look and resonates with them. I've traveled a lot and consider myself an "adventure junkie"... so I think my passion for life and photography helps me tell the story of their adventure.

Back cover photos also provided by Ashley Kelemen Photography.
Wedding Dress by Thorne Artistry and Florals by Sweet Marie Designs.

What Makes Us Different?

We do most of your homework for you.

1. We actually visit the venues in *Here Comes The Guide*.

We check out 95% of our event sites in person before we include them in The Guide.

2. We write every venue description with you in mind.

Each site description is based on our personal experience, so it's informative, accurate and often entertaining.

3. We provide real pricing for venues, along with nitty-gritty details about each site's capacity, services and amenities.

This makes it easy to create a list of your top contenders, and by the time you call or visit a location you're totally informed!

4. We save you a ton of time.

By putting so much comprehensive information all in one place, we save you hours...days...maybe months of searching for event locations and professionals. And, you can actually do most of your planning without leaving home!

HereComesTheGuide.com has it ALL:

- **Virtual Tours**

  Most of the event sites we feature on **HereComesTheGuide.com** have virtual tours! It's *the* way to explore wedding locations on your own time (and in your pajamas).

- **Photos of Hundreds of Wedding Venues and Services**

  Each location and event professional has their own photo gallery.

- **Fee Info for Every Venue**

  HereComesTheGuide.com provides pricing for facility rental, catering and other costs.

- **CERTIFIED BY THE GUIDE Event Services**

  We don't just feature any old caterer or DJ. We've carefully checked out each event professional.

- **Local Bridal Shows**

  Find out what events are happening near you, like fab food tastings and fashion shows. Did you have something better to do this weekend?

- **Wedding Dress Trunk Shows and Samples Sales Calendar**

  Want to browse an entire collection of the latest designer wedding dresses? How about a discount on an in-stock bridal gown? This is the place to find special designer and sales events.

- **MyGuide**

  Log in to organize your **HereComesTheGuide.com** search results. You can save and share your favorite locations and event services (and we won't give out your email address—period).

- **Guest Accommodations, Honeymoon Locations & Rehearsal Dinner Venues**

  Need to book a block of rooms for your out-of-town guests? Looking for the perfect honeymoon or rehearsal dinner spot? Find them all on HereComesTheGuide.com.

Our website also includes many venues that are so new they aren't even in this book!

What People Say

"This is a wonderful website, with all the details that a bride looks for when she's searching for a reception location. It's well organized and incredibly useful. I wish there were more sites like this one. THANK YOU!!!"

—*Amy, Bride*

"I have finally found a website that has it all! I'm planning my wedding from out of state and your event locations search is the best! I've been looking for a website that has all the information in one place. Thank you!!!"

—*Sarah, Bride*

"I'm in the process of helping my daughter research sites for her wedding reception and your website has been hugely helpful! The location information is thorough and consistent, making comparing the different locations so easy. We have found places to check out that we never would have thought of on our own. Thanks so much for all the work you must have done to put all this information together!"

—*Gail C., Mother of the Bride*

"I went out and spent the money on your book without hesitation. I'm so glad I did! I've gotten some great ideas and was able to create an outline for my budget. Not only did I find great reception locations in your book, but I think I found my rehearsal dinner place as well. It was a gold mine!"

—*Liz Davis, Bride*

"I got married in August and cannot stress enough how much help *HereComesTheGuide.com* was to me. I was often able to receive more information from your site than from my contacts with the actual locations and vendors! Especially since I was planning a Southern California wedding from Northern California, you saved me A TON of legwork."

—*Jamie Juster, Bride*

"I just had to let you know how WONDERFUL your website is. I was amazed to finally find a website with REAL information. Other wedding websites just gave me names and phone numbers, and I still had to do all the research on my own. Yours gave me all the nitty-gritty stuff I needed to know to find locations and vendors. With only two sessions at your website, my wedding was planned. Amazing!"

—*Christina R., Bride*

About Here Comes The Guide

"I have to tell you, I was blown away by your website. It's so beautiful and professionally done. The detail you provide is just enough so that the browser doesn't get bogged down in minutiae. **Your site is such a great resource that I've started telling everybody about it.** I've seen tons of wedding sites, so I know that you've come up with something that's really different."

—Kimberly P., Bride

"I went to about ten locations that are in your book and found that the site descriptions were pretty accurate. **I'm amazed at how well you were able to capture the feeling of a place and put it into words.**"

—Stephanie Stevensen, Bride

"Having recently gotten married, I have a special appreciation for *Here Comes The Guide.* It was extremely helpful during my time of planning. **The quick descriptions painted a beautiful picture of each and every venue, and were very helpful in narrowing down the search by budget, criteria and location.** I feel this is a very important tool for every busy bride and still recommend it to all my engaged friends."

—A Southern California Bride

"I completely love your website and look forward to the book. **This is the only resource that is so detailed on California sites, and it makes it so much easier to plan from a long distance.** *Here Comes The Guide* is the best source of information."

—Jocelyn, Bride

"**I absolutely love your website. It's warm, feminine and has what one might call 'simple elegance.'** Great job! I refer friends to your website all the time—for weddings, showers and of course, birthdays. Keep up the fabulous work."

—Maria, Bride

"I love your site! Most other sites that I visited seemed to have a hidden agenda to steer me towards only what benefited them. **This site is non-biased and easy to use. Thank you!**"

—Elisa Parra, Bride

"Thanks for providing this invaluable resource! **I'll be using the site for corporate event planning**—I don't know what I did without it!"

—Mary, Corporate Planner

We Need Your Help

- **Tell venues that you're using *Here Comes The Guide*.**

  When you call the places we feature, let them know that you heard about them through *The Guide*.

- **Help us keep our information current.**

  We'd appreciate it if you'd contact us with your comments, corrections, suggestions and complaints. Your feedback helps us maintain the accuracy of our information.

- **Let us know if you discover a great venue that's not featured in *Here Comes The Guide*.**

  Please call or email us if you find an event site you think we should include in our book and on our website.

Hopscotch Press, Inc.

930 Carleton Street, Berkeley CA 94710

510/548-0400   fax 510/548-0144

info@HereComesTheGuide.com
HereComesTheGuide.com

Information Is Always Changing

Everything changes:
pricing, services, décor,
landscaping and even ownership.

We've tried to make the information in this book completely accurate, but it's not possible. Locations change ownership or management, revamp their pricing and policies, and sometimes go out of business. Truth is, things in the event industry can turn upside down overnight.

So how can you make sure that you're getting correct information? It's simple:

- When you tour venues, bring your book with you or use your smartphone or tablet to quickly refer to each location's page on **HereComesTheGuide.com** for the most up-to-date info.

- When you contact a location, show or read the information in *Here Comes The Guide* to the facility's representative to verify that it's still current.

- Get everything that's been agreed on in writing, and review it carefully before you sign any contract!

Here Comes The Guide

Fourteenth Edition

Copyright ©2016–2017
Published by Hopscotch Press, Inc.
Printed in the U.S.A.

Here Comes The Guide, Southern California®

Fourteenth Edition

Jan Brenner, Co-Author/Editor-in-Chief
Jolene Rae Harrington, Co-Author/Editor

Meredith Monday Schwartz, Chief Operating Officer
Sharon Carl, Production Director
Jennifer Ahearn, Online Media Director
Angela Mullan, Regional Sales Manager
Maggie Munki, Production Specialist
Morgan Lambert, Regional Sales Manager
Jessica Robins, Regional Sales Manager

Lynn Broadwell, Publisher

Inside Illustrations: *Jon Dalton and Michael Tse*

Library of Congress Control Number: 2015952280
ISBN 978-1-885355-23-2

Here Comes The Guide®

Fourteenth Edition

Acknowledgments

Our deepest appreciation goes to our writers, Jolene Rae Harrington (also an invaluable editor), Laurie Turner and Annie Cooper. Without them none of our books would ever get written.

Our artist, Jon Dalton, penned all the new illustrations for this edition of *Here Comes The Guide*. Using both computer graphics and fine art skills, he transformed photographs of the facilities into the distinctive line drawings that give *The Guide* its unique style.

And as always, we are eternally grateful to our clients and our readers. Your support year in and year out keeps *Here Comes The Guide* a popular resource.

Table of Contents

Really Really Important Information

Questions To Ask

Event Venues

Regional Areas and Cities

Eastern Sierras

Central Coast

Santa Barbara Area

Ventura County

San Fernando Valley

Orange County

Mountain Lakes Area

Riverside/Inland Empire

San Diego Area

Greater Palm Springs

Maps

Indexes

Preface

When I graduated from college, I thought I'd never have to do another endless research project again. Boy, was I wrong. Compared to looking for a place to get married, term papers were a piece of cake. I began my quest optimistically enough, but after a couple of days of frantic and fruitless networking (my wedding date was a mere three months down the road!), the enormity of my task started to sink in. It had taken me 33 years to find the right guy, and it was beginning to look like it might take an equally long time to find the right place.

Going into high gear, I reached out and touched just about everyone I knew, along with quite a few total strangers. Friends and friends of friends didn't have any recommendations that suited our particular needs, and although wedding consultants had information, they were reluctant to part with their lists of sites unless I hired them to plan my wedding. I even called some caterers, florists and cake makers, but they were usually too busy to give me in-depth descriptions of places over the phone. Some chambers of commerce had organized wedding location lists ready to mail out; others had nothing and knew nothing.

After days of phoning, all I had was a patchwork quilt of information. I still hadn't found *the* place, and finally had to face the painful truth: there was no central resource or comprehensive, detailed list. I became anxious. With a full-time job I was hardly free to conduct an exhaustive search, and I realized that I would never be able to find out about the vast majority of interesting or unusual wedding sites, let alone thoroughly evaluate them! My frustration was exacerbated by the fact that it was August and the wedding date in October was drawing closer with each passing day.

As luck would have it, my sister mentioned that her hairdresser had gotten married on a yacht in San Francisco Bay. Hallelujah! That's it! I cried. What a great idea! I'd never even thought about a floating wedding and had no idea you could do such a thing.

We got married on a hot, sunny day behind Angel Island in San Francisco Bay. The captain performed the ceremony on the bow, and afterwards the yacht tooted its horn, the crew let loose multicolored balloons, and a "Just Married" sign was thrown over the stern. As we swept past Alcatraz Island, Sausalito and the Golden Gate and Bay Bridges, our guests relaxed in the sun, enjoying drinks and hors d'oeuvres. What a wonderful day! Even my parents' friends had a great time, and wrote us after the wedding to let us know how much they'd loved their outing on the water.

Serendipity was largely responsible for making my wedding memorable, but you don't have to rely on luck. I created *Here Comes The Guide* so that others wouldn't have to experience what I went through, and I hope it makes your search for the perfect location easy and painless.

Lynn Broadwell
Publisher

Really Really Important Information

Introduction

Little did we know when we wrote *Here Comes The Guide, Northern California* in 1989 that we would receive such an overwhelming response from our readers. The first edition sold out in less than a year, and as public demand grew we launched our Southern California edition. Thanks to our enthusiastic readership of engaged couples, savvy party hostesses and event planners, *The Guide* continues to be a bestseller!

So what makes this book so popular?

We've done most of your homework for you.

We present comprehensive, solid information: a full description and illustration of each location, plus details about fees, capacities and services. Our wide selection of facilities includes delightful places that you might not have found on your own.

This book cuts your search time by 90%.

Instead of having to call or email dozens of facilities and ask the same questions over and over again, you can look up many of the answers in *The Guide*. Once you've narrowed down your list of potential sites, you can contact them to schedule an in-person visit. Not only does *The Guide* save you time, it often saves you money by letting you comparison shop!

We screen our venues.

We personally evaluate almost every property in *Here Comes The Guide,* sending a professional writer to 95% of our sites to make sure they meet our criteria. (Yes, we actually turn down locations that don't satisfy our requirements.)

We're experienced.

We've been writing and publishing *Here Comes The Guide* since 1989. We're proud that our publication has become the essential resource for weddings—and just about any kind of event in California.

If you can't find the perfect venue in *Here Comes The Guide,* check out our website at HereComesTheGuide.com.

You'll have access to all the information in the *Here Comes The Guide* book online and a lot more:

- **More Southern California venues,** along with photo gallery slideshows and virtual tours. You'll be able to tour hundreds of sites in your pajamas.

- **Even more venues** in other regions of the U.S., like Northern California, New England, Chicago and Hawaii, just to name a few.

- **Plenty of event services,** with lots of photos of floral designs, cakes, makeup and hair—you name it!

- **Trunk Shows & Sample Sales Calendar** for the latest wedding attire styles and savings.

- **Bridal Fair Calendar** with details about upcoming extravaganzas and wedding showcases.

- **Venues for rehearsal dinners, etc.** Need a place to hold your rehearsal dinner, bridal shower, day-after brunch or other intimate gathering? We've got lots of suggestions (with photos and details, of course!)

- **Guest accommodations/room block options** plus photos and details.

- **Honeymoon destinations,** including romantic photos and practical info.

Navigation is a snap, and our searchable database lets you find event sites by city, type, capacity, view, etc., and event professionals by company name, region or service category. A special *MyGuide* feature lets you save your favorites and share them with friends and family.

And check back often—we regularly update our website with event locations and services that are not featured in the book!

Understanding Our Information

Explanation of Main Headings

Each venue description in *Here Comes The Guide* follows the same format. To help you understand the information presented, we've provided an explanation of the main headings in the same order as they appear.

Description

Once you've selected a geographical area and you're clear about your needs, then thoroughly review all the sites listed in your area of preference. The descriptions are written to give you a sense of what places are like, from ambiance to physical layout. However, before reading the descriptions, you may want to check the *Capacity* and *Fees & Deposits* sections to determine which places seem to be a good fit from a size and budget perspective. If a facility is still a viable option after you've read the entire two-page editorial, flag it for easy reference when planning to contact and visit sites later on. You can also go to our website, HereComesTheGuide.com, and log in to MyGuide to save and share your favorites.

Ceremony Capacity

Standing and seated capacities are sometimes included for ceremonies since these numbers may be totally different than the corresponding numbers for receptions.

Reception Capacity

By now you should have a rough idea of how many people will be attending. If not, it's time to zero in on the number, since many facilities want a deposit based on an estimated head count. Look at the capacity figures for each event location. Seated or sit-down capacity refers to guests seated at tables. Standing capacity refers to a function where the majority of guests are not formally seated, such as a champagne/hors d'oeuvres reception (though there may be cocktail tables and/or lounge furniture). Keep track of those facilities that are compatible with your guest count, or add them to your MyGuide favorites. If you're planning well in advance and don't have your guest list whittled down yet, then you'll just have to estimate and refine the count as the date draws near. There is a world of difference in cost and planning effort between an intimate party of 60 and a large wedding with over 200 guests, so pin down your numbers as soon as you can.

Meeting Capacity

In general, the seated capacity for meetings is listed as a range or a maximum. Sometimes, specific spaces are named along with their individual capacities. Occasionally, seating configurations are also provided: *theater-style* (auditorium row seating with chairs arranged closely together), *classroom-style* (an organized table-and-chair arrangement, usually in rows) and *conference-style* (seating around tables).

Fees and Deposits

We've tried to make the information regarding costs as accurate as possible. However, keep in mind that we can't list the fees for all of the services a venue offers. Also, while packages tend to be more inclusive, they may not cover the full cost of your event—especially when you add in extras like appetizers or rentals. It's important to find out as soon as possible exactly what is—and isn't—included with any service or package you're considering in order to accurately assess how your venue choice will impact your budget.

It's a good idea to confirm pricing with the facility you're calling. If you're planning far in advance, anticipate price increases by the time you contract with a venue. Once you're definite about your location, you should lock in your fees in a contract, protecting yourself from possible rate increases later. Make sure you ask about every service provided and are clear about all of the extras that can really add up. Facilities may charge you for tables, chairs, linens, plateware and silverware, glassware and additional hours. Don't be surprised to see tax and service charges in fixed amounts applied to the total bill if the facility provides restaurant or catering services. Although it may seem redundant to include the phrase "tax, alcohol and service charge are additional" in each entry, we find that most people forget (or just don't want to accept the painful reality) that 23–33% will be applied to the food & beverage total.

> **Look at the information regarding fees and deposits and remember that these figures change regularly and usually in one direction—up!**

Sometimes a deposit is nonrefundable—a fact you'll definitely want to know if the deposit is a large percentage of the total bill. And even if it's refundable, you still need to read the cancellation policy thoroughly. Make sure you understand the policies that will ensure you get your cleaning and security deposit returned in full and, again, get everything in writing.

Food costs vary considerably. Carefully plan your menu with the caterer, event consultant or chef. Depending on the style of service and the type of food being served, the total food bill can vary dramatically—even if you're getting quotes from the same caterer. If, for example, you're having a multi-course seated meal, expect it to be the most expensive part of your event.

Alcohol is expensive, too, and you may be restricted in what you can serve and who can serve it. Some venues don't allow you to bring your own alcoholic beverages, and even if they do permit it you may be limited to beer, wine or champagne. Many places discourage you from bringing your own (BYO) by charging an exorbitant corkage fee to remove the cork and pour. Other places have limited permits that don't allow them to serve alcohol or restrict them from serving certain kinds; some will let you or the caterer serve alcohol, others require someone with a license. Make sure you know what's allowed. Decide what your budget is for alcohol and determine what types you're able to provide. And keep in mind that the catering fees you are quoted rarely include the cost of alcohol. If you provide the alcohol, make sure you keep your purchase receipts so you can return any unopened bottles.

So how much will your event cost? Hopefully not more than you can afford! There are a lot of variables involved in coming up with an estimated total for your event. Just make sure you've included them all in your calculations and read all the fine print before you sign any contract.

Availability

Some facilities are available 7am to 2am; others offer very limited "windows." If you'd like to save some money, consider a weekday or weeknight reception, or think about having your event in the off-season (often November, or January through March, but varies depending on the region). Even the most sought-after places have openings midweek and during non-peak months—and at reduced costs. Facilities want your business and are more likely to negotiate terms and prices if they have nothing else scheduled. Again, read all the fine print carefully and mark those facilities that have time slots that meet your needs. If the date you have in mind is already booked, it doesn't hurt to ask if someone actually confirmed that date by paying a deposit or signing a contract. If they haven't, you may be in luck.

Services/Amenities and Restrictions

Most facilities provide something in the way of services and many have limitations that may affect your function. For instance, they may not allow you to have amplified music outdoors or bring your own caterer.

We've attempted to give you a brief description of what each venue has to offer and what is restricted. Because of space limitations, we've shortened words and developed a key to help you follow our abbreviated notations. Once you're familiar with our shorthand, you'll be able to read through all the data outlined at the bottom of each entry and flag each facility that meets your requirements.

Services/Amenities Key

CATERING

- **in-house:** the facility provides catering (for a fee)
- **in-house, no BYO:** the facility provides catering; you cannot bring in your own
- **preferred list:** you must select your caterer from the facility's approved list
- **in-house or BYO:** the facility will provide catering or you can select an outside caterer of your own
- **BYO, licensed:** arrange for your own licensed caterer

KITCHEN FACILITIES

- **ample** or **fully equipped:** large and well-equipped with major appliances
- **moderate:** medium-sized and utilitarian
- **minimal:** small with limited equipment; may not have all the basic appliances
- **setup** or **prep only:** room for setup and food prep, but not enough space or utilities to cook food
- **n/a:** not applicable because facility provides catering or doesn't allow food

TABLES & CHAIRS

- **some provided** or **provided:** facility provides some or all of the tables and chairs
- **BYO:** make arrangements to bring your own

LINENS, SILVER, ETC.

- same as above

RESTROOMS

- **wheelchair accessible** or
- **not wheelchair accessible**

DANCE FLOOR

- **yes:** an area for dancing (hardwood floor, cement terrace, patio) is available
- **CBA, extra charge:** a dance floor can be brought in for a fee

BRIDE'S & GROOM'S DRESSING AREA

- **yes:** there is an area for changing
- **no:** there's no area for changing
- **limited:** smaller space, not fully equipped as changing room
- **CBA:** can be arranged

PARKING

- **CBA:** can be arranged
  other descriptions are self explanatory

ACCOMMODATIONS

If overnight accommodations are available on site, the number of guest rooms is listed.

- **CBA:** the facility will arrange accommodations for you

OUTDOOR NIGHT LIGHTING

- **yes:** there is adequate light to conduct your event outdoors after dark
- **access only** or **limited:** lighting is sufficient for access only

OUTDOOR COOKING FACILITIES

- **BBQ:** the facility has a barbecue on the premises
- **BBQ, CBA:** a barbecue can be arranged through the facility
- **BYO BBQ:** make arrangements for your own barbecue
- **n/a:** not applicable

CLEANUP

- **provided:** facility takes care of cleanup
- **caterer:** your caterer is responsible
- **caterer or renter:** both you and/or your caterer are responsible for cleanup

AUDIOVISUAL/MEETING EQUIPMENT

- **full range:** facility has a full range of audiovisual equipment
- **no:** no equipment is available
- **BYO:** bring your own equipment
- **CBA:** equipment can be arranged
- **CBA, extra fee:** equipment can be arranged for an extra fee

VIEW

We've described what type of view is available for each facility.

- **no:** the facility has no views to speak of

OTHER

Description of any service or amenity that is not included in above list.

Restrictions Key

ALCOHOL

- **in-house, no BYO:** the facility provides alcoholic beverages (for a fee) and does not permit you to bring your own
- **BYO:** you can bring your own alcohol
- **corkage, $/bottle:** if you bring your own alcohol, the facility charges a fee per bottle to remove the cork and pour
- **WCB only:** (*or any combination of these three letters*) only wine, champagne and beer are permitted
- **licensed server:** the server of alcohol must be licensed

SMOKING

- **allowed:** smoking is permitted throughout the facility
- **outside only:** smoking is not permitted inside the facility
- **not allowed:** smoking is not permitted anywhere on the premises
- **designated areas:** specific areas for smoking have been designated

MUSIC

Almost every facility allows acoustic music unless stated otherwise. Essentially, restrictions refer to amplified music.

- **amplified OK:** amplified music is acceptable without restriction
- **outside only:** no amplified music allowed inside
- **inside only:** no amplified music permitted outside
- **amplified OK with limits or restrictions:** amplified music is allowed, but there are limits on volume, hours of play, type of instruments, etc.

WHEELCHAIR ACCESS

Accessibility is based on whether the event areas (not necessarily the restrooms) of a facility are wheelchair accessible or not.

- **yes:** the facility is accessible
- **limited:** the facility is accessible but with difficulty (there may be a step at the entrance, for example, but all of the rooms are accessible)
- **no:** the facility is not accessible

INSURANCE

Many facilities require that you purchase and show proof of some insurance coverage. The type and amount of insurance varies with the facility, and some facilities offer insurance for a minimal charge.

- **liability required, certificate required** or **proof of insurance required:** additional insurance is required
- **not required:** no additional insurance is required
- **may be required:** sometimes additional insurance is required

Valuable Tips

Selecting an Event Venue

Before you jump into the venue descriptions in *Here Comes The Guide,* identify what kind of celebration you want and establish selection criteria early. Here are some basics:

Your Venue's Geographical Location

For many couples, it's important that the location they select is easy for the majority of their guests to get to. However, whether you're hosting your event close to home or planning a destination wedding in another city, state or country, you need to think about the logistics of getting everyone to your event site.

Special Considerations in Southern California

Guests may be traveling a considerable distance by car to your party destination. Sure, they can use Google Maps or their vehicle's GPS to get directions to your venue, but those resources aren't always 100% reliable. Given the Southern California freeway system and traffic congestion, you'll save your guests lots of time and trouble if you provide, along with the invitation, specific directions on a separate map drawn to scale. Include symbols indicating north, south, etc. and the names of the appropriate off-ramps. If you're not sure about exits, landmarks or street names, take a dry run of the route to make sure everything on your map is accurate and easy to follow. If your function occurs after dark, do the test drive at night so you can note well-lit landmarks that will prevent your guests from getting lost—both coming to your event and going home.

If you're having a Friday evening event, take commuters into account, especially if your event site is in an area that gets bumper-to-bumper traffic. One solution is to schedule your get-together after 7pm when freeways are less congested.

Even if you have few constraints when picking a location, it's still worth considering the total driving time to and from your destination. When it's more than two hours, an overnight stay may be necessary, and you may be limited to a Saturday night event, since your nearest and dearest won't be able to spend hours on the road during the week. If you're going to need lodging for some of your guests during your celebration, be sure to check out the "Guest Accommodations/Room Blocks" section on HereComesTheGuide.com for suggestions and info. If you have guests arriving by plane, it's certainly helpful if there's an airport nearby, and if your co-workers, friends or family enjoy drinking try to house them close to the event site or have contact numbers handy for transportation via taxis or Uber.

There's no reason why you can't contemplate a special event in the San Diego mountains or in a wine cave in Santa Ynez. Just remember that if you're planning a wedding that's not local, a venue's on-site coordinator or a wedding planner can really help: Many are experienced in handling destination events and can be a great asset.

Budget

Many couples aren't very experienced with event budgeting and don't know how to estimate what locations, products and services will ultimately cost. If you're not sure what you can realistically afford, we recommend talking to a professional event planner or wedding coordinator early in the planning stages. You don't have to make a big financial or time commitment to use a professional; many will assist you on an hourly basis for a nuts-and-bolts session to determine priorities and to assign costs to items on your wish list.

Part of being realistic involves some simple arithmetic. Catering costs, for example, are usually calculated on a per-person basis. The couple who has $10,000 and wants to invite 250 guests should know that $40 per guest actually won't go very far. Tax and gratuity combined usually consume 23–33% of the food & beverage budget. If you subtract that 30% from $40, you have $28 left. If you also serve alcohol at $12/person, you're down to $16/person for food. That's usually not enough for appetizers and a seated meal, let alone location rental fees, entertainment, flowers, printed invitations, photography, etc.

Before you make any major decisions or commit any of your funds for specific items, take a serious look at your total budget, make sure it can cover all your anticipated expenses, and leave a little cushion for last-minute items. If your budget doesn't cover everything, it's time for some hard decisions. If you have a very large guest list and a small pocketbook, you may need to shorten the list or cut back on some of the amenities you want to include. No matter who foots the bill, be advised that doing the homework here really counts. Pin down your costs at the beginning of the planning stage and get all estimates in writing.

> **The important point is that if you know what kind of event you want and are clear about your budget, your search will be faster and easier.**

Style

Do you know what kind of event you want? Will it be formal or informal? A traditional wedding or an innovative party? Will it be held at night or during the day? Indoors or outdoors? Is having a garden ceremony or gourmet food a deal breaker? By identifying the geographical area and the most important elements of your dream wedding before you start looking for a venue, you can really narrow down your search.

Guest Count

How many people are anticipated? Many facilities request a rough estimate 60–90 days in advance of your function—and they'll want a deposit based on the figure you give them. A confirmed guest count or guarantee is usually required 72 hours prior to the event. It's important to come up with a solid estimate of your guest list early on in order to plan your budget and select the right ceremony or reception spot.

It's also important to ensure that the guest count you give the facility *before* your event doesn't change *during* your event. Believe it or not, it's possible to have more people at your reception than you expected. How? Some folks who did not bother to RSVP may decide to show up anyway. In one case we know of, the parents of the bride got an additional bill for $1,200 on the event day because there were 30 "surprise" guests beyond the guest count guarantee who were wined and dined. To prevent this from happening to you—especially if you're having a large reception where it's hard to keep track of all the guests—it's a good idea to contact everyone who did *not* RSVP. Let them know as politely as possible that you will need to have their response by a given date to finalize food & beverage totals.

Seasonal Differences

Southern California, for all its (pardon the expression) faults, has got some great advantages weather-wise. Outdoor special events, ceremonies and receptions can take place throughout most of the year, and from September to November you can anticipate sunny skies and warm temperatures. However, when the mercury rises in inland areas, watch out. A canopy or tables with umbrellas are essential for screening the sun. In fact, you should ask each facility manager about the sun's direction and intensity with respect to the time of day and month your event will take place. Guests will be uncomfortable facing into the sun during a ceremony, and white walls and enclosed areas bounce light around and can hold in heat. If your event is scheduled for midday in July, for example, include a note on your location map to bring sunglasses, hat and sunscreen. If you also mention words like "poolside," "yacht deck" or "lawn seating" on the map, it will help guests know how to dress. In summer, you might want to consider an evening rather than a midday celebration. Not only is the air cooler, but you may also get an extra bonus—a glorious sunset.

If you're arranging an outdoor party November through April, or in the foothills or mountain areas, expect cooler weather and prepare a contingency plan. Despite our region's favorable Mediterranean climate, it has rained in May, June and July, so consider access to an inside space or a tent (and factor in any additional cost that might require).

Special Requirements

Sometimes places have strict rules and regulations. If most of your guests smoke, then pick a location that doesn't restrict smoking. If alcohol is going to be consumed, make sure it's allowed and find out if bar service needs to be licensed. If dancing and a big band are critical, then limit yourself to those locations that can accommodate them and the accompanying decibels. Do you have children, seniors or disabled guests, vegetarians or folks who want kosher food on your list? If so, you need to plan for them, too. It's essential that you identify the special factors that are important for your event before you sign a contract.

Locking in Your Event Date

Let's say it's the first day of your hunt for the perfect spot, and the second place you see is an enchanting garden that happens to be available on the date you want. You really like it but, since you've only seen two locations, you're not 100% sure that this is *the* place. No problem. You decide to keep your options open by making a tentative reservation. The site coordinator dutifully pencils your name into her schedule book and says congratulations. You say thanks, we have a few more places (like 25) to check out, but this one looks terrific. Then off you go, secure in the knowledge that if none of the other sites you visit pans out, you still have this lovely garden waiting for you.

The nightmare begins a couple of weeks, or perhaps months, down the road when you've finished comparison-shopping and call back the first place you liked to finalize the details. So sorry, the coordinator says. We gave away your date because a) oops, one of the other gals who works here erased your name by mistake (after all, it was only *penciled* in), b) we didn't hear back from you soon enough, or c) you never confirmed your reservation with a deposit.

For the tiniest instant you picture yourself inflicting bodily harm on the coordinator or at least slapping the facility with a lawsuit, but alas, there's really not much you can do. Whether a genuine mistake was made or the facility purposely gave your date to another, perhaps more lucrative party (this happens sometimes with hotels who'd rather book a big convention on your date than a little wedding), you're out of luck. To avoid the pain (and ensuing panic) of getting bumped, here's what we suggest: Instead of just being penciled in, ask if you can write a refundable $100–250 check to hold the date for a limited time. If the person in charge is willing to do this but wants the full deposit up front (usually nonrefundable), then you'll need to decide whether you can afford to lose the entire amount if you find a more appealing location later on. Once the coordinator or sales person takes your money, you're automatically harder to bump. Make sure you get a receipt that has the event date, year, time and space(s) reserved written on it, as well as the date your tentative reservation runs out. Then, just to be on the safe side, check in with the facility weekly while you're considering other sites to prevent any possible "mistakes" from being made. When you finally do commit to a place, get a signed contract or at least a confirmation letter. If you

> **If you try to pick a venue before you've made basic decisions, selection will be a struggle and it will take longer to find a spot that will make you happy.**

don't receive written confirmation within a week, hound the coordinator until you get it, even if you have to drive to the sales office and stand there until they hand it over to you. And even after you've plunked down your money and have a letter and/or contract securing your date, call the coordinator every other month to reconfirm your reservation. It pays to stay on top of this, no matter how locked in you think you are. If you don't hear back from your contact in a reasonable time frame despite repeated attempts, you should contact the facility or catering sales department directly to confirm that your coordinator still works there. If she/he doesn't, find out who is responsible for managing your event, and verify that your contract (and the must-have details) are still in place.

Parking

Parking is seldom a critical factor if you get married outside an urban area, but make sure you know how it's going to be handled if you're planning a party in a parking-challenged place like downtown Los Angeles, Pasadena or Santa Monica.

A map is a handy supplement to any invitation, and there's usually enough room on it to indicate how and where vehicles should be parked. Depending on the location, you may want to add a note suggesting carpooling or mention that a shuttle service or valet parking is provided. If there's a fee for parking, identify the anticipated cost per car and where the entry points are to the nearest parking lots. The last thing you want are surprised and disgruntled guests who can't find a place to stash their car, or who are shocked at the $20–40 parking tab.

Professional Help

If you're a busy person with limited time to plan and execute a party, pick a facility that offers complete coordination services, from catering and flowers to decorations and music. Or better yet, hire a professional event or wedding coordinator. Either way, you'll make your life much easier by having someone else handle the details. And often the relationships these professionals have with vendors can end up saving you money, too.

Food and Alcohol Quality

Food and alcohol account for the greatest portion of an event's budget; consequently, food & beverage selections are a big deal. Given the amount of money you will spend on this category alone, you should be concerned about the type, quantity and quality of what you eat and drink. If in-house catering is provided, we suggest you sample different menu options prior to paying a facility deposit. If you'd like to see how a facility handles food setup and presentation, ask the caterer to arrange a visit to someone else's party about a half hour before it starts. It's wise to taste wines and beers in advance, and be very specific about hard alcohol selections.

Hidden Costs

This may come as a surprise, but not all services and event equipment are covered in the rental fee, and some facilities hide the true cost of renting their space by having a low rental fee. It's possible to get nickeled and dimed for all the extras: tables, chairs, linens, dance floor, cake cutting, valet service and so forth. You can also end up paying more than you expected for security and cleanup. All these additional charges can really add up, so save yourself a big headache by understanding exactly what's included in the rental fee and what's not before you sign any contract.

Bonus Info

If you're not sure what to ask potential venues and event professionals, check out our "QUESTIONS TO ASK" section starting on page 21. We've put together lists of questions that come in very handy when you're interviewing potential event locations, photographers, caterers, etc.

Tips for Previewing a Venue

Make Appointments.

If you liked what you read about a venue in *The Guide,* then we recommend you make an appointment to see that location rather than just driving by. Sometimes an unremarkable-looking building will surprise you with a secluded garden or hidden courtyard. And sometimes the opposite is true—you'll love the stunning façade, but the interior isn't your style.

Incidentally, we've withheld the addresses of privately owned properties. Should you happen to know where any of these facilities is located, we urge you to respect the owner's or manager's privacy and make an appointment instead of stopping by.

When you do call for an appointment, don't forget to ask for specific directions, including cross streets. You can also look up the location on *HereComesTheGuide.com* and print out a detailed street map. Try to cluster your visits so that you can easily drive from one place to another without backtracking. Schedule at least an hour per facility and leave ample driving time. You want to be efficient, but don't over-schedule yourself. It's best to view places when you're fresh and your judgment isn't clouded by fatigue.

Bring along *The Guide* or use your phone or tablet to access our website.

We've listed the street address for each site, and our illustrations in the book often make it easier to identify the venues you're planning to see. And if you bring the book or use your smartphone or tablet to look up venues on HereComesTheGuide.com, you can double-check our information with the site representative.

Bring a notebook—paper or digital!

You can make notes in your copy of *Here Comes The Guide,* but have a small notebook or digital device handy, too. Keep track of the date, time and name of the person providing the information, and then read back the info to the site representative to confirm that what you heard is correct. Remember to have your notes with you when you review your contract, and go over in detail what you were told versus what's in the contract before you sign anything.

Take pictures.

Video is particularly useful for narrating your likes, dislikes and any other observations while you're shooting a venue. However, if you're just taking still photos, make sure you have a system for matching shots to their respective locations. You'd be surprised how easy it is to confuse photos. Make sure your phone or other gear is charged and bring whatever else you need to make it all work properly.

File everything.

Many facilities will hand you pamphlets, menus, rate charts and other materials. Develop a system for sorting and storing the information that keeps your notes, photos and handouts together, clearly labeled and easily accessible.

Bring a checkbook or credit card.

Some of the more attractive venues book a year to 18 months in advance. If you actually fall in love with a location and your date is available, plunk down a deposit to hold the date.

Working With a Venue

Confirm All the Details

When you make the initial phone call or email, confirm that the information presented in *Here Comes The Guide* is still valid. Show or read the information in our book to the site's representative, and have him or her inform you of any changes. If there have been significant increases in fees or new restrictions that you can't live with, cross the place off your list and move on. If the facility is still a contender, request a tour.

Once you've determined that the physical elements of the place suit you, it's time to discuss details. Ask about services and amenities or fees that may not be listed in the book and make a note of them. Outline your plans to the representative and make sure that the facility can accommodate your particular needs. If you don't want to handle all the details yourself, find out what the facility is willing and able to do, and if there will be an additional cost for their assistance. Venues often provide planning services for little or no extra charge. If other in-house services are offered, such as flowers or wedding cakes, inquire about the quality of each service provider and whether or not substitutions can be made. If you want to use your own vendors, find out if the facility will charge you an extra fee. For more help with working with a location, see our "Questions to Ask a Wedding Venue" on page 26.

The Importance of Rapport

Another factor to consider is your rapport with the person(s) you're working with. Are you comfortable with them? Do they listen well and respond to your questions directly? Do they inspire trust and confidence? Are they warm and enthusiastic or cold and aloof? If you have doubts, you need to resolve them before embarking on a working relationship with these folks—no matter how wonderful the facility itself is. Discuss your feelings with them, and if you're still not completely satisfied, get references and call them. If at the end of this process you still have lingering concerns, you may want to eliminate the facility from your list even though it seems perfect in every other way.

On the other hand, don't let your rapport with a banquet coordinator or site rep sway you to book a venue you aren't in love with—there's a lot of turnover in the hospitality industry, and you may call Brittany one day only to—surprise!—be referred to Brian. So if Brittany was your main reason for choosing this place, you could be in for a big disappointment if you and Brian don't hit it off and suddenly the venue's shortcomings really stand out.

Signing a Contract

It's easy to get emotionally attached to a location, but remember that it's not a done deal until you sign a contract. Now's the time to be businesslike and put your emotions aside. If you can't do that, get a non-emotional partner, friend or relative to help you review the small print and negotiate changes before you sign. Remember all those notes you took when you first visited the site? Compare them with what's actually written in the contract. No matter what someone told you about the availability of a dance floor, the price of pastel linens, or the ceremony arch, you can't hold the facility to it until the contract is signed. Places revise their prices and policies all the time, so assume that things may have changed since you originally saw the site or talked to a site representative.

If you're not happy with the contract, prepare to negotiate. Before your appointment with whoever has the power to alter the contract, make an itemized list, in order of importance, of the changes you want. Decide what you're willing to give up, and what you can't live without. If in the end the most important things on your list cannot be addressed to your satisfaction, this is probably not the right place for you. It's better to find another location than to stay with a facility that isn't willing to work with you.

Insurance Considerations

Nowadays, if someone gets injured at an event or something is damaged at or near the event site, it's likely that someone will be sued.

In order to protect themselves and spread the risk among all parties involved, facilities often require additional insurance and/or proof of insurance from service professionals and their clients.

Event sites and service professionals (such as caterers) are very aware of their potential liability and all have coverage of one kind or another. Many of the properties we represent will also require you, the renter, to get extra insurance.

What's funny (or not so funny) is that as more and more event sites require extra liability and/or a certificate of insurance, fewer insurance companies are willing to issue either one—even if you're covered under a homeowner's policy. At this point, insurance carriers don't want to attach extra clauses to your policy to increase coverage for a single event, and most, if not all, companies are unwilling to add the event site's name to your existing policy as an additional insured.

Don't despair. Even though it's hard to come by, you can get extra insurance for a specified period of time, and it's relatively inexpensive.

Obtaining Extra Insurance

- **The first thing to do is read your rental contract carefully.** Make sure you understand exactly *what's* required and *when* it's required. Most facilities want $1,000,000–2,000,000 in extra liability coverage. If you don't pay attention to the insurance clauses early in the game, you'll have to play catch-up at the last moment, frantically trying to locate a carrier who will issue you additional insurance. And, if you don't supply the certificate to the facility *on time*, you may run the risk of forfeiting your event site altogether.

- **The second thing is to ask your event site's representative if the site has an insurance policy through which you can purchase the required extra coverage.** If the answer is yes, then consider purchasing it—that's the easiest route (but not necessarily the best!). The facility's extra insurance coverage may not be the least expensive and it may not provide you with the best coverage. What you need to ask is: "If one of my guests or one of the professionals working at my event causes some damage to the premises or its contents, will this extra insurance cover it?" If the answer if yes, get it in writing.

- **The third thing, if the answer is no, is to find your own coverage.** We suggest you avoid random searches online and call one of these two insurance providers:

    1) WedSafe at 877/723-3933. This company insures weddings and private events. You can reach them at their toll free number or online at wedsafe.com. They offer coverage for wedding cancellation and/or liability.

2) WedSure®, a division of R.V. Nuccio & Associates, Inc. at 1-800-ENGAGED or www.WedSure.com. They specialize in insuring special events. Their website FAQs outline what's offered, and you can also contact them to clarify details and get a personalized quote.

Coverage starts at $95 for a wedding; the total cost will depend on what you want. Rob Nuccio's coverage is underwritten by Fireman's Fund.

Here are some of the items a typical policy might cover:

- Cancellation or postponement due to: weather, damage to the facility, sickness, failure to show of the caterer or officiant, financial reasons—even limited change-of-heart circumstances!

- Photography or videography: failure of the professional to appear, loss of original negatives, etc.

- Lost, stolen or damaged gifts

- Lost, stolen or damaged equipment rentals

- Lost, stolen or damaged bridal gown or other special attire

- Lost, stolen or damaged jewelry

- Personal liability and additional coverage

- Medical payments for injuries incurred during the event

If you use this service, call or email to let us know whether you're happy with them. We'd love to get your feedback.

It Can't Happen To Me

Don't be lulled into the notion that an event disaster can't happen to you. It could rain when you least expect it. Or your well-intentioned aunt might melt your wedding dress while ironing out a few wrinkles. Wouldn't it be nice to know that your dress, wedding photos, equipment rentals and gifts are covered? Naturally, a New Year's Eve party or a high school prom night is riskier than a wedding, but we could tell you stories of upscale parties where something did happen and a lawsuit resulted.

So even if extra insurance is not required, you may still want to consider additional coverage, especially if alcohol is being served. *You are the best predictor of your guests' behavior.* If you plan on having a wild, wonderful event, a little additional insurance could be a good thing.

Recycling

Do Your Part!

If you're wondering why we're including a brief item about recycling in a book like *Here Comes The Guide,* it's because parties and special events often generate recyclable materials as well as leftover food and flowers.

You and your caterer can feel good by donating the excess, and recycling plastic bottles, glass, paper, etc. An added benefit is that food donations are tax deductible for either you or the caterer. And if you recycle, the cost for extra garbage bins can be eliminated or reduced. Call your local recycling center to arrange a pickup.

Food donations can be distributed to teenage drop-in centers, youth shelters, alcoholic treatment centers, rescue missions, and AIDS hospices, as well as senior, homeless and refugee centers. Flowers will brighten the day of patients or residents at your favorite local hospital, hospice or senior center.

IMPORTANT: There are regulations that apply to the kinds of foods that can be donated and how they need to be packaged. If you plan to donate your leftovers, it's best to talk to your caterer about it or call the places where you'd like to donate *prior* to your event to find out what their requirements for preparation and drop-off are.

We've provided a list of some well-known Southern California food banks, but you can also look online to find others that may be more convenient for you.

For more valuable tips about going green, read our article "It's A Nice Day for a Green Wedding." You'll find it in the Wedding Ideas section on HereComesTheGuide.com!

Working With Event Professionals

Hiring a Caterer: Get References and Look for Professionalism

If you're selecting your own caterer, get references from friends and acquaintances or, better yet, contact any of the caterers featured on HereComesTheGuide.com. We've thoroughly screened these companies and can assure you that they're in the top 5% of the industry in terms of quality and service. We keep all of their references on file, so you can contact us and ask questions about them.

Every caterer is different. Some offer only pre-set menus while others will help you create your own. Menus and prices vary enormously, so try to have a good idea of what you want and what you can spend before interviewing prospective caterers. After you've talked to several caterers and have decided which ones to seriously consider, request references from each one and call them. Ask not only about the quality of the food, but about the ease of working with a given caterer. You'll want to know if the caterer is professional—fully prepared and equipped, punctual and organized. You may also want to know if the caterer is licensed, prepares food in a kitchen approved by the Department of Health, or carries workmen's compensation and liability insurance. And don't forget to inquire about the cleanup—did the staff remove all the equipment and garbage in a matter that was acceptable? Although this level of inquiry may seem unnecessary, responses to these questions will give you a more complete picture of how a caterer runs his or her business, and will help you determine which one is best suited for your event.

Facility Requirements for Caterers

Facilities often have specific requirements regarding caterers—they may have to be licensed and bonded, out by 11pm or fastidiously clean. Before you hire a caterer, make sure that he or she is compatible with your site. In fact, even if the facility does not require it, it's a good idea to have your caterer visit the place in advance to become familiar with any special circumstances or problems that might come up. You'll notice throughout *Here Comes The Guide* the words "in-house" or "select from list" after the word *Catering*. Sites that have an exclusive caterer or only permit you to select from a preferred list do so because each wants to eliminate most of the risks involved in having a caterer on the premises who is not accustomed to working in that environment. Exclusive or preferred caterers have achieved their exalted status because they either provide consistently good services or they won the catering contract when it went out to bid. Whether you're working with one of your facility's choices or your own, make sure that your contract includes everything you have agreed on before you sign it.

Working with an Event Planner or Wedding Coordinator

Opting to hire a professional planner may be a wise choice. A good consultant will ask you all the right questions, determine exactly what you need, and take care of as much or as little of your affair as you want. If you'd like to feel like a guest at your own event, have the consultant manage everything, including orchestrating the day of the event. If you only want some advice and structure, hire a planner on a meeting-by-meeting basis.

Most of the principles used in selecting a caterer apply to hiring an event coordinator. Try to get suggestions from friends or facilities, follow up on references the coordinators give you, compare service fees and make sure you and the coordinator are compatible. The range of professionalism and experience varies greatly, so it really is to your advantage to investigate each coordinator's track record. You can save a lot of time by starting with the coordinators featured on HereComesTheGuide.com.

Again, once you've found someone who can accommodate you, get everything in writing so that there won't be any misunderstandings down the road. Although engaging a professional to "manage" your event can be a godsend, it can also be problematic if you turn the entire decision-making process over to them. Don't forget that it's your party, and no one else should decide what's right for you.

For lists of questions to ask potential wedding venues and vendors, go to page 21 in this book. You can also find them on HereComesTheGuide.com.

Questions To Ask
Venues and Event Professionals

(including Here Comes The Guide's Wedding Checklist)

Here Comes The Guide's Wedding Checklist

10–12 Months To Go...

☑ Visit HereComesTheGuide.com and start planning your wedding!

☐ Work out your budget and establish your top priorities—where to save/where to splurge.

☐ Find ideas. Start browsing bridal blogs and magazines (or visit Pinterest.com/HCTG) to identify your wedding style and color palette.

☐ Compile your preliminary guest list (you'll need that guest count!).

☐ Choose your wedding party—who do you want by your side at the altar?

☐ Find a venue for your ceremony and reception, and reserve your date.

☐ Now that you have a date, tell everyone to save it! For destination weddings or weddings around a holiday, consider sending out Save-the-Date cards or emails. Or create your own wedding website, and let your invitees know about it.

☐ Find a dress and begin assembling the perfect accessories. Need inspiration? Attend a bridal fair or trunk show.

☐ Already feeling overwhelmed? Consider hiring a Wedding Coordinator.

☐ Assemble an all-star vendor team. We'd start with:
  - Caterer
  - Photographer/Videographer
  - Officiant

  When you hire a vendor, get all the details in writing!

☐ Another way to minimize stress: Start dreaming up your honeymoon...and check out our "Plan A Honeymoon" section on HereComesTheGuide.com.

6–9 Months To Go...

☐ Continue researching, interviewing and booking vendors. And don't forget, when you hire one make sure to put everything in writing!

- Decide on arrangements with your Floral Designer.
- Do a tasting and choose your wedding cake with your Cake Designer.
- Hire the DJ/Entertainment for your ceremony, cocktail hour and reception.
- Discuss the style and wording of your wedding invitations with a Stationer.

☐ Create your gift registry (and don't forget to update your wedding website!).

☐ Arrange hotel room blocks for out-of-town guests and book your own suite for the wedding night. See HereComesTheGuide.com for room block options.

☐ Shop for bridesmaid/flower girl dresses and give your attendants clear instructions on how to place their orders.

☐ Arrange and book any necessary transportation.

☐ Go over bridal shower/bachelorette details and the guest list with the person(s) hosting your party.

3–5 Months To Go...

☐ Book the rehearsal and rehearsal dinner locations (see HereComesTheGuide.com for rehearsal dinner options). If you're including entertainment or specialty details like a groom's cake, now's the time to lock in these elements.

☐ Put together your rehearsal dinner guest list.

☐ Make childcare arrangements for your guests' kids.

☐ Reserve all necessary party rentals and linens.

☐ Order wedding favors for your guests.

☐ Shop for and reserve men's formalwear.

☐ Concentrate on finalizing the:
  - Guest list. Get everyone's mailing address.
  - Invitation wording. Confirm your invitation text with the Stationer, and consider additional stationery (programs, menu cards, place cards, thank-you cards, etc.).

Schedule a pickup date for your invites.

- Ceremony readings and vows.
- Menu, beverage and catering details.
- Timeline of the reception formalities.

☐ Do a Makeup & Hair trial and book your stylists. While you're at it, come up with your own beauty and fitness regimen to be camera-ready for the big day.

☐ Shop for and purchase your wedding rings.

☐ Finalize honeymoon plans and obtain all necessary documents (are you sure your passports are up to date?).

6–8 Weeks To Go…

☐ You're getting close…mail out those invitations! Have a game plan for recording the RSVPs and meal choices.

☐ Touch base with your vendors to confirm date, deposits and details.

☐ Start researching marriage license requirements and name-change paperwork.

☐ Begin your dress fittings. Be sure to buy the appropriate undergarments beforehand.

☐ So you think you *can't* dance? Consider taking a dance lesson with your fiancé—a good way to break in your bridal shoes!

☐ Give the wedding party a nudge—make sure they've ordered all necessary attire.

☐ Write thank-you cards for shower gifts and any early wedding gifts received.

3–5 Weeks To Go…

☐ Send out rehearsal dinner invitations. If your get-together will be informal, feel free to send an Evite.

☐ Finalize and confirm:

- Wedding vows and readings with your Officiant.
- Shot list with your Photographer/ Videographer.
- Song list for ceremony, cocktail hour and reception with your DJ and/or Band/ Musicians.

- Timeline for the reception and who's giving the toasts.
- Wedding night and honeymoon accommodations.

☐ Obtain marriage license and complete name-change documents, if applicable.

☐ Pick up your wedding rings and proofread any engraving!

☐ If you're the traditional type, do you have something old, new, borrowed and blue?

☐ Purchase your guest book, toasting flutes, cake servers, unity candle, and all that good stuff.

☐ Buy gifts (optional) for the wedding party and parents of the bride and groom.

☐ Have your final dress fitting. Bring your shoes and accessories for the full impact.

☐ Sigh. Hunt down whoever hasn't RSVP'd yet.

1–2 Weeks To Go…

☐ Give your caterer/venue the final guest count.

☐ Arrange seating and create the seating chart and/or place cards.

☐ Pick up your gown. Swoon.

☐ Confirm arrival times and finalize the wedding timeline with vendors and the wedding party—make sure your MOH has a copy, too.

☐ Put together your own Bridal Emergency Kit.

☐ Speaking of emergencies: Check the weather report, and if things look iffy contact your venue to make sure a contingency plan is in place.

☐ Start packing for your honeymoon. (See "weather report" above.)

☐ In desperate need of a facial or massage? Now's the time to squeeze one in.

The Day Before...

☐ Make sure all wedding-day items are packed/ laid out and ready to go! (Don't forget the rings and marriage license!)

☐ Figure out tips and final payments for vendors. Put them in clearly marked envelopes and give them to the Best Man or another person you trust to hand out at the reception.

☐ Assign someone to pack up your gifts/ belongings after the reception (don't forget the top tier of your cake!).

☐ Thank your BFF for agreeing to return your groom's tux and other rental items the day after the wedding.

☐ Enjoy a mani-pedi.

☐ Attend the rehearsal and dinner. Now's the time to give out wedding party gifts.

☐ Try to go to bed early...you need your beauty sleep tonight.

Wedding-day advice

☐ Allow plenty of time to get ready.

☐ Do the rounds at your wedding—greet everyone and thank them for coming.

☐ Take a deep breath. Stop to appreciate your new spouse and the day that you spent so much time planning!

After the Honeymoon/Back to Reality...

☐ Write and send thank-you cards. (Don't procrastinate!)

☐ Complete your registry and exchange any unwanted or duplicate gifts.

☐ Have your wedding dress cleaned and preserved by a reputable company.

☐ Keep in touch with your Photographer/ Videographer to work on albums, DVDs, etc.

☐ Enjoy wedded bliss...

Questions to Ask a Wedding Venue

Here Comes The Guide is a fantastic resource to help you find the location to host your wedding, rehearsal dinner or company party. Even with all the info we provide, though, you'll need to address your specific needs with each venue you visit to come up with a winner.

The following list of questions and tips will help you navigate through your location search (for a printable version, go to HereComesTheGuide.com). Use them as a guide while you're talking with a site contact or reviewing a site information packet. Feel free to add questions that relate to your particular event (e.g. "Can my dog be the ring bearer in my ceremony?") Make sure to get everything in writing in your final contract!
Don't forget to have a notebook, digital device or your planning binder handy so that you can record answers to all these questions.

1. What dates are available in the month I'm considering?

2. How many people can this location accommodate?

3. What is the rental fee and what is included in that price? Is there a discount for booking an off-season date or Sunday through Friday?

4. How much is the deposit, when is it due, and is it refundable? What's the payment plan for the entire bill?

5. Can I hold my ceremony here, too? Is there an additional charge? Is the ceremony site close to the reception site? Are there changing areas for the bride and groom? How much time is allocated for the rehearsal?

6. Is the site handicap accessible? (To be asked if you have guests with mobility issues.)

7. What's the cancellation policy? *NOTE: Some places will refund most of your deposit if you cancel far enough in advance, since there's still a chance they can rent the space. After a certain date, though, you may not be able to get a refund—at least not a full one.*

8. What's your weather contingency plan for outdoor spaces?

9. How long will I have use of the event space(s) I reserve? Is there an overtime fee if I stay longer? Is there a minimum or maximum rental time?

10. Can I move things around and decorate to suit my purposes, or do I have to leave everything as is? Are there decoration guidelines/restrictions? Can I use real candles? *TIP: Keep the existing décor in mind when planning your own decorations so that they won't clash. If your event is in December, ask what the venue's holiday décor will be.*

11. What time can my vendors start setting up on the day of the wedding? Is it possible to start the setup the day before? How early can deliveries be made? How much time will I have for décor setup? Does the venue provide assistance getting

gifts or décor back to a designated car, hotel room, etc. after the event has concluded?

12. Do you provide a coat check service (especially important for winter weddings)? If not, is there an area that can be used and staffed for that purpose?

13. Is there an outdoor space where my guests can mingle, and can it be heated and/or protected from the elements if necessary? Is there a separate indoor "socializing" space?

14. Do you have an in-house caterer or a list of "preferred" caterers, or do I need to provide my own? Even if there is an in-house caterer, do I have the option of using an outside caterer instead?

15. If I hire my own caterer, are kitchen facilities available for them? *NOTE: Caterers charge extra if they have to haul in refrigerators and stoves.*

16. Are tables, linens, chairs, plates, silverware and glassware provided, or will I have to rent them myself or get them through my caterer?

17. What is the food & beverage cost on a per-person basis? What is the tax and service charge?

18. Can we do a food tasting prior to finalizing our menu selection? If so, is there an additional charge?

19. Can I bring in a cake from an outside cake maker or must I use a cake made on the premises? Is there a cake-cutting fee? If I use a cake made on site is the fee waived? Do you provide special cake-cutting utensils?

20. Can I bring my own wine, beer or champagne, and is there a corkage fee if I do? Can I bring in other alcohol?

21. Are you licensed to provide alcohol service? If so, is alcohol priced per person? By consumption? Are there additional charges for bar staff? Is there a bar minimum that must be met before the conclusion of the event? What is the average bar tab for the number of people attending my event? *NOTE: Some facilities (private estates and wineries in particular) aren't licensed to serve hard*

alcohol. You may need to get permission from the location to bring in an outside beverage catering company.

22. Are there restrictions on what kind of music I can play, or a time by which the music must end? Can the venue accommodate a DJ or live band? *TIP: Check where the outlets are located in your event space, because that will help you figure out where the band can set up and where other vendors can hook up their equipment. You don't want the head table to block the only outlet in the room.*

23. Is there parking on site? If so, is it complimentary? Do you offer valet parking, and what is the charge? If there is no parking on site, where will my guests park? Are cabs easily accessible from the venue? ? If a shuttle service is needed, can you assist with setting it up? *TIP: You should have the venue keep track of the number of cars parked for your event and add the total valet gratuity to your final bill so that your guests won't have to tip.*

24. How many restrooms are there? *TIP: You should have at least 4 restrooms per 100 people.*

25. Do you offer on-site coordination? If so, what services are included and is there an additional charge for them? Will the coordinator supervise day-of? How much assistance can I get with the setup/décor?

26. What security services do you offer? Do I need to hire my own security guards, or does the site hire them or have them on staff? *TIP: In general, you should have 2 security guards for the first 100 guests and 1 more for every additional 100 guests.*

27. Does the venue have liability insurance? *NOTE: If someone gets injured during the party, you don't want to be held responsible—if the site doesn't have insurance, you'll need to get your own. For info on insurance go to page 16.*

28. Can I hire my own vendors (caterer, coordinator, DJ, etc.), or must I select from a preferred vendor list? If I can bring my own, do you have a list of recommended vendors? *TIP: Check out the prescreened vendors featured on HereComes-TheGuide.com. They're all top event professionals who have passed our extensive "Certified By The Guide" reference check.*

29. What overnight accommodations do you provide? Do you offer a discount for booking multiple rooms? Do you provide a complimentary room or upgrade for the newlyweds? What are the nearest hotels to the venue? *TIP: Some venues have partnerships with local hotels that offer a discount if you book a block of rooms.*

30. Do you have signage or other aids to direct guests to my event?

31. Do you have a recycling policy?

More Tips:

- If you really love the site, ask the venue representative to put together a proposal with all the pricing and policies—including the tax and service charge—so you have an idea of the basic cost.

- Use your cell phone (or a digital camera) to take photos or videos of the locations you visit, so that you have a record of what you liked or didn't like about them. And if you're planning to visit more than a few venues, it's a good idea to snap a photo of each one's sign when you arrive—that way you won't get confused about which place is which when you review your photos later.

- Pay attention to the venue as a whole: Check out everything, including the restrooms, the foyer, the dressing rooms, the outdoor lighting and even the kitchen. You want to be sure your vision can be realized at this location. If possible, make arrangements with the site representative to visit the venue when it's set up for a wedding.

- GET EVERYTHING IN WRITING. Your date is not officially reserved until you sign a contract and, in many cases, give a deposit—even if a site contact says you don't need to worry about it. Once you've found THE PLACE, make sure you ask what is required to get your booking locked in and then follow through on satisfying those requirements. And don't assume that just because the site coordinator said you can have 4 votive candles per table you'll get them. Before you sign a contract, read the fine print and make sure it includes everything you and the site contact agreed on. As new things are added or changed in your contract, have the updated version printed out and signed by you and the site representative. Also, document all your conversations in emails and keep your correspondence.

For PDF versions of these QUESTIONS TO ASK, visit www.HereComesTheGuide.com

Questions to Ask a Wedding Photographer

You've put so much time and effort into planning your wedding you'll want every special moment captured for your photo album. But how do you know which photographer is right for you? Whether you're considering any of our *Certified By The Guide* wedding photographers or another professional, you need to do your homework.

Here are the questions you should ask those photographers who've made your short list, to ensure that the one you ultimately choose is a good fit for you and your wedding.

The Basics

1. Do you have my date available? *NOTE: Obviously, if the answer is NO and you're not willing or able to change your date, don't bother asking the rest of these questions.*

2. How far in advance do I need to book with you?

3. How long have you been in business?

4. How many weddings have you shot? Have you done many that were similar to mine in size and style?

5. How would you describe your photography style (e.g. traditional, photojournalistic, creative)? *NOTE: It's helpful to know the differences between wedding photography styles so that you can discuss your preferences with your photographer. For descriptions of the various styles, see the next page.*

6. How would you describe your working style? *NOTE: The answer should help you determine whether this is a photographer who blends into the background and shoots what unfolds naturally, or creates a more visible presence by taking charge and choreographing shots.*

7. What do you think distinguishes your work from that of other photographers?

8. Do you have a portfolio I can review? Are all of the images yours, and is the work recent?

9. What type of equipment do you use?

10. Are you shooting in digital or film format or both? *NOTE: The general consensus seems to be that either format yields excellent photos in the hands of an experienced professional, and that most people can't tell the difference between film and digital images anyway. However, film takes longer to process than digital.*

11. Do you shoot in color and black & white? Infrared? *NOTE: Photographers who shoot in a digital format can make black & white or sepia versions of color photos.*

12. Can I give you a list of specific shots we would like?

13. Can you put together a slideshow of the engagement session (along with other photos the couple provides) and show it during the cocktail hour? What about an "instant" slideshow of the ceremony?

14. What information do you need from me before the wedding day?

15. Have you ever worked with my florist? DJ? Coordinator, etc.? *NOTE: Great working relationships between vendors can make things go more smoothly. It's especially helpful if your videographer and photographer work well together.*

16. May I have a list of references? *NOTE: The photographer should not hesitate to provide this.*

The Shoot

17. Are you the photographer who will shoot my wedding? If so, will you have any assistants with you on that day? If not, who will be taking the pictures and can I meet them before my wedding? *NOTE: You should ask the questions on this list of whoever is going to be the primary photographer at your event, and that photographer's name should be on your contract.*

18. Do you have backup equipment? What about a backup plan if you (or my scheduled photographer) are unable to shoot my wedding for some reason?

19. If my wedding site is out of your area, do you charge a travel fee and what does that cover?

20. Are you photographing other events on the same day as mine?

21. How will you (and your assistants) be dressed? *NOTE: The photographer and his/her staff should look professional and fit in with the style of your event.*

22. Is it okay if other people take photos while you're taking photos?

23. Have you ever worked at my wedding site before? If not, do you plan to check it out in advance? *NOTE: Photographers who familiarize themselves with a location ahead of time will be prepared for any lighting issues or restrictions, and will know how best to incorporate the site's architectural elements into the photos.*

24. What time will you arrive at the site and for how long will you shoot?

25. If my event lasts longer than expected, will you stay? Is there an additional charge?

Packages, Proofs and Prints

26. What packages do you offer?

27. Can I customize a package based on my needs?

28. Do you include engagement photos in your packages?

29. What type of album designs do you offer? Do you provide any assistance in creating an album?

30. Do you provide retouching, color adjustment or other corrective services?

31. How long after the wedding will I get the proofs? Will they be viewable online?

32. What is the ordering process?

33. How long after I order my photos/album will I get them?

34. Will you give me the negatives or the digital images, and is there a fee for that?

Contracts and Policies

35. When will I receive a written contract? *TIP: Don't book a photographer—or any vendor—who won't provide a written contract.*

36. How much of a deposit do you require and when is it due? Do you offer a payment plan?

37. What is your refund/cancellation policy?

38. Do you have liability insurance?

Questions to Ask Yourself:

1. Do I feel a connection with this photographer as well as his/her photos? Are our personalities a good match?

2. Am I comfortable with this person's work and communication style?

3. Has this photographer listened well and addressed all my concerns?

Check references. *Ask the photographer for at least 5 references, preferably of couples whose weddings were similar to yours in size and/or style. Getting feedback from several people who have actually hired the photographer in question can really help you decide if that person is right for you. Be sure to check out the photographers on HereComesTheGuide.com. They're some of the best in the business and have all been Certified By The Guide.*

Photography Style Glossary

Though there are no standard "dictionary definitions" of photographic styles, it's still a good idea to have an understanding of the following approaches before you interview photographers:

Traditional, Classic: The main idea behind this timeless style is to produce posed photographs for display in a portrait album. The photographer works from a "shot list," ensuring he or she covers all the elements the bride and groom have requested. To make sure every detail of the shots is perfect, the photographer and his/her assistants not only adjust their equipment, but also the background, the subject's body alignment, and even the attire.

Photojournalism: Originally favored by the news media, this informal, reality-based approach is the current rage in wedding photography. Rather than posing your pictures, the photographer follows you and your guests throughout the wedding day, capturing events as they unfold to tell the story of your wedding. He or she has to be able to fade into the background and become "invisible" in order to snap these candid or unposed photos, and must also possess a keen eye and a willingness to do what it takes to get the shot.

Illustrative Photography: This style, which is often used for engagement photos, is a pleasing blend of traditional and photojournalistic, with an emphasis on composition, lighting and background. The photographer places subjects together in an interesting environment and encourages them to relax and interact. Illustrative captures some of the spontaneity of candids, while offering the technical control of posed shots.

Portraiture: Traditional photographers generally excel at the precision required in portraiture—formal, posed pictures that emphasize one or more people. Couples interested in a more edgy result may prefer Fine Art Portraiture, with its dramatic lighting, unique angles and European flavor.

High Fashion: Commercial photographers excel at creating striking, simple photographs that dramatize the subject—and, of course, her clothes! Though not a style generally included in wedding photography, you may want to choose a photographer with high fashion experience if looking artsy and glamorous while showing off your dress is important to you.

Natural Light: Rather than using a camera flash, photographers use the natural light found in a setting, usually daylight. The look is warm and, well, natural—yet the photographer must be skilled to deal with shadows and other lighting challenges.

Questions to Ask a Wedding Planner

In the first flush of joy after your engagement, you probably began browsing wedding websites, social media sites like Pinterest, and magazines. If you soon felt buried by a blizzard of checklists and a daunting array of decisions, you and your fiancé might want to think about hiring a professional wedding planner.

Depending on your budget and needs, you can contract:

- a full-service planner to arrange every detail

- someone to assist you only in choosing your wedding location and vendors

- a day-of coordinator (which really means 30 days before your wedding)

NOTE: Many locations have in-house coordinators, but make sure you're clear on exactly what level of service they provide. Venue coordinators usually just handle day-of issues and offer a list of their preferred vendors, so having your own planner may still be a great help.

Even though hiring a planner is an added cost, they often end up saving you money in the long run. And no doubt about it—the right wedding planner can definitely save you time and stress (priceless!).

Before interviewing potential wedding planners, you and your fiancé should have an idea of:

- How much money you have in your budget

- How many people you would like to invite

- Your preferred wedding date

- Your vision for your wedding *(NOTE: If you aren't sure yet don't worry—getting help with this is one of the reasons why you're hiring a wedding planner!)*

After each interview is complete, ask yourselves:

- Did we feel heard?

- Does the planner understand our vision?

- Did we get a strong sense he/she will work with our budget?

- Was there a good connection and did our personalities mesh well?

Listen to your gut. If an interview doesn't feel right, then maybe that person just isn't a good fit for you. Your wedding planner is the vendor you'll be spending the most time with, so it's important to pick someone who's compatible with you and your fiancé.

Now, here are THE QUESTIONS!

Getting to Know a Planner

1. Do you have our wedding date open? If so, do you anticipate any issues with the date such as weather, travel for our guests, difficulty booking a venue, etc.?

2. What made you want to be a wedding planner?

3. Describe the most challenging wedding you planned and how you handled the problems that came up.

4. How would you rate your problem-solving skills?

5. How would you rate your communication skills?

6. Are you a certified wedding planner? If so, where did you get certified? What is your educational background?

7. Are you a member of any wedding association(s)? If so, does your association require you to satisfy yearly education requirements?

8. How long have you been in business? Do you have a business license?

9. How many full-scale weddings have you planned? When was your last one?

10. How many wedding clients do you take on in a year? How many do you expect to have during the month of our wedding?

11. Is wedding planning your full-time job? If it's part-time, what is your other job?

Working With the Venue

12. Have you ever worked at the venue we've chosen?

13. If our event is outdoors, what contingency plan would you have for bad weather? (Describe an event where you had weather issues and how you resolved them.)

Hiring Other Vendors

14. Are we required to book only the vendors you recommend or do we have the freedom to hire someone even if you haven't worked with them before?

15. Do you take a commission or discount from any of the vendors you would refer us to?

16. Will you be present at all of the vendor meetings and will you assist us in reviewing all of the vendor contracts and making sure everything is in order?

17. Will you invoice us for all the vendor fees or will we need to pay each one of them ourselves?

18. For the vendors who will be on site the day of our wedding, can I provide you with checks for final payment that you will distribute to them?

19. If issues arise with the vendors before, during or after our wedding, will you handle them or are we responsible for this?

Scope of Work

20. What kind planning do you offer? Logistical only (i.e. organizational—handling things like the timeline and floor plan) or Design and Logistical (i.e. bringing a client's vision to life as well as taking care of all the organizational aspects of the wedding)?

21. If you just do logistical planning, can you refer us to a vendor who can assist us with event design? *(NOTE: Floral designers often do full event design, as do vendors who specialize in design.)*

22. Will you handle every aspect of the planning or can we do some things on our own? In other words, what parts of the planning will we be responsible for?

23. Will you be the person on site the day of our wedding or will it be another planner? How many assistants will you have?

24. In case of an emergency that prevents you from being at our wedding, who will be the backup planner? What are their qualifications?

25. What time will you arrive and depart on the day of our wedding?

26. Will you stay on site after our wedding to make sure everything has been broken down and all vendors have left the location?

27. Will you provide us with a timeline of the wedding and a floor plan of the wedding venue?

28. Do you offer different package options or is everything customized based on what we're looking for?

29. How many meetings and phone calls are included in our package?

30. Is the wedding day rehearsal included in your services?

31. Do any of your packages include planning the rehearsal dinner and/or post-wedding brunch? If not, would you provide that service and what would be the extra cost to include it in our contract?

32. Do any of your packages include honeymoon planning? If not, would you provide that service and what would be the extra cost to include it in our contract?

33. Do any of your packages include assistance with finding my wedding dress and wedding party attire? If not, would you provide that service and what would be the extra cost to include it in our contract?

Getting Down to Business

34. Once we book with you, how quickly can we expect to receive the contract?

35. After we give you our budget, will you provide us with a breakdown of how the money is going to be allocated?

36. As changes are made to our plans, will you update us with a revised estimate and updated contract?

37. How do you charge for your services? Hourly, percentage of the wedding cost, or flat rate?

38. Can you provide a detailed list of all the items included in your fee?

39. What is your payment policy? Do you accept credit cards?

40. How much of a deposit is required to book your services? When is the final payment due?

41. Are there any fees that won't be included in your proposal that we should be aware of?

42. What is your refund or cancellation policy?

43. Can you provide a list of references? *NOTE: Any experienced coordinator should be able to give you plenty of references. For a list of Coordinators/ Wedding Planners you can trust, see the ones we've featured on HereComesTheGuide.com. They've all passed our difficult certification process with flying colors! Brides and grooms told us how much they loved working with them, so we wanted to recommend them to you.*

44. Can you provide us with a portfolio and/or video of weddings you have done?

Questions to Ask a Caterer

Besides your location, the food and drink for your wedding bash will probably consume the largest portion of your wedding budget. Catering costs are usually presented as "per-person" charges, sometimes abbreviated in wedding brochures as "pp" after the amount. But be aware—the per-person charge often doesn't include everything: Tax and the gratuity (sometimes called the "service charge") might be extra, and there may also be separate per-person charges for the meal, drinks, hors d'oeuvres, and even setup. So your actual per-person charge might end up being considerably more than you expect. Bring your calculator along when meeting with potential caterers to help you arrive at the real bottom line.

There's more to consider. Nowadays, many caterers offer a range of services in addition to catering. Some are actual "event producers," providing props, special effects, décor—in other words, complete event design. They might also be able to assist in finding a location, coordinating your affair, or lining up vendors. One thing a caterer can't do, however, is cook up a 5-course Beef Wellington dinner for $20 per person. When planning your menu, be realistic about what you can serve given your budget and the size of your guest list.

A lot of factors come into play when selecting a caterer, so don't be afraid to ask as many questions as you need to. You can refer to the following list, whether your potential caterer works at your event facility or you're hiring them independently.

The Basics

1. Do you have my date open?

2. How many weddings do you do per year, and how long have you been in business?

3. Have you done events at my location? *TIP: If you haven't chosen your location yet, ask the caterer if they can help you select one.*

4. Are you licensed by the state of California? Are you licensed to serve alcohol?

5. Will I need any permits for my event? If so, will you handle obtaining them?

6. Will you provide a banquet manager to coordinate the meal service or an on-site coordinator who will run the entire event?

7. Can you assist with other aspects of the wedding like selecting other vendors, event design (e.g. specialty lighting, elaborate décor, theme events, etc.)?

Food & Presentation

8. Given my budget, guest count and event style, what food choices would you recommend? Do you specialize in certain cuisines?

9. Do we have to work off a preset menu or can you create a custom menu for our event? If I have a special dish I'd like served, would you accommodate that?

10. Do you offer event packages or is everything à la carte? What exactly do your packages include?

11. Do you use all fresh produce, meat, fish, etc.? Can you source organic or sustainably farmed ingredients?

12. Can you accommodate dietary restrictions, such as kosher, vegan, etc.?

13. What décor do you provide for appetizer stations or buffet tables?

14. Do you offer package upgrades such as chocolate fountains, ice sculptures, espresso machines or specialty displays?

15. Can you do theme menus (e.g. barbecue, luau, etc.)? Would you also provide the décor?

16. What's the difference in cost between passed appetizers and appetizer stations? What's the price difference between a buffet and a sit-down meal? If we have a buffet, are there any stations that cost extra, like a carving station? *NOTE: Don't automatically assume that a buffet is going to be the less expensive option. Ask your caterer which type of service is more affordable for you, given the menu you're planning.*

17. How much do you charge for children's meals?

18. How much do you charge for vendor meals?

19. Do you do wedding cakes? If so, is this included in the per-person meal price or is it extra?

20. Can you show me photos of cakes you've done in the past?

21. If I decide not to serve cake, can you provide a dessert display instead?

22. If we use an outside cake designer, do you charge a cake-cutting fee?

23. Do you do food tastings and is there an extra charge for this?

24. Do you handle rental equipment such as tables, chairs, etc.?

25. What types of linens, glassware, plates and flatware do you provide? *NOTE: Some low-budget caterers have basic packages that use disposable dinnerware instead of the real thing, so make sure you know exactly what you'll be getting.*

26. Can you provide presentation upgrades such as chair covers, lounge furniture, Chiavari chairs, etc.? What would be the additional fees?

27. What is your policy on cleanup? *TIP: Be very clear about what "cleanup" means and who's responsible for handling it—and be sure to get it in writing. We've heard many tales about caterers that left dirty dishes, trash and uneaten food behind. In most cases, when you rent a location it will be YOUR responsibility to leave the place in acceptable condition. You want to spend your wedding night with your honey, not picking up empty bottles from the lawn!*

28. If there is leftover food from my event, can we have it wrapped up for guests to take home or have it delivered to a local shelter?

Drink

29. Do you provide alcoholic beverages and bartenders? Can you accommodate specialty cocktails?

30. What brands of alcohol will be served?

31. Can we provide the alcohol and you provide the bar labor?

32. Do you charge a corkage fee if we provide our own wine or champagne?

33. How do you charge for alcoholic and non-alcoholic beverages? Per consumption or per person? Which is more cost-effective?

34. Is the champagne toast after the ceremony included in your meal packages or is it extra?

35. Will your staff serve the wine with dinner?

36. How long will alcohol be served?

37. Is coffee and tea service included with the per-person meal charge? What brands of each do you offer and do they include decaf and herbal tea options?

Business Matters

38. What is the ratio of servers to guests?

39. How will the servers be dressed?

40. How is your pricing broken down (e.g. food, bar, cake-cutting, tax, gratuity)? *NOTE: Usually tax and a service charge are tacked on to your final cost. The service charge, which can range 18–23%, is used to tip the staff. And in many states, the service charge itself is taxable.*

41. How much time do you require for setting up and breaking down my event, and are there extra fees for this?

42. If my event runs longer than contracted, what are your overtime fees?

43. What is the last date by which I can give you a final guaranteed guest count?

44. What is your payment policy? Do you accept credit cards?

45. How much of a deposit is required to hold my date? When is the final payment due?

46. Are there any fees that won't be included in the proposal that we should be aware of?

47. Once we book with you, how quickly can we expect a contract? And if we make changes to menu choices or other items, will you update us with a revised estimate and contract?

48. What is your refund or cancellation policy?

49. Can you provide a list of recent references? *TIP: See the caterers we feature on HereComesTheGuide. com. These pre-screened companies provide great food and service, and they all passed our rigorous certification process with flying colors.*

Questions to Ask a Floral Designer

Floral designers do much more than just supply the bouquet! They help create the look and mood for your wedding ceremony, as well as centerpieces and other table decorations for the reception. They add the floral flourishes for the wedding party (don't forget that corsage for Grandma!), and some may even work with your cake designer to provide embellishments.

Before sitting down with a floral designer, you should already have reserved your ceremony and reception venue. That way you'll be able to discuss how much additional floral décor will be needed to either achieve a specific look at your site or complement an existing garden and/or room aesthetic.

Another must: Don't design the wedding bouquet until you've ordered your wedding dress. Since that task will hopefully be completed at least 6 months before your wedding date (hint, hint!), you should have plenty of time to work out the details of both your accessories and floral décor.

So where to start? Do a little research prior to interviewing floral artists by visiting the websites or shops of vendors you're considering. You want to know that whomever you hire can create bouquets and arrangements that suit your style. And do explore our "Brides Want to Know: Bouquet Brainstorm" article on HereComesTheGuide.com for more GUIDElines and inspiration.)

Once you've compiled your short list of contenders, use these questions to zero in on your final choice:

The Basics

1. Do you have my date open?

2. Have you done events at my ceremony and reception location(s) before? If not, are you familiar with the sites?

3. How long have you been in business?

4. How many weddings have you done?

5. Where did you receive your training?

6. How many other weddings or events will you schedule on the same day?

7. Will you be doing my arrangements yourself or would it be another floral designer?

8. What design styles (e.g. ikebana, traditional, modern, trendy, European, Oriental) do you work in?

9. Can you work with my budget?

10. What recommendations can you give me to maximize my budget?

11. Do you offer specific packages or is everything customized?

12. Can you provide me with 3–4 recent brides that I can contact for references?

The Flowers

13. What flowers are in season for the month I am getting married?

14. Based on my color scheme and budget, what flowers do you recommend?

15. Is there a difference in price if I use one type of flower vs. a mixed arrangement or bouquet?

16. If I request it, can you provide any organic, pesticide-free or sustainably grown varieties? *TIP: Organic roses cost more, but last so much longer!*

17. What are the different kinds of wraps (called "collars" in florist-speak) you can do for my bouquet?

18. What about coordinating boutonnières, bridesmaid flowers, and centerpieces? Can you suggest anything special to coordinate with the theme/venue/season of my event?

19. What other décor can you provide (aisle runner, candelabras, trees, arches, votives, mirrors, etc.)? How will these items affect the overall cost?

20. If I give you a picture of a bouquet and/or arrangement that I like, can you recreate it?

21. Do you have photos or live examples of florals designed in the style I want?

22. Can you do sketches or mockups of the arrangements you've described before I sign the contract? If so, is there an additional fee for this?

23. Will you work with my cake designer if I decide to add flowers to my wedding cake? If so, is there an additional setup fee for this?

24. How far in advance of the wedding will you create the bouquets and arrangements, and how are they stored?

25. Can you assist me in the preservation of my bouquet after the wedding? If not, can you recommend someone?

The Costs

26. Do you charge a delivery fee?

27. Do you have an extra charge for the setup and breakdown of the floral décor?

28. Is there an extra fee if I need you to stay throughout the ceremony to move arrangements to the reception site?

29. Are there any additional fees that have not already been taken into account?

The Contract

30. How far in advance do I need to secure your services? What is the deposit required to secure my date?

31. Will you provide me with an itemized list of all the elements we've discussed, along with prices?

32. When can I expect to receive my contract from you?

33. What is your refund policy if for some reason I need to cancel my order?

Useful Tips:

• Prior to meeting with potential floral designers: have your color scheme finalized; create a list of the kinds of flowers you like; and have some examples (pictures from magazines, the web, etc.) of the kind of bouquets and arrangements that appeal to you.

• After you've met with each floral designer ask yourself, "Did the florist answer all my questions to my satisfaction?" "Do I feel like the florist really listened and understood my vision?" "Am I comfortable with this person?"

• Once you've booked your floral designer you'll want to provide them with a picture of your dress and swatches or photos of the bridesmaids dresses and the linens you'll be using.

Don't forget to browse our Floral Designers on HereComesTheGuide.com! They all got rave reviews during our rigorous certification process, and received the Certified By The Guide seal of approval.

For PDF versions of these QUESTIONS TO ASK, visit www.HereComesTheGuide.com

Questions to Ask a Cake Designer

Next to your dress, the cake is probably a wedding's most important icon. And whether you want a traditional multi-tiered confection, a miniature Statue of Liberty (hey, that's where he proposed!) or a cupcake tower, your wedding cake should reflect your personality. Use the following questions as a guide when evaluating a potential cake designer. If you're not familiar with cake terms, please see the cake glossary on page 37.

Business Matters

1. Do you have my wedding date open?

2. How many wedding cakes do you schedule on the same day? *NOTE: You want to feel comfortable that your designer is sufficiently staffed to handle the number of cakes they've scheduled to deliver and set up on your date.*

3. How do you price your cakes? By the slice? Does the cost vary depending on the design and flavors I choose?

4. What is your minimum per-person cake cost?

5. What recommendations can you give me to maximize my budget?

6. Do you have a "menu" of cakes and prices that I can take with me?

7. What are the fees for delivery and setup of the cake? Do you decorate the cake table, too?

8. What do you do if the cake gets damaged in transit to or at my reception site?

9. Do you provide or rent cake toppers, a cake-cutting knife, cake stands, etc.? What are the fees?

10. How far in advance should I order my cake?

11. How much is the deposit and when is it due?

12. When is the final payment due?

13. Are there any additional fees that I should be aware of?

14. What is your refund policy if for some reason I need to cancel my order? What if I'm not happy with the cake?

15. When can I expect to receive my contract from you?

Background Check

16. How long have you been in business? Are you licensed and insured?

17. How many weddings have you done?

18. Where did you receive your training?

19. Can you provide me with 3–4 recent wedding clients that I can contact for references? *TIP: Check out the cake vendors featured on* HereComesTheGuide.com. *They're some of the best cake designers in Southern California and they've all been Certified By The Guide.*

The Cake

20. Do you have a portfolio of your work I can view, and did you make all the cakes in it?

21. What are your specialties?

22. Can you design a custom cake to match my theme, dress or color scheme, or do I select from set designs?

23. If I provide you with a picture of what I'd like, can you recreate it? Does it cost extra for a custom design?

24. I have an old family cake recipe. Can you adapt it for my wedding cake?

25. If I don't have a clear vision of what I would like, can you offer some design ideas based on my theme and budget?

26. What flavors and fillings do you offer?

27. What are the different ingredients you typically use? Do you offer all organic or vegan options? *TIP: Quality ingredients cost more, but the investment is worth it—the cake will taste better.*

28. Do you have cake tastings? Is there a charge?

29. Do you do both fondant and buttercream icing?

30. Are there any other icing options I should consider? Which do you recommend for my cake design?

31. Can you create sugar paste, gum paste or chocolate flowers? If I decide to have fresh flowers on my cake will you work with my florist or will you obtain and arrange the flowers yourself?

32. Will you preserve the top tier of my cake for my first wedding anniversary or do you provide a special cake for the occasion?

33. Can you make a groom's cake? Is this priced the same as my wedding cake?

34. How much in advance of the wedding is the cake actually made? Do you freeze your cakes? *NOTE: Wedding cakes usually take at least a couple of days to make.*

Useful Tips:

- Arrange a consultation with your potential cake designer in person, and do a tasting before you sign a contract. *NOTE: Not all cake tastings are complimentary.*

- Make sure your cake designer specializes in wedding cakes. A wedding cake is generally much more elaborate than a birthday cake from your local bakery. Your cake professional should have special training in constructing this type of cake.

- In general, you should order your cake 6–8 months prior to your wedding.

- You might be able to save money by choosing one overall flavor for your cake, or by having a small cake for display and the cake cutting accompanied by a sheet cake to serve to your guests. Some cake designers may even offer a "dummy" or fake cake layer (usually made from styrofoam) to add an extra tier (or more) to your cake without too much extra expense. Talk to your cake designer to see how you can get the most bang for your wedding cake buck.

Wedding Cake Glossary

Icings

Buttercream: It's rich and creamy, is easily colored or flavored, and is used for fancy decorations like shells, swags, basketweaves, icing flowers, etc. Since it's made almost entirely of butter (hence the name), buttercream has a tendency to melt in extreme heat, so it's not recommended for outdoor weddings.

Fondant: Martha Stewart's favorite. This icing looks smooth and stiff and is made with gelatin and corn syrup to give it its helmet-like appearance (it's really very cool looking). It looks best when decorated with marzipan fruits, gum paste flowers, or a simple ribbon, like Martha likes to do. Although not as tasty as buttercream or ganache, fondant does not need refrigeration so it's the perfect icing to serve at your beach wedding.

Royal Icing: A mix of confectioner's sugar and milk or egg whites, royal icing is what the faces of gingerbread men are decorated with. It's white, shiny and hard, and does not need to be refrigerated. It's used for decorations like dots and latticework.

Ganache: This chocolate and heavy cream combination is very dark, and has the consistency of store-bought chocolate icing. It can be poured over cakes for a glass-like chocolate finish or used as filling (it stands up wonderfully between cake layers). Due to the ingredients, however, it's unstable—don't use it in hot or humid weather or the icing will slide right off the cake.

Whipped Cream: Delicious, but by far the most volatile, fresh whipped cream is usually not recommended for wedding cakes because they have to be out of the fridge for so long. If you really want to use it (it looks extremely white and fresh, which goes beautifully with real flowers) just keep it in the fridge until the very last second.

Decorations

Marzipan: An Italian paste made of almonds, sugar and egg whites that is molded into flowers and fruits to decorate the cake. They're usually brightly colored and very sugary. Marzipan can also be used as icing.

Gum Paste: This paste, made from gelatin, cornstarch, and sugar, produces the world's most realistic, edible fruit and flower decorations. Famous cake designers like Sylvia Weinstock are huge fans of gum paste. One nice benefit: these decorations last for centuries in storage.

Piping: Piping is ideal for icing decorations like dotted Swiss, basketweave, latticework, and shells. It comes out of a pastry bag fitted with different tips to create these different looks, which can range from simple polka dots to a layered weave that you'd swear is a wicker basket.

Pulled Sugar: If you boil sugar, water, and corn syrup it becomes malleable and the most beautiful designs can be created. Roses and bows that have been made from pulled sugar look like silk or satin—they're so smooth and shiny.

Dragees: These hard little sugar balls are painted with edible gold or silver paint, and they look truly stunning on a big ol' wedding cake.

Questions to Ask a DJ or Live Entertainment

Too often choosing the entertainment is left to the end of your overwhelming "Wedding To-Do List"—but it shouldn't be. Not only does music set the appropriate mood, but a skilled Master or Mistress of Ceremonies will gracefully guide your guests from one spotlight moment to another. And practically speaking, the best performers are often booked well in advance—so shake your groove thing, or you may be stuck doing the chicken dance with Uncle Edgar.

To get you started, we've put together this list of questions that will help you evaluate a DJ, band, or other entertainer. Note that rather than interviewing a specific performer or DJ yourself, you might be dealing with an entertainment agency rep.

The Basics

1. Do you have my date open?

2. Have you done events at my ceremony and/or reception location before? If not, are you familiar with them?

3. How long have you been in business? *NOTE: If you are interviewing a live band, you'll want to ask how long the musicians have played together. However, if you work with a reputable agency, instead of booking a specific band you'll most likely be getting seasoned professionals brought together for your event. Even though all the band members may not have played together before, they're professional musicians who are able to work together and sound fantastic anyway. The key is to make sure you book the specific singer and/or bandleader that you liked in the demo. The players will take their cues from them.*

4. How many weddings have you done? How many do you do in an average weekend?

5. What sets you apart from your competition?

6. Are there any other services that you provide, such as lighting design?

7. How far in advance do I need to secure your services?

8. Can you provide me with 3–4 recent wedding clients that I can contact for references?

Pricing and Other Business Details

9. What is your pricing? Does this include setup and breakdown between ceremony and reception locations?

10. How much is the deposit and when is it due? When is the final payment due?

11. If the event lasts longer than scheduled, what are the overtime charges?

12. What is the continuous music charge? *NOTE: For bands, bookings traditionally run for 4 hours divided into 4 sets, each lasting 45 minutes with a 15-minute break. If you want "continuous music," i.e. with band members trading breaks, there is usually an additional charge.*

13. When can I expect to receive my contract from you?

14. Are there any additional fees that could accrue that I am not taking into account, like travel expenses or charges for special musical requests? (One performer was asked to prepare an entire set of songs from *Phantom of the Opera!* Yes, he charged extra.)

15. What is your refund policy if for some reason I need to cancel or alter my date?

16. Do you carry liability insurance? *NOTE: This usually only applies to production companies that also supply lighting, effects, etc.*

17. If I hire musicians for the ceremony and want them to play at the wedding rehearsal, what is the extra charge?

The Music

18. Do you have a DVD of your music or a video link to a prior wedding where you performed?

19. Can you assist me in choosing the music for my processional, recessional, father-daughter dance, etc.?

20. How extensive is your music library or song list? What genres can you cover? Can I give you a specific list of songs I want or don't want played?

21. Are we guaranteed to have the performer(s) of our choice at our event? *SEE NUMBER 3 ABOVE. As mentioned, many bands hired by an agency are made up of members who may not play together regularly. Even set bands often have substitute players. If there are specific performers (singer, harpist, guitarist, etc.) that you want, make sure that your contract includes them. Of course, illness or other circumstances may still preclude their being able to perform at your event.*

22. If the DJ or one of the band members scheduled for my event is unable to perform for some reason, do you have a backup replacement ready to go?

23. Can you provide wireless mics for the ceremony?

24. Does any of your equipment require special electrical outlets that I need to inform my wedding site about?

25. Do you bring backup equipment?

26. What kind of space or stage do you require for the DJ or band? If my site doesn't provide what you need, will you make arrangements for the stage or am I responsible for renting it? *NOTE: a band will require a specific amount of square feet per band member.*

27. How much time will you need for setup, sound check and breakdown on the day of the event?

28. What music will be provided during the breaks? *NOTE: If you have a preference, make it known. If you want them to play your own digital music mix, be sure to inquire about system compatibility with your CD, iPod, etc.*

29. How many people will you staff for my event?

Useful Tips:

- Discuss with your site manager any restrictions that might affect your event, like noise limits, a music curfew and availability/load of electrical circuits. Also check with your facility and caterer about where and what to feed the performers.

- All professional entertainers have access to formalwear (if they don't, that's your first clue they're not professionals!) However, it is YOUR responsibility to be specific about how you expect your performers to be dressed. Any extraordinary requests (period costumes, all-white tuxes, etc.) are normally paid for by the client.

- Make notes of your general music preferences before you meet with your DJ, bandleader, etc. For example: "Classical for the ceremony, Rat Pack-era for the cocktail hour and a set of Motown during the reception." Not only will this help you determine which entertainment professionals are a good match for you, it will guide them in preparing your set list. *TIP: The DJs and Entertainers on HereComesTheGuide.com are first-rate. They all got great reviews during our certification process, and we're happy to recommend them.*

Questions to Ask When Ordering Your Wedding Invitations

*Letterpress, thermography, engraved, matte, jacquard, glassine...*ordering invites will mean learning a few new vocabulary words (see page 42). You'll also need to learn about all the components that you might want to include in your invitation, as well as what other printed materials could be part of your wedding scenario. With so many details to consider, you'll depend on a creative wedding invitation professional to clue you in on the jargon, and guide you in choosing invites that reflect your wedding style. After all, nothing sets the tone for an event like an impeccably designed wedding invitation.

This list of questions has been compiled to help ensure that no detail is left unaddressed (no pun intended), whether you're working with a stationery boutique, an online vendor, or a graphic designer.

Getting To Know Your Invitation Professional

1. How long have you been in business?

2. What is your design background? *NOTE: This may or may not involve formal training. Remember, "good taste" isn't necessarily something that can be taught!*

3. What types of printing processes do you offer and which do you specialize in? Which do you recommend for my budget and style?

4. Is your printing done in-house or do you outsource it? *NOTE: Printing is usually less expensive if it's outsourced. However, a possible benefit of in-house printing is a quicker turnaround time, which could come in especially handy if any reprinting (say, due to an error) is required.*

5. Do you offer custom invitations as well as templated styles? Is there a fee if I want to order a sample of either an existing invitation style or a custom design? If so, how much?

6. If I choose a custom wedding invitation, what are my options for color, paper type, ink and fonts? What is the word limit for the text?

7. Can I also order my table numbers, place cards, escort cards, ceremony programs, menus, etc. from you?

8. Do you offer a package or a discounted price if I order all of the invitation components at the same time? (For a complete list of what might be included, see the next page.)

9. If I want to include a picture or graphic on my save-the-date card or invitation, can you accommodate that? If so, does the image need to be saved in a specific format? Do you have photo retouching available, and if so, what is the price range? Can your photo specialist also convert color images to black & white or sepia? Is there an additional cost?

10. Are there any new styles, trends and color combinations I might consider? Which are the most popular? What kinds of handmade or artisanal paper do you offer? *NOTE: The answers to these questions will give you a sense of how creative and up-to-the-minute your invitation professional is.*

11. Can my invitations be printed on recycled paper and/or with soy-based ink?

12. Based on the paper I select and the number of pieces involved, what would it cost to mail my wedding invitation? *NOTE: If you use a non-standard sized envelope, postage may be more expensive.*

Getting Down To Business

13. Once I place my order, how long will it take to have the completed invitations delivered? Do you have rush-order available and what are the extra fees? If you are ordering from an online company, ask: What are the shipping methods available to me, and their respective costs?

14. If the invitation involves multiple pieces, can you assemble them? If so, is there an additional fee? How will the assembly affect my delivery date?

15. Do you offer an invitation addressing service? If so, what is the charge for this? What lettering style options are available? Will the lettering push back my delivery date?

16. When is payment due?

17. I will have an opportunity to sign off on my invitation proof before you send my order to print, right?

18. Once I've signed off on the proof, I expect the printed invitations to match the approved sample. If they don't (i.e. an error was made after I signed off on the proof), will my invitations be corrected and reprinted at no additional cost? How much additional time will it take to redo my order if there is a problem with it?

19. What is your refund policy if for some reason I need to cancel my order?

20. When can I expect to receive my contract from you?

21. Can you provide me with the contact information of 3–4 recent wedding clients who I can call or email for references?

Possible Printed Invitation Components

(Don't panic... most of the extra elements are OPTIONAL!!)

- Save-the-Date Cards

- Wedding Announcement

- Wedding Invitation Components:
  - Outer Envelope
  - Optional Inner Envelope
  - Optional Belly Band
  - Invitation
  - Reception Card, if held at a different location than the ceremony
  - Directions/Map
  - Response Card & SASE (self-addressed stamped envelope)

- Thank-You Cards

- Shower Thank-You Cards

- Other Invites:
  - Engagement Party
  - Shower
  - Bachelor/Bacherlorette Party
  - Rehearsal Dinner
  - After Party

- Wedding Program

- Pew Cards

- Place Cards

- Table Cards

- Menus

- Napkins, Matchbooks or Labels for favors

Useful Tips:

- Ordering your invitations over the phone increases the possibility of mistakes, so order in person if possible. If you order your invitations from an online company, make sure your contract states that they will correct mistakes they make for free.

- Insist on getting a proof. Have at least two other people review all your proofs before you sign off on them—it's amazing what a fresh pair of eyes will see!

- If ordering online, remember that color resolution can vary drastically between computers. The best way to guarantee the exact color you want is to ask that a sample be snail-mailed to you.

- Order 20–30 extra save-the-dates and/or invitations with envelopes in case you have to add to the guest list or you make a mistake when assembling or addressing the envelopes.

- Save-the-date cards should be sent out 6–9 months prior to your wedding.

- Invitations should be sent out 6–8 weeks prior to your wedding.

- Consider working with one stationer or graphic designer for all of your printed materials. He or she will guide you in making sure all of the components convey a consistent design concept. Not that they have to be identical, but as Joyce Scardina Becker observes in *Countdown to Your Perfect Wedding,* "It's like making a fashion statement: All of the accessories in your wardrobe should coordinate and fit together nicely."

- To Evite or not to Evite? For the main event, even we progressives at *Here Comes The Guide* come down on the side of tradition and say go with real paper and snail mail—even if your budget determines that you have to DIY. However, if your overall wedding style is relaxed and casual, then we think Evites are fine for the supporting events, such as your Bachelorette Party. We like Evite's built-in RSVP system and creative style options.

Invitations Glossary

A glossary of common printing terms.

Printing Terms

Letterpress: Letterpress printing dates back to the 14th century, and involves inking the raised surface of metal type or custom-engraved plates and then applying the inked surface against paper with a press. When used with the right paper (thick, softer paper results in a deeper impression), typefaces and colors, letterpress creates an elegant product with a stamped, tactile quality. This process offers lots of options, but can cost more than other methods. Also, photographs and metallic inks generally don't work well with letterpress.

Embossing: Using a metal die, letters and images are pressed into the paper from behind, creating a raised "relief" surface, imparting added dimension to the invitation design. Usually used for large initials or borders. Ink or foil may be applied to the front of the paper so that the raised letters and images are colored.

Blind embossing: No ink or foil is applied, so the embossed (raised) image is the same color as the paper.

Thermography: This popular printing method uses heat to fuse ink and resinous powder, producing raised lettering. Though it looks almost exactly like engraved printing, thermography is much less expensive. This process will not reproduce detail as sharply as engraving will. The powder is added after the ink is applied, generally with an offset press, so the use of paper or metal offset plates affects quality here, too.

Engraving: Engraving is generally the most formal and expensive printing option. The image is etched into a metal plate, and the ink held in the etched grooves is applied to the paper with a press. The resulting raised image is comprised entirely of ink sitting on the surface of the paper. The ink applied is opaque, making it possible to print a lighter colored ink on a darker colored paper. Engraving is not the best printing choice if you have a photo or illustration that requires a screen.

Offset printing: Most printing these days is offset, which means the original image is transferred from a plate to a drum before it is applied to the paper. This process produces print that sits flat on the surface. There are many levels of quality with this method: If your printer uses paper printing plates, the job will cost less but the result may be fuzzy, inconsistent lettering. Metal plates yield much sharper, crisper type.

Digital printing: In this method the computer is linked to the printing press and the image is applied to paper or another material directly from a digital file rather than using film and/or plates. Digital is best for short-run, quick jobs. This can also be a good option if you want to use full color.

Foil stamping: Foil is applied to the front side of the paper, stamped on with a metal die. Foils can be metallic or colored, shiny or dull. They are usually very opaque, and this is a great way to print white on a dark colored paper.

Calligraphy: This is the perfected art of writing by hand. Often associated with fancy, curlicue script, calligraphy can be done in several genres and styles.

Paper Terms

Matte: A paper coating that's flat and non-reflective (no gloss).

Jacquard: Screen-printed paper that creates an illusion of layering; for example, paper that looks like it's overlaid with a swatch of lace.

Parchment paper: This paper is somewhat translucent and often a bit mottled to mimic the appearance of ancient, historical documents made out of animal skin. It's excellent for calligraphy.

Linen finish: Paper with a surface that actually mimics linen fabric. If you look closely, you see lines of texture going both horizontally and vertically on the surface.

Rice paper: Not actually made of rice, this paper is extremely thin and elegant.

Glassine: A very thin, waxy paper. Thinner than vellum (see below), its surface is slick and shiny, whereas vellum is more translucent. Glassine is best suited for envelope use, while vellum is sturdy enough to be printed on directly for invitation use.

Vellum: A heavier, finely textured, translucent paper made from wood fiber. Similar to parchment, it was originally made from the skin of a calf, lamb or baby goat and used for writing and painting during the pre-printing age.

HereComesTheGuide.com

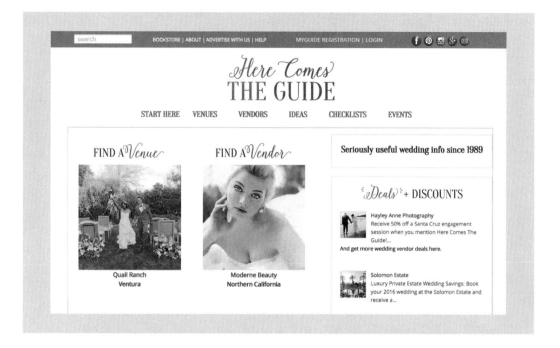

You've gotta visit our website!
Here's what you'll find:

- A fast and easy way to search for the perfect venues and vendors.

- Information about new venues that aren't in the book!

- Lots of locations for rehearsal dinners, honeymoons and accommodations (room blocks!) for your event.

- More great wedding and special event services!

- Direct links to the event venues and vendors we feature.

- Tons of photos and videos. Real Wedding galleries, too!

- Virtual tours of most venues.

- Information about bridal fairs.

- Wedding dress trunk shows and sample sales calendar.

Event Venues

Southern California

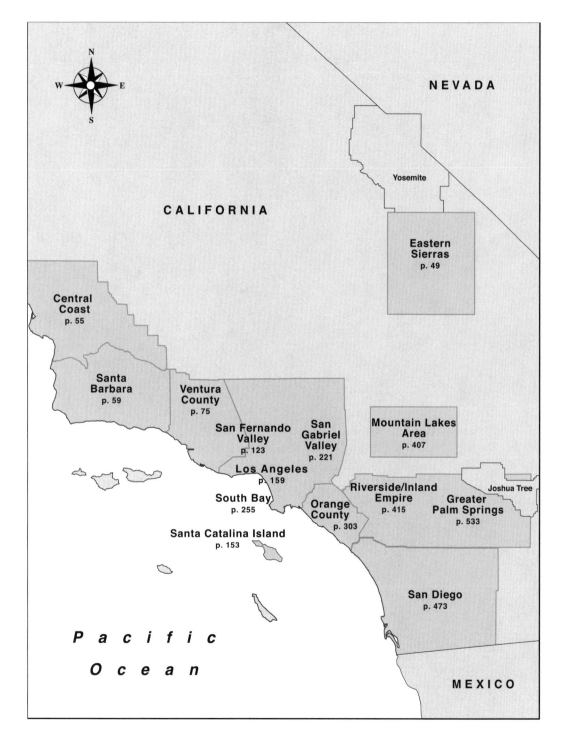

NEVADA

CALIFORNIA

Yosemite

Eastern
Sierras
p. 49

Central
Coast
p. 55

Santa
Barbara
p. 59

Ventura
County
p. 75

San Fernando
Valley
p. 123

San
Gabriel
Valley
p. 221

Mountain Lakes
Area
p. 407

Los Angeles
p. 159

South Bay
p. 255

Orange
County
p. 303

Riverside/Inland
Empire
p. 415

Greater
Palm Springs
p. 533

Joshua Tree

Santa Catalina Island
p. 153

San Diego
p. 473

P a c i f i c

O c e a n

MEXICO

Eastern Sierras

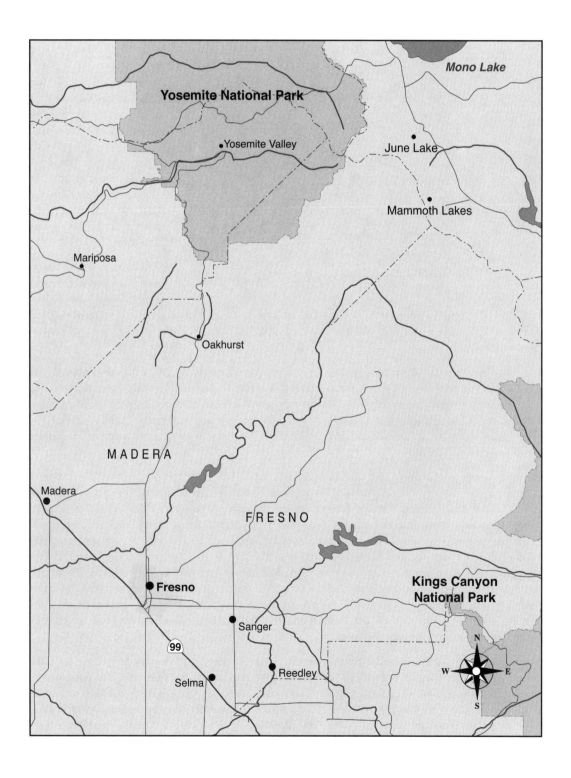

Mammoth Resorts

Mountain Resort

10001 Minaret Road, Mammoth Lakes
800/MAMMOTH (800/626-6684), 760/934-2571 X2220
www.mammothmountain.com/weddings
weddings@mammothresorts.com

● Rehearsal Dinners	● Corporate Events
● Ceremonies	● Meetings
● Wedding Receptions	● Film Shoots
● Private Parties	● Accommodations

The Eastern Sierra isn't just for skiers anymore. In fact, leisure-seekers flock to this alpine oasis year-round for golf, fishing, and hiking—or to just kick back in the serene environment. Still others, enticed by the dramatic terrain and the deluxe amenities, come here to wed.

Mountain resorts extend from Mammoth Lakes to neighboring June Mountain, and offer a vast assortment of lodges and event venues, each with its own distinctive appeal. The knowledgeable resort staff will assist in customizing your destination celebration to suit your personal style.

For an experience as exhilarating as falling in love, the adventurous say "I do" atop Mammoth's 11,053-foot summit—one of the highest peaks in California. In keeping with this wild wedding scenario, newlyweds can even ski down the mountain, the bride's wedding veil trailing behind like a flurry of snowflakes. Or treat guests to a champagne gondola ride for an authentic bird's-eye view of the town below. Disembark mid-mountain at Parallax, an elegant restaurant with soaring windows on two sides.

On Mammoth's northwest fringe, rustic romance flourishes at Tamarack Lodge and Resort, whose cabins overlook the crystalline shores of Twin Lakes. Sporting high-beamed ceilings and the warm patina of the past, Tamarack's wood-frame cabins are spread throughout the forest where chipmunks and mule deer meander among lodgepole pines and fir trees. Here, you can bask in the ever-changing hues of the seasonal foliage, from autumn's orange-red aspens to a spring palette of deep blue lupine and the burnished reds and golds of Indian paintbrush. In winter, everything is frosted in white. After an invigorating day on the slopes, cozy up in front of the fireplace with your sweetheart as a light snow falls outside. Views from Tamarack stretch across the lakes, and from summer through fall you can cross the footbridge that leads to a tiny islet holding the Forest Chapel. Have an intimate ceremony beneath a log trellis, then celebrate your union at one of Mammoth's many great reception sites.

For ultimate exclusivity, consider renting nearby June Mountain for the day. It boasts the same majestic setting, glacial lakes and "big sky" 360-degree panoramas as Mammoth, but with a more intimate, laid-back vibe. The lakeside town is known for its friendly atmosphere, and this mountain dazzles year-round, too, with its myriad of all-weather outdoor activities and changing tableau of snowcapped peaks, colorful wildflowers, and blazing golden aspens. Weddings here begin with a 10-minute chairlift ride to the awe-inspiring Scenic Overlook (other transportation options are available, too.) The ceremony takes place against unparalleled mountain vistas, aquamarine lakes and distant waterfalls. Receptions unfold in the adjacent June Meadows Chalet, whose several window-lined event spaces lend a wonderful flow to your festivities. Start with cocktails by the Great Room's huge stone fireplace, followed by dinner in the appropriately named View Room. Dance the night away in the Main Room (outfitted with AV amenities) and then wander out onto the Chalet Deck to take in the vast, star-spangled heavens.

Indeed, the sky's the limit in the Eastern Sierra. Whether you envision a sophisticated soirée, a casual get-together or a thrilling adventure, Mammoth Resorts will inspire your imagination. The range of breathtaking ceremony and reception sites, combined with *Mammoth Catering's* outstanding service, will take your wedding dream to new heights.

CEREMONY, EVENT/RECEPTION & MEETING CAPACITY: Event spaces hold from 20 to 250 guests, seated or standing.

FEES & DEPOSITS: For special events, a nonrefundable deposit is required when booking a site. Rental fees range $250–2,900 depending on the guest count and the space reserved. Wedding packages start at $55/person. Tax, alcohol and a 20% service charge are additional.

AVAILABILITY: Year-round, daily.

SERVICES/AMENITIES:

Catering: in-house, no BYO

Kitchen Facilities: n/a

Tables & Chairs: provided

Linens, Silver, etc.: provided

Restrooms: wheelchair accessible

Dance Floor: CBA

Bride's & Groom's Dressing Areas: CBA, extra fee

AV/Meeting Equipment: CBA, extra fee

Parking: ample, complimentary

Accommodations: 625 guest rooms and cabins

Outdoor Night Lighting: no

Outdoor Cooking Facilities: BBQ CBA

Cleanup: provided

View: mountains, lakes, forest, meadows

Other: on-site coordinator

RESTRICTIONS:

Alcohol: in-house, or BYO with corkage fee

Smoking: outside only

Music: amplified OK

Wheelchair Access: yes

Insurance: not required

This is important! Tell locations you're reading HERE COMES THE GUIDE and ask if our information is still current.

The Westin Monache Resort, Mammoth

Mountain Resort

50 Hillside Drive, Mammoth Lakes
760/934-0454

www.westinmammoth.com
sales@westinmammoth.com

- Rehearsal Dinners
- Ceremonies
- Wedding Receptions
- Private Parties
- Corporate Events
- Meetings
- Film Shoots
- Accommodations

The breathtaking alpine scenery of the Eastern Sierras makes an incomparable backdrop for a wedding, and the Westin Monache Resort perfectly showcases both the setting and your event. Mammoth Lakes' only full-service, luxury hotel offers relaxed elegance and first-class amenities, from en suite fireplaces and in-room massages to gourmet dining and a seasoned staff to help you plan an unforgettable celebration. In short, everything you'd expect from a Westin—just taken to a higher elevation.

A true, all-seasons resort, this venue basks in nature's spectacular display year-round. Whether you prefer a winter wonderland, golden aspens or early summer wildflowers, a stunning tableau awaits just outside your door. But you don't have to leave the hotel to savor the area's boundless beauty: Even the sleek two-story lobby, designed with slate floors, lots of natural wood, and floor-to-ceiling windows framing the gorgeous landscape, brings the scenery inside.

Majestic vistas are part of the ceremony site as well. You and your guests gather on the pool deck, which has been reserved exclusively for your party. You'll exchange vows on a raised platform against a background of towering pines and quaking aspens, with high mountain peaks visible between the trees. Afterwards, if you want to linger a bit longer in the clean fresh air, serve cocktails and hors d'oeuvres poolside, too.

Many couples, however, choose to host their cocktail hour in the private Gallery Room or the Whitebark Bar & Lounge. These intimate spaces exude a modern rustic vibe, accompanied by amazing views of the surrounding forest!

Dinner unfolds in the restaurant itself, a place that feels warm and cozy thanks to an abundance of reclaimed wood throughout and flickering fireplaces at each end of the venue. The cuisine, which will delight even the most discriminating "foodies" on your guest list, features a wide range of American fare with an emphasis on seasonal and regional ingredients.

Following a fabulous meal, dance the night away in the bar and lounge, or move your wedding across the hall to the Foxfir & Redfir Banquet Rooms which provide additional options for dining, dancing or both. With high ceilings and a neutral color palette, they allow you to create the ambiance that matches your vision.

The local airport makes Mammoth easier than ever to reach, and odds are you and your guests will want to turn your event into a mini-vacation. Since the Westin is located within the lively Mammoth Village, shopping, dining and entertainment are only a short walk away…or you can simply board the picturesque gondola that departs across the street from the hotel and be whisked up the mountain where you can ski, hike, bike or just enjoy the ride.

CEREMONY CAPACITY: The site holds 100 standing guests outdoors (limitations may apply in the winter).

EVENT/RECEPTION CAPACITY: Banquet spaces can accommodate 110 seated or 120 standing guests indoors, and 65 seated or 150 standing outdoors.

MEETING CAPACITY: Spaces hold 110 seated.

FEES & DEPOSITS: 25% of the total event cost is required to reserve your date. An additional 50% is due 60 days prior to the event and the balance is due 30 days prior. The rental fee ranges $500–2,000 depending on the season. Meals start at $45/person. Tax, alcohol and a 21% service charge are extra.

AVAILABILITY: Year-round, daily, 10am–midnight.

SERVICES/AMENITIES:

Catering: in-house
Kitchen Facilities: n/a
Tables & Chairs: provided
Linens, Silver, etc.: provided
Restrooms: wheelchair accessible
Dance Floor: CBA
Bride's & Groom's Dressing Areas: CBA
AV/Meeting Equipment: provided

Parking: valet required
Accommodations: 230 guest rooms
Outdoor Night Lighting: yes
Outdoor Cooking Facilities: BBQ on site
Cleanup: provided
View: forest, hills, mountains, pool area
Other: spa services, event coordination

RESTRICTIONS:

Alcohol: in-house
Smoking: not allowed
Music: amplified OK with restrictions

Wheelchair Access: yes
Insurance: not required

Central Coast

King City • 198 • Huron
Coalinga •
Salinas River
101
1
Avenal •
41
Paso Robles • 46
Cambria • 46
Templeton
Cayucos •
Atascadero
41
Morro Bay •
San Luis Obispo •
Avila Beach •
Arroyo Grande • Cuyama River
Pismo Beach •
Shell Beach •
Santa Maria •
1
Mission Hills •
Lompoc • Santa Ynez River 101
Solvang •

P a c i f i c

O c e a n

Cambria Pines Lodge and Gardens

Historic Lodge

2905 Burton Drive, Cambria

805/924-3353

www.cambriapineslodge.com
bethanya@moonstonehotels.com

- Rehearsal Dinners
- Ceremonies
- Wedding Receptions
- Private Parties
- Corporate Events
- Meetings
- Film Shoots
- Accommodations

As you settle into the relaxed garden setting of this hilltop lodge, it's hard to believe that it was established in 1927 for an eccentric European baroness who wanted her own personal resort within visiting distance of Hearst Castle. Unfortunately, her plans for an opulent American lifestyle were cut short by her husband back in Europe, who demanded that she choose between him and her lodge. She chose the baron, and sold her home to the Cambria Development Company, which used the lodge as a gathering place for prospective buyers of local land. Since that time, the Main Lodge building has been replaced, and the property has added world-class gardens as well as accommodations ranging from rustic rooms to deluxe suites.

Although the current Main Lodge resembles a huge, modern-day log cabin, the grounds behind it bring to mind a beautiful English garden. Rows of sculpted hedges separated by paths, bushes and beds of vibrantly colored flowers meander among Monterey pines. Next to the garden, a broad lawn serves as both ceremony and reception site for outdoor weddings. Couples get married in a lovely gazebo at one end, and dance on a patio in front of a covered bandstand at the other; the entire expanse of grass in between is turned into an al fresco dining room filled with linen-covered tables.

Indoor receptions are held in the Peacock Room. With wall coverings of rosy beige, it derives additional warmth from an abundance of pine wainscoting and trim. Other pluses are a high ceiling, movable dance floor, adjustable lighting and a built-in, granite-topped pine bar. After the celebration, you and your guests can chat it up in the Lounge, where a fire blazes in the floor-to-ceiling river rock fireplace, and chandeliers glow overhead.

If you're fortunate enough to be here for a few days, there's a world of things to do outside the Lodge, too. Cambria itself is a quaint village, noted for its local artists and craftspeople and filled with shops, galleries and boutiques. Hearst Castle is a mere nine miles to the north, the beach is minutes away, and wine tasting has become a popular pastime in Cambria and the surrounding San Luis Obispo County. Alas, the baroness may have left the country so quickly that she never had time to truly enjoy either her lodge or her surroundings. We suggest you don't make the same mistake: When you have your garden wedding here, plan to stay long enough to take full advantage of all that this friendly, family-oriented venue and the Central Coast have to offer.

CEREMONY CAPACITY: The garden/gazebo area holds 250 seated.

EVENT/RECEPTION CAPACITY: For an outdoor ceremony plus reception, the garden/gazebo area holds 200 seated. Indoors, the Peacock Room (which can be divided into 2 sections) accommodates up to 250 with a dance floor. Each half of the room can hold 90 seated with a dance floor.

MEETING CAPACITY: Several spaces seat 40–300 guests.

FEES & DEPOSITS: To hold your date, the entire site rental fee is due at booking: $1,000–2,000 for the garden, Peacock Room, or half of the Peacock Room. A guest count guarantee is due 11 days prior to the event, and the food & beverage balance is payable at the event's conclusion. Cambria Pines Lodge offers a varied menu, with luncheons ranging $23–33/person and dinners $26–50/person; alcohol, tax and a 20% service charge are additional. A $1,000 ceremony charge covers the use of the gazebo, chairs, setup/takedown service and rehearsal.

For meetings, the Sycamore, Treetop and Peacock rooms are available. Please call for pricing.

AVAILABILITY: Indoor events, year-round, daily. Outdoor events, year-round, optimally mid-April to late October. Ceremonies and receptions take place outdoors 11am–4pm, and indoors 11:30am–4pm or 6:30pm–11pm. Other times may be arranged; call for more information.

SERVICES/AMENITIES:

Catering: in-house, no BYO
Kitchen Facilities: n/a
Tables & Chairs: provided; Chiavari chairs CBA, extra charge
Linens, Silver, etc.: provided
Restrooms: wheelchair accessible
Dance Floor: outdoor patio or indoor portable provided
Bride's Dressing Area: CBA, extra charge
AV/Meeting Equipment: full range

Parking: large lots
Accommodations: 152 guest rooms and suites
Outdoor Night Lighting: CBA, extra charge
Outdoor Cooking Facilities: BBQs CBA
Cleanup: provided
View: gardens, woods and hills

RESTRICTIONS:

Alcohol: in-house, or corkage $15/bottle
Smoking: designated areas only, not in the gardens
Music: amplified OK with volume restrictions

Wheelchair Access: yes
Insurance: not required
Other: no rice, birdseed, glitter or confetti; flames restricted

Santa Barbara Area

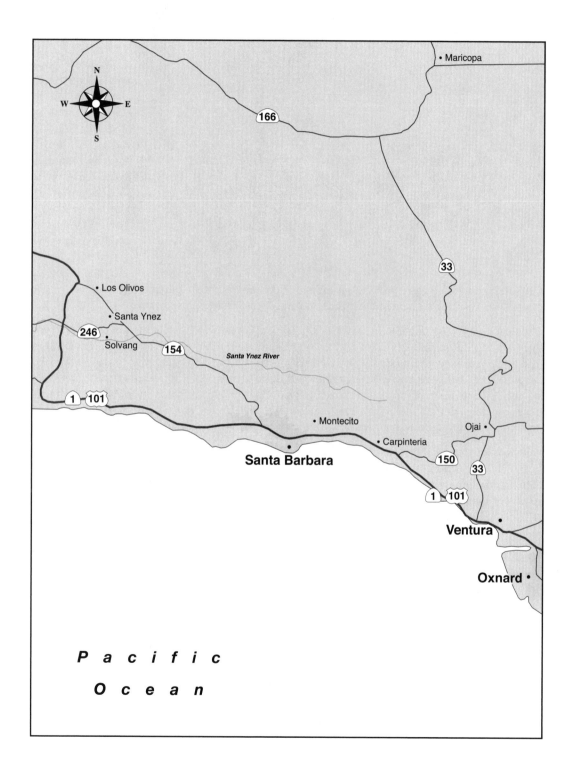

Rincon Beach Club

3805 Santa Claus Lane, Carpinteria
805/566-9933

www.rinconbeachclub.com
sales@rinconcatering.com

Waterfront Event Facility

- Rehearsal Dinners
- Ceremonies
- Wedding Receptions
- Private Parties
- Corporate Events
- Meetings
- Film Shoots
- Accommodations

The Rincon Beach Club, located in the seaside community of Carpinteria just south of Santa Barbara, is bound to make you smile as soon as you arrive: The club resides on "Santa Claus Lane" amid a quaint row of colorful shops and cafés along the Carpinteria coastline. We're pretty sure smiles will continue throughout your time at Rincon, a gracious, private setting with mountain vistas and an easy, coastal sophistication.

The Beach Club has two main event areas: the Dining Room, which exudes a quiet elegance; and the Wedding Garden, a leafy courtyard awash in sunlight during the late afternoon. Enclosed by dense green foliage, the garden is finished with grass-fringed flagstone. At one end, a wooden pergola laced with white roses tops an elevated deck, a pretty spot for ceremonies. A flowering shade tree leans in from one side as if listening closely, while the bridal party, dressed to impress, poses on the stairs. As the couple exchanges vows, loved ones watching from below are close enough to feel an intimate connection with the proceedings.

Guests enjoy the cocktail hour on the West Patio, which wraps around the exterior of the Dining Room. In one section, a mahogany bar, couches and chairs are a comfortable improvisation of an al fresco lounge; just around the corner, café tables form a cozy enclave next to a trickling fountain. As dusk descends, the sweet scent of star jasmine mingles with refreshing sea breezes, and antique-style heat lamps keep everyone toasty. Twinkle lights add their glow beneath a starfilled night sky.

For a formal reception, invite guests into the Dining Room, where French doors on two sides let in the garden view. The room's clean, uncluttered palette is a refined backdrop for personalized décor. The Club has a collection of furniture, props and other accoutrements to create whatever atmosphere you envision. Unique banquet chairs with a faux-pewter finish and classy up-lighting enhance the aura of refinement, while a skylit foyer showcases the buffet.

At Rincon Beach Club, you get much more than a picturesque venue: Expert planning, event production and palate-pleasing cuisine are also part of the package. This full-service approach is not only a time- and money-saver—it also results in a more cohesive expression of your vision. Rincon's experienced professionals know how to craft a celebration that reflects your style and taste. This is especially evident when it comes to your menu, which they'll customize from aperitif to dessert. If you want to honor your heritage, choose from among Rincon's many global-inspired delicacies: blinis with caviar, Beef Copenhagen, Greek Mousaka—not even escargot intimidates these culinary artists! More contemporary dishes include favorites like Seared Ahi on Sugar Cane with Wasabi Cream Sauce or Apricot Spiced Ginger Chicken Wontons.

Minutes from Santa Barbara, yet "miles from conventional," Rincon Beach Club and Catering's impressive presentation and devotion to details really sets them apart. As one satisfied bride put it: "I was so relaxed—I just showed up and had fun!"

CEREMONY CAPACITY: The site holds 350 seated guests outdoors.

EVENT/RECEPTION CAPACITY: The club can accommodate 130 seated or 350 standing guests indoors, and 300 seated or 350 standing outdoors.

MEETING CAPACITY: The club can accommodate up to 350 guests.

FEES & DEPOSITS: A deposit is required to reserve your date. Deposits range $3,100–5,750 depending on the day of the week rented. 50% is due 4 months prior, and the balance is due 2 weeks prior to the event. Rental fees range $350–5,750 depending on the day of the week of the event. Meals range $41–75/person. Tax, gratuity and beverages are additional, but included in a complete estimate.

AVAILABILITY: Year-round, daily, anytime.

SERVICES/AMENITIES:

Catering: in-house
Kitchen Facilities: n/a
Tables & Chairs: provided
Linens, Silver, etc.: provided
Restrooms: wheelchair accessible
Dance Floor: portable provided
Bride's & Groom's Dressing Areas: yes
AV/Meeting Equipment: some provided, CBA
Other: in-house wedding cake, groom's lounge, event coordination, day-of and full-service wedding planning

Parking: on street
Accommodations: no guest rooms
Outdoor Night Lighting: provided
Outdoor Cooking Facilities: BBQ on site; food action stations available
Cleanup: provided
View: coastline, fountain, garden, landscaped grounds, mountains, ocean

RESTRICTIONS:

Alcohol: full in-house bar
Smoking: allowed on patio only
Music: amplified OK

Wheelchair Access: yes
Insurance: liability required

Canary Hotel Santa Barbara

Resort & Spa

31 West Carrillo Street, Santa Barbara
805/879-9144
www.canarysantabarbara.com
elizabeth.duffy@canarysantabarbara.com

- Rehearsal Dinners
- Ceremonies
- Wedding Receptions
- Private Parties
- Corporate Events
- Meetings
- Film Shoots
- Accommodations

Santa Barbara, one of the most beautiful towns in the world, welcomes a gorgeous new venue: Canary Hotel, an upscale boutique hostelry that reigns from the historic city center, between the sparkling-blue Pacific and the tree-studded Santa Ynez foothills. This strategic location puts you steps from what the New York Times dubbed "shopping Nirvana," as well as theaters, galleries, and the exciting nightlife of State Street. Like the balmy tropical islands the Canary is named after, Santa Barbara boasts miles of sun-kissed beaches, as well as an artistic spirit and a convivial, laid-back attitude—qualities that are embodied by this very sophisticated hotel.

Canopied walkways lead inside this urban oasis, where lush native plantings blend with the indigenous sounds of exotic birds, tree frogs, lizards and crickets from the Canary Islands. This sultry ambiance is also reflected in the décor. Exotic North African textures combine with luxurious Spanish-Colonial style for a fashionably fun, yet plush, interior. Wainscoted walls, hand-carved woods and wrought-iron details complement carpets, upholstery and tile in rich shades evocative of fine Madeira. The hotel's restaurant and bar, Finch & Fork, is a popular Santa Barbara gathering spot. There's a lovely private dining room for rehearsal dinners, and all your event dining is catered by the accomplished culinary team, who specialize in New American cuisine paired with wonderful wines from around the world.

The hotel's most unique event locale is found atop its five stories: an exclusive rooftop pool and terrace. Already it's "a scene" for Hollywood types and celebs drawn to the phenomenal 360-degree view, which encompasses the red-tiled roofs of the "American Riviera" and spectacular sunsets over the ocean. The terrace is also attracting couples with weddings on their minds. Wicker resort furniture outfitted with comfy cushions and a Mission-style hearth transform the area into a spacious outdoor room. A profusion of greenery and terracotta pots brimming with flowers create a pretty garden milieu for ceremonies and open-air gatherings. A short staircase inlaid with Spanish tiles holds court between the terrace and the pool, making it a natural focal point for tying the knot. A pair of pergolas flanks the upper landing, where the cocktail hour flourishes around a swimming pool that mirrors the blue of the Pacific beyond.

Formal soirées take place in one of five banquet rooms that surround an elegant foyer on the hotel's lower level. They all have a warm, inviting character, including the largest venue, the Riviera Ballroom. Your "after-party for two" unfolds in your cozy, yet refined, guest suite. With a CD of

Spanish guitar music playing and ultra-soft robes to slip into, you'll feel as if you're indulging in a romantic Mediterranean honeymoon. While your friends and family hop the beach shuttle or hit the gym next door, you order in-room spa treatments or snuggle between deluxe linens. Go ahead and extend your siesta as long as you want—after all, in this delightful haven, room service is available 24 hours a day!

CEREMONY CAPACITY: The Terrace holds 130 seated guests, indoor spaces up to 130 seated guests.

EVENT/RECEPTION CAPACITY: Indoors, the site holds up to 130 seated or 200 standing guests; outdoors 130 seated or 175 standing guests. Several combinations of indoor and outdoor seating are available; call for details.

MEETING CAPACITY: Several spaces are available that accommodate up to 130 seated guests.

FEES & DEPOSITS: A deposit is required to reserve your date. The balance is due 30 days prior to the event. Rental fees range $300–2,500 depending on space rented and guest count. Meals range $75–175/person. Tax, alcohol and a 22% service charge are additional.

AVAILABILITY: Year-round, daily, anytime.

SERVICES/AMENITIES:

Catering: in-house, no BYO

Kitchen Facilities: n/a

Tables & Chairs: provided

Linens, Silver, etc.: provided

Restrooms: wheelchair accessible

Dance Floor: provided

Bride's Dressing Area: yes

AV/Meeting Equipment: CBA, extra charge

Parking: valet and adjacent public garage

Accommodations: 97 guest rooms

Outdoor Night Lighting: yes

Outdoor Cooking Facilities: no

Cleanup: provided

View: ocean, mountains, cityscape

Other: coordination, spa services

RESTRICTIONS:

Alcohol: in-house, no BYO

Smoking: not allowed

Music: amplified OK indoors with restrictions

Wheelchair Access: yes

Insurance: liability required

Overwhelmed? Use the search criteria on www.HereComesTheGuide.com to narrow down your choices.

63

Elings Park

Park

1298 Las Positas Road, Santa Barbara
805/569-5611

www.elingspark.org
cfranquet@elingspark.org

● Rehearsal Dinners	● Corporate Events	
● Ceremonies	● Meetings	
● Wedding Receptions	● Film Shoots	
● Private Parties	Accommodations	

Located in beautiful Santa Barbara, Elings Park is a 230-acre nonprofit park blessed with incredible city, mountain and ocean views. This recreational paradise encompasses sports fields, picnic grounds, tennis courts, a hang-gliding hill, a sculpture garden, a Veteran's Memorial Walk—plus hiking and biking trails galore. However, Elings also has two lovely sites for romantic wedding celebrations.

To reach the first, take a short curvy drive up to Godric Grove, an estate-like venue at the park's summit. You're only 400 feet above sea level here, but the multifaceted perspective makes you feel like you're on top of the world: From one direction, the grove surveys velvety-green park meadows; from another, the Santa Barbara cityscape unfolds against the silhouette of the Santa Ynez Mountains—and whichever way you face, a ribbon of ocean winks in the distance.

Wedding ceremonies make the most of this dynamic vista at the Grove's stone amphitheater, gently terraced into the hillside overlooking a forest of oaks. The amphitheater is completely secluded, blissfully quiet (save for the occasional birdcall or rustle of leaves), and harmonizes with the surrounding landscape. The adjacent reception area is just as pleasing. A large free-form redwood deck is spread out along the rim of a plateau. Gnarled oak trees grow up right through the deck and around its perimeter, providing dappled shade for your cocktail hour and reception. Next to the deck there's a sizable patio with built-in barbecues that's just right for a buffet or dancing. A cozy, treelined lawn nearby also has event possibilities. From spring to summer, cheery matilija poppies are in bloom around the lawn, while in the autumn the liquid amber trees put on a colorful show.

The second site, Singleton Pavilion, provides a more expansive setting with its own special charms. The centerpiece of Singleton is a sweep of lawn that can easily accommodate both your ceremony and reception seating. At one end, a copse of trees on a slight rise makes a leafy milieu for exchanging vows; or say "I do" in front of a handsome gazebo at the opposite end. A path partly encircles the lawn and culminates in a stone terrace poised at the edge of the hillside. Here a petite grove of saplings creates a magical atmosphere for intimate dining or a novel cocktail hour. And one more (wonderful) thing about Singleton: It also boasts serene city and mountain vistas, as well as peeks of the Pacific Ocean.

Both Godric Grove and Singleton Pavilion can accommodate large canopies, and site rental includes dedicated parking along with a Park Host. You can also reserve time on one of the playing fields for friendly competitions among families—think a genial round of croquet or softball. The Events Director will help with ideas and finding quality local vendors.

This spectacular, unspoiled setting can be styled as elegantly as you please, but you really don't need to add a single flower, plant or ribbon because Nature has provided all the decoration.

CEREMONY, EVENT/RECEPTION & MEETING CAPACITY: The site holds up to 325 guests outdoors.

FEES & DEPOSITS: The full rental fee is required to reserve your date. A credit card number is required to keep on file for any damages at the venue. Rental fees range $1,400–4,500 depending on the season and the space selected.

AVAILABILITY: Year-round, daily starting at 8am. All events must end by 10pm with cleanup completed by 11pm, with extended cleanup available until midnight upon request.

SERVICES/AMENITIES:

Catering: BYO

Kitchen Facilities: none

Tables & Chairs: through caterer or BYO

Linens, Silver, etc.: through caterer or BYO

Restrooms: wheelchair accessible

Dance Floor: BYO

Bride's Dressing Area: none

AV/Meeting Equipment: BYO

Parking: large lot

Accommodations: no guest rooms

Outdoor Night Lighting: BYO

Outdoor Cooking Facilities: BBQ on site

Cleanup: renter

View: panorama of ocean, mountains and cityscape; park, garden, landscaped grounds

Other: picnic area

RESTRICTIONS:

Alcohol: through caterer or BYO

Smoking: not allowed

Music: select from approved vendor list

Wheelchair Access: yes

Insurance: liability required

Hyatt Santa Barbara

Waterfront Hotel

1111 E. Cabrillo Boulevard, Santa Barbara
805/879-1319

www.santabarbara.hyatt.com
krista.kurosaki@hyatt.com

- ● Rehearsal Dinners
- ● Ceremonies
- ● Wedding Receptions
- ● Private Parties
- ● Corporate Events
- ● Meetings
- ○ Film Shoots
- ○ Accommodations

Santa Barbara embodies the perfect balance of small-town charm and big-city attractions, and its irresistible mix of sun, surf and sand has earned it the nickname "The American Riviera." If a beautiful oceanview venue on the coast tops your wedding wish list, then consider Hyatt Santa Barbara your fairy godmother.

The historic hotel first opened its doors in 1931, and its Spanish Colonial architecture and décor, including antique tilework and wrought-iron embellishments, all add up to classic Santa Barbara style. Although a recent makeover combines sleek, contemporary refinement with the latest amenities, the Hyatt Santa Barbara's enviable location is timeless—three landscaped acres commanding a prime spot across from East Beach, bordered by a treelined park.

It's just a short stroll from the hotel to the breathtaking ceremony site, right on the soft sand. Your event manager has thoughtfully arranged all the details: A refreshment station greets your guests, who will be seated on white wooden chairs accented with starfish. The wedding aisle is lined with seashells and a white trellis frames you and your fiancé against a backdrop of gentle waves—everything you need for a dreamy beach wedding! But if you have your heart set on tying the knot at one of the town's other scenic parks or gardens, then Hyatt's event pros are happy to take your ceremony there.

The cocktail hour is simply sublime back at Hyatt's wraparound Vista Terrace, which, as its name implies, treats everyone to picture-postcard scenery. French doors open to the Vista Ballroom, a smartly decorated space in pleasing earth tones with windows that look out to the ocean on one side and to the hills on the other. An adjoining alcove can hold a buffet, gift table or photo booth. Leave the doors open to the evening sea breezes and wander outside with your sweetheart for some romantic stargazing.

Yes, it all sounds divine, but there's another glamorous ballroom to consider. From its second story vantage, Cabrillo's panoramas are even more sweeping and dynamic. One wall showcases the Pacific and another overlooks a park towards the hills. The Gazebo, a curved, windowed annex, is a novel setting for an intimate indoor ceremony or cocktails.

The smallest of the hotel's three banquet spaces, La Cantina, also boasts the most Old World character, thanks to hand-stenciled ceiling beams, dark wood trim and huge candelabra chandeliers. Arched windows capture swaying palms and a ribbon of ocean, while a soaring cut-stone fireplace just begs for a cozy winter wedding or rehearsal dinner.

The Hyatt's enticing banquet menus are fully customizable and their wedding packages feature lots of extras, including a complimentary oceanview room for the newlyweds. Of course, staying here is half the fun: The beach-facing pool deck with bar and fire pit, the plush guest rooms, plus the restaurant and bar provide plenty of creature comforts … and a waterfront shuttle offers easy access to the area's many activities. Invite your friends and family to a destination wedding at this luxurious venue and they'll experience the best of Santa Barbara along with your memorable celebration.

CEREMONY CAPACITY: The facility holds 250 seated guests indoors or outdoors.

EVENT/RECEPTION CAPACITY: Indoors, the hotel can accommodate 250 seated or 320 standing guests; outdoors 60 seated or 150 standing.

MEETING CAPACITY: The site holds 250 seated guests.

FEES & DEPOSITS: A $1,000 deposit is required to reserve your date and the balance is due 1 month prior to the event. Rental fees range $0–10,000 depending on the day of the event, guest count and the space(s) reserved. Meal packages start at $42/person. Tax, alcohol and a 24% service charge are additional.

AVAILABILITY: Year-round, daily, 8am–11pm.

SERVICES/AMENITIES:

Catering: in-house
Kitchen Facilities: n/a
Tables & Chairs: provided
Linens, Silver, etc.: provided
Restrooms: wheelchair accessible
Dance Floor: portable provided
Bride's Dressing Area: yes
AV/Meeting Equipment: some provided

Parking: valet only
Accommodations: 195 guest rooms
Outdoor Night Lighting: CBA
Outdoor Cooking Facilities: BBQ CBA
Cleanup: provided
View: panorama of ocean, coastline and mountains; pool area, park
Other: centerpieces, complimentary room for the bride & groom, event coordination

RESTRICTIONS:

Alcohol: full in-house bar
Smoking: outdoors only
Music: amplified OK with restrictions

Wheelchair Access: yes
Insurance: not required

Santa Barbara Zoological Gardens

Waterfront Zoological Gardens

500 Ninos Drive, Santa Barbara
805/566-9933

www.zoocateringbyrincon.com
angie@rinconcatering.com

● Rehearsal Dinners	● Corporate Events
● Ceremonies	Meetings
● Wedding Receptions	● Film Shoots
● Private Parties	Accommodations

Sure, plenty of zoos have the requisite elephant or lion… but the Santa Barbara Zoo has something more: 30 acres of lush gardens laced with majestic ocean views. This isn't your typical wedding venue, and this isn't a typical zoo, either. For one thing, the meticulously maintained park rests between the beach and a bird sanctuary. For another, it's got a surprisingly pleasant aroma, a mixture of roses, jasmine and the sea. This zoo also has experienced event pros who are particularly attentive and enthusiastic about helping make your day special. Oh, and one more huge plus—privacy! When the public leaves at 5pm, the entire place becomes your exclusive wedding playground.

Arriving wedding guests are escorted along a landscaped path to Palm Garden, a stunning ceremony site tucked away in a sunken, grassy courtyard. Surrounded by palm trees, agapanthus and leafy green thickets, it has the exotic air of a tame jungle hideaway. Couples tie the knot in front of a cluster of palms, sometimes adding a *chuppah* or bamboo arch, with a hint of ocean in the distance.

Next, while you and your wedding party pose for photos in the park's scenic gardens, your guests take refreshments on nearby Lower Hilltop, a broad grassy "porch" set with cocktail tables and a bar. To make this time even more memorable, you might arrange some novel entertainment: Invite some flamingoes to join the party; hire the zoo train to take everyone on a tour (cocktails welcome); or have guests take turns feeding Michael, Audrey and Betty Lou, Masai giraffes who unfurl long purple tongues as they gently accept their food. Now that's something most wedding guests don't get to experience!

When it's time to serve dinner to your friends and family, a short flight of stone steps leads to Upper Hilltop, a circular expanse of lawn gorgeously arrayed for the reception. Since the field is so spacious, the event staff creates "outdoor rooms" to lend a feeling of intimacy, using a variety of optional amenities—a dance floor, tenting, chandeliers, market lights, heat lamps, specialty linens, lounge furniture and props. They stage the festivities either overlooking Lower Hilltop, which offers glimpses of the Pacific through the palm fronds in one direction and the Santa Ynez Mountains in the other; or on the interior section, which enjoys two different Pacific vistas plus a pergola and splashing fountain. The event team will personalize your wedding, whether you prefer traditionally elegant styling or something imaginative. (One couple recently had an Alice in Wonderland-themed gala!) Pretty much anything you can dream up, the zoo staff will help you pull off.

The same is true of the cuisine. *Zoo Catering Services by Rincon (ZCS)* boasts "Wild Flavors with Civilized Service," and they're equally adept at delivering a relaxed barbecue or a sophisticated candlelit affair, global fusion or the freshest California cuisine. You're in good hands with these culinary superstars!

The Santa Barbara Zoological Gardens is a private, nonprofit organization, which is perfect for green weddings—your special event fees help support the zoo's conservation and education efforts. With its picturesque setting and impeccable service, this unique location is a "natural" for out-of-the-ordinary celebrations.

CEREMONY CAPACITY: The facility holds up to 250 seated guests outdoors.

EVENT/RECEPTION CAPACITY: The site can accommodate 600 seated or 1,000 standing outdoors.

MEETING CAPACITY: Meetings do not take place at this facility.

FEES & DEPOSITS: Two fees are required at the time of booking your event at the zoo. The first is 50% of the site fee plus a $500 zoo security deposit and the second is $2,000 payable to *Catering by Rincon*. The balance of the estimated total is due 60 days prior to the event. The site rental fee is $4,000. Meals range $31–72/person. Tax, alcohol and an 18% service charge are additional. Custom menus are available; pricing may vary, especially for smaller events, so please inquire.

AVAILABILITY: Year-round.

SERVICES/AMENITIES:

Catering: in-house
Kitchen Facilities: n/a
Tables & Chairs: CBA
Linens, Silver, etc.: CBA
Restrooms: wheelchair accessible
Dance Floor: CBA
Bride's Dressing Area: yes
AV/Meeting Equipment: CBA
Other: picnic area, event coordination, animal options, zoo train options

Parking: provided, large lot
Accommodations: no guest rooms
Outdoor Night Lighting: CBA
Outdoor Cooking Facilities: BBQ on site; food action stations available
Cleanup: provided
View: fountain, garden, courtyard, landscaped grounds; panorama of hills, mountains, ocean and coastline

RESTRICTIONS:

Alcohol: in-house
Smoking: designated areas only
Music: amplified OK

Wheelchair Access: yes
Insurance: liability required

Unitarian Society of Santa Barbara

Historic Church & Event Facility

1535 Santa Barbara Street, Santa Barbara

805/965-4583 X223

www.ussb.org/love
facilities@ussb.org

- Rehearsal Dinners
- Ceremonies
- Wedding Receptions
- Private Parties
- Corporate Events
- Meetings
- Film Shoots
- Accommodations

Directly across from the blossom-filled Alice Keck Park Memorial Garden is the Unitarian Society of Santa Barbara, a historic, nondenominational church with a long tradition as a wonderful wedding location. Their beautiful Sanctuary evokes a peaceful sense of divine mystery, and the congregation's inclusive philosophy makes this venue a congenial gathering place, perfectly suited for life's celebrations. Unitarian Universalists support one another on their various spiritual paths, and are nonjudgmental, compassionate and socially conscious. As you and your soul mate begin your own lifelong journey together, consider letting the tranquil surroundings of the Unitarian Society provide you with a memorable send-off.

The Unitarian Society campus includes the Sanctuary, a Reception hall, a Terrace and two Gardened Courtyards. Designed and built in 1930 in the city's signature Spanish-Revival style, the Sanctuary's rustic glamour is enhanced by antique architectural elements: Vintage lantern-style light fixtures are suspended from the vaulted ceiling's open beams. The original wooden pews are flanked by lofty, rectangular stained-glass panels in subdued shades of pale blue and honey, each inscribed with the name of a famous Unitarian freethinker like essayist Ralph Waldo Emerson. At the front of the Sanctuary, the chancel is softly illuminated by a breathtaking stained-glass rose window in radiant jewel tones; a smaller rose window looks out over balcony seating at the rear. The Sanctuary conveys a momentous yet joyful ambiance, and its quality acoustics make music sound even more dramatic. Hire one of their recommended musicians, and walk down the aisle to the impressive sound of the Sanctuary's genuine 1,500-pipe organ or Steinway concert piano. Couples of any faith or sexual orientation are invited to pledge their love in this glorious space, a welcome solution for interfaith marriages and same-sex unions.

Following the ceremony, guests often enjoy an open-air social hour in the pretty Jefferson Courtyard. A brick patio flanked by twin lawns crowned with olive saplings is a delightful spot to toast the newlyweds; then, while refreshments are served, bridal parties can sneak across the street for photos in the park. A second-story terrace lets guests survey the festivities below. Tucked in one corner of the courtyard, a semiprivate enclave with a labyrinth and small amphitheater invites cozy conversations.

Outdoor receptions are usually held in the Parish Courtyard at the front of the facility. Lovely and serene, this bricked garden plaza offers a spacious yet intimate environment for up to 200 guests. Well-placed foliage provides filtered shade, and at the right time of year a grand magnolia tree shows off delicately fragrant flowers. A triple-arched breezeway is a perfect place for the bar and, once the sun sets, ambient lighting lends a romantic luster to the idyllic setting.

Through the breezeway lies the newly refurbished Parish Hall, an attractive banquet room with high ceilings. Earth-toned walls bring out the room's Mission-style flavor and complement a large stained-glass window (similar to the Sanctuary panels). The hardwood floor is great for dancing, and a proscenium stage puts the entertainment on display. Recent upgrades include an audiovisual system, and behind the scenes your caterer cooks up a feast in a professional kitchen.

Flexible, welcoming and aesthetically pleasing, the Unitarian Society continues its legacy as host to unforgettable events.

CEREMONY CAPACITY: The Sanctuary holds 285 seated guests; the courtyard 200 seated.

EVENT/RECEPTION CAPACITY: Indoors, the site holds up to 110 seated; outdoors 200 seated.

MEETING CAPACITY: Spaces are available that accommodate up to 150 seated guests.

FEES & DEPOSITS: A $500 deposit is required to reserve your date, and the balance is due 6 months prior to the event. Rental fees range $1,250–3,850 depending on the space and hours reserved. For meetings or memorial services, please call for a quote. To tour this facility, call or email ahead to arrange a site visit.

AVAILABILITY: Year-round, daily. Monday–Saturday 9am–10pm; Sunday 3pm–10pm.

SERVICES/AMENITIES:

Catering: select from list or BYO
Kitchen Facilities: new commercial kitchen
Tables & Chairs: CBA
Linens, Silver, etc.: BYO
Restrooms: wheelchair accessible
Dance Floor: provided indoors
Bride's Dressing Area: yes
AV/Meeting Equipment: some provided

Parking: on street and valet CBA
Accommodations: no guest rooms
Outdoor Night Lighting: CBA
Outdoor Cooking Facilities: BBQ CBA
Cleanup: CBA
View: gardens, park, mountains
Other: grand piano; vocalists and organist CBA

RESTRICTIONS:

Alcohol: BYO, licensed server only
Smoking: not allowed
Music: amplified OK with restrictions

Wheelchair Access: yes
Insurance: one-day liability policy required

The wedding vendors on our website are the best in the business. How do we know? Read page 577.

71

Gainey Vineyard and Ranch

Winery

3950 East Highway 246, Santa Ynez
805/688-0558

www.gaineyvineyard.com
events@gaineyvineyard.com

● Rehearsal Dinners	● Corporate Events
● Ceremonies	● Meetings
● Wedding Receptions	● Film Shoots
● Private Parties	Accommodations

Although its setting in the rolling, oak-studded hills of Santa Barbara's wine country is a picturesque one, Gainey Vineyard has earned a reputation for something other than its native good looks. With its year-round program of tastings, tours and concerts, the winery has become a purveyor of both fine wine and culture. The combination has met with success: All of Gainey's varietal wines have won coveted gold medals, while big names like Randy Newman, Count Basie, Emmylou Harris, Diana Krall, Lucinda Williams and Al Jarreau have been among the acts providing the music. Gainey Vineyard has over 25 years of experience hosting special events and weddings. The site's natural beauty can't help but attract couples from miles around, and when they get here, the bride and groom will find a supportive and energetic staff.

As you approach the winery, you get your first glimpse of its visual appeal. Over 90 acres of premium grapevines spread out on either side of the long entry drive, which ends in a sweep around a circular courtyard in front of the hacienda-style winery building. The Tasting Room inside is a handsome space for intimate gatherings. Spanish tile floors, dramatic lighting and a grand-scale fireplace give it a country-casual ambiance. Adjacent to the Tasting Room is the Wine Cellar, a long room whose walls are stacked with floor-to-ceiling bottles of aging wine. Add tables outfitted with linens, candelabras and bowls of fruit for a glowing Tuscan-style reception, or follow your own vision. The spacious Barrel Room, lined with casks of aging wine, is another option for a warm, elegant dinner.

Receptions also take place right outside on the Patio, a grassy open-air courtyard bordered on one side by a grapevine-covered trellis. At the end of the trellis, a barbecue and kitchen prep area make outdoor catering easy. Leafy rows of Sauvignon Blanc and Merlot grapes frame the Patio's uphill side, where two stately heritage oaks create a majestic focal point.

The Vineyard View Picnic Area, with its two massive oaks and commanding vistas, is the facility's most popular site for ceremonies. Couples say their vows on a raised knoll beneath one of the oaks, while their guests enjoy not only the moment but the view: acres of vineyards and the Santa Ynez Mountains in the distance.

Gainey's oldest event site is The Old Homestead, built in the 1890s. Located a half mile from the winery, this rustic barn is a terrific spot for dancing, and the expansive area around it makes a wonderful setting for either a western-style celebration or an upscale casual affair. Rolling hills, a nearby creek and shady oaks provide the scenery.

If Gainey Vineyard sounds like the kind of place where you'd like to get married or throw a party, come by for a wine tasting and take in a concert. After you've sampled its wine, song and pastoral surroundings, Gainey is sure to rank high on your list.

CEREMONY CAPACITY: The Vineyard View Picnic Area holds up to 300 seated guests; the Patio accommodates up to 200 seated.

EVENT/RECEPTION CAPACITY: The Courtyard holds up to 400 seated or standing guests; the Tasting Room 50; the Patio up to 200 seated; the Wine Cellar 50 seated and the Barrel Room 125 seated. The Barn grounds accommodate up to 500 guests.

MEETING CAPACITY: The Conference Room adjacent to the Patio holds 10 seated.

FEES & DEPOSITS: For weddings, a $5,000 nonrefundable deposit is required to book the site. The site rental fee for a BBQ wedding is $2,500 Monday–Thursday, $4,500 on Friday and $5,500 on Saturday and Sunday. For a catered wedding the site rental fee is $3,000 Monday–Thursday, $5,000 on Friday and $6,000 on Saturday and Sunday. The Barn rental fee is $3,000, which includes use of the Barn and grounds. The Conference Room rental fee is $200/day.

Sophisticated barbecues start at $38/person and include tableware, linens, tables and chairs. If you don't use the in-house caterer, you'll have to supply all event rentals. The event balance is payable 2 weeks prior to the function. With prior arrangement, the sophisticated kitchen may be used.

AVAILABILITY: Year-round, daily except major holidays, 10am–10pm. The Tasting Room, Wine Cellar and Barrel Room are available 5pm–10pm only.

SERVICES/AMENITIES:
Catering: in-house or BYO
Kitchen Facilities: fully equipped
Tables & Chairs: provided or BYO
Linens, Silver, etc.: provided or BYO
Restrooms: wheelchair accessible
Dance Floor: BYO
Bride's Dressing Room: lounge available
AV/Meeting Equipment: BYO

Parking: large lot, valet required
Accommodations: no guest rooms
Outdoor Night Lighting: yes
Outdoor Cooking Facilities: BBQ
Cleanup: provided or caterer
View: vineyards, rolling hills
Other: coordination, extra fee

RESTRICTIONS:
Alcohol: Gainey Vineyard wines only; beer also available
Smoking: outside only
Music: amplified OK

Wheelchair Access: yes
Insurance: certificate required
Other: no rice or confetti

Ventura County

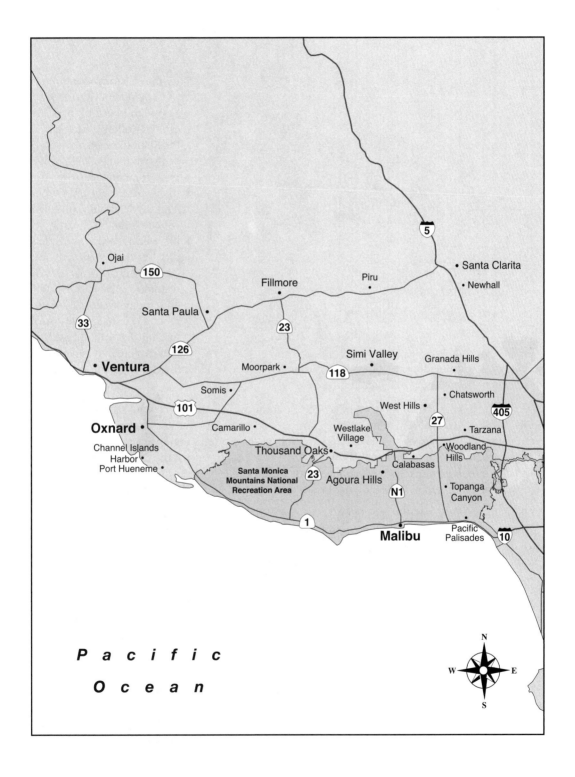

Camarillo Ranch

Historic Mansion and Ranch

201 Camarillo Ranch Road, Camarillo
805/389-8182

www.camarilloranch.org
events@camarilloranch.org

● Rehearsal Dinners		● Corporate Events	
● Ceremonies		● Meetings	
● Wedding Receptions		● Film Shoots	
● Private Parties		Accommodations	

In the pastoral community of Camarillo, a historic mansion with peaceful, park-like grounds offers a rare setting for all kinds of events—especially weddings. The product of a romantic gesture, this turn-of-the-century Queen Anne-style estate was built in 1892 by Adolfo Camarillo for his wife Isabella. The splendid heritage structure and its remaining 4.5 acres were restored by the city in 2001, and today visitors tour the ranch's original stables, stroll through the beautiful gardens, and explore a living museum expertly reconstructed inside the mansion. Your own friends and family can enjoy the same diversions when they attend special gatherings here.

If you come to wed at the ranch, you may choose from among several pleasant sites. One possibility is the West Garden, a manicured lawn surrounded by palm trees and luxuriant foliage. Stage your ceremony in front of a vine-covered archway at the garden's entrance or a splashing, triple-tiered stone fountain in the center of the garden. On the other side of the mansion the commodious East Garden features its own fountain and a lush border of trees. Or marry on the mansion's wraparound front porch, whose ornate façade and carved balustrades form an elegant backdrop.

Follow the ceremony with a cocktail hour in one of the gardens, or invite your guests inside the mansion to explore its antique décor and vintage furnishings. A grand staircase in the foyer is a wonderful place to stage group photos, and an alcove opposite features stained glass and scroll-work. You'll also appreciate the Bride's Room, a feminine and floral salon where you can put the finishing touches to your finery.

Outdoor receptions are hosted on the expansive Front Lawn, beneath the scattered shade of magnificent mature trees. One specimen, a fabulous Moreton Bay fig tree, displays an intricate root system—symbolic of a knot well tied! The Front Lawn holds 600 or more guests, and takes on many different moods or themes—from a posh garden soirée to a festive hoedown—depending on how you have it decorated.

If you prefer to bring the party inside, then you'll love the ranch's Red Barn. Originally constructed in 1905, a recent renovation has preserved the look of the classic American structure, complete with a brick-red façade trimmed in white and a whimsical weathervane on top. And although the barn's ambiance is rustic, it's been outfitted with 21st century amenities. A catering kitchen, lighting and AV capabilities (including flat screen TVs, a sound system and projection screen), and modern, tiled restrooms mean your guests won't have to rough it. The neutral décor and soaring wooden rafters beg for your own embellishments—tulle swags, antique chandeliers or icicle lights, for example. Spacious enough to hold 250 for a reception and still allow for dancing on the sealed concrete floor, the barn also boasts two sets of double doors and windows that can be opened to the country breeze.

Camarillo Ranch is run by a nonprofit foundation, committed to preserving the ranch's historical traditions. Whether you envision a nostalgic Victorian-inspired fête or a casual barbecue, this facility provides a flexible, scenic venue for a landmark celebration.

CEREMONY CAPACITY: The Front Lawn accommodates 1,000 seated guests; other outdoor sites are available. Indoors, the Red Barn can hold 250.

EVENT/RECEPTION & MEETING CAPACITY: The Front Lawn holds 1,000 seated or standing guests; Indoors, the Red Barn accommodates 250 seated or 600 standing guests.

FEES & DEPOSITS: 50% of the rental fee and a signed contract are required to reserve your date. The remaining site rental balance and a $1,000 refundable damage deposit are due 90 days prior to the scheduled event. Wedding packages range $5,000–6,500 and cover an all-day, 16-hour time block (9am–1am) that includes use of the Red Barn and lawns, a Bridal Suite, and escorted access to the Victorian Home for wedding photography. Please inquire about seasonal wedding package discounts. A 10% discount for active-duty military is available. For details on corporate, nonprofit and other special event package rates, contact the venue.

Note that Camarillo Ranch is a location-only venue. Clients are responsible for equipment, setup/cleanup and contracting/coordinating all vendors; a professional day-of event coordinator and security are required. Catering, bartending, equipment rentals, lighting, décor and security are contracted through the ranch's preferred vendors unless a $500 buyout option is requested. The Ranch can provide vendor recommendations for additional categories.

AVAILABILITY: Year-round, daily, 9am–1am.

SERVICES/AMENITIES:

Catering: BYO
Kitchen Facilities: prep only
Tables & Chairs: CBA, extra fee or through caterer
Linens, Silver, etc.: through caterer
Restrooms: wheelchair accessible
Dance Floor: no
Bride's & Groom's Dressing Areas: yes
AV/Meeting Equipment: CBA, extra fee

Parking: 30-car lot on site; more CBA
Accommodations: no guest rooms
Outdoor Night Lighting: CBA
Outdoor Cooking Facilities: BBQ CBA
Cleanup: renter or caterer
View: mountains, garden, fountain, landscaped grounds
Other: picnic area

RESTRICTIONS:

Alcohol: BYO, licensed server
Smoking: not allowed
Music: amplified OK

Wheelchair Access: yes
Insurance: liability required

McCormick Home Ranch

Private Ranch

2034 East Fifth Street, Camarillo
805/482-1549
www.mccormickhomeranch.com
mccormickhomeranch@verizon.net

	Rehearsal Dinners	●	Corporate Events
●	Ceremonies	●	Meetings
●	Wedding Receptions	●	Film Shoots
●	Private Parties		Accommodations

If only a real country wedding will do, then get on over to the McCormick Home Ranch in Camarillo. Built in 1918, this historic home is set on 11 verdant acres, eight of them devoted to avocado trees. The Ranch is surrounded by miles of farmland, where everything from strawberries to onions grows almost effortlessly in a fertile plain at the base of the Conejo foothills. That's what prompted Irish immigrant Thomas McCormick to settle in Camarillo back in 1888, and McCormick Home Ranch has been the scene of family weddings and parties for four generations. Now Sally McCormick, the current matriarch, invites you to experience a little bit o' country charm by staging your special event on the picturesque grounds.

Trees, flowers, and greenery of all kinds make this venue cheery and welcoming. Guests drive onto the property and park in an ample lot behind some shrubs to the side. Then it's just a short walk to the front of the main house, a white wood-frame Colonial with a trio of dormer windows and a broad brick veranda edged in fragrant star jasmine. A portico extends from one side of the house; on the other, Sally's old wooden wagon holds your wedding gifts, and her vintage white iron stand supports your guest book.

The gravel driveway in front of the house encircles a large lawn, where the newlyweds hold their reception. There's plenty of room for a bar, buffet area, or even a band or DJ. Couples have the option of setting a portable dance floor on either the gravel or the grass. Flowers are everywhere—some in pots, some growing wild like a delicate dusting of confetti. Dining tables face a thicket of colorful jacarandas, palms, pine trees and all manner of leafy foliage. At night, Tivoli lights twinkle through the jasmine, and Japanese lanterns glow softly like candlelight.

An exceptionally pretty place for a ceremony is the Garden, reached by a small flagstone path next to the house. A spacious brick patio bordered by trees extends from the side of the house, which has a charming, countrified feel thanks to trails of trumpet vine hugging its windows. At the patio's far corner, a permanent arch brimming with honeysuckle frames the couple as they exchange vows. The center of the Garden holds a stone birdbath encircled with lacy blooms, and the fluttering of sparrow wings and the occasional butterfly make it seem like spring any time of year.

Behind the house, yet one more brick patio and garden is available for your ceremony or cocktail hour. An arbor laced with vines and nestled amongst the lush landscaping is an inviting spot to say "I do." Quaint outdoor furniture, birdhouses, and a swing with room enough for two make everyone feel right at home.

Throughout the property, delightful discoveries, like distressed watering cans tucked in garden nooks and a genuine cistern pump, contribute to the old-fashioned mood. McCormick Home Ranch recaptures the rustic appeal of bygone days, and is bound to make your wedding a historic event.

CEREMONY, EVENT/RECEPTION & MEETING CAPACITY: The site accommodates up to 250 guests.

FEES & DEPOSITS: Half of the rental fee is a nonrefundable deposit required to reserve your date. The balance is due 2 weeks prior to the event. Rental fees range $3,800–4,000 for Friday, Saturday and Sunday. A $500 refundable cleaning and security deposit is additional. Tables, chairs, linens, etc. and vintage furnishings & décor are all provided by the ranch at an additional fee.

AVAILABILITY: Spring–Fall, daily, 11am–11pm.

SERVICES/AMENITIES:

Catering: BYO, licensed caterer; licensed server for alcohol
Kitchen Facilities: no
Tables & Chairs: provided
Linens, Silver, etc.: linens provided; BYO tableware
Restrooms: wheelchair accessible, portable
Dance Floor: provided
Bride's & Groom's Dressing Areas: yes
AV/Meeting Equipment: BYO

Parking: large lighted lot
Accommodations: no guest rooms
Outdoor Night Lighting: yes
Outdoor Cooking Facilities: no
Cleanup: caterer or renter
View: trees, garden

RESTRICTIONS:

Alcohol: BYO
Smoking: allowed
Music: amplified OK, curfew 10:30pm

Wheelchair Access: yes
Insurance: required

Wedgewood Sterling Hills

901 Sterling Hills Drive, Camarillo
866/966-3009

www.wedgewoodbanquet.com
events@wedgewoodbanquet.com

- Rehearsal Dinners
- Ceremonies
- Wedding Receptions
- Private Parties
- Corporate Events
- Meetings
- Film Shoots
- Accommodations

Camarillo lies at the heart of Pleasant Valley, cradled by the richly forested Las Posas Mountains. With arguably the best weather in the country, it's become one of the most desirable areas for living out the Southern California lifestyle. Wedgewood Sterling Hills perfectly reflects Camarillo's congenial attitude and idyllic surroundings.

The country road up to Sterling Hills winds past strawberry fields and orange groves and, as you crest the first rise, the handsome Sterling Hills clubhouse suddenly makes its appearance. The building is a sleek example of Mediterranean chic, with a red-tile roof and a double-arched portico supported by classical columns. Crowning the circular driveway is a grand stone fountain flanked by young palm trees. The glass-and-mahogany front door opens into a dramatic vaulted rotunda. Sunlight peeks through lofty arched windows, and an elaborate wrought-iron chandelier suspended from the cupola adds a nighttime glow. Further on is the banquet room and lounge, distinguished by an air of attractive refinement and an open floor plan. A working fireplace keeps things cozy, while a long row of windows treats guests to a vision of the emerald fairways of Sterling Hills Golf Course and picturesque countryside.

The outdoor wedding site is lovely, with the bridal couple silhouetted against the gently rolling greens. As the pink gauze of sunset veils the horizon, feathery clouds hover over the slopes along the valley's eastern edge, completing the romantic picture.

Cocktails are poured at the mahogany bar in the lounge, but guests usually wander outside to enjoy the central fountain terrace, set with the hors d'oeuvres display. A delicious dinner is served back in the banquet room and, as the evening progresses, guests spill out onto the south terrace facing the ninth hole. Here, lanky marsh grass and a thicket of reeds surround a small pond, from which a chorus of frogs often serenades the guests.

Like the rest of Wedgewood's popular banquet centers, this one at Sterling Hills is not only beautiful, but convenient as well. Their thoughtful and comprehensive wedding packages are a terrific value, and make it easy for you to put your event details together.

Whether your wedding is a formal affair or a casual get-together of family and friends, the personalized service, appealing amenities and sophisticated country club setting of Wedgewood Sterling Hills will make you and your guests feel utterly indulged.

CEREMONY, EVENT/RECEPTION & MEETING CAPACITY: The site accommodates up to 225 seated or standing guests.

FEES & DEPOSITS: 25% of the estimated total event cost is required to reserve your date. An additional 25% is due 120 days prior to the event and the balance (based on your final guest count) is due 10 days prior. All payments are credited towards your final balance and are nonrefundable and nontransferable. All-inclusive, completely customizable wedding packages start at $43/person. Tax, alcohol and a 21–22% service charge are additional.

AVAILABILITY: Year-round, daily, 7am–1am.

SERVICES/AMENITIES:

Catering: in-house
Kitchen Facilities: n/a
Tables & Chairs: provided
Linens, Silver, etc.: provided
Restrooms: wheelchair accessible
Dance Floor: provided
Bride's Dressing Area: yes
AV/Meeting Equipment: provided

Parking: large lot
Accommodations: no guest rooms
Outdoor Night Lighting: yes
Outdoor Cooking Facilities: no
Cleanup: provided
View: fairways, Santa Paula Mtns., orchards

RESTRICTIONS:

Alcohol: in-house
Smoking: outdoors only
Music: amplified OK

Wheelchair Access: yes
Insurance: not required
Other: no rice, confetti or glitter; no open flames

Want to know WHAT TO ASK a potential location or vendor? Check out our Questions to Ask starting on page 21..

Eden Gardens Weddings

Garden

Address withheld to ensure privacy. Moorpark
805/208-3098

www.edengardensweddings.com
edengardensweddings@gmail.com

●	Rehearsal Dinners	●	Corporate Events
●	Ceremonies	●	Meetings
●	Wedding Receptions	●	Film Shoots
●	Private Parties		Accommodations

Wanted: True Romantics to wed in fragrant garden paradise. Must love the sounds of flowing water and birdsong. Desire for unique celebration with family and friends a definite plus!

Equal parts enchanted forest and tropical oasis with a large helping of event-friendly amenities, Eden Gardens is two acres of "wow" from your first step inside the private gates. An arched entryway beckons you deep into fairyland. Lush, meandering paths canopied in greenery yield surprises at every turn: a waterfall that feeds a running brook…vintage birdcages aglow with luminarias…urns brimming with blooms…a covey of wedding-white peacocks. Down one walkway, you'll find yourself among a series of fantastical aviaries alive with sound and color. Vivid parrots engage in friendly chatter (Arturo se habla espanol!), while lovebirds and rosy-cheeked cockatiels trill a sweet serenade. A clearing serves as a pre-event welcome station, where guests quaff lemonade amid the fluttering of doves' wings. And you haven't even arrived at the Ceremonial Garden yet!

A series of twinkle-lit archways entwined with blush-pink Eden roses leads to a breathtaking vision: a picturesque pond dotted with blooming lily pads and fountain sprays. Spread along the bank, a pair of manicured lawns flanks a spacious stage which is elevated to allow views of the bridal couple from every angle. Behind them, an uplit waterfall cascades around a classical statue; in front of them, the sunset's reflection turns the pond into a scintillating waterscape. "Dreamy" doesn't begin to describe this storybook setting.

The myriad of photogenic backdrops lures the wedding party away during the social hour, but guests won't mind—they're busy exploring the several pondside terraces set with cocktail tables. As evening descends, your gathering moves on to the open-air Amphitheater, a swathe of grass with a low, colorfully lit waterfall along the perimeter. Overhead, market lights merge with the starscape for maximum magic. A raised demilune stage that looks as if it was made of alabaster is perfect for showcasing the sweetheart table and wedding cake or your entertainment.

Down a nearby path, the lofty whitewashed Pavilion, adorned with flower baskets, has the feel of an open-sided barn. A dollhouse porch off to one side is a fun spot to serve late-night snacks or the wedding cake.

With so many delights competing for your attention, it's easy to overlook Eden Gardens' practical enhancements. For example, an abundance of specialty lighting accentuates the nighttime glamour of each fountain and event area, and many of the tree trunks are wrapped with twinkle lights. Your choice of music fills the air, thanks to a sound system discreetly wired throughout the grounds.

Eden Gardens' chosen caterer, *Command Performance,* is "Certified by The Guide." Experienced and caring with an expert staff, the company boasts a knowledgeable catering coordinator as well as chefs who specialize in exciting food station receptions and theme menus. Their wedding packages offer both convenience and flexibility, and customization is welcome.

For true romantics, Eden Gardens will be love at first sight, but anyone who appreciates natural beauty and exceptional services will fall under its spell.

CEREMONY CAPACITY: The site holds 300 seated guests outdoors.

EVENT/RECEPTION CAPACITY: The site accommodates 300 seated or 400 standing guests outdoors.

MEETING CAPACITY: Meeting spaces seat 400 guests outdoors.

FEES & DEPOSITS: A $1,750 deposit is required to reserve your date, and the balance is due 14 days prior to the event. Rental fees for use of the ceremony and reception area are $3,450 for Friday and $4,450 for Saturday or Sunday. There is an additional charge of $5/person for all Saturday events. Guest count minimums vary depending on the day of the week, and holiday rates may apply on certain dates. Valet, security and special event insurance are required.

Catering packages are available through *Command Performance Catering* and start at $72/person. A $1,000 deposit is required. Tax and a 20% service charge are extra. Alcohol is not included in catering packages; contact the catering coordinator for details. *Rental and catering fees are subject to change.*

AVAILABILITY: Year round, daily, 8am–11pm.

SERVICES/AMENITIES:

Catering: in-house
Kitchen Facilities: n/a
Tables & Chairs: CBA
Linens, Silver, etc.: CBA
Restrooms: wheelchair accessible
Dance Area: provided
Bride's Dressing Area: yes
AV/Meeting Equipment: CBA

Parking: large lot
Accommodations: no guest rooms
Outdoor Night Lighting: CBA
Outdoor Cooking Facilities: none
Cleanup: provided
View: creek, fountain, garden, lagoon, land-scaped grounds and waterfall
Other: event coordination

RESTRICTIONS:

Alcohol: BYO
Smoking: designated areas only
Music: amplified OK outdoors

Wheelchair Access: yes
Insurance: liability required

Rancho de las Palmas

Private Estate

3566 Sunset Valley Road, Moorpark
805/529-6699
www.ranchodelaspalmas.com
ranchodelaspalmas@gmail.com

- Rehearsal Dinners
- Ceremonies
- Wedding Receptions
- Private Parties
- Corporate Events
- Meetings
- Film Shoots
- Accommodations

In describing an event facility, the word "oasis" gets thrown around pretty loosely, but Rancho de las Palmas, with its spring-fed lagoon, thousands of palm trees and 15 fountains, comes as close as we've ever seen to fitting the literal definition. Personally designed and executed over nearly two decades by the Cassar family, this unique, 420-acre private estate is also a registered turtle sanctuary and botanical garden. Everything here is handmade and reflects the family's seemingly unlimited creative energy.

The focal point of Rancho de Las Palmas is the huge lagoon, with three sparkling fountains and a marvelous island connected to the shore by a bridge. Weeping willows and stalwart palm trees make for a tropical setting on the shore, and a spacious serpentine deck—any part of which can be set up for entertaining—borders the lagoon. This is a great spot to sip a mai tai with friends and enjoy the view.

Couples get married in front of the double-tier waterfall, on the grass beneath a lovely bronze arch, or on the short flight of brick stairs facing the large lagoon. The stairs have an overhead arch and side railings fashioned in ornate wrought iron, perfect for twining with flowers. From here, it's only a few steps to the Pavilion for the reception. This circular space is quite charming—organza draped from the top of the center pole is embedded with glowing twinkle lights, creating a romantic ambiance. When the sun goes down, this place really comes alive!

If you're planning a large ceremony, you'll be thoroughly delighted by the estate's newest wedding site. Here, the bride walks down a 100-foot-long aisle and through a series of five ornate archways, all of which can be festooned with flowers and tulle. Vows are exchanged beneath the last arch against a backdrop of tropical foliage.

One of the greatest pleasures of being at Rancho de las Palmas is taking a stroll around the grounds. As you do, notice the unique architectural details: On the deck, wood railings change to wrought iron, and pathways that start out brick turn to cobblestone, then to concrete poured in imaginative designs. Classical fountains rub shoulders with abstract stone structures made of river rock and brick, some decorated with leaping dolphins. However, if you think this sounds like an artistic hodgepodge, you're in for a treat. It all harmonizes beautifully—the man-made structures seem to have grown as naturally as the palms, pepper trees and flowers that surround them. And if children are included in your celebration, they'll be enchanted (and occupied!) by a Swiss Family Robinson-style tree house, complete with slide and swings.

Incidentally, the Rancho only holds one event per day, so you and your bridal party are welcome to start setting up in the morning, and spend a little time relaxing before the festivities. In addition to weddings, Rancho de las Palmas has hosted numerous movie shoots, luaus, casino nights, bar mitzvahs, birthday and graduation parties, swing dances, memorial services, auctions and fundraisers. If you can't stand the thought of renting a stuffy ballroom or crowded banquet hall for your event, try Rancho de Las Palmas—it's as refreshing as an oasis in the desert!

CEREMONY CAPACITY: Ceremony areas hold 230 seated guests.

EVENT/RECEPTION & MEETING CAPACITY: The covered Pavilion can accommodate up to 230 seated guests. For corporate events, the site holds up to 230 guests.

FEES & DEPOSITS: For weddings, a $3,000 nonrefundable deposit is payable when reservations are confirmed; the balance is due 2 weeks prior to the event. The rental fee is $3,000 on Saturday, $2,000 on Sunday and $1,500 on Friday evening. Wedding packages start at $60/person, and include use of the property, a buffet or dinner, hors d'oeuvres, unlimited social bar and champagne toast, chairs, tables and tableware. Tax and a 17% service charge are additional.

For corporate events a nonrefundable deposit totaling 50% of the estimated event total is payable when reservations are confirmed; the balance is due 2 weeks prior to the event. The rental fee varies depending on guest count, day of week and event type; call for more information.

AVAILABILITY: Year-round, daily including holidays, 9am–10pm.

SERVICES/AMENITIES:
Catering: in-house, no BYO
Kitchen Facilities: n/a
Tables & Chairs: provided
Linens, Silver, etc.: provided
Restrooms: wheelchair accessible
Dance Floor: rental available
Bride's Dressing Area: yes
AV/Meeting Equipment: BYO

Parking: large, lighted lot
Accommodations: no guest rooms
Outdoor Night Lighting: yes
Outdoor Cooking Facilities: through caterer
Cleanup: caterer
View: tropical botanical gardens, freshwater lake, turtle rescue sanctuary, palm trees, fountains

RESTRICTIONS:
Alcohol: in-house, or BYO
Smoking: designated areas
Music: amplified OK outdoors

Wheelchair Access: mostly yes
Insurance: extra insurance CBA
Other: no rice or confetti

Wedgewood at The Tower Club

Special Events Facility

300 East Esplande Drive, Oxnard
866/966-3009

www.wedgewoodbanquet.com
events@wedgewoodbanquet.com

- Rehearsal Dinners
- Ceremonies
- Wedding Receptions
- Private Parties
- Corporate Events
- Meetings
- Film Shoots
- Accommodations

Even if you're usually a casual "t-shirts and jeans" type of couple, for your wedding you'll want to entertain in style. One of the most sophisticated settings in Ventura County is Wedgewood at The Tower Club, where you'll be treated to delectable cuisine, courtly service and a million-dollar view.

This sophisticated venue occupies the 22nd floor of the Morgan Stanley Building, an impressive black glass citadel overlooking the city. Founded in 1987, The Tower Club has established a tradition of providing superb hospitality for members and nonmembers alike who wish to celebrate in its swanky surroundings. Recently, Wedgewood Wedding and Banquet Centers joined forces with the Tower Club, bringing expertise, flexibility and affordability to this local landmark—a winning combination sure to please engaged couples!

One of the privileges enjoyed by wedding guests is the "members only" elevator that whisks them to the uppermost floor. A chandelier-lit hallway leads past a glass-enclosed wine cellar to a black-tiled foyer, where guests can mingle.

The club's event areas are a semicircular series of adjoining salons which all boast the same fabulous feature: large picture windows that showcase a panorama of city and sea all the way to the Channel Islands. The area just beyond the foyer is sometimes used for intimate ceremonies. Guests are seated facing those soaring windows, which make a stunning backdrop for heartfelt vows. Another ceremony spot, the East Room, is actually down the hall and accommodates 75 guests. In either space, couples often bring in a decorated arch that frames them in front of that spectacular view. Couples can also say "I do" outside in the garden plaza atop a raised dais, with the soaring skyscraper in the background.

Social hours convene in the snazzy Sky Lounge at the club's farthest corner. Loaded with all the retro-chic attitude of a Rat Pack-era night club, Sky Lounge is outfitted with white leather banquettes and club chairs huddled around low cocktail tables. Even the long bar is upholstered in white leather. A large flat screen TV, a built-in sound system and a piano provide plenty of entertainment options. A fireplace separates Sky Lounge from the main dining rooms, where receptions unfold amid classic elegance.

Unlike some private clubs, whose dark wood paneling feels too masculine and heavy, these rooms are light-filled and welcoming, thanks to the windows and white ceilings inset with burnished bronze. As the ultimate VIPs, newlyweds have their choice of either cuddling at a sweetheart table or presiding over a head table facing the windows. A dance floor is set amidst the diners, so no matter where they're sitting they can get a good look at the action. Everyone also has a front-row seat for the skyline's magical transformation from sunset to nightfall, as stars and city lights combine in a glittering carpet to the sea.

Both the tablesettings and the meals are pleasing to the eye, and the Wedgewood banquet team will work with you to create your culinary vision. They're so helpful, in fact, you can even include details like invitations and florals with your wedding package, for ultimate convenience. The Tower Club is an exceptional choice for rehearsal dinners, too, as well as bridal showers or other noteworthy occasions.

An oasis of courteous attention, palate-pleasing fare and breathtaking views, Wedgewood at The Tower Club is one of the area's most wedding-worthy venues.

CEREMONY, EVENT/RECEPTION & MEETING CAPACITY: The site holds up to 250 seated or standing guests.

FEES & DEPOSITS: 25% of the estimated total event cost is required to reserve your date. An additional 25% is due 120 days prior to the event and the balance (based on your final guest count) is due 10 days prior. All payments are credited towards your final balance and are nonrefundable and nontransferable. All-inclusive, completely customizable wedding packages start at $43/person. Tax, alcohol and a 21–22% service charge are additional.

AVAILABILITY: Year-round, daily, 7am–2am.

SERVICES/AMENITIES:

Catering: in-house
Kitchen Facilities: n/a
Tables & Chairs: provided
Linens, Silver, etc.: provided
Restrooms: wheelchair accessible
Dance Floor: yes
Bride's Dressing Area: yes
AV/Meeting Equipment: provided

Parking: large lot, garage nearby
Accommodations: no guest rooms
Outdoor Night Lighting: yes
Outdoor Cooking Facilities: no
Cleanup: provided
View: garden, landscaped grounds, courtyard; panorama of cityscape, coastline, ocean
Other: in-house wedding cake and florals, clergy on staff, event coordination

RESTRICTIONS:

Alcohol: in-house
Smoking: outdoors only
Music: amplified OK

Wheelchair Access: yes
Insurance: not required
Other: no rice, confetti or glitter; no open flames

Newhall Mansion

829 Park Street, Piru
805/398-5042

www.newhallmansion.com
guestrelations@newhallmansion.com

Historic Mansion & Garden

● Rehearsal Dinners	● Corporate Events
● Ceremonies	Meetings
● Wedding Receptions	● Film Shoots
● Private Parties	● Accommodations

Despite its decades-long popularity as a location for film and TV shoots, you've probably never heard of Piru before. Yet the quiet agricultural community on the Eastern fringe of scenic Heritage Valley is a mere 10 minutes from Valencia's Magic Mountain. The town is emerging from its relative obscurity, however, thanks to the spectacular renovation of its crown jewel, Newhall Mansion. This enchanting Queen Anne-style hilltop residence, set on nine landscaped acres, was originally built in 1890 by Piru's founder, publishing magnate David C. Cook, as a gift for his wife. The ensuing years saw a series of owners, a fire and two earthquakes, until at last the mansion was rescued in 2013. The current proprietors have completely transformed the Ventura County landmark, adding modern amenities, lush gardens and exquisite décor that accentuates its vintage glamour.

Passing through the mansion's imposing wrought-iron gates, you're greeted by a citrus grove flanking a long, rose-lined promenade. Next comes the Park, a lovely hedged lawn in front of the mansion with a splashing fountain and panoramic mountain view. The estate's fairy-tale façade, featuring wraparound verandas, intricate scrollwork and a stone tower, makes a grand backdrop for exchanging vows.

A stroll to the backyard reveals a tiled Courtyard that's a delightful locale for dining and dancing under the stars. Extras include a fire pit, a swimming pool with white cabanas, and an old-fashioned pagoda to showcase the wedding cake, sweetheart table or bar. Specialty lighting throughout the grounds adds to the evening's magic. The terraced gardens and rolling lawns that overlook the Courtyard hold more wedding options. An illuminated stairway makes a dramatic wedding aisle, and the couple exchanges vows in front of a twinkle-lit arch. Groves of olive, pomegranate, apricot and fig trees form a leafy background, a legacy of David Cook's "Second Garden of Eden." In the tranquil twilight, the romantic milieu does seem a lot like paradise.

The best way to indulge in all the mansion's luxuries is to spend the weekend, which also lets you expand your event into the breathtaking 12,000-square-foot interior. Each room is lavished with period details, antiques and artistic restorations. The Ballroom's magnificent stained-glass transom frames a glorious view, and is a favorite spot for bridal portraits. The Dining Room, with its stunning coffered ceiling, and the stately fire-lit Library offer classic Victorian elegance. And the new Bridal Hospitality Suite provides 3,000 square feet of seclusion and queenly comforts.

The mansion's most imaginative entertainment option is the Tavern, an underground man-cave whose circular stone entryway recalls a Gothic castle. A series of brick-walled salons radiate an aura of mystery, and a giant flat-screen TV, custom redwood bar and cool stylings make the Tavern a novel setting for a cocktail reception, bachelor party or rehearsal dinner. A hidden bedroom will have you feeling like characters in a romance novel. Seven sumptuous bedrooms in the main house boast a collective assortment of deluxe treats: a fireplace, an extravagant stone shower with carved mermaids, a wooden Jacuzzi and a huge stained-glass oriel window.

Newhall Mansion welcomes you to celebrate in complete privacy amid nostalgic opulence, all while surrounded by nature. Not only has this historic charmer put Piru on the map—it's also a treasure of a wedding venue.

CEREMONY & EVENT/RECEPTION CAPACITY: The facility can accommodate 100 seated or standing guests indoors and 300 seated or standing outdoors.

MEETING CAPACITY: Meetings do not take place at this facility.

FEES & DEPOSITS: 25% of the total event cost is required to reserve your date. Three additional payments of 25% each are due 180 days, 90 days, and 30 days prior to the event. Flexible payment terms are available. The rental fee ranges $8,000–16,000 depending on the day of the week and customizable options such as interior access and overnight accommodations. The Wedding Weekend Package includes full use of the property from Friday noon to Sunday noon for your rehearsal dinner, wedding, and day-after brunch, accommodations for up to 20 adults, plus free parking. Note that indoor usage is only available when overnight accommodations are booked. Please contact the site for your personalized quote.

AVAILABILITY: Year-round, daily, 10am–11pm.

SERVICES/AMENITIES:

Catering: BYO with approval

Kitchen Facilities: limited

Tables & Chairs: provided

Linens, Silver, etc.: through caterer or BYO

Restrooms: wheelchair accessible

Dance Area: provided

Bride's Dressing Area: yes

AV/Meeting Equipment: n/a

Other: picnic area

Parking: large complimentary lot

Accommodations: 8 guest rooms, including a new 3,000 sq. ft. bridal suite

Outdoor Night Lighting: provided

Outdoor Cooking Facilities: BBQ on site

Cleanup: caterer or renter

View: canyon, forest, fountain, garden, landscaped grounds, pool, vineyards

RESTRICTIONS:

Alcohol: BYO

Smoking: designated areas only

Music: amplified OK with restrictions

Wheelchair Access: yes

Insurance: liability required

Want to find more venues and services? Check out our informative website, www.HereComesTheGuide.com.

89

Limoneira Ranch

1141 Cummings Road, Santa Paula
805/525-5736
www.limoneiraranchweddings.com
jason@platedevents.com

Historic Ranch & Garden

● Rehearsal Dinners	● Corporate Events
● Ceremonies	● Meetings
● Wedding Receptions	● Film Shoots
● Private Parties	Accommodations

The historic township of Santa Paula in Heritage Valley presents a refreshing contrast to the urban bustle just an hour away. Visitors warm to its slower pace and small-town charms, which include vintage homes, antique airplanes and a train depot that dates to 1887. Acres upon acres of fruit groves in this "Citrus Capital of the World" are hugged by oak-studded hillsides and rugged mountain peaks. A center of silent film production in the 1920s, the picturesque region still attracts Hollywood filmmakers…and lately, engaged couples who've discovered an authentic venue for staging their own wedding masterpiece.

Limoneira Ranch perfectly embodies the valley's rich legacy. Founded in 1893, the 7,300-acre spread remains the county's largest producer of oranges, avocados, and, of course, lemons. Limoneira may have one foot in the past, but the other is firmly set in a very green future—innovations like their solar orchard demonstrate their commitment to a sustainable natural lifestyle.

Entering the property between rows of fir trees, you inhale the pleasing aroma of ripening fruit and sweet lemon blossoms. To your right stands the handsome Craftsman-style Ranch Lobby building; on your left, the original Sunkist lemon packinghouse—an architectural award-winner—conveys a timeless allure. Between their two striking facades, Limoneira's event team creates a festive setting with an open-sided tent, market lights, floral displays, tables and lounge seating, food stations, and whatever else it takes to realize your reception vision. The many balmy months make outside entertaining inviting throughout much of the year, and guests often enjoy their cocktails on the adjacent garden breezeways and nearby flower-dappled lawns.

Limoneira's lush grounds offer several appealing spots, but for an all-in-one wedding locale, the North Lawn can't be beat. Set against the backdrop of fragrant lemon groves traced by mountain silhouettes, the Lawn's approach holds 12 bocce ball courts (a terrific ice-breaker activity for cocktail hours or rehearsal dinners). Crowning the scene, steps lead to a broad landing, a dramatic place to exchange vows. Just above, a grassy expanse provides plenty of room for a lavish reception, including dancing under an explosion of stars.

With so much to arrange, couples can count on the ranch's experienced event coordinator, Jason Collis of *Plated Events.* They're lucky: Not only is Jason a chef extraordinaire, he's also passionate about helping them make the most of the ranch's many attributes.

Steeped in nostalgia, this green wedding venue brings together Nature's splendor and heartwarming family celebrations. After over 100 years, Limoneira is still keeping it real.

CEREMONY, EVENT/RECEPTION & MEETING CAPACITY: Outdoors, the site can accommodate 75–1,000 seated or up to 3,000 standing guests on the North Lawn or in the Front Office Courtyard.

FEES & DEPOSITS: A $500 deposit is required to reserve your date and the balance is due 30 days prior to the event. Rental fees range $500–2,000 depending on the day of the event and the space rented. Meals range $20–125/person. Tax, alcohol and a 20% service charge are additional.

AVAILABILITY: Year-round, daily, until midnight.

SERVICES/AMENITIES:

Catering: in-house
Kitchen Facilities: n/a
Tables & Chairs: through caterer
Linens, Silver, etc.: through caterer
Restrooms: wheelchair accessible
Dance Floor: provided
Bride's Dressing Area: yes
AV/Meeting Equipment: provided
Other: picnic area, day-of vendor coordination

Parking: large lot
Accommodations: no guest rooms
Outdoor Night Lighting: CBA
Outdoor Cooking Facilities: BBQ CBA
Cleanup: provided
View: fountain, garden, creek, landscaped grounds, waterfall; panorama of mountains, ocean, and valley

RESTRICTIONS:

Alcohol: in-house
Smoking: designated areas only
Music: amplified OK

Wheelchair Access: yes
Insurance: liability required

Quail Ranch

Private Ranch

Address withheld to ensure privacy. Simi Valley
805/328-4928
www.quailranchevents.com
joanne@quailranchevents.com

● Rehearsal Dinners		● Corporate Events	
● Ceremonies		● Meetings	
● Wedding Receptions		● Film Shoots	
● Private Parties		Accommodations	

Perched high on a hill, Quail Ranch is a hidden retreat set in the midst of a working 70-acre avocado ranch.

Built in 1933 by one of Simi Valley's founding families, the Ranch House has everything you love about Spanish-Revival architecture: red-tile roofs, huge picture windows (that happen to frame the glorious grounds), and a hacienda-style layout complete with splashing tiled fountains. The present-day proprietress has a deft hand at decoration, and her efforts have resulted in a serene world of rustic elegance that showcases the ranch's historic character and charm.

Nature plays a beautiful role in all of the event spaces. The first one is an expansive courtyard in front of the Ranch House, shaded by a stupendous ancient oak. An idyllic gathering spot for arriving guests, it offers a natural canvas for your personal touches: hand-drawn signs, welcome refreshments, café lights, a chandelier…The courtyard also hosts lively parties (its brick surface makes a unique dance floor!) In the far corner, the barn-style Carriage House can house games, a fabulous 1920s-style bar and nightclub-like amenities—whatever your imagination can come up with!

Alongside the Ranch House lies Star Pine Lawn, where an intimate garden wedding is oh-so-pretty framed by lush greenery and pops of lavender and purple salvia. Tall pines at one end make a lovely backdrop for tying the knot. The neighboring Fountain Courtyard, a quaint rose-scented patio with climbing vines and tropical palms accenting a wrought-iron balcony, hosts a delightful al fresco brunch or cocktail hour.

Larger ceremonies unfold on the sprawling 5,000-square-foot Lemon Blossom Terrace, created specifically with romantic "I do"s in mind. For her grand entrance, the bride descends a dramatic stairway flanked by olive trees and bougainvillea to the brick terrace below. The fragrance of lemon and lavender is in the air as vows are exchanged beneath a majestic oak, or under a decorated wrought-iron arch overlooking the terrace.

The other side of the home holds even more possibilities. Serve cocktails beneath the cozy Wisteria Arbor, followed by a reception on an adjoining manicured lawn crowned by a towering oak. The original stone fireplace, a fire pit (perfect for late-night s'mores!) and a hand-painted tiled fountain ringed with jasmine enhance the picturesque scene. Flagstone steps ascend to a classic turquoise swimming pool and deck, just the place to sip champagne while a rosy sunset spreads across the horizon. At the Poolside Retreat, which is reserved for the bridal party, French doors open to a chic interior with a stunning floor-to-ceiling stone fireplace and luxe furnishings. The groom has his own hideaway, too—The Lodge, a comfortable masculine space outfitted with leather sofas, a flagstone hearth, a pool table and even a private patio.

Fresh, imaginative cuisine is also part of the Quail Ranch experience. Delicious farm-to-table dishes featuring locally grown produce are exquisitely presented by their exclusive "Certified By The Guide" caterer, *Command Performance*. Menus are customized with each client's tastes and budget in mind.

While every inch of the property is meticulously maintained, there's a seductive ease about the place that ensures relaxed entertaining. Infused with nostalgia, gracious living and warm hospitality, Quail Ranch is an inspiring choice for your landmark celebration.

CEREMONY & EVENT/RECEPTION CAPACITY: The facility holds up to 300 seated or standing guests outdoors.

MEETING CAPACITY: Meeting spaces can seat up to 100.

FEES & DEPOSITS: A $2,500 deposit is required to reserve your date, and the balance is due 30 days prior to the event. The venue rental fee starts at $4,500 and varies depending on the guest count and the day of the event. Catering packages start at $79/person. Tax, alcohol and service charge are additional.

AVAILABILITY: Year round, daily. Hours are flexible.

SERVICES/AMENITIES:

Catering: in-house
Kitchen Facilities: n/a
Tables & Chairs: provided
Linens, Silver, etc.: provided
Restrooms: not wheelchair accessible
Dance Floor: yes
Bride's & Groom's Dressing Areas: yes
AV/Meeting Equipment: BYO
Other: groom's room with pool table and private patio; fire pit, fireplaces, swimming pool; event coordination available, extra fee

Parking: valet required
Accommodations: no guest rooms
Outdoor Night Lighting: CBA
Outdoor Cooking Facilities: no
Cleanup: caterer or renter
View: fountain, garden, landscaped grounds, fields; panorama of orchards, cityscape, hills and mountains

RESTRICTIONS:

Alcohol: BYO
Smoking: not allowed
Music: amplified OK outdoors with restrictions

Wheelchair Access: limited
Insurance: liability required

The Vineyards

2525 Stow Street, Simi Valley
805/583-2525
www.thevineyardsimi.com
soroor@thevineyardsimi.com

Garden Event Facility

- Rehearsal Dinners
- Ceremonies
- Wedding Receptions
- Private Parties
- Corporate Events
- Meetings
- Film Shoots
- Accommodations

Hidden among the Simi Valley foothills on 8 acres, The Vineyards is a lavish special event oasis that includes almost every romantic element you can imagine: sunsets and starlight, grapevines and gardens, waterfalls and whimsical fountains, as well as glamorous interiors that make you feel like movie stars. Yet perhaps the venue's most standout attribute is their service-oriented banquet managers, who thoughtfully orchestrate each phase of your celebration, right from your guests' arrival at the main center's waterfall entryway.

The friendly staff (and the personalized signage) directs them to either a rustic or contemporary ceremony site, depending on your preference. A stroll to the former follows a serpentine garden path shaded by twinkle-lit, vine-covered arbors down a hillside to a forested dell. As fragrant blooms perfume the air, you exchange vows in front of a profusion of lush greenery and willowy trees. The namesake vineyards are spread out below the garden, and newlyweds are often photographed holding hands among the grapevines.

For a different yet equally invigorating experience, wed on the Waterfall Terrace atop a stunning stone stage framed by a redwood pergola, to the hypnotic accompaniment of rushing water. Behind you, water spills over two landscaped stone tiers that flank the stage steps where your bridal party holds court. Your loved ones enjoy this refreshing tableau, seated beneath café lights and portable white-wood pergolas fashioned with adjustable canopies and sheer drapes—an innovation that's both practical and pretty.

Several enchanting patios encircle the main building, each lending its own charms to al fresco gatherings (think fire tables, custom-built fountains, a fetching footbridge and more!) Or bring the social hour inside to the ultra-swanky Mountain View Room, whose décor epitomizes unique chic. Outfitted in the venue's signature creamy white (always in style, darling), the bi-level room dazzles with crystal chandeliers, luminarias and sparkly accents. On the upper level, silver banquettes dressed with retro fur pillows are the perfect spot to admire breathtaking wraparound windows that double as transparent water walls, a clever design that elevates the space's hip factor.

Elegant galas are sure to impress in the neighboring Grandview Room, which boasts a similar aesthetic—taken up a notch. Chiffon ceiling canopies entwined with rope lights showcase dining tables and gold Chiavari chairs. A built-in stage stands ready for your entertainment, and theatrical lighting delivers a range of color enhancements that add dramatic flair to your reception.

The venue's most novel space is the rotunda-shaped Star View Room, centered around a circular copper bar ringed with trendy acrylic stools. Overhead, an elaborate chandelier hangs from a soaring coved ceiling that displays a scintillating faux starscape. With its nightclub attitude and intimate white leather-clad enclaves, the Star View's mood is at once sultry and cool, just the thing for cocktails, an after-party or an out-of-the-ordinary rehearsal dinner.

If it's all a bit dizzying, don't worry. The Vineyards' seasoned event pros will skillfully integrate your vision with their value-filled packages. Versatile, original and accommodating, this is definitely one of those places you have to experience to fully appreciate, so be sure it's on your "must see" list. You won't be disappointed.

CEREMONY & MEETING CAPACITY: The facility holds 200 seated guests indoors and 300 seated outdoors.

EVENT/RECEPTION CAPACITY: The facility can accommodate up to 300 seated indoors and 300 seated or standing outdoors.

FEES & DEPOSITS: A nonrefundable $1,500 deposit is required to reserve your date and the balance is due 10 days prior to the event. All-inclusive wedding packages range $70–99/person (50-guest minimum). Packages include meals, alcohol, facility, coordinator; and may include photographers, DJ, florist & cake. Tax and a 20% service charge are additional.

AVAILABILITY: Year-round, daily, 9am–midnight.

SERVICES/AMENITIES:
Catering: in-house
Kitchen Facilities: n/a
Tables & Chairs: provided
Linens, Silver, etc.: provided or through caterer
Restrooms: wheelchair accessible
Dance Floor: yes
Bride's Dressing Area: yes
AV/Meeting Equipment: CBA
Other: in-house event coordination, wedding cake, florals, photographer and DJ

Parking: large complimentary lot; valet available, extra fee
Accommodations: no guest rooms
Outdoor Night Lighting: yes
Outdoor Cooking Facilities: BBQ CBA
Cleanup: caterer or renter
View: canyon, forest, fountain, garden, landscaped grounds, waterfall, vineyards; panorama of hills and mountains

RESTRICTIONS:
Alcohol: in-house
Smoking: outdoors only
Music: amplified OK

Wheelchair Access: yes
Insurance: liability required

Wood Ranch Golf Club

Golf Club

301 Wood Ranch Parkway, Simi Valley
888/998-6396

www.countryclubreceptions.com
www.woodranchgc.com
eventdirector@woodranchgc.com

● Rehearsal Dinners	● Corporate Events
● Ceremonies	● Meetings
● Wedding Receptions	● Film Shoots
● Private Parties	Accommodations

Framed by the rugged Santa Susanna Mountains, the upscale Simi Valley community of Wood Ranch, located a stone's throw from the Reagan Library, is prized for its quiet lifestyle, wide boulevards and manicured lawns. At its center lie the verdant greens of the exclusive Wood Ranch Golf Club and its striking contemporary clubhouse, reminiscent of Frank Lloyd Wright.

Masterfully marrying nature and architecture, the building's exterior incorporates elements of Wright's enduring designs, such as cast cement bricks, wood beams and strong, clean lines softened by feathery ferns and colorful blooms. Step under the porte-cochère and you'll feel like you're visiting a sleek, private lodge. That feeling is enhanced when a greeter welcomes your guests and directs them down the walkway to the left, which takes them to a scenic knoll for your ceremony. Shaded from the afternoon sun by a tall stand of trees and brightened by an ever-changing landscape of flowering plants, the site's large lawn and gazebo overlook a glistening lake below.

Once vows have been exchanged, it's time to move inside to the beautifully appointed clubhouse. The foyer's cool slate floor and the enormous barrel-shaped skylight overhead set the tone for the Arts and Crafts touches throughout each room. The Main Lobby, where cocktails are served, makes generous use of luxury materials for an understated elegance: The slate and marble fireplace, for example, is adorned with a large metallic artwork and contributes a modern focal point to the room. Mahogany accents not only add richness to the space, but also mirror the warm wood of the grand piano. A massive chandelier hangs from the high ceiling and reflects the best of Craftsman style in burnished copper, which is picked up again in the room's distinctive copper-and-glass-enclosed wine cellar to your right. The entire room is flooded with light filtering in from the Grand Ballroom, just beyond the tall silk drapes that separate the two spaces (but allow your guests a peek at what's in store for them during the reception).

The Ballroom's most arresting feature is its wall of floor-to-ceiling windows. Over 20 feet tall, they provide a panorama of the golf course below, fringed by the mountains beyond it. For smaller groups, there's the Lakeview Room to the left, which has an outdoor terrace overlooking the gazebo, lawns and lakes of the signature 18th hole.

Wood Ranch Golf Club's seamless combination of timeless design, modern sensibilities, and first-class service creates a beautiful setting for a most memorable wedding celebration.

CEREMONY CAPACITY: The Gazebo Lawn holds up to 350 seated guests; the Ballroom up to 220 seated.

EVENT/RECEPTION & MEETING CAPACITY: The Club accommodates up to 220 seated or 400 standing guests indoors or outdoors.

FEES & DEPOSITS: A nonrefundable deposit, which is applied to your food & beverage total, is required to reserve your date. The amount of the deposit varies depending on how far in advance you book. Payment terms for the balance also vary, and may be arranged on an individual basis. Food & beverage minimums will apply. Wedding packages start at $59/person and food & beverage minimums may apply. Tax, alcohol and service charge are additional. Menus and packages can be customized to fit your needs and budget. Call for details.

AVAILABILITY: Year-round, daily, anytime. Closed on Christmas Day.

SERVICES/AMENITIES:

Catering: in-house or BYO
Kitchen Facilities: n/a
Tables & Chairs: provided
Linens, Silver, etc.: provided
Restrooms: wheelchair accessible
Dance Floor: provided
Bride's Dressing Area: provided
AV/Meeting Equipment: some provided

Parking: large lot, valet required for parties over 100 guests
Accommodations: no guest rooms
Outdoor Night Lighting: access only
Outdoor Cooking Facilities: BBQ
Cleanup: provided
View: fairways, hills, lakes, landscaped grounds
Other: grand piano, secluded gazebo, reception lawn

RESTRICTIONS:

Alcohol: in-house
Smoking: outside only
Music: amplified OK

Wheelchair Access: yes
Insurance: not required

This is important! Tell locations you're reading HERE COMES THE GUIDE and ask if our information is still current.

97

Hartley Botanica

Botanical Gardens

4465 Balcom Canyon Road, Somis
805/532-1997
www.hartleybotanica.com
rj@hartleybotanica.com

● Rehearsal Dinners	● Corporate Events
● Ceremonies	● Meetings
● Wedding Receptions	● Film Shoots
● Private Parties	Accommodations

Just beyond the hills of Camarillo in the peaceful Las Posas Valley you'll find the small hamlet of Somis, home to generations of family farmers. Somis has so far managed to escape the pressure of development, and boasts one post office, one store, and the oldest wooden gas station in California. It's the kind of place that makes you want to slow down for a while, stop and smile at a stranger, and breathe in the fresh country air that seems to make all that grows here flourish.

At Hartley Botanica, not only do the plants and flowers thrive, they also end up in beautiful shapes and clever arrangements. That's because this Somis nursery doubles as a landscaping company, and throughout the property you'll discover artistic examples of garden design. Nowhere is this more impressive than in the wedding area, a spectacular garden oasis that owes its creation to a proud father's love.

It all started when owner Barbara Goodrich took over the place in 1995. Her interest in landscaping came from her parents, creative types whose 30 years of experience include such notable clients as Janet Jackson and Michael Landon. When Barbara got engaged, Mom offered to make her a fabulous wedding gown. Not to be outdone, Dad took advantage of the nursery's natural beauty to create a dream ceremony and reception site for his daughter's wedding. Now Barbara wants to share her fantasy garden with you for your own wedding or special event.

Party guests are free to explore the nursery's novelties, like its rock waterfall with grotto, peacocks, and sculptured rose garden. Yet the celebration grounds themselves are shielded from the public by custom-designed metal gates. The bride has her own changing room to prepare for the walk down the aisle—and you've never seen an aisle quite like this one!

A dramatic, sweeping promenade winds around an expanse of verdant lawn. Along the way you pass under no fewer than 18 vine-covered archways set in bases of flowering stone urns. The rosecolored walkway is embellished with real leaves pressed into the concrete, and caged songbirds add to the magical effect. To the left, a pond featuring an aquatic garden and a cascading waterfall accompany you until you reach the final stretch of the aisle. Then a delicate canopy of tree branches laden with honeysuckle leads to your groom, standing at the center of an enormous daisy permanently etched right into the aisle. (A smaller daisy just beyond can hold an accompanist.) Your guests enjoy the spectacle from the lawn, with the rolling hills as a picturesque backdrop.

A row of shrubs marks the rear of the Ceremony Garden, and on the other side lies the reception area, an even larger swath of lawn dotted with trees, decorative statuary, and pots overflowing with colorful flowers. A stand of Chinese pistachio trees shelters a long bar fashioned of smooth stones; its countertop, embedded with leaves, is the ideal spot to serve drinks and a buffet. Each botanical treatment features built-in seating areas, and some offer intriguing surprises: In the center of the lawn, for example, a lush forest environment of eucalyptus trees serves as a natural aviary for cockatiels and doves.

After a short time at the Gardens, your cares seem to float away on a gentle rose-scented breeze. Everything here is fresh, green and blossoming—an enchanting environment for a celebration of new beginnings.

CEREMONY CAPACITY: The Wedding Area holds 375 guests.

EVENT/RECEPTION CAPACITY: The Reception Area holds 375 guests.

MEETING CAPACITY: Several spaces accommodate up to 375 guests.

FEES & DEPOSITS: A $3,000 nonrefundable deposit is required to secure your date; the event balance is payable 60 days prior to the event along with a refundable security/cleanup deposit. Wedding packages start at $72/person and include use of the property, valet parking, catering, 4 to 4½ hours of beverage service, catering staff and bartender, linens, tableware and event coordination. Tax and an 18% service charge are additional.

AVAILABILITY: Year-round, Saturday or Sunday, 8am–2:30pm or 3:30pm–midnight.

SERVICES/AMENITIES:

Catering: in-house
Kitchen Facilities: n/a
Tables & Chairs: provided
Linens, Silver, etc.: provided
Restrooms: wheelchair accessible
Dance Floor: provided
Bride's Dressing Area: yes
AV/Meeting Equipment: BYO

Parking: valet parking
Accommodations: no guest rooms
Outdoor Night Lighting: yes
Outdoor Cooking Facilities: no
Cleanup: caterer or renter
View: gardens, waterfalls, foothills, pond
Other: DJ, florist, cake

RESTRICTIONS:

Alcohol: BYO, no corkage fees
Smoking: designated areas
Music: amplified OK outdoors

Wheelchair Access: yes
Insurance: liability required
Other: no rice, birdseed or confetti

Saticoy Country Club

Golf Club

4450 Clubhouse Drive, Somis
805/485-4956
www.saticoycountryclub.com
alex@saticoycountryclub.com

● Rehearsal Dinners	● Corporate Events
● Ceremonies	● Meetings
● Wedding Receptions	● Film Shoots
● Private Parties	Accommodations

The road that leads to Saticoy Country Club gently winds its way up the hillside, and as you approach your destination you're likely to pass acres of colorful foliage in full bloom.

Upon arrival, you may notice the faint aroma of strawberries, carried on a light sea breeze. A tranquil landscape of farmland spreads out below, with the Pacific coastline in the distance. As you take in the beauty of your surroundings, it's easy to understand why the club's founders chose this scenic spot.

The first country club in Ventura County, Saticoy opened in 1921 and over the ensuing decades has become a social center for distinguished residents and visiting celebrities. Given its illustrious pedigree, visitors are pleasantly surprised by Saticoy's welcoming, unpretentious atmosphere—just one of the things that make it a standout venue for affordable weddings and events.

Arriving guests gather in the traditionally elegant Dining Room Foyer before being escorted to one of three ceremony sites. Intimate vows are celebrated on a garden lawn just below the Dining Room Terrace. A rose-petal aisle and floral arrangements to mark the altar are included with all ceremony packages. Larger groups convene on a neighboring knoll, which overlooks a picturesque pond and treelined fairways. A short walk away, the most popular ceremony site is poised on a bluff ringed by lofty hedges. Guests looking on from a lush lawn enjoy a spectacular panorama of miles of bountiful fields beneath a gorgeous sunset. On a clear day, the ocean view stretches all the way to the Channel Islands! Backdrops like all of these make Saticoy Country Club a truly lovely place for tying the knot.

As the newlyweds explore the grounds for photo ops, friends and family mingle on the Terrace, where lounge furniture and golf course vistas create a congenial social hour. Two adjustable monitors are often used to display slideshows of the bride and groom. When it's time to dine, everyone steps inside the spacious Dining Room, which boasts a high, open-beamed ceiling and graceful chandeliers. A tulle-and-light canopy can be added for extra glamour, but a wall of windows that captures the setting sun and starry skies offers plenty of visual appeal. The head table gets prime placement in front of a huge picture window at the room's far end, and a sizable dance floor encourages everyone to show off their best moves.

The cornerstone of the Club's excellent reputation is its service-oriented philosophy. Food & Beverage Manager Alex Galaviz has worked here for over 20 years, and treats everyone as if they were guests in his own home. Known for his careful consideration of each couple's particular wishes, Alex oversees your event from your first meeting through the big day. During your complimentary tasting, courtesy of the club's award-winning chef, he'll guide you towards menu selections and wine pairings that suit your palate and budget. Linens in a range of colors (satins, too!) are included with your booking, and Alex even provides a tablescape preview: "We want to make sure our couples get exactly what they've envisioned," he says.

Such high-caliber service at a premier venue usually comes with a high price, but at Saticoy Country Club you'll be delighted by the reasonable cost. And the personal attention and staff smiles are always on the house!

CEREMONY CAPACITY: The facility holds 100 seated guests indoors and 265 seated outdoors.

EVENT/RECEPTION CAPACITY: The facility can accommodate 300 seated or 325 standing indoors and 75 seated or 150 standing outdoors. Dancing can be held outdoors for up to 300 guests (a dance floor is included with the rental).

MEETING CAPACITY: Meeting spaces hold up to 150 guests.

FEES & DEPOSITS: A nonrefundable $2,000 deposit is required to reserve your date, and the balance is due 7 days prior to the event. The rental fee ranges $350–2,000 depending on the spaces reserved. Meals start at $34/person. Tax, alcohol and a 20% service charge are additional.

AVAILABILITY: Year-round, daily.

SERVICES/AMENITIES:

Catering: in-house
Kitchen Facilities: n/a
Tables & Chairs: provided
Linens, Silver, etc.: provided
Restrooms: wheelchair accessible
Dance Floor: portable provided
Bride's Dressing Area: yes
AV/Meeting Equipment: some provided

Parking: large lot, on street
Accommodations: no guest rooms
Outdoor Night Lighting: yes
Outdoor Cooking Facilities: BBQ CBA
Cleanup: provided
View: hillsides, fairways; panorama of Pacific coastline and cityscape

RESTRICTIONS:

Alcohol: in-house or BYO with corkage fee
Smoking: outdoors only
Music: amplified OK with restrictions

Wheelchair Access: yes
Insurance: not required
Other: no rice, birdseed or confetti

The Gardens at Los Robles Greens

Garden Golf Club

299 South Moorpark Road, Thousand Oaks
805/495-6421
www.thegardensatlosrobles.com
cpaul@arcisgolf.com

- Rehearsal Dinners
- Ceremonies
- Wedding Receptions
- Private Parties
- Corporate Events
- Meetings
- Film Shoots
- Accommodations

One minute you're exiting the 101 freeway, and the next you exchange the urban bustle for the tranquil, park-like setting of Los Robles Greens. Sheltered by the Santa Monica Mountains, the elegant clubhouse is perched on a rise overlooking scenic fairways down below. The contemporary Mediterranean-inspired architecture pays a nod to the area's Spanish heritage, with a red-tile roof, butterscotch-hued façade and artfully employed natural materials. Walking paths meander through the lovely grounds, revealing Nature's paintbrush: Blooms of the season provide pops of lavender and coral against the earthy shades of native landscaping, while chirping blue jays and yellow finches flutter between graceful tree branches. Arrive late in the day, and behold the transformation of the usually blue sky into a magnificent rainbow sunset.

If you're thinking this lush oasis would be a perfect place for a wedding, you're right! Outside the clubhouse, a fetching terrace with a spectacular panorama of the rolling greens can host a ceremony-with-a-view, a cocktail party or even an open-air rehearsal dinner. Some couples wed right on the golf course's 10th tee alongside a picturesque pond (horse-and-carriage can be arranged!), before moving up to the terrace for the social hour. Then step inside to the spacious Sunset Ballroom for a grand reception, where floor-to-ceiling windows and an adjoining veranda serve up a birds-eye vantage of the golf course and evening sky.

But the best is yet to come: Tucked in one corner of the property, a pair of ornate wrought-iron gates open to The Gardens. This self-contained haven combines privacy with gorgeous outdoor environs, ringed with pepper trees, oaks, sycamores and the summertime show of purple jacaranda. A dramatic ceremony site is anchored around a long wooden pergola that frames the wedding aisle. The couple exchanges vows in front of an arched cherrywood door at the center of an earth-tone plaster wall, a backdrop that lends a bit of rustic flair. On both sides of the door, curved alcoves edged with tiles are ready-made for floral arrangements or candelabras. Feathery treetops bending in the breeze complete the romantic tableau.

Champagne and congratulations are offered on an adjacent terrace, while a splashing fountain recalls the convivial atmosphere of an Old World village plaza. A two-sided bar also services a larger reception terrace, where a variety of tempting dishes and the wedding cake are beautifully arrayed under an arbor with flowering vines. Your loved ones dine beneath glowing bistro lights and fairy-lit trees, a truly magical experience.

The *pièce de résistance,* however, is the neighboring garden lawn, which boasts a stunning rock waterfall cascading into a reed-lined pool. Naturally this is a favorite spot for enchanting photos, but many couples also place the dance floor on the lawn along with fashionable lounge seating so their guests can savor the balmy starlit evenings, Los Robles style.

From start to finish, planning for your celebration at Los Robles is overseen by their experienced wedding director, dedicated to satisfying both your vision and budget. Whether you opt for a formal ballroom gala or al fresco festivities, you'll be charmed by Los Robles' warm hospitality and variety of congenial venues.

CEREMONY, EVENT/RECEPTION & MEETING CAPACITY: The facility can accommodate 300 seated or standing indoors and 500 seated or 800 standing outdoors.

FEES & DEPOSITS: A refundable $1,000 deposit is required to reserve your date. 50% of the estimated event total is due 60 days prior to the event and the balance is due 10 days prior. The ceremony site fee starts at $1,000 and varies depending on the space reserved. Reception packages range $60–120/person and include alcohol. Tax and a 20% service charge are additional.

Rates for business functions, meetings or other types of events vary. Please contact the venue for more details.

AVAILABILITY: Year-round, daily, 6am–midnight.

SERVICES/AMENITIES:

Catering: in-house
Kitchen Facilities: n/a
Tables & Chairs: provided
Linens, Silver, etc.: provided
Restrooms: wheelchair accessible
Dance Floor: yes
Bride's Dressing Area: yes
AV/Meeting Equipment: some provided

Parking: large lot
Accommodations: no guest rooms
Outdoor Night Lighting: yes
Outdoor Cooking Facilities: no
Cleanup: provided
View: fountain, lake, landscaped grounds, valley, waterfall; panorama of hills, mountains, gardens and fairways

RESTRICTIONS:

Alcohol: in-house
Smoking: designated areas only
Music: amplified OK with restrictions

Wheelchair Access: yes
Insurance: not required

Palm Garden Hotel

Hotel

495 North Ventu Park Road, Thousand Oaks
805/716-4200

www.palmgardenhotel.com
sales@palmgardenhotel.com

● Rehearsal Dinners	● Corporate Events
● Ceremonies	● Meetings
● Wedding Receptions	Film Shoots
● Private Parties	● Accommodations

First-time visitors to Palm Garden Hotel are always pleasantly surprised to discover this suburban oasis tucked amidst a busy commercial district a mere minute from the 101. The hustle and bustle instantly melts away once you step inside the marble-clad lobby, where you're greeted by an electronic grand piano playing familiar tunes. This is your first taste of Palm Garden's arts and music motif: Veteran Big Band leader Harry Selvin purchased the boutique hotel in 2012, and began a loving transformation that has all the hallmarks of pride of ownership. From grounds to guest rooms, the jazzy décor reflects an Old Hollywood vibe that's both jaunty and elegant.

The hotel is built around a sun-washed garden courtyard that encircles a sparkling swimming pool and spa, with plush loungers and cabanas beckoning from the pool deck. Landscaped pathways pass a whimsical bronze statue of a trio of child musicians that's sure to bring a smile. Continue on to two hospitality suites that serve as basecamp for your wedding weekend. The guys gather in the Hollywood Suite, where a legendary pool table once belonging to late comedian George Burns holds court in the front room. Framed black & white photos of Burns' celebrity billiard buddies line one wall, a testament to their having played on—and autographed—this very table. Two flatscreen TVs, a bar, kitchen and bedroom enhance the suite's fun factor, as does the putting green just outside.

Meanwhile, the bride and her attendants prepare in the lovely Garden Suite, which includes a comfortably furnished living room, kitchen, and garden-view bedroom (where the newlyweds spend their wedding night). Brides especially appreciate the roomy walk-in closet and makeup area, as well as the window that lets them watch the guests taking their seats for the ceremony on the Garden Lawn. This lush setting, sheltered by greenery, palm trees and trellises entwined with bougainvillea and fragrant jasmine, is pure romance. A built-in wedding aisle ends at a spacious white wood gazebo. Trimmed with fairy lights and white roses, it's a picturesque backdrop for exchanging vows.

Afterwards, guests stroll over to the Garden Room and Patio for cocktails. The bar is usually set inside the cheerful, airy space, which is also a popular choice for bridal showers and rehearsal dinners. Keep the French doors open and the party flows out onto the patio, where cushioned seating clustered around copper-lined fire pits invites conversation.

Receptions are held in the Palm Ballroom, outfitted with whitewashed shutters, potted palms and abstract chrome fixtures, all of which create a breezy sophistication. Catering is provided by the hotel's on-site restaurant, Brendan's Irish Pub, known for its fine food. Their chefs can whip up delicious dishes in a range of culinary styles—just ask! Brendan's semi-private dining room, featuring rich dark woods and folksy Irish décor, is another rehearsal dinner option.

Palm Garden Hotel makes it easy to gather loved ones (and their pets!) under one roof for an extended celebration, from welcome cocktails to day-after brunch. And with all the freebies—WiFi, banquet equipment, AV, full hot breakfast, parking and more—it's a great value, too. Add its convenient location and effortless charm, and the new Palm Garden seems destined to become a classic.

CEREMONY, EVENT/RECEPTION & MEETING CAPACITY: The facility holds 200 seated guests indoors or outdoors.

FEES & DEPOSITS: A $500 deposit is required to reserve your date and the balance is due 1 week prior to the event. Event space rental fees start at $500 and vary depending on the space reserved. Meals range $25–75/person. Tax, alcohol and a 19% service charge are additional.

AVAILABILITY: Year-round, daily, anytime.

SERVICES/AMENITIES:

Catering: in-house

Kitchen Facilities: n/a

Tables & Chairs: provided

Linens, Silver, etc.: provided

Restrooms: wheelchair accessible

Dance Floor: portable provided

Bride's Dressing Area: yes

AV/Meeting Equipment: provided

Parking: large lot

Accommodations: 150 guest rooms

Outdoor Night Lighting: provided

Outdoor Cooking Facilities: none

Cleanup: provided

View: garden, landscaped grounds, mountains, pool area

RESTRICTIONS:

Alcohol: full in-house bar

Smoking: outdoors only

Music: amplified OK

Wheelchair Access: yes

Insurance: not required

Overwhelmed? Use the search criteria on www.HereComesTheGuide.com to narrow down your choices.

105

Sherwood Country Club

Country Club

320 West Stafford Road, Thousand Oaks
805/496-3036
www.sherwoodcatering.com
hsims@sherwoodcc.com

●	Rehearsal Dinners	●	Corporate Events
●	Ceremonies	●	Meetings
●	Wedding Receptions	●	Film Shoots
●	Private Parties		Accommodations

Your name has to be "on the list" to gain entrance to the gated, ultra-exclusive Lake Sherwood neighborhood. We felt privileged to be admitted, but the geese that waddled across our path seemed to take their VIP status for granted. This lush, luxe enclave tucked against the Santa Monica Mountains is indeed nature-friendly, even while impressive celebrity-owned mansions line its serene lanes.

Sherwood owes its name to the 1922 film, *Robin Hood,* when the picturesque, oak-covered grounds where the club would later be built, doubled as Sherwood Forest. With such a cinematic pedigree, it's not surprising that Sherwood Country Club itself, opened in 1989, is often featured in movies, too, including (appropriately) the hit comedy, *Bridesmaids.* In real life, the club is also a sought-after wedding location.

A grand circular drive leads to the Clubhouse, a stunning example of classic Georgian architecture. The immaculate bricked façade and stately white-columned portico create a pronounced sense of occasion, a feeling that increases inside the elegant lobby: Tastefully curated antiques and paintings lining the walls are perfectly complemented by a herringbone-patterned wood floor and a coved ceiling awash in *trompe l'oeil* clouds.

The ambiance is even more heavenly outside on the Canopy Terrace, a favorite ceremony spot with a romance all its own: A semi-circular, cream-colored colonnade forms a rotunda, topped with a pergola and overhead canopy that provides year-round shade. Star jasmine perfumes the perimeter, and chandeliers, garlands, or draping can easily be added. Guests gaze out on a panorama of green fairways, rolling hillsides and blue horizon, all of which makes an enchanting backdrop for wedding vows.

While the bridal party strolls to the members-only rose garden for photos in front of a cascading waterfall, friends and family enjoy the cocktail hour on the sun-splashed brick Garden Patio adjacent to the terrace. For guests who prefer to mingle inside, French doors open into the Conservatory, a refined hideaway outfitted with a baby grand piano, fireplace and plush furnishings.

Outdoor receptions are staged on the Croquet Lawn, an expanse of crisply trimmed grass below the patio, edged with manicured hedgerows and twinkle-lit trees. The space adapts well to tents, lounge furniture, string lights and whatever other décor you fancy, but whether it's decorated or left au naturel, guests are treated to a rosy-pink sunset above the hills and after-dinner dancing under glittering stars.

Yet once you get a look at Sherwood's pretty-as-a-picture ballroom, you might decide to host the party indoors instead. Not your typical square banquet space, this ballroom has a curved wall of windows that frame the club's lovely views. Dazzling beaded crystal chandeliers, suspended from the coffered ceiling, cast an ethereal glow over your reception. At the room's far end, a separate lounge area is just the place to add a cappuccino bar. Consider heightening the magic with the club's customizable lighting packages or other event enhancements. From wedding-cake spotlights to signature cocktails, the accomplished event managers will help you sort through all the options—including Sherwood's enticing menus.

Every inch of Sherwood Country Club is meticulously maintained, and weddings here receive the same careful attention to detail. Even your most selective guests will be impressed, and all you and your new spouse have to do is enjoy being the center of attention.

CEREMONY CAPACITY: The site seats 200 guests indoors and 1,000 outdoors.

EVENT/RECEPTION CAPACITY: The facility can accommodate 280 seated or 500 standing indoors and 1,000 seated or standing outdoors.

MEETING CAPACITY: Meeting spaces hold 300 seated guests.

FEES & DEPOSITS: 25% of the estimated event cost is required to reserve your date. Another 25% is due 6 months prior to the event and the balance is due 14 days prior. Wedding packages start at $100/person and may include bar packages, hors d'oeuvre reception, served meal, complimentary self-parking, tables, chairs, linens and silver, and time for your rehearsal. Tax and a 20% service charge are additional.

Pricing varies for other kinds of events, including social and corporate events, business meetings, and golf tournaments. Call for more details.

AVAILABILITY: Year-round, daily. Call for details.

SERVICES/AMENITIES:
Catering: in-house, or BYO
Kitchen Facilities: fully equipped
Tables & Chairs: provided
Linens, Silver, etc.: provided
Restrooms: wheelchair accessible
Dance Floor: portable provided
Bride's Dressing Area: yes
AV/Meeting Equipment: provided, CBA
Other: grand piano, event coordination

Parking: large lot
Accommodations: no guest rooms
Outdoor Night Lighting: CBA
Outdoor Cooking Facilities: BBQ CBA
Cleanup: provided
View: forest, fountain, garden, pond, landscaped grounds, waterfall; panorama of fairways and Santa Monica mountains

RESTRICTIONS:
Alcohol: in-house
Smoking: designated areas only
Music: amplified OK with restrictions

Wheelchair Access: yes
Insurance: liability required

Sunset Hills Country Club

Country Club

4155 Erbes Road North, Thousand Oaks
888/998-6386
www.countryclubreceptions.com
events@sunsethillsclub.com

● Rehearsal Dinners	● Corporate Events
● Ceremonies	● Meetings
● Wedding Receptions	● Film Shoots
● Private Parties	Accommodations

Nestled in the rolling hills of Thousand Oaks, Sunset Hills Country Club is just outside Los Angeles but feels like it's worlds away. The club is spread over 85 lush acres, whose gently rolling hills are dotted with majestic oaks, mature elms, and a wealth of other trees. In addition to a clubhouse and golf shop, the property features an 18-hole golf course and an Olympic-sized swimming pool.

Situated on three separate levels with interconnecting stairways, the two clubhouse buildings and Pro Shop are arranged in a horseshoe around the sparkling pool. With their arched façades and red-tile roofs, these one-story stuccos reflect a contemporary melding of California and Spanish architecture.

Sunset Hills welcomes events of all kinds—weddings, birthday parties, and golf tournaments to name a few. If marriage is on your mind, two sites are available for ceremonies. For a big wedding, the best place to tie the knot is in a flat green valley surrounded by stately oaks that affords ample room for theater-style seating. More intimate ceremonies take place at the crest of a little hill beneath overarching alder branches.

After saying "I do" outdoors, bring your festivities inside the Sunset Hills Ballroom, located on the clubhouse's upper level. This spacious, L-shaped venue comes with a parquet dance floor and features an arching, adobe-style brick fireplace. Wrought-iron chandeliers and sconces illuminate earth-tone walls adorned with Tuscan-style artwork, imparting a tasteful elegance. If your event calls for more space, a movable wall rolls easily aside, allowing the ballroom and the lounge to combine into a single large room overlooking the patio and pool.

Sunset Hills offers a variety of wedding packages, all of which can be customized. Their executive chef is happy to personalize your menu, and the on-site coordinator and catering manager will work with you and/or your wedding planner to choreograph your affair from start to finish.

The team at Sunset Hills Country Club is experienced at hosting all types of celebrations. Their expertise and marvelous *esprit de corps* will ensure that yours will be a resounding success.

CEREMONY CAPACITY: The lawn area holds 200 seated guests.

EVENT/RECEPTION CAPACITY: The Ballroom accommodates 200 seated with dance floor.

MEETING CAPACITY: The Ballroom holds 200 guests seated theater-style.

FEES & DEPOSITS: A nonrefundable deposit, which is applied to your food & beverage total, is required to reserve your date. The amount of the deposit varies, depending on how far in advance you book. Payment terms for the balance also vary, and may be arranged on an individual basis. Luncheons start at $15/person, dinners at $25/person. Tax, alcohol and service charge are additional. Menus and packages can be customized to fit your needs and budget. Call for details.

For business meetings, rates vary depending on the services required; call for details.

AVAILABILITY: Year-round, daily, 6pm–midnight. Earlier events can be arranged.

SERVICES/AMENITIES:

Catering: in-house
Kitchen Facilities: n/a
Tables & Chairs: provided
Linens, Silver, etc.: provided
Restrooms: wheelchair accessible
Dance Floor: yes
Bride's Dressing Area: yes
AV/Meeting Equipment: CBA, extra fee

Parking: ample, large lots
Accommodations: no guest rooms
Outdoor Night Lighting: yes
Outdoor Cooking Facilities: none
Cleanup: provided
View: pool

RESTRICTIONS:

Alcohol: in-house or BYO with corkage fee
Smoking: outside only
Music: amplified OK indoors, outdoors with restrictions

Wheelchair Access: yes
Insurance: not required

Crowne Plaza Ventura Beach Hotel

Hotel

450 East Harbor Boulevard, Ventura

805/652-5108

www.cpventura.com
sales@cpventura.com

● Rehearsal Dinners	● Corporate Events
● Ceremonies	● Meetings
● Wedding Receptions	● Film Shoots
● Private Parties	● Accommodations

Living is easy in Ventura, California, a laid-back coastal town midway between the hectic Los Angeles scene and pricey Santa Barbara resorts. Ventura's beaches are picturesque even when the morning fog swirls above the breakers; on its many sunny days, beachcombers can spy the Channel Islands— a necklace of atolls—etched on the horizon.

As the only beachfront hotel in Ventura, this Crowne Plaza provides everything you need for a beach wedding ceremony right on the powdery sand. Their event team will arrange white folding chairs beside the aisle, and set a ceremonial arch in front of the surf so that you can exchange vows just steps from the shore—a microphone and speaker are included, too. Afterwards, your photographer captures shots of the two of you walking off into a glorious sunset, while friends and family begin the party on the Lanai Patio, a private terrace that faces the sea. As twilight descends, everyone moves indoors for your reception.

The versatile San Miguel Ballroom is conveniently located right on the first floor, and can accommodate a party of 200 or be sectioned off for more intimate gatherings. Alternatively, take the elevator 12 stories up to the most spectacular ballroom in the county. The circular Top of the Harbor Ballroom looks out on a captivating panorama through floor-to-ceiling glass: the Ventura hills in one direction and the sinuous shoreline in the other. At twilight, wisps of mist play along the crashing waves; as night descends, the city lights and the illuminated Ventura pier vie with a star-filled indigo sky in a contest of sparkle. The ballroom's contemporary styling, like the rest of the hotel, is both relaxed and confident and suits the soothing surroundings.

The venue's catering packages include many amenities that enhance your celebration at a very good value, such as custom floral centerpieces, table linens, chair covers, wine with dinner, custom wedding cake and an oceanview bridal suite. If you want to pamper your guests even more, consider adding hand-rolled cigars, an espresso cart or a decadent chocolate fountain—or save these treats for your rehearsal dinner or post-wedding brunch. The California-inspired cuisine showcases fresh, local ingredients complemented by an outstanding wine list. We were delighted with the meal we sampled, and bet your guests will be, too. (And yes, the chef is happy to customize your menu!) Other dining temptations include the new NOM Tequila Grill, which offers casually upscale authentic Mexican cuisine for any of your guests staying for the weekend.

Speaking of staying here: Guests will appreciate their oceanview accommodations, which feature the Crowne's "Seven Layers of Comfort" bed. As the newlyweds, you get to sleep in and then enjoy room service delivery of your complimentary breakfast. Eventually, though, you'll want to venture forth and explore the area's attractions. The hotel is walking distance to downtown, and you can also take an easy stroll along the promenade and watch the surfers ply the waves. Other diversions include kayaking around the Channel Islands (adventurous) or renting an on-site bicycle (fun), visiting the hotel's art gallery (cultured), or simply lounging by the oceanfront swimming pool (sublime!).

Every step of the way, the Crowne Plaza Ventura Beach will contribute to a scenic and stress-free wedding weekend.

CEREMONY CAPACITY: The hotel holds 400 seated guests, indoors or out.

EVENT/RECEPTION CAPACITY: The hotel accommodates 350 seated.

MEETING CAPACITY: Meeting spaces seat 400 guests indoors.

FEES & DEPOSITS: 15% of the food & beverage minimum is required to reserve your date and the balance is due 10 days prior to the event. Rental fees start at $2,500 and vary depending on the day and time of the event and the space rented. Meals range $45–120/person. Tax and a 22% service charge are additional.

AVAILABILITY: Year-round, daily, hours vary depending on event.

SERVICES/AMENITIES:

Catering: in-house
Kitchen Facilities: fully equipped
Tables & Chairs: provided
Linens, Silver, etc.: provided
Restrooms: wheelchair accessible
Dance Floor: provided
Bride's Dressing Area: yes
AV/Meeting Equipment: some provided

Parking: large lot, covered garage
Accommodations: 258 guest rooms
Outdoor Night Lighting: yes
Outdoor Cooking Facilities: BBQ
Cleanup: provided
View: pool area, cityscape and panorama of the ocean, coastline and mountains
Other: beach ceremonies

RESTRICTIONS:

Alcohol: in-house
Smoking: outdoors only
Music: amplified OK

Wheelchair Access: yes
Insurance: required for vendors only

San Buenaventura Mission and Gardens

Historic Mission

211 East Main Street, Ventura

805/525-5736

www.venturamissionevents.com
jason@platedevents.com

- Rehearsal Dinners
- Ceremonies
- Wedding Receptions
- Private Parties
- Corporate Events
- Meetings
- Film Shoots
- Accommodations

The seaside community of Ventura offers an irresistible combination of picturesque scenery and unpretentious charm, and visitors flock to the quaint shops, antique malls and trendy eateries on its vibrant Main Street. Yet the most venerable attraction is the stunning Mission, a graceful reminder of the town's origins.

Founded in 1782 by Father Junipero Serra (and the last mission he would personally dedicate in his lifetime), the four-acre complex is tucked against a hillside facing the ocean. Its Spanish-Colonial architecture and signature cross-topped bell tower reflect the area's rich history—even the 135-year-old twin pines at the entrance are designated landmarks. Marriages have been consecrated here since the early 1900s, and Catholic ceremonies are still welcomed inside the beautiful chapel, whose original adobe walls speak to longevity and commitment.

Mission celebrations are overseen by *Plated Events,* an experienced local catering team who've thoughtfully arranged several additional ceremony options beyond the Mission's grounds. Across the street is Figueroa Plaza, a treelined promenade flanked by the colorfully vintage Peirano's grocery building and a lush green park. Couples say their vows between two tiled fountains with a ribbon of ocean in the distance. Opt for the Beach Wedding Package, and the staff will stage your "I do"s alongside the Ventura Pier just a few blocks away. Another romantic choice is Serra Cross Park, a nearby aerie with Pacific vistas stretching to the Channel Islands. These enticing outdoor spots include city permits, your choice of seating, an aisle runner strewn with rose petals, sound system, wedding arch and even a beverage station to welcome your guests!

The cocktail hour in the enchanting Mission Gardens is a not-to-be-missed experience. Guests mingle among the flowers, ornamental palms, and bougainvillea-lined loggias. A magnificent Old World fountain burbles at the center, and fragrant blooms perfume the sea air. Historic markers detail the Mission's heritage, and a stone grotto dedicated to Our Lady has a spiritual resonance, no matter what your faith. Twinkle lights and sunset-kissed skies enhance the magical ambiance, and your loved ones will want to linger until after dark.

But it's time to kick up the action with a delicious dinner followed by dancing! Behind the mission, spacious and contemporary O'Brien Hall boasts a lofty ceiling, clerestory windows and a minimalist aesthetic, and it easily transforms into an elegant and grand space, whatever your design and color scheme. The hall is also outfitted with the latest technical capabilities, including a built-in stage to showcase your entertainment and specialty lighting to help personalize your reception. Best of all, a row of street-side windows and a veranda afford spectacular birds-eye views of the Bell Tower, bustling downtown and the surrounding hills and coastline.

Plated Events specializes in farm-to-table cuisine and is known for their mouthwatering, customizable meals. They work with each couple to interpret their wedding vision—all at an affordable price. For added convenience, the Mission is mere steps from nightlife options (after-party, anyone?), and close to a range of local hotels.

Combining the best of the old and new, the inspiring San Buenaventura Mission and Gardens is the perfect setting for building something that's meant to last.

CEREMONY CAPACITY: The Mission Church seats 336. A beach ceremony may also be arranged at the nearby Ventura Pier for up to 700 seated guests.

EVENT/RECEPTION CAPACITY: Several rooms accommodate 40–350 seated or 75–700 standing guests. The Mission Gardens hold 125 seated or 200 standing outdoors.

MEETING CAPACITY: O'Brien Hall seats 500 conference-style, and the Bonaventure Room seats 75.

FEES & DEPOSITS: A deposit of 50% of the site fee is required to reserve your date, and the balance is due 30 days prior to the event. The site fee ranges $500–2,000, depending on the space rented, day of the week and event date. Meals range $20–125/person. Tax, alcohol and service charge are additional. Beach Wedding Ceremony packages start at $450 plus $4 per guest, and include permit fee, setup, arbor, chairs, rose-petal aisle runner, beverage station and more.

This venue is brought to you exclusively by *Plated Events*. The Mission is also available for quinceñeras, parties, concerts, meetings and other gatherings.

AVAILABILITY: Year-round. Reception venues are open to all. However, the church is reserved for Catholic sacred liturgies such as wedding ceremonies, quinceñeras, baptisms, etc. The Mission Gardens are available for photos anytime, or for outdoor non-seated events Monday–Friday and Sunday evening. Please inquire about the Gardens' availability for Saturday cocktail receptions.

SERVICES/AMENITIES:

Catering: in-house

Kitchen Facilities: n/a

Tables & Chairs: provided

Linens, Silver, etc.: provided

Restrooms: wheelchair accessible

Dance Floor: yes

Bride's Dressing Area: yes

AV/Meeting Equipment: provided

Other: event coordination, clergy on staff, picnic area, elevator service

Parking: large lot, valet available

Accommodations: no guest rooms

Outdoor Night Lighting: yes

Outdoor Cooking Facilities: BBQ CBA

Cleanup: provided

View: fountain, garden, landscaped grounds, park, mountains; panorama of Historic Mission Belltower, downtown Ventura, coastline and ocean

RESTRICTIONS:

Alcohol: in-house or BYO

Smoking: designated areas only

Music: amplified OK

Wheelchair Access: yes

Insurance: liability required

The wedding vendors on our website are the best in the business. How do we know? Read page 577.

Serra Cross Park

Oceanview Park

Brakey Road, Ventura
805/223-5505
www.serracrosspark.org
amber@amberweir.com

Rehearsal Dinners		Corporate Events	
● Ceremonies		Meetings	
● Wedding Receptions		● Film Shoots	
● Private Parties		Accommodations	

What California bride doesn't fantasize about getting married in a beautiful, natural setting with a sweeping ocean view? Yet for some couples, it seems that the right to gaze out to sea during their most important celebration is reserved for those with a lavish budget. Don't despair! You'll feel like you've landed on Easy Street when you learn about our latest discovery: Serra Cross Park, a hilltop aerie with a breathtaking coastal panorama, a modest pricetag, and a rich history.

It all started back in 1782. Shortly after Father Junipero Serra founded the San Buenaventura Mission, a large wooden cross was placed on a neighboring hillside as a guidepost for travelers. Over the years, the original cross and a series of replacements were lost to the elements, but locals never gave up. The current cross has stood atop its circular stone pedestal since 1941, and today the Serra Cross Conservancy and community volunteers are committed to maintaining and improving the park for everyone's enjoyment. Serra Cross Park also has a romantic legacy—throughout the years, countless couples have been married here, making this a particularly cherished piece of local heritage.

From a side street behind Ventura's handsome City Hall, the short but sinuous drive to the park begins. Once you and your guests reach the top, expect wide eyes and open mouths as the awe-inspiring view unfolds. In one direction, a curve of beach embraces the crashing surf; in another, the Channel Islands are etched against a billowing stretch of blue; behind you are the multilayered contours of chaparral-cloaked hills. Taking it all in from your exalted perch, you're filled with a sense of humility and wonder—even reverence. For many, these powerful feelings are symbolized by the simple wooden cross, poised atop its stone platform.

It's on this small stage that you'll exchange your vows, with a filigree of olive trees and the watery vista in the background. Champagne toasts follow, and if you want to continue the party, you'll be treated to a magnificent sunset. As evening falls, the moon, the stars and the city lights set the horizon aglow. Reserve the park in the month of August, and you'll get the best seat in the house for a stunning fireworks display, courtesy of the Ventura County Fair! It's hard to imagine a more exhilarating finale than this exuberant, multicolored spectacle.

With its dramatic vantage, friendly pricing and enduring tradition, Serra Cross Park just might be the answer to your wedding prayers.

CEREMONY & EVENT/RECEPTION CAPACITY: The site holds 300 seated or 450 standing outdoors.

MEETING CAPACITY: Meetings do not take place at this location.

FEES & DEPOSITS: The rental fee is required to reserve your date. Site rental fees range $450–1,500 and vary depending on the hours reserved and type of event.

AVAILABILITY: Year-round, daily, 10am–8pm in set blocks of time.

SERVICES/AMENITIES:

Catering: BYO, recommendations available
Kitchen Facilities: n/a
Tables & Chairs: through caterer
Linens, Silver, etc.: through caterer
Restrooms: not wheelchair accessible
Dance Floor: CBA
Bride's & Groom's Dressing Areas: no
AV/Meeting Equipment: n/a

Parking: large lot
Accommodations: no guest rooms
Outdoor Night Lighting: access only, additional through caterer
Outdoor Cooking Facilities: BBQ CBA
Cleanup: through caterer
View: garden, landscaped grounds; panorama of coastline, hills, canyon and mountains
Other: site coordination

RESTRICTIONS:

Alcohol: through caterers
Smoking: not allowed
Music: amplified OK outdoors with restrictions

Wheelchair Access: limited
Insurance: $1 million liability policy required for catered events
Other: security required for large events

Wedgewood Ventura

5880 Olivas Park Drive, Ventura
866/966-3009
www.wedgewoodbanquet.com
events@wedgewoodbanquet.com

Special Events Facility

- Rehearsal Dinners   • Corporate Events
- Ceremonies   • Meetings
- Wedding Receptions   • Film Shoots
- Private Parties   Accommodations

Between Ventura's sandy beaches and wooded hillsides lie acres of farmland, where everything from strawberries to snapdragons flourishes in the pleasant climate. Such an appealing locale has naturally attracted many golf courses to the area, and the first public course in the county is the San Buenaventura, whose manicured greens, billowing treetops and small-town friendliness have been courting customers for decades. Sound like a picture-perfect setting for a special event? It is, and Wedgewood Ventura, which shares the scenic grounds with the golf course, not only ensures your celebration will unfold effortlessly, they'll do it all for a reasonable price.

The banquet center is perched on a gentle rise overlooking the sweeping fairways and the Ceremony Rose Garden just below. In the garden, palm trees encircle a splash of lawn, and star jasmine and rose blossoms adorn the air with their sweet perfume. The bride begins her entrance by descending the stairway from the center's banquet room. Then she glides along the wedding aisle to her groom, who waits in front of an arched wooden pergola. You can add embellishments like tulle and flowers, but with the rolling greens and the pretty landscaping little else is needed.

The same is true of the banquet room itself, designed with sophisticated touches that contribute to a sense of classic comfort and ease. Just inside the room, a blazing fireplace provides warmth. Guests have a birds-eye view of the golf greens, thanks to windows that run the length of the banquet room. There's nothing like a serene vista to help folks unwind, except maybe a champagne toast in the Lounge next to the foyer. Here an old-fashioned built-in bar makes your cocktail hour a breeze. Then, when it's time to dine, guests adjourn to tables set in the center of the banquet room. The wedding party takes the place of honor on a raised level opposite the windows.

A built-in dance floor separates diners from a stage area, a prime spot for a formal head table or to showcase the band. However, most of Wedgewood's patrons prefer the services of their dynamic DJs, who hold court from a state-of-the-art sound booth, discreetly styled to blend in with the rest of the room. These outgoing songsters expertly MC your reception, and entertain with a customized song list. And here's the kicker—this service is included as part of your wedding package, along with a choice of wedding invitations, floral centerpieces and engraved champagne flutes.

With a variety of packages to fit most budgets and tastes, Wedgewood seems to have thought of everything (so you won't have to!). The popular Gold Package, for example, offers extra goodies like personalized cocktail napkins, a deluxe wedding cake selected from a premier local bakery and a wedding night hotel room for the bridal couple. Upgrade to the Millennium Package, and treat your guests to custom uplighting, chocolate-covered strawberries and a real-time photo booth!

Wedgewood Ventura has one more specialty offering: They'll arrange your wedding ceremony right on the beach. Their chosen spot is just 10 minutes away on a stretch of coastline adjacent to Ventura Harbor. The staff will arrange chairs for your guests right on the sand, facing a wooden arch with the rolling waves as the backdrop. Then, while family and friends head back to the banquet center for cocktails, the newlyweds have some time to capture scenic wedding photos before the reception. Wedgewood Buenaventura is clearly user friendly, and the staff truly accommodating—all you have to do is sit back and enjoy the day.

CEREMONY, EVENT/RECEPTION & MEETING CAPACITY: The site accommodates up to 300 seated or standing guests.

FEES & DEPOSITS: 25% of the estimated total event cost is required to reserve your date. An additional 25% is due 120 days prior to the event and the balance (based on your final guest count) is due 10 days prior. All payments are credited towards your final balance and are nonrefundable and nontransferable. All-inclusive, completely customizable wedding packages start at $35/person. Tax, alcohol and a 21–22% service charge are additional.

AVAILABILITY: Year-round, daily, 6am–1am.

SERVICES/AMENITIES:

Catering: in-house
Kitchen Facilities: n/a
Tables & Chairs: provided
Linens, Silver, etc.: provided
Restrooms: wheelchair accessible
Dance Floor: provided
Bride's Dressing Area: yes
AV/Meeting Equipment: some provided

Parking: ample parking
Accommodations: no guest rooms
Outdoor Night Lighting: yes
Outdoor Cooking Facilities: no
Cleanup: provided
View: fairways, landscaped grounds, beach, ocean
Other: in-house wedding cake and florals, clergy on staff, event coordination

RESTRICTIONS:

Alcohol: in-house
Smoking: outdoors only
Music: amplified OK

Wheelchair Access: yes
Insurance: not required
Other: no rice, confetti or glitter; no open flames

Hyatt Westlake Plaza in Thousand Oaks

Hotel

880 South Westlake Boulevard, Westlake Village
805/557-4650
www.hyattwestlake.com
westl-rfp@hyatt.com

● Rehearsal Dinners	● Corporate Events
● Ceremonies	● Meetings
● Wedding Receptions	● Film Shoots
● Private Parties	● Accommodations

Hyatt Westlake Plaza feels like a secluded world of European opulence and serenity, thanks to lush landscaping and a captivating ambiance. The hotel's architecture and interior design reflect Westlake's Spanish heritage, as well as a dash of contemporary Mediterranean elegance. Colorful murals flank the foyer, and the spacious, airy lobby features a spectacular five-story skylit atrium with indoor verandas curving around a central plaza. Everywhere you turn, intriguing elements catch your eye: a rustic wall sconce, chandeliers that appear hand-wrought and striking floral arrangements. A splashing limestone fountain at the center of the plaza casts a refreshing refrain over the scene.

In all, fourteen different event spaces, each comfortable and tastefully appointed, are available for bridal luncheons, company parties or elaborate galas. A favorite option for intimate get-togethers is the Vista Ballroom, which is lined with windows that bring in natural light while capturing views of the hotel gardens.

In fact, if you've always fantasized about a garden wedding, then Hyatt Westlake can make your dreams a reality. Picture your guests seated on a swath of lawn, basking in the warm California sunshine as they await your appearance. At last, you begin the walk down the aisle alongside a waterfall cascading over rocks into a placid pond. You join your love at a white gazebo under the shade of lofty evergreens. What a perfect place for exchanging vows or taking romantic photos! The social hour and even receptions can be enjoyed right in the garden, too.

Or retire indoors to the Grand Ballroom, the largest one in the county, which displays the same attention to detail as the rest of this Hyatt. Ornate beveled mirrors and a coordinating cornice around the perimeter lend the ballroom a sophisticated air of distinction. Alabaster dome-shaped lighting fixtures with faux candles hang from the recessed ceiling, and the addition of customizable lighting effects and draping heighten the glamour. The Grand Ballroom Foyer, with one wall of windows, has a gracious formality that makes it an appealing option for a cocktail reception or staging a buffet.

You'll dine on exceptional gourmet fare, and any of their menus can be adapted to suit your tastes. This fine hotel specializes in accommodating the unique event requirements of a variety of cultures, and although their creative chefs are skilled with many types of cuisine, outside ethnic caterers are allowed with approval. Hyatt Westlake is also TAG Approved®, and proud to welcome LGBT events.

Friends and family spending the weekend will appreciate the hotel's inviting guest rooms, decorated with rich, warm tones, sumptuous fabrics, and every amenity for an enjoyable stay, including a garden swimming pool. The new Harvest Kitchen and Bar serves up delicious local, sustainable fare—and even has private rooms for your rehearsal dinner. Or let your personal wedding consultant arrange a casual pre-wedding gathering around the patio's fire pit, finished off with a round of decadent s'mores!

A luxurious full-service venue with all the grace and tranquility of a Mediterranean villa, Hyatt Westlake Plaza comes dressed to impress, making it a smart choice for any landmark celebration.

CEREMONY CAPACITY: The Grand Ballroom holds up to 800 seated guests; the garden area up to 350 seated or 500 standing.

EVENT/RECEPTION & MEETING CAPACITY: The Grand Ballroom accommodates up to 450 seated or 900 standing guests; the garden up to 350 seated or 500 standing.

FEES & DEPOSITS: 25% of the estimated event total is required to reserve your date with the remaining balance due 10 days prior to your event. Wedding packages include 4 passed hors d'oeuvres, choice of meal, wine with dinner, champagne toast, cake cutting and a complimentary guest room for the bride and groom. Package prices start at $74/person. Tax and service charge are additional.

Other options for your event include, but are not limited to, hosted bar, chair covers, chargers, audiovisual equipment and specialty lighting. Please call for details!

AVAILABILITY: Year-round, daily; 6am–midnight indoors, 8am–10pm outdoors.

SERVICES/AMENITIES:

Catering: in-house or select from approved ethnic caterers
Kitchen Facilities: fully equipped
Tables & Chairs: provided
Linens, Silver, etc.: provided
Restrooms: wheelchair accessible
Dance Floor: portable provided
Bride's Dressing Area: yes
AV/Meeting Equipment: full range

Parking: large lot, self-parking and valet are available
Accommodations: 263 guest rooms
Outdoor Night Lighting: yes
Outdoor Cooking Facilities: no
Cleanup: provided
View: pool, garden, hills, manicured grounds, cascading waterfalls
Other: grand piano, spa services

RESTRICTIONS:

Alcohol: in-house
Smoking: outside in designated areas
Music: amplified OK with restrictions

Wheelchair Access: yes
Insurance: required for vendors such as caterers and entertainment

Westlake Yacht Club

Yacht Club

32123 Lindero Canyon Road, Westlake Village
805/624-9350
www.cpcatering.com
annettekirkhuff@cpcatering.com

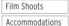

● Rehearsal Dinners	● Corporate Events
● Ceremonies	● Meetings
● Wedding Receptions	● Film Shoots
● Private Parties	Accommodations

Just a half hour north of Los Angeles sits Westlake Village, an idyllic, upscale neighborhood cradled by the Santa Monica Mountains and acres of greenspace. The centerpiece of this serene enclave is its scenic 125-acre lake, the site of the newly remodeled Westlake Yacht Club. Founded in 1969 as a private sporting hub, these days the casually elegant venue plays host to unforgettable waterfront celebrations for members and nonmembers alike.

The jaunty, Cape Cod-inspired clubhouse is perched on a landscaped knoll overlooking the lake promenade. Arriving guests might be greeted by a scampering white-tailed rabbit or a few geese, but you can provide a more conventional welcome by placing signage beneath the club's bright blue awning.

The recently enlarged interior features oak walls and soaring ceiling beams sporting colorful maritime flags. The nautical motif is subtle enough that formal and laid-back get-togethers work equally well, and the décor easily adapts to your own stylings. In one corner of the room, steps lead up to a private bridal loft, sweetly outfitted with mirrors and an antique vanity. Most impressive, however, are the tall windows along the three sides that bathe the space in natural light and contribute to its expansive ambiance. French doors opposite the entry frame a view of the lake and open onto the roomy club deck.

Most wedding couples can't resist holding a ceremony out here: The picturesque lakefront panorama is edged with forested hills and almost perennial blue skies. A parade of sailboats and watercraft, along with a variety of shorebirds, provides a tranquil yet invigorating vista. The setting is made all the more dreamy by the sight of graceful swans gliding along the water. Time your vows for dusk, and a magnificent sunset will complete the picture-postcard backdrop.

After the first kiss, the bridal party poses for fun photos on the boardwalk. Meanwhile guests meander toward the other side of the deck for a twilight cocktail hour. Friends and family can also mingle around a large bar that commands a corner of the clubhouse, a convivial spot for refreshments and conversation.

Receptions spread out inside the spacious clubhouse, with ample room for 200 guests and a dance floor. But if you can't resist dining al fresco, then have your social hour around the bar while the staff prepares the deck for dinner under the stars.

Speaking of dinner, your loved ones are in for a treat: Banquets here are managed by *Command Performance Catering*, Certified By The Guide professionals that deliver crowd-pleasing cuisine and exemplary service. They're also experienced event producers, so if you're fantasizing about a themed bash—luau, anyone?—or require specialty upgrades, they'll gladly orchestrate your wishes.

And while you're envisioning the possibilities, think beyond the wedding…the club's deck is also a great place for a romantic rehearsal dinner or anniversary party. In fact, we can imagine many couples getting married here, and then returning for their 10th, 25th or even 50th-year celebration to relive the wonderful memories!

CEREMONY CAPACITY: The facility holds 150 seated guests indoors and 300 seated outdoors.

EVENT/RECEPTION & MEETING CAPACITY: The facility accommodates up to 200 guests, either indoors or outdoors. It holds up to 300 when the indoor and outdoor spaces are combined.

FEES & DEPOSITS: 50% of the estimated venue rental fee plus 10% of the estimated catering total are required to reserve your date. The balance of the venue rental fee is due 30 days prior to your event, and the catering balance is due 1 week prior. The venue rental fee ranges $1,250–3,250, depending on the day of the week. The venue rental fee for meetings starts at $500. Catering packages run $50–100/person. A wide range of hosted and non-hosted alcohol packages are available. Tax, alcohol and an 18% service charge are additional.

AVAILABILITY: Year-round, daily, 7am–10pm outdoors and until midnight indoors. Availability on Friday nights is limited.

SERVICES/AMENITIES:

Catering: in-house
Kitchen Facilities: n/a
Tables & Chairs: some provided
Linens, Silver, etc.: provided
Restrooms: wheelchair accessible
Dance Floor: yes
Bride's Dressing Area: yes
AV/Meeting Equipment: some provided

Parking: large complimentary lot; valet CBA, extra fee
Accommodations: no guest rooms
Outdoor Night Lighting: yes
Outdoor Cooking Facilities: BBQ on site
Cleanup: caterer
View: panorama of lake and hills
Other: complete event production (styling, specialty furnishings, lighting & décor) call for details; event coordination, extra fee

RESTRICTIONS:

Alcohol: in-house
Smoking: outdoors only
Music: amplified OK with restrictions

Wheelchair Access: yes
Insurance: liability required

Want to know WHAT TO ASK a potential location or vendor? Check out our Questions to Ask starting on page 21.

San Fernando Valley

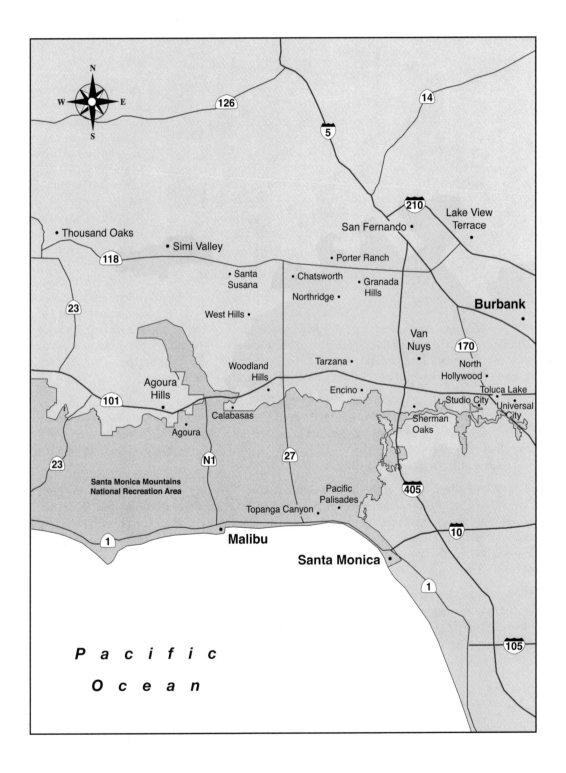

Malibou Lake Mountain Club

Private Lakeside Club

29033 Lake Vista Drive, Agoura

818/753-6772

www.maliboulakeclub.com
www.trulyyourscatering.com
laura@trulyyourscatering.com

● Rehearsal Dinners	● Corporate Events
● Ceremonies	● Meetings
● Wedding Receptions	Film Shoots
● Private Parties	Accommodations

Two natural rock pillars frame the entryway to the Malibou Lake Mountain Club, a private club nestled in the Santa Monica Mountains. A rustic colonial façade with a wide front veranda leads you into the clubhouse, and once inside the spacious main room, it's easy to envision a terrific event here. Wood walls are finished in a whitewashed gray with white trim, providing a neutral backdrop for any color scheme. The warm glow from a fireplace adds a homey touch. On the right side of the room a huge bay window flanked by French doors overlooks a gently sloping lawn, bordered by eucalyptus and pine trees. The stage in front of the window can be used for a band, making toasts or even an indoor ceremony.

Given its neutral décor, you can have a field day decorating the club. One group had an elegant black-and-white affair, with guests garbed in tuxedos and snazzy dresses; another staged a western-themed party, with bales of hay, white foam horses on the tables and a barbecue reception on the lawn. Still a third hosted a renaissance gala, complete with period costumes, wandering minstrels and rounds of croquet and bocce ball.

Most weddings take place at the far end of the lawn, overlooking the lake. Feel free to customize your ceremony too, by adding an arch, gazebo, tent or any other element you choose. Afterwards, your guests can mingle on the grass and admire the view of the sparkling lake with the Santa Monica mountains in the distance. The lawn also lends itself to lively company picnics, reunions or anniversary parties—there's plenty of room for all kinds of interactive games, sports or carnival activities.

The beauty of this place—aside from its country setting—is that you have carte blanche (within reason) to design whatever celebration you desire. No two parties are alike here, so if you want plenty of control over your event, come to the Malibou Lake Mountain Club and have the creative time of your life.

CEREMONY CAPACITY: The lawn holds up to 400 guests.

EVENT/RECEPTION CAPACITY: Indoors, the facility holds up to 200 seated. A smaller room is available for 10–50 guests.

MEETING CAPACITY: The facility can accommodate 175 seated theater-style or 200 conference-style.

FEES & DEPOSITS: A nonrefundable $2,000 deposit and signed contract are required to secure your date. 20% of the food & beverage cost is due within 90 days of booking, and the balance is due 12 days before the event. The rental fee for Monday–Thursday is $250/hour with a 4-hour minimum; Friday, $2,300; Saturday, $5,300; and Sunday, $3,300. Wedding packages start at $44/person and include food, beverage and some rentals.

AVAILABILITY: Year-round: Sunday–Thursday until 10pm, Friday–Saturday until 11pm.

SERVICES/AMENITIES:

Catering: provided by *Truly Yours Catering*
Kitchen Facilities: n/a
Tables & Chairs: provided through caterer
Restrooms: wheelchair accessible
Linens, Silver, etc.: provided through caterer
Dance Floor: wood floor provided
Bride's & Groom's Dressing Areas: yes
AV/Meeting Equipment: BYO

Parking: 2 large lots
Accommodations: no guest rooms
Outdoor Night Lighting: twinkle lights in trees
Outdoor Cooking Facilities: provided through caterer
Cleanup: caterer or renter
View: lake, an island and mountains
Other: event coordination, outdoor lounge-style furniture, and draping

RESTRICTIONS:

Alcohol: BYO or through caterer
Smoking: outdoors only
Music: amplified OK indoors, Sunday–Thursday until 10pm, Friday–Saturday until 11pm; acoustic only outdoors

Wheelchair Access: yes
Insurance: required for DJ or live band

Calamigos Equestrian

Equestrian Center

480 Riverside Drive, Burbank
818/972-5940

www.calamigosequestrian.com
info@calamigosequestrian.com

Rehearsal Dinners	●	Corporate Events
● Ceremonies	●	Meetings
● Wedding Receptions	●	Film Shoots
● Private Parties		Accommodations

Set against the scenic backdrop of the Santa Monica Mountains on 75 beautifully landscaped acres, the L.A. Equestrian Center has hosted everything from celebrity-studded polo matches to Elizabeth Taylor's perfume launch, and has been used for filming hit movies like *Pretty Woman*.

What you'll find here are charming ceremony locations for bridal couples, and an appealing variety of upscale event spaces for celebrants of all kinds—even those with only a passing interest in horses. As an added bonus, the event producers of Calamigos Ranch (best known for hosting decades of special events at their facility in Malibu) have recently brought their experience to this unique locale. So relax and let them coordinate your entire celebration!

One of the favorite sites is the Little White House and Garden Courtyard in the middle of Hunt Field, a vast expanse of lawn enclosed by a traditional white picket fence. From the parking lot, guests stroll along a path that winds through majestic sycamore trees. Some couples like to say their vows under the trees' graceful boughs, and the entire field can be set up for cocktails for up to a thousand guests. The Little White House, which provides a private dressing room for the bride, is a quaint cottage with French doors that open to the Garden Courtyard, bordered by fragrant rose bushes.

Another option for tying the knot is the raised demi-gazebo at the far end of the Courtyard, where the soothing strains of songbirds accompany a cascading waterfall. And for added romance, many couples opt to come through the Courtyard gates on an old-fashioned horse-drawn carriage! After the ceremony, guests amble back across Hunt Field to one of the Center's private rooms for a formal reception.

Beautiful wrought-iron gates invite you into the Equestrian Ballroom, a sophisticated space with chandeliers and a large bar. Panel doors swivel open to the Equestrian terrace, a lovely spot for post-reception mingling or a garden ceremony among California pines. The garden atmosphere is enhanced by a jasmine-covered trellis, rock waterfall, and views of Griffith Park and the distant mountains. For a different feel, the Grand Prix Room offers a more formal setting with rich red and gold carpeting, spectacular chandeliers and an impressive wood-burning fireplace.

The Polo Room has a comfortable bar and lounge separate from its casually elegant dining room. French doors open onto a veranda, enabling guests to enjoy cocktails outdoors or wander off to observe the equestrian competitions. The horses and the grounds are all impeccably maintained, so everything will be fresh and clean for your event.

Calamigos has prepared an array of tempting event packages that include plenty of extras, and their in-house caterers will happily customize your menu with delicious offerings. All this, and horses too!

CEREMONY CAPACITY: The Little White House holds up to 350 seated, Hunt Field Lawn up to 1,000 guests and the Equestrian Terrace up to 250 seated guests.

EVENT/RECEPTION CAPACITY: The facility has a variety of areas that accommodate up to 550 seated or 1,200 standing indoors, and 250 to 5,000 seated outdoors.

MEETING CAPACITY: The Equestrian Ballroom (divisible into 4 sections) holds 120–800 guests. The Grand Prix Room (divisible into 3 sections) holds 800 guests. The Little White House can accommodate up to 500 guests, seated theater-style.

FEES & DEPOSITS: A $1,500 nonrefundable deposit is required to reserve your date. 50% of the estimated event total is due 6 months prior to the event; the balance is payable 10 days prior. Wedding packages range $59–101/person and include a half-hour wedding rehearsal, a seated or buffet meal, room rental fees, cake-cutting and a 3-hour hosted champagne, wine and beer package. Tax and a 20% service charge are extra. For other kinds of special events, prices range $50–85/person. Tax, alcohol and a 20% service charge are additional. Meetings start at $55/person and include continental breakfast, lunch, room rental fees and 2 breaks with beverages and snacks.

AVAILABILITY: Year-round, daily, 7am–1am.

SERVICES/AMENITIES:

Catering: in-house, no BYO
Kitchen Facilities: n/a
Tables & Chairs: Chiavari chairs provided
Linens, Silver, etc.: provided
Restrooms: wheelchair accessible
Dance Floor: provided
Bride's Dressing Area: yes
AV/Meeting Equipment: some provided, extra CBA

Parking: ample lot
Accommodations: no guest rooms
Outdoor Night Lighting: yes
Outdoor Cooking Facilities: CBA
Cleanup: provided
View: mountains, horse arena, landscaped grounds
Other: coordination, horse-drawn carriage

RESTRICTIONS:

Alcohol: in-house
Smoking: outdoors only
Music: amplified OK indoors, outdoors with restrictions

Wheelchair Access: yes
Insurance: liability required for vendors

Pickwick Gardens

Garden

1001 West Riverside Drive, Burbank

818/845-5300 x171

www.pickwickgardensconferencecenter.com
info@pickwickgardens.com

● Rehearsal Dinners	● Corporate Events
● Ceremonies	● Meetings
● Wedding Receptions	● Film Shoots
● Private Parties	Accommodations

For anyone who only knows Pickwick Gardens from their sign on Riverside Drive, walking through the wrought-iron gate in the back will be a revelation, because this has to be one of the most idyllic outdoor wedding spots in the San Fernando Valley.

This area was once the bustling aquatic section of a public recreation complex, but today it's an expansive, two-and-halfacre, woodland oasis that's at the very heart of any event at Pickwick Gardens. Paved walkways lit by old-fashioned street lamps meander through the lawns. The varied landscape of this bucolic retreat combines towering pines, graceful jacarandas, spiky palms and majestic oak trees. Old stone fountains serve as multi-tiered planters, and colorful flowerbeds punctuated with rose bushes and seasonal blooms line the walkways. At the center of the garden is a huge tented pavilion with overhead fans. A raised stage at one end is anchored by a curving, river rock wall that would make a beautiful altar backdrop for your ceremony...or you can exchange vows on a lawn, shaded by trees. Afterwards, serve cocktails under the pavilion as the late afternoon and evening breezes come off the Santa Monica Mountains in nearby Griffith Park.

Bordering the gardens are several banquet rooms, each with a private bridal room where you and your attendants can get ready. Most have full-on, outdoor views and awning-covered patios. The very popular Rose Garden Room features a unique rotunda and circular parquet dance floor set against tall windows, while the charming, newly renovated Magnolia Terrace Room is bright with a white, woodbeamed ceiling, white wainscoting and golden candelabra chandeliers. Just outside the Magnolia Terrace Room windows sits a bubbling fountain in its own private mini-garden, separated from the main gardens by a low wall of natural stone.

If your guest list truly includes *all* your nearest and dearest, there's the 8,500-squarefoot Royal Ballroom, which can comfortably accommodate 550 guests for a sit-down dinner and dancing. Decorated in rich tones of garnet and gold paisley, its regal ambiance is further established by windows draped with swags and valances, and huge chandeliers dripping with crystals.

Whether you desire a formal dinner, a buffet with ethnic specialties or more casual fare for a bridal shower or rehearsal dinner, an executive chef is on site to help you customize your menu. And if you feel like arranging a fairy-tale entrance on horseback or by horse-drawn carriage from the neighboring Equestrian Center, a full-time wedding planner can assist you in tailoring your event to make it suit you perfectly.

CEREMONY CAPACITY: The site holds 1,000 seated guests indoors and 1,200 seated outdoors.

EVENT/RECEPTION CAPACITY: The site accommodates 550 seated or 1,000 standing guests indoors and 1,200 seated or 2,000 standing outdoors.

MEETING CAPACITY: Meeting spaces hold 1,000 seated guests.

FEES & DEPOSITS: A $500–2,500 deposit is required to reserve your date and the balance is due 30 days prior to the event. Rental fees range $1,500–8,500 depending on the guest count. Meals range $30–90/person. Tax, alcohol and a 21% service charge are additional.

AVAILABILITY: Year-round, daily, 7am–1am.

SERVICES/AMENITIES:

Catering: in-house
Kitchen Facilities: n/a
Tables & Chairs: provided
Linens, Silver, etc.: provided
Restrooms: wheelchair accessible
Dance Floor: provided
Bride's Dressing Area: yes
AV/Meeting Equipment: provided

Parking: large lot
Accommodations: no guest rooms
Outdoor Night Lighting: yes
Outdoor Cooking Facilities: BBQ
Cleanup: provided
View: garden, mountains, fountain, landscaped grounds
Other: picnic area, ceremony coordinator, meeting planner

RESTRICTIONS:

Alcohol: in-house
Smoking: in designated areas only
Music: amplified OK with restrictions

Wheelchair Access: yes
Insurance: liability required

Agoura Hills/Calabasas Community Center

Community Center

27040 Malibu Hills Road, Calabasas

818/880-2993

www.ahccc.org
jenna@ahccc.org

●	Rehearsal Dinners	●	Corporate Events
●	Ceremonies	●	Meetings
●	Wedding Receptions	●	Film Shoots
●	Private Parties		Accommodations

Nestled in the Santa Monica foothills, the family-friendly towns of Calabasas and Agoura Hills are among the most desirable places to live in Southern California. Some longtime residents were lured here by the wide-open spaces that welcomed their horses, while many newcomers fled the confines of the city for exclusive, creekside neighborhoods. It's quiet here, but not too quiet, with plenty of upscale shopping and trendy dining to content erstwhile urbanites. Now this pleasant enclave has one more enviable feature: a Community Center that's part health club, part "activities central," and part special event facility. Lucky for you, you don't have to be a resident to enjoy what the Center has to offer.

During normal business hours, both the young and the young-at-heart indulge in a potpourri of fun at the Center, including Swing Salsa lessons, youth camps, belly dancing classes, rock-climbing lessons, and annual events like the St. Patrick's Day Community Barbecue. However, on most weekends you can hold a private celebration here.

Set back against the hills and surrounded by attractive landscaping, the Center is housed in a contemporary building boasting a huge, avant-garde arch over the entryway. The lobby is bright and airy, thanks to the double-tall windows and a vaulted atrium that let in the sunshine, nourishing the potted plantation ferns. Everything here is "quality"—even the vending machine serves fresh-ground Starbuck's cappuccinos! Party planners and brides find this space so welcoming they often use it for their cocktail hour.

On the outdoor patio, which runs the length of the Community Room, banks of African violets, French lavender and native grasses border one side, and several faux brick planters hold graceful saplings. Guests can enjoy their champagne and hors d'oeuvres while lounging on teak garden furniture, and when it's time for the reception they simply walk through a set of doors that open right into the Community Room.

The Community Room holds up to 300, but can be divided into three sections for smaller groups. The high, barrel-vaulted ceiling—made of open beams and wooden planking—coordinates with the floor, polished to a gleam. A row of accent tiles marks the floor's perimeter, but other than that, neutral earth tones keep the look light and accessible. If you're planning a gala-sized affair, the 10,000-square-foot Gymnasium accommodates 800 guests with ease.

With two generous spaces you can decorate nearly any way you like, you're free to design a thoroughly original event. One bride enlisted a local nursery to transform the Community Room into an enchanted forest with potted trees, garlands of greenery, and hanging floral baskets. Another inspired client hung draping from the ceiling to separate five themed areas inside the Gymnasium.

The folks at the Center encourage your creativity, and there are no limitations on catering, so they say YES! to specialty cuisine. You'll appreciate their friendly, helpful attitude, and the way they make you feel like part of the community, even if you visit from afar.

CEREMONY CAPACITY: The Community Room holds 308 seated guests.

EVENT/RECEPTION & MEETING CAPACITY: The Community Room holds 308 seated or standing guests and can be divided into 3 smaller sections. The Patio holds up to 50 guests.

FEES & DEPOSITS: A deposit ranging $175–500 is required to reserve your date; the balance is due 30 days prior to the event. Community room rental fees range $55–255/hour. A security guard is required, whether alcohol is served or not, at an additional charge.

AVAILABILITY: Year-round, daily, 6am–2am.

SERVICES/AMENITIES:

Catering: BYO
Kitchen Facilities: large warming kitchen
Tables & Chairs: provided
Linens, Silver, etc.: BYO
Restrooms: wheelchair accessible
Dance Floor: wood floor
Bride's Dressing Area: no
AV/Meeting Equipment: wireless internet, projector, PA system, microphones

Parking: large lot
Accommodations: no guest rooms
Outdoor Night Lighting: yes
Outdoor Cooking Facilities: BYO BBQ
Cleanup: provided or through renter
View: mountains and hills
Other: limited event coordination

RESTRICTIONS:

Alcohol: BYO
Smoking: not allowed
Music: amplified OK indoors

Wheelchair Access: yes
Insurance: liability required
Other: no rice, glitter, confetti or birdseed, no duct tape or anything that mars walls

---

Want to find more venues and services? Check out our informative website, www.HereComesTheGuide.com.

Saddle Peak Lodge

Restaurant

419 Cold Canyon Road, Calabasas
818/222-3888 x14

www.saddlepeaklodge.com
sean@saddlepeaklodge.com

● Rehearsal Dinners	● Corporate Events
● Ceremonies	● Meetings
● Wedding Receptions	● Film Shoots
● Private Parties	Accommodations

Saddle Peak Lodge is one of the more intriguing event sites we've ever seen. Steeped in California history, this turn-of-the-century hunting lodge began over 100 years ago as a small one-room cabin where cowboys, miners, fishermen and oil riggers imbibed the local "Hillbilly Punch" and swapped tall stories. Later the lodge carved a new identity, first as a way-stop and general store and then as a summer resort. In the '30s and '40s, Saddle Peak became the in-vogue hangout for movie stars such as Errol Flynn, Clark Gable and Charlie Chaplin. Today it prospers as a restaurant specializing in exotic game, and is renowned as an extraordinary place to host any special occasion.

As you enter the lodge, the antler door pulls and three-hoofed lamp in the foyer signal that you're in for a unique dining experience. The provocative aroma of roasting elk, venison, buffalo and mesquite lingers in the air—so tantalizing it gives you pangs of hunger in anticipation.

With its rough-hewn, tall-timbered interior, Saddle Peak is warm and elegantly rustic in its décor. An antique pistol collection gleams in a display case, while old western saddles and riding tack are slung casually over large beams. Populating the wood walls is an amusing mix of mounted trophy heads—deer, moose, pronghorn, eland—as well as authentic saloon paintings from the 1800s.

Saddle Peak's log-cabin ambiance lends itself beautifully to weddings: With hurricane lamps glowing on white tablecloths and a fire crackling in the Main Dining Room's massive rock hearth, the lodge is a wildly romantic setting.

Most weddings are celebrated on the lodge's picturesque and secluded Far Patio, just a short walk from the Main Dining Room. Couples exchange vows on a circular, two-tiered slate rock area that overlooks a spectacular view of Santa Monica Mountains' rolling hills and canyons. Note that as an added perk when you buy out the lodge, the third-floor Loft is transformed into a bridal suite where the bride can get ready for her walk down the aisle. French doors open to a stone walkway that leads past a cascading waterfall to the ceremony site.

Post ceremony, guests sip wine under the shade of pine and eucalyptus trees, or relax fireside in the dining room in handsome, handmade willow chairs. Small parties may want to savor hors d'oeuvres in the upstairs Den or Library—cozy pine-paneled rooms lined with windows and eclectically decorated with collectibles, antique books, and relics of the Old West. Dinner and dancing take place in the Main Dining Room, or al fresco on the Main Patio under a canopy of trees with the natural sounds of the nearby waterfall in the background.

The restaurant's extensive menu includes seafood, poultry, lamb and beef in addition to game, and they're perfectly happy to prepare vegetarian entrées as well. Not only is the food award winning (earning "best-of" honors from the *Los Angeles Times* and *Conde Nast Traveler,* as well as the highest ratings from ZAGAT, DiRoNA and Four Diamond AAA), but the lodge also boasts an award-winning domestic wine collection. Plus the staff are incredibly friendly and accommodating, making you feel like you're part of the Saddle Peak family.

From their distinctive cuisine and impeccable service to the incredible vistas, Saddle Peak Lodge earns rave reviews.

CEREMONY & EVENT/RECEPTION CAPACITY: The facility holds 150 seated or 175 standing guests indoors and 150 seated or 200 standing outdoors.

MEETING CAPACITY: Meeting spaces seat 90 guests indoors.

FEES & DEPOSITS: A $200–750 deposit is required to reserve your date. The food & beverage minimum varies depending on the space(s) needed and day of the week. Meals range $35–75/person. Tax, beverages and a 20% service charge are additional. There are no rental or site fees; setup, takedown and resets throughout the event are included in the F&B minimum.

AVAILABILITY: Year-round. Daytime and evening events may be scheduled.

SERVICES/AMENITIES:

Catering: in-house
Kitchen Facilities: n/a
Tables & Chairs: provided
Linens, Silver, etc.: provided
Restrooms: wheelchair accessible
Dance Floor: provided, CBA
Bride's Dressing Area: yes
AV/Meeting Equipment: CBA
Other: in-house florals

Parking: large lot, valet only
Accommodations: no guest rooms
Outdoor Night Lighting: provided
Outdoor Cooking Facilities: no
Cleanup: provided
View: canyon, fountain, garden, landscaped grounds; panorama of mountains, forest and hills

RESTRICTIONS:

Alcohol: full in-house bar
Smoking: designated areas only
Music: amplified OK with restrictions

Wheelchair Access: yes
Insurance: not required

Knollwood Country Club

Country Club

12024 Balboa Boulevard, Granada Hills
888/991-5042

www.countryclubreceptions.com
privateeventdirector@knowllwoodgc.com

● Rehearsal Dinners	● Corporate Events
● Ceremonies	● Meetings
● Wedding Receptions	● Film Shoots
● Private Parties	Accommodations

When Granada Hills was founded in 1927, town members chose the name "Granada" after its sister city Granada, Spain. Although separated by thousands of miles, the two communities have similarities: Both are in the foothills of mountain ranges, and both have temperate climates—a quality making them prime candidates for outdoor weddings.

One of this city's best-known wedding locations is Knollwood Country Club, an affordable public golf course and clubhouse with a friendly attitude. Ceremonies are held outside on a trim lawn backed by pine trees and the rolling fairways. You can say your vows under the open sky beneath a metal arch that can be ornamented with flowers, tulle or even pine boughs. And, speaking of pines, there are so many around here you can almost imagine you're getting married in a quiet mountain meadow.

After the ceremony, guests walk over to the clubhouse, an unpretentious fieldstone-faced building with three event spaces. Here, they sip cocktails in the private bar area while you and your new spouse have your pictures taken under the trees. The reception follows in the spacious Granada Room. With its unadorned white walls, this room easily adapts to your event theme and color scheme. Light streams in through floor-to-ceiling windows during the day, while faux-candle fixtures hanging from the high ceiling provide illumination at night. The Granada Room also has its own large built-in dance floor with a mirrored ball overhead.

If your event is more intimate or you need additional space, there are two other smaller banquet rooms: the Gallery and the Fairway. Both are neutral-toned with floor-to-ceiling windows; the larger Gallery Room also has a fieldstone wall and its own bar.

Next to the relaxed golf-club setting, it's the ease of planning an event here that draws couples to Knollwood. Wedding packages include your choice of linens, tray-passed hors d'oeuvres, and the cake (with cutting). Choose the Platinum Package, and you'll also receive an open bar and assorted pastries! Although Knollwood provides a wide selection of packages, the catering staff is happy to customize one to meet your specific needs.

Knollwood offers another perk that's especially popular with the men in your group: You can integrate a little golf into your event! Grooms frequently schedule a morning tee time to loosen up with family and friends on the wedding day.

Granada Hills is known as the "Valley's Most Neighborly Town," and you might say that Knollwood is its most neighborly wedding site. You don't have to be a member—or even a golfer—to get married here, and they take such good care of you, you may end up feeling that you've definitely hit a wedding hole in one.

CEREMONY CAPACITY: The lawn holds 250 seated guests; the indoor areas hold 300 seated.

EVENT/RECEPTION&MEETINGCAPACITY: The clubhouse accommodates 300 seated or 400 standing guests.

FEES & DEPOSITS: A nonrefundable deposit, which is applied to your food & beverage total, is required to reserve your date. The amount of the deposit varies, depending on how far in advance you book. Payment terms for the balance also vary, and may be arranged on an individual basis. Inclusive packages start at $47/person. Tax, alcohol and service charge are additional. Food & beverage minimums may apply. Menus and packages can be customized to fit your needs and budget. Call for details.

AVAILABILITY: Year-round, daily.

SERVICES/AMENITIES:
Catering: in-house
Kitchen Facilities: n/a
Tables & Chairs: provided
Linens, Silver, etc.: provided
Restrooms: wheelchair accessible
Dance Floor: provided
Bride's Dressing Area: yes
AV/Meeting Equipment: some provided

Parking: large complimentary lot
Accommodations: no guest rooms
Outdoor Night Lighting: CBA
Outdoor Cooking Facilities: no
Cleanup: provided
View: fairways, mountains, garden
Other: event coordination

RESTRICTIONS:
Alcohol: in-house
Smoking: outside only
Music: amplified OK, subject to management approval

Wheelchair Access: yes
Insurance: not required

Middle Ranch

Country Club

11700 Little Tujunga Canyon Road, Lake View Terrace
818/897-4029
www.middleranch.com
middle.ranch@hotmail.com

	Rehearsal Dinners	●	Corporate Events
●	Ceremonies	●	Meetings
●	Wedding Receptions	●	Film Shoots
●	Private Parties		Accommodations

Surrounded by the San Gabriel Mountains and bordered by the Angeles National Forest on three sides, Middle Ranch's civilized lawns and attractive buildings are a pleasant surprise in the midst of this rugged landscape.

The 650-acre property, known primarily as an exclusive equestrian country club, is also a spectacular place for a wedding. Ceremonies are held on the expansive front lawn with a backdrop of trees and mountains. The venue's main building, the award-winning Lodge, harmonizes nicely with its surroundings and has been recognized for its architectural style. Beneath its Spanish tile roof you'll find a large "living room" that's ideal for socializing over cocktails and hors d'oeuvres. The ambiance here is very relaxed, with a lofty, open-beamed ceiling, an abundance of warm natural wood, terracotta-tile floors and a handsome, two-sided fieldstone fireplace. Leather couches and chairs, along with antique Oriental carpets, complete the décor.

French doors open out to a lovely and spacious garden patio. Partly shaded by fragrant eucalyptus trees, it's an intimate spot for an al fresco reception. A few steps uphill, there's a pool with a large deck backed by an untamed hillside. You and your guests can sit by the water enjoying cocktails, or dine at tables set up on the patio.

The contrast between the wild, natural setting and the effortless elegance of the venue itself makes Middle Ranch a very special—and distinctly Californian—place to celebrate.

CEREMONY CAPACITY: The grass field can accommodate up to 225 seated guests. The Patio holds up to 100 seated, 150 standing.

EVENT/RECEPTION CAPACITY: The Lodge accommodates 150 seated, 175 standing; the Patio holds 225 seated or standing guests. From late fall through early spring there is a 150-guest maximum.

MEETING CAPACITY: The Lodge holds 150 seated, the conference room up to 30 seated.

FEES & DEPOSITS: A nonrefundable $1,000 deposit is required to reserve your date. 50% of the total estimated event cost is due 180 days prior to the event; the balance is payable 14 days prior. The facility rental fee is $28/person (minimum $2,240) and includes tables, chairs, linens and choice of linen color, place settings, facility personnel, and 6 hours of facility rental time. The ceremony fee is $700 and includes an additional half hour of rental time, your choice of oakwood or white chairs, wedding arch, bridal dressing room, and rehearsal time.

AVAILABILITY: Year-round, daily, until midnight.

SERVICES/AMENITIES:

Catering: select from approved list
Kitchen Facilities: fully equipped
Tables & Chairs: provided
Linens, Silver, etc.: linens, silver and china provided
Restrooms: wheelchair accessible
Dance Floor: CBA, extra fee: $225
Bride's & Groom's Dressing Areas: yes
AV/Meeting Equipment: BYO

Parking: large lot
Accommodations: no guest rooms
Outdoor Night Lighting: yes
Outdoor Cooking Facilities: n/a
Cleanup: provided
View: landscaped patio and pool area; Angeles Forest

RESTRICTIONS:

Alcohol: in-house, no BYO
Smoking: not allowed
Music: amplified OK

Wheelchair Access: yes
Insurance: not required for social functions; required for business functions

Ca' Del Sole Ristorante

Italian Restaurant

4100 Cahuenga Boulevard, Toluca Lake
818/753-8889
www.cadelsole.com
events@cadelsole.com

- Rehearsal Dinners
- Ceremonies
- Wedding Receptions
- Private Parties
- Corporate Events
- Meetings
- Film Shoots
- Accommodations

Welcome to Ca' Del Sole—"House of the Sun"—where life is good, the food even better, and the setting sublime. When you visit this updated version of an authentic trattoria, the tantalizing aroma of fresh roasted garlic and herbs mingled with an infectious mood of contentment will make you want to linger as long as possible.

Ca' Del Sole was fashioned after a Venetian country inn. Details like dark wooden beams and the double-sided fireplace in the main dining rooms recall an Old World village where strangers are wined and dined, and even the most trivial milestone is cause for celebration.

However, a recent remodel brings contemporary chic to the rustic décor, artfully realized in the two adjoining private banquet rooms: the Gondolier and the Venetian. A new floor has a walnut patina that may make you think of a renovated Tuscan farmhouse, and a distressed white hutch displaying vintage ceramics lends a handcrafted touch. Italian Mod lounge furniture in tomato-red and marine-blue adds a colorful contrast to accents like oversized rough-hewn bowls adorning dove-gray walls. The eclectic blend all comes together beautifully, and provides a clean and classy canvas for your own event stylings.

At the far end of the Venetian, French doors lead you onto an L-shaped, brick terrace enclosed by smooth plaster walls. Vibrant bougainvillea spills from the top of a slanted wooden awning, while leafy trees, espaliered jasmine and creamy-white urns brimming with flowers transport you to a balmy Mediterranean garden. In the corner of the terrace, water cascades from a triple-tiered stone fountain, a refreshing backdrop for you and your fiancé to exchange wedding vows. An al fresco cocktail hour and reception are also divine out here, with cafe umbrellas for shade or heat lamps to ward off any chill.

An extra "wow factor" comes courtesy of the striped olive-and-white curtained cabanas along one wall, each sporting a stunning glass chandelier. These glamorous tents are ripe with event possibilities: You can showcase your wedding cake in one, your sweetheart table in the other, and a distinctive head table in the spacious center cabana. Next to the terrace, Ca' Del Sole's new bar patio is so cool that it's already a local hotspot. Also cool: There are no room charges at Ca' Del Sole, so feel free to use the event spaces for everything from your bridal shower to the most lavish gala.

Whatever type of gathering you host here, count on a chorus of satisfied "oohs" and "aahs" from your guests after their first bite of the tantalizing cuisine. The light Northern Italian fare lets classic Mediterranean flavors shine through—garlic and capers, parmesan and polenta—each dish is a feast for the senses. The fresh, imaginative creations taste like the ingredients were plucked from the sun-kissed hills of Veneto. And if there's any special food you require, just ask.

The ristorante's approach is extremely professional, yet guests are able to relax amid a joyous atmosphere. "We at Ca' Del Sole want to make everyone feel comfortable," assures co-owner Signor Costella. Your event at the "House of the Sun" will have guests so comfortable that they won't want to leave!

CEREMONY CAPACITY: The patio holds up to 15 seated guests.

EVENT/RECEPTION CAPACITY: The restaurant holds up to 150 seated both inside in the private dining rooms and outside on the private patio. The private patio alone accommodates 120 seated.

MEETING CAPACITY: The Gondolier Room holds up to 30, the Venetian Room up to 40. Combined, these rooms accommodate up to 80 seated guests.

FEES & DEPOSITS: For weddings, a $500 deposit is required to reserve your date. 50% of the estimated event total is due 2 weeks prior to the event; the balance is payable 3 days prior. Meals range $35–55/person; alcohol, tax and service charges are additional. A $300 ceremony setup fee is extra, as is a $1.50/person cake-cutting fee.

For other kinds of functions, a $300 deposit is required to reserve the date, and full payment is due on the day of the event.

AVAILABILITY: Year-round, daily, 11am–midnight.

SERVICES/AMENITIES:

Catering: in-house, no BYO
Kitchen Facilities: n/a
Tables & Chairs: provided
Linens, Silver, etc.: provided
Restrooms: wheelchair accessible
Dance Floor: provided, extra charge
Bride's & Groom's Dressing Areas: no
AV/Meeting Equipment: CBA or BYO

Parking: valet or self-parking on street
Accommodations: no guest rooms
Outdoor Night Lighting: yes
Outdoor Cooking Facilities: CBA
Cleanup: provided
View: garden setting with fountain
Other: event coordination

RESTRICTIONS:

Alcohol: in-house, no BYO
Smoking: outdoors only
Music: amplified music OK indoors with volume restrictions, outdoors acoustic only

Wheelchair Access: yes
Insurance: not required

This is important! Tell locations you're reading HERE COMES THE GUIDE and ask if our information is still current.

139

Porter Valley Country Club

Country Club

19216 Singing Hills Drive, Porter Ranch
818/360-1071 x231/232

www.portervalley.com
contactus@portervalley.com

●	Rehearsal Dinners	●	Corporate Events
●	Ceremonies	●	Meetings
●	Wedding Receptions	●	Film Shoots
●	Private Parties		Accommodations

Nestled in the foothills of the Santa Susana Mountains, Porter Valley Country Club is a lushly land-scaped private club surrounded by green rolling hills. As you survey the property, an abundance of trees, flowers, lawns, and water features makes you feel like you're in paradise.

Weddings take place at your choice of two locations: The first is the rose garden at the west end of the clubhouse. Here, most couples exchange vows under an arbor adorned with flowers, tim-ing the ceremony to coincide with a beautiful sunset. Seating on the lawn and Clubhouse Ter-race affords guests an excellent view of the fairways as well as the nearby lake with its sparkling fountain. The second ceremony site is on the first tee overlooking the lake. This option gives the bride a more dramatic entrance, as all eyes are on her as she walks from the clubhouse down a path and up a long aisle to the elevated tee.

After the ceremony the bride and groom are welcome to pose for photographs on the greens or alongside the club's impressive arched portico with the lake in the background. At the same time, guests can get ready for the reception in the Pinehurst Room, a setting that's both classic and elegant. Painted in pale cream hues and with a wall of west-facing windows, it opens directly onto the Terrace through glass doors. English country chandeliers and handsome wooden pillars buttressing a coffered ceiling lend an air of quiet dignity. Large enough for a 36-piece band and dance floor, this room is suitable for small to midsize gatherings. Need more space? Simply pull back the Pinehurst's retractable wall and expand into the equally appealing Homestead Room, which has swimming pool and golf course views.

Porter Valley's expertise is definitely proven. Their staff has a reputation for being warm and welcoming, and they're especially adept at hosting large events. They've orchestrated hundreds of weddings, corporate functions, private parties and, of course, golf tournaments, so you know you'll be in skilled hands.

CEREMONY CAPACITY: The outdoor Terrace holds up to 300 seated guests; the Homestead Room holds 150 seated.

EVENT/RECEPTION CAPACITY: Outdoors, the Pool Area holds up to 150 seated guests. Indoors, several spaces hold 25–300 seated guests.

MEETING CAPACITY: There are 3 areas that accommodate 20–300 seated guests.

FEES & DEPOSITS: For weddings, a nonrefundable $2,000 deposit is required to secure your date. 50% of the estimated total is due 60 days prior to the event, and the balance and final guest count are due 2 weeks prior. Several wedding packages can include: hors d'oeuvres, wine and beverages, bar service, champagne toast, cake, 2-course meal, and coffee or tea. Tax and a 20% service charge are additional. Luncheon packages start at $60/person, dinner packages at $64/person; à la carte luncheons start at $27/person and dinners start at $29/person. For business functions or meetings, room rental fees vary depending on the time frame. Food & beverage services are provided; call for more specific information.

AVAILABILITY: Year-round, daily. Luncheons 11am–4pm, 11:30am–4:30pm or noon–5pm; dinners 6:30pm–11:30pm or 7pm–midnight. Additional hours are available for a nominal fee. Business functions or meetings can take place anytime; private golf tournaments can be held on Mondays.

SERVICES/AMENITIES:

Catering: in-house, no BYO
Kitchen Facilities: n/a
Tables & Chairs: Chiavari chairs provided for reception
Linens, Silver, etc.: provided
Restrooms: wheelchair accessible
Dance Floor: provided
Bride's Dressing Area: CBA
AV/Meeting Equipment: LCD screen, VCR, TVs, flip charts, microphone, podium

Parking: complimentary large lot, valet CBA, security provided
Accommodations: no guest rooms, hotels nearby
Outdoor Night Lighting: yes
Outdoor Cooking Facilities: BBQ
Cleanup: provided
View: fairways, lake with wildlife, Santa Susana Mountains
Other: photo booth, coordination, flowers, vendor referrals

RESTRICTIONS:

Alcohol: in-house
Smoking: outside only
Music: amplified OK with volume limits

Wheelchair Access: yes, elevator
Insurance: not required
Other: no rice, confetti, glitter, or birdseed; votive candles OK, decorations must be approved

Hummingbird Nest

2940 Kuehner Drive, Santa Susana
805/579-8000

www.hummingbirdnestranch.com
info@hummingbirdnestranch.com

Private Estate & Garden

● Rehearsal Dinners	● Corporate Events
● Ceremonies	● Meetings
● Wedding Receptions	Film Shoots
● Private Parties	● Accommodations

Far from the hustle and bustle of city life, the Hummingbird Nest ranch is an oasis of tranquility and beauty. Extending over 140 acres, the estate's landscape transitions from the earth tones of the Santa Susana Mountains that surround it to the vibrantly colored blooms of the native plants lining its curving roadways and lush green pastures.

There are so many things here that please the eye and inspire the soul, among them bubbling fountains, meandering pathways, hidden gazebos and spectacular mountain vistas. This is truly an extraordinary location for events ranging from weddings and formal dinners to awards ceremonies and charity balls. Corporations also find that Hummingbird's serene environment is conducive to successful meetings and seminars.

Presiding over the property at the top of a hill is the sprawling, 17,000-square-foot Spanish Colonial-style villa. Arched entryways, curved columns, tiled staircases and the prodigious use of fancy ironwork add grace and drama to the crisp white façade. At the front of the building, the main circular court with its central fountain has such a lovely view that it's often used during the ceremony as a backdrop to the bride's dramatic entrance down the front steps of the villa.

Just to the left of the main entrance, there's a wrought-iron gate that leads to a garden, complete with a natural stone waterfall and a Spanish-tiled gazebo—another favorite ceremony backdrop. To the right, a multilevel patio with fountains, iron lanterns and an array of palms offers enormous flexibility for receptions, whether large scale or more intimate. From this vantage, you can look down over the sweeping acreage to the vast Grand Prix Lawn below, which can be tented and is perfect for very large weddings, music festivals and other grand events. Hummingbird Nest's newest area is the expansive Lake Lawn. Bordering a tranquil lake, it makes a beautiful area for celebrations as well as an excellent backdrop for bridal photos.

Yet, there are still more tempting options to explore on the park-like grounds. At a recent wedding, guests had cocktails on the patio, then strolled along a paved pathway to a large open field that can easily accommodate 1,000. The bride and groom, in keeping with the pastoral surroundings, arrived by horse-drawn carriage.

For a very romantic setting that draws upon the history of the property, there's the secluded original 1920s ranch house, known as "Sitting Bull." Utterly charming, the brick-and-adobe building is shaded by century-old eucalyptus and olive trees. It features a cobblestone courtyard (where you can add a dance floor), a sizeable garden, and a sparkling pool area.

To complete the experience, extend your stay in one of several fully equipped three to four bedroom cottages. Hummingbird Nest Ranch takes you away from your daily routine, providing a place to relax, laugh and just let go. By the time you leave, you'll feel enriched, refreshed and looking forward to returning for future events.

CEREMONY, EVENT/RECEPTION & MEETING CAPACITY: Various locations accommodate 100–1,000 seated or standing guests outdoors.

FEES & DEPOSITS: A nonrefundable $5,000 deposit is required to reserve your date, and the balance is due 30 days prior to the event. The site fee starts at $7,000 and varies depending on the day and area(s) reserved. Security, parking management and valet are required, and are contracted exclusively through Hummingbird Nest. All service providers must be insured, as well as approved by Hummingbird Nest, to perform services on the property. Discounts on packages are available when Hummingbird Nest's preferred vendors are used.

AVAILABILITY: Year-round, until 2am. The site is shown by appointment only.

SERVICES/AMENITIES:

Catering: select from preferred list, or BYO with approval
Kitchen Facilities: satellite kitchen required
Tables & Chairs: BYO
Linens, Silver, etc.: BYO
Restrooms: wheelchair accessible in some areas
Dance Floor: BYO
Bride's & Groom's Dressing Areas: yes
AV/Meeting Equipment: BYO
Other: events may run until 2am

Parking: valet required, extra fee
Accommodations: four guest houses are available to rent with a total of 13 bedrooms
Outdoor Night Lighting: limited
Outdoor Cooking Facilities: no
Cleanup: caterer and renter
View: cityscape, fountain, garden, hills, lake, landscaped grounds, meadows, mountains, pool area, valley

RESTRICTIONS:

Alcohol: licensed server required
Smoking: designated outside areas only
Music: amplified OK

Wheelchair Access: limited
Insurance: liability required

Sportsmen's Lodge Events Center

Event Center

12833 Ventura Boulevard, Studio City
818/755-5000

www.sportsmenslodge.com
weddings@sportsmenslodge.com

● Rehearsal Dinners		● Corporate Events	
● Ceremonies		● Meetings	
● Wedding Receptions		● Film Shoots	
● Private Parties		● Accommodations	

The fantastic renovation of the iconic Sportsmen's Lodge Events Center, an artful blending of historic charm and updated flair, proves that the classics never go out of style.

This unique property, once a rustic playground for Hollywood's most famous players, like John Wayne, Clark Gable, Bogey & Bacall and Tracy & Hepburn, was never your typical Tinseltown watering hole. Water, however, was definitely part of its appeal. Long before the movie industry even began, travelers making the journey on dirt roads through rural San Fernando Valley would stop at this oasis, catch their own trout in the spring-fed lake and have the chef cook it up for dinner. As the valley grew and the pace quickened along Ventura Boulevard, countless visitors continued to embrace this landmark where they'd often celebrate life's memorable moments.

Devoted exclusively to special events now, the popular center is like a world unto itself. Spread out over eight acres, this enchanting retreat combines century-old trees, bucolic gardens, romantic bridges, outdoor patios and elegant interior venues with views of the legendary ponds and waterways. The sprawling Events Center building retains its familiar mid-century lodge architecture, but has been completely refreshed in sparkling white, from the large porte-cochère to the welcoming front lobby, outfitted with chic white leather seating and antique mirrored sconces.

There are two heavenly outdoor ceremony sites. The Waterfall Gazebo overlooks the south pond and provides a picture-perfect moment as the bride crosses a wrought-iron bridge to join her groom and exchange vows against a woodsy backdrop of towering eucalyptus, redwoods and Monterey pines. The expansive Garden Gazebo at the back of the property is a huge plaza, lushly landscaped on both sides. A center aisle runs between two rows of mature trees for a very dramatic entry by the bridal party. Both sites include ample room for post-ceremony toasting—especially the Garden Gazebo, where the bar faces a delightful scene of a blooming island in the nearby pond.

Options abound when it comes to reception areas. There are 10 of them, ranging from a cozy fireplace room for an intimate affair to spectacular, flowing spaces, several of which can be combined. The Cascade-Starlight-Waterfalls combination is the most requested and it's easy to see why. Floor-to-ceiling windows frame a soothing tableau of fountains, a footbridge arching over a rose garden and water cascading over natural stone and moss. (Nature's white, cream and soft green tones are often repeated in the interiors.) The Starlight Ballroom adds a touch of pizzazz with a raised stage and a step-down dance floor encircled by an ornate iron railing.

If you dream of full-out glamour, then you'll love the Empire-Regency Ballroom's regal proportions, dazzling crystal-drop chandeliers, crown molding, curtained stage and built-in bar. The luxe atmosphere carries over into the adjacent Rear Lobby, an impressive grand foyer with a gracious, curving, two-story staircase—an absolute "must" for some great wedding photos.

For more than a hundred years, Sportsmen's Lodge has held a special place for generations of Angelenos. Now, updated and better than ever, its legacy continues—along with the tradition followed by many newlyweds of coming back to celebrate future anniversaries, too.

CEREMONY CAPACITY: The site features two outdoor decks in garden settings with two gazebos. The South Garden seats 150 and the North Garden seats 600.

EVENT/RECEPTION CAPACITY: The center can accommodate 800 seated indoors and 600 seated outdoors.

MEETING CAPACITY: Meeting spaces hold 1,000 seated guests.

FEES & DEPOSITS: 25% of the total event cost is required to reserve your date and the balance is due 14 days prior to the event. Wedding packages range $49–99/person. Tax and a 20% service charge are additional. Kosher catering is available, and outside ethnic caterers are welcome with approval.

AVAILABILITY: Year-round, daily, 6am–midnight

SERVICES/AMENITIES:

Catering: in-house
Kitchen Facilities: n/a
Tables & Chairs: provided
Linens, Silver, etc.: provided
Restrooms: wheelchair accessible
Dance Floor: portable provided
Bride's Dressing Area: yes
AV/Meeting Equipment: some provided
Other: spa services, garden ceremonies, complimentary event coordination

Parking: large lot, complimentary self-parking, valet $10/car
Accommodations: 191 guest rooms
Outdoor Night Lighting: yes
Outdoor Cooking Facilities: no
Cleanup: provided
View: fountain, garden, lagoon, landscaped grounds, waterfall

RESTRICTIONS:

Alcohol: in-house
Smoking: outdoors only
Music: amplified OK

Wheelchair Access: yes
Insurance: required for vendors

Braemar Country Club

Country Club

4001 Reseda Boulevard, Tarzana
818/345-6520
www.braemarclub.com
contactus@braemarclub.com

● Rehearsal Dinners	● Corporate Events
● Ceremonies	● Meetings
● Wedding Receptions	● Film Shoots
● Private Parties	Accommodations

Nestled in the canyons and arroyos along the northern slopes of the Santa Monica Mountains, Braemar Country Club offers an oasis of peace away from the hustle and bustle of the city. The beautifully designed clubhouse is an elegant, modern setting for all types of events. One walks on cool, creamy marble through an open floor plan flooded with natural light. There are graceful columns along every hallway, lots of French doors, and a tiled deck that wraps around the entire structure. The pleasing architectural elements are perfectly complemented by the natural colors of the carpeting and comfortable furniture.

Just a short walk from the clubhouse is the Cypress Lawn, a serene outdoor ceremony site. This secluded spot is sheltered on one side by a stand of tall cypress trees and on the other by a tree-covered hillside. Guests seated on the grass enjoy watching you exchange vows against a lovely backdrop of the rolling hills in the distance.

Open-air ceremonies are also held on the brick terrace, which works well for receptions, too. This space offers a breathtaking panoramic view of the Masters Course and San Fernando Valley. During evening celebrations, city lights glitter in the distance, and for more sparkle you may want to add candles and twinkle lights. Customized cocktail bars and buffet stations can be set up on the terrace, making it the perfect place for guests to mingle on a balmy night. The terrace is also popular for al fresco rehearsal dinners. Other dining options are the clubhouse's Main Dining Room or poolside.

The best location for an indoor ceremony is a versatile suite of three rooms, each of which overlooks the same spectacular view available from the terrace: the emerald hills of the golf course in the foreground, the Santa Susana and San Gabriel mountains in the background. Laid out in an L-shape with floor-to-ceiling windows, the rooms can be opened up to allow for very large parties or partitioned into five separate spaces that collectively serve as ceremony site, cocktail area, and banquet hall with dance floor.

Flexibility is the name of the game here, and no matter how you orchestrate your celebration nature is always within reach.

CEREMONY CAPACITY: The Club holds 50–300 seated guests outdoors, and 50–250 seated indoors.

EVENT/RECEPTION CAPACITY: The Main Dining Room holds 200 seated or 300 standing. The entire Clubhouse holds 300 seated or 500 standing.

MEETING CAPACITY: 3 areas accommodate 10–250 seated guests.

FEES & DEPOSITS: For weddings, 25% of the estimated event total (nonrefundable) is required to hold your date. 50% is payable 60 days prior to the event; the balance and a guest count guarantee are due 10 days prior. Reception luncheons run approximately $19–30/person, dinners $35–53/person, luncheon buffets $31–34/person and dinner buffets $45/person. Hors d'oeuvres, alcohol, tax and a 20% service charge are additional. Wedding receptions are held in 5-hour blocks; overtime is $250/hour. Pricing includes the ceremony, dance floor, room rental, linens and cake-cutting fee. The ceremony includes rehearsal, white folding chairs, wired microphone, and speakers.

For business functions or meetings, a nonrefundable deposit is required to hold your date. All-day meeting packages, including breakfast, lunch and afternoon snack, start at $19/person. A $50–800 cleanup/setup fee, depending on the room and menu, is extra.

AVAILABILITY: Year-round, daily, in 5-hour blocks.

SERVICES/AMENITIES:

Catering: in-house; outside caterers may be permitted

Kitchen Facilities: n/a

Tables & Chairs: provided

Linens, Silver, etc.: provided

Restrooms: wheelchair accessible

Dance Floor: provided

Bride's & Groom's Dressing Areas: yes

AV/Meeting Equipment: full range

Parking: valet or self-parking

Accommodations: no guest rooms

Outdoor Night Lighting: yes

Outdoor Cooking Facilities: BBQs CBA

Cleanup: provided

View: golf course, valley and distant mountains

Other: full event planning and coordination

RESTRICTIONS:

Alcohol: in-house, no BYO

Smoking: outdoors only

Music: amplified OK

Wheelchair Access: yes

Insurance: not required

Other: no rice or birdseed outdoors

Overwhelmed? Use the search criteria on www.HereComesTheGuide.com to narrow down your choices.

147

Sheraton Universal

Hotel

333 Universal Hollywood Drive, Universal City
818/509-2726 Catering Department

www.sheratonuniversal.com
sciccarelli@sheratonuniversal.com

- Rehearsal Dinners
- Ceremonies
- Wedding Receptions
- Private Parties
- Corporate Events
- Meetings
- Film Shoots
- Accommodations

A gleaming tower that rises up from the back lot of famed Universal Studios Hollywood, the Sheraton Universal has provided a swank place to stay for an impressive roster of actors and actresses. Celebrity patrons have earned it the nickname "The Hotel of the Stars," and a similar moniker could be applied to its most spectacular wedding spot—the Starview Room on the 21st floor. In this case, however, "The Wedding Site of the Stars" derives its sparkle not from Hollywood's brightest, but from the heavenly bodies glittering in the night sky.

A botanical haven, the Starview Room is a glassed-in aerie with wraparound views of the Hollywood Hills and the San Fernando Valley as far as the eye can see. At night, twinkling lights in the ceiling compete with the great L.A. Basin light show.

If a sky-high perch isn't what you had in mind, the first floor offers a series of handsome banquet facilities, starting with the Grand Ballroom. It features rich woodwork, beveled mirrors, sparkling chandeliers, and carpeting in subdued shades of taupe and ocean blue. The Ballroom's foyer—aptly named the Great Hall—is a terrific prefunction space, with six crystal chandeliers and floorto-ceiling windows framed in flowing, sheer white fabric. They overlook a garden ringed with magnolia trees. You can tie the knot in the Grand Ballroom, although some couples prefer to have their ceremony outside in the garden.

There are several other spacious banquet rooms, all with a similarly refined décor. And for a small wedding, you might want to reserve the Terrace Room, which opens onto a terracotta patio next to the pool.

The Sheraton Universal offers a full range of gourmet menus that can be customized for each client—and it's one of the few event sites in L.A. that can provide glatt kosher catering. As we discovered, there's a great deal of choice and flexibility here, and this is one place where the sky is, quite literally, the limit.

CEREMONY CAPACITY: The Starview Room seats 300 guests indoors and the Ballroom Garden seats 500 outdoors.

EVENT/RECEPTION CAPACITY: Indoor spaces accomodate 150–850 seated or 250–1,200 standing. Outdoors, the site holds up to 500 seated or 600 standing.

MEETING CAPACITY: 3 areas accommodate 150–1,200 seated guests.

FEES & DEPOSITS: For weddings, a nonrefundable $4,500 deposit is payable within 10 days of your receipt of the contract. The guest count guarantee and the balance of all estimated charges are due 4 days before the event. Each event is customized; reception luncheons start at $44/person, dinners at $54/person. Alcohol, tax and a 22% service charge are additional. For ceremonies, there is a $1,000 charge.

For business functions and meetings, rental fees vary depending on room(s) and services selected, guest count and time frame; call for more specific information.

AVAILABILITY: Year-round, daily. Meetings take place 8am–5pm; weddings are held noon–4pm or 6:30pm–12:30am.

SERVICES/AMENITIES:

Catering: in-house, no BYO

Kitchen Facilities: n/a

Tables & Chairs: provided

Linens, Silver, etc.: provided

Restrooms: wheelchair accessible

Dance Floor: provided

Bride's & Groom's Dressing Areas: yes

AV/Meeting Equipment: full range, in-house audiovisual company

Parking: self-parking or valet, extra charge

Accommodations: 451 guest rooms

Outdoor Night Lighting: yes

Outdoor Cooking Facilities: no

Cleanup: provided

View: city view from Starview Room; San Fernando Valley skyline, Hollywood Hills skyline

Kosher: glatt kosher kitchen

Other: event coordination

RESTRICTIONS:

Alcohol: in-house, no BYO

Smoking: outside only

Music: amplified OK indoors

Wheelchair Access: yes

Insurance: liability required

Woodland Hills Country Club

Golf Course

21150 Dumetz Road, Woodland Hills

818/347-1511

www.woodlandhillscc.org
rebecca@woodlandhillscc.org

- Rehearsal Dinners
- Ceremonies
- Wedding Receptions
- Private Parties
- Corporate Events
- Meetings
- Film Shoots
- Accommodations

In the early 1920s, Victor Girard saw the hills and open land of the west San Fernando Valley and decided to develop his dream city there. A showman to the core, he wanted something extra to lure homeowners so he imported 120,000 trees and built a golf course and clubhouse. Although his grand city vision was never realized, the trees and clubhouse remain: The former shade the streets of what is now Woodland Hills, and the latter has evolved into the Woodland Hills Country Club, a beautiful wedding site offering some of the best panoramic views in the valley.

Drive through the iron gates and up the long curved road and you'll immediately see Girard's legacy: towering, mature Eucalyptus trees giving way to tantalizing peeks of the golf course. At the top of the hill sits the clubhouse (rebuilt three times since the 1920s) with a prominent porte-cochère covered in climbing vines and surrounded by flowering shrubs. There are flowers and greenery everywhere, and since all plants throughout the property are replaced seasonally, there will always be fresh, colorful blooms to greet you.

Directly across from the clubhouse is the peaceful Ceremony Garden. Its expansive lawn overlooking the 18th green features a magnificent wrought-iron gazebo, as well as a raised concrete area that's perfect for a small musical ensemble or whatever you choose to personalize and enhance your event. A grove of oak, pepper and eucalyptus trees runs the length of the garden, providing shade from the afternoon sun. If you'd like, you can hold an al fresco cocktail reception for 300 people here, or move inside to one of several venues.

The Main Lobby and adjoining Trophy Hall, displaying 80 years of the club's history, can be staged with chairs and couches for a cocktail lounge effect. Afterwards, your guests will be welcomed to the Terrace Ballroom for your main reception. This spacious banquet area has a built-in dance floor and raised stage for your band, DJ or cake table display. Decorated in muted, neutral tones, the room boasts a marble-topped bar where friends and family can mingle for conversation, as well as a small back patio with red roses, overlooking the putting green and surrounding hills.

If you're planning a more intimate affair, the Sunset Room on the opposite side of the clubhouse is a little gem. A warmly inviting spot with a wall of natural stone and floor-to-ceiling windows, it's ideal for a rehearsal dinner. It can also be used as a cocktail and/or dance area for the larger, adjacent Oak Room, replete with oak-beamed ceilings and breathtaking views. Just outside is the wraparound Back Terrace, a very popular location for enjoying those fabulous vistas that extend all the way to Warner Center.

Myriad photo opportunities take advantage of the views and scenic backdrops from the terraces, or you can arrange to pose beside picturesque sites on the fairways, like a stone bridge, waterfall or pond floated with lily pads.

There are many options available in planning your celebration here, and the staff takes pride in helping each bride determine her ideal wedding—and stay within her budget. After all, this was a location built on dreams.

CEREMONY CAPACITY: The site holds 160 seated guests indoors and 300 seated outdoors.

EVENT/RECEPTION CAPACITY: The facility accommodates 250 seated or 325 standing guests indoors and 300 seated or 400 standing outdoors.

MEETING CAPACITY: Meeting spaces hold up to 325 seated guests.

FEES & DEPOSITS: A $2,000 deposit is required to reserve your date and the balance is due 7 days prior to the event. Wedding packages range $45–114/person, and may include the room rental, meals, liquor and linens (depending on which package is chosen). Tax and a service charge are additional.

AVAILABILITY: Year-round, daily.

SERVICES/AMENITIES:

Catering: in-house
Kitchen Facilities: n/a
Tables & Chairs: provided
Linens, Silver, etc.: provided
Restrooms: wheelchair accessible
Dance Floor: provided
Bride's Dressing Area: yes
AV/Meeting Equipment: some provided, more CBA

Parking: large lot
Accommodations: no guest rooms
Outdoor Night Lighting: CBA
Outdoor Cooking Facilities: BBQ CBA
Cleanup: provided
View: garden patio; panorama of mountains, valley, cityscape, hills and fairways; fountain, landscaped grounds
Other: coordination, grand piano, in-house florals

RESTRICTIONS:

Alcohol: in-house
Smoking: outdoors only
Music: amplified OK

Wheelchair Access: yes
Insurance: not required

Santa Catalina Island

Casino Ballroom
A Santa Catalina Island Company Wedding Venue

1 Casino Way, Avalon
877/778-9399 Sales
www.visitcatalinaisland.com
weddings@scico.com

- Rehearsal Dinners
- Ceremonies
- Wedding Receptions
- Private Parties
- Corporate Events
- Meetings
- Film Shoots
- Accommodations

"…Twenty-six miles across the sea, Santa Catalina is waitin' for me"

This once exclusive isle still beckons those in search of "fun in the sun" in a tranquil setting free of pollution, skyscrapers, and yes, cars (golf carts are the vehicle of choice here). Make your destination wedding an extended vacation by inviting your friends and family to celebrate amidst this island paradise, just over an hour from the mainland by express boat. The staff at the fabulous Santa Catalina Island Company will gladly help you arrange everything, including transportation, tours, golf, accommodations, dining and, of course, all the event details. They'll even help you select the wedding site that's right for you!

Catalina Island's most famous venue is the Casino Ballroom, a grand, Art Deco landmark built in 1929. The Casino Ballroom wasn't actually a gambling house, but rather a spectacular dance pavilion that attracted thousands of well-dressed socialites from the mainland. Today the aura of elegance still lingers around this historic treasure, and its glamorous legacy is carried on by 21st-century event hosts seeking the maximum amount of panache.

Located on a rocky harbor break at the edge of Avalon Cove, the Casino is a huge, 12-story circular building. The forum-like structure boasts a red-tile roof and an impressive triple-arched portico. Above the entryway a tiled mural portrays a fetching underwater sea sylph who welcomes light-hearted revelers inside. Downstairs, flamboyant murals in vibrant hues decorate the walls of the Casino's sumptuous movie theater, where visitors can still enjoy nightly cinematic diversions while relaxing in red-velvet seats.

However, you and your guests are headed up to the top floor to the Casino's crowning glory: an enormous ballroom that retains its original style—a lavish medley of rose-hued walls, black Art Deco reliefs, and an arching 50-foot ceiling. No less than five resplendent Tiffany chandeliers illumine the crowd, and curving windows capture postcard views of the aqua sea. The ballroom is so spacious that you can set up an altar and theater-style seating for a wedding ceremony in one area, then host a sit-down reception on raised seating areas that surround the dance floor. A vintage full-service bar in the back serves up refreshments, and an elevated stage is just the spot for the entertainment.

An outdoor veranda encircles the ballroom and overlooks the protected coves of Avalon Bay; from here the fabulous view of the mainland sometimes stretches all the way from Ventura to San Diego. In the twilight it's still possible to see seals, dolphins and brightly colored fish splashing about in the clear waters of the cove. At night the scenery takes on an air of dreamy mystery, with an endless starscape sparkling in the surf.

The Santa Catalina Island Company has two more outstanding and very different event venues: The Descanso Beach Club is great for a casual outdoor party or relaxed rehearsal dinner, while the Catalina Country Club exudes Old World charm and sophistication. For more details on all three locations, please visit the Santa Catalina Island Company website.

CEREMONY CAPACITY: The Ballroom accommodates up to 600 seated guests.

EVENT/RECEPTION & MEETING CAPACITY: The Ballroom holds up to 600 seated or 1,000 standing guests; the balcony up to 25 seated or 100 standing.

FEES & DEPOSITS: The venue rental fee is required to reserve your date, and the balance is due 1 month prior to the event. The rental fee ranges $5,000–10,000 depending on the space reserved and guest count. Meals range $50–90/person. Tax, alcohol and a 21% service charge are additional.

AVAILABILITY: Year-round, daily, anytime.

SERVICES/AMENITIES:

Catering: in-house, no BYO
Kitchen Facilities: n/a
Tables & Chairs: provided
Linens, Silver, etc.: some provided
Restrooms: wheelchair accessible
Dance Floor: provided
Bride's Dressing Area: CBA
AV/Meeting Equipment: some provided

Parking: on street, limited
Accommodations: 3 Santa Catalina Island Company hotels and other local options
Outdoor Night Lighting: access only
Outdoor Cooking Facilities: yes
Cleanup: provided
View: Pacific Ocean, bay, coast, hills

RESTRICTIONS:

Alcohol: in-house
Smoking: outside only
Music: amplified OK indoors with restrictions

Wheelchair Access: yes
Insurance: liability required

Descanso Beach Club
A Santa Catalina Island Company Wedding Venue

Beach Club

1 Descanso Canyon Road, Avalon
877/778-9399 Sales
www.visitcatalinaisland.com
weddings@scico.com

● Rehearsal Dinners	● Corporate Events
● Ceremonies	● Meetings
● Wedding Receptions	● Film Shoots
● Private Parties	Accommodations

If your wedding fantasy involves sipping mai tais on the beach under the California sun, then come to the Descanso Beach Club, a little slice of paradise on Catalina Island. This idyllic haven is less than an hour from the mainland by ferry or private boat; visitors disembark in Avalon, which is more laid-back beach town than tourist metropolis—there are no cars, no malls, and not one single billboard! A scenic 10-minute stroll along the shore takes you past the historic Catalina Casino and on to Descanso Beach, a peaceful curve of shoreline that the club calls home.

Beachfront weddings are popular on the club's Terraced Lawn, a series of three spacious grass plateaus sloping down towards the water's edge. Ceremonies are held on the lower terrace, where couples say their vows against a backdrop of the azure ocean.

Outdoor receptions take place on the upper terraces of the lawn, which offer the same wonderful view of the beach and the sea, complete with yachts bobbing on the water and the landmark Catalina Casino just up the coastline. Here, you can enhance the natural elements with your own creative touches, like dressing tables with upscale linens and luminarias for a sophisticated soirée.

Descanso's newest venue, Catherine's Terrace, is actually the entire second floor of the club. Its elevated vantage makes the most of the sublime setting, affording spectacular panoramic bay vistas. The Ballroom, which can be divided into two, is light and airy, with a creamy-white interior. A wall of floor-to-ceiling retractable folding doors slide open completely to reveal a timeless tableau of palm trees backed by sparkling blue water extending to the horizon. Sea breezes waft inside, and guests can step out onto the long terrace, an ideal spot for al fresco cocktails or simply savoring the view. The cozy adjoining Living Room features a fireplace, and is often used for food stations, a bar setup, dancing, or overflow seating.

Though weddings are traditionally evening events, luncheon receptions take best advantage of the club's views and refreshing atmosphere. You're surrounded by lush greenery, and with the boundless Pacific stretching out in front of you the urban hustle and bustle feels a million miles away.

However you envision your event, the club's event pros are eager to help; they've got the scoop on local vendors, as well as lodging and transportation. They've also got you covered when it comes to cuisine, offering a variety of banquet menus created by their world-class, in-house chefs. And if you don't see what you want, just ask!

One more benefit of a destination wedding on Catalina: You and your family and friends are in such close proximity for the weekend that you end up spending quality time with each other ... and since everyone is in a vacation state of mind, the mood is relaxed and lighthearted. By celebrating at the Descanso Beach Club, you're inviting your guests to share a true Catalina experience.

CEREMONY CAPACITY: The Terraced Lawn area holds 200 seated guests.

EVENT/RECEPTION CAPACITY: The Terraced Lawn area accommodates 200 seated or 1000 standing. Catherine's Terrace Ballroom holds up to 120–150 seated or 200 standing.

MEETING CAPACITY: The Lawn seats up to 200 outdoors and Catherine's Terrace Ballroom seats 120–150 indoors.

FEES & DEPOSITS: The venue rental fee is required to reserve your date, and the balance is due 1 month prior to the event. The rental fee ranges $3,000–$15,000 and varies depending on the season and the space reserved. Meals range $50–80/person. Tax, alcohol and a 21% service charge are additional.

AVAILABILITY: Year-round, daily, anytime.

SERVICES/AMENITIES:

Catering: in-house, no BYO
Kitchen Facilities: n/a
Tables & Chairs: some provided
Linens, Silver, etc.: provided
Restrooms: wheelchair accessible
Dance Floor: n/a
Bride's Dressing Area: CBA
AV/Meeting Equipment: CBA

Parking: large lot
Accommodations: 2 Santa Catalina Island Company hotels and other local options
Outdoor Night Lighting: CBA
Outdoor Cooking Facilities: BBQ
Cleanup: provided
View: panoramic view of ocean and coastline

RESTRICTIONS:

Alcohol: in-house
Smoking: outdoors only
Music: amplified OK outdoors with restrictions

Wheelchair Access: yes
Insurance: liability required

The wedding vendors on our website are the best in the business. How do we know? Read page 577.

Los Angeles Area

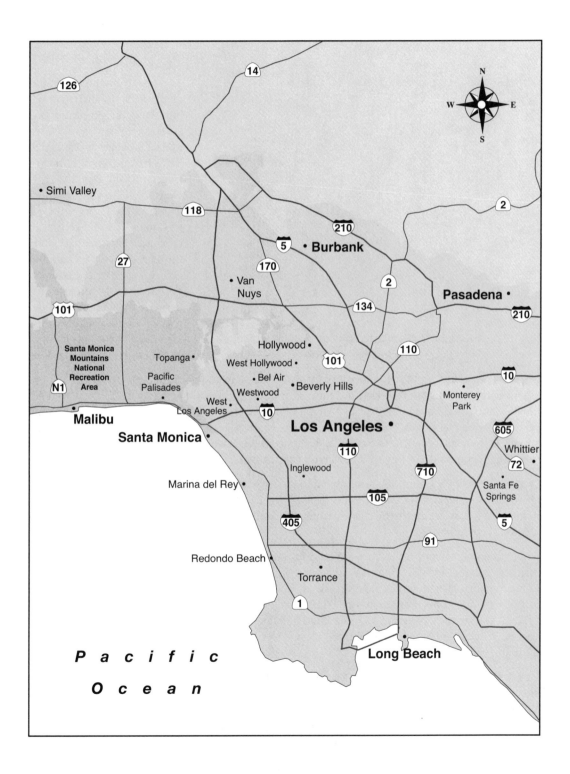

Lawry's The Prime Rib

Restaurant

100 N. La Cienega Boulevard, Beverly Hills
310/360-6281 x4
www.lawrysonline.com/lawrys-primerib/beverly-hills
efremaux@lawrysonline.com

- Rehearsal Dinners
- Ceremonies
- Wedding Receptions
- Private Parties
- Corporate Events
- Meetings
- Film Shoots
- Accommodations

Not far from the glitz and glamour of Hollywood you'll find the other red carpet: one steeped in seven decades of Los Angeles history, rich British/American culinary tradition and Beverly Hills elegance. Lawry's The Prime Rib combines the comforts of home—if you lived in an expansive English estate along the Thames—with a sumptuous dining experience executed flawlessly by professional servers who treat you like royalty. And if you're worried that this venue's famed Restaurant Row location or opulent English Edwardian décor puts it out of your league, don't be—Lawry's The Prime Rib provides classic sophistication with Old World prices.

Step inside the foyer and the contemporary world fades away into a timeless, softly lit realm of amenable luxury. Tasteful period furniture in the cocktail room and adjacent bar area complements wainscoted, jewel-toned walls. Antique chandeliers and sconces illuminate eye-catching polished silver pieces and gold-framed paintings of English nobles, dignitaries and countryside scenes. Despite its formal accoutrements, the atmosphere is warm and relaxed—perfect for guests mingling over hors d'oeuvres while awaiting your arrival.

Double doors open to reveal a step-down into the brilliant, emerald-colored Oak Room, a popular choice for smaller celebrations. Here, a bust of the Duke of Wellington and a bas-relief of William Shakespeare adorn the fireplace mantel, while the mixed-shade parquet flooring highlights a colorful coat of arms.

Larger ceremonies and receptions are held in the spacious main dining room, where a pair of majestic wooden lions evocative of regal courtyards presides over your grand entrance. An uplit, domed ceiling casts a subtle glow on the dark wooden columns and beveled glass, lending a festive nighttime ambiance at any hour. The sweetheart table is housed in the "garden," a central space that features a sweeping hand-painted mural overhead. The adjacent Vintage Room, a private wine cellar, can be used as a bride's room or for rehearsal dinners and post-reception family traditions, including tea ceremonies.

Lawry's The Prime Rib's reputation for great food has stood the test of time. One of the oldest single-family-owned restaurants in Los Angeles, it has served its signature British-style dinner of slow-roasted Midwestern prime beef, mashed potatoes and Yorkshire pudding alongside flavorful gravy, horseradish, and its original seasoning salt since 1938. The almost-theatrical tableside service includes spinning salad prepared on a bed of ice and a carving of the roast from a 500-pound silver cart inspired by London's famous Simpsons-in-the-Strand restaurant. The meal finishes with a selection of traditional British and American desserts, including an ice cream sundae made with C.C. Brown's hot fudge sauce, a secret recipe bought by the Lawry family from Hollywood's most legendary but now-defunct ice cream parlor.

From their family to yours, Lawry's The Prime Rib serves up the most authentic Anglo-British (and award-winning) culinary experience this side of the pond, lending its cherished traditions to your celebration.

CEREMONY CAPACITY: The restaurant can accommodate 250 seated guests indoors.

EVENT/RECEPTION & MEETING CAPACITY: The restaurant holds 450 seated or standing guests indoors.

FEES & DEPOSITS: 20% of the total event cost is required to reserve your date and the balance is due the day of the event. There is a ceremony fee of $350. Meals range $47–62/person. Tax, alcohol and a 20% service charge are additional.

AVAILABILITY: Year-round, daily, 4pm–11pm, except Christmas. Luncheon hours are Monday–Friday 7am–4pm, Saturday 7am–3:30pm and Sunday 7am–3pm. Off-Site Catering: anytime except December 25th.

SERVICES/AMENITIES:
Catering: in-house
Kitchen Facilities: n/a
Tables & Chairs: provided
Linens, Silver, etc.: provided
Restrooms: wheelchair accessible
Dance Floor: provided
Bride's Dressing Area: yes
AV/Meeting Equipment: provided

Parking: large lot, valet required
Accommodations: no guest rooms
Outdoor Night Lighting: CBA
Outdoor Cooking Facilities: no
Cleanup: provided
View: no
Other: clergy on staff, event coordination

RESTRICTIONS:
Alcohol: in-house
Smoking: not allowed
Music: amplified OK indoors

Wheelchair Access: yes
Insurance: not required

Chester Washington Golf Course

Golf Club

1930 West 120th Street, Los Angeles
888/227-5795

www.countryclubreceptions.com
privateeventmanager@chesterwashington.com

- Rehearsal Dinners
- Ceremonies
- Wedding Receptions
- Private Parties
- Corporate Events
- Meetings
- Film Shoots
- Accommodations

Chester Washington Golf Course offers amenities you won't find at most big L.A. hotels: a beautiful outdoor ceremony site, a banquet room with verdant views and plenty of natural light, great rates and ample free parking.

Ceremonies take place in the gazebo, against a backdrop of rolling green hills and mature trees. Afterwards, cocktails and hors d'oeuvres are served on the clubhouse patio, just off the bar/ lounge. The congenial lounge is a far cry from the stuffy, dark bars you find at some golf clubs. There's an oak bar and tall, floor-to-ceiling windows inset with doors that open to the patio, permitting your event to flow seamlessly indoors and out.

You also have exclusive use of the foyer when you celebrate here. This space connects to both the bar and the banquet room, so in addition to being a handy location for place card and gift tables it can host your cocktail reception if the weather doesn't cooperate.

The banquet room's recent remodel accentuates its natural assets: a high ceiling and tall windows on three sides, all of which create a light and airy ambiance. On one side, floor-to-ceiling windows and sliding glass doors form a long curved wall overlooking manicured lawns, lofty eucalyptus trees, and pines. Cream-colored walls, amber wood wainscoting, chandeliers with diminutive silk shades, and a built-in parquet dance floor make the space even more inviting. Since nothing about the décor is heavy handed, you can dress it up any way you want. With its clean, crisp look, this room is handsome enough that you don't need to be a set designer to make it look good.

In addition to its appealing event spaces, the venue has a rich history. Back in 1928 when it was built, this part of L.A. was just fields of corn and beans. Later this facility would become one of the most important courses available to African-American golfers in the United States. Not only did a number of the great African-American golf players of the era make this course their home base, other famous African-Americans could be found swinging their clubs here too, like heavyweight champion Joe Louis and baseball great Jackie Robinson.

In 1982, the course was renamed to honor one of its habitués: award-winning African-American journalist Chester Washington. Today the players at Chester Washington Golf Course are as ethnically diverse as the surrounding neighborhoods. Golf lovers and history buffs may have a special connection to this place, but you don't have to be either to appreciate this lovely spot, which scores high in our book.

CEREMONY CAPACITY: The ceremony site holds up to 300 seated guests, indoors or outdoors.

EVENT/RECEPTION & MEETING CAPACITY: Indoor spaces accommodate up to 300 seated or 350 standing guests.

FEES & DEPOSITS: A nonrefundable deposit, which is applied to your food & beverage total, is required to reserve your date. The amount of the deposit varies depending on how far in advance you book. Payment terms for the balance also vary, and may be arranged on an individual basis. Meals start at $25/person. Tax, alcohol and service charge are additional. Menus and packages can be customized to fit your needs and budget. Call for details.

AVAILABILITY: Year-round, daily, 8am–1am.

SERVICES/AMENITIES:

Catering: in-house, no BYO

Kitchen Facilities: n/a

Tables & Chairs: provided

Linens, Silver, etc.: provided

Restrooms: wheelchair accessible

Dance Floor: yes

Bride's Dressing Area: CBA

AV/Meeting Equipment: CBA, extra charge

Parking: large lot

Accommodations: no guest rooms

Outdoor Night Lighting: CBA

Outdoor Cooking Facilities: no

Cleanup: provided

View: fairways, garden, landscaped grounds

RESTRICTIONS:

Alcohol: in-house

Smoking: outside only

Music: amplified OK

Wheelchair Access: yes

Insurance: not required

City Club Los Angeles

Private Club

555 Flower Street, 51st Floor, Los Angeles
213/620-9662
www.cityclubla.com
ernest.nicodemus@clubcorp.com

● Rehearsal Dinners	● Corporate Events
● Ceremonies	● Meetings
● Wedding Receptions	Film Shoots
● Private Parties	Accommodations

One look is worth a thousand words, so if you're planning a wedding or special event in Los Angeles you definitely want to check out this stylish, new 51st-floor venue that delivers jaw-dropping views of city and coastline.

After 25 years on Bunker Hill and a multimillion-dollar reinvention, the City Club Los Angeles has relocated to the Gold LEED Certified City National Plaza Tower situated in the heart of L.A.'s thriving central business district. Your guests will love exploring this area, which is home to the fabulous Staples Center and the L.A. Live entertainment complex with its glamorous theaters, restaurants and hotels.

Step into the City Club itself and you enter a world of privacy and exclusivity—one where all of the spaces reflect a unique interpretation of Los Angeles' diverse districts. Elevators whisk guests up to the dramatic lobby, whose chic furnishings, art, and 3-D jewel-toned wall convey the spirit of the Jewelry District.

The spectacular Angeles Ballroom is truly a room with a view: 280 degrees of top-of-the-world vistas through its floor-to-ceiling windows. Chandeliers that look like delicate clusters of stars drop from the beautiful white, coffered ceiling. The room's brilliant mélange of posh and trend-setting touches, no doubt inspired by the nearby Fashion District, includes luxurious champagne and icy blue colorations, as well as striking wall and carpet designs whose intersecting lines and angles suggest the freeway system that crisscrosses L.A.

If you use the entire ballroom, its vast dimensions make it ideal for ultra-grand functions with multiple bars, stages, dining areas and dance floors, but it also breaks into three more intimate chambers, each overlooking the tower's picturesque surround. The Santa Monica Room, Harbor Room and Hollywood Ballroom can be used individually or in combination to create varying environments for your function. You might start by exchanging vows in the Harbor Room with its Pacific or sunset views, and then progress to the Hollywood Ballroom and Santa Monica Room for cocktails and/or dining enhanced by the gorgeous nighttime cityscape glittering all around you. State-of-the-art lighting and audiovisual systems let you fine-tune each room's ambiance at the touch of a button (think colored LED and GOBO lights).

If you're planning a weekend extravaganza, there are additional entertainment areas you can add to the mix. The club's vibrant Anytime Lounge, outfitted with "spotlight" chandeliers, a bar top that resembles a grand piano, and a lush red wall framing a giant TV screen, brings to mind the Theater District. In the Private Dining Room, which looks out on the Hollywood sign, walls "blooming" with faux orchids evoke the Flower District. Even the hallway leading to the lounge showcases art from the private collections of L.A. residents—a nod to the city's Art Walk.

And don't forget, City Club Los Angeles has 25 years of experience in superior service and fine dining. You can sample your proposed menu's mouthwatering selections at a private tasting.

What more can you ask for? Oh, yes, a great time before, during, and after your party! Whether you and your guests are locals or out-of-towners, we guarantee you'll find plenty of terrific places to stay and loads of fun things to do in this club's one-of-a-kind setting.

CEREMONY CAPACITY: The Angeles Room holds 380 seated guests. The Harbor Room accommodates up to 250 for a ceremony. The Hollywood Ballroom accommodates up to 400 for a ceremony.

EVENT/RECEPTION CAPACITY: The Santa Monica, Hollywood and Harbor Rooms combined hold up to 360 guests seated with a dance floor or 600 for a cocktail reception. They can also be broken out to accommodate a smaller more intimate wedding.

MEETING CAPACITY: 11 rooms can accommodate 5–600, including a screening room that seats 15.

FEES & DEPOSITS: For weddings and special events, a $2,000 nonrefundable and nontransferable deposit is required to secure your date; 50% is due 60 days prior to the event and the balance is payable 10 working days prior. Menus can be customized. Wedding receptions start at $100/person; alcohol/beverages, tax and service charges are additional. For all events, there is a food & beverage minimum, not including tax and service charge.

AVAILABILITY: Year-round, daily including holidays, 7am–2am.

SERVICES/AMENITIES:

Catering: in-house, no BYO
Kitchen Facilities: n/a
Tables & Chairs: provided
Linens, Silver, etc.: provided
Restrooms: wheelchair accessible
Dance Floor: available
Bride's & Groom's Dressing Areas: yes
AV/Meeting Equipment: full range
Other: full event coordination, private screening room

Parking: in-house garage, valet on weekdays, self-park on weekends
Accommodations: no guest rooms, hotels nearby
Outdoor Night Lighting: n/a
Outdoor Cooking Facilities: n/a
Cleanup: provided
View: panorama of Los Angeles

RESTRICTIONS:

Alcohol: in-house
Smoking: not allowed
Music: amplified OK

Wheelchair Access: yes
Insurance: required for vendors only

The Ebell of Los Angeles

4400 Wilshire Boulevard, Los Angeles

323/931-1277

www.ebelloflosangeles.com
inquiry@ebelloflosangeles.com

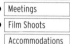

Rehearsal Dinners	● Corporate Events
● Ceremonies	● Meetings
● Wedding Receptions	● Film Shoots
● Private Parties	Accommodations

A visual delight, The Ebell of Los Angeles was built in the late 1920s to house the nation's most prestigious women's club. Arched doorways, including an intricately crafted wrought-iron main entrance, lead into sunny galleries and lofty salons, all of which have their own intriguing details.

The large, pleasant Main Dining Room features a series of carved columns with arches supporting its high ceiling, and a bank of tall French doors opens onto the adjacent courtyard, flooding the room with light.

Enclosed by picturesque arcades, flowering shrubs and trees, it's no surprise that this serene courtyard garden is the preferred spot for ceremonies. Exchange vows in front of a fountain topped with an appealing bronze statue or under the tall arched doorway of the Art Salon. This unique gallery, with its draped archways, is hung with original paintings by local artists. It serves as a foyer for the larger Lounge, a magnificent space with a striking carved Italian ceiling, wrought-iron chandeliers, dramatic floor-to-ceiling windows, a grand piano, plus a mezzanine and grand staircase from which to look down on it all!

Both elegance and functionality were important to the leading society women who designed this extraordinary social center, and The Ebell bears the marks of their good judgment and distinguished taste in every detail.

CEREMONY CAPACITY: The Garden holds approximately 150 seated guests, and up to 400 standing. Indoors, the Lounge can seat 260 in rows, and for a wedding-in-the-round can accommodate 150.

EVENT/RECEPTION & MEETING CAPACITY: Indoor spaces hold 100–250 seated with dance floor; the garden accommodates up to 150 seated or 400 standing guests.

FEES & DEPOSITS: A refundable $2,000 security deposit is required to book the event date. Estimated balance will be divided into three separate payments. Final payment is due 10 business days prior to the event. Average price for all-inclusive Ebell services ranges $185–250/person. This estimated price includes menus, bar and beverages, personnel, setup fee, room rental fee, tasting, security, lighting, linens, place settings, in-house tables and banquet chairs. Sales tax and a 21% service charge are additional.

AVAILABILITY: Year-round, anytime until midnight.

SERVICES/AMENITIES:

Catering: in-house
Kitchen Facilities: fully equipped
Tables & Chairs: provided
Linens, Silver, etc.: provided
Restrooms: wheelchair accessible
Dance Floor: hardwood floors
Bride's Dressing Area: yes
AV/Meeting Equipment: some provided

Parking: ample
Accommodations: no guest rooms
Outdoor Night Lighting: limited
Outdoor Cooking Facilities: no
Cleanup: provided
View: no

RESTRICTIONS:

Alcohol: in-house, or wine corkage $15/bottle, $20/magnum
Smoking: outside only
Music: amplified OK; time restrictions on patio

Wheelchair Access: yes
Insurance: certificate required
Other: no rice, birdseed, glitter or confetti

Want to know WHAT TO ASK a potential location or vendor? Check out our Questions to Ask starting on page 21.

Hilton Los Angeles Airport

Hotel

5711 West Century Boulevard, Los Angeles
310/410-6128
www.losangelesairport.hilton.com
gloria.guillen@hilton.com

● Rehearsal Dinners	● Corporate Events
● Ceremonies	● Meetings
● Wedding Receptions	● Film Shoots
● Private Parties	● Accommodations

Standing at the gateway to California's largest and arguably most diverse city, the Hilton Los Angeles Airport combines a soothing sophistication with artistic flourishes. Located just a quarter mile outside of LAX and within an easy drive to downtown, the beaches or Beverly Hills, it's the perfect destination for gathering your far-flung friends and relatives for an upscale wedding celebration.

This world-class hotel, while managed by the Hilton organization, is privately owned and much of the décor has been hand-picked by the owners. That attention to detail is evident as soon as you enter the lobby, which balances its three-story-high proportions with lots of human-scaled conversation areas. Gleaming marble floors and granite consoles are softened with richly patterned rugs and velvet armchairs, all layered in a neutral palette of cream, gold and honey. At the far end of the lobby an impressive center staircase, all glass and gold railings, makes a stellar backdrop for wedding photos.

Just beyond the staircase are two of the hotel's premier banquet rooms, which are often used together for a seamless affair. If you have your ceremony on site, the palatial-sized International Ballroom is an excellent choice—it has ample room for a traditional or ethnic ceremony, even when divided in two. Done in warm shades of wine and gray with silver accents, it's a modern and quite elegant space. The high, coffered ceiling enhances the dramatic impact of the enormous, rectangular, icicle-crystal chandeliers.

After you've said "I do," invite everyone across the foyer to the similarly themed (same colors) but smaller Pacific Ballroom, a somewhat more intimate setting for mingling over cocktails. Then it's back to the International Ballroom for a sumptuous dinner and dancing, taking advantage of the venue's full 11,000 square feet of splendor. (Although the hotel has an extensive catering menu, you're free to bring in ethnic or specialty foods from an outside caterer.)

For something quite different, head up to the La Jolla Room and Foyer on the mezzanine level. Along the way, take a moment to enjoy the aerial views of the lobby below, then check out the display of dazzling accoutrements that you pass en route to the event spaces: a framed golden brocade, Asian tapestries and gorgeous geodes of amethyst and crystal—all arranged using the principles of Feng Shui. Cocktails and hors d'oeuvres are served in the warmly inviting La Jolla Foyer, followed by dinner in the La Jolla Room, which is adorned with unusual chandeliers that look like flower petals descending from the ceiling, and mirrored French doors along the back wall.

There are several other options for weddings of 50 or fewer, and the staff will happily work with you to design an event that suits your style and budget. Your out-of-town guests can relax at the hotel (there's a pool, sports bar, fitness center and restaurants) or they can visit many of the local attractions. And when their stay at the Hilton is over, it's just a quick trip back to the airport.

CEREMONY CAPACITY: The site seats 450 guests, indoors or outdoors.

EVENT/RECEPTION CAPACITY: The facility can accommodate 800 seated or standing guests indoors, and up to 600 standing outdoors.

MEETING CAPACITY: Meeting spaces hold up to 1,000 seated guests.

FEES & DEPOSITS: 25% of the total event cost is required to reserve your date and the balance is due 72 hours prior to the event. The venue rental ranges $800–5,000 depending on the space reserved. Meals range $40–100/person. Tax and alcohol are additional.

AVAILABILITY: Year-round, daily.

SERVICES/AMENITIES:
Catering: in-house, or BYO
Kitchen Facilities: limited
Tables & Chairs: provided
Linens, Silver, etc.: provided
Restrooms: wheelchair accessible
Dance Floor: portable provided
Bride's Dressing Area: CBA
AV/Meeting Equipment: available

Parking: large lot, self park or valet available
Accommodations: 1,234 guest rooms
Outdoor Night Lighting: yes
Outdoor Cooking Facilities: no
Cleanup: provided
View: no

RESTRICTIONS:
Alcohol: in-house, or BYO with glass rental
Smoking: outdoors only
Music: amplified OK indoors

Wheelchair Access: yes
Insurance: liability required

The Legendary Park Plaza

607 South Park View Street, Los Angeles

213/381-6300 x103

www.parkplazala.com
tawni@parkplazala.com

● Rehearsal Dinners	● Corporate Events
● Ceremonies	● Meetings
● Wedding Receptions	● Film Shoots
● Private Parties	Accommodations

An architectural tour de force, the opulent Park Plaza embodies the rich and decadent boom-town times of Los Angeles before the 1929 stock market crash. Built in 1925 (it was originally an Elks Lodge), the Hotel languished into a lamentable state of disrepair during the 80s and 90s. Fortunately, it's been rescued from ruin by the same folks who refurbished the Oviatt. Finishing touches on the extensive facelift were completed in October of '99.

Don't expect to hold a shy and demure event here. The sheer scale and splendor of the building calls for affairs on the grander end of the spectrum. Big weddings, band premieres and corporate Christmas parties are equal to the Park Plaza's sensibility.

Hold onto your hat when exploring this location, because much of your time will be spent with head tipped back, ogling its many wonders. Occupying almost an entire city block, the building's façade is embellished by a series of arches, pilasters, cornices and majestic friezes featuring intriguing statuary of Roman women. This neoclassical motif is carried over to the inside as well. Enchanting you from the moment you step across the transom is the Park Plaza Lobby, a cathedral-like space with a Romanesque vaulted ceiling at least three stories high. Sunlight streams through the immense Palladian glass doorway and fanlight, burnishing the Tennessee-rose granite floor.

The Park Plaza offers a plethora of exhilarating event sites. On the ground floor is the Gold Ballroom, the Park's most intimate space. Just right for cocktails or small seated dinners, this space boasts dark wood wainscoting, tasseled antique chandeliers and Corinthian pilasters whose tops are crowned in gleaming gold leaf. Equally gorgeous is the Bronze Ballroom, featuring burgundy wall-to-wall carpeting, a mammoth Art Deco bar, hand-stenciled ceiling beams and fantastic columns gilded in copper leaf. On the room's south side, glass doors open out onto the Tuscan Garden. This private open-air courtyard, filled with greenery and flower planters, is a beautiful setting for exchanging vows.

Take the magnificent stairway up from the Lobby, turn left and you'll encounter our favorite event site—the Grand Ballroom. It is, in a word, spectacular. On either side of the room twin colonnades create a linear dynamism, drawing the eye along the length of the room. The meticulously restored beamed ceilings showcase hand-painted floral designs, patterned after a palace ceiling in Florence. Chandeliers suspended from the beams spotlight these amazing works of art. Not to be outdone is the Terrace Room, the hotel's most capacious ballroom. Art Deco in motif, and featuring elaborate wall sconces and a ceiling of dizzying height, this vast multilevel space can accommodate almost any kind of pageantry you can dream up.

One of Los Angeles' best kept secrets, the Park Plaza has become the place for film shoots, record launchings, wrap parties and Hollywood bashes. In fact, at a birthday party for a "recently arrived" star, the hotel was packed with glitterati. And even these jaded, been-everywhere-done-everything luminaries could be overheard exclaiming, "I never knew this place existed; it's SO beautiful!"

The secret is out....

CEREMONY CAPACITY: The Gold Ballroom seats 90, the Bronze Ballroom 250, the Grand Ballroom 250, the Terrace Ballroom 550, and the Tuscan Garden 400.

EVENT/RECEPTION CAPACITY: Indoor spaces accommodate 80–490 seated or 145–750 standing. Outdoors, the garden holds 275 seated or 450 standing.

MEETING CAPACITY: Several spaces hold 80–750 seated guests.

FEES & DEPOSITS: A signed contract plus a nonfundable deposit equal to 20% of the estimated event total are required to secure your date. 60% of the event total is due 90 days prior to the event, and the balance is due 30 days prior. A 20% refundable security deposit is due 14 days prior. Catering packages are available, and range $115–210/person including staff and rentals.

AVAILABILITY: Year-round, daily, until 2am.

SERVICES/AMENITIES:

Catering: in-house or BYO
Kitchen Facilities: fully equipped, kosher kitchen CBA
Tables & Chairs: provided, or BYO
Linens, Silver, etc.: provided, or BYO
Restrooms: wheelchair accessible
Dance Floor: provided
Bride's & Groom's Dressing Areas: yes
AV/Meeting Equipment: CBA, extra fee

Parking: valet parking or nearby public lots
Accommodations: no guest rooms
Outdoor Night Lighting: yes
Outdoor Cooking Facilities: yes
Cleanup: provided, extra fee
View: downtown cityscape and park
Kosher: kosher catering provided, or BYO
Other: event coordination

RESTRICTIONS:

Alcohol: in-house, no BYO
Smoking: outdoors only
Music: amplified OK indoors; outdoors OK with volume limits

Wheelchair Access: yes
Insurance: liability required for social functions
Other: some decorations require approval

Luxe Sunset Boulevard Hotel

Hotel

11461 Sunset Boulevard, Los Angeles
310/691-7510 Special Events

www.luxesunset.com
specialevents@luxehotels.com

- Rehearsal Dinners
- Ceremonies
- Wedding Receptions
- Private Parties
- Corporate Events
- Meetings
- Film Shoots
- Accommodations

It's not always easy to find tranquility in Los Angeles, but the Luxe Sunset Boulevard Hotel will make you feel like you've gotten away from it all. Occupying seven hilltop acres, this boutique property is a secluded oasis that happens to be a stone's throw from the Getty Center and a short drive to other favorite L.A. sites like Santa Monica Beach, UCLA, and the Skirball Cultural Center.

When you have your wedding here, your event is the only one taking place at that time so it receives top priority. The hotel also has some of the most appealing event spaces in West Los Angeles, most notably the elegant Luxe Sunset Ballroom. Designed like a home away from home, it's sophisticated, yet inviting. The neutral color scheme—shades of taupe, cream and bronze—compliments almost any decoration, and the room is dramatically lit with modern chandeliers, recessed lighting and wall sconces. If you have a particular ambiance in mind, state-of-the-art audiovisual equipment is available to help you create just the right mood.

For a *plein air* ceremony or cocktails under the stars, the adjacent patio is a true urban garden. Olive trees shade conversational seating areas, while fountains lend a pleasing background sound. A unique feature of the garden is the Luxe Sunset Terrace. As you walk down the central aisle of this intimate courtyard, lacy elm trees provide a natural canopy and frame views of the "fountain wall" backdrop. An upper patio makes a lovely spot for mingling and casual drinks.

Your out-of-town guests will find the hotel an extremely comfortable, enjoyable place to stay. All of its superior and deluxe rooms, as well as most of their suites, have windows or doors that open to the outside, and they're decorated in warm, natural shades, with custom-made furniture. Additional amenities include free WiFi and high-speed internet, designer bedding, and a Keurig Single Cup Brewer with complimentary coffee and tea. In-room dining is available 24 hours a day, and Luxe also offers daily turndown service and plush cotton robes.

Far from the madding crowd, the Luxe Hotel is a stylish L.A. getaway. Have your celebration here, or come for a weekend "vacation." Stroll through the gardens, go for a swim, and luxuriate in the full-service spa. After you unpack your bags, the soothing setting and accommodating staff will quickly help you relax and unwind.

CEREMONY & EVENT/RECEPTION CAPACITY: The Luxe Sunset Ballroom holds 300 seated guests and the Luxe Terrace holds 250 seated guests.

MEETING CAPACITY: Three rooms accommodate 12–300 seated guests.

FEES & DEPOSITS: A nonrefundable $5,000 deposit is required when the space is booked. Half the anticipated total is due 90 days prior to the event; the final payment is due 72 hours prior. There are 3 wedding packages ranging $110–175/person for lunch and $125–200/person for dinner. Tax and a 20% gratuity are additional.

AVAILABILITY: Year-round, daily, 6am–midnight.

SERVICES/AMENITIES:

Catering: in-house, no BYO
Kitchen Facilities: n/a
Tables & Chairs: provided
Linens, Silver, etc.: provided
Restrooms: wheelchair accessible
Dance Floor: CBA, $600 fee
Bride's & Groom's Dressing Areas: yes
AV/Meeting Equipment: full range, extra fee
Other: off-site catering also provided

Parking: valet only, $10/car
Accommodations: 162 guest rooms
Outdoor Night Lighting: yes
Outdoor Cooking Facilities: n/a
Cleanup: provided
View: garden
Kosher: kosher catering provided; has kosher kitchen

RESTRICTIONS:

Alcohol: in-house, or wine corkage $25/bottle
Smoking: outside only
Music: amplified OK indoors, until 10pm outdoors

Wheelchair Access: yes
Insurance: liability required
Other: no rice or birdseed

Matteo's Restaurant

Restaurant

2321 Westwood Boulevard, Los Angeles

310/475-4521

www.matteosla.com
www.facebook.com/matteosla
events@matteosla.com

● Rehearsal Dinners	● Corporate Events
● Ceremonies	● Meetings
● Wedding Receptions	● Film Shoots
● Private Parties	Accommodations

Since it first came onto the scene in 1963, Matteo's in West L.A. has been the epitome of cool. Maybe it was because Frank Sinatra (an old pal of Matty "Matteo" Jordan's from back home in Hoboken) often came to dinner along with his rat pack crowd. Maybe it was the great Italian food, served in an upscale supper club atmosphere. Or maybe it was just because no matter who you were, you were greeted like a friend as you enjoyed your dinner next to a Who's Who of Hollywood movers and shakers. What's amazing is that more than 50 years and a whole new generation later, the restaurant, recently renovated, still has that winning combination of homey and hip.

Their unique wedding spot, dubbed The Townhouse, gives you that same feeling in a city sophisticated way. Head up the private stairs and it's as if you've arrived at a chic New York brownstone. The first thing that greets your guests is a smart little lounge, complete with its own bar, where they can check in. The entire upstairs is yours to enjoy, so you can create whatever flow works best for you. Perhaps you'd like to start by inviting everyone out to the rooftop terrace for an open-air ceremony or cocktail reception. The tile floor and textured plaster walls embellished with green latticework panels give this cosmopolitan space a country charm. Huge planters with flowering shrubs and a weathered lion's head fountain set into a niche in the wall add to the sense of an in-town getaway.

When you're ready for dinner, the French doors will be opened to reveal the Townhouse Dining Room, decorated like a spacious penthouse drawing room. This lovely venue takes full advantage of both natural and reflected light: A pale blue, barrel ceiling features a skylight as well as drop chandeliers, and the mirror over a beautifully crafted antique hutch shimmers behind an array of flickering candles.

The Townhouse menu includes all the great Italian fare from the restaurant downstairs, and the chef is also quite open to whipping up innovative ethnic or cultural dishes on request. After dinner, continue your festivities with dancing al fresco under the stars as well as hundreds of twinkling lights strung overhead.

In addition to all its other assets, one of The Townhouse's greatest perks is that the resident event manager will work with you from your initial consultation to the end of your event, making sure the space fits your needs and your vision.

CEREMONY CAPACITY: The banquet room holds 78 seated guests indoors and 28 seated outdoors.

EVENT/RECEPTION CAPACITY: Upstairs, the banquet room holds 78 seated or 100 standing indoors and the adjoining patio seats 28 outdoors. Downstairs, the restaurant can accommodate 145 seated or standing guests with a buyout.

MEETING CAPACITY: Meeting spaces hold up to 78 seated guests.

FEES & DEPOSITS: A $500–1,000 deposit is required to reserve your date and the balance is due on the date of the event. Rental fees are waived if the food & beverage minimums are met. Meals range $35–65/person. Tax, alcohol and a 20% service charge are additional.

AVAILABILITY: Year-round, daily, 6am–2am.

SERVICES/AMENITIES:

Catering: in-house
Kitchen Facilities: n/a
Tables & Chairs: provided
Linens, Silver, etc.: provided
Restrooms: wheelchair accessible
Dance Floor: provided
Bride's & Groom's Dressing Areas: yes
AV/Meeting Equipment: provided

Parking: on street, valet required, garage nearby
Accommodations: no guest rooms, hotel nearby
Outdoor Night Lighting: yes
Outdoor Cooking Facilities: BBQ CBA
Cleanup: provided
View: sky view from patio
Other: coordination, grand piano, in-house wedding cake and florals

RESTRICTIONS:

Alcohol: in-house
Smoking: outdoors only
Music: amplified OK indoors

Wheelchair Access: limited
Insurance: not required

Want to find more venues and services? Check out our informative website, www.HereComesTheGuide.com.

175

MountainGate Country Club

Country Club

12445 Mountaingate Drive, Los Angeles
888/995-7937

www.countryclubreceptions.com
privateeventdirector@mtngatecc.com

● Rehearsal Dinners	● Corporate Events
● Ceremonies	● Meetings
● Wedding Receptions	● Film Shoots
● Private Parties	Accommodations

Situated at the gateway to the Santa Monica Mountains, at the top of a scenic road that heightens expectations as you ascend, MountainGate does not disappoint. The country club—the jewel of a private residential development—is a breath of fresh air for L.A. brides and grooms seeking panoramic views and a location that's convenient to both Beverly Hills and the Valley.

Fronted by a cobblestone entryway and a white porte-cochere, the clubhouse is embraced by a grove of tall conifers and native trees. The building evokes Frank Lloyd Wright's aesthetic, with its geometric configuration and interior use of natural wood and glass. In contrast to the angular architectural lines, the entry walkway is surrounded by cascading waterfalls, ferns, bougainvillea, azaleas, birds of paradise, and other tropical plants. It's a calming and inviting environment, and guests take time to appreciate it before stepping into the building's foyer. Needless to say, this gorgeous setting is a favorite for individual or group photos.

The best spot for outdoor ceremonies is a picturesque, perfectly manicured tee box at the edge of an expansive golf course that constitutes MountainGate's backyard. The ceremony site, which overlooks a serene panorama of rolling hills, is shaded by a cluster of birch trees. It's also backed by dozens of multicolored roses that lend a heavenly fragrance to the air during the early summer.

Indoor receptions are held in the club's stunning Dining Room, designed with a vaulted ceiling and wraparound floor-to-ceiling windows. The room is done in earth tones and appointed with rustic, wrought-iron chandeliers. Depending on where you place your sweetheart table, you'll have a double-sided fireplace or windows facing the terrace as your backdrop. An adjacent lounge and bar, featuring granite counters and cherrywood accents, enjoys a view of trees, the endless golf course, and the Santa Monica Mountains.

MountainGate is known for its outdoor garden areas. The North Lawn, set with cocktails tables and hors d'oeuvres prepared by the on-site chef, is ideal for mingling. Afterwards, guests head to the romantic Garden Terrace to continue the festivities. Lined with trees, flowers and a wall of greenery, it's a lovely canvas on which to create whatever style reception you envision. At night, bistro string lights and a sky full of glittering stars provide a glowing finishing touch.

In addition to the smart architecture and attractive landscaping, what really makes a MountainGate wedding so memorable is the hospitable attitude that prevails among staffers: Everyone goes out of his or her way to make your event feel special. And, thanks to the club's policy of hosting only one wedding at a time, you'll receive the personal attention that every couple deserves.

CEREMONY CAPACITY: The site can accommodate up to 250 seated guests indoors or 350 outdoors.

EVENT/RECEPTION CAPACITY: The Main Dining Room holds 180 seated guests with a dance floor, 200 without, or 350 standing guests. The Garden Terrace (which can be tented) accommodates 375 seated with a dance floor, and 400 without.

MEETING CAPACITY: The Main Dining Room can accommodate 100 guests classroom-style or 200 theater-style.

FEES & DEPOSITS: A nonrefundable deposit, which is applied to your food & beverage total, is required to reserve your date. The amount of the deposit varies depending on how far in advance you book. Payment terms for the balance also vary, and may be arranged on an individual basis. Wedding packages start at $85/person on Fridays or $105/person on Saturdays and Sundays. Tax, alcohol and service charge are additional. Food & beverage minimums may apply. Menus and packages can be customized to fit your needs and budget. Call for details.

AVAILABILITY: Year-round, Tuesday, Friday and Saturday evenings, with some exceptions. The first Sunday evening of the month is also available.

SERVICES/AMENITIES:

Catering: in-house or BYO
Kitchen Facilities: fully equipped
Tables & Chairs: provided
Linens, Silver, etc.: provided
Restrooms: wheelchair accessible
Dance Floor: provided
Bride's & Groom's Dressing Areas: yes
AV/Meeting Equipment: microphone, screen

Parking: on site; valet included with some packages
Accommodations: no guest rooms
Outdoor Night Lighting: yes
Outdoor Cooking Facilities: n/a
Cleanup: provided
View: hills, golf fairways and city skyline
Other: event coordination, wedding cake

RESTRICTIONS:

Alcohol: in-house
Smoking: outside only
Music: amplified OK until midnight

Wheelchair Access: yes
Insurance: not required
Other: no rice, glitter or birdseed

Natural History Museum of L.A. County

Museum

900 Exposition Boulevard, Los Angeles
213/763-3221
www.nhm.org/specialevents
specialevents@nhm.org

●	Rehearsal Dinners	●	Corporate Events
●	Ceremonies	●	Meetings
●	Wedding Receptions	●	Film Shoots
●	Private Parties		Accommodations

Frankly, after strolling through the Natural History Museum of Los Angeles County, other venues seem, well, quite tame in comparison. Where else can you entertain 500 guests alongside a massive American bison silhouetted against a prairie sunset? Or be brazen enough to enjoy a cocktail in front of a herd of African elephants? Or dance among the dinosaurs?

With its incredible array of dramatic settings, the museum is one of the most thrilling places we've encountered. No matter what kind of event you're planning—be it a wedding, corporate affair, or birthday party—this amazing site has a space for you.

The museum's historic 1913 Beaux Arts building houses the iconic Haaga Family Rotunda, lined with marble columns and crowned by a 58-foot-high dome with a 20-foot stained-glass skylight at its center. As you enter this soaring space, your eye is drawn to Julia Bracken Wendt's graceful statue of the "Three Muses," representing the disciplines of art, history and science. The Rotunda is ideal for a wedding ceremony, as well as any kind of private or corporate reception. It comes with a view of Exposition Park's Rose Garden through glass doors, and is even more wonderful when used in conjunction with the museum's Nature Gardens.

If you'd like to have a gigantic guest at your ceremony, get married upstairs at the Otis Booth Pavilion, where you can exchange vows beneath a 163-foot fin whale skeleton in front of a 5-story wall of glass with nothing but the sky behind you. The clean-lined event space on the ground floor is a *tabula rasa* that can be transformed any way you like. Plus, it opens to the gardens for an indoor/outdoor experience.

Then there's the Grand Foyer, a remarkable reception space that boasts twin half domes, marbled columns, travertine marble floors…and enormous dueling dinosaurs—a *Tyrannosaurus rex* and a *Triceratops* engaged in fierce battle. (With centerpieces like this, who needs decorations?)

The Nature Gardens are a total surprise: 3.5 serene acres in the middle of L.A. that contain an edible garden, a wildflower pasture, and a pond. Receptions are held in a long open area flanked by tall trees. To one side, there's a patio with a deck for observing the birds that congregate here; on the other side is the Urban Water Feature, where couples often say "I do" on one of its tiered platforms.

Other exotic backdrops for large parties include the African Mammal Hall or one of the two North American Mammal Halls. With gleaming, polished cork floors (the perfect surface for dancing), and magnificent dioramas of the world's animals, these rooms take you on an adventure around the globe.

More intriguing possibilities are offered as well: You can have a museum expert give a special talk at your festivities, or tour an area of the museum like the Gem and Mineral Hall, which houses glittering jewels that will surely make your guests feel like royalty.

Sound extraordinary? It is! See for yourself—drive over to Exposition Park and take a walk on the wild side.

CEREMONY CAPACITY: The Rotunda and Grand Foyer each seat 150 guests; the African and North American Mammal Halls each seat 340; and the Otis Booth Pavilion 2nd floor accommodates 125.

EVENT/RECEPTION CAPACITY: The Rotunda and Grand Foyer each hold 120 seated or 250 standing guests; the African Mammal Hall holds 280 seated or 500 standing; and the North American Mammal Hall holds 300 seated or 500 standing. Halls can be used in conjunction with each other, allowing a standing capacity of 800–1,100 and a seated capacity of up to 650. The Nature Gardens seat up to 600 guests; the Otis Booth Pavilion ground floor accommodates 160 seated and 350 standing and the 2nd floor holds 70 seated and 125 standing.

MEETING CAPACITY: Small meeting spaces hold up to 80 guests, depending on the configuration.

FEES & DEPOSITS: A nonrefundable deposit of 50% of the estimated total is required at the time the contract is signed to reserve your date; the balance is due 45 days prior to the event. The rental fee starts at $10,000 and varies depending on the number of guests and the spaces used. It covers an 8-hour time block including setup and cleanup (4pm load-in to midnight), a 1-year VIP membership to the Natural History Museum Family of Museums, operations, security, housekeeping, event management staffing, and all taxes and service charges. A portion of the fee is tax deductible.

AVAILABILITY: Year-round, daily, 6pm–11pm, extended hours are available.

SERVICES/AMENITIES:
Catering: Select from list or BYO, extra fee
Kitchen Facilities: none
Tables & Chairs: some provided
Linens, Silver, etc.: through caterer
Restrooms: wheelchair accessible
Dance Floor: some areas available for dancing
Bride's & Groom's Dressing Area: no
AV/Meeting Equipment: provided in Meeting Room only

Parking: complimentary for event guests in adjacent lots
Accommodations: no guest rooms
Outdoor Night Lighting: access only
Outdoor Cooking Facilities: through caterer
Cleanup: caterer or renter
View: nature gardens, pond, nearby rose garden
Other: museum tours; "Dinosaur Encounters" CBA, extra fee

RESTRICTIONS:
Alcohol: licensed server and permit required
Smoking: not allowed
Music: amplified OK

Wheelchair Access: yes
Insurance: required for renters and vendors

Oviatt Penthouse

Penthouse of Landmark, Art Deco Building

617 South Olive Street, Los Angeles
213/379-4172
www.oviatt.com
weddings@trulyyourscatering.com

● Rehearsal Dinners	● Corporate Events
● Ceremonies	● Meetings
● Wedding Receptions	● Film Shoots
● Private Parties	Accommodations

Seldom does Old Hollywood meet New Hollywood as spectacularly as at the Oviatt Penthouse, an exclusive 13th-story aerie of Art Deco splendor. Once the private residence of James Oviatt, the dapper haberdasher behind the building of this 1927 landmark, the penthouse now lends its sophisticated elegance—and a 360-degree view of the downtown L.A. skyline—to weddings and other special events.

The moment you enter the building's lobby, you get a hint of what awaits you in the Penthouse. Many of the glass and metal features you see here—the windows, doors, pillars and ceiling—are the work of the famous Parisian glassmaker, René Lalique. His genius is also evident in the Penthouse's light fixtures and glasswork. The elevator that whisks you up to the 13th floor might as well be a time machine, because when the doors open and you step into the Penthouse foyer, you find yourself in another world, one that's a virtual time capsule from the 1930s.

As you and your guests wander among the Penthouse's seven rooms, notice the extraordinary details: the arched hallway ceiling, painted like a starry night sky and edged with Lalique light fixtures; the autographed photos of Mr. Oviatt's wonderfully dressed movie star clients; the Saddier et Fils Art Deco bar in the dining room; the living room's parquet floor fashioned from precious woods; and the bathroom, which has a sunken marble tub and glazed terracotta tiles etched with a palm-leaf design. The entire penthouse is incredibly sensual and tactile, tempting you to stroke the rose-colored, velvet-covered chairs and the cool surface of the marble fireplace. Even the powder room's commode and lavatory basin are veneered in burled maple and upholstered with cut velvet.

As though all this weren't enough, the splendor extends to the outdoors as well on the terrace. This breathtaking space has a slightly Moorish feel, with a colorful tiled fountain and arabesques of wrought iron adorning staircases and rooftops. A Spanish-tiled stairway leads you up to the Martini Lounge, a chic new area for up to 25 guests. Formerly just an observation deck that had been closed to the public for 15 years, it's now outfitted with lounge furniture, draperies and dramatic uplighting. This is *the* place to host an intimate private party on a warm summer night, with the glittering city spread out beneath you—especially if you enhance the space with gobos, twinkle lights or other mood lighting.

Truly Yours Catering, the company handling events at the Penthouse, has been working with the Los Angeles Conservancy to preserve the space, returning some of the original antiques, and repainting the interior. They've also built their own kitchen on site so that all their fabulous food arrives the way it was prepared: fresh and hot.

In addition to being a one-of-a-kind location for weddings, rehearsal dinners and brunches, the Penthouse has become a prime spot for bridal mixers (where brides meet each other over drinks and desserts and share ideas) and seminars (free events where brides can meet with wedding vendors). Check with *Truly Yours* to find out what's scheduled!

The Oviatt Penthouse is truly an extraordinary venue that makes an indelible impression on everyone who sees it, so no matter what event you host at this "castle in the air" it's bound to be unforgettable.

CEREMONY, EVENT/RECEPTION & MEETING CAPACITY: The site—indoor areas and terrace combined—holds 120 people, maximum. The terrace can seat 120.

FEES & DEPOSITS: A nonrefundable deposit of 100% of the total site fee is required to secure your date. The rental fee ranges $800–5,800 depending on the day of the week. For filming fees, please contact the venue. Wedding packages range $10,000–18,000 and include the site, food, rentals and lighting.

AVAILABILITY: Year-round.

SERVICES/AMENITIES:

Catering: provided by *Truly Yours Catering*
Kitchen Facilities: n/a
Tables & Chairs: provided
Linens, Silver, etc.: through caterer
Restrooms: wheelchair accessible
Dance Floor: no
Bride's & Groom's Dressing Areas: yes
AV/Meeting Equipment: BYO

Parking: valet CBA; adjacent fee lots
Accommodations: no guest rooms
Outdoor Night Lighting: yes
Outdoor Cooking Facilities: yes
Cleanup: $250 fee per event
View: stunning 360-degree L.A. cityscape from terrace
Other: stereo system provided indoors, outdoor heaters

RESTRICTIONS:

Alcohol: in-house or BYO
Smoking: terrace only
Music: amplified OK

Wheelchair Access: limited
Insurance: liability required

Petersen Automotive Museum
and Rooftop Penthouse

Automotive Museum

6060 Wilshire Boulevard at Fairfax, Los Angeles
323/964-6348

www.petersenevents.org
privateevents@petersen.org

●	Rehearsal Dinners	●	Corporate Events
●	Ceremonies	●	Meetings
●	Wedding Receptions	●	Film Shoots
●	Private Parties		Accommodations

With millions of dollars' worth of beautiful cars, the Petersen Automotive Museum has always been an amazing setting for glamorous celebrations. But, after its 2015 total transformation inside and out, it's become a positively astounding place for weddings, as well as corporate parties, conferences, product launches, and more.

The gleaming new façade is an absolute show-stopper: An ingeniously designed series of undulating silver steel ribbons wrap around the building, symbolizing streams of air waves generated by a speeding car. As jaw-dropping as this is, though, it's just an introduction to all the spectacular features you'll find inside.

For weddings, the Rooftop Penthouse & Terrace is the most popular choice. Occupying the entire 4th floor, it's an architecturally intriguing space: an all-glass "room" surrounded by a smooth, slate patio. You can have your ceremony on one side of the patio and host a seated reception on the other, using the glass-enclosed penthouse itself for cocktails and dancing. You're free to choreograph your celebration any way you like, and no matter where you are in this thoroughly modern aerie you'll be cooled by passing breezes and enjoy panoramic vistas of the Hollywood Hills and Century City, along with a birds-eye view of Miracle Mile. At night, Los Angeles becomes a sea of glittering lights, lending a romantic sparkle to your evening soirée.

More than 20 galleries on the other three floors are also available. The museum's contemporary interior—white walls paired with stainless steel and glass accents—provides a neutral backdrop for highlighting both the cars on display and your event.

The 1st floor is dedicated to the ARTISTRY of cars, as inspiration and as a canvas for artistic expression. One of this floor's key attributes is a 160-foot wall where you can project event-enhancing images such as a sunset, starry night sky, or personal photos. On the 2nd floor, the focus is INDUSTRY. Here you'll see how a car is created from concept to completion…and have an opportunity to shift your event into high gear: For an additional fee, you can let your guests live out their race car driver fantasies in the interactive Forza Racing simulation room. The HISTORY of cars is explored on the 3rd floor, which is perhaps most notable for its famous film and celebrity cars, like the Batmobile, Laurel and Hardy's Model T, and the 1966 Ford Thunderbird convertible from *Thelma and Louise*. Everyone will love the photo op section where you can have your picture taken posing in one of the cars from the museum's fabulous collection!

When you book a floor, your reservation includes access to all the galleries on that floor. However, exhibits or activities on other floors can be added for an extra charge. Guided tours may also be arranged—even for the Vault, the lower-level "garage" where hidden automotive gems are stored.

The Petersen Automotive Museum is a remarkable place whether you're hosting an event or just visiting. One of the perks of having your wedding here is a one-year membership for the newlyweds, including unlimited free admission, invitations to members-only special events and a 10% discount in the museum store. Whether you party in the Penthouse or on another floor, your guests will be thanking you for an unforgettable experience.

CEREMONY CAPACITY: The 4th-floor Penthouse/Terrace holds 200 seated; the 2nd-floor Gallery seats 200; and the 1st-floor Grand Salon seats 400.

EVENT/RECEPTION CAPACITY: The Museum can accommodate 400 seated or 650 standing on the 1st floor; 300 seated or 600 standing on the 2nd floor; 120 seated or 300 standing on the 3rd floor; and 200 seated or 300 standing in the 4th-floor Penthouse/Terrace.

MEETING CAPACITY: The Penthouse seats 150 theater-style; the Founder's Lounge seats 60 theater-style or 20 conference-style.

FEES & DEPOSITS: 50% of the total event cost is required to reserve your date and the balance is due 30 days prior to the event. The rental fee ranges $2,500–15,000 depending on the space(s) reserved and the guest count.

AVAILABILITY: Year-round, daily; 6pm–2am for the museum interior, 9am–2am for the 4th-floor Penthouse/Terrace.

SERVICES/AMENITIES:

Catering: provided exclusively by *Celestino Drago Catering*; outside ethnic caterer allowed with approval, extra fee
Kitchen Facilities: prep only CBA, extra fee
Tables & Chairs: CBA, extra fee
Linens, Silver, etc.: through caterer
Restrooms: wheelchair accessible
Dance Floor: CBA, extra fee
Bride's Dressing Area: CBA
AV/Meeting Equipment: some provided

Parking: large lot
Accommodations: no guest rooms
Outdoor Night Lighting: yes
Outdoor Cooking Facilities: CBA
Cleanup: provided
View: panoramic city views

RESTRICTIONS:

Alcohol: through caterer
Smoking: outside only
Music: amplified OK indoors; no amplified on the 4th-floor Penthouse/Terrace after 10pm

Wheelchair Access: yes
Insurance: liability required
Other: no rice, birdseed, confetti or glitter; candles allowed on 4th-floor terrace only

Taglyan Cultural Complex

1201 Vine Street, Los Angeles

323/978-0005

www.taglyan.com
info@taglyancomplex.com

- Rehearsal Dinners
- Ceremonies
- Wedding Receptions
- Private Parties
- Corporate Events
- Meetings
- Film Shoots
- Accommodations

Opened to great fanfare in 2008, the Taglyan Arts and Cultural Complex offers a dazzling combination of Old World opulence and cutting-edge audiovisual technology. Located mere blocks from the world-famous intersection of Hollywood and Vine, this venue may be new to the event scene, but with its stately limestone façade it looks like it's been part of the neighborhood for years.

As soon as you enter the massive iron gates on a quiet side street, you feel like you've been transported to a European villa. Italian cypress, magnolia and olive trees, along with vintage-look streetlamps, dot the property. Immediately on your right is the formal brick courtyard, anchored by the kind of huge two-tiered fountain you might find in an Italian piazza, complete with figural fish and turtles spouting water. A formal garden containing white roses encircles the fountain, creating a very romantic spot for wedding ceremonies. As an added enhancement, the historic French Normandy-style building across the street acts as a charming backdrop. Taglyan's upper patio, which could serve as an alternate ceremony site or for cocktails, overlooks the courtyard and has its own cherub fountain with two small gardens and marble pillars.

Inside the building itself, it's obvious that no expense has been spared in workmanship or materials. The dramatic Grand Foyer is a feast for the eyes, highlighted by an Italian marble floor inlaid with various patterns—the first one symbolizing eternity, which seems rather fitting for couples who've just exchanged vows. This palatial-sized space has natural light streaming in through tall windows draped in rich green velvet, as well as filtering in through stained-glass inserts in the high, coffered ceiling. Along one wall you can set up couches in front of faux fireplaces, creating a cozy area for small-group mingling. Another option for intimate conversation is the outdoor flagstone patio, which makes a perfect bar and lounge setting.

But the *pièce de résistance* is the Main Ballroom—truly a "grand" ballroom. Set off by green marble pillars and elaborate, cascading crystal chandeliers, its 5,000-square-foot, circular stained-glass ceiling is flat-out, jaw-droppingly beautiful. And as if its artistry alone wasn't mesmerizing enough, it can even be programmed to shift colors with an elaborate lighting system. In fact, the entire facility incorporates state-of-the-art audiovisual equipment, including scrims and projectors with screens that descend around the room so you can screen personal movies, then take it up a notch by bathing the stage and dance floor in sound and light.

Taglyan Complex has devoted just as much attention to every detail behind the scenes as well, from its two top-of-the-line kitchens to the ample underground parking and luxurious bridal room (and large groom's room). Their exclusive in-house caterer, *Divine Food & Catering,* will customize your menu whether you desire a multicultural meal, Continental fare, or something in between. When you're here, all you have to do is relax, revel in your surroundings and get ready for a very memorable event.

CEREMONY CAPACITY: The Complex holds 250 seated guests in the foyer and 250 seated in the garden.

EVENT/RECEPTION CAPACITY: The site accommodates 500 seated or 800 standing guests in the ballroom, 400 standing in the foyer, and 400 standing in the garden.

MEETING CAPACITY: Meeting rooms hold up to 25 seated guests.

FEES & DEPOSITS: A minimum $5,000 deposit is required to reserve your date, and the balance is due 7 days prior to the event. Packages that include venue rental, furniture, linens, and in-house catering start at $115/person. Tax, alcohol and an 18% service charge are additional. There's a $25,000 minimum required for a Friday or Sunday event, and a $40,000 minimum for a Saturday event.

AVAILABILITY: Year-round, daily.

SERVICES/AMENITIES:

Catering: in-house or BYO
Kitchen Facilities: fully equipped
Tables & Chairs: provided
Linens, Silver, etc.: provided
Restrooms: wheelchair accessible
Dance Floor: portable provided
Bride's Dressing Area: yes
AV/Meeting Equipment: provided

Parking: large lot, valet required
Accommodations: no guest rooms
Outdoor Night Lighting: yes
Outdoor Cooking Facilities: BBQ CBA
Cleanup: provided
View: garden courtyard, landscaped grounds

RESTRICTIONS:

Alcohol: in-house
Smoking: in designated areas only
Music: amplified OK with restrictions

Wheelchair Access: yes
Insurance: not required
Other: coordination, in-house wedding cake and florals, clergy on staff

---

This is important! Tell locations you're reading HERE COMES THE GUIDE and ask if our information is still current.

Vibiana

214 South Main Street, Los Angeles
213/626-1507

www.vibiana.com
info@vibiana.com

● Rehearsal Dinners		● Corporate Events
● Ceremonies		● Meetings
● Wedding Receptions		● Film Shoots
● Private Parties		Accommodations

They say there are no second acts in life, but the magnificent Vibiana has an exciting new focus under the direction of husband-and-wife restaurateurs Neal Fraser and Amy Knoll Fraser, along with partner Bill Chait. Neal has long been one of L.A.'s premier chefs, having worked with culinary luminaries such as Thomas Keller and Wolfgang Puck. He's also the first California chef to win the prestigious Iron Chef America TV show. Together, the Frasers bring their handcrafted approach to food and event services to this full-service venue that's a star in its own right: Not only is Vibiana an architectural treasure, it's also a "take your breath away" setting for weddings, concerts and special occasions.

Designed in the Spanish Baroque style and patterned after San Miguel Del Mar in Barcelona, Vibiana (originally St. Vibiana's Cathedral) was built in 1876 as the Catholic Archdiocese in Los Angeles. Over the next century it flourished—until the 1994 Northridge earthquake, when it suffered some severe damage. Eventually, one of L.A.'s most respected developers began a long and expensive process to completely retrofit, redefine and revitalize Vibiana.

Mindful of maintaining the integrity of this landmark, the developer strengthened and secured the building while keeping its original beauty and appearance intact. At first glance, the limestone exterior may still resemble a church, but the site has been desanctified and its massive double doors thrown open to welcome celebrants of all backgrounds, faiths and persuasions. In short, it's now secular heaven.

The foyer entryway is dazzling with its gold embellished barrel ceilings and black-and-white marble floor. To your left are massive glass-and-iron doors that lead to a beautiful garden on the property's grounds at Main and Second. Surrounded by tall wrought-iron fencing and enough greenery to ensure privacy, it has a long center aisle that ends at a landscaped island, a natural spot for exchanging your vows. From this verdant vantage point, you can look up and see such notable buildings as City Hall and the historic L.A. Times Building, both of which light up at night making the cityscape come alive.

But it's Vibiana's interior and its truly grand proportions that make this a one-of-a-kind wedding location. It's an architectural marvel with soaring gilded ceilings, an abundance of white marble, and clerestory windows that let in natural light. Long rows of white columns on either side stand in contrast to the deeply burnished dark wood floors. At the far end, the old altar is now an impressive white marble stage with plenty of space to set up your sweetheart table, make toasts or bring in a band (the acoustics here are great). While the grandeur of the old cathedral can be seen in the scale of the venue, some features have been re-imagined in fun new ways, like the old confessionals, which can be turned into photo booths for your guests. Perhaps it's this combination of putting a modern spin on Old World beauty that's made Vibiana such a runaway success since the day it opened.

CEREMONY CAPACITY: The site holds 600 seated guests indoors and 300 seated outdoors.

EVENT/RECEPTION & MEETING CAPACITY: The facility can accommodate 600 seated or 789 standing guests indoors, and 300 seated or 500 standing outdoors.

FEES & DEPOSITS: 50% of the venue rental fee and a $2,500 food & beverage deposit are required to reserve your date. 50% of the estimated food & beverage total is due no later than 60 days after booking your event. The remaining balance is due 14 days prior to the event along with a $1,000 refundable damage deposit. Rental fees range $4,000–8,000 depending on the event date.

AVAILABILITY: Year-round, daily, 9am–2am.

SERVICES/AMENITIES:
Catering: in-house
Kitchen Facilities: n/a
Tables & Chairs: provided
Linens, Silver, etc.: provided
Restrooms: wheelchair accessible
Dance Floor: provided, extra fee
Bride's & Groom's Dressing Areas: yes
AV/Meeting Equipment: BYO

Parking: valet available
Accommodations: no guest rooms
Outdoor Night Lighting: yes
Outdoor Cooking Facilities: BBQ CBA
Cleanup: provided
View: cityscape, garden

RESTRICTIONS:
Alcohol: in-house
Smoking: allowed outside in the garden
Music: amplified OK with restrictions

Wheelchair Access: yes
Insurance: liability required

Wilshire Loft

Event Facility

700 Wilshire Boulevard, Los Angeles
213/259-9573
www.wilshireloft.com
events@wilshireloft.com

Rehearsal Dinners	●	Corporate Events
● Ceremonies	●	Meetings
● Wedding Receptions	●	Film Shoots
● Private Parties		Accommodations

You could say that Wilshire Loft was built from the ground up, except that the creative team behind it—as well as some of southern California's most popular venues and high-profile events—actually started at the top. They painstakingly transformed the entire 7th floor of office space into this glam, expansive penthouse with a huge terrace and to-die-for views right in the heart of downtown.

A private elevator takes you up to a large, open entry filled with natural light from a wall of windows. Throughout the whole loft-like space, you'll find a cool vibe generated by clean, modern lines paired with the best eye-catching elements of 70s décor. For example, the spacious Bridal Room sports boldly colored walls, faux fur chairs and sleek mirrored tables, while the chic Lounge embodies low-key elegance with its creamy tones, coved ceiling and glittery chandelier.

This seamless melding of different eras is nowhere more evident than on the fabulous terrace. As friends and family gather here for the ceremony, they're surrounded by the vibrancy of Los Angeles with a birds-eye view of high-rises dating from the 60s to today. Vows are exchanged against a skyline that juxtaposes the glass-clad U.S. Bank, California's tallest building, right next to the low-slung, Art Deco L.A. Public Library. Now, if seeing two unique entities like these standing side by side in beautiful harmony isn't a metaphor for a good marriage, we don't know what is!

The celebration continues inside the bar, where you can still savor the city vistas through a wall of glass. Adorning the ceiling is an undulating, kinetic light fixture that runs nearly the length of the room and seems more like a work of art than a chandelier. Not to be outdone for visual artistry, the cocktails and appetizers are equally worthy of your attention. Highly acclaimed *Truly Yours Catering* has developed a wide variety of specialty libations and hors d'oeuvres that range from short rib quesadillas and ahi tuna sliders to mac n' cheese topped with broccoli and black truffles. Their dinner menu is even more extensive (actually over 20 pages long!) with new twists on old favorites and a focus on organic and locally sourced ingredients, plus Asian, Middle Eastern, Mexican, Vegetarian and Indian selections. Fortunately, they have a very knowledgeable culinary team that can help you plan your meal and personalize it.

The dining room layout is flexible, so you can choreograph your event to suit your needs. (If you're hosting dinner for a more intimate group, you might even be able to arrange it on the terrace.)

And if you thought the cityscape looked great at sunset, you'll love the city lights at night—they'll really make your wedding album pictures pop.

CEREMONY CAPACITY: The site holds 140 seated indoors and 160 seated outdoors.

EVENT/RECEPTION CAPACITY: The site can accommodate 160 seated or 200 standing guests indoors.

MEETING CAPACITY: Meeting spaces seat 200 guests.

FEES & DEPOSITS: A nonrefundable deposit of the venue fee is required to reserve your date, and the balance of the estimated event total is due 10 days prior to the event. The venue rental fee ranges $4,550–6,750 and varies depending on the day of the week. Meals range $55–75/person.

Rates for business functions, meetings or other types of events vary. Please contact the venue for more details.

AVAILABILITY: Year-round, daily.

SERVICES/AMENITIES:

Catering: in-house
Kitchen Facilities: n/a
Tables & Chairs: provided
Linens, Silver, etc.: provided
Restrooms: wheelchair accessible
Dance Floor: portable provided
Bride's Dressing Area: yes
AV/Meeting Equipment: some provided, more CBA

Parking: large lot, on street, valet available
Accommodations: no guest rooms
Outdoor Night Lighting: yes
Outdoor Cooking Facilities: no
Cleanup: provided
View: 360-degree panorama of L.A. cityscape
Other: club-style venue lighting package

RESTRICTIONS:

Alcohol: BYO
Smoking: designated areas only
Music: amplified OK indoors

Wheelchair Access: yes
Insurance: liability required

Calamigos Ranch Malibu

327 South Latigo Canyon, Malibu
818/889-6280

www.calamigos.com
weddings@calamigos.com

Ranch and Conference Center

- Rehearsal Dinners
- Ceremonies
- Wedding Receptions
- Private Parties
- Corporate Events
- Meetings
- Film Shoots
- Accommodations

Although Calamigos bills itself as a country ranch set amongst 130 acres of rolling hills, verdant meadows, lakes, ancient oaks, and its own vineyard, most of its event facilities are far from rustic.

There are four different outdoor ceremony options, each with its own reception site. The Garden Patio near the ranch's entrance is an expansive lawn with picturesque waterfalls at each end. Guests are seated on either side of a stone aisle, facing a redwood arbor adorned with flowers where the bride and groom exchange vows. Shaded by trees, it's a peaceful and private area. From here it's just a few steps to the Lodge, a delightful, sun-filled space thanks to light streaming in through "walls" of French doors. One of the room's remarkable features is the romantic "waterfall," a curtain of water that descends like a light rain just outside the glass doors.

The Oaks Deck is popular for intimate ceremonies. Rows of chairs are set up in front of a wood arbor with a rock waterfall directly behind it, and a backdrop of eucalyptus, pine and oak trees. Couples who get married here usually have their reception in the dining room nearby. Like the Lodge, it uses French doors to maximize light and views of the outdoors. Crisp white table linens contrast nicely with the warm pine ceiling beams and doorframes, and ferns and ficus trees provide indoor greenery. Buffets are often served on the adjoining redwood deck, which is partially shaded by oak branches.

A third option is the Cottage and Pavilion, a secluded little meadow ringed by trees and natural landscaping. Couples tie the knot on an earthen terrace beneath a majestic spreading oak, or in front of a clear pond at the base of a river rock waterfall. Afterwards, guests are invited to the reception under an elegant white tent draped with sheer fabric and twinkle lights.

Lastly, the Secret Garden is a charming venue designed for more intimate gatherings. Ceremonies unfold on a grassy field bordered by roses, plum trees and a large cascading waterfall. The reception can be held on the private, multilevel deck nearby. Surrounded by nature, including a couple of streams, this spot is beautiful and calm. Sunset and evening events are lovely here, especially when the thousands of twinkle lights lacing the trees add their sparkle.

And if you've come to the ranch for one of their legendary western-style celebrations (including Barn Mitzvahs!), check out The Barn. It's the real thing: The floor is covered with sawdust, bales of hay are scattered about, and it's painted—you guessed it—bright red.

The newest addition to the ranch, the Calamigos Resort and Spa, lets you extend your stay with 36 luxurious guest rooms that bring you closer to nature. Each one has its own terrace—some offer a mountain view and others are designed as enclosed interior spaces that are open to the sky and stars.

We were pleasantly surprised by the ranch's reception facilities and the Calamigos staff, who are true professionals when it comes to helping you plan your wedding. They'll design your event to suit your special needs, and coordinate everything down to the last detail.

CEREMONY CAPACITY: Indoors, the ranch holds up to 400 seated guests; outdoors up to 800 seated.

EVENT/RECEPTION CAPACITY: Indoor areas accommodate 75–500 seated or 150–600 standing guests. The smallest site has a 75-guest minimum.

MEETING CAPACITY: The site accommodates 35–500 guests for conferences.

FEES & DEPOSITS: For weddings, a nonrefundable $1,500 deposit is required to reserve your date and is applied to the final bill; the balance is payable 3 days prior to the event. A variety of wedding packages (including customized ones) are available, with prices starting at $121/person.

For day conferences, all-inclusive packages start at $55/person.

AVAILABILITY: Year-round, daily, including holidays. Conferences and other corporate events are by arrangement.

SERVICES/AMENITIES:

Catering: in-house, or BYO, buyout required
Kitchen Facilities: fully equipped
Tables & Chairs: provided
Linens, Silver, etc.: provided
Restrooms: wheelchair accessible
Dance Floor: provided
Bride's Dressing Area: yes; groom's CBA
AV/Meeting Equipment: CBA, extra fee

Parking: large lot, free valet
Accommodations: 36 guest rooms
Outdoor Night Lighting: yes
Outdoor Cooking Facilities: BBQs
Cleanup: provided
View: Santa Monica Mountains
Other: ceremony coordination & rehearsal

RESTRICTIONS:

Alcohol: in-house, BWC corkage $10/bottle
Smoking: outdoors only
Music: amplified OK until 11pm

Wheelchair Access: yes
Insurance: liability required
Other: no rice, confetti or sparklers

Overwhelmed? Use the search criteria on www.HereComesTheGuide.com to narrow down your choices.

191

Cypress Sea Cove

33572 Pacific Coast Highway, Malibu
310/589-3344

www.cypressseacove.com
info@cypressseacove.com

Private Beachfront Estate

- Rehearsal Dinners
- Ceremonies
- Wedding Receptions
- Private Parties
- Corporate Events
- Meetings
- Film Shoots
- Accommodations

Poised on a flat bluff overlooking the wide blue backdrop of the Pacific, this two-acre, oceanfront private estate is an exceptionally dramatic locale for any occasion. Beauty greets you at every turn: Majestic Monterey cypress are silhouetted against the sky, an acre of velvety lawn spreads all the way to the end of the bluff, and on summer nights the cliff-edge gazebo is backlit by the setting sun. The nautical white Victorian home, reminiscent of the East Coast Hamptons, is generally not available for events, but the gorgeous grounds, festooned with roses and multicolored blooms, leave little to be desired.

Most celebrations are held on the bluff's expansive lawn. Here a large brick patio beneath towering cypress trees works perfectly for a buffet setup, and every table on the grass has an ocean view. The white gazebo, spacious enough for the bride and all her bridesmaids, also serves as a classic frame for wedding photos as well as displaying and cutting the cake.

For smaller receptions or seaside ceremonies, walk down through Palm Canyon to the secluded beach patio, where young Marilyn Monroe attended many luaus. As you descend, you'll see hundreds of phoenix, Mexican fantail and date palms, some of them over 150 feet tall! The tropical-style beach bar and patio, really a series of three lushly landscaped brick and adobe terraces that end on the sand, is an intimate and romantic spot to exchange vows. The couple stands with their backs to the crashing surf, while guests seated on the palm-shaded lawn have a view of the sea. The patio also boasts a delightful bamboo cabana. With canvas rollback windows and wired for sound, it's a sublime place to spend an evening listening to your favorite music, sipping mai tais and watching the moon drop into the sea.

Cypress Sea Cove hosts many types of events, including corporate barbecues and private parties, but the estate's owners have a particular fondness for weddings and provide a cottage just for the bride. In addition, they can suggest several experienced wedding and special event planning companies that will help make your event worry-free. A _New York Times_ pick as one of the best wedding locations in the U.S., this stunning waterfront venue is truly a little piece of paradise found.

CEREMONY, RECEPTION & MEETING CAPACITY: The formal lawn holds up to 300 seated guests. The lower beach patio can accommodate up to 50 guests.

FEES & DEPOSITS: The rental fee ranges $8,000–20,000 depending on the season, date selected and group size. A cleaning fee may be additional.

AVAILABILITY: Year-round, daily, including holidays.

SERVICES/AMENITIES:

Catering: BYO

Kitchen Facilities: prep area for outdoor caterers

Tables & Chairs: BYO

Linens, Silver, etc.: BYO

Restrooms: wheelchair access CBA

Dance Floor: BYO

Bride's Dressing Area: Bridal Cottage with restroom

AV/Meeting Equipment: BYO, wireless internet provided

Parking: shuttle or valet

Accommodations: no guest rooms

Outdoor Night Lighting: yes

Outdoor Cooking Facilities: yes

Cleanup: caterer

View: 180-degree panorama of Pacific Ocean and beach; palm trees and sunsets

RESTRICTIONS:

Alcohol: BYO

Smoking: not restricted

Music: amplified OK with time & volume restrictions

Wheelchair Access: yes

Insurance: liability required

Duke's Malibu

Oceanfront Restaurant

21150 Pacific Coast Highway, Malibu
310/317-6204
www.dukesmalibu.com
events@dukesmalibu.com

- Rehearsal Dinners
- Ceremonies
- Wedding Receptions
- Private Parties
- Corporate Events
- Meetings
- Film Shoots
- Accommodations

Duke's enviable waterfront location, fun-loving yet professional staff, and elegant event spaces will tempt you to celebrate right here on Malibu's famous shores. This supremely popular restaurant and its private banquet rooms enhance all types of occasions—wedding ceremonies, receptions, rehearsal dinners, day-after brunches, and more—with gracious hospitality and gorgeous Pacific panoramas. It's the perfect atmosphere for old friends and new families to come together.

Duke's Malibu was inspired by the memory of the legendary Duke Kahanamoku and the benevolent values that he personified. This extraordinary Olympic athlete set numerous swimming records and is credited with popularizing the sport of surfing. In his twilight years, Duke served as Hawaii's official "Ambassador of Aloha." He also had a profound impact on the beach culture of Southern California, so Malibu is an ideal site for a restaurant in his honor.

The "aloha" spirit embraces guests as they're welcomed through a private entrance and ushered into the Ocean Room. This lovely space has two walls of beachfront windows that are just steps away from the splashing surf. The other walls, paneled in the rare and valuable Hawaiian koa wood, give off a rich luster. In addition, doors open onto a balcony situated over the sand where guests may enjoy a quiet moment away from the festivities—perhaps to take in one of Malibu's extraordinary sunsets. At Duke's Malibu, you can create a casual celebration or transform the room into a stylish affair limited only by your imagination.

For more intimate celebrations, like bridal and baby showers, Duke's Malibu can accommodate your group in its "Board" Room (as in surfboard). This private, oceanview room is located in the restaurant and seats 36. As with the Ocean Room, mahogany Chiavari chairs, a choice of linens in various colors, and votive candles are provided for your event.

Just as satisfying as the view, Duke's coastal-inspired menus feature Hawaiian-influenced fresh fish and premium steaks, offered in both plated and buffet options.

When you desire to treat guests to an oceanfront experience, Duke's Malibu is the ideal spot for a truly unique and memorable gathering.

CEREMONY CAPACITY: The Ocean Room holds 150 seated guests.

EVENT/RECEPTION CAPACITY: The Ocean Room holds up to 250 seated or 400 standing guests.

MEETING CAPACITY: The Ocean Room holds 250 seated, the Board Room 36 seated.

FEES & DEPOSITS: A $2,000 nonrefundable deposit for the Ocean Room ($500 for the Board Room) is required to guarantee a specified date, time and space for an event. A food & beverage minimum is required for certain times and dates. Luncheons start at $30/person, dinners at $45/person; alcohol, tax and a 20% service charge are additional.

AVAILABILITY: Year-round, daily, until midnight. Closed Christmas Day.

SERVICES/AMENITIES:

Catering: in-house, no BYO
Kitchen Facilities: n/a
Tables & Chairs: provided
Linens, Silver, etc.: provided
Restrooms: wheelchair accessible
Dance Floor: CBA, extra charge
Bride's Dressing Area: yes
AV/Meeting Equipment: CBA or BYO

Parking: valet
Accommodations: no guest rooms
Outdoor Night Lighting: access lighting only
Outdoor Cooking Facilities: n/a
Cleanup: provided
View: 180-degree panorama of Pacific Ocean and beach; palm trees and sunsets

RESTRICTIONS:

Alcohol: in-house; wine and champagne corkage $20/750 ml bottle, $35/1.5 L bottle
Smoking: designated area outdoors
Music: amplified OK indoors

Wheelchair Access: yes
Insurance: not required

Malibu West Beach Club

Private Beach Club

30756 W. Pacific Coast Highway, Malibu

310/457-0195

www.malibuwestbeachclub.com
events@malibuwestbc.com

- Rehearsal Dinners
- Ceremonies
- Wedding Receptions
- Private Parties
- Corporate Events
- Meetings
- Film Shoots
- Accommodations

Standing at the edge of the ocean between Zuma State Beach and Broad Beach, the Malibu West Beach Club presides over one of the most desirable slices of real estate in Southern California. Glorious white sand stretches 200 yards from the clubhouse to the breaking surf, and from the second-floor deck there's a 180-degree panorama of the vast Pacific and miles of Malibu coastline. When it's clear, you can even see all the way to Catalina Island and the Channel Islands! As an added treat, whales migrate close to shore in the winter months, and almost daily you'll spot dolphins leaping out of the water as they swim by.

The unassuming two-story structure is partially screened from the street behind some hot pink bougainvillea and evergreen trees; you'd never know it was there if you didn't go looking for it. The large event space, which occupies the top floor and opens onto the spacious deck, is a bright and airy room with a high vaulted and arched ceiling. Its clean, simple interior is as unadorned as can be—truly a blank canvas where you can create your own decoration. Of course, the sunsets, visible through the club's glass façade, complement any décor.

Ceremonies are held on the 50-foot deck, with that glorious ocean panorama as a backdrop. Afterwards, the newlyweds may go down to the beach for photos, while their guests remain on the deck to mingle during the cocktail hour and savor the view.

Dinner and dancing take place inside, where everyone can enjoy the fabulous ocean vista through the wall of floor-to-ceiling glass that separates the banquet room from the deck. And throughout the evening, diners are free to step outside to sip wine or champagne, linger over the setting sun or watch the stars come out in the night sky.

In addition to the banquet room, Malibu West also offers a versatile bride's room. The club has outfitted it with thoughtful amenities to help the ladies primp and prepare—mirrors, vanities, dress racks—and there's even an ocean view! After the ceremony, it's also a quiet retreat where the bride and groom can have a moment alone together before the festivities begin; and during the reception this space can be set up as a kiddies' play area.

As if all this weren't enough, Malibu West also boasts a knowledgeable, friendly staff that will assist you in selecting vendors that match your vision and your budget. Given its beachfront location, genial ambiance and affordable prices, the Malibu West Beach Club is understandably in demand.

CEREMONY CAPACITY: The oceanview deck holds 150 seated guests.

EVENT/RECEPTION & MEETING CAPACITY: The site holds up to 170 seated or 250 standing guests. 150 or fewer is suggested for weddings, if you want everyone in the same room at the same time.

FEES & DEPOSITS: For events, 50% of the rental fee is a nonrefundable deposit required to reserve your date. The remaining balance and a $1,000 refundable security deposit are payable 60 days prior to the event. Weekend and holiday rental fees range $5,250–7,450 depending on guest count. An on-site representative is required for the duration of the event and is included in the rental fee. Midweek rates start at $2,850.

AVAILABILITY: Year-round, daily, 8am–1am, in 12-hour blocks.

SERVICES/AMENITIES:

Catering: select from extensive list
Kitchen Facilities: most appliances
Tables & Chairs: provided, 150 chairs and tables for up to 200 guests
Linens, Silver, etc.: caterer or BYO
Restrooms: two are wheelchair accessible
Dance Floor: included
Bride's Dressing Area: yes
AV/Meeting Equipment: BYO

Parking: limited on-street, 7 spaces at the club; valet or shuttle required for larger parties
Accommodations: no guest rooms
Outdoor Night Lighting: access lighting only
Outdoor Cooking Facilities: BYO
Cleanup: through caterer
View: panoramic ocean views and sunsets, Catalina and Channel Islands, Malibu coastline
Kosher: kosher kitchen CBA

RESTRICTIONS:

Alcohol: BYO; server bonded and licensed
Smoking: outdoors only
Music: amplified OK indoors until 10pm, volume reduced until midnight

Wheelchair Access: ramp
Insurance: required for caterers not on preferred list
Other: no rice, staples, nails, birdseed or confetti

Saddlerock Ranch and Vineyard

Ranch

Address withheld to ensure privacy. Malibu

818/889-0008 x27

www.malibufamilywines.com
weddings@malibufamilywines.com

- Rehearsal Dinners
- Ceremonies
- Wedding Receptions
- Private Parties
- Corporate Events
- Meetings
- Film Shoots
- Accommodations

Touted as "one location, a million scenes," this thousand-acre privately owned estate in the hills of Malibu is a much sought-after film site. Which isn't surprising: Saddlerock Ranch and Vineyard has views of the Conejo Valley, and is itself a veritable cornucopia of visual delights, with fruit and avocado orchards, acres of vineyards and pastureland dotted with heritage oaks and grazing herds of horses, cattle and llamas. Craggy rocks—including a landmark outcropping shaped like a saddle—jut up from vineyard-covered slopes, and ribbons of white fences meander alongside fields and tree-shaded driveways. Look carefully, and you'll see a few peacocks or even a camel or zebra as you wind your way through the ranch.

Happily for you, all this scenic beauty is available for special events. Four separate areas lend themselves to wedding ceremonies: the rose garden adjacent to the estate's main house; under the cascading fronds of a willow tree next to the rose garden; beneath a willow tree that overlooks a bucolic horse pasture (imagine mares and foals frolicking in the sun as morning mist rises from the fields); and lastly, under the branches of a 250-year-old oak, centered in a large grassy clearing surrounded by thickets of trees. Twinkle lights in the oak and nearby trees make this a spectacular spot for evening affairs, although the natural grandeur of the ranch doesn't need much adornment.

Many couples like the convenience of having their reception on one of the expansive level lawns at each of the wedding sites, but there are numerous other possibilities. One couple covered the tennis courts near the oak tree with AstroTurf, decorated it with lights, and hosted a black-tie reception for 500. Another couple opted for a country western theme—they rode horses to their ceremony, and then celebrated with a barbecue.

Saddlerock's newest event site is Chateau Le Dome, located on a hilltop in the middle of the ranch's vineyards. The Chateau in this case is an octagonal stone house, set on a manicured lawn that's large enough for a ceremony and reception. From this elevated vantage, you have panoramic views of the surrounding vineyards, valleys and pastures. As the bride prepares inside the house, guests take their seats for a ceremony on one side of the lawn. In keeping with the natural setting, vows are exchanged beneath a fallen oak-tree arch, entwined with grapevines. Afterwards, as friends and family dine in the serenity of their secluded perch, they'll feel like they're on top of the world.

Another appealing gathering area is the Malibu Wines Tasting Room, an expansive and artfully landscaped outdoor venue. Instead of the usual cocktail hour, why not treat your guests to an array of savory local vintages? The Tasting Room's temperate hilltop climate and gorgeous views are the perfect accompaniments to a glass of Saddlerock Chardonnay or their award-winning Semler Merlot.

At Saddlerock Ranch you start with a breathtaking backdrop and add whatever props you like. Fill the sky with butterflies or doves, bring in an elephant, or wave goodbye to your guests from a helicopter or hot-air balloon. Virtually anything is possible here, where you get to be the star in a fantasy uniquely your own.

CEREMONY CAPACITY: There are several spots on the grounds surrounding the Main House; each can accommodate hundreds of guests.

EVENT/RECEPTION & MEETING CAPACITY: The site holds 10–2,500 guests.

FEES & DEPOSITS: Half of the rental fee is required upon booking; the balance plus a refundable $1,000 security deposit are due 10 days prior to the event. The rental fee for the Ranch starts at $12,000 for up to 400 guests, plus $25/person for each person over 400. The rental fee for Chateau Le Dome is $6,000 for up to 100 guests; for Camp Cabernet, $7,500 for up to 300 guests; for the Oak Grove, $9,000 for up to 400 guests; and for the Garden Setting, $12,000 for up to 400 guests. For guest counts over 400 in the Garden and the Oak Grove, there is a $25/person charge for each additional guest. Security and valet parking are required; all service providers must be insured to perform services on the property.

AVAILABILITY: Year-round, daily, anytime.

SERVICES/AMENITIES:

Catering: select from preferred list or BYO, extra fee
Kitchen Facilities: prep only
Tables & Chairs: through caterer or preferred rental company
Linens, Silver, etc.: through caterer or preferred rental company
Restrooms: wheelchair access CBA
Dance Floor: BYO
Bride's & Groom's Dressing Areas: yes
AV/Meeting Equipment: CBA, extra charge

Parking: valet required, extra fee
Accommodations: no guest rooms
Outdoor Night Lighting: access only
Outdoor Cooking Facilities: CBA
Cleanup: caterer and renter
View: mountains, orchards, lawns and pastures, rose garden, vineyards

RESTRICTIONS:

Alcohol: wines purchased through Saddlerock
Smoking: not allowed
Music: amplified OK

Wheelchair Access: yes
Insurance: liability required
Other: security required, extra fee

The wedding vendors on our website are the best in the business. How do we know? Read page 577.

Serra Retreat

3401 Serra Road, Malibu
310/456-6631
www.premierepartyrents.com/serra-retreat
reservations@serraretreat.com

Franciscan Retreat Center

Rehearsal Dinners	● Corporate Events
● Ceremonies	● Meetings
● Wedding Receptions	Film Shoots
● Private Parties	Accommodations

Perched on a coastal bluff high above Malibu, Serra Retreat is a community of Spanish Mission-style buildings that has been home to the Franciscan Friars of California for over half a century. Although this facility was once available only for retreats, the Franciscans have opened their gates to couples who wish to wed in a place of great natural and spiritual beauty.

Named for Father Junipero Serra, the retreat encompasses 26 acres of pines, eucalyptus, flowering gardens and untamed wilderness. Meditative walking paths meander throughout the estate, leading the thoughtful wanderer to contemplative spots such as the Shrine of Fatima or a peaceful wooden bench overlooking the headlands.

Although Serra Retreat offers any number of nooks, courtyards and gardens for ceremonies, two sites stand out as sensational: the Chapel and the Junipero Serra Gardens. If you're leaning towards a traditional wedding, then the Serra Chapel will appeal to you. Designed in the round, with enormous windows set into every wall and blond pine beams supporting a lofty ceiling, this hilltop sanctuary affords spectacular views of the Santa Monica Mountains and the Pacific. Overhead, light cascades through a cupola skylight, burnishing the Mexican-tile floor.

A short stroll away are the Junipero Serra Gardens, one of the most breathtaking sites we've seen. Here brides make their entrance via a Malibu-tile staircase, stepping out onto a grassy promontory awash in flowers and shaded by towering pines. A quaint cobbled path running around the perimeter of the point makes a perfect bridal promenade. Couples say their vows at the west end of the gardens in front of a tall crucifix and statue of Junipero Serra. Apres ceremony, guests will naturally be drawn to the white stucco balustrade at the promontory's edge, delighting in the dizzying 360-degree view of the eastern mountains, wooded canyons and the sea's wide blue horizon.

While it is possible to host receptions in the Junipero Serra Gardens, your best bet is to stage festivities in the Bell Garden, closer to the hub of the retreat. Featuring an iron bell and cross, potted palms and intricate iron railings, this large sunny patio overlooks a bright blooming terrace garden. Indoor receptions can be held in the Mediterranean-style Serra or Dining Rooms, both of which provide views of the ocean and gardens. What's nice about the Serra Room (which was once the chapel in the original 1920s home) is the colorful and ornate Malibu tilework, set inside handcarved wood frames along one wall of the room.

Although Serra Retreat is a Catholic retreat center, people of all faiths are welcome here; the Franciscans ask only that guests remain mindful of the quiet beauty and grace that embody the spirit of this lovely place.

CEREMONY, EVENT/RECEPTION & MEETING CAPACITY: The site can accommodate 120 guests, maximum. The Dining Room seats 100 with room for a small dance area; the Serra Room seats 120. Slightly higher guest counts may be accommodated on a case by case basis.

FEES & DEPOSITS: For weddings and social events, a nonrefundable deposit of 50% of the site rental donation is required when the agreement is signed. The balance is due 60 days prior to the event. The tax deductible rental donation is $5,000 for the use of the entire property for a ceremony and reception, $2,000 for use of the Point or Chapel for a ceremony, and $3,500 for use of the Fountain Court for a reception. Professional event coordination is required. An 18% site representative charge is additional. Security and parking fees apply if the guest count is over 50.

AVAILABILITY: Year-round; Saturdays on a limited basis, Sundays 4–10pm.

SERVICES/AMENITIES:

Catering: select from preferred list
Kitchen Facilities: fully equipped
Tables & Chairs: provided, extra charge
Linens, Silver, etc.: provided, extra charge
Restrooms: wheelchair accessible
Dance Areas: provided, extra charge
Bride's & Groom's Dressing Areas: yes
AV/Meeting Equipment: CBA, extra charge

Parking: large lot; valet with over 100 guests
Accommodations: no guest rooms
Outdoor Night Lighting: access only
Outdoor Cooking Facilities: no
Cleanup: provided
View: 360-degree vista of mountains, ocean, canyons and gardens with creek

RESTRICTIONS:

Alcohol: provided by *Liquid Catering*
Smoking: designated area only
Music: amplified OK until 10pm

Wheelchair Access: yes
Insurance: certificate required
Other: no rice, birdseed, glitter or confetti; decorations restricted; cannot pick garden's flowers; children under 10 must be supervised

The Sunset Restaurant

6800 Westward Beach Road, Malibu

310/589-2027

www.thesunsetrestaurant.com
eventscoordinator@thesunsetrestaurant.com

Waterfront Restaurant

- Rehearsal Dinners
- Ceremonies
- Wedding Receptions
- Private Parties
- Corporate Events
- Meetings
- Film Shoots
- Accommodations

You can have it all—a romantic setting, delectable cuisine, and gracious service—at the Sunset Restaurant, tucked against the Malibu bluffs just steps from Zuma Beach. Housed in an updated version of a classic beach bungalow, the two-story restaurant breathes with space and light, thanks to the expanse of windows along the ocean-facing front wall. One of the many benefits of staging your wedding at the Sunset is the ease of having everything in one package. This venue is particularly event-friendly, with distinct areas that coordinate with each phase of a wedding celebration.

First, say your marriage vows right on the beach. For a fee that includes the city permit, the Sunset arranges a platform walkway, runner and a wood stage area with the blue Pacific as a vibrant backdrop. Other elements further enhance this idyllic place: Sailboats drift across the horizon...dolphins play in the surf...the sound of the waves is in soothing harmony with the music of your accompanist. As you walk down the aisle, a light breeze lifts your veil, which floats around you like sea foam. Your guests are entranced, and the fun is only beginning. (This writer knows from personal experience: She had her wedding here, and the guests are still raving!)

After the ceremony, your photographer captures dramatic photos of the bridal party during one of Malibu's jewel-toned sunsets. Meanwhile, your friends and family gather on the outdoor patio that adjoins the Event Room. Here they enjoy the cocktail hour and scrumptious hors d'oeuvres, while mingling around cocktail tables or relaxing on couches. You can add your own festive touches with colored paper lanterns, string lights or vibrant throw pillows.

When it's time for the reception, everyone moves into the Event Room. Simple, yet classy, its understated décor adapts easily to your own vision...but this room has a couple of tasteful features that add to your celebration: The white fabric lining the ceiling lends a wavy softness to the space, and a row of view-filled windows curves shoreward, like a long ripple in the nearby surf. At some point during your festivities, you might drift outside with your sweetheart to stroll on the sugary sand and soak up a bit of moonlight.

Two cozy upstairs venues, the North and South Rooms, prove that the views are even more spectacular from the second floor. Picture windows keep these spaces bathed in golden daylight, when the warm, cheery ambiance is perfect for wedding brunches or showers; at night, star-filled horizons and city-light vistas are sparkling additions to rehearsal dinners.

The Sunset Restaurant, which is open for weekend brunch as well as lunch and dinner every day, has a large number of regular (and often celebrity!) clientele and attracts more loyal fans every day. After paying a visit to this divine seaside locale, you're bound to become a regular, too.

CEREMONY CAPACITY: The beach site holds up to 150 seated guests.

EVENT/RECEPTION & MEETING CAPACITY: Indoors, the restaurant holds 120 seated with a dance floor or 150 without, or 200 standing guests. Outdoors the parking lot may be tented for 200 seated or 300 standing. The entire restaurant can be rented for larger parties.

FEES & DEPOSITS: 10% of the estimated event total (or $1,500) is required to reserve your date and another 50% is due 4 months prior to the event. Both deposits are nonrefundable. Rental fees range $500–10,000 depending on space and time rented and guest count. Meals range $45–110/person and there is a beverage minimum of $20/person. Tax, a 20% administration fee, and mandatory valet charges are additional.

AVAILABILITY: Year-round.

SERVICES/AMENITIES:

Catering: in-house; outside kosher caterer may be allowed, call for details
Kitchen Facilities: fully equipped
Tables & Chairs: provided
Linens, Silver, etc.: provided
Restrooms: wheelchair accessible
Dance Floor: yes
Bride's Dressing Area: CBA
AV/Meeting Equipment: BYO

Parking: valet
Accommodations: no guest rooms
Outdoor Night Lighting: CBA
Outdoor Cooking Facilities: CBA
Cleanup: provided
View: Malibu coastline, ocean
Other: beach ceremony

RESTRICTIONS:

Alcohol: in-house only, no BYO
Smoking: outside only
Music: amplified OK

Wheelchair Access: yes
Insurance: not required

California Yacht Club

Yacht Club

4469 Admiralty Way, Marina del Rey
310/448-4771 Catering Department
www.calyachtclub.com
cycater@calyachtclub.net

● Rehearsal Dinners	● Corporate Events
● Ceremonies	● Meetings
● Wedding Receptions	● Film Shoots
● Private Parties	Accommodations

Cleverly designed in an octagonal shape with glass walls that showcase a panoramic view of the harbor, California Yacht Club is a great place for a waterside wedding.

Lovers of the sea will naturally want to get married as close to the ocean as possible, and the Club has a stellar site: a triangular expanse of lawn that advances from the building and tapers to a rounded point in front of the water's edge. Couples exchange vows here, while their guests enjoy the sea air, glittering Pacific and the colorful parade of boats that pass by just beyond the point. After the ceremony, everyone strolls over to the adjacent patio for cocktails and hors d'oeuvres.

The Club itself is a handsome, two-story building that devotes its entire first floor to celebrations. Receptions take place in the spacious Fireside Room, named for its beautiful brick fireplace, which is set into a wall of windows. Before the dining begins, all eyes are on the bride, who makes a dramatic entrance as she gracefully descends a sweeping atrium staircase. The room's décor is completely up to your imagination—anything from a Polynesian buffet with tiki torches, hula dancers and a fire show (held outdoors), to a formal Black & White Ball. No matter where you sit you're virtually on the water, and the 180-degree view allows every guest to watch the sun set over the ocean.

For very large events, a custom-ordered tent can seat up to 250 beneath a 40-foot ceiling. This expansive space is a blank slate: Hang swags of fabric, add colored gel lights, or bring in a stage for a show or a 10-piece band. And no matter how you design the interior, a view of the water is always available.

The accommodating staff will customize every detail, so you'll get the event that you want along with a lovely location. This is a place where water surrounds you, flocks of sea birds fly overhead, and ships slip quietly in and out of the harbor. Set sail together at California Yacht Club.

CEREMONY CAPACITY: The Club's outdoor lawn holds 250 seated; the indoor Fireside Room 175 seated guests.

EVENT/RECEPTION CAPACITY: The Fireside Room can accommodate 175 seated with a dance floor or 250 for a cocktail reception. The Tent can hold up to 400 guests for cocktail reception or 270 for dining and dancing.

MEETING CAPACITY: The Gallery Room holds up to 36 seated; the Fireside Room up to 175 seated guests.

FEES & DEPOSITS: A nonrefundable deposit equal to the facility fee plus a percentage of the food & beverage minimum is required to secure your date and is applied to the event balance. The balance is due 10 days prior to the event. Luncheons range $38–48/person, dinners or buffets $42–65/person; alcohol, tax and a 20% service charge are additional.

AVAILABILITY: Year-round, daily, 9am–midnight. The Club is closed on Mondays and Tuesdays and is available for buyouts on those days.

SERVICES/AMENITIES:

Catering: in-house
Kitchen Facilities: yes
Tables & Chairs: provided
Linens, Silver, etc.: provided
Restrooms: wheelchair accessible
Dance Floor: portable provided, extra fee
Bride's & Groom's Dressing Areas: yes
AV/Meeting Equipment: CBA, extra fee

Parking: valet parking required
Accommodations: no guest rooms
Outdoor Night Lighting: access only
Outdoor Cooking Facilities: BBQs CBA
Cleanup: provided
View: marina, Pacific Ocean

RESTRICTIONS:

Alcohol: in-house, or corkage $15/bottle
Smoking: outdoors only
Music: amplified OK indoors until midnight, outdoors until 11:30pm

Wheelchair Access: yes
Insurance: required of all vendors
Other: no rice or birdseed

Hornblower Cruises & Events

Yachts

13755 Fiji Way, Marina del Rey
310/301-6000
www.hornblower.com
mdr@hornblower.com

● Rehearsal Dinners	● Corporate Events
● Ceremonies	● Meetings
● Wedding Receptions	● Film Shoots
● Private Parties	● Accommodations

If boats could talk, what tales the Hornblower Cruises and Events fleet could tell! Collectively, the five Marina del Rey-based yachts have entertained movie stars, politicians, playboys, and proletariat alike.

Set foot on an Hornblower Cruises and Events yacht and you encounter a classy operation: Each vessel is meticulously main-tained—it's as sleek and well-groomed as a thoroughbred. Mahogany and teak boiseries gleam; brass railings sparkle. Quality is the byword here. It defines all aspects of a Hornblower Cruises and Events event, from the gracious uniformed staff to the meals, which are exquisite in taste as well as presentation.

Weddings on board are exhilarating—exchange vows dockside or while the yacht's underway, plying the harbor's gentle waters. And if you want to take full advantage of the maritime motif, enlist the ship's captain to perform your ceremony.

Entertainer boasts two large, fully enclosed decks, each with a full bar and dance floor. With a full galley, high-quality sound system, and open-air lounge deck, she can accommodate 400 guests for seated dining or 550 for cocktails and a buffet. The aft deck provides a "back porch," additional deck space for guests who want to take in the sea air or dance under the stars!

Hornblower's nostalgic *Zumbrota* is a Roaring Twenties masterpiece rich in history: Mae West and Douglas Fairbanks both took their turns at ownership. The *Zumbrota* is a truly majestic vessel, showcasing walls paneled in Burmese teak, a bar with whimsical brass elephant-head fixtures and the wheelhouse's original compass.

Also available for events is the *Dream On*. This custom-built beauty, with a large main salon and comfortable bow area, provides all the modern features you might expect of a luxury liner. Guests can dine and dance on the roomy and fully enclosable upper deck, while taking in the spectacular view of the Marina del Rey harbor. Nice touches like wide staircases and a private "bride's cabin" right next to the ceremony area make having a wedding on board a breeze.

Hornblower Cruises and Events has other luxurious yachts in its fleet, so if none of these seems to fit your needs, let them match you up with just the right vessel for your celebration. Through the years, the seasoned Hornblower Cruises and Events staff has hosted more than 50,000 events!

And besides, what better way to begin life's journey together than with a buoyant send-off on a beautiful boat? It doesn't get much better than this.

CEREMONY & EVENT/RECEPTION CAPACITY: The yachts can accommodate 10–550 guests.

MEETING CAPACITY: The yachts can accommodate up to 350 seated guests.

FEES & DEPOSITS: A $1,000–8,000 deposit (depending on the vessel's size) is required to book a boat; the balance is payable 30 days prior to the event. Hornblower Cruises and Events offers wedding packages starting at $73/person that include boat rental, food, cake, non-alcoholic beverages and a ceremony by the captain. Hourly boat rental rates and à la carte services can also be arranged.

AVAILABILITY: Year-round, daily.

SERVICES/AMENITIES:

Catering: in-house, no BYO
Kitchen Facilities: n/a
Tables & Chairs: provided
Linens, Silver, etc.: provided
Restrooms: wheelchair access varies
Dance Floor: provided
Bride's & Groom's Dressing Areas: some yachts
AV/Meeting Equipment: provided

Parking: fee lots near dock
Accommodations: available on some yachts
Outdoor Night Lighting: yes
Outdoor Cooking Facilities: no
Cleanup: provided
View: ocean, bay views
Other: event coordination

RESTRICTIONS:

Alcohol: in-house, no BYO
Smoking: outdoors only
Music: amplified OK

Wheelchair Access: limited
Insurance: not required

Want to know WHAT TO ASK a potential location or vendor? Check out our Questions to Ask starting on page 21.

Casa del Mar

Oceanfront Hotel

1910 Ocean Way, Santa Monica

310/581-5533

www.hotelcasadelmar.com
sfriddle@hotelcasadelmar.com

- Rehearsal Dinners
- Corporate Events
- Ceremonies
- Meetings
- Wedding Receptions
- Film Shoots
- Private Parties
- Accommodations

During the Roaring Twenties, Santa Monica was the heart of California's Gold Coast, the chic stretch of beach that became the personal playground of L.A.'s elite. Of the many lavish beach clubs that were built during this era, Club Casa Del Mar was the uncontested Grande Dame. The building's Renaissance Revival architecture fed designers' imaginations.

Hand-painted ceilings, bronze statuary, and the poshest of furnishings gave the club an unrivaled elegance. The lively social scene, led by Hollywood celebrities and business magnates, tempted everyone who was anyone to take part in the excitement.

Casa del Mar survived the Depression, but World War II finally closed this stylish landmark. Now, a dedicated team of hotel developers has restored the Grande Dame to her former magnificence. This lavish restoration evokes the glamour and creative spirit of the hotel's glory days, while incorporating modern amenities that the discriminating guest has come to expect from a premier facility.

First, notice the brick-and-sandstone façade, decorative sculpted accents and the Mediterranean flair of a red-tile roof and iron balconies. The beautiful hotel is separated from the sand by palm trees and a promenade, but you enter streetside through an exquisite two-story door made of ornate stained glass. The foyer is a grand rotunda dominated by a wrought-iron chandelier and twin sweeping staircases inlaid with mosaic tiles. As you make your way up to the lobby, you hear the faint strains of a ragtime piano from a distant past as you're caught up in the magical ambiance. Your eyes take in the gorgeous rugs, intriguing Art Nouveau-inspired lighting fixtures and gold-inlaid ceilings before resting on the scintillating seascape visible through the tall windows lining the far wall. Design details throughout are an artful mix of the casual and the refined, ranging from Miami-style furnishings in the seaside restaurant to plush chairs and velvet sofas in the lobby living room. Warm fruitwood paneling and the soothing tones of peach, marine blue, and sage predominate. Comfort, a top priority here, is easy to come by: Enjoy a cocktail while lounging on the oceanside terrazza, unwind in the full-service spa, or curl up by one of the many fireplaces.

If you've come for a celebration, let the good times roll in the Casa's stunning ballroom, the Colonnade. Two-tiered Venetian glass chandeliers suspended from the sculpted ceiling gently illuminate the pale walls. Silk draperies in celadon and gold frame a wall of windows that reveal breathtaking Pacific sunsets. Open the doors, step out onto the loggia, and let a refreshing ocean breeze caress your cheek. The Colonnade can easily be divided into smaller sections to suit the size of your event, and several other well-appointed spaces are available for intimate dinners, business meetings, or conferences.

The entire restoration blends quality craftsmanship with nostalgic elegance. For a special event as original as the setting, experience the romance of Hotel Casa Del Mar.

CEREMONY & EVENT/RECEPTION CAPACITY: The Oceanview Colonnade holds 320 seated (with dance floor) or 500 standing guests.

MEETING CAPACITY: The Boardroom holds up to 18 guests seated conference-style. The Crimson Room holds up to 50 seated guests.

FEES & DEPOSITS: For weddings, a nonrefundable deposit of 40% of your food & beverage minimum is due to reserve your date. 40% of the anticipated event total is due 60 days prior to the event; the remaining balance is due 10 working days prior. Wedding packages start at $195/person for lunch, and range $245–280/person for dinner; alcohol, tax and a 22% service charge are included. A wedding planner is required for all weddings, and must be chosen from the venue's preferred list.

For meetings or business functions, room rental fees vary depending on room and/or services selected, and may be waived with food & beverage minimums or overnight accommodation minimums. A conference coordinator and business center are available.

AVAILABILITY: Year-round, daily, anytime until 1am.

SERVICES/AMENITIES:

Catering: in-house, no BYO
Kitchen Facilities: n/a
Tables & Chairs: provided
Linens, Silver, etc.: provided
Restrooms: wheelchair accessible
Dance Floor: provided, wood floor
Bride's & Groom's Dressing Areas: no
AV/Meeting Equipment: full AV, additional charge

Parking: on-site valet, extra charge
Accommodations: 129 guest rooms
Outdoor Night Lighting: yes
Outdoor Cooking Facilities: no
Cleanup: provided
View: Pacific Ocean, from Palos Verdes to Malibu

RESTRICTIONS:

Alcohol: in-house, no BYO
Smoking: nonsmoking hotel
Music: amplified OK indoors, acoustic only outdoors on the Ballroom Terrace

Wheelchair Access: yes
Insurance: hold harmless waiver required
Other: no rice

Le Méridien Delfina Santa Monica

Hotel

530 Pico Boulevard, Santa Monica
310/309-8020
www.lemeridiendelfina.com
delfina.sales@lemeridiendelfina.com

● Rehearsal Dinners	● Corporate Events
● Ceremonies	● Meetings
● Wedding Receptions	● Film Shoots
● Private Parties	● Accommodations

Le Méridien Delfina Santa Monica may remind you of that friend you secretly envy, the cosmopolitan and creative traveler who always seems to know about the hot gallery opening and latest dining craze…a veritable design diva who throws together an eye-catching outfit at a moment's notice. Always chic, always confident, she's the most interesting guest at a dinner party.

Like your hip friend, Le Méridien Delfina Santa Monica is a paragon of cutting-edge style. Perched on a gentle rise, this urban sanctuary commands a spectacular view of bustling Santa Monica and the ocean just a few blocks away. Its double-tall lobby instantly sets a fashion-forward tone: The interiors are a triumph of eclectic artistry, combining textures, shapes and global influences into an intriguing style matrix that nevertheless breathes soothing simplicity.

Coastal soirées often gather around the hotel's beautiful swimming pool for drinks and finger food. A trio of cabanas is wonderful for showcasing dramatic presentations of culinary masterpieces or your favorite VIPs—or use one of them as a cozy enclave for intimate conversation.

For the ultimate Le Méridien Delfina Santa Monica experience, bring your guests up to the top floor, where the Delfina Ballroom & Penthouse Foyer are the toast of the town. Stepping into the Foyer, your eyes go first to a row of windows that take in the city stretched out below and the coastline to the south. Handpicked artworks dress up the walls. Tastefully understated, the space is equally suitable for a corporate meet-and-greet or a classy cocktail reception. The Foyer might also be used in conjunction with the adjoining Lucina Room; cocktails go down just fine here as well, and your guests still enjoy that sweeping view.

Then for the main event, open the doors to the Delfina Ballroom. The hotel's signature décor perfectly complements the astounding view: A tapestry of breathtaking coastline, ocean waves, and rugged mountains in the distance fills two long walls of windows. As twilight fades to a rainbow-hued sunset, the stars and the city lights begin to sparkle on the horizon, adding extra pizzazz to your festivities.

Le Méridien Delfina Santa Monica offers wedding packages that include an oceanview Honeymoon Suite, so you and your spouse can sleep late while your out-of-town guests explore Santa Monica's many attractions.

Remember your trendsetting friend? She's about to announce that she's having her next private party here. It sure will be fun to see the look on her face when she hears that you've already booked the luxurious Le Méridien Delfina Santa Monica for your own upcoming wedding celebration!

CEREMONY CAPACITY: The Lucina Room holds up to 120 guests. Outdoors, the Terrazza Garden accommodates 120 and the ballroom seats up to 300 guests.

EVENT/RECEPTION CAPACITY: The Delfina Ballroom holds up to 300 seated or 500 standing guests, the Lucina Room holds up to 100 seated or 130 standing.

MEETING CAPACITY: The venue accommodates up to 500 guests.

FEES & DEPOSITS: 25% of the estimated event total is required to reserve your date; the balance is due 30 calendar days prior to the event. Wedding packages start at $124/person and include food, beverage and custom wedding cake. Tax and service charge are additional.

For meetings or business functions, meeting room costs are based on food, beverage and guest room requirements.

AVAILABILITY: Year-round, daily, 7am–midnight. Additional hours can be arranged.

SERVICES/AMENITIES:

Catering: in-house, or BYO with approval, extra fee
Kitchen Facilities: fully equipped
Tables & Chairs: provided
Linens, Silver, etc.: provided
Restrooms: wheelchair accessible
Dance Floor: provided
Bride's Dressing Area: yes
AV/Meeting Equipment: CBA

Parking: valet parking
Accommodations: 310 guest rooms
Outdoor Night Lighting: yes
Outdoor Cooking Facilities: no
Cleanup: provided
View: cityscape, mountains, ocean
Other: event coordination

RESTRICTIONS:

Alcohol: in-house, or wine and champagne only with corkage fee
Smoking: outdoors only
Music: amplified OK indoors with restrictions

Wheelchair Access: yes
Insurance: proof of insurance required for outside vendors

Shutters on the Beach

Oceanfront Hotel

1 Pico Boulevard, Santa Monica
310/587-1726

www.shuttersonthebeach.com
bhochberger@shuttersonthebeach.com

- Rehearsal Dinners
- Ceremonies
- Wedding Receptions
- Private Parties
- Corporate Events
- Meetings
- Film Shoots
- Accommodations

With an oceanfront address as stylish as its chic, unpretentious décor, Shutters outclasses most of the nearby hotel competition. Its crisp gray and white exterior, enlivened with flower-covered trellises and balconies, brings to mind an upscale version of the classic clapboard beach cottage. Inside, the attractive lobby gives guests their first experience of Shutters' snappy appeal. Original artwork, comfy sofas, and a stenciled ceiling contribute to an atmosphere that's both sophisticated and relaxed. A few steps from the lobby you'll find the pool, and one of the nicest outdoor terraces we've seen anywhere. Sunny, but sheltered, this spacious stone tiled deck commands a panoramic view of the ocean. Ceremonies are held here at day's end, just as the sun is setting and the sky is awash in color.

For receptions, Shutters offers function rooms of various sizes, all practical and attractively decorated in pale pastels with unique handcrafted light fixtures. The Grand Salon is the largest and most luxurious of the rooms, creating a refined ambiance for special celebrations. A floor-to-ceiling marble mantel holds a handsome fireplace, flanked by alternating panels of antiqued beveled mirrors and French moiré satin. The Grand Salon also boasts five spectacular Venetian chandeliers made of hand-blown glass "leaves."

The more intimate Promenade Room divides into three spaces, each of which opens onto an outdoor terrace. Another "room with a view" is the Beachside Room. Adjacent to Shutters' popular Coast Café & Bar, Beachside features hardwood flooring and wood millwork throughout, giving the space a warm and cozy feel with a spectacular view of the sea and sand. Rehearsal dinners, bridal and baby showers taking place in this room are unique and refreshing.

Shutters' many attractions include its resort-like accommodations. Rooms have sliding shuttered doors that open to a balmy Pacific breeze, and suites also include a fireplace lined with handmade tiles, and wood floors adorned with thick rugs. Marble baths with windows to the outside, and a host of thoughtful amenities make you feel like you're a guest in someone's exclusive beach house.

At the romantic Shutters, you can stage your entire wedding—from rehearsal dinner to honeymoon—right on one of the most beautiful beaches in the world.

CEREMONY CAPACITY: The Oceanview Pacific Terrace seats 220 for a ceremony; the Promenade Room and Terrace accommodate 140 seated or 200 standing.

EVENT/RECEPTION CAPACITY: The Grand Salon accommodates 220 seated (with dance floor) or 400 standing; the Pacific Terrace, 150 seated or 300 standing; the Promenade Room holds 140 seated or 200 standing. Beachside holds 90 seated or 150 standing guests.

MEETING CAPACITY: Several spaces hold 20–400 seated guests.

FEES & DEPOSITS: For weddings, a nonrefundable deposit of 40% of the food & beverage minimum is required to reserve your date; 40% of the estimated event total is due 60 days prior to the event and the remaining balance is due 10 working days prior. Wedding packages start at $195/person for lunch, and range $245–280/person for dinner. Alcohol, tax and a 22% service charge are included. A wedding planner is required for all weddings, and must be chosen from the venue's preferred list.

Room rental fees for business functions or meetings vary depending on room and/or services selected, and may be waived with food & beverage minimums or overnight accommodation minimums. Shutters has both a conference coordinator and a business center plus in-house audiovisual services.

AVAILABILITY: Year-round, daily, anytime until 1am.

SERVICES/AMENITIES:

Catering: in-house
Kitchen Facilities: n/a
Tables & Chairs: provided
Linens, Silver, etc.: provided
Restrooms: wheelchair accessible
Dance Floor: parquet floor
Bride's Dressing Area: no
AV/Meeting Equipment: full range; AV in-house

Parking: on-site valet, extra charge
Accommodations: 198 guest rooms
Outdoor Night Lighting: minimal provided
Outdoor Cooking Facilities: no
Cleanup: provided
View: Pacific Ocean, Santa Monica Mountains, Santa Monica Pier

RESTRICTIONS:

Alcohol: in-house, no BYO
Smoking: limited, outdoors only
Music: amplified OK indoors, acoustic outdoors

Wheelchair Access: yes
Insurance: hold harmless waiver required
Other: no rice or birdseed

The Victorian

2640 Main Street, Santa Monica
310/392-4956
www.thevictorian.com
info@thevictorian.com

Special Event Location

● Rehearsal Dinners	● Corporate Events
● Ceremonies	● Meetings
● Wedding Receptions	● Film Shoots
● Private Parties	Accommodations

Santa Monica is famous for trendy boutiques and bistros, oceanview resorts and powder-sand beaches … it's probably the last place you would expect to find a historic Victorian home and garden. Yet tucked inside Heritage Square on Santa Monica's Main Street, a pale yellow shingled mansion lends a turn-of-the-century gentility to the lively seaside town. This unexpected juxtaposition of old-fashioned glamour in a contemporary coastal milieu makes The Victorian a delightfully intriguing venue for formal banquets, family get-togethers and all sorts of parties—bridal couples in particular are drawn to the home's heirloom look and storied elegance.

Originally built near the Hotel Miramar in 1892 as the residence of one the neighborhood's founding families, the two-story building was moved to its current location in 1973. Heritage Square is a prime pocket of nostalgic architecture, with the California Heritage Museum and its sprawling lawn on one side and The Victorian on the other. Completely and carefully renovated, The Victorian has had its main rooms enlarged and added an exclusive speakeasy for a total of 15,000 square feet of event space including the landscaped grounds.

A brick path leading to the front door (and lined with candles and twinkle lights at night) curves among oak trees, blooming flowers and outdoor seating. As you enter, you're greeted by a polished oak bar, a congenial spot for cocktails, as are the home's two patios. Throughout, the décor is characteristic of the late 19th century—a mixture of fine antique furnishings, classical artwork and candles.

Couples often exchange vows upstairs in a lovely room with a built-in bar for champagne toasts and a covered veranda for pre-ceremony mingling. Open-air ceremonies are held on the Heritage Museum lawn or even on the beach, a short walk from here.

There's plenty of room both indoors and out for a sit-down reception or elegant buffet. The intimate main dining room features an octagonal enclave framed by tall windows at one corner, perfect for the bride and groom's table or to showcase the wedding cake. A line of French doors opens to a terrace, where guests sit among trees that seem to grow right up from the wooden floor and through the canopy. The terrace is enclosed for warmth and comfort, and guests are soothed by the sound of a nearby waterfall.

The Victorian boasts an experienced staff that will help you make the most of this unique property. They've even put together an inclusive wedding package that covers: meal service by their in-house caterer; beer, wine, champagne and soft bar; rental fee; on-site parking; a spacious dance floor; tables, linens and Chiavari chairs; and setup and breakdown—in other words, an easy and stress-free way to entertain.

The quaint home and its tranquil garden are awash in vintage charm, yet the salty tang in the air reminds visitors that the rolling waves are just one block away. With plenty of lodging options close by, your out-of-town guests will be thrilled with the opportunity to explore the local scene. Whether you fancy a cozy gathering or a lavish gala, the hospitality offered by The Victorian will lend your celebration the romantic sophistication of a bygone era.

CEREMONY CAPACITY: The Main Room holds 200 seated guests, the Museum Lawn up to 400, and the Upstairs Room up to 130 seated. A beach ceremony is also an option.

EVENT/RECEPTION CAPACITY: Indoors, the house accommodates 24–200 seated or 40–450 standing. Outdoors, the lawn holds 300 seated or 400 standing guests.

MEETING CAPACITY: Several spaces hold 30–200 seated guests.

FEES & DEPOSITS: A $1,500 nonrefundable deposit is required upon booking to secure your date. An additional $1,500 (also nonrefundable) is due 1 month from the initial deposit, 50% of the estimated event total is due 6 months prior and the remaining 50% is due 2 months prior to the event. Holiday rates apply. Guaranteed guest count is due 14 days prior and final payment is due 10 business days prior to the event.

Wedding packages run approximately $121/person depending on menu selected and guest count; the package price includes the site rental, sit-down dinner, dance floor, linens, Chiavari chairs, valet parking, and 3-hour bar service. Other special events begin at approximately $80/person for seated or cocktail-style receptions; tax, alcohol and a 20% service fee are additional. An extra fee applies to events on Saturday nights (and there is a food & beverage minimum). An outside coordinator is required.

Full-day meeting packages start at approximately $65/person including breakfast buffet, lunch, afternoon snack and unlimited nonalcoholic beverage service.

AVAILABILITY: Year-round, daily, anytime.

SERVICES/AMENITIES:

Catering: in-house
Kitchen Facilities: n/a
Tables & Chairs: provided
Linens, Silver, etc.: provided
Restrooms: wheelchair accessible 1st floor only
Dance Floor: provided
Bride's Dressing Area: provided
AV/Meeting Equipment: CBA

Parking: 100-car lot with attendant, valet CBA
Accommodations: no guest rooms
Outdoor Night Lighting: yes
Outdoor Cooking Facilities: no
Cleanup: provided
View: no
Kosher: outside kosher caterer with approval

RESTRICTIONS:

Alcohol: available
Smoking: outdoors only
Music: amplified OK indoors until 1:30am

Wheelchair Access: main floor only
Insurance: liability required
Other: no rice or sparklers

Want to find more venues and services? Check out our informative website, www.HereComesTheGuide.com.

215

Inn of the Seventh Ray

Restaurant

128 Old Topanga Canyon Road, Topanga

310/455-1311

www.innoftheseventhrayweddings.com
kellyhancock@innoftheseventhray.com

●	Rehearsal Dinners	●	Corporate Events
●	Ceremonies	●	Meetings
●	Wedding Receptions	●	Film Shoots
●	Private Parties		Accommodations

Looking for a unique garden setting for your special celebration? Consider the Inn of the Seventh Ray, voted L.A.'s most romantic restaurant for 20 years. Combining its natural surroundings with market-driven menus featuring fresh organic foods and wines, the Inn is one of California's original culinary agents for change, serving up much more than standard fare for four decades.

Minutes from the city in the heart of Topanga Canyon, the Inn hugs the bank of a gently flowing creek and is surrounded by greenery. Huge oak and pine trees grow through and over the restaurant's two terraces, filtering sunlight and creating a sense of intimacy. Looking at this bucolic setting, it's hard to believe that when owners Lucy and Ralph Yaney found it in 1973, it was a defunct auto junkyard. Undaunted, they walked over piles of old tires to the center of the site, where they felt an intense energy. The feeling was so strong they immediately decided to buy the property, even though they had absolutely no idea what they would do with it. Over the next couple of years, they developed an interest in natural food and a desire to do something that would benefit society, and although neither one had any experience running a restaurant, they opened the Inn of the Seventh Ray.

The name comes from the seventh ray of the colorful spectrum you see when light passes through a prism—it's the violet ray, signifying change. And since getting married constitutes a significant change in most people's lives, it seems perfectly fitting that the Inn hosts weddings. Ceremonies are held in the Fountain Courtyard, a brick-and-stone terrace with an elevated, wisteria-covered gazebo. After they exchange vows, the bride and groom join their guests seated below for the reception. The courtyard is enclosed by a wild mix of canyon foliage on three sides and the Garden Room on the fourth. Tables are arranged around a white fountain, and beneath a lattice wood trellis laced with honeysuckle. Although the Garden Room is generally used just for the bar, it's also a quasi-rustic setting for indoor receptions, with a glass ceiling, latticed walls, tall plants, and a fireplace.

The Creekside Patio, not surprisingly, sits just above the creek and stretches along it for about a hundred feet. A narrow version of the Fountain Courtyard, it's framed by sycamores, and bordered by bushes and a low brick wall. Just behind the patio is the Church Room, the Inn's original structure. Once a gospel church, it's also rumored to have been Aimée Semple MacPherson's private mountain retreat in the '30s. Now a dining room, this ivy-covered building still feels a little like a country chapel, with its steeply peaked, open-beamed ceiling and arched stained-glass windows.

A series of clear, UV-rated, octagonal tents are placed over the patios. Open on the sides in summer and heated during winter months, they give diners access to everything around them and permit outdoor celebrations any time of year. Meals are pesticide- and additive-free, and the food is 80–95% organic, including the free-range meat and poultry. Fish is wild, and fresh seasonal vegetables come from local organic farms. The restaurant has a staunchly loyal clientele whose allegiance is spiritual as well as gastronomical: The Inn's unique bookstore is stocked with books that inspire, and the gazebo—purported to have a special energy—is considered a charmed spot for ceremonies. The soul-satisfying union of uplifting garden atmosphere and high-quality food puts the Inn of the Seventh Ray in a class by itself.

CEREMONY CAPACITY: The Fountain Courtyard and Creekside Patio combined hold up to 225 guests.

EVENT/RECEPTION CAPACITY: Indoors, the Inn accommodates 48–65 guests. Outdoor areas hold 70–220 seated or 80–260 standing guests.

MEETING CAPACITY: Meeting space is available for 135 seated guests.

FEES & DEPOSITS: A rental fee deposit plus a $1,000 coordinator fee are required to reserve your date, and the balance of the estimated total is due 2 weeks prior to the event. The rental fee ranges $1,200–6,500 depending on the day, date and time of the event, and the guest count. Meals start at $46/person for a brunch buffet and $55/person for plated dinners and full service. Tax, alcohol and a 20% service charge are additional.

AVAILABILITY: Year-round.

SERVICES/AMENITIES:

Catering: in-house
Kitchen Facilities: n/a
Tables & Chairs: provided
Linens, Silver, etc.: provided
Restrooms: wheelchair accessible
Dance Floor: patio
Bride's Dressing Area: yes
AV/Meeting Equipment: microphone available

Parking: valet
Accommodations: nearby bed & breakfast inns
Outdoor Night Lighting: yes
Outdoor Cooking Facilities: n/a
Cleanup: provided in fees
View: Topanga Creek and mountains
Other: event coordination

RESTRICTIONS:

Alcohol: BWC provided or BYO
Smoking: designated area outdoors
Music: amplified OK with volume limits

Wheelchair Access: yes
Insurance: not required
Other: no rice

Friendly Hills Country Club

Country Club

8500 South Villaverde Drive, Whittier
562/698-0331 X303

www.friendlyhillscc.com
bakuramoto@friendlyhillscc.com

●	Rehearsal Dinners	●	Corporate Events
●	Ceremonies	●	Meetings
●	Wedding Receptions	●	Film Shoots
●	Private Parties		Accommodations

This green oasis on Whittier's north side is everything you expect in a traditional country club: A curving pine-and-oleander lined road whisks you up to its gate, and there's a sea of trees at the entrance and a feeling of leafy quiet once you arrive. When you do hear sounds, they're the happy shouts of children romping around the club pool while their moms and dads laze about chatting and laughing.

The clubhouse exterior is creamy white stucco with wide chocolate-colored wood beams and trim. Its look is one of simple sophistication, with Craftsman-style good proportions. But the focus here is on the outdoors, where all wedding ceremonies are held (yes, the weather is that good). They take place on a tiled terrace whose backdrop, the golf course's 1st and 18th holes, is easily the visual highlight of Friendly Hills. The fairways rise, side by side, up a commanding slope that disappears into the distance. Between them, a long cascade of water, with willows, firs and sycamores strung along its course, spills its way over large boulders to a small lake next to the terrace. The lake, populated with plump swans and ducks, can be reached via an elegant stonefaced bridge that makes a perfect photo op site.

You can't help but constantly gaze at this combination of water, greenery and dramatic ascent, which is why few brides choose to wed under an arch here. The backdrop is all the decoration you need.

Friendly Hills has two excellent places to hold a post-ceremony party: a downstairs banquet room, and an upper reception area that can be used alone or in combination with an adjacent sleek bar. The downstairs space has a wall of tall windows facing the club's signature first and last holes, and a full-service bar at the far end of room. Flattering indirect lighting along with natural light from outside keeps the place wonderfully well lit. Glass doors lead to the terrace, which is dotted with canopies for sheltering guests.

The upper reception area, off the clubhouse's elegant lobby, has white truss ceilings and big windows looking onto the course. Just a few steps down from it is an elegant bar, finished in warm brown tones of leather and wood. Invitingly soft leather lounge seats are arranged beside a bank of 10-foot-high windows, offering perhaps the best view in the house. The bar—subdued, simple and classy—is a very agreeable place where guests can lift heartfelt toasts to the newlyweds.

Whoever designed Friendly Hills understood the dynamics of heat and light. Southern California's almost year-round equable climate and golden sun make this club a bright, exhilarating wedding venue. Yet, when the excitement of the day is done and cooling shadows creep over the terrace, your psyche is gently tugged into a restful, stress-free zone. You quietly chat with your guests, watching the sunset's light burnish the fairways, taking in a memorable moment and scene. Heavenly!!!

CEREMONY, EVENT/RECEPTION & MEETING CAPACITY: The location holds 250 seated or 400 standing guests.

FEES & DEPOSITS: A $2,500 deposit is required to reserve your date, and the balance is due 7 days prior to the event. The event minimum ranges $1,000–8,000 depending on the space, day and time rented, and guest count. Meals range $22–90/person. Tax, alcohol and a 20% service charge are additional. A buyout option is available.

AVAILABILITY: Year-round, daily.

SERVICES/AMENITIES:

Catering: in-house, no BYO
Kitchen Facilities: n/a
Tables & Chairs: provided
Linens, Silver, etc.: provided
Restrooms: wheelchair accessible
Dance Floor: provided
Bride's Dressing Area: yes
AV/Meeting Equipment: some provided, more CBA

Parking: large complimentary lot
Accommodations: no guest rooms
Outdoor Night Lighting: yes
Outdoor Cooking Facilities: BBQ
Cleanup: provided
View: waterfall, lake, forest, fountain, hills
Other: event coordination, grand piano

RESTRICTIONS:

Alcohol: in-house, BYO wine & champagne with corkage fee
Smoking: outside only
Music: amplified OK

Wheelchair Access: yes
Insurance: not required

San Gabriel Valley

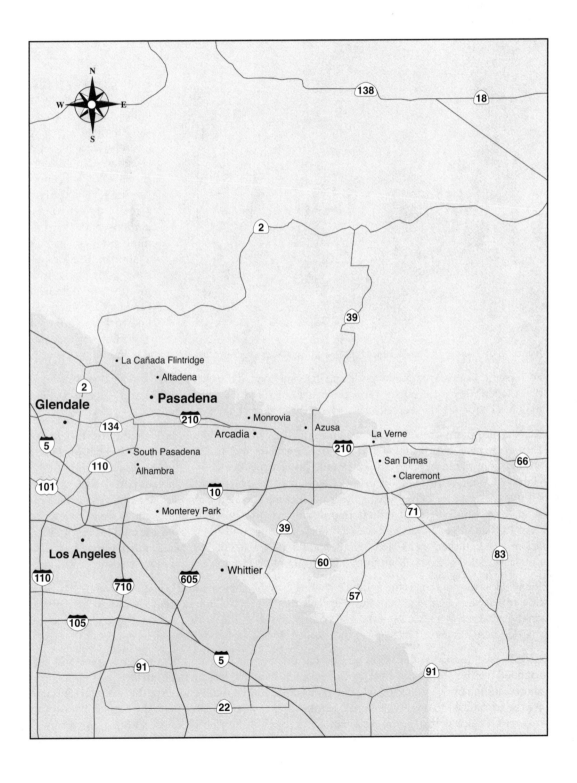

Altadena Town & Country Club

Country Club

2290 Country Club Drive, Altadena
626/794-7163
www.altaclub.com
sandy@altaclub.com

● Rehearsal Dinners	● Corporate Events
● Ceremonies	● Meetings
● Wedding Receptions	● Film Shoots
● Private Parties	Accommodations

Residing at the foot of the San Gabriel Mountains is the serenely beautiful Altadena Town & Country Club. It's hard to believe that this gorgeous estate—encompassing several verdant acres of tennis courts, gardens and a swimming pool—began as a simple, Craftsman-style bungalow. Built in 1910, the Altadena Country Club (as it was known then) weathered a stormy adolescence; floods, Santa Anas and the Great Depression nearly caused its ruin at several points along the way.

Fortunately, in 1946 community pride and ingenuity ended the club's run of bad luck. Rechristened the Altadena Town & Country Club, the facility matured into what it is today: a gracious, gabled multilevel structure that serves as a very stylish place to hold a celebration.

A handsome porte-cochère directs you through the club's front doors and into the Foyer. Here, it's easy to imagine guests sinking into the cozy armchairs and musing to the melodies of Cole Porter issuing from the black baby grand. Double doors on either side of the Foyer swing open to the club's ballrooms—the Mendocino and Victorian Rooms. Depending on your party's size, you can reserve these spaces either separately or in tandem. The Mendocino Room features a Craftsman-style wood-paneled ceiling and enormous windows that provide ample light as well as views of the San Gabriel Mountains and the club's expansive grounds. More sophisticated is the Victorian Room, distinguished by its blond hardwood floors, ornamental fireplace and charming bay window. Parties may also spill out from the Victorian Room onto the club's lovely covered veranda.

Right below the veranda is the South Lawn. Enclosed by tall trees, and bordered by stone benches, flowerbeds and an arbor, it's a private enclave that works well for a ceremony. Guests can mingle on the grass, enjoying views of the golf course as well as the garden setting. If you choose to get married here, it's just a few steps to the adjacent Victorian Room for your reception.

Couples also marry on the Wedding Court, a pristine patio shaded by a towering pine and surrounded by lawn, roses and crisp green hedges. A stairway descending from the club's upper level showcases the bride's entrance, while a trellis at the court's south end serves as an exquisite frame for the exchange of vows. One more reception area is also available here: the Terrace Room with a spacious balcony that shows off a panoramic view of the club grounds. Sporting green canvas umbrellas and an abundance of bright blooming terracotta pots, the Terrace's refreshing open-air atmosphere makes it a popular event spot.

The Altadena Town & Country Club has also been a favorite site for a number of film shoots. *Wonder Years, Speechless, Dirty Dancing* and *Starsky & Hutch* have all taken advantage of this classy backdrop. Why not follow their cue and reserve the club for your own production?

CEREMONY CAPACITY: The outdoor area holds 240 seated or standing guests; a variety of rooms inside the Clubhouse can accommodate 50–240 seated.

EVENT/RECEPTION CAPACITY: Several areas accommodate 100–240 seated guests.

MEETING CAPACITY: Several spaces accommodate 20–240 seated guests.

FEES & DEPOSITS: For weddings, a nonrefundable $1,000–1,500 deposit per room is required to secure your date. The rental fee for the Wedding Court or South Lawn is $1,000. For other spaces, the setup charges run $5/person/room. Half of the estimated total is payable 90 days prior to the event, an additional 25% is due 60 days prior, and the balance is due 30 days prior.

Wedding packages range $70–85/person and include hors d'oeuvres, complete meal, wedding cake, champagne toast, wine with dinner, bartender and bar setup, room setup, parking security guard, a night's stay for the bride and groom at one of the participating hotels, service charges and tax. À la carte menus run $30–42/person plus alcohol, tax and a 20% service charge. For business functions or meetings, rates will vary depending on the rooms and services selected. Call for additional information.

AVAILABILITY: Year-round, daily. Ceremonies take place before sunset only. Closed on Christmas and New Year's Eve.

SERVICES & AMENITIES:

Catering: in-house, no BYO
Kitchen Facilities: n/a
Tables & Chairs: provided
Linens, Silver, etc.: provided
Restrooms: wheelchair accessible
Dance Floor: hardwood floors provided
Bride's & Groom's Dressing Areas: yes
AV/Meeting Equipment: CBA, extra fee

Parking: large lots, valet
Accommodations: no guest rooms
Outdoor Night Lighting: no
Outdoor Cooking Facilities: CBA
Cleanup: provided
View: San Gabriel Mountains, golf course, landscaped grounds and pool area

RESTRICTIONS:

Alcohol: in-house, no BYO
Smoking: designated areas
Music: amplified OK with volume limits; acoustic music only on the south lawn

Wheelchair Access: yes
Insurance: not required
Other: no rice or open flames

Lindley-Scott House and Gardens

Private Estate

710 & 720 East Foothill Boulevard, Azusa
626/334-5215

www.lindleyscotthouse.com
historicallindleyscotthouse@gmail.com

	Rehearsal Dinners	●	Corporate Events
●	Ceremonies	●	Meetings
●	Wedding Receptions	●	Film Shoots
●	Private Parties		Accommodations

What is it that draws us to vintage houses? Maybe it's their grace and elegance, which reminds us of a bygone era when artisans had pride in their work and people took their time. One such place is the historic Lindley-Scott House and Gardens, a serene private estate in the San Gabriel foothills.

The Georgian-style home was built in 1911 by famed architect Robert D. Farquhar, and it's sheltered from the outside world by tall trees, green hedgerows and wrought-iron gates. A curving driveway climbs to the stately two-story home, painted a cheery yellow with green shutters and white trim. A garden setting surrounds the house, featuring a wide expanse of lawn with a majestic cypress, a California live oak and other lush foliage.

In keeping with the home's nostalgic feeling, some brides make their grand entrance in a horse-drawn carriage or an antique auto. But most often the bride and her attendants prepare upstairs in the Victorian-style dressing room. From here she descends the classic staircase in the Lindley-Scott foyer, then steps outside and follows a walkway between the trees to meet her groom at a storybook staging area—an arched arbor bordered by a pair of white picket fences with potted plants and flowers. Another romantic site for saying "I do" is near the Carriage House—it's a secluded white gazebo standing on a carpet of manicured grass ringed with hedges and trees.

After vows are exchanged, the bridal party makes use of the picturesque grounds for photos. One of the most photogenic spots is the Rose Garden, filled with fragrant blooms that serve as a natural—and colorful—backdrop. Guests enjoy coming here, too: There's a lawn bordered by Jacaranda trees where they can mingle…or simply stop to smell the roses!

Receptions take place in the magnificent Carriage House. Its white-columned portico welcomes family and friends into an elegant ballroom, where vintage-style chandeliers suspended from the lofty ceiling illuminate the dining and dancing. An abundance of natural light flows in through a wall of windows and French doors, which open to a cozy patio overlooking the beautifully landscaped grounds.

In contrast to events at many private estates, a celebration at Lindley-Scott House and Gardens is "one-stop shopping": Everything you'll need for a stylish reception is included in your wedding package, like a choice of wedding cakes and linen colors—even a keyboardist! All you'll have to do is thank your guests for coming and receive their enthusiastic compliments.

CEREMONY CAPACITY: The garden holds up to 200 seated.

EVENT/RECEPTION & MEETING CAPACITY: The facility accommodates 200 seated guests indoors in the Carriage House.

FEES & DEPOSITS: A 25% nonrefundable deposit is required to reserve your date. 50% of the total is due 90 days prior, and the balance is due 1 month prior to the event. Meals range $47–65/person; tax, alcohol and a 20% service charge are additional. There's also a $950 ceremony setup fee.

AVAILABILITY: Year-round, Friday, Saturday, Sunday, until midnight.

SERVICES/AMENITIES:

Catering: in-house
Kitchen Facilities: n/a
Tables & Chairs: provided
Linens, Silver, etc.: provided
Restrooms: wheelchair accessible
Dance Floor: oak parquet floor
Bride's Dressing Area: yes
AV/Meeting Equipment: CBA, extra fee

Parking: on-site or street
Accommodations: no guest rooms
Outdoor Night Lighting: yes
Outdoor Cooking Facilities: CBA
Cleanup: provided
View: landscaped grounds, lawns and garden
Other: bar service, event coordination, organist for ceremonies, PA system

RESTRICTIONS:

Alcohol: in-house
Smoking: outside only, designated areas
Music: amplified OK

Wheelchair Access: yes
Insurance: not required
Other: no rice, birdseed, confetti or open flames

This is important! Tell locations you're reading HERE COMES THE GUIDE and ask if our information is still current.

225

Descanso Gardens

1418 Descanso Drive, La Cañada Flintridge

818/949-4291

www.descansogardens.org
weddings@descansogardens.org

Rehearsal Dinners	● Corporate Events
● Ceremonies	● Meetings
● Wedding Receptions	● Film Shoots
● Private Parties	Accommodations

As you drive down the quiet, oak-lined residential street that leads to the Gardens, you get your first taste of this facility's peaceful seclusion. Living up to its name (*descanso* means "rest" in Spanish), Descanso Gardens is indeed a tranquil, verdant oasis at the foot of the arid San Gabriel Mountains.

Once a large private estate, the Gardens occupy over 150 acres, offering a wide variety of enchanting sites for weddings. One favorite is a quintessential California setting—a broad, open lawn under wide-spreading coast live oaks that convey a rustic simplicity.

Another option is the Magnolia Lawn. A wall of lattice entwined with crabapple vines and ruby-red buds marks the entrance, and guests pass beneath a pretty archway before taking their seats facing a pair of mature magnolia trees. The trees serve as a natural altar for the bride and groom, while their creamy white flowers evoke a feminine grace. The surrounding greenery is punctuated by seasonal surprises—think cheery tulips in April and perfumed paperwhites in late autumn—enhance the picturesque environs.

If you're exchanging vows with a few family and friends looking on, then consider the serene Japanese Garden. Your guests cluster along the bank of a koi-filled stream as you share your first kiss in front of the Full Moon Tea House. An orange footbridge and springtime show of pink cherry blossoms create a colorful, exotic milieu for photos.

And who can resist the romance of a rose garden? Descanso's five-acre International Rosarium boasts over 4,000 rosebushes. Couples can wed at the wrought-iron Rose Garden gazebo, and continue their outdoor celebration in a timber-and-stone pavilion bordered by fragrant blooms.

Seated receptions can also be held in the classic Boddy House, poised at the edge of the oak forest. Larger gatherings convene in Van de Kamp Hall, which is situated near the Garden's main entrance. This Craftsman-style building boasts a lofty open-beamed ceiling and French doors that open onto a lovely and expansive tiled courtyard flanked by flowerbeds and a bubbling natural-rock fountain.

With its shade-dappled lawns, brilliant flowers, majestic camellia forests and secluded woodland clearings, Descanso Gardens is just the right wedding spot for any nature-loving couple. But whether you get married here or not, a visit to the gardens is a tonic to urban stresses and—dare we suggest it—frayed prenuptial nerves. You can breathe easy in this serene setting, or, as they say in Spanish, *aquí puede usted descansar.*

CEREMONY CAPACITY: Various outdoor locations hold up to 300 seated guests.

EVENT/RECEPTION CAPACITY: Van de Kamp Hall holds 180 seated; the Rose Garden Pavilion holds 180 seated guests. The Boddy House seats 50 guests indoors or 90 guests outdoors.

MEETING CAPACITY: Van de Kamp Hall holds 250 seated theater-style or 125 conference-style; Classrooms Maple and Birch each hold 50 seated theater- or conference-style, and Minka Room holds 20 seated.

FEES & DEPOSITS: The rental fee starts at $3,600 for a ceremony only, $4,600 for a reception only, or $6,200 for both. Discounted rates are available on Friday and Sunday.

For ceremonies or receptions, a nonrefundable $1,000 deposit is required when the date is booked. Half the rental fee is due 6 months prior to the event; the balance is payable 2 months prior. For other special events, a 50% deposit is required with a signed contract; the balance is due 30 days prior to the event. The site has an in-house caterer. Wedding packages start at $100/person. Tax and service charge are included, alcohol is additional.

For meetings, rental fees run $425–2,500, depending on room, guest count, day of week and time frame. Half of the estimated event total is required to reserve your date; the balance is payable 1 month prior to the event.

AVAILABILITY: Indoors year-round, daily, except Christmas. Business meetings, 8am–4pm or 5pm–10pm; wedding ceremonies 5pm–7pm. Evening receptions, 5pm–10pm; at Van de Kamp Hall, the time can be extended until 11pm on Fridays and Saturdays for an additional fee.

SERVICES/AMENITIES:

Catering: in-house
Kitchen Facilities: n/a
Tables & Chairs: provided
Linens, Silver, etc.: provided
Restrooms: wheelchair accessible
Dance Floor: provided
Bride's Dressing Area: yes
AV/Meeting Equipment: PA system, 2 microphones

Parking: two large complimentary lots
Accommodations: no guest rooms
Outdoor Night Lighting: yes
Outdoor Cooking Facilities: n/a
Cleanup: provided
View: rose garden, stream and koi pond, lawns, woods, estate home

RESTRICTIONS:

Alcohol: in-house
Smoking: not allowed
Music: amplified OK

Wheelchair Access: yes
Insurance: liability required

Wedgewood Sierra La Verne

Event Center

6300 Country Club Drive, La Verne
866/966-3009

www.wedgewoodbanquet.com
events@wedgewoodbanquet.com

● Rehearsal Dinners	● Corporate Events
● Ceremonies	● Meetings
● Wedding Receptions	● Film Shoots
● Private Parties	Accommodations

This peaceful oasis of green, nestled in the foothills of the San Gabriel Mountains, has always held an allure for wedding couples. And, since Sierra La Verne Country Club is part of the Wedgewood family of event venues, there's the added value and convenience of knowing that everything for your big day will be handled perfectly from start to finish.

Tucked away at the end of a quiet residential street, this private golf club encompasses more than 100 verdant acres of rolling hills, manicured fairways and two very different spots for outdoor ceremonies, each with its own distinctive charms.

The Garden Ceremony Site near the main entry feels like a secret hideaway, with its tall hedges and white wooden canopy that welcomes you and your guests. A paved center aisle cuts through the wide swath of grass and leads to a red-roofed gazebo where you can exchange vows. The nice variety of lush plantings, enhanced by twinkle lights entwined in the hedges, create a soft, romantic mood.

If your idea of romance runs a bit more to a rustic, natural setting, then the Scenic Ceremony Site is for you. Like a clearing in the woods, it's a large grassy dell bordered by a mix of palm, oak and birch trees with the majestic mountains rising in the background. Anchoring this "great outdoors" space is a wonderful old wrought-iron arch where you can hang crystals, flowering vines—even mason jars for a bohemian look. Complete the scene with scattered rose petals down the center aisle.

Once everyone's ready to celebrate, head to Sierra La Verne's sprawling, multilevel clubhouse. The red brick exterior is highlighted with hunter green awnings, pillars festooned with lights, and a long breezeway. (Photo op alert: Snap a few pix snuggled on a vintage bench framed by one of the brick arches or a take a group shot atop the lobby's staircase).

The club's Terrace Room, which includes a foyer, boasts a wall of glass doors that not only provide lots of natural light and great golf course and pond views, but also lead out to an expansive, wraparound terrace—perfect for late night stargazing! Inside, you'll appreciate the large hardwood dance floor (with a mirrored ceiling) and raised stage for your DJ or sweetheart table.

Or opt for the Sierra View Room, where picture windows offer bird's-eye vistas of the golf course, treetops and those awesome mountain peaks. This high-ceilinged, flexible space, complete with fireplace, works for intimate receptions, bridal showers, and even an indoor ceremony.

Whichever spot you choose, their experienced staff can help you pick the best package for your budget. It's really simple: start with a beautiful venue, add a company known for reliable service, then relax and enjoy your day.

CEREMONY, EVENT/RECEPTION & MEETING CAPACITY: The site holds up to 250 guests.

FEES & DEPOSITS: 25% of the estimated total event cost is required to reserve your date. An additional 25% is due 120 days prior to the event and the balance (based on your final guest count) is due 10 days prior. All payments are credited towards your final balance and are nonrefundable and nontransferable. All-inclusive, completely customizable wedding packages start at $42/person. Tax, alcohol and a 21–22% service charge are additional.

AVAILABILITY: Year-round, daily, 6am–midnight.

SERVICES/AMENITIES:

Catering: in-house
Kitchen Facilities: n/a
Tables & Chairs: provided
Linens, Silver, etc.: CBA
Restrooms: wheelchair accessible
Dance Floor: yes
Bride's Dressing Area: yes
AV/Meeting Equipment: provided
Other: in-house florals and wedding cake; clergy on staff; event coordination

Parking: large lot
Accommodations: no guest rooms
Outdoor Night Lighting: yes
Outdoor Cooking Facilities: no
Cleanup: provided
View: garden, fountain, lake, landscaped grounds; panorama of trees, fairways, hills and San Gabriel Mountains

RESTRICTIONS:

Alcohol: in-house
Smoking: outdoors only
Music: amplified OK

Wheelchair Access: yes
Insurance: not required
Other: no rice, confetti or glitter; no open flames

Brookside Golf Club

Golf Club

1133 Rosemont Avenue, Pasadena

888/212-4652

www.countryclubreceptions.com
www.brooksidegc.com
privateevents@brooksidegc.com

● Rehearsal Dinners	● Corporate Events
● Ceremonies	● Meetings
● Wedding Receptions	● Film Shoots
● Private Parties	Accommodations

If you think golf clubs are haughty and pretentious, then you haven't been to Brookside. Nestled in the picturesque arroyo next to Pasadena's famed Rose Bowl, and surrounded by palm trees and two championship golf courses, this impeccably maintained golf club will enfold you in its warm hospitality. From its humble beginnings in 1920, Brookside has grown into one of Southern California's most popular golf courses.

When you plan a special event at the completely renovated club, you have several distinctive options to choose from. The largest is the Mediterranean Room. Combining a clean, contemporary feel with Spanish details, it works equally well for weddings, fundraisers and corporate events. Recessed antiqued-brass chandeliers provide nighttime illumination, while sunshine streams in through glass walls during the day. One "wall" looks directly out onto a verdant golf course; another faces the adjacent patio with its panorama of emerald fairways in the background. Many couples exchange vows beneath a flower-festooned pergola on the patio, and then bring their guests inside for a seated reception.

Adjoining the Mediterranean Room is an inviting suite for the bride, outfitted with a vanity, comfortable couches and floral accents. There's plenty of space for her entourage, and while they're all preparing for the ceremony they're fortified with champagne and hors d'oeuvres. This room also doubles as a lounge for guests who want a bit of private relaxation during the festivities.

Brookside Restaurant, in a separate location on the club's grounds, is also extremely popular for receptions, rehearsal dinners and parties. Its centerpiece is a floor-to-ceiling, double-sided river rock fireplace that warms the entire space. Arched picture windows along two walls frame views of the manicured greens as well as the San Gabriel Mountains in the distance. The adjoining covered patio lets guests dine al fresco while savoring the beautiful surroundings.

Several other spaces at the club are perfect for smaller events like rehearsal dinners, business meetings, wedding showers or luncheons. Each one offers a unique ambiance: The Arroyo Room reflects Pasadena's history with black & white photos from the turn of the century; the Madrid

Room features floor-to-ceiling windows with wonderful views of the Rosemont Avenue hills; and the Rose Room showcases classic paintings that depict great moments from the Tournament of Roses. All of these spaces can be outfitted with a full range of audiovisual equipment.

Whether you want a casual celebration right on the golf course or a five-course gourmet banquet, you can bet that the Brookside family will treat you like one of their own.

CEREMONY CAPACITY: Outdoors, the Mediterranean Patio accommodates up to 250 seated guests. Indoors, the Mediterranean Room holds 300 seated.

EVENT/RECEPTION & MEETING CAPACITY: The Mediterranean Room holds 300 seated for dining, 400 for standing receptions, and 200 seated classroom-style. Seated capacities for other spaces are: the Brookside Restaurant, 150; the Arroyo Room, 80; the Madrid Room, 50; and the Rose Room, 50.

FEES & DEPOSITS: A nonrefundable deposit, which is applied to your food & beverage total, is required to reserve your date. The amount of the deposit varies depending on how far in advance you book. Payment terms for the balance also vary, and may be arranged on an individual basis. Wedding packages start at $48/person. Tax, alcohol and service charge are additional. Food & beverage minimums may apply. Menus and packages can be customized to fit your needs and budget. Call for details.

AVAILABILITY: Year-round, daily.

SERVICES/AMENITIES:
Catering: in-house, or BYO
Kitchen Facilities: n/a
Tables & Chairs: provided
Linens, Silver, etc.: provided
Restrooms: wheelchair accessible
Dance Floor: portable available, nominal charge
Bride's and Groom's Dressing Area: provided
AV/Meeting Equipment: nominal fee for screens, podiums, large-screen TV and microphones; all other equipment CBA

Parking: lots, street, complimentary
Accommodations: no guest rooms
Outdoor Night Lighting: yes
Outdoor Cooking Facilities: BBQ
Cleanup: provided
View: flower garden; overlooking golf course and Arroyo
Other: event coordination

RESTRICTIONS:
Alcohol: in-house, or BYO wine or champagne only with corkage fee
Music: amplified OK outdoors until 10pm and indoors until 1am.

Smoking: outdoors only, at least 20 feet away from the building
Wheelchair Access: yes
Insurance: required for vendors

Castle Green

99 South Raymond Avenue, Pasadena
626/793-0359
www.castlegreen.com
events@castlegreen.com

Historic Landmark

Rehearsal Dinners	● Corporate Events
● Ceremonies	● Meetings
● Wedding Receptions	● Film Shoots
● Private Parties	Accommodations

The ornate rooftops of this inviting Pasadena landmark soar high above Old Pasadena, advertising Castle Green as a unique place to hold a special event. Once a posh hotel, this grand 1898 building is designed in an unusual style called Moorish Colonial, an arresting mixture of European and Middle Eastern architectural elements. Several towers capped with red domes and wrought-iron balconies lend the castle its handsome and distinctive silhouette. Also of visual interest is a whimsical bridge that extends from the main façade and connects the two wings of the historic building.

If you get married here, your ceremony can be held in the Ballroom or in the surrounding garden, which is landscaped with tall, graceful palms and a tranquil fountain that trickles into a lily pool, evoking a feel of Old World romance.

The castle's interior displays a wealth of late Victorian splendor, like a pair of massive oak doors that invite guests into a lofty lobby with a sweeping marble staircase and crystal chandelier. To the left you'll find a cluster of impressive "sitting" rooms, including the spacious Main Salon and the circular Moorish Room. These now possess their original, turn-of-the-century colors of deep rose, soft green and ochre. The original antique furnishings, warm wood mouldings, and extraordinary fireplaces complete the lovely and singular décor.

A grand hallway takes you to the Ballroom, where silent movie stars Rudolph Valentino and Lilian Gish once danced the night away by the light of the moon, streaming in through a wall of arched windows. The room is in shades of cream, with a high ceiling, pale stone-tiled floors and majestic alabaster pillars—all providing an elegant and sophisticated backdrop. Further enhancing the entire main floor is lavish carpeting that replicates the beautiful colors and patterns of the 1898 original. Just imagine holding your reception in this magnificent space, or strolling its broad verandas and park-like grounds!

Weddings here enjoy exclusive access to this one-of-a-kind privately owned estate. However, Castle Green is also an intriguing venue for any type of event: corporate gala, fundraiser, family reunion, or retirement party. This historic treasure will captivate you with an abundance of visual delights, so arrange for a tour and see why it's one of Pasadena's favorite places to celebrate.

CEREMONY CAPACITY: The Ballroom holds 250 seated guests. The Garden seats 300.

EVENT/RECEPTION CAPACITY: The Ballroom holds 220 seated or 300 standing guests; the Garden/Veranda 300 seated or 400 standing. The Grand Salon accommodates up to 300 standing.

MEETING CAPACITY: Several areas accommodate 20–220 seated guests.

FEES & DEPOSITS: Half the facility rental fee and a refundable $1,000 damage deposit are required to secure your date. The remaining balance is due 60 days prior to the event. The rental fee is $5,200 on Friday and Sunday, $7,200 on Saturday, and $3,700 Monday through Thursday evenings. Weekend rental pricing includes: the use of up to twenty 60-inch round tables; 200 gold Chiavari chairs; 2 portable bars; and a complimentary 1-hour rehearsal time. There is no food & beverage minimum or cake-cutting fee. You may provide your own alcohol with no corkage fee.

AVAILABILITY: Year-round, daily. Weddings usually take place Fridays, Saturdays and Sundays. Weekday business meetings take place 10am–7pm. Only one event is booked per day.

SERVICES/AMENITIES:

Catering: select from approved list
Kitchen Facilities: no
Tables & Chairs: provided indoors
Linens, Silver, etc.: through caterer
Restrooms: wheelchair accessible
Dance Floor: provided indoors, CBA outdoors
Bride's and Groom's Dressing Area: yes
AV/Meeting Equipment: BYO
Other: wood fireplace in salon, 2 grand pianos, 50" TV, children's room

Parking: large lot nearby, $6/car; or guest-provided valet
Accommodations: no guest rooms; discounts at nearby hotels
Outdoor Night Lighting: limited to bridge & veranda
Outdoor Cooking Facilities: yes
Cleanup: caterer
View: garden

RESTRICTIONS:

Alcohol: BYO, but caterer must serve; no corkage fee
Smoking: outdoors only, in designated areas
Music: amplified OK indoors with volume limits, outdoors with City of Pasadena rules

Wheelchair Access: limited
Insurance: liability required from caterer
Other: no sparklers, rice or birdseed; open-flame candles require permit; decorations restricted; children must be supervised

Overwhelmed? Use the search criteria on www.HereComesTheGuide.com to narrow down your choices.

233

Fenyes Estate Garden
at Pasadena Museum of History

470 West Walnut Street, Pasadena
626/600-1661

www.pasadenahistory.org
specialevents@pasadenahistory.org

Historic Garden

● Rehearsal Dinners
● Ceremonies
● Wedding Receptions
● Private Parties
● Corporate Events
● Meetings
● Film Shoots
○ Accommodations

A garden wedding is hard to resist, especially when it's held on the beautifully landscaped grounds of the Fenyes Mansion, the centerpiece of the Pasadena Museum of History. And, as an added bonus, they only allow one event per day so you have exclusive use of this gorgeous setting and plenty of time to enjoy all it has to offer.

Built in 1906, the Beaux Arts landmark impresses with its pearl-white façade, ornate balustraded balconies, and columned portico. Presiding over a two-acre garden, it lends your celebration a nostalgic grandeur and provides a fabulous backdrop for your festivities *and* your wedding photos.

The garden, which features a flowing brook and rock waterfall, expansive lawns and a wide variety of trees, flowers, and other greenery, can be used in the way that best suits your event. Ceremonies usually begin with the bride making her entrance via a long pathway lined with palm trees that leads to the mansion's magnificent staircase. Here, the couple exchanges vows on the broad steps in full view of their guests seated on the lawn below. Afterwards, cocktails are served on the adjacent North Lawn & Patio, a wonderful spot bordered by rose bushes and fragrant jasmine.

Receptions on the South Lawn are quite magical, with tables arranged beneath the spreading fronds of two enormous palms. There's a built-in concrete dance floor off to one side, and the elegant presence of the mansion on the other. If you like, add twinkle lights or lanterns in the evening for a romantic glow.

Although the garden is popular for formal affairs, it works equally well for a casual barbecue or an al fresco rehearsal dinner. Many couples also personalize their event by bringing in lounge furniture or other décor, and creating special "retreats" for mingling and conversation. For example, a bark-covered space near the entrance is easily transformed with a few plush couches and armchairs into a welcome area for arriving guests.

Speaking of special retreats, brides have their own place to get ready—or get away: the charming Drawing Room of the Curtin House, another of the museum's historic buildings. The room has hardwood floors, a decorative fireplace, and windows overlooking a small courtyard. It's outfitted with a full-length mirror and tables for makeup and accessories, but you're free to bring in additional furnishings to make it your own private haven.

At the turn of the century, an invitation to Fenyes Mansion on Pasadena's "Millionaires' Row" meant you had "arrived". Today, you'll be the one sending out the invitations! Simply host your wedding in the lovely estate garden and you and your guests will experience the timeless allure of this Gilded Age gem.

CEREMONY CAPACITY: The Fenyes Garden Estate holds 200 seated or standing guests.

EVENT/RECEPTION & MEETING CAPACITY: The Garden accommodates 200 seated or standing guests. The Giddings Conference Room and the Curtin House Drawing Room each hold 50 seated.

FEES & DEPOSITS: A nonrefundable $1,000 deposit is required to reserve your date, and the balance is due 60 days prior to the event. The rental fee for the garden ranges $3,000–6,000. Meeting rooms are available starting at $400; call for details.

AVAILABILITY: Year-round, daily, anytime. All events must conclude by 10pm.

SERVICES/AMENITIES:

Catering: BYO, licensed
Kitchen Facilities: none
Tables & Chairs: BYO
Linens, Silver, etc.: BYO
Restrooms: wheelchair accessible
Dance Floor: patio
Bride's & Groom's Dressing Areas: provided
AV/Meeting Equipment: some available

Parking: complimentary lot and unmetered street parking
Accommodations: no guestrooms
Outdoor Night Lighting: minimal
Outdoor Cooking Facilities: BYO
Cleanup: through caterer
View: historic mansion and gardens

RESTRICTIONS:

Alcohol: BYO, licensed server
Smoking: designated outdoor area
Music: amplified OK with restrictions

Wheelchair Access: yes
Insurance: liability required
Other: no rice or confetti

The Grand Ballroom
at the Pasadena Convention Center

300 East Green Street, Pasadena
626/817-5635

www.pasadenacenter.com
lcotton@pasadenacenter.com

Historic Theatre & Convention Center

- Rehearsal Dinners
- Ceremonies
- Wedding Receptions
- Private Parties
- Corporate Events
- Meetings
- Film Shoots
- Accommodations

The Pasadena Convention Center is a spectacular boutique venue for galas, weddings and special events. It offers a wide variety of event sites, so, brides, whatever style of celebration you have in mind they can make it happen!

Guests are impressed as soon as they arrive: As they walk across the 22,000-square-foot plaza, which spreads out along the front of the historic Civic Auditorium, they're treated to a wonderful view of the San Gabriel Mountains in the distance and City Hall as the backdrop. The plaza's beautiful tiled surface is perfect for a ceremony, an al fresco cocktail reception, or a convenient valet drop-off before moving inside for the main festivities.

The 25,000-square-foot Grand Ballroom—the largest one in the San Gabriel Valley—can be divided into 10 separate sections to comfortably accommodate an intimate gathering of 100 or a party for over 1,000 guests. Its neutral, modern interior is a blank canvas on which you can paint your own vision. The ballroom is also equipped with state-of-the-art audio and lighting systems and provides internet and WiFi access. Another plus: it opens to an 11,000-square-foot lobby with a sparkling terrazzo floor and artistic, free-form chandeliers. This foyer is ideal for cocktails and hors d'oeuvres, and can be turned into an inviting lounge area.

Weddings may be held in the main conference building's lower level, which houses another chic, contemporary event space. Done in soft grays and off-white, it complements almost any color scheme. Hang swags of fabric from the ceiling for an element of softness and movement, or add whimsical string lighting for a dramatic effect. Brides enjoy tossing their bouquet over the sleek metal railing on the upper level.

On the second floor of the Civic Auditorium you'll find the elegant Gold Room, featuring a rosette ceiling and elaborate moldings. It's a lovely choice for a smaller wedding ceremony and reception.

Recently restored, the Historic Exhibition Hall/Ballroom boasts a 30-foot ceiling, tall arched windows, and chandeliers original to the building. With over 17,000 square feet, it can easily host a large affair.

The Pasadena Convention Center's in-house culinary professionals are happy to customize your menu. They specialize in California cuisine with a focus on fresh, locally grown ingredients. The center has also implemented a host of "go green" initiatives, which should please environmentally conscious couples.

In addition to being a unique place for your event, the Center is a great destination for your guests! The facility is close to the Burbank and Los Angeles airports and just blocks from Old Pasadena, a historic area filled with shops, boutiques, restaurants, clubs, and hotels, all within walking distance. Museums, golf and live theater are nearby as well.

CEREMONY AND EVENT/RECEPTION CAPACITY: Several flexible indoor and outdoor event spaces accommodate more intimate gatherings to large extravaganzas for over 1,000 guests. With a dance floor and banquet-style seating, the Gold Room accommodates 150; the Lower Level Conference Building and Historic Exhibition Hall C, 500 each; and the Grand Ballroom 1,000 (2 sections are ideal for 150 each). Without a dance floor, the capacities for these spaces are greater. Please contact the catering department for more details.

MEETING CAPACITY: The Exhibition Hall seats 5,400 guests. Small to large events may be held in several flexible meeting spaces.

FEES & DEPOSITS: A nonrefundable deposit equal to 10% of the estimated food & beverage minimum is required along with a signed contract. An additional deposit of 65% of the total estimated food & beverage balance is required 30 days prior to the event. The remaining balance is due 5 business days prior. A 22% service charge and sales tax applies to all services. The rental fee varies depending on the space(s) reserved.

AVAILABILITY: Year-round, daily.

SERVICES/AMENITIES:

Catering: in-house, or BYO with approval
Kitchen Facilities: n/a
Tables & Chairs: provided
Linens, Silver, etc.: provided, specialty linens available for additional fee
Restrooms: wheelchair accessible
Dance Floor: yes
Bride's & Groom's Dressing Areas: yes
AV/Meeting Equipment: CBA

Parking: large lot, valet CBA
Accommodations: no guest rooms; premium hotels nearby
Outdoor Night Lighting: yes
Outdoor Cooking Facilities: CBA
Cleanup: provided
View: cityscape, mountains
Other: event coordination

RESTRICTIONS:

Alcohol: in-house, no BYO
Smoking: outside, in designated areas only
Music: amplified OK

Wheelchair Access: yes
Insurance: liability required

Happy Trails Garden

Historic Garden

207 South Fair Oaks Avenue, Pasadena

626/796-9526

www.happytrailscatering.com
events@happytrailscatering.com

●	Rehearsal Dinners	●	Corporate Events
●	Ceremonies	●	Meetings
●	Wedding Receptions		Film Shoots
●	Private Parties		Accommodations

Who would ever guess that behind the *Happy Trails Catering Company's* narrow storefront is one of the best-kept event location secrets in Pasadena? Well, we certainly didn't, and were pleasantly surprised when we left the sun-soaked main street and walked down a short driveway into the cool shade of an expansive, park-like courtyard.

Here you'll find soft grass underfoot, high ivy-covered walls, palm trees, bamboo stands and a formidable, century-old camphor tree that rises from the garden's center like an enormous protective umbrella. As you approach the tree you can't help but notice the boards and pipes embedded in its trunk. They're left over from a plumber's shop that occupied this spot a hundred years ago. Apparently the tree had grown right through the wall and roof of the shop, and when it was pulled down, the parts of the building that had been absorbed into the living flesh of the tree simply remained for posterity.

An elevated wooden deck has been built around the trunk of the tree, and some couples exchange vows here; others prefer to get married in front of a tall stand of bamboo against the back wall of the courtyard. Tables are set up on the grass for the reception, their white linens and colorful centerpieces contrasting beautifully with the green surroundings. Soft night lighting is provided by Craftsman-style lanterns hanging from the tree, and you can dance beneath them on the deck or on the patio next to the quaint brick building that houses the catering kitchen.

Happy Trails Catering is dedicated to fresh, exciting food. When they customize your menu they pull out all the stops: They'll incorporate family recipes, take the garlic (or other seasonings) out of dishes if you request it, or whip up a completely vegetarian meal if that's what you want. And being a full-service caterer, they'll coordinate all the details so that you'll have very little to do.

CEREMONY CAPACITY: The location holds up to 200 seated guests.

EVENT/RECEPTION CAPACITY: The garden holds 200 seated guests.

MEETING CAPACITY: The brick patio holds 50 seated theater-style, the lawn area holds 200 seated in a circular theater-style configuration, and the raised deck accommodates 30 with additional bench seating around the edge.

FEES & DEPOSITS: To reserve your date for a wedding, 50% of the event total and a completed contract are required; the final balance is due the day of the event. The rental fee is $3,500 for the entire day. Catering, which is provided, runs $100–150/person and includes a full menu, staff, most rentals (e.g. tables, chairs, linens, china, etc.), and gratuity.

AVAILABILITY: Weddings and special events, April 1st–November 30th, 9am–midnight, one function per day. Business meetings, weekdays, 9am–5pm.

SERVICES/AMENITIES:

Catering: in-house, no BYO

Kitchen Facilities: n/a

Tables & Chairs: provided

Linens, Silver, etc.: provided

Restrooms: wheelchair accessible

Dance Floor: on wood deck or brick patio

Bride's & Groom's Dressing Areas: yes

AV/Meeting Equipment: PA system, podiums, special lighting, heaters extra charge

Parking: on-street or valet service

Accommodations: no guest rooms

Outdoor Night Lighting: CBA, extra fee

Outdoor Cooking Facilities: BBQs CBA

Cleanup: provided

View: of enclosed garden

Other: some coordination

RESTRICTIONS:

Alcohol: in-house, or BYO with corkage fee

Smoking: allowed

Music: amplified OK

Wheelchair Access: mostly accessible

Insurance: not required

The Langham Huntington, Pasadena

Hotel

1401 South Oak Knoll Avenue, Pasadena

626/585-6244

www.langhamhuntingtonweddings.com
tllax.weddings@langhamhotels.com

- Rehearsal Dinners
- Ceremonies
- Wedding Receptions
- Private Parties
- Corporate Events
- Meetings
- Film Shoots
- Accommodations

How do you define elegance? One possible answer is The Langham Huntington, Pasadena. Since its unveiling in 1907, this legendary hotel has been a favorite for high-profile events, celebrity soirées and discerning world travelers. Lavishly renovated in the early '90s by Ritz-Carlton, the Huntington legacy continues to flourish under its new owner, Langham Hotels International, one of the oldest and most prestigious hoteliers in the world.

Couples planning their once-in-a-lifetime event might begin in the Horseshoe Garden behind the hotel. Originally the main entrance, today it's the most striking vantage point from which to appreciate the Huntington's imposing architecture: The building's stone façade and balustrades strike a classical pose against the contour of the San Gabriel foothills, which echo the hotel's timeless grandeur. Center stage is a broad stone landing with twin staircases that sweep down toward a sprawling manicured lawn. This spectacular park-like enclave, dotted with colorful blooms, swaying palm trees and lush greenery, invites you to dream large for your wedding ceremony—make a fairy-tale entrance in a horse-drawn carriage, a classic Rolls Royce, or even atop a beribboned elephant!

In contrast, the sequestered Japanese Garden has a quiet, almost mystical beauty. A step-down waterfall pond is spanned by a curved footbridge, a charming spot for an intimate ceremony. Here, whispered endearments mingle with the sound of trickling water, evoking an aura of enchantment. Overlooking the garden's border, the weathered wooden trestle of the old Picture Bridge lends a turn-of-the-century nod to the serene setting.

Yet there's nothing understated about the hotel's posh interior. A stroll along marbled hallways takes you past priceless artwork and antiquities—Chinese porcelain, portraits from the era of Gainsborough, and hand-painted ceiling murals, for example. Several glass-walled corridors frame a view of the Courtyard, an outdoor haven where blossoming pear trees fringe a tranquil pond. Relaxed yet refined, the Courtyard is the just the place for a chic cocktail hour.

Next, host an impeccably serviced reception in one of the hotel's sumptuous ballrooms. The historic Georgian Ballroom feels palatial, with its soaring arched ceiling, stained-glass windows, and gorgeous pear-shaped chandeliers, each one fashioned of thousands of brilliant crystals and ringed with candelabra-style lights. Or consider the storied Viennese Ballroom, featuring a vaulted ceiling edged in gold and a glittering constellation of crystal chandeliers designed by the same atelier that crafted the chandeliers in the palace of King Ludwig II of Bavaria. If you prefer the natural glow of stars and moonlight, then stage your festivities on the Viennese Terrace, an open-air expanse that takes advantage of Pasadena's warm summer nights. The hotel's newest addition is the super-sized Huntington Ballroom that lets you fête 750 guests in swanky style. Many a high-society gala has graced these ballrooms over the decades, and it takes no imagination at all to envision the gleam of silver and fine china, the swirl of satin gowns and the lighthearted laughter that will accompany your own celebration at such an incomparable establishment.

Add to this cornucopia of luxury even more delights! The award-winning Chuan Spa pampers with signature treatments inspired by traditional Chinese medicine and cutting-edge skincare technology. Then there's the outstanding dining offered by the Royce Wood-fired Steakhouse and the Terrace, as well as afternoon tea in the Lobby Lounge. And, of course, the plush accommodations provide serene havens for your guests. Yes, The Langham Huntington, Pasadena does indeed seem like the quintessential definition of elegance.

CEREMONY CAPACITY: The hotel holds up to 300 seated guests indoors, and 650 seated outdoors.

EVENT/RECEPTION CAPACITY: The hotel accommodates 650 seated or 1,400 standing indoors and 650 seated or 1,400 standing outdoors.

MEETING CAPACITY: Meeting spaces seat 1,000 guests.

FEES & DEPOSITS: 25% of the food & beverage minimum, along with the site fee, is required to reserve your date. An additional 25% of the food & beverage minimum is due 90 days prior to the event. The final anticipated balance plus an additional 10% of the food & beverage minimum to cover any unexpected costs is due 21 days prior. The rental fee ranges $750–$5,000 depending on the day and number of hours of the event. Weddings start at $150/person. A 22% service charge and sales tax are extra. The food & beverage minimum varies depending on the size of ballroom, day of the week and time of day.

AVAILABILITY: Year-round, daily

SERVICES/AMENITIES:

Catering: in-house
Kitchen Facilities: n/a
Tables & Chairs: provided
Linens, Silver, etc.: provided
Restrooms: wheelchair accessible
Dance Floor: portable provided
Bride's & Groom's Dressing Areas: CBA
AV/Meeting Equipment: CBA
Other: in-house wedding cake, spa services, event coordination, WiFi, fitness center, nearby golf and bike-riding

Parking: valet required
Accommodations: 380 guestrooms
Outdoor Night Lighting: CBA
Outdoor Cooking Facilities: BBQ CBA
Cleanup: provided
View: garden patio; panorama of hills, landscaped grounds, mountains, garden, fountain, waterfall

RESTRICTIONS:

Alcohol: in-house
Smoking: outdoors in designated areas
Music: amplified OK indoors

Wheelchair Access: yes
Insurance: required for vendors only

Noor

300 East Colorado Boulevard, Suite 200, Pasadena
626/793-4518
www.noorevents.com
sales@noorevents.com

● Rehearsal Dinners	● Corporate Events
● Ceremonies	● Meetings
● Wedding Receptions	● Film Shoots
● Private Parties	Accommodations

Ah, Noor! This dramatic event venue in the historic heart of Old Pasadena seems to have the power to elevate any occasion and surround it in magic. Named "Winner Best Event Venue" for 2011, 2012, 2013 and 2014 by the readers of *Pasadena Weekly,* this function-dedicated property features a collection of elegant spaces designed specifically with transcendent celebrations in mind.

Indoors, you'll find two stunning ballrooms with fabulous foyers. Outdoors, there's a room-sized second-story balcony overlooking views of City Hall and the San Gabriel Mountains, plus a spectacular terrace spacious enough for a grand open-air gala.

Heads will turn and eyes will widen when guests step into the Sofia Ballroom's lavish 1920s-inspired foyer. The long, burnished wood bar, high ceilings, and magnificent chandeliers will transport them to a world of glamour and gaiety. From here, your party can flow to the Sofia Ballroom, with its Art Nouveau styling and city and mountain views or onto the Sofia Balcony, a sophisticated al fresco lounge where you can practically reach out and touch the city skyline.

Like the Sofia Foyer and Ballroom complex, the Ella Foyer and Ballroom have their own fashionable entrance. Big black double doors welcome you from the patio out front into what feels like a very chic Hollywood club. Art Deco-imbued touches—the shiny black bar, Venetian plaster walls sculpted to look like tufted dove-gray leather, the wraparound black leather banquette, and the ethereal "ghost" chandeliers—enhance the luxurious vibe. It's a striking introduction to the Ella Ballroom. Not quite as vast as the Sofia, this room's more intimate "members only" atmosphere conjures up an era of opulence and prestige.

You have a lot of options here, and the staff, who are experts in hospitality, will help you select the spaces, menu and services that best suit your vision. You'll see why politicians, celebrities, and individuals from all walks of life have enjoyed entertaining and being entertained at Noor. From relaxed to formal, traditional to the unexpected, Noor is committed to creating a personalized event that is both exquisite and uniquely yours.

CEREMONY CAPACITY: The Noor Terrace holds 300 seated guests outdoors.

EVENT/RECEPTION CAPACITY: The Ella Ballroom can accommodate 156 seated or 250 standing, the Sofia Ballroom 352 seated or 600 standing indoors, and the Noor Terrace 170 seated or 300 standing guests.

MEETING CAPACITY: Meeting spaces hold up to 300 seated.

FEES & DEPOSITS: 25% of the food & beverage minimum is required to reserve your date. An additional 25% of the estimated event total is due 4 months after booking, 25% is due 4 months prior to the event, and the remaining balance is due 14 days prior. The food & beverage minimum varies depending on the spaces reserved, time of event and day of the week. For weekday evening events (Monday–Thursday, 5pm–12am) the food & beverage minimum is $6,000; for weekend events (Friday, Saturday and Sunday, 5pm–2am) it's $8,400 for the Ella Ballroom and $26,200 for the Sofia Ballroom. Luncheons start at $45/person and dinners start at $75/person. Tax, room rental, and service fee are included. Alcohol, AV, lighting, packages and valet service are additional.

AVAILABILITY: Year-round, daily.

SERVICES/AMENITIES:

Catering: in-house, or BYO with approval
Kitchen Facilities: fully equipped
Tables & Chairs: provided
Linens, Silver, etc.: provided
Restrooms: wheelchair accessible
Dance Area: provided
Bride's Dressing Area: yes
AV/Meeting Equipment: provided

Parking: large lot, validation and hosted valet available
Accommodations: no guest rooms
Outdoor Night Lighting: provided
Outdoor Cooking Facilities: no
Cleanup: provided
View: cityscape, mountains
Other: photobooth, DJ services; day-of coordination available, extra fee; recommended vendor list will be provided

RESTRICTIONS:

Alcohol: full in-house bar
Smoking: designated areas only
Music: amplified OK

Wheelchair Access: yes
Insurance: liability required

The wedding vendors on our website are the best in the business. How do we know? Read page 577.

Sheraton Pasadena

Hotel

303 Cordova Street, Pasadena
626/449-4000 x142

www.sheraton.com/pasadena
fiorella@sheratonpasadena.com

● Rehearsal Dinners	● Corporate Events
● Ceremonies	● Meetings
● Wedding Receptions	● Film Shoots
● Private Parties	● Accommodations

The Sheraton Pasadena, ideally located just blocks from Old Town, has been a magnet for out-of-towners and locals alike for more than 30 years. Gracing one end of a wide, treelined pedestrian plaza, with the new Convention Center on one side and the landmark 1930s Civic Auditorium on the other, the hotel offers almost 12,000 square feet of event and banquet space, including one of the most open, airy and utterly romantic places you could choose for a wedding.

The Piazza Ballroom is positively luminous. Natural light filters in through sheer-draped, glass doors topped with fan-shaped glass arches and a dramatic, peaked skylight that runs virtually the length of the room. Spanish tile floors, a soaring ceiling, and ironwork chandeliers fitted with dozens of glass shades convey the feeling of an elegant hacienda.

While there's ample space to have your ceremony *and* reception here, the Piazza is actually part of a multilevel private event area that gives you enormous flexibility in creating your dream celebration. For example, a raised mezzanine, set apart by a fancy scrollwork railing, provides another great spot for exchanging vows, making toasts or even placing the head table. But if you really want to expand the festivities, go for all out drama: After cocktails, open the mirrored, arched doors on the mezzanine to reveal Justine's, an elegant dining room with antiqued brass chandeliers. While your guests enjoy a beautifully presented sit-down dinner, the Piazza is turned into a dance floor with DJ or band setup on the mezzanine...or, as in one recent African-themed wedding, a stage for a Fire Dancer. Whether it's fire or ice (as in transforming the space into a winter wonderland for another wedding), the event staff will be happy to work with you to make your wedding unique. Want to go beyond a simple waltz as your first dance? They're open to helping you unleash your inner Michelle Kwan by arranging your first dance at the ice skating rink next door.

For smaller gatherings or for rehearsal dinners, there's Soleil, the hotel's restaurant. Done in muted shades of cream and cocoa, it has a cozy private room in the back with a terrace that overlooks the pool.

CEREMONY, EVENT/RECEPTION & MEETING CAPACITY: The hotel can accommodate 250 seated or 350 standing guests.

FEES & DEPOSITS: 25% of the total event cost is required to reserve your date. A portion is due 90 days prior to the event and the balance is due 72 hours prior. Meals range $68–87/person. Tax and a 21% service charge are additional.

AVAILABILITY: Year-round, daily, 6am–midnight.

SERVICES/AMENITIES:

Catering: in-house or BYO
Kitchen Facilities: fully equipped
Tables & Chairs: provided
Linens, Silver, etc.: provided
Restrooms: wheelchair accessible
Dance Floor: provided
Bride's Dressing Area: yes
AV/Meeting Equipment: provided

Parking: garage
Accommodations: 311 guest rooms
Outdoor Night Lighting: CBA
Outdoor Cooking Facilities: no
Cleanup: provided
View: none
Other: coordination, in-house wedding cake

RESTRICTIONS:

Alcohol: in-house or BYO wine with corkage fee
Smoking: outdoors only
Music: amplified OK indoors

Wheelchair Access: yes
Insurance: not required

Westminster Presbyterian Church

Historic Church

1757 North Lake Avenue, Pasadena
626/794-7141
www.wpcpas.org
weddings@wpcpas.org

- Rehearsal Dinners
- Ceremonies
- Wedding Receptions
- Private Parties
- Corporate Events
- Meetings
- Film Shoots
- Accommodations

Visible for miles, the magnificent Westminster Presbyterian Church rises above Pasadena like the mirage of a fantastic sand castle. Unlike the ephemeral sand castle, however, this awesomely graceful church has been a rock solid part of the community since 1928. Its enduring appeal as a wedding location is evident in the fact that the church has performed ceremonies for daughters and granddaughters of brides who've exchanged their vows here.

Stretching one square block on Lake Avenue, the church compels you to take a moment and admire its beauty and workmanship. Designed in the French Gothic style, it was patterned after the medieval cathedrals of Metz, Beauvais and Amiens. (Its 150-foot bell tower resembles that of the Église St. Maclou in Rouen.) Constructed of cement blocks with intricately carved adornments, the massive structure stands like a citadel on its corner.

Enter the church through three arches connected by block pillars. From this shaded portico, three sets of dark wood-and-iron doors lead into the narthex, an impressive vestibule. With its beamed ceilings, filigree iron chandeliers and stone archways framing stained-glass windows, it lends the proper tone to your solemn, yet joyous, occasion.

The sanctuary itself is breathtaking. Dark mahogany pews and polished stone floors contrast with the soaring vaulted ceilings of deep azure and crimson. Rendered in the fresco style by master stone painter Julian Gurnsey, they depict a starry heaven, incorporating crosses and fleurs-de-lis. Several antique brass-and-glass chandeliers suspended from the joists create a golden glow throughout the church. Along both sides, six original 1920s stained-glass devotional windows by Judson Studios are accentuated by stone archways leading to the enormous triptych centerpiece up front. The church is laid out in the classic T-shaped cruciform with a long center aisle, and can accommodate 1,000 people. Gleaming pipes from the original (and well-maintained) Reuter Organ frame the chancel area, where additional pews are available for the choir, although many couples opt for a string quartet or soloist.

There's a charming bridal room for you and your attendants to use downstairs, while upstairs, the groom's party has their own lounge. When you're ready, you'll make your dramatic entrance down that long aisle, which can be dressed with flowers or candles. In a lovely touch symbolizing the start of your new life together, you and your groom will be invited by the pastor to light a unity candle. Then, after you've pledged your troth and walked back down the aisle as husband and wife, you can re-enter through a side door to take pictures inside.

If you're hosting your reception here, too, Morrison Hall, a large wood-paneled room in the adjoining building, has a stage with velvet curtains and a service kitchen for your caterer. If you're continuing your celebration in one of the hotels or restaurants nearby, be sure to take full advantage of the church grounds for your wedding album photos. One day, they may inspire your own daughter to get married at this same venerable church and carry on the tradition.

The sanctuary has been featured extensively in film and on television as well as in *People* and *US* magazines.

CEREMONY CAPACITY: The Sanctuary holds 500 seated guests on the main floor.

EVENT/RECEPTION & MEETING CAPACITY: Morrison Hall holds up to 350 seated guests.

FEES & DEPOSITS: A nonrefundable $500 deposit is required to reserve your date. The balance is due 30 days prior to the event. The $2,200 wedding fee includes a minister and premarital counseling, both of which are required. Co-officiation is common. The reception rental fee ranges $1,500–1,800.

AVAILABILITY: Fridays, Saturdays and Sundays. The Church is decorated for Christmas from Thanksgiving through New Year's Day. No weddings during Easter week or Christmas week.

SERVICES/AMENITIES:

Catering: BYO
Kitchen Facilities: prep only
Tables & Chairs: provided
Linens, Silver, etc.: BYO
Restrooms: wheelchair accessible
Dance Floor: provided
Bride's Dressing Area: yes
AV/Meeting Equipment: provided

Parking: lot and street parking
Accommodations: no guest rooms
Outdoor Night Lighting: yes
Outdoor Cooking Facilities: no
Cleanup: provided
View: hills
Other: coordination and clergy available; grand piano

RESTRICTIONS:

Alcohol: BYO champagne and wine only
Smoking: outside only
Music: amplified OK indoors, no recorded music

Wheelchair Access: yes
Insurance: not required

Oneonta

1515 Garfield Avenue, South Pasadena
626/799-6161

www.oneontawed.com
oneontawed@gmail.com

Church & Banquet Hall

● Rehearsal Dinners	○ Corporate Events
● Ceremonies	● Meetings
● Wedding Receptions	● Film Shoots
● Private Parties	○ Accommodations

Oneonta, set on a wide swath of green in South Pasadena, offers a peaceful oasis for Christian weddings. Established more than a century ago, the property's signature Congregational Church was rebuilt after WWII and instantly garnered awards for its Mid-Century Modern architecture. The cast stone façade, so eye-catching from the outside, is inlaid with stained-glass windows that convey various biblical stories when viewed from inside.

Your guests will first be welcomed into the cool breezeway filled with chic mid-century furniture, where they can mingle before taking their seats for your ceremony. The Sanctuary's awe-inspiring ceiling features a soaring, gravity-defying design of massive Douglas Fir beams arched to resemble the ribs of an upended ship or ark. Along the walls are large, vertical glass panels that allow for lots of natural light, and a wide, center brick aisle that leads to the impressive chancel. And while the clean, timeless aesthetic of the surroundings are so lovely that most brides opt to add only the simplest of floral adornments, you'll appreciate the drama of their gleaming organ accompanying your walk to the altar. Expansive enough to seat 450, the Sanctuary also works very well for smaller groups.

However if you're looking for something more intimate, you should check out the rustic Redwood Chapel. It boasts dark paneling, light wood floors, a crossbeam ceiling, and an indoor rock and water garden. But if your heart is set on exchanging vows al fresco, you're going to absolutely love the grassy Courtyard! This beautifully landscaped lawn provides a choice of backdrops, including a lush canopy of camellias and a wall of colorful vines. Dotted with shade trees and accented with a sweetheart bench, it's a quiet garden setting for a champagne toast and reception—and plenty of photo ops.

Just beyond lies the covered Terrace (another nice spot for cocktails) and Gray Hall. This spacious indoor venue sports a vaulted ceiling, arched beams and a full wall of sliding glass doors. With a large stage, grand piano and pull-down screen, you can easily incorporate a live band or home movies into your celebration.

There are a lot of options to choose from, and happily you'll have a wedding coordinator to help you navigate through them…but if you're interested in hosting a very unique rehearsal dinner, ask about the circular Tower Room, topped with a conical roof. Although it's usually reserved for Tea Ceremonies (Oneonta has a long-established, warm relationship with the Asian community), dining here can be an auspicious way to start your marriage.

CEREMONY CAPACITY: The facility seats 450 guests indoors and 200 outdoors.

EVENT/RECEPTION & MEETING CAPACITY: The facility holds 200 seated or standing guests indoors and 300 seated or standing outdoors.

FEES & DEPOSITS: A nonrefundable deposit of 25% of the rental fee is required to reserve your date. The remaining balance is due 30 days prior to the event. The rental fee starts at $2,000 and varies depending on spaces reserved. All food and alcohol must be served by a licensed caterer.

AVAILABILITY: Year-round.

SERVICES/AMENITIES:

Catering: BYO
Kitchen Facilities: prep only
Tables & Chairs: some provided
Linens, Silver, etc.: BYO
Restrooms: not wheelchair accessible
Dance Floor: yes
Bride's Dressing Area: yes
AV/Meeting Equipment: BYO

Parking: large lot
Accommodations: no guest rooms
Outdoor Night Lighting: access only
Outdoor Cooking Facilities: BBQ CBA
Cleanup: caterer or renter
View: panorama of gardens and landscaped grounds
Other: grand piano, clergy on staff, picnic area

RESTRICTIONS:

Alcohol: BYO
Smoking: not allowed
Music: amplified OK with restrictions

Wheelchair Access: limited
Insurance: liability required

Want to know WHAT TO ASK a potential location or vendor? Check out our Questions to Ask starting on page 21.

Puddingstone Resort

Resort

1777 Campers View Road, San Dimas
909/592-2221

www.hottubsresort.com
info@hottubsresort.com

Rehearsal Dinners	Corporate Events
● Ceremonies	● Meetings
● Wedding Receptions	● Film Shoots
Private Parties	Accommodations

Set high on a hilltop, Puddingstone is a tranquil oasis where you can truly unwind. Stroll down brick paths that meander through stands of pines and eucalyptus…listen to the trees rustling in the breeze…and admire the spectacular panoramic lake and valley vistas spread out before you. You also have a choice of two different event sites, so you can choreograph your wedding in a variety of ways.

The Vista Site offers three ceremony options, all with impressive views of Puddingstone Lake and the San Gabriel Valley. The large Gazebo, which can be draped with fabric or decorated with flowers, provides a shady spot to exchange vows. Alternatively, you can get married on the Gazebo Lawn, seating your guests in a circle around a central arch. Lastly, there's the Deck at the edge of the lawn, a "floating" aerie where you'll feel like you could take off and soar out over the shimmering lake below.

The celebration continues with hors d'oeuvres and cocktails at the Hilltop Reception Area, just steps from all three ceremony locations. While everyone mingles on this expansive terrace, the adjacent lawn is arranged with tables for dining. The DJ sets up nearby, and a dance floor is placed on the lawn.

Over the years, the resort has hosted Hawaiian luaus with fire dancers, Renaissance weddings, and even a traditional African wedding where the bride was carried in on a carriage-like sedan chair on the shoulders of four men. And, in keeping with Puddingstone's goal to soothe all guests, the bride has her own changing room, a cool and relaxing hideaway.

Puddingstone's second event area is the secluded Mesa Site. Hidden away on a lush mountaintop mesa with views of the San Gabriel Valley, this serene setting is perfect for a couple who wants a private location with a more intimate atmosphere. Couples say "I do" beneath a crisp white canopy, and a quaint room close by allows the bride to calm her nerves before the walk down the aisle.

No matter which event area you choose, you're likely to be rewarded with one more perk: a gorgeous sunset that turns the sky into a breathtaking backdrop. People actually drive up to Puddingstone just to watch the sun go down in an amazing blaze of color!

If all this isn't enough to put you at ease, tucked discreetly among the trees are plenty of three-sided cabanas with hot tubs overlooking the lake and valley. You and your honey can soak in private, while you contemplate your future together.

CEREMONY, EVENT/RECEPTION & MEETING CAPACITY: The Vista facility holds up to 250 seated guests, the Mesa facility up to 150.

FEES & DEPOSITS: A deposit ranging $500–1,500 is required to reserve the date. 30% of the rental fee is due 6 months prior to the event, 30% is due 3 months prior, and the remaining balance is due 30 days prior. Rental fees range $1,000–8,500 depending on space and time reserved, guest count, and type of function.

AVAILABILITY: Year-round, daily, 6am–1am.

SERVICES/AMENITIES:

Catering: BYO, must be insured
Kitchen Facilities: no
Tables & Chairs: provided
Linens, Silver, etc.: provided, extra charge
Restrooms: wheelchair accessible
Dance Floor: yes
Bride's Dressing Area: yes
AV/Meeting Equipment: CBA

Parking: large lot
Accommodations: no guest rooms
Outdoor Night Lighting: yes
Outdoor Cooking Facilities: BBQs
Cleanup: provided, extra charge or through renter
View: Puddingstone Lake, valley, cityscape

RESTRICTIONS:

Alcohol: BYO
Smoking: outdoor only
Music: amplified OK

Wheelchair Access: yes
Insurance: not required
Other: no rice, confetti or birdseed

San Dimas Canyon Golf Course

Golf Club

2100 Terrebonne Avenue, San Dimas
888/998-6126

www.sandimasgc.com
www.countryclubreceptions.com
privateeventdirector@sandimasgc.com

●	Rehearsal Dinners	●	Corporate Events
●	Ceremonies	●	Meetings
●	Wedding Receptions	●	Film Shoots
●	Private Parties		Accommodations

While some wedding venues have only one attribute that makes brides say "Yes!" right away, San Dimas Canyon Golf Course has several. For starters, it offers a beautiful location at the base of the San Gabriel Mountains, a tranquil ceremony area that's just steps away from the banquet room, and a seasoned private event staff.

But the thing that most endears brides to this place may well be the terrace adjoining the banquet facility. It's like a broad tropical veranda—open, airy and decorated with small fan palms. From here you have quite a view: a putting green along with the fairways, plus some of the grandest peaks of the San Gabriels. The tree-dotted golf course slopes gently down to a seasonal creek that descends from the mountains in winter. This is a lovely vista, both for its geology and its Inland Empire palette of greens, browns, golds and soft grays.

The recently refurbished banquet room features stylish chandeliers and sconces as well as custom uplighting, plus rich chocolate-colored carpets and molding that give the space an uptown feel. Renovated even more recently, the enclosed ceremony site has become a charming, private garden area. Guests are seated on a long lawn facing the new wedding "arch," a spacious, white pergola bordered by flowers, blooming bushes, and other greenery. A sweet, two-tiered fountain fills one corner of the garden, and there's another wonderful grace note: three handsome eucalyptus trees that soar like living sculptures over the far end of the lawn.

San Dimas has two lakes on site—perfect for wedding photos—but keep in mind that they're accessible only to the couple and their photographer. For shots involving larger groups and the rest of the wedding party, the favorite spot is under a pair of massive oaks standing a stone's throw from the banquet room. The wedding pavilion and ceremony lawn are also preferred and convenient places for posing.

If you're hoping for a free hand with decorations, you're in luck here. Aside from requesting that you refrain from using confetti or glitter to shower the newlyweds, they have very few restrictions. Besides the terrace and the views, brides who've had their wedding at San Dimas laud the staff's catering prowess and general helpfulness. Menus are varied, and choices range from simple to elaborate. The club can also recommend reliable, experienced vendors.

From the setting and décor to the service and amenities, you'll find that San Dimas really does provide many of the things that make a bride say "Yes!"

CEREMONY CAPACITY: Ceremony spaces hold 200 seated guests outdoors.

EVENT/RECEPTION CAPACITY: The site accommodates 200 seated or 250 standing guests indoors, and 120 seated or standing outdoors.

MEETING CAPACITY: Meeting spaces can seat up to 200 guests.

FEES & DEPOSITS: A nonrefundable deposit, which is applied to your food & beverage total, is required to reserve your date. The amount of the deposit varies depending on how far in advance you book. Payment terms for the balance also vary, and may be arranged on an individual basis. Meals start at $25/person. Tax, alcohol and service charge are additional. Menus and packages can be customized to fit your needs and budget. Call for details.

AVAILABILITY: Year-round, daily.

SERVICES/AMENITIES:

Catering: in-house or BYO
Kitchen Facilities: not available to outside caterers
Tables & Chairs: provided
Linens, Silver, etc.: provided
Restrooms: wheelchair accessible
Dance Floor: provided
Bride's & Groom's Dressing Areas: yes
AV/Meeting Equipment: some provided

Parking: large lot
Accommodations: no guest rooms
Outdoor Night Lighting: provided
Outdoor Cooking Facilities: no
Cleanup: provided
View: canyon, forest, garden, fairways, hills, landscaped grounds; panorama of mountains and valley
Other: in-house wedding cake, event coordination

RESTRICTIONS:

Alcohol: in-house
Smoking: designated areas only
Music: amplified OK

Wheelchair Access: yes
Insurance: not required

South Bay

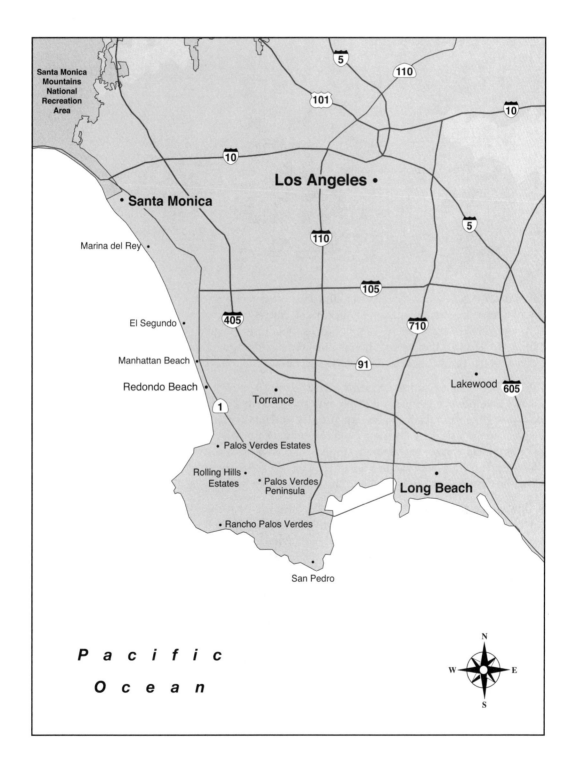

Lakewood Country Club

Country Club

3101 Carson Street, Lakewood
888/993-6396

www.lakewoodgolfcc.com
www.countryclubreceptions.com
privateeventdirector@lakewoodgolf.net

● Rehearsal Dinners		● Corporate Events	
● Ceremonies		● Meetings	
● Wedding Receptions		● Film Shoots	
● Private Parties		Accommodations	

Lakewood Country Club is both a delightful and convenient venue for gathering family and friends. Though mere minutes from a major airport, the club is tucked away on a quiet residential street, surrounded by 11 verdant acres of golf greens. Built in 1930 when golf was still an elite sport, the club now welcomes the public. Though hints remain throughout the property of its gracious past, Lakewood has been completely updated to accommodate the contemporary bride.

Lakewood's historic Spanish-style clubhouse adjoins a sprawling garden lawn encircled by lush foliage. Outdoor ceremonies are lovely on this manicured expanse, with flowering borders and trees providing natural adornment. An archway or the décor of your choice sets the stage for your walk down the aisle. You'll begin your grand entrance from the spacious bridal suite on the second floor of the clubhouse, where you've prepared in comfort and style. A musical cue is your signal to descend an exterior wrought-iron and stone staircase to the garden below. If you prefer a lake view, the first-tee box offers a more intimate space in a gorgeous setting.

Following the ceremony, you and your new spouse will be whisked away to pose for photos amid the beautiful lakes and greenery. Meanwhile, guests are invited inside the Saltillo-tiled foyer for cocktails and hors d'oeuvres. This vintage-influenced interior courtyard leads to three separate, and quite different, room options for your reception.

Host an impressive gala in the spacious Ballroom, where your nearest and dearest can celebrate beneath ornate brass chandeliers. Tall windows overlook the golf course, and the view of the emerald fairways is like an artfully rendered landscape painting. More modest affairs are held in the Hacienda Room, a wonderfully airy and light-filled space, thanks to an open-beamed cathedral ceiling. For something cozier, the marvelous Fireside Room retains many details of the original building, including a decorative hearth—place flickering candles on it for a romantic glow. The angular lines of an interior roof, complete with eaves and Spanish tiles, add to this room's nostalgic ambiance.

With its rustic atmosphere, attention to detail, and competitively priced wedding packages, the Lakewood Country Club deftly answers the needs of today's brides.

CEREMONY, EVENT/RECEPTION & MEETING CAPACITY: The location holds up to 300 guests, indoors or outdoors. Reception spaces each accommodate 20–250 people.

FEES & DEPOSITS: A nonrefundable deposit, which is applied to your food & beverage total, is required to reserve your date. The amount of the deposit varies depending on how far in advance you book. Payment terms for the balance also vary, and may be arranged on an individual basis. Wedding packages start at $37/person. Tax, alcohol and service charge are additional. Food & beverage minimums may apply. Menus and packages can be customized to fit your needs and budget. Call for details.

AVAILABILITY: Year-round, daily.

SERVICES/AMENITIES:

Catering: in-house
Kitchen Facilities: n/a
Tables & Chairs: provided
Linens, Silver, etc.: provided
Restrooms: wheelchair accessible
Dance Floor: provided
Bride's Dressing Area: yes
AV/Meeting Equipment: CBA

Parking: large complimentary lot
Accommodations: no guest rooms
Outdoor Night Lighting: yes
Outdoor Cooking Facilities: BBQ
Cleanup: provided
View: fairways, lake, landscaped grounds
Other: house centerpieces and wedding cake are included

RESTRICTIONS:

Alcohol: in-house
Smoking: outside only
Music: amplified OK

Wheelchair Access: yes
Insurance: not required

Aquarium of the Pacific

Aquarium and Event Facility

100 Aquarium Way, Long Beach
562/951-1663

www.aquariumofpacific.org/plan_your_event
aquariumofpacific@lbaop.org

- Rehearsal Dinners
- Ceremonies
- Wedding Receptions
- Private Parties
- Corporate Events
- Meetings
- Film Shoots
- Accommodations

You're exchanging vows in a place like no other: Behind you slivers of light filter down through three stories of liquid turquoise, illuminating tall flowing sea plants and the iridescent sea creatures that are your audience. As your senses take in the enveloping hush and the gentle sway of the blue water, you feel at once serene and enlivened.

Such is the magical effect of the brilliant Blue Cavern, the ceremony site of choice at the Aquarium of the Pacific in Long Beach. Receptions are held in this area as well, but there are a variety of other options. One favorite is the intimate Rooftop Veranda, where gorgeous sunsets are a regular occurrence. Sheltered on three sides and half-shaded by a canvas cover, it boasts a 180-degree view of the water that encompasses Rainbow Harbor, the lighthouse, and even the *Queen Mary*. It's perfect for rehearsal dinners, bridal showers, and cocktail receptions. Smaller gatherings also take place in Café Scuba, which opens onto a terrace overlooking the docks.

Larger events unfold in The Great Hall, an exciting space featuring multiple skylights and a life-size suspended blue whale that presides majestically over the festivities. The hall is equipped with an 8-screen projection system and state-of-the-art sound and video. Automated screens, which cover the skylights at the touch of a button, enable you to project your own slideshow or videos—as well as the Aquarium's award-winning short films—around the room for all to see.

The space can be "designed" to create whatever mood suits you, from low-key to theatrical. For something fun, go with a more fanciful theme, like silhouettes of hammerhead sharks and penguins swimming by amidst blue and green swirling lights.

Depending on the arrangements you've made with the museum, guests can wander among aquarium exhibits and marvel at the wonders of the deep. Many remarkable habitats and ecosystems are represented here in engaging watery displays. Amber forests of giant swaying kelp beds, multihued tropical coral reefs, and translucent floating sea life grab your attention and ignite the imagination. Watch playful otters, sea lions and harbor seals…delight in the penguins that meet and mate for life. One is instantly immersed in the enchantment of the sea and its fascinating inhabitants.

Located adjacent to Rainbow Harbor in downtown Long Beach, the Aquarium is truly a one-of-a-kind event location with incredible marine views and spectacular exhibits. For ocean lovers or those just looking for a truly singular environment for their celebration, this is a magnificent place. Its sights and sounds will transport you and your guests to an underwater fantasy come to life.

CEREMONY CAPACITY: The Blue Cavern seats 300 guests.

EVENT/RECEPTION & MEETING CAPACITY: The Great Hall accommodates 500 seated, and the Rooftop Veranda seats 120. When the venue is reserved in its entirety, it can host a reception-style event for up to 2,500 guests, indoors and out.

FEES & DEPOSITS: 25% of the event total is required to reserve your date. An additional 25% payment is due 90 days prior, and the balance is due 14 days prior to the event. Wedding packages, which require a 150-guest minimum, start at $79/person. Tax, alcohol, and a 22% service charge are additional. Pricing for smaller groups varies; custom menus are available.

AVAILABILITY: Year-round, daily. Events in the Great Hall may begin at 7pm; on the Veranda, they can be hosted during the day or evening.

SERVICES/AMENITIES:

Catering: in-house

Kitchen Facilities: n/a

Tables & Chairs: some provided, CBA

Linens, Silver, etc.: some provided, CBA

Restrooms: wheelchair accessible

Dance Area: yes, slate floor

Bride's & Groom's Dressing Areas: yes

AV/Meeting Equipment: provided, extra fee

Parking: garage nearby

Accommodations: no guest rooms

Outdoor Night Lighting: CBA

Outdoor Cooking Facilities: BBQ CBA

Cleanup: provided

View: cityscape, coastline, harbor

Other: picnic area

RESTRICTIONS:

Alcohol: in-house

Smoking: not permitted

Music: amplified OK

Wheelchair Access: yes

Insurance: liability required

Want to find more venues and services? Check out our informative website, www.HereComesTheGuide.com.

259

Earl Burns Miller Japanese Garden

Japanese Garden

California State University, Long Beach

Earl Warren Drive, Long Beach

562/985-8889

www.csulb.edu/~jgarden
jgcoordinators@csulb.edu

● Rehearsal Dinners	● Corporate Events
● Ceremonies	● Meetings
● Wedding Receptions	● Film Shoots
● Private Parties	○ Accommodations

Breathe deep, relax, and let yourself fall into the lush embrace of the Earl Burns Miller Japanese Garden. Situated in a tranquil enclave on the campus of Cal State Long Beach, the Miller Garden melts away any stress associated with hosting an important celebration. Not only are you instantly enveloped in beauty, you're relieved of any lingering concerns by your experienced in-house event coordinator.

The same careful attention is bestowed on the meticulously maintained garden. Rocks and plants are artistically transformed into poetic compositions of form and texture; living things play amidst a harmonious world of earth and water, light and shadow. This powerful place enhances your appreciation of subtle aesthetics, like the velvety lavender of bearded irises or the rustle of the breeze through the weeping willows. In this state of heightened awareness, the joy shared with your friends, family, and that "special someone" seems almost tangible.

Arriving guests gather in a rectangular courtyard outside the main garden. A row of lemon eucalyptus trees screens the courtyard from the outside world and flavors the air with a tangy aroma. Bonsai trees are grouped around the perimeter, and a wooden entry gate is flanked by stone "lion dogs." Lest they seem threatening, a cluster of bamboo bends gently towards the entrance and beckons you inside.

Spread before you is a vision of nature's nirvana: A pathway winds around a curvaceous pond rippling with the movement of over 200 brightly colored koi. Nearby, the graceful branches of a Chinese flame tree frame the wedding cake, dynamically showcased by a spotlight hidden within the leaves. Other decorative accents whisper rather than shout—stone lanterns peek out from lacy greenery; a three-tiered pagoda rests among rare black-stemmed bamboo; an ebony-pebbled beach glistens in the sunlight. Seasonal offerings include a springtime rhapsody of rainbow blooms, and a fall aria by the flame tree, bursting into scarlet song.

The garden's structural elements help define your celebration. At the far end of the pond a Moon Bridge arches across a waterfall that cascades down moss-covered rocks. Dressed with tulle and garlands, or unadorned against the watery backdrop, the Moon Bridge puts the bridal party on dramatic display. While the immediate family is seated at the base of the bridge, the rest of the guests have a view across the pond from the wooden Zig Zag Bridge alongside another waterfall. Feel free to add multicultural flourishes. For example, one bride had African-American "prayer dancers" parade through the crowd, and a Jewish *chuppah* is a standout on the Moon Bridge.

During the cocktail hour, guests adjourn to the courtyard while the garden is set up for the reception. When everyone reconvenes at the pond, guests are wined and dined around the water's edge, while the newlyweds snuggle at a sweetheart table on their own pondside platform. As dusk falls, the bridges and pathways come aglow with romantic lighting.

The garden invites creative adaptations to the usual wedding rituals: Whether or not you hail from the Land of the Rising Sun, you might get into the spirit at the Tea House (reached from a small side path), and greet your guests with a steaming cup of tea. The adjacent Zen Garden, featuring loose gravel in patterns resembling the sea, is a peaceful spot for a hired masseuse to give guests a few minutes of pampering. Rather than showering the newlyweds with rice, loved ones toss food to the *koi,* symbols of strength and longevity. The possibilities are virtually endless, and so are the memories created at this very special place.

CEREMONY CAPACITY: The Garden holds 200 seated guests.

EVENT/RECEPTION & MEETING CAPACITY: The Garden accommodates 150 seated or 200 standing guests.

FEES & DEPOSITS: For ceremonies, a $900 deposit is required to reserve your date; for receptions and other social functions, a $1,100 deposit is required. The balance is due 60 days prior to the event. Rental fees are $2,400 for a ceremony and $4,500 for a wedding and reception plus the cost of catering and equipment. Special rates are available on Friday and Sunday evenings and Saturday mornings. Meals by *Thank Goodness its Sofia, Choura Venue Services* and *Jay's Catering* range $38–80/person. Tax, alcohol and a 20% service charge are additional.

AVAILABILITY: Year-round, daily, anytime.

SERVICES/AMENITIES:

Catering: provided by *Thank Goodness its Sofia, Choura Venue Services* and *Jay's Catering*
Kitchen Facilities: n/a
Tables & Chairs: available
Linens, Silver, etc.: through caterer
Restrooms: wheelchair accessible
Dance Floor: available
Bride's Dressing Area: yes
AV/Meeting Equipment: available

Parking: ample, included in packages
Accommodations: no guest rooms
Outdoor Night Lighting: yes
Outdoor Cooking Facilities: CBA
Cleanup: provided
View: garden, waterfall
Other: site coordinator

RESTRICTIONS:

Alcohol: provided by *Thank Goodness its Sofia, Choura Venue Services* and *Jay's Catering*
Smoking: outside of garden gates only
Music: amplified OK with volume restrictions

Wheelchair Access: yes
Insurance: included in packages
Other: no rice, birdseed, confetti or rose petals

El Dorado Park Golf Course

Golf Course

2400 N. Studebaker Road, Long Beach
888/876-8247

www.eldoradoparkgc.com
www.countryclubreceptions.com
privateeventmanager@eldoradoparkgc.com

● Rehearsal Dinners		● Corporate Events
● Ceremonies		● Meetings
● Wedding Receptions		● Film Shoots
● Private Parties		Accommodations

Set in the quiet El Dorado Park neighborhood of Long Beach, this historic golf course—once the site of the Queen Mary Open and now home to the prestigious Long Beach Open—is a favorite event location for locals and visitors alike. The lovely public park that surrounds the landscaped course frames it with even more trees, pretty paths and picturesque waterways—all ideal for beautiful day-of-portraits of the bride and groom.

Couples can exchange vows outdoors on the Garden Ceremony Lawn overlooking the 18th green and gorgeous views of the course. Towering trees act as green "umbrellas," providing natural shade. There's also a "Winner's Board" here that often serves as a backdrop for a mini stage where wedding party photos can be taken.

Cocktail receptions and dinner dances are held just a few steps away in the airy, white Garden Pavilion, a dramatic tented venue. Set apart from the clubhouse, it features a private Garden Patio entrance and a high, peaked ceiling with elegant draping; at night, chandeliers and twinkle lights contribute to a magical, fairy-tale atmosphere.

The space is incredibly flexible, which helps explain its widespread appeal. In addition to wedding receptions, this affordable and immensely popular setting accommodates corporate events, bar and bat mitzvahs, quinceañeras, sweet sixteen parties, anniversary celebrations—even auctions, mini-festivals and tournaments! El Dorado will provide all of your tables, chairs, linens, glassware, flatware and more. However, you can also bring in lounge furniture, decorations, special uplighting and floral arrangements to personalize the environment and create an ambiance that suits your party style.

Require more space? Inside the recently renovated clubhouse, you'll find additional options. The handsome restaurant treats diners to floor-to-ceiling windows that showcase patio and golf course vistas, while the private dining room with coffered ceilings, mood lighting, and stained-glass accents is ideal for rehearsal dinners or smaller functions. When schedules permit, both can be used to expand and enhance your function.

El Dorado's on-site Private Event Manager and experienced staff will make sure your every expectation is met. Come see why those who have hosted their important celebrations here call their experiences "unforgettable."

CEREMONY CAPACITY: The facility holds 95 seated guests indoors and 350 seated outdoors.

EVENT/RECEPTION & MEETING CAPACITY: Indoors, the facility accommodates 95 seated or 150 standing guests. Outdoors, it accommodates 350 seated or 400 standing.

MEETING CAPACITY: Meeting spaces seat 350 guests.

FEES & DEPOSITS: A nonrefundable deposit, which is applied to your food & beverage total, is required to reserve your date. The amount of the deposit varies depending on how far in advance you book. Payment terms for the balance also vary, and may be arranged on an individual basis. Meals start at $20/person and wedding packages start at $39/person. Tax, alcohol and service charge are additional. Menus and packages can be customized to fit your needs and budget. Call for details.

AVAILABILITY: Year-round, daily, anytime.

SERVICES/AMENITIES:

Catering: in-house
Kitchen Facilities: n/a
Tables & Chairs: provided
Linens, Silver, etc.: provided
Restrooms: wheelchair accessible
Dance Floor: portable provided
Bride's Dressing Area: CBA
AV/Meeting Equipment: CBA

Parking: large lot, on-street
Accommodations: no guest rooms
Outdoor Night Lighting: provided
Outdoor Cooking Facilities: BBQ CBA
Cleanup: provided
View: forest, garden; panorama of fairways and park
Other: event coordination

RESTRICTIONS:

Alcohol: full in-house bar
Smoking: designated areas only
Music: amplified OK with restrictions

Wheelchair Access: yes
Insurance: not required

Queen Mary

1126 Queens Highway, Long Beach
562/499-1749
www.queenmary.com/weddings
weddings@queenmary.com

Historic Ship & Wedding Chapel

● Rehearsal Dinners	● Corporate Events
● Ceremonies	● Meetings
● Wedding Receptions	● Film Shoots
● Private Parties	● Accommodations

Celebrate in a place that is like no other—aboard the *Queen Mary*. Permanently docked in Long Beach Harbor, this luxury ocean liner-turned-hotel/attraction offers the perfect venue for your wedding as well as breathtaking views.

The legendary *Queen Mary* set out on her maiden voyage from Southampton, England to New York City in 1936 and was considered the only way to travel for the world's rich and famous. As soon as you step onto the ship, you get a sense of the glamour of that bygone era. She's a treasure trove of Art Deco design, with event facilities guaranteed to wow your guests.

Fourteen luxurious salons are available for your reception, and collectively feature a wealth of handcrafted touches including exquisite paneling, unique light fixtures, etched-glass doors, original murals and carved marble fireplaces. And while you and your guests are appreciating the splendid surroundings, the *Queen Mary's* full-service catering staff will take excellent care of everyone.

The *Queen Mary* also provides both outdoor and indoor options for your ceremony. To take advantage of the sunshine or sunset, get married on the bow or stern, under the Gazebo or on one of the decks. For a more traditional setting, the finely crafted Royal Wedding Chapel is a stunning choice.

An on-site wedding specialist can help you plan every detail of your wedding, from invitations to entertainment, as well as your rehearsal dinner, ceremony, reception, and even the breakfast before your honeymoon.

When the festivities have ended and the moon has risen over the harbor, retire to one of the ship's original first-class staterooms for a romantic and peaceful night. It's no mystery why every year hundreds of couples have their wedding on this extraordinary landmark: The *Queen Mary* sets the stage for an unforgettable experience.

CEREMONY CAPACITY: The Royal Wedding Chapel holds 150 seated. The Sun Deck Gazebo holds 100 seated. The Verandah Deck holds 350 seated.

EVENT/RECEPTION CAPACITY: The ship has 14 rooms that can accommodate 20–1,500 seated guests. With a tent in the Queen Mary Park, receptions of up to 2,000 may be held (a minimum of 800 is required for the tent, and additional rental fees and permits are required).

MEETING CAPACITY: There is 45,000 square feet of meeting space and 50,000 square feet of exhibit space. Up to 500 seated guests can be accommodated.

FEES & DEPOSITS: For weddings, a nonrefundable/nontransferable deposit is required to hold your date. The estimated event total is payable 30 days prior to the event date. Reception packages start at $60/person (ceremony cost is additional). Tax, beverages and a 22% service charge are additional.

AVAILABILITY: Year-round, daily, including holidays.

SERVICES/AMENITIES:

Catering: in-house
Kitchen Facilities: n/a
Tables & Chairs: provided
Linens, Silver, etc.: provided
Restrooms: wheelchair accessible
Dance Floor: provided
Bride's Dressing Area: in Chapel only
AV/Meeting Equipment: full range, extra charge

Parking: hosted and non-hosted parking available
Accommodations: 346 guest rooms
Outdoor Night Lighting: CBA
Outdoor Cooking Facilities: no
Cleanup: provided
View: Long Beach Harbor and city skyline
Other: event coordination and wedding planning services

RESTRICTIONS:

Alcohol: in-house, no BYO
Smoking: on deck only
Music: amplified OK

Wheelchair Access: limited (no wheelchair access to Verandah Deck)
Insurance: not required
Other: security optional

Recreation Park 18 Golf Course

Golf Club

5001 Deukmejian Drive, Long Beach
888/998-3560

www.countryclubreceptions.com
privateeventdirector@recreationparkgc.com

●	Rehearsal Dinners	●	Corporate Events
●	Ceremonies	●	Meetings
●	Wedding Receptions	●	Film Shoots
●	Private Parties		Accommodations

From its earliest days, Recreation Park Golf Course has been *the* place for Long Beach residents to get away from it all. Back in 1909, as a beautiful-but-rugged country club, it attracted golfers who were willing to take a train from town, and then hike to the course where the "greens" were actually made of slicked-down sand. Eventually the club approved a horse and buggy to shuttle the players, which vastly improved the golfers' experience and no doubt increased membership.

Today, even with a wide boulevard circling the grounds, you still get that sense of leaving the city behind once you enter this full-service park. As you drive in you first notice the lawn bowlers enjoying their genteel pastime. Then you pass a long row of tennis courts, and turn up a hill where the white Spanish Colonial clubhouse, with its columned portico and red-tile roof, basks in the peaceful views of the surrounding property. Built in 1926 by the Bixby family, this historic landmark was deeded to the city of Long Beach in 1980 for one dollar, in what has to be one of the better real estate deals of the century.

Only one wedding is held in the clubhouse at a time, so you and your guests have free rein of the facilities. Begin your affair in the circular Rose Garden, a delightful ceremony spot featuring a 75-foot garden pathway leading you to a beautiful gazebo encased with rosebushes. Afterwards, serve cocktails right there on the lawn or follow the short pathway to an intimate hedged patio festooned with twinkle lights. At the appointed time three sets of French doors just off the patio open to reveal the grandly proportioned Main Ballroom.

Here, architectural details, like soaring ceilings and the original dark wood crossbeams with period chandeliers, evoke the lifestyle of the wealthy in the 1920s. A gilded *trompe l'oeil* balcony accentuates the room's height and lends a European ambiance. Above it, artisan stained-glass windows set off a subtle interplay of light, as the rays from the setting sun softly stream in while tiny runner lights begin to glitter just below the beams. A large built-in dance floor in front of a massive decorative fireplace provides ample room for a band or DJ.

Since the entire place is yours to enjoy, take advantage of the adjacent parlor for quiet conversation by a cozy hearth…as a retreat for the bridal party…or as a separate children's room. You can also step out onto the front portico to savor the night air. At the end of the evening, when your celebration has wound down and you drive back through the park's entrance, you'll find it hard to believe you were so close to the city all this time.

CEREMONY CAPACITY: The Rose Garden holds 250 seated guests; indoor spaces hold up to 200 seated guests.

EVENT/RECEPTION & MEETING CAPACITY: The Garden holds up to 300 seated or 350 standing guests; the Main Ballroom accommodates 180 seated or 200 standing.

FEES & DEPOSITS: A nonrefundable deposit, which is applied to your food & beverage total, is required to reserve your date. The amount of the deposit varies depending on how far in advance you book. Payment terms for the balance also vary, and may be arranged on an individual basis. Meals range $37–75/person. Tax, alcohol, and a 20% service charge are additional. Food & beverage minimums may apply. Menus and packages can be customized to fit your needs and budget. Call for details.

AVAILABILITY: Year-round, daily, 6am–1am.

SERVICES/AMENITIES:

Catering: provided
Kitchen Facilities: n/a
Tables & Chairs: provided
Linens, Silver, etc.: provided
Restrooms: wheelchair accessible
Dance Floor: provided
Bride's Dressing Area: yes
AV/Meeting Equipment: projector and screen

Parking: large lot and on street
Accommodations: no guestrooms
Outdoor Night Lighting: yes
Outdoor Cooking Facilities: BBQ CBA
Cleanup: provided
View: park, fairways, landscaped grounds

RESTRICTIONS:

Alcohol: provided
Smoking: outside only
Music: amplified OK

Wheelchair Access: yes
Insurance: not required

This is important! Tell locations you're reading HERE COMES THE GUIDE and ask if our information is still current.

267

Skylinks at Long Beach

Golf Club

4800 East Wardlow Road, Long Beach
888/625-6682

www.countryclubreceptions.com
privateeventmanager@skylinksgc.com

● Rehearsal Dinners	● Corporate Events
● Ceremonies	● Meetings
● Wedding Receptions	● Film Shoots
● Private Parties	Accommodations

The sky's the limit at Skylinks Golf Course when it comes to satisfying every wish, dream and special request for your wedding. You want doves released after the ceremony? No problem. Tents set up outside? Consider it done! In fact, it's hard to find a more accommodating staff than the one at Long Beach's premier public golf course.

While you're thinking up ways to let your creativity run wild, you'll be pleased to know that the event spaces here—whether in the clubhouse or on the golf course itself—are easy to customize. They've hosted all kinds of celebrations, from a casual cocktail reception to the most formal plated dinner and everything in between!

Their ceremony site is a thing of beauty. Couples say "I do" beneath a white, trellised arch set against a striking backdrop: a free-form rock waterfall and cascading pools, surrounded by a lush landscape of palm trees, flowering bushes and other greenery. As vows are exchanged, guests look on from their lawn seating, arranged in rows on either side of a petal-strewn aisle.

Receptions are held in the expansive Sky Room, whose vaulted ceiling makes it feel even more spacious. A wall of windows overlooks the property's signature waterfall, which is dramatically lit up at night. Just outside the Sky Room, a comfortable patio is yours to enjoy as well, with the nearby greens and the glorious waterfall balancing nature and artistry.

However, if you happen to have a guest list of 200 or more, consider having your festivities in a custom-designed tent on the driving range. In most cases, you can still have your ceremony in front of the gorgeous waterfall just a few yards away. Tenting the grass is also popular for corporate parties and fundraisers.

Providing numerous choices and flexibility, the Skylinks banquet staff functions like an attentive concierge—diligently translating what you imagine into the wedding you've always wanted.

CEREMONY CAPACITY: The Waterfall Lawn accommodates up to 200 seated guests.

EVENT/RECEPTION CAPACITY: The Sky Room accommodates up to 200 seated guests. Outdoors, the site holds 500 seated.

MEETING CAPACITY: Several spaces seat up to 200 guests.

FEES & DEPOSITS: A nonrefundable deposit, which is applied to your food & beverage total, is required to reserve your date. The amount of the deposit varies depending on how far in advance you book. Payment terms for the balance also vary, and may be arranged on an individual basis. Rental fees vary depending on the day of the event and guest count. Meals start at $40/person. Tax, alcohol and service charge are additional. Food & beverage minimums may apply. Menus and packages can be customized to fit your needs and budget. Call for details.

AVAILABILITY: Year-round, daily, 6am–midnight.

SERVICES/AMENITIES:

Catering: in-house
Kitchen Facilities: n/a
Tables & Chairs: provided
Linens, Silver, etc.: provided
Restrooms: wheelchair accessible
Dance Floor: yes
Bride's Dressing Area: no
AV/Meeting Equipment: some provided, more CBA

Parking: large lot, on street
Accommodations: no guest rooms
Outdoor Night Lighting: provided
Outdoor Cooking Facilities: CBA
Cleanup: provided
View: waterfall, garden, pond, fairways
Other: some coordination

RESTRICTIONS:

Alcohol: in-house
Smoking: outdoors only
Music: amplified OK

Wheelchair Access: yes
Insurance: not required

Shade Hotel

Hotel

1221 North Valley Drive, Manhattan Beach
310/546-4995
www.shadehotel.com
events@shadehotel.com

● Rehearsal Dinners	● Corporate Events
● Ceremonies	● Meetings
● Wedding Receptions	● Film Shoots
● Private Parties	○ Accommodations

If event sites were rated by their "cool" factor, Shade would be off the charts. This luxuriously hip, five-star boutique hotel perfectly captures the breezy, laid-back essence of its seaside community. Shade's super-convenient location at the edge of Metlox Plaza puts you just two blocks from the beach and steps away from a wide variety of shops and restaurants.

As you walk through the hotel, the trappings of "cool" are everywhere, from the flower-filled vases that seem to float like magic in front of the mirrored wall in the lounge to the eye-catching cyclone fireplaces in many of the guest rooms. Accents such as handmade sea urchin chandeliers and an artful display of sea ferns are visual links to the nearby ocean.

The setting is an inspired one for a destination wedding (not to mention a wrap party, corporate bash or product launch). Although you can reserve individual areas for your event, we recommend "The Ultimate Wedding" package: booking the entire hotel—including its 38 guest rooms—for the weekend. You'll not only have a fabulous home-to-die-for all to yourselves, you'll be free to choreograph your celebration exactly as you like, taking advantage of the dynamic flow between Shade's unique spaces.

You might want to kick things off with cocktails on the slate-tiled rooftop Skydeck, where your guests can mingle over martinis and mojitos while checking out the view of Manhattan Beach and the Pacific, spread out below. Then everyone gathers downstairs for your ceremony in the Courtyard, Shade's signature space. Enclosed on three sides by the hotel, this versatile open-air venue works well for daytime or evening events. Couples exchange vows on the tile-and-stone steps at the far end, with a striking 20-foot-high stone waterfall behind them. Walls of ivy framing the waterfall and planters sprouting bright green bamboo add natural bursts of color. Fabric banners or colored lighting can be strung overhead for a dramatic effect, and brides often use one of the second-story balconies facing the Courtyard for the bouquet toss.

Après-ceremony, the party moves into the Zinc Lounge for hors d'oeuvres and more drinks while the Courtyard is reset for the reception. The mix of warm cherrywood, cool steel, and soft lighting creates a sultry atmosphere. Folding glass doors open to the Zinc Terrace, the perfect al fresco spot for nursing that sub-zero martini (in a glass made of ice) and people-watching in the plaza below.

Dinner is served back in the Courtyard, which has been transformed into as casual or elegant a scene as you wish. And if you need more space for that extra-long guest list, additional seating can be arranged in the Green Room upstairs. It overlooks the Courtyard, so celebrants on both floors will still feel connected.

The staff at Shade are finicky about everything, and they almost never say "no" to anything. They'll help you plan your dream wedding, including a customized menu based on the freshest, highest quality products. They'll even replicate your grandmother's Swedish meatballs!

In the curious alchemy of perfection, all the elements at Shade—the fluid design, the exquisite details, the people and the very air—come together in a harmonious environment that, well, makes people happy. Very happy. So give yourself the most sublime wedding gift of all: a day—or three!—in the Shade.

CEREMONY & EVENT/RECEPTION CAPACITY: The hotel holds 150 seated or 200 standing guests indoors and outdoors.

MEETING CAPACITY: Meeting spaces seat 60 guests indoors.

FEES & DEPOSITS: 50% of the event minimum is required to reserve your date and the balance is due 10 days prior to the event. The minimum ranges $2,000–25,000 depending on the date and time of the event. Meals range $35–100/person. Tax, alcohol and a 22% service charge are additional.

AVAILABILITY: Year-round, daily, noon–midnight.

SERVICES/AMENITIES:

Catering: in-house
Kitchen Facilities: n/a
Tables & Chairs: provided
Linens, Silver, etc.: provided
Restrooms: wheelchair accessible
Dance Floor: CBA
Bride's Dressing Area: CBA
AV/Meeting Equipment: some provided

Parking: valet available
Accommodations: 38 guest rooms
Outdoor Night Lighting: yes
Outdoor Cooking Facilities: BBQ CBA
Cleanup: provided
View: garden, cityscape, coastline, pool area, fountain
Other: event coordination, custom décor, chair covers, ice carvings, lounge furniture, photo booth

RESTRICTIONS:

Alcohol: in-house or BYO with corkage fee
Smoking: outdoors only
Music: amplified OK with restrictions

Wheelchair Access: yes
Insurance: liability required

Verandas Beach House

401 Rosecrans Avenue, Manhattan Beach

310/546-7805

www.verandasbh.com
info@verandasmb.com

Special Events Facility

● Rehearsal Dinners	● Corporate Events
● Ceremonies	● Meetings
● Wedding Receptions	● Film Shoots
● Private Parties	Accommodations

We love beach chic for a Southern California wedding, and that's exactly what this two-story, Cape Cod-style confection of a Manhattan Beach venue serves up—along with fabulous service and outstanding fare. Tucked away in a private garden just a short walk from the sandy shore (where beach ceremonies are an option), Verandas Beach House and its coastal ambiance will make you feel as if the honeymoon has already begun.

An ornate wrought-iron gate invites you behind the high white walls and into a fragrant little oasis, complete with manicured lawn and pathways, trellises, two petite waterfalls an exquisite koi pond full of flowering water plants and jewel-bright fish. Sunlit and dazzling by day, trimmed in twinkling lights at night, it's an entrancing setting for a wedding ceremony or a garden party.

A grand staircase, ideal for dramatic entrances and group photos, leads from the garden to the patio lounge upstairs. Furnished with comfortable outdoor sofas, it's perfect for chilling and chatting al fresco. Then, when you set foot inside the house, you'll think you've been swept away to some faraway sun-drenched place: Design details like soft seashell colorations against crisp white contrasts, luxurious fabrics, and surprising textures suggest the sand and the sea.

Have a champagne cocktail or some other specially concocted libation in the enticing white wainscoted vestibule with its driftwood accents and black marble bar, then step into a capacious chamber with handsome French hardwood flooring and a beautiful lounge area with expansive windows that frame an ocean view. A wonderful environment for exchanging vows, a cocktail reception, dining or dancing, it will elevate any event and infuse it with a fresh, easy elegance.

From here, another stunning staircase (there's an elevator as well) descends to more lovely spaces, but you might want to pause on the landing—which is large enough to seat a string quartet and a super spot for photos—to bask in the opulent atmosphere. Downstairs the "swept away" experience continues. The exquisitely appointed bride's room and restrooms have a gracious spa-like ambiance, but the real show-stopper is the large skylit banquet room in which flashes of white play against sophisticated neutral shades, sumptuous textures and coastal details to create a rich yet contemporary tone.

The final element that makes this luxurious beach house an extraordinary event site is *New York Food Company,* renowned for their talented catering team and brilliantly presented cuisine. These creative professionals will have you and your guests believing, for an enchanted moment in time, that you're the very fortunate residents of your own seaside estate.

CEREMONY CAPACITY: Verandas Beach House holds up to 250 seated, indoors or outdoors.

EVENT/RECEPTION & MEETING CAPACITY: The entire facility can accommodate up to 250.

FEES & DEPOSITS: For weddings: A $4,000 payment, which is applied toward the event total, is required to book the site. A second payment for half the estimated total is due 6 months prior to the event, and the balance and guaranteed guest count are due 9 days prior. Event pricing starts at $70/person. The venue rental fee, tax, alcohol and a 23% production fee are additional. The venue rental fee ranges $2,500–9,500 depending on the day of the week and time frame. There's an additional $1,700 charge for a ceremony in conjunction with a reception. For a ceremony-only, which can be held Monday–Friday, the charge is $2,500. During the off-season (November 1st–June 30th), significant discounts are offered on the rental fee. All-inclusive midweek wedding packages start at $159/person.

For business functions: Breakfast meetings start at $15/person, luncheon meetings at $18/person. A $1,500 room rental fee and an $850 food minimum apply for events taking place Monday–Thursday, 8am–5pm.

AVAILABILITY: Weddings take place year-round, daily, 11am–4pm or 6pm–11pm. Additional hours can be accommodated for an extra fee.

SERVICES/AMENITIES:

Catering: provided by *New York Food Company*
Kitchen Facilities: n/a
Tables & Chairs: provided
Linens, Silver, etc.: provided
Restrooms: wheelchair accessible
Dance Floor: provided
Bride's Dressing Area: yes
AV/Meeting Equipment: CBA, extra fee

Parking: attended lot
Accommodations: no guest rooms
Outdoor Night Lighting: yes
Outdoor Cooking Facilities: no
Cleanup: provided
View: ocean and garden
Other: event design and coordination; sound system

RESTRICTIONS:

Alcohol: in-house or BYO
Smoking: outside only
Music: amplified OK indoors

Wheelchair Access: yes
Insurance: required for all vendors

La Venta Inn

796 Via Del Monte, Palos Verdes Estates

310/373-0123

www.laventa.com
info@laventa.com

Banquet Facility with Garden

● Rehearsal Dinners	● Corporate Events
● Ceremonies	● Meetings
● Wedding Receptions	● Film Shoots
● Private Parties	Accommodations

Early South Bay developers designed La Venta Inn as an exclusive retreat to entertain prospective land buyers, and it occupies a prime spot on a hill overlooking the sweep of the Palos Verdes Peninsula.

Built in the 1920s, its Spanish-style architecture is set off by a distinctive tower, red-tiled roofs and, in front, a court-yard with a bubbling fountain enclosed by a bougainvillea-covered arbor. At one time, La Venta Inn was used as a personal residence, and it has all the warmth and convenience of a private estate.

Inside, the rooms are spacious and airy, with wood floors and cream-colored walls that evoke vintage elegance and provide a neutral backdrop for decorations. The large main ballroom has lofty open-beamed ceilings, antique wrought-iron chandeliers and a handsome fireplace with a carved stone mantelpiece. French doors open out onto a Palos Verdes stone patio that spans the length of the house, commanding stunning views of the entire L.A. Basin and Santa Monica Bay below. Two steps lead down onto a broad semicircle of lawn surrounded by flowering shrubs and palm trees. A classic white gazebo stands at the lawn's edge, with the sweep of the coastline as a dramatic backdrop. The developers chose this site well—it has a view that makes you want to stay here long after your celebration.

CEREMONY CAPACITY: La Venta Inn can accommodate up to 250 guests.

EVENT/RECEPTION CAPACITY: La Venta Inn holds 250 seated or standing guests.

MEETING CAPACITY: The venue seats up to 125 theater-style.

FEES & DEPOSITS: For weddings: A $4,000 payment, which is applied toward the event total, is required to book the site. A second payment for half the estimated total is due 6 months prior to the event, and the balance and guaranteed guest count are due 9 days prior. The rental fee ranges $4,000–12,500 depending on the day of the week and time frame. During the off-season (November 1st–June 30th), it ranges $2,500–7,000. There's an additional $2,250 charge for a ceremony. Catering pricing, which also includes exclusive use of the property, a personal event coordinator and complimentary parking, starts at $70/person for food and $16/person for beverages.

For business functions and meetings, fees vary depending on the guest count and food service. Please call for details.

AVAILABILITY: For weddings: Year-round, daily, 10am–3pm or 5pm–10pm. Functions are in 5-hour blocks, with 2 events per day. Additional hours and all-day events can be accommodated for an extra fee.

For business functions: Meeting space is available Monday–Thursday in blocks of 4, 6 or 8 hours.

SERVICES/AMENITIES:

Catering: provided by *New York Food Company*

Kitchen Facilities: n/a

Tables & Chairs: provided

Linens, Silver, etc.: provided

Restrooms: wheelchair accessible

Dance Floor: provided

Bride's & Groom's Dressing Areas: yes

AV/Meeting Equipment: full range, extra fee

Parking: valet or attended parking provided

Accommodations: no guest rooms

Outdoor Night Lighting: yes

Outdoor Cooking Facilities: no

Cleanup: provided

View: Santa Monica Bay, L.A. Basin and coastal vistas

Other: event coordinator, state-of-the-art sound system

RESTRICTIONS:

Alcohol: in-house, or BYO

Smoking: outdoors only

Music: vendors require approval

Wheelchair Access: limited access; call for details

Insurance: required for all vendors

Overwhelmed? Use the search criteria on www.HereComesTheGuide.com to narrow down your choices.

275

Palos Verdes Golf Club

Country Club

3301 Via Campesina, Palos Verdes Estates

310/375-2533

www.pvgc.com
catering@pvgc.com

● Rehearsal Dinners	● Corporate Events
● Ceremonies	● Meetings
● Wedding Receptions	● Film Shoots
● Private Parties	Accommodations

With its commanding ocean, city and mountain views, this location is a stunner. The rural surroundings also add a peaceful quality to the setting: picturesque stables nearby, horses walking down the street, and woods everywhere you look. Although the rambling Mediterranean Revival-style clubhouse has recently undergone an $11 million renovation, all of its rustic touches—wrought-iron gates and chandeliers, wood-beamed ceilings, and distressed furniture—have been preserved. The result? Palos Verdes Golf Club is more fabulous than ever for hosting an ultra-glam event.

When the club opened in 1924 it was an instant success, immediately attracting film stars and celebrities to the beautiful Palos Verdes Peninsula. Today, the venue specializes in weddings and other celebrations, offering a grand collection of handsomely appointed indoor and outdoor spaces for large or small extravaganzas.

The brilliant blue Southern California sky, the Spanish tile roof, the stately palms, and the bougainvillea-draped hillside will make your feel as if you have just stepped into a painting. Here, you're front and center for the best vista ever: breathtaking views of the Queen's Necklace—the sparkling curve of coastline between Rancho Palos Verdes and Malibu, visible from the event spaces as well as the outside areas. Have your ceremony against that backdrop in the broad Wedding Garden, followed by cocktails and hors d'oeuvres on the clubhouse's spacious Patio Terrace—your photographer's camera will definitely be clicking.

For an indoor variation on the picture-perfect theme, let guests head into the Lunada Bay Room. Elegantly furnished and large enough for banquet tables, food stations, a quartet, or strolling performers—there's even a grand piano—it looks out onto the Wedding Garden and can also serve as the Palos Verdes Ballroom foyer for larger celebrations. The adjacent Palos Verdes Ballroom, with its high open-beam ceiling, floor-to-ceiling windows, and spectacular Veranda Terrace, affords more ocean and golf course panoramas as well as plenty of room for dining and whirling around the dance floor.

That's not all. For more intimate occasions like rehearsal dinners, the Monte Malaga Room, where unobstructed views, terrace access, mood lighting and great audio are *de rigueur,* is an excellent choice. And if you combine it with the adjacent Malaga Cove Dining Room, you nearly double its size. With a property of this magnitude there are additional areas that can be used alone or in combination, not to mention special spots like the Altamira Tower—a bride's retreat with an adorable Juliet balcony. The club's on-site specialists will be delighted to walk you through the many possibilities.

Naturally, Palos Verdes Golf Club also delivers flawless service and superb cuisine. Their talented chef—a member of the internationally renowned *Confrerie de la Chaine des Rotisseurs*—has prepared pages and pages of mouthwatering menu options. After decades of catering to high expectations, the event experts here know how to throw a phenomenal party—plus they love weddings and it shows. You and your guests will undoubtedly rave, like so many who have come before you, about your wonderful experience at this dazzling country club.

CEREMONY CAPACITY: The site seats 500 guests indoors and 300 outdoors.

EVENT/RECEPTION CAPACITY: The facility can accommodate 350 seated or 600 standing guests indoors and 125 seated or 300 standing outdoors.

MEETING CAPACITY: Meeting spaces hold up to 600 seated guests.

FEES & DEPOSITS: A deposit is required to reserve your date. Wedding packages start at $100/person. Personalized and à la carte menus are available.

AVAILABILITY: Year-round, daily, 6am–midnight.

SERVICES/AMENITIES:

Catering: in-house or BYO ethnic caterer with approval
Kitchen Facilities: fully equipped
Tables & Chairs: provided
Linens, Silver, etc.: provided
Restrooms: wheelchair accessible
Dance Floor: portable provided
Bride's & Groom's Dressing Areas: yes
AV/Meeting Equipment: provided

Parking: large complimentary lot
Accommodations: no guest rooms
Outdoor Night Lighting: CBA
Outdoor Cooking Facilities: BBQ on site
Cleanup: included
View: panorama of ocean, mountains, and coastline; cityscape, garden, landscaped grounds, fairways and lake
Other: grand piano, picnic area

RESTRICTIONS:

Alcohol: full in-house bar
Smoking: outdoors only
Music: amplified OK

Wheelchair Access: yes
Insurance: not required

South Coast Botanic Garden

Garden

26300 Crenshaw Boulevard, Palos Verdes Peninsula
310/544-1948
www.southcoastbotanicgarden.org
events@southcoastbotanicgarden.org

● Rehearsal Dinners		● Corporate Events	
● Ceremonies		● Meetings	
● Wedding Receptions		● Film Shoots	
● Private Parties		Accommodations	

Gardenias, lilies, iris, honeysuckle and more than 1,600 rosebushes are only a tiny part of the spectacular floral display at South Coast Botanic Garden. And flowers are just one of the attractions here: With 87 acres of over 150,000 plants and trees—accompanied by arbors, ponds, fountains, meadows, and terraces of every shape and size—this horticultural wonderland is unquestionably one of the most scenic outdoor wedding sites in Los Angeles County.

Whatever the event, your guests will enjoy congregating in the trellised Cornish Courtyard, named after one of the early supporters of this flowering paradise. The small gift shop here is a great place to look for your botanically inspired party favors or for guests to select their own mementos of a celebration they won't want to forget.

From the courtyard, a cart path and walkways lead to a series of garden environments of surprising variety and dimension. The spacious upper meadow features two pergolas and broad lawns with sightlines that draw your attention to a lacy gazebo set like a gemstone in a flowery surround with sweeping views of the rest of the property. This area is roomy enough for any kind of large-scale entertaining—picnics to garden parties to swank nighttime affairs—tented or *en plein air*. The lower meadow, which can be used by itself or in tandem with the upper meadow, has another gazebo and a much more intimate feel.

But this is one location where there are no walls and every short walk takes you to extraordinary places … so why not explore more of the many possibilities? In the children's garden, set between the meadows, young and old will appreciate an enchanting oasis full of bowers and butterflies—it even has its own little bridge. Imagine treating your guests to the magic of a cactus garden at twilight, or watching them happily mingle in an award-winning rose garden full of fragrant paths and special gathering spots. If a stage is in order, consider using the amphitheater, where a border of star jasmine, flowering cherries, white camellias and angel's trumpets will frame any kind of production to perfection. Prefer a setting that's simple and serene? A petite patio complete with koi pond, stone lanterns, and plantings reminiscent of a Japanese garden might be exactly what you're looking for.

Of course there are nonstop photo ops throughout the grounds, but you'll also find lots of practical amenities like an assembly hall, prep kitchen for the caterers, classrooms, and plenty of parking. This foundation- and county-run property is a testament to the power of community and a definite labor of love. With its endless array of bloom-filled event options, as well as a happy and supportive staff that aims to please, South Coast Botanic Garden is a venue that feels as good as it looks.

CEREMONY CAPACITY: The facility holds 350 seated guests indoors and 1,000 seated outdoors.

EVENT/RECEPTION CAPACITY: Several event spaces can accommodate 250 seated or 500 standing indoors and 1,000 seated or 2,000 standing outdoors.

MEETING CAPACITY: The facility holds 400 seated guests.

FEES & DEPOSITS: A $100–1,000 deposit (depending on the space reserved) is required to reserve your date and the balance is due 30 days prior to the event. Event space rental fees start at $500 and vary depending on the spaces reserved, day and time of the event, and the guest count.

AVAILABILITY: Year-round, daily, 9am–10pm.

SERVICES/AMENITIES:

Catering: select from preferred list
Kitchen Facilities: prep only
Tables & Chairs: some provided, more CBA
Linens, Silver, etc.: some provided, more CBA
Restrooms: wheelchair accessible
Dance Floor: CBA
Bride's Dressing Area: yes
AV/Meeting Equipment: CBA

Parking: large lot
Accommodations: no guest rooms
Outdoor Night Lighting: CBA
Outdoor Cooking Facilities: CBA
Cleanup: renter or caterer
View: garden, forest, fountain, courtyard, landscaped grounds, pond, meadow
Other: picnic area, gazebo, event coordinator, extra fee

RESTRICTIONS:

Alcohol: BYO licensed server
Smoking: designated areas only
Music: amplified OK with restrictions

Wheelchair Access: limited
Insurance: liability required

Los Verdes Golf Course

Golf Club

7000 West Los Verdes Drive, Rancho Palos Verdes
888/995-4503

www.countryclubreceptions.com
privateeventdirector@losverdesgc.com

● Rehearsal Dinners	● Corporate Events
● Ceremonies	● Meetings
● Wedding Receptions	● Film Shoots
● Private Parties	○ Accommodations

"The promise of paradise fulfilled" is how one author describes Rancho Palos Verdes, a chic community nestled on a picturesque peninsula. In this coastal Eden, dream homes built on rugged bluffs enjoy panoramas of lush hillsides, crashing surf and spectacular sunsets. Grazing cattle and family farms once inhabited this beautiful 13-square-mile neighborhood, but in 1913 banker Frank Vanderlip began transforming it into a "fashionable and exclusive residential colony." He envisioned an enclave in harmony with its natural surroundings, and during the few minutes it takes to drive through Rancho Palos Verdes you realize how well Vanderlip succeeded.

One of the most striking sites belongs to Los Verdes Golf Course, a private event venue perched on the crest of a gentle slope. If you fantasize about a wedding with the ocean as your backdrop, but are daunted by sky-high prices and attitudes to match, then meet the accommodating folks at Los Verdes—they call the regulars by name and welcome newcomers like they're old friends. On-site event experts offer advice, such as design tips for the reception or the most romantic spots for memorable photographs. They'll also match you up with the cream of the local vendors, who have worked together for years and also know their way around Los Verdes—all of which ensures that your event will come off without a hitch.

And as for getting hitched…Los Verdes has a truly inspiring spot for a wedding ceremony. A circular driveway leads to a pair of wrought-iron gates that open onto the Catalina Terrace, which is flanked by towering pines on one side and glass doors leading to the newly renovated Vista Ballroom on the other. Overlooking the golf greens, the Terrace will seduce your guests with a sweeping view of rolling fairways dotted with blossoms and evergreens, and the azure Pacific beyond. In fact, Los Verdes Golf Course boasts an ocean view from every hole, and couples can wed right on the scenic 10th or 11th tee. At any of the ceremony sites, wedding guests are treated to a captivating scene—stretching from Malibu to Catalina Island—of tranquil ocean, soaring seabirds, and graceful sailboats.

Amidst all this beauty, everyone will want to stay outdoors a little bit longer, so hors d'oeuvres can be set up under the shade of the Terrace's awning. When it's time for the reception, guests flow into the Vista Ballroom, where two walls of floor-to-ceiling windows keep that gorgeous view at hand. Adjoining the Vista is a smaller meeting space that can be sectioned off for restless kids and their toys.

If you're planning a corporate golf tournament or theme party, consider taking over the entire country club. Whatever your celebration requires, Los Verdes delivers with fine cuisine, reasonable prices, and lovely surroundings.

CEREMONY CAPACITY: The Ceremony Terrace seats 175, and the 10th tee 350.

EVENT/RECEPTION CAPACITY: The Vista Ballroom holds 375 seated or 500 standing guests. The Catalina Terrace holds 120 seated or 250 standing.

MEETING CAPACITY: The Vista Ballroom holds 350 seated theater-style or 200 classroom-style.

FEES & DEPOSITS: A nonrefundable deposit, which is applied to your food & beverage total, is required to reserve your date. The amount of the deposit varies depending on how far in advance you book. Payment terms for the balance also vary, and may be arranged on an individual basis. Wedding packages start at $68/person. Tax, alcohol and service charge are additional. Food & beverage minimums may apply. Menus and packages can be customized to fit your needs and budget. Call for details.

For corporate, golf-related or other special events, call for pricing details.

AVAILABILITY: Year-round, daily.

SERVICES/AMENITIES:
Catering: in-house or BYO
Kitchen Facilities: fully equipped
Tables & Chairs: provided
Linens, Silver, etc.: provided
Restrooms: wheelchair accessible
Dance Floor: provided
Bride's & Groom's Dressing Areas: yes
AV/Meeting Equipment: CBA, extra fee
Other: ceremony coordination

Parking: large lots, no fee
Accommodations: no guest rooms
Outdoor Night Lighting: yes
Outdoor Cooking Facilities: CBA, extra fee
Cleanup: provided
View: panorama of ocean, Catalina Island and Malibu; golf fairways
Kosher: off-site kosher caterer allowed

RESTRICTIONS:
Alcohol: in-house or wine corkage $12/bottle
Smoking: outdoors only
Music: amplified OK indoors or outdoors

Wheelchair Access: yes
Insurance: not required
Other: no glitter, birdseed, rice or confetti

Terranea Resort

Oceanfront Resort & Spa

100 Terranea Way, Rancho Palos Verdes
310/265-2883
www.terranea.com
terraneacatering@destinationhotels.com

● Rehearsal Dinners	● Corporate Events
● Ceremonies	● Meetings
● Wedding Receptions	● Film Shoots
● Private Parties	● Accommodations

Prepare to fall in love ... with this magnificent 102-acre coastal resort, situated on a bluff overlooking the sea at the very tip of the stunning Palos Verdes Peninsula. If you're searching for an earthly paradise, you're bound to find it here, where every meandering path transports you to new and varied delights. Built on land that once served as the exotic setting for numerous films and TV shows, this vast oceanside sanctuary is designed to capture hearts and instill indelible memories. In fact, just checking this venue out is a treat you won't want to miss.

Terranea Resort is definitely the location for postcard-perfect celebrations. Promontories with jaw-dropping vistas abound on grounds landscaped to showcase native vegetation and ecology. Catalina Point, with its hilltop trellis, broad lawn, and sightlines all the way to its namesake island, is ideal for open-air vows. The nearby Ocean Lawn also boasts views that will set your heart racing. If your guest list numbers in the high hundreds, scenic Palos Verdes Meadows offers a vast expanse for a ceremony or an affair *en plein air* with a backdrop that features the Point Vicente lighthouse, the sky-blue-meets-sea-blue horizon and a glorious sunset.

Inside Terranea's seven-story central complex, the choices are similarly compelling. You can't help but be dazzled by this wonderland of possibilities! There are multiple ballrooms of varying dimensions, all grand, impressive, and splendidly appointed. Whether your choice is the casual grace of the Catalina Ballroom, the warmth and sophistication of the Marineland Ballroom, or the elegance and scale of the Palos Verdes Grand Ballroom, your selection can be personalized to create just the right frame for your special occasion. All are teamed with Terranea's lovely terraces, allowing seamless transitions from indoor pleasures to al fresco cocktails and dining. Up on the sixth floor, the same refined sensibility and service can be yours in a series of suites with oceanview balconies—some ample enough to accommodate a small ceremony—that work well for welcome receptions, rehearsal dinners, post-wedding brunches and countless other social or business events. A legion of handsome Point Rooms on the second floor may also be combined with the Mediterranean-inspired Point Terrace and Lawn for a sun-splashed or star-lit gathering with a garden and seascape surround.

Once the festivities are over, let the leisure begin. Indulge in soothing treatments at their signature spa mere steps from the ocean's edge ... sample the fabulous fare at any of the six restaurants—including several with celebrity status ... savor unhurried walks along the shoreline ... play a round of golf on their award-winning 9-hole, par-3 course, The Links. A host of gorgeous accommodations, ranging from luxurious guest rooms and suites to beautifully outfitted freestanding casitas and villas, will entice you to extend your stay. And with so many divine opportunities for pampering, relaxing, and alone time, Terranea is *the* place for a romantic honeymoon. But we warn you: Book early. This resort made *Conde Nast Travelers'* Gold List as one of the Best Places on Earth for a reason. Once you see it, you'll know why.

CEREMONY CAPACITY: The resort holds 900 seated guests indoors or outdoors.

EVENT/RECEPTION & MEETING CAPACITY: The facility can accommodate 900 seated or 1,100 standing guests indoors and 600 seated or standing outdoors.

FEES & DEPOSITS: 30% of the food & beverage minimum is required to reserve your date, and the balance is due 30 days prior to the event. The rental fee ranges $250–8,000 depending on the space(s) used, and the day and time of the event. Meals range $70–200/person. Tax, alcohol and a 23% service charge are additional.

AVAILABILITY: Year-round, daily.

SERVICES/AMENITIES:

Catering: in-house
Kitchen Facilities: n/a
Tables & Chairs: provided
Linens, Silver, etc.: provided
Restrooms: wheelchair accessible
Dance Floor: portable provided
Bride's Dressing Area: yes
AV/Meeting Equipment: CBA
Other: grand piano

Parking: valet required
Accommodations: 582 guest rooms, suites, bungalows, casitas and villas
Outdoor Night Lighting: CBA
Outdoor Cooking Facilities: BBQ CBA
Cleanup: renter
View: panorama of Pacific Ocean, coastline, beach cove, bluffs and Catalina Islands

RESTRICTIONS:

Alcohol: in-house
Smoking: designated areas only
Music: amplified OK indoors

Wheelchair Access: yes
Insurance: not required

The wedding vendors on our website are the best in the business. How do we know? Read page 577.

Wayfarers Chapel

Chapel

5755 Palos Verdes Drive South, Rancho Palos Verdes
310/377-1650
www.wayfarerschapel.org
joanm@wayfarerschapel.org

Rehearsal Dinners	Corporate Events
● Ceremonies	Meetings
Wedding Receptions	● Film Shoots
Private Parties	Accommodations

Panoramic ocean views and a spectacular "glass church" set high on a seaside bluff amidst redwood groves and landscaped gardens should be enough to entice you to this awe-inspiring wedding venue, but the Wayfarer's Chapel has so much more to offer.

Designed by noted landscape and structural architect Lloyd Wright, son of Frank Lloyd Wright, this exquisite glass chapel and its setting are known not just for their startling physical beauty, but for a spiritual grace that is every bit as compelling. For over 50 years this citadel of the Swedenborgian Church has welcomed individuals from all religious backgrounds and beliefs to celebrate their weddings, memorials, baptisms and other important life-affirming occasions in an elegant nature-inspired sanctuary.

Your experience begins as soon as you drive up the hill. The grounds themselves are stunning: Tranquil and serene, they consist of 3.5 meticulously landscaped acres. Arriving guests can congregate briefly in front of the recently constructed Visitors Center before taking the stone walkway from the parking lot past a meditation pond, gardens and stately pines to the chapel entrance. Some might want to linger on the way to chat beneath the trees in an adjacent glade or gaze out contemplatively over the glittering sea. From this high vantage, you can see Catalina Island on a clear day and watch dolphins leap through the waves or pelicans sweep over the ocean swells far below.

The church itself may be even more breathtaking than the grounds. Framed in timber and steel, but walled and roofed in glass, the many-faceted building gleams like a gem. The soaring walls and ceiling, whose panes are slanted at 30- and 60-degree angles, catch the light and illuminate every event, no matter what time of day, in a shower of sunshine, moonlight or candlelight. And there's no need for additional flowers: The interior of the church, like the outside, is garlanded in living greenery and furnished in wood and local Palos Verdes stone. Here the master artist is nature. For example, the massive circular window above the altar creates a living tableau of the surrounding trees and the ever-changing sky.

Within this transparent cloister every moment is picture-perfect, but comfort and ease are also a huge part of the property's attraction. The bride and groom each have quarters where they can retire with their respective entourages and get ready for the ceremony. Just beyond these, a breezy colonnade with Pacific views is another gloriously situated spot where the bridal party and guests often relax for conversation and photos or listen for the carillon set in the crown of the chapel's handsome Hallelujah Tower. It rings after each and every celebration, sending its joyous message out over land and sea.

CEREMONY CAPACITY: The Chapel accommodates 100 seated guests.

EVENT/RECEPTION & MEETING CAPACITY: Receptions and meetings do not take place at this facility.

FEES & DEPOSITS: A $100 nonrefundable reservation fee is required to reserve your date and the balance is due 15 days after the reservation is made. Event space contributions range $1,500–3,400 depending on the day of the week and the time of day.

AVAILABILITY: Year-round.

SERVICES/AMENITIES:

Catering: no catering allowed
Kitchen Facilities: n/a
Tables & Chairs: n/a
Linens, Silver, etc.: n/a
Restrooms: wheelchair accessible
Dance Floor: no dancing allowed
Bride's & Groom's Dressing Areas: yes
AV/Meeting Equipment: n/a

Parking: large lot
Accommodations: no guest rooms
Outdoor Night Lighting: yes
Outdoor Cooking Facilities: no
Cleanup: n/a
View: fountain, garden, landscaped grounds; panorama of ocean and coastline
Other: chapel musician, wedding director and minister provided

RESTRICTIONS:

Alcohol: no alcohol permitted
Smoking: designated areas only
Music: acoustic only

Wheelchair Access: yes
Insurance: not required

Bluewater Grill

Restaurant

665 North Harbor Drive, Redondo Beach

310/318-3474

www.bluewatergrill.com
vdye@bluewatergrill.com

- Rehearsal Dinners
- Ceremonies
- Wedding Receptions
- Private Parties
- Corporate Events
- Meetings
- Film Shoots
- Accommodations

Bluewater Grill isn't just a local favorite—it's also a hotspot for rehearsal dinners, wedding receptions and lots of private parties. The reason for its popularity is obvious to anyone who dines here: It offers a picturesque waterfront location and the kind of food that keeps people coming back again and again.

Sitting right at the edge of King Harbor, the restaurant overlooks the water. Guests seated inside or out on the deck are treated to a fantastic, up-close view of hundreds of colorful boats either passing by or bobbing at their moorings. The ambiance in the main dining room is comfortably casual, with vintage photos of fishermen and their prize catches adorning the walls, teak floors, and polished brass fixtures throughout. But if you're planning a special celebration, you'll want to reserve one of their two private dining rooms.

Both versatile rooms offer harbor vistas and can accommodate a wide range of events, from a birthday bash to a business meeting. The intimate Captain's Cabin is ideal for a rehearsal dinner or small reception. Its unique interior features an abundance of wood in the barrel ceiling and wainscoting, as well as floor-to-ceiling windows that let in lots of natural light along with a harbor view. On cool evenings, a fireplace at one end adds a warm glow. The room works equally well for an informal gathering or a sophisticated soirée.

The Avalon Room upstairs hosts larger groups, and this is where most wedding receptions take place. Wraparound windows and a high, peaked ceiling lend this space an open, airy quality. It's easy to transform this room into whatever style you have in mind: Go festive with vibrant table settings and balloons floating overhead, or host an elegant sit-down dinner with custom linens and stunning centerpieces. No matter what ambiance you create inside, you'll always be able to look out onto the harbor scene and, if you're lucky, a glorious sunset.

The on-site Event Coordinator will help you plan your celebration from start to finish. And although this eatery specializes in fresh, sustainable fish, their banquet menus offer a wide range of dishes that will satisfy everyone in your group.

Bluewater Grill is within walking distance of many Redondo Beach hotels and beaches, making it convenient not just for events but for a great lunch or dinner out while you and your guests are staying in town. Drop by, relax with an exotic martini, and enjoy a quintessential beach city experience at one of the area's best loved restaurants.

CEREMONY & MEETING CAPACITY: The restaurant can accommodate 100 seated guests.

EVENT/RECEPTION CAPACITY: The Captain's Cabin holds 60–70 seated or 80 standing guests, and the Avalon Room holds 100–120 seated or 150 standing.

FEES & DEPOSITS: A $2,000 deposit is required to reserve your date. A portion of the anticipated total is due 90 days prior to the event and the balance is due at the end of the event. There are no separate rental fees, but food & beverage minimums may apply. Meals start at $30/person for luncheon and range $45–55/person for dinner. Tax, alcohol and a 20% service charge are additional.

AVAILABILITY: Year-round, daily, 11am–11pm.

SERVICES/AMENITIES:

Catering: in-house

Kitchen Facilities: n/a

Tables & Chairs: provided

Linens, Silver, etc.: provided

Restrooms: wheelchair accessible

Dance Floor: portable provided

Bride's Dressing Area: no

AV/Meeting Equipment: some provided

Parking: large lot, valet required

Accommodations: no guest rooms

Outdoor Night Lighting: yes

Outdoor Cooking Facilities: none

Cleanup: provided

View: ocean, marina, coastline

Other: wedding coordinator

RESTRICTIONS:

Alcohol: in-house

Smoking: outdoors only

Music: amplified OK indoors

Wheelchair Access: yes

Insurance: not required

Chart House Redondo Beach

Oceanfront Restaurant

231 Yacht Club Way, Redondo Beach
310/798-7666

www.chart-house.com
ebrack@ldry.com

- Rehearsal Dinners
- Ceremonies
- Wedding Receptions
- Private Parties
- Corporate Events
- Meetings
- Film Shoots
- Accommodations

This is a true story: The Chart House of Redondo Beach can trace its origins to a 1960s surf-safari. That's right—legendary longboarders Buzzy Bent and Joey Cabell surfed their way down the West Coast on an enviable twofold mission: to find the best surf in California and a stellar restaurant location. When the duo reached the Redondo Beach breakwaters, they knew they'd hit pay dirt—they had not only discovered a surfing paradise, but also a building with unsurpassed ocean views and beach access.

After an extensive remodel by the noted architect Kendrick Bangs Kellog, the Chart House opened in 1969 and has enjoyed renown as both an exceptional restaurant and event venue for over three decades.

Built on sturdy piers, the Chart House is a contemporary, low-profile, cream stucco building with a red-tile hipped roof. Huge beams and pillars define the restaurant's newly renovated, smartly dressed interior, while a ribbon of tinted windows around the perimeter heightens the sense of space and provides guests with a breathtaking seascape. Diners enjoy a rare 180-degree view of the Pacific Ocean from anywhere in the house. During winter's high tides, a window seat is a giddy ride, as the surf thunders and splashes against the glass. On chillier days, a fireplace in the restaurant's lounge area adds warmth and comfort.

If you're having a large event, reserve the entire restaurant so guests can mingle freely and enjoy the facility's amenities: an upscale circular bar with snazzy lighting fixtures, new furnishings with royal blue accents, and a wall hung with sepias of lifeguards, red cars and images of Redondo Beach in a more innocent era. We particularly liked the hand-blown glass art situated near the entry.

Smaller-scale parties can raise their glasses for a toast in the Sunset Room, a private space offering an expansive view of the north coast. This room can be completely separated from the rest of the dining area by simply closing its glass doors.

The Chart House is one of the only places in the South Bay where you can get married on the beach, and weddings here are conducted with ease. As you might imagine, sunset is often the preferred hour for ceremonies, with couples exchanging vows barefoot, right on the sand. It's a glorious tableau, with the sun's last shimmering light preserving the moment in a golden glow.

CEREMONY CAPACITY: Indoors, overlooking the ocean, the site seats up to 100 guests; outdoors, the beach holds up to 300 seated.

EVENT/RECEPTION & MEETING CAPACITY: For daytime receptions when the restaurant is closed, the venue can accommodate up to 225 seated indoors. Evening receptions are held in a private room that seats up to 90 guests (65 with a dance floor) or up to 100 for a rehearsal dinner or other nighttime special event.

FEES & DEPOSITS: A nonrefundable deposit is required at the time of booking to reserve your date. The reception package is $850. For an indoor ceremony, add $10/person. Beach ceremony packages range $2,200–2,500. Plated entrées range $41–85/person and buffets range $51–61/person. Tax, alcohol, and service charge are additional. Food & beverage minimums may apply to specific times, days and rooms.

AVAILABILITY: Year-round, daily, 11am–4pm, 5pm–10pm or 6pm–11pm.

SERVICES/AMENITIES:

Catering: in-house, no BYO
Kitchen Facilities: n/a
Tables & Chairs: provided
Linens, Silver, etc.: provided
Restrooms: wheelchair accessible
Dance Floor: provided, extra fee
Bride's Dressing Area: CBA
AV/Meeting Equipment: CBA
Other: event coordination

Parking: included during the day; valet only at night, $4/car
Accommodations: no guest rooms
Outdoor Night Lighting: yes
Outdoor Cooking Facilities: no
Cleanup: provided
View: 180-degree ocean view, coastline vistas, Redondo Beach Harbor and sailboats

RESTRICTIONS:

Alcohol: in-house, no BYO
Smoking: designated area only
Music: amplified OK

Wheelchair Access: yes
Insurance: not required

Crowne Plaza Redondo Beach
and Marina Hotel

Marina Hotel

300 North Harbor Drive, Redondo Beach
310/318-8888

www.cpredondobeachhotel.com
courtney.fishman@ihg.com

● Rehearsal Dinners	● Corporate Events
● Ceremonies	● Meetings
● Wedding Receptions	● Film Shoots
● Private Parties	● Accommodations

Located in the heart of the Redondo Beach Marina, the Crowne Plaza is just a few steps away from the Redondo Beach Pier and within walking distance of many local attractions.

The hotel's proximity to the water makes it popular for weddings, and their second-floor Harbor Terrace is a stunning spot for an outdoor ceremony. This expansive area gives you a 180-degree panorama of the sailboats in the marina as well as the Pacific beyond, and on clear days you can see Catalina Island. A refreshing sea breeze keeps things cool as you exchange vows, with the glittering ocean as a backdrop. And because you're so high up, a gorgeous sunset is practically guaranteed to add a romantic glow to the occasion.

Reception possibilities abound. Medium-sized events work well in the Seascape Ballroom and the adjacent Coral Foyer. We love the high planked-wood ceiling here, an unusual touch for a hotel ballroom. A wall of glass lets in natural light, and French doors open out onto a private patio. Large events are held in the Coral Ballroom, which features modern chandeliers and comes with its own foyer. Since this ballroom divides into three sections, it provides a lot of flexibility.

The completely private Promenade Ballroom on the mezzanine level is an attractive choice for smaller weddings, vow renewals or rehearsal dinners. Serve cocktails in the private foyer, and then move into the room itself for dinner and dancing. Large windows on two sides overlook the ocean, and at night the view sparkles with lights from the boats in the marina.

Splash, the hotel's California/Mediterranean restaurant, offers a completely different ambiance for events. Its sophisticated private room (it has a high black ceiling and fireplace) can be used on its own or with an adjoining patio for your rehearsal dinner or farewell brunch. We also can't resist the fun of the Chef's Table, which seats 10 in the exhibition kitchen. After the staff has helped personalize your menu (they'll even create specific dishes just for you), you and your guests will have the pleasure of watching the chef cook dinner right before your eyes!

The hotel takes maximum advantage of its ocean exposure, so 85% of their stylish guest rooms have water views and private balconies, while special room packages and suite options give you amenities usually found only in boutique hotels. Their European day spa will tempt you with a couple's treatment room, and there's even a package for your entire bridal party. You won't have to worry about finding a wedding planner, DJ or makeup artist, because the hotel has personally selected its own topnotch vendors and they're all housed on site. And if you're experiencing any pre-wedding jitters, you can work them out at the newly renovated gym, complimentary to hotel guests.

The Crowne Plaza Redondo Beach staff take care of everything: Not only can they customize one of their all-inclusive wedding packages to fit your budget and style, an Event Manager will assist you from the planning stage through the end of your reception.

CEREMONY CAPACITY: Indoors up to 800 seated guests; outdoors up to 500 seated.

EVENT/RECEPTION & MEETING CAPACITY: Indoor spaces hold up to 500 seated or 1,000 standing guests, outdoors up to 400 seated or 800 standing.

FEES & DEPOSITS: A nonrefundable $1,500 deposit is required to reserve your date. A second deposit may be required. The balance is due 8 business days prior to the event. The ceremony site rental fee starts at $1,900. Wedding packages range $87–175/person. Tax, alcohol, and a service charge are additional.

AVAILABILITY: Year-round, daily, 6am–1am. Harbor Terrace (the outdoor venue) is available until 8pm with some acoustic music allowed. Call for details.

SERVICES/AMENITIES:
Catering: in-house or BYO ethnic caterer with approval
Kitchen Facilities: fully equipped
Tables & Chairs: provided
Linens, Silver, etc.: provided
Restrooms: wheelchair accessible
Dance Floor: provided
Bride's Dressing Area: CBA
AV/Meeting Equipment: provided

Parking: valet & garage available, fees apply
Accommodations: 342 guest rooms and suites
Outdoor Night Lighting: no
Outdoor Cooking Facilities: BBQ CBA
Cleanup: provided
View: coastline, cityscape, marina, ocean, patio
Other: event coordination, spa services, DJ, wedding planner, makeup artist

RESTRICTIONS:
Alcohol: in-house or BYO wine with corkage fee
Smoking: outside only
Music: amplified OK with restrictions

Wheelchair Access: yes
Insurance: liability required

Want to know WHAT TO ASK a potential location or vendor? Check out our Questions to Ask starting on page 21.

The Portofino Hotel & Marina

Hotel & Marina

260 Portofino Way, Redondo Beach

310/798-5874

www.hotelportofino.com
weddings@hotelportofino.com

- Rehearsal Dinners
- Ceremonies
- Wedding Receptions
- Private Parties
- Corporate Events
- Meetings
- Film Shoots
- Accommodations

If Redondo Beach, with its sunshine and balmy ocean breezes epitomizes the Southern California lifestyle, then the Portofino Hotel & Marina is the perfect place to enjoy it. Set on a lush private peninsula, it offers guests a chance to relax, let loose, and embrace the "endless summer" experience.

The venue has the unassuming intimacy of a boutique hotel, and its casual, nautical-chic ambiance makes you feel immediately at home. The inviting lobby is actually dubbed "the Living Room," although we don't know too many people who have a three-story atrium in their house—or such an astounding view! Tall, multipaned windows overlook King Harbor, where kayaks and yachts regularly make their way out to sea. There's no sign of land, only rippling sapphire-blue water, so you have the impression of floating on some elaborate houseboat. It's a remarkably soothing vision, and between the soft jazz playing on the sound system and the cocktail you're served from the bar tucked discreetly in one corner, you might want to lounge in the comfortable Living Room chairs indefinitely.

But there's a celebration afoot, beginning with a Seaside Lawn ceremony. It's surprising how many guests this intimate area can accommodate, but up to 200 of your friends and family can watch you exchange vows under an archway or gazebo with the water as the backdrop. The tropical garden atmosphere and the refreshing scent of sea spray provide natural adornments.

A short stroll from the hotel proper takes you to the Pavilion, a crisp contemporary building with two distinctive ballrooms for receptions. The sophisticated Bayside Ballroom has a 180-degree view of the ocean, and at night the twinkling stars and the lights of the Palos Verdes Peninsula cast a dreamy shimmer on the water. Next door, the Pacific Ballroom features floor-to-ceiling windows that take in the action of the lagoon and the cityscape beyond. Step out to the Pacific Terrace for cocktails or a whiff of sea air, and perhaps you'll spy dolphins cavorting in the ocean waves.

Your Portofino wedding package includes a room for your wedding night so that you can snuggle under the covers and savor your ocean view a while longer. With first-class service, a long list of amenities and a spectacular setting, it's no wonder The Portofino Hotel & Marina has become one of California's most desirable spots for weddings, vacations and romantic getaways.

CEREMONY CAPACITY: The Pacific or Bayside Ballrooms each hold 250 seated. Outdoors, the Seaside Lawn holds 200 seated.

EVENT/RECEPTION CAPACITY: The Bayside Ballroom accommodates 250 seated or 350 standing. The Pacific Ballroom holds 140 seated or 250 standing.

MEETING CAPACITY: The Pacific or Bayside Ballrooms hold 200–300 seated, depending on the seating configuration.

FEES & DEPOSITS: 40% of the estimated event total is required to reserve your date; partial payments are due 6 months and 4 business days prior to the event. Wedding packages run $120–199/person and include a custom wedding cake and an oceanside room for the bridal couple. Tax and a 23% service charge are additional.

A $2,800 ceremony setup fee is extra, as is hosted valet or self-parking at $15/car. Special discounted room rates for overnight hotel accommodations are available.

AVAILABILITY: Year-round, daily, 11am–4pm and 6pm–midnight.

SERVICES/AMENITIES:

Catering: in-house
Kitchen Facilities: n/a
Tables & Chairs: provided
Linens, Silver, etc.: provided
Restrooms: wheelchair accessible
Dance Floor: provided
Bride's Dressing Area: provided
AV/Meeting Equipment: full range AV, extra fee

Parking: large lots, $15/car valet or self-parking
Accommodations: 161 guest rooms
Outdoor Night Lighting: access only
Outdoor Cooking Facilities: n/a
Cleanup: provided
View: ocean and coastline
Other: event coordination

RESTRICTIONS:

Alcohol: in-house
Smoking: outdoors only
Music: amplified indoors with restrictions

Wheelchair Access: yes
Insurance: not required
Other: no rice, birdseed or smoke/fog machines

The Redondo Beach Historic Library

Oceanfront Historic Library

309 Esplanade, Redondo Beach

310/937-6844

www.rbhistoriclibrary.com
info@rbhistoriclibrary.com

● Rehearsal Dinners	● Corporate Events
● Ceremonies	● Meetings
● Wedding Receptions	● Film Shoots
● Private Parties	Accommodations

Book lovers that we are, it was a foregone conclusion that the Redondo Beach Historic Library would capture our hearts. Whether you're a bibliophile or not, however, the library is bound to appeal to you and all who walk through its impressive double wooden doors.

Local architect Lovell Pemberton built the library in 1930, positioning it to command a view of both the Pacific and the sprawling lawn of Veterans' Park.

Combining both Spanish and Dutch colonial styles, the library is a handsome three-story ivory stucco building with arched windows, a red-tile roof and straight-edged gables peaking on its north and south wings. Ornamental ironwork on the windows and Art Deco moldings on the front façade spice up the architectural mix still further. Shading the library is its gorgeous companion—a giant Moreton Bay Fig, itself a registered landmark.

Guests stepping out onto the library's main floor will undoubtedly be a little in awe of the expansive, illumined space that greets them. With windows set in almost every wall and skylights opening up the ceiling, the main floor is radiant in light—ideal for large celebrations. Cream-colored walls offset by a dusky burgundy-and-blue carpeting impart a simple elegance. Overhead, arches and dark wood beams echo the Spanish motif. Although renovated throughout, some of the library's original amenities remain, namely the circular brass lamps suspended from the ceiling and the wooden bookshelves bracketing three walls—an excellent showcase for memorabilia, pictures, votive candles or flowers.

Most couples say their vows during sunset's lavish light, in front of a quartet of ocean-facing windows on the main floor. Other possible ceremony sites include the long stretch of lawn directly behind the library or on the Veterans' Park concert green, situated on the building's north side. If it's a more intimate fête you're hosting—perhaps a communion or baby shower—then you'll want to reserve one of the library's smaller spaces: either the overflow room or the third floor mezzanine, which also affords a glorious ocean view.

Since its opening in 1996 as an event venue, the library has proved to be one of the most popular event facilities in Redondo Beach, booking almost every weekend. Call to make an appointment to visit this site, and chances are you'll sign their dance card too.

CEREMONY CAPACITY: The outdoor ceremony area holds 320 seated, the indoor ceremony area 150 seated.

EVENT/RECEPTION CAPACITY: The site accommodates up to 320 seated or standing guests indoors.

MEETING CAPACITY: The main room holds 320 seated. There are 3 smaller rooms that seat up to 50 guests each.

FEES & DEPOSITS: A nonrefundable $3,000 deposit is required to secure your date, and 75% of the estimated total is due 6 months prior to your event. All balances and guest counts are due 10 business days prior to your event. Inclusive wedding packages start at $17,000. Customized events are always available. No additional service charges apply to any events with a guest count exceeding 100.

AVAILABILITY: Year-round, daily, anytime.

SERVICES/AMENITIES:

Catering: by *Spectrum Catering,* no BYO
Kitchen Facilities: n/a
Tables & Chairs: provided, including Chiavari chairs
Linens, Silver, etc.: provided
Restrooms: wheelchair accessible
Dance Floor: provided
Bride's Dressing Area: yes
AV/Meeting Equipment: CBA, extra charge

Parking: valet included in package
Accommodations: no guest rooms
Outdoor Night Lighting: access lighting only
Outdoor Cooking Facilities: CBA
Cleanup: provided
View: Pacific Ocean, Redondo Beach Pier, Palos Verdes Peninsula and nearby park
Other: event coordination, theme events

RESTRICTIONS:

Alcohol: in-house, no BYO
Smoking: outside only
Music: amplified OK

Wheelchair Access: yes
Insurance: not required
Other: no confetti or glitter

Shade Hotel Redondo Beach

Hotel

655 North Harbor Drive, Redondo Beach
310/546-4995
www.shaderb.com
events@shadehotel.com

- Rehearsal Dinners
- Ceremonies
- Wedding Receptions
- Private Parties
- Corporate Events
- Meetings
- Film Shoots
- Accommodations

Redondo Beach is affectionately known as the "Hollywood Riviera" for its uncrowded beaches and laid-back, coastal vibe. It's Los Angeles County's southernmost beach city, and the quaint community has earned a reputation as a waterfront playground with casual California style and a flair for the artistic.

Shade Hotel Redondo Beach, like its sister property a few miles north in Manhattan Beach, embodies the best elements of its hometown, while providing a sleek, sophisticated haven that's welcoming to locals and visitors alike. It occupies an absolutely prime spot on King Harbor Marina, (one of Southern California's most picturesque waterfronts and an amazing place for photos), and boasts two separate buildings—one designed exclusively for weddings and corporate events that also houses their restaurant, and one dedicated to the boutique hotel's 54 guest suites and meeting rooms.

Ceremonies are held on the event building's rooftop "Skydeck," and you won't find a more breathtaking place for exchanging vows—the spacious top-floor terrace is open to the sky, and overlooks the sparkling harbor and Redondo Beach's vivid sunsets. The celebration continues downstairs in the second-floor Marina View Room, which is outfitted with wood flooring and white Chiavari chairs. Here, floor-to-ceiling glass walls slide open to an airy balcony, allowing guests to flow freely indoors and out while taking in the glorious ocean views.

Like the hotel itself, the event spaces seamlessly blend a relaxed coastal style with refined, cosmopolitan elements. The combination of "living walls" (vertically planted with succulents), mesmerizing fire features, waterwalls, and intimate lighting creates an effect that's both unexpected and urbane, yet the color palette is neutral enough for your own decorations to fit right in.

You'll love the chic restaurant, too. With fabulous food and indoor/outdoor seating, it's a great setting for a rehearsal dinner.

Up on the top floor of the hotel building, the divine rooftop pool area is the perfect spot to unwind with your guests or wedding party before or after the festivities. Here you can sip finely crafted cocktails, soak up the sun, or snuggle with your sweetie by a fire pit.

For a special treat, consider turning your wedding into a destination weekend by doing a hotel buyout—you'll have full use of the event facilities, as well as all 54 suites for your nearest and dearest. And, we have to say, the accommodations here are truly special. All suites face the harbor and are appointed with the best amenities around, like Tempur-Pedic beds, Keurig espresso machines, and luxurious soaps and lotions. Most incredible, though are the bathtubs, which sit on private balconies open to the balmy sea breezes (with privacy screens, of course!).

The event staff is dedicated to making each wedding reflect the couple's unique style, and they'll happily create customized menus, assist with specialized décor requests, provide excellent vendor recommendations, and be there on the big day to ensure things go exactly as planned. When it comes to helping you realize your vision, the team at Shade have a wonderful habit of saying "Yes!" to almost anything you have in mind.

CEREMONY & EVENT/RECEPTION CAPACITY: The hotel holds 250 seated or 300 standing guests indoors and outdoors.

MEETING CAPACITY: Meeting spaces seat 40 guests indoors.

FEES & DEPOSITS: 50% of the food & beverage minimum is required to reserve your date, and the balance is due 10 days prior to the event. The food & beverage minimum ranges $3,000–35,000 depending on the day and time of the event. Meals range $50–200/person. Wedding packages start at $150/person. Tax and a 22% service charge are additional.

AVAILABILITY: Year-round, daily, 8am–midnight.

SERVICES/AMENITIES:

Catering: in-house
Kitchen Facilities: n/a
Tables & Chairs: provided
Linens, Silver, etc.: provided
Restrooms: wheelchair accessible
Dance Floor: portable CBA
Bride's Dressing Area: CBA
AV/Meeting Equipment: CBA

Parking: large lot, on street; valet available
Accommodations: 54 guest rooms
Outdoor Night Lighting: yes
Outdoor Cooking Facilities: BBQ CBA
Cleanup: provided
View: coastline, ocean, pool area, waterfall; panorama of marina
Other: event coordination

RESTRICTIONS:

Alcohol: in-house or BYO with corkage fee
Smoking: designated areas only
Music: amplified OK with restrictions

Wheelchair Access: yes
Insurance: not required

Michael's Tuscany Room

Restaurant

470 West 7th Street, San Pedro

310/519-7100

www.michaelstuscanyroom.com
michaeltuscanyroom@att.net

● Rehearsal Dinners	● Corporate Events	
● Ceremonies	● Meetings	
● Wedding Receptions	● Film Shoots	
● Private Parties	Accommodations	

Exciting things are happening in San Pedro these days. Thanks to a spruced up waterfront and a resurgent downtown, locals and tourists alike are flocking to this vibrant area where the First Thursday art walk brings a party atmosphere to the newly created cultural district. Right in the midst of this dynamic neighborhood, supporting unique mom-and-pop stores as well as hip art galleries, is Michael's Tuscany Room, a beautiful and very romantic wedding and event venue.

Wrought-iron gates and slender trees in terracotta pots adorn the outside of the building, where three sets of French doors are topped with magnificent stained-glass windows. Step inside and you feel like you've been transported to an upscale, yet rustic, country home somewhere in Tuscany.

As you take in this soaring, 30-foot-high space, your eye is drawn up to the open-beamed ceiling with its pyramid-shaped skylights and mix of ornate Old World chandeliers. Once one of Mr. Cutri's warehouses, the room has been lovingly refashioned to capture the charms of his homeland. The walls are sandblasted weathered brick, punctuated with rows of French doors in a rich dark wood. There's a decorative balcony that runs the length of both sides of the room, creating the illusion of being in an outdoor courtyard. Faux windows and flower boxes brim with colorful blooms, and the fancy wrought-iron railing is laced with green, cascading vines.

Near the back of the room is a gracious, curving staircase that leads up to the mezzanine. Entwined with twinkle lights, it's perfect for the bride making her grand entrance for a ceremony at the base of the stairs.

Afterwards, guests mingle on the main floor and up on the mezzanine, as they raise a glass of bubbly and toast to *amore*. Dinner is served at tables set around the central dance floor. The mezzanine, which is decorated with a bucolic countryside mural and fireplace, can also be used for your band/DJ or set up as a lounge or even a photo booth area.

As captivating as this place is, it's not just a feast for the eyes. With an owner whose first love was the culinary arts (which he studied in Tuscany), you'd expect a lot of care to go into the cuisine and you won't be disappointed. A truly mouth-watering array of dishes—most with an Italian influence—is offered, but menus can also be customized for your particular event and budget.

CEREMONY CAPACITY: The site holds 150 indoors for a non-traditional yet lovely ceremony with guests seated at their table.

EVENT/RECEPTION CAPACITY: The facility can accommodate 250 seated or 300 standing guests indoors.

MEETING CAPACITY: Meeting spaces hold 300 seated guests.

FEES & DEPOSITS: For daytime and weeknight events, a $500 deposit is required to reserve your date. For Friday and Saturday evening events, $1,000 or $10/person (whichever is greater) is required. 50% of the event cost is due 60 days prior to the event; final guest count and the remaining balance is due 2 weeks prior. A $300 rental fee is required only if the time reserved exceeds the standard hours. There is an additional fee for a ceremony. Luncheon wedding packages start at $28/person and dinner packages start at $38/person. Tax, alcohol and a 20% service charge are extra.

AVAILABILITY: Year-round. Lunch: 11am–3pm, daily; Dinner: Sunday–Thursday, 5–10pm and Friday–Saturday 6–11pm. Additional hours can be arranged; rental fee will apply.

SERVICES/AMENITIES:

Catering: in-house
Kitchen Facilities: n/a
Tables & Chairs: provided
Linens, Silver, etc.: provided
Restrooms: wheelchair accessible
Dance Floor: provided
Bride's Dressing Area: CBA
AV/Meeting Equipment: BYO

Parking: large lot, on street
Accommodations: no guest rooms
Outdoor Night Lighting: access only
Outdoor Cooking Facilities: no
Cleanup: provided
View: no
Other: event coordination

RESTRICTIONS:

Alcohol: beer and liquor in-house, or BYO wine or champagne with corkage fee
Smoking: outdoors only
Music: amplified OK indoors with restrictions

Wheelchair Access: yes
Insurance: not required

Want to find more venues and services? Check out our informative website, www.HereComesTheGuide.com.

299

Torrance Cultural Arts Center

Arts Center

3330 Civic Center Drive, Torrance
310/781-7150
www.tcac.torranceca.gov
tcac@torranceca.gov

● Rehearsal Dinners	● Corporate Events
● Ceremonies	● Meetings
● Wedding Receptions	● Film Shoots
● Private Parties	Accommodations

Since its 1991 inauguration, the Torrance Cultural Arts Center has become a mecca for all types of events, including thousands of bridal showers, wedding receptions, parties and dinners. With its many different event venues, this unique complex easily sparks the imagination of many a bride or event planner. The spacious facilities spread out in a series of lofty buildings joined together by open spaces, such as a sweeping entry plaza, a large courtyard and a serene Japanese Garden.

The most popular reception room is the Toyota Meeting Hall. This room has high ceilings and a bright foyer for pre-dinner gatherings. An entire wall of glass doors opens onto the Torino Festival Plaza, an inner courtyard that accommodates tented seating or simply affords diners a place to mingle in the fresh air. A fully equipped professional kitchen is accessible to any licensed caterer.

The Ken Miller Recreation Center offers two event spaces with a shared kitchen connected by an open lobby. The Auditorium benefits from lots of natural light, and its stage will accommodate a DJ or small band with ease. The adjoining Assembly Room features hardwood floors and track lighting.

Couples getting married here often like to have their ceremony in the natural environment of the Pine Wind Japanese Garden, which contains two waterfalls, a small stream and a pond. As you enter this diminutive world (it holds approximately 60 people), you're greeted by the sound of rushing water. The wide modern fountain by the entrance releases a continuous sheet of falling water; the more romantic rock-lined waterfall in the garden's center serves as a beautiful backdrop for a ceremony or formal photo shoot. Guests may sit on redwood risers in the small amphitheater, or stand above the garden on an overlooking walkway. Afterward, they'll enjoy wandering along a circular pathway of stepping stones leading through a landscape of dainty bonsai, maple trees and bamboo.

Adjacent to the garden, the Garden Room provides a more intimate space for a bridal shower, or preparation for a wedding party holding their ceremony at the center. A custom wall divider and two separate entrances allow flexibility in the room setup, and guests will appreciate the view of the Pine Wind Japanese Garden through large picture windows.

With an easy, accessible location, free parking, competitive rental rates, and a professional staff, the Torrance Cultural Arts Center promises to make your event a success.

CEREMONY CAPACITY: The Pine Wind Japanese Garden holds 60 seated guests; the Toyota Meeting Hall can accommodate 250 seated; the outdoor Torino Festival Plaza 530 seated.

EVENT/RECEPTION CAPACITY: Indoors, the center holds up to 300 seated or 350 standing. Outdoors, the site accommodates 530 seated or 600 standing.

MEETING CAPACITY: Indoor facilities can accommodate up to 502 guests theater-style, 150 conference-style or classroom-style.

FEES & DEPOSITS: A $500 refundable deposit is required to secure your date. For events where alcohol is served, 2 Torrance police officers are required at an additional hourly fee, as is an additional $500 deposit and alcohol insurance. There's a small fee to use the Toyota Meeting Hall or Ken Miller Recreation Center kitchens. Liability insurance is required for all events. The rental fee for wedding functions ranges $78–197/hour depending on the space and length of time reserved. Setup and staff charges are additional. Please call for specific information.

AVAILABILITY: Year-round, daily, until midnight.

SERVICES/AMENITIES:

Catering: Toyota Meeting Hall requires licensed caterer; BYO for Ken Miller Recreation Center

Kitchen Facilities: 2 available

Tables & Chairs: provided

Linens, Silver, etc.: caterer or renter

Restrooms: wheelchair accessible

Dance Floor: varies per space

Bride's & Groom's Dressing Areas: CBA

AV/Meeting Equipment: full range

Parking: large complimentary lot

Accommodations: no guest rooms

Outdoor Night Lighting: some, call for details

Outdoor Cooking Facilities: through caterer

Cleanup: caterer and renter

View: Torino Festival Plaza and Pine Wind Japanese Garden

Other: grand piano, PA system, video projector, free WiFi

RESTRICTIONS:

Alcohol: BYO BWC only; licensed and insured server required

Smoking: outside only

Music: amplified OK indoors, OK outdoors with restrictions

Wheelchair Access: yes

Insurance: liability required

Other: no birdseed, rice, glitter, confetti or open flames

Orange County

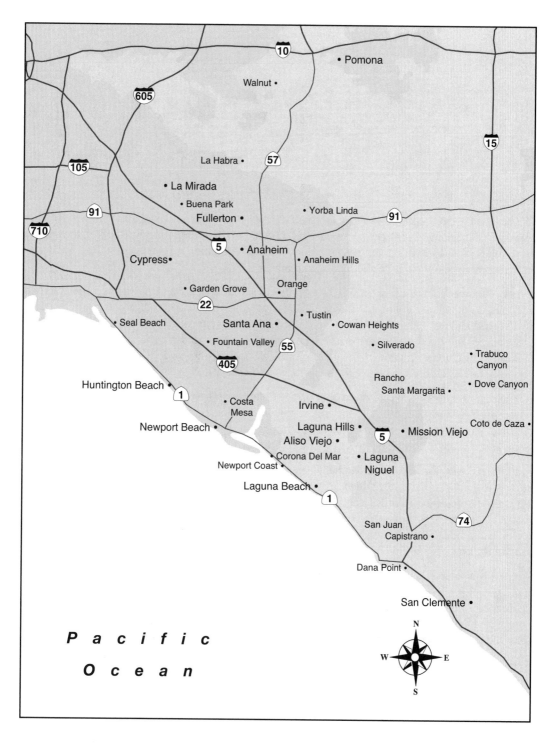

Aliso Viejo Country Club

Golf Club

33 Santa Barbara Drive, Aliso Viejo
949/609-3305
www.alisogolf.com
chrislynn.vanskiver@ourclub.com

- Rehearsal Dinners
- Ceremonies
- Wedding Receptions
- Private Parties
- Corporate Events
- Meetings
- Film Shoots
- Accommodations

Its gracious hacienda-like architecture hints at California's past, but in personality and performance this distinctive venue is stylishly contemporary. Located in the rolling hills overlooking the Saddleback Valley, the Aliso Viejo Country Club is a warm and welcoming special event setting that serves up memorable celebrations of all kinds with panache.

One of Orange County's newest private country clubs (and boasting one of the only two Jack Nicklaus-designed golf courses in the region), its little lakes and woods are home to a plethora of small woodland creatures. Kingfishers, green herons, snowy egrets, and western meadowlarks are just a few of the many wonderful birds that can be seen around the waterways and well-tended fairways and greens. Fragrant herbs and colorful blooms fill the gardens. Balconies, bell towers and elegant French doors open onto the terraces and courtyards.

Ceremonies and receptions are often held on the Celebration Lawn, where both the graceful arbor framed by beds of white roses and the well-manicured course provide applause-worthy backdrops for any festivity. Whether your event is a wedding, a brunch, a baby shower, a corporate shindig, or an anniversary dinner, it will be well placed and beautifully served.

Indoors, an elevator and a handsome wrought-iron staircase off the lobby take you up to an attractive second-story foyer, which adjoins a series of lovely salons where guests can unwind, sip cocktails and dine in private and unhurried bliss. The Bell Tower Room serves as an elegant lounge. Here, French doors open onto a small half-moon-shaped Juliet balcony in the clubhouse tower. Its arched, brick window openings looking out over the grounds create an ultra-romantic frame for photos of the bride and groom.

Also on this floor is a rustic living room with a Spanish-style fireplace and comfortable furnishings, as well as a versatile private dining room. It features a full granite bar, a vaulted, beamed ceiling, two outdoor terraces suitable for dining and dancing, and panoramic views of the golf course and valley. After a dinner of delicious California fusion cuisine, you may want to step out onto the terraces to watch night fall over the Saddleback Valley.

The spectacular spa-caliber ladies room is a bonus. Just the place for prepping and pampering, it has club chairs, leather ottomans, a beamed ceiling, carpeted and tumbled travertine marble floors, and a four-station granite vanity with sinks. Rumor has it the gentlemen's locker room is equally plush.

And, of course, there's the golf course—a stunning location for those joyful wedding pictures. You're sure to be flushed with happiness and wearing big smiles because your wedding here is the best one…ever.

CEREMONY & EVENT/RECEPTION CAPACITY: The facility accommodates 180 seated or 250 standing guests indoors or outdoors.

MEETING CAPACITY: Meeting spaces seat 80 indoors.

FEES & DEPOSITS: 20% of the estimated event cost is required to reserve your date. 40% is due 60 days prior to the event and the balance is due 10 days prior. The rental fee starts at $400 and varies depending on the day and time of the event, guest count, and space reserved. Meals start at $35/person. Tax, alcohol and a 21% service charge are additional.

AVAILABILITY: Year-round, daily, 6am–midnight.

SERVICES/AMENITIES:

Catering: in-house
Kitchen Facilities: n/a
Tables & Chairs: provided
Linens, Silver, etc.: provided
Restrooms: wheelchair accessible
Dance Floor: provided
Bride's Dressing Area: yes
AV/Meeting Equipment: CBA

Parking: large lot
Accommodations: no guest rooms
Outdoor Night Lighting: CBA
Outdoor Cooking Facilities: BBQ CBA
Cleanup: provided
View: cityscape, courtyard, fairways, hills, mountains, landscaped grounds
Other: event coordination

RESTRICTIONS:

Alcohol: in-house
Smoking: designated areas only
Music: amplified OK with restrictions

Wheelchair Access: yes
Insurance: not required

Wedgewood Aliso Viejo

Banquet Center

31 Santa Barbara Drive, Aliso Viejo
866/966-3009

www.wedgewoodbanquet.com
events@wedgewoodbanquet.com

- Rehearsal Dinners
- Ceremonies
- Wedding Receptions
- Private Parties

- Corporate Events
- Meetings
- Film Shoots
- Accommodations

"The Place with Panoramic Views of the Saddleback Valley and a Gorgeous Golf Course" might be a more apt name for Wedgewood Aliso Viejo, peacefully perched above the valley and adjacent to the Aliso Viejo Country Club. Although its serene setting makes you feel like you're far from the city, this lovely venue is easily accessible from the freeway and other main thoroughfares.

A standout facility in South Orange County, Wedgewood Aliso Viejo is equally enticing for corporate and social events, especially weddings. Ceremonies are held on the Fireside Lawn, named for the tall stone fireplace that anchors one end of this congenial spot. Couples say their vows in front of the hearth, surrounded by the views of the emerald fairways and the natural beauty of the Saddleback Valley. With such a scenic backdrop, little decoration is needed—and the Mediterranean-style buildings, palm trees and seasonal flowers provide a pleasing landscape to complement any color scheme and style, from casual to opulent.

While the photographer is capturing the couple's post-ceremony smiles and kisses, the festivities kick into high gear with the cocktail hour on the spacious patio, enhanced with fire pits and market lights. From here, the vista could not be more picturesque: As guests toast the newlyweds, they gaze out past manicured greens into the valley.

The patio connects to the ballroom, allowing a smooth transition to the reception. Natural light flowing in through multiple glass doors and windows gives the room its open, airy feeling. The vaulted, wood-beamed ceiling and ivory walls lend considerable warmth to the space. There's plenty of room for dancing indoors, but on a balmy evening guests are more likely to head for the patio, where they can enjoy the starry night sky.

As with all of Wedgewood's fine locations, they make it easy for couples to create a celebration that matches their vision as well as their budget. Wedding packages are fully customizable and include a range of event extras like florals, music and invitations to help ensure a stress-free and fun wedding-planning experience.

Whether your special occasion is simply elegant or elegantly simple, Wedgewood Aliso Viejo's event specialists will give it the attention it deserves.

CEREMONY CAPACITY: The Fireside Lawn holds 280 seated guests.

EVENT/RECEPTION CAPACITY: The Ballroom accommodates 280 seated or standing guests.

MEETING CAPACITY: Meeting spaces seat 280 guests indoors.

FEES & DEPOSITS: 25% of the estimated total event cost is required to reserve your date. An additional 25% is due 120 days prior to the event, and the balance (based on the final guest count) is due 10 days prior. All payments are credited towards the final balance and are nonrefundable and nontransferable. All-inclusive, completely customizable wedding packages start at $55/person. Tax, alcohol and a 21–22% service charge are additional.

AVAILABILITY: Year-round, daily, 7am–11pm.

SERVICES/AMENITIES:

Catering: in-house
Kitchen Facilities: n/a
Tables & Chairs: provided
Linens, Silver, etc.: provided
Restrooms: wheelchair accessible
Dance Floor: yes
Bride's Dressing Area: yes
AV/Meeting Equipment: some provided

Parking: large lot
Accommodations: no guest rooms
Outdoor Night Lighting: yes
Outdoor Cooking Facilities: none
Cleanup: provided
View: fairways; panorama of valley, hills and mountains
Other: coordination, in-house wedding cake and florals, clergy on staff

RESTRICTIONS:

Alcohol: in-house
Smoking: designated areas only
Music: amplified OK

Wheelchair Access: yes
Insurance: not required
Other: no rice, confetti or glitter; no open flames

Anaheim Majestic Garden Hotel

Hotel

900 South Disneyland Drive, Anaheim
714/778-1700
www.majesticgardenhotel.com
catering@majesticgardenhotel.com

- Rehearsal Dinners
- Ceremonies
- Wedding Receptions
- Private Parties
- Corporate Events
- Meetings
- Film Shoots
- Accommodations

If you live in Southern California, you've probably passed the Tudor-style Anaheim Majestic Garden Hotel hundreds of times as you've made your way north or south along the I-5 Freeway. And if you stopped to check out the hotel, there's a good chance you were impressed by its stylish porte-cochère entryway, majestic fireplace, and charming outdoor courtyards. But if you haven't visited recently, you'll be delighted by all the enhancements at this centrally located landmark.

After passing through the attractive lobby, you arrive at a picturesque outdoor koi pond surrounded by giant ferns, with a bubbling waterfall as a focal point. This is a lovely spot for photographs after you've tied the knot!

Adjacent to the pond is the Pond Courtyard, a manicured enclave where couples exchange vows. Enclosed by the quaint façades of the hotel buildings, with their stone and brick turrets, and high- and low-pitched roofs, it's a peaceful, private space with an enchanting gazebo. And since the gazebo is located just off the bridal changing room, you won't have far to venture after the last hair is put in place.

More intimate ceremonies are hosted in the Rose Garden, where you can say "I do" under a rustic archway entwined with rose vines and festooned with fragrant blooms. A two-tier fountain adds a romantic element to the setting.

All the reception rooms are accented with cream-colored damask stripes, crown molding, dome-shaped chandeliers and wall sconces. No matter which area you select, you can count on fine cuisine and flawless service overseen by the Banquet Director and Executive Chef, who've been with the hotel for more than 40 years combined.

Convenient to airports and attractions in both Los Angeles and Orange counties, the Anaheim Majestic Garden Hotel caters to your out-of-town visitors' comfort. It boasts the largest guest rooms in town (typically more than 500 square feet). And just so no one's bored after your big event, the hotel offers complimentary transportation and a concierge desk to assist with purchasing multiple-day passes to neighboring Disneyland Resort.

Oh yes, one more thing about being so close to the Magic Kingdom—if fireworks from the park happen to light up your celebration, no one need know they're not intended for you!

CEREMONY CAPACITY: The banquet rooms hold up to 600 seated guests, the courtyard up to 300.

EVENT/RECEPTION CAPACITY: The location accommodates up to 600 seated or 1,000 standing guests indoors and up to 250 seated or 350 standing outdoors.

MEETING CAPACITY: Spaces seat up to 800 guests.

FEES & DEPOSITS: A percentage of the estimated event total is required to reserve your date. The balance is due in 2 installments with the final payment being made 15 days prior to the event. Rental fees range $1,000–1,500 depending on space, day and time rented and guest count. Meals range $34–75/person. Tax, alcohol and a service charge are additional.

AVAILABILITY: Year-round, daily, anytime.

SERVICES/AMENITIES:

Catering: in-house, no BYO
Kitchen Facilities: n/a
Tables & Chairs: provided
Linens, Silver, etc.: provided
Restrooms: wheelchair accessible
Dance Floor: provided
Bride's Dressing Area: yes
AV/Meeting Equipment: full range

Parking: complimentary for guests during event
Accommodations: 489 oversized guest rooms
Outdoor Night Lighting: yes
Outdoor Cooking Facilities: no
Cleanup: reception area by hotel; ceremony area by renter
View: fountain, garden, pond, pool, fireworks, landscaped grounds, garden courtyard

RESTRICTIONS:

Alcohol: in-house, no BYO
Smoking: outdoors only
Music: amplified OK with restrictions

Wheelchair Access: yes
Insurance: not required

This is important! Tell locations you're reading HERE COMES THE GUIDE and ask if our information is still current.

Hotel Ménage

Boutique Hotel

1221 South Harbor Boulevard, Anaheim

714/400-9085

www.hotelmenage.com
kevin.anawati@interstatehotels.com

- Rehearsal Dinners
- Ceremonies
- Wedding Receptions
- Private Parties
- Corporate Events
- Meetings
- Film Shoots
- Accommodations

There are a lot of hotels that host weddings, but you won't find another one like the Hotel Ménage. Located in the heart of Orange County, this must-see venue offers a unique mix of elegance, affordability, variety and fun—along with a tropical flair. Anaheim's first true boutique hotel is a play-scape that will make any event exciting.

As you enter, you're welcomed by the lobby's rich, mahogany-hued interior and sophisticated vibe. Just a few steps to your left is a delightful outdoor scene—a sprawling complex of terraces, lawns, shady lounges, and a lushly landscaped pool.

The festive spirit begins in the Palapa Bar & Lounge, where a traditional palm-covered palapa and ample seating make mingling easy. Follow the winding stone walkway past graceful palms and other tropical plantings to the Palm Court. Ideal for a ceremony, cocktail reception or seated dinner (highlighted by comfort food from the hotel's restaurant, American Tavern Eatery & Drink), its gently curving shape mirrors the footprint of the nearby pool and creates a sense of movement and flow. The sunny South Lounge nearby, also well-suited for both ceremonies and receptions, can be used in combination with other outdoor and indoor spaces to extend your party. The North Lounge on the opposite side of the spa and pool area is surrounded by towering palms, has a beautiful fountain, and offers still more room for your dining and dancing delight.

Indoors, the Main Ballroom puts an innovative spin on the ballroom concept. The look is upscale and contemporary, with warm wood-paneled walls, modern lighting fixtures and a soothing earth-tone color scheme. It's also outfitted with a full bar at one end as well as a white stone fireplace. Sliding glass doors open to the Palm Court, providing an indoor/outdoor experience. Designed with the utmost flexibility in mind, the "ballroom" can be configured in whatever way you like: as a lounge, a reception room with dance floor, or both.

A variety of smaller event spaces and meeting rooms are also available for intimate cocktail receptions and private parties. Guest rooms feature luxurious touches like leather headboards, executive desks, fridges, coffee makers and 42-inch high-def plasma TVs. But we're going to bet that your guests won't be spending much time in them. Disneyland is only a 10-minute walk, while Knott's Berry Farm, Universal Studios and the seashore are also within a short drive.

And in the evening, as you lounge by the only 24-hour pool in Anaheim, you'll get to enjoy the magic of Disneyland's Fireworks from the very best seats in the county.

CEREMONY CAPACITY: The hotel holds 180 seated guests indoors and 200 seated outdoors.

EVENT/RECEPTION CAPACITY: The hotel can accommodate 150 seated or 200 standing guests indoors, and 200 seated or 500 standing outdoors.

MEETING CAPACITY: Meeting spaces hold 200 seated guests.

FEES & DEPOSITS: 30% of the total event cost is required to reserve your date and the balance is due 72 hours prior to the event. The rental fee ranges $250–1,000 depending on the space reserved. Meals range $39–59/person. Tax, alcohol and a 21% service charge are additional.

AVAILABILITY: Year-round, daily, 8am–11pm.

SERVICES/AMENITIES:

Catering: in-house
Kitchen Facilities: n/a
Tables & Chairs: provided
Linens, Silver, etc.: provided
Restrooms: wheelchair accessible
Dance Floor: CBA
Bride's Dressing Area: no
AV/Meeting Equipment: provided

Parking: valet required
Accommodations: 246 guest rooms
Outdoor Night Lighting: CBA
Outdoor Cooking Facilities: no
Cleanup: provided
View: landscaped grounds, pool area
Other: event coordination

RESTRICTIONS:

Alcohol: in-house
Smoking: outdoors only
Music: amplified OK with restrictions

Wheelchair Access: yes
Insurance: not required

Sheraton Park Hotel
at the Anaheim Resort

Resort Hotel

1855 South Harbor Boulevard, Anaheim

714/750-1811

www.sheraton.com/anaheimresort
oromero@sheratonparkanaheim.com

- Rehearsal Dinners
- Ceremonies
- Wedding Receptions
- Private Parties
- Corporate Events
- Meetings
- Film Shoots
- Accommodations

Located within easy walking distance of Disney's Magic Kingdom, the Sheraton Park Hotel at the Anaheim Resort creates a bit of magic itself with a dazzling array of event spaces to suit virtually every bride's fairy-tale dreams. Having recently undergone a $50 million renovation, this bustling hotel offers sophisticated elegance in its ballrooms, yet maintains a "family friendly" atmosphere that is sure to please out-of-town guests.

The hotel consists of several buildings laid out resort-style around a landscaped pool. The Tiffany Terrace, an utterly charming, architecturally unique structure with a domed roof, occupies a prime spot right near the pool. This jewel of a wedding locale has an adjoining free-form outdoor space, the Tiffany Terrace Patio, from which your friends and family can take in the soothing sounds of a gurgling fountain along with great views of the glass-clad elevators ascending the nearby guest room tower. You can have your ceremony on the sun-dappled patio beneath the trees, or just enjoy cocktails al fresco before going inside for a very romantic dinner under an amazing arched canopy of stained glass. The homage to famed French designer Louis Tiffany continues with colorful stained-glass chandeliers, re-created in his distinctive Art Nouveau style. The entire front wall of this self-contained building is glass enhanced with wood-beam framing, which lends a wonderful, Parisian turn-of-the-century, "greenhouse in the park" atmosphere to your festivities.

Another indoor-outdoor option is the Garden Room, featuring crystal chandeliers that descend like inverted pyramids and tall windows that look out onto the room's own patio. This flagstone ceremony/cocktail area is covered with a striped awning and surrounded by a lawn bordered by palm trees for privacy.

If you have something more traditional in mind, there are several luxuriously appointed ballrooms in the main building. Enter the double glass doors to a grand lobby with cream-colored marble floors. To the right is a large and very comfortable earth-toned lounge; to your left is the Palm Ballroom, adorned with crystal chandeliers hanging from the coffered ceiling and carpeting in serene brown and linen hues. Further down the hall are two other ballrooms, both opening up to the El Prado Foyer, a prefunction space for cocktails and hors d'oeuvres. Done in light shades of gold and brown, it provides a lovely view to a small outdoor rotunda and lawn. When you're ready for dinner and dancing, you can opt for either the Park or Plaza Ballroom. Both have grand proportions, high ceilings and dramatic crystal chandeliers, and each can be divided into smaller, more intimate spaces if desired.

With all it has to offer, the Sheraton Park Hotel at the Anaheim Resort is something of a magic kingdom in its own right.

CEREMONY CAPACITY: The hotel holds 1,000 seated guests indoors and 500 seated outdoors.

EVENT/RECEPTION CAPACITY: The hotel accommodates 700 seated or 900 standing guests indoors and 500 seated or standing outdoors.

MEETING CAPACITY: Meeting spaces seat 1,200 guests.

FEES & DEPOSITS: 33% of the estimated event total is required to reserve your date. An additional deposit is due 90 days prior to the event and the balance is due 30 days prior. Ceremony rental fees range $1,800–2,500. Meals range $65–85/person. Tax, alcohol and a 21% service charge are additional.

AVAILABILITY: Year-round, daily.

SERVICES/AMENITIES:

Catering: provided
Kitchen Facilities: n/a
Tables & Chairs: provided
Linens, Silver, etc.: provided
Restrooms: wheelchair accessible
Dance Floor: provided
Bride's Dressing Area: CBA
AV/Meeting Equipment: CBA

Parking: large lot, valet also available
Accommodations: 490 guestrooms
Outdoor Night Lighting: CBA
Outdoor Cooking Facilities: BBQ CBA
Cleanup: provided
View: fountain, garden, pool, garden areas

RESTRICTIONS:

Alcohol: provided
Smoking: in designated areas only
Music: amplified OK with restrictions

Wheelchair Access: yes
Insurance: not required

Anaheim Hills Golf Course Clubhouse

Golf Club & Restaurant

6501 E. Nohl Ranch Road, Anaheim Hills
714/998-3041 x3
www.hillsclubhouse.com
catering@hillsclubhouse.com

● Rehearsal Dinners	● Corporate Events
● Ceremonies	● Meetings
● Wedding Receptions	● Film Shoots
● Private Parties	Accommodations

With its clean-lined Spanish Mediterranean style and desert landscaping, the Anaheim Hills Golf Course Clubhouse could be a villa in Palm Springs or along Spain's Costa del Sol. Instead, it's in upscale Anaheim Hills, a city of rolling knolls, pastoral vistas and cool valleys in the bosom of central Orange County. A local favorite, this 30,000-square-foot facility is a top pick for brides seeking casual elegance in a contemporary setting.

Although built on City property, the facility is independently run and staffed by full-service wedding and special event coordinators. They'll assist you with everything from favors, linens and place cards to the wedding cake and décor—all in keeping with the style and colors of your celebration. In addition, they offer a long list of referrals for DJs, musicians, florists, photographers, videographers and even officiants, and are happy to help guide you in your selections.

Getting ready on the Big Day is a breeze, thanks to a spacious bridal dressing room with a quartet of mirrors and a private restroom. While you prepare to make your entrance, guests step through the arched entryway of the clubhouse into a gracious lobby with a high, beamed ceiling. Another set of arched double doors leads to the Terrace, an expansive patio where umbrella-shaded tables and portable cocktail bars can be set up for your party.

Outdoor ceremonies are also held on the Terrace, which overlooks the course's rolling fairways, punctuated with stands of oaks and sycamores. A pair of columns provides a focal point, while a multi-tiered fountain adds Mediterranean flair. Before or after saying your vows, you can opt to take photos in a sheltered enclave of the course, shaded by tall greenery—your ivory gown will be beautifully highlighted against the emerald lawn.

The Grand Ballroom is an impressive space for a large wedding ceremony, reception or corporate affair. A high, coffered ceiling, ironwork chandeliers, tied-back draperies, and a Byzantine-motif carpet set a sophisticated tone. Light flows in through three walls of floor-to-ceiling arched windows that also afford panoramic views of the golf course.

The Anaheim Hills Golf Course is not just another golfing facility that does weddings. This is a venue that really knows how to host the 'Big Day,' from their expert staff and smartly designed clubhouse (the layout is perfect for events) to the topnotch food and abundant free parking. The Clubhouse gets great word-of-mouth from satisfied couples saying things such as, "The Catering Manager and Wedding Day Coordinator were awesome—simply amazing at getting all the details ironed out and working with us on the pricing and menu," and "Wow! Great customer service still exists!" One bride summed up her experience this way: "If you choose this venue, you will not be disappointed."

CEREMONY & EVENT/RECEPTION CAPACITY: The clubhouse holds 350 seated with a dance floor, or 650 standing guests indoors. Outdoors the ceremony site can accommodate 275 seated or 450 standing.

MEETING CAPACITY: Meeting spaces hold 500 seated guests.

FEES & DEPOSITS: A deposit is required to reserve your date. 50% of the estimated event total is due 90 days prior to the event, and the balance is due 7 days prior. Rental fees are waived with a minimum food purchase. All-inclusive wedding packages range $49–113/person. Tax and service charge are additional.

AVAILABILITY: Year-round, daily except Sunday morning, 10am–4pm or 6pm–midnight.

SERVICES/AMENITIES:
Catering: in-house or BYO
Kitchen Facilities: fully equipped
Tables & Chairs: provided
Linens, Silver, etc.: provided
Restrooms: wheelchair accessible
Dance Floor: portable provided
Bride's Dressing Area: yes
AV/Meeting Equipment: provided

Parking: large lot, free self-parking
Accommodations: no guest rooms, hotels nearby
Outdoor Night Lighting: provided
Outdoor Cooking Facilities: CBA
Cleanup: yes
View: fairways, hills, landscaped grounds
Other: on-site coordination, wedding cake, chair covers, dropdown screen

RESTRICTIONS:
Alcohol: in-house
Smoking: allowed outdoors only
Music: amplified OK indoors

Wheelchair Access: yes
Insurance: liability required with outside catering

Los Coyotes Country Club

8888 Los Coyotes Drive, Buena Park
888/995-4188
www.countryclubreceptions.com
eventdirector@loscoyotescc.com

●	Rehearsal Dinners	●	Corporate Events
●	Ceremonies	●	Meetings
●	Wedding Receptions		Film Shoots
●	Private Parties		Accommodations

The two things people ooh and aah the most about at Los Coyotes Country Club are the food and the facility's good looks. The Executive Chef, along with his culinary team, has given this site a reputation for consistently serving gourmet meals. And the club's Mission-style architecture—with its tiled roofs, arched colonnades and beautiful vantage atop a small hill—is a bragging point among regulars.

But there's a third thing to tout here, and it may be just as important as the other two: the golf course itself. It's probably best viewed from the grand flagstone-paved terrace along one side of the clubhouse. Here, you look out over a putting green and beyond toward three long verdant fairways, each separated from the others by lines of mature trees. And while you're gazing off at those fairways—even though you know there are millions of people and all the trappings of modern civilization within a few miles of where you stand—you'd swear the green earth goes on forever. The sense of being away from the Southland's pressure-cooker environment is both palpable and soothing.

The terrace, part of which is shaded under an archway, adjoins a spacious ballroom featuring an 18-foot-high ceiling, six-lamp chandeliers, and beautiful wall sconces. The terrace-facing side of the ballroom, as well as another side that looks out onto a small manmade lake, are lined with picture windows and French doors. The room can be divided into three sections, but most couples decide to reserve the entire space. They love this ballroom's drama—it looks impressive (because of its height) and inviting (thanks to its big, sun-loving windows) at the same time.

Los Coyotes' lush setting inspires many al fresco ceremonies and offers two options for exchanging vows: The Lakeside Ceremony Site, bordered by a tranquil lake on one side and a large putting green on another, provides the quintessential golf course experience. The Terrace affords the convenience of saying "I do" and then stepping right into the ballroom for the reception. During those rare times when the weather is inclement, or for smaller parties seeking an indoor setting, the Cypress Palm Room, with its French door-framed view of the lake, is popular.

Located down the hall from the ballroom, the bride's dressing room is a posh extension of Los Coyotes' stylish décor. It's nicely appointed with an oversized oak-trimmed vanity mirror, a sink, a large closet and a wall mirror.

Even the drive up to Los Coyotes has appealing touches: The curving road sweeps through a well-landscaped neighborhood of large ranch-style houses, and the tall palms along the median strip evoke an almost resort-like feel. When you reach the club, the banquet room's dramatic porte-cochère entrance only reinforces that feeling of refinement. Ah, if a day can unfold so agreeably just getting to Los Coyotes, you can be confident it will continue that way long after you've arrived.

CEREMONY CAPACITY: The Lakeside site and the Terrace hold up to 300 seated guests. Indoors, the Cypress Palm Room seats up to 150.

EVENT/RECEPTION & MEETING CAPACITY: The Ballroom holds 350 seated with a dance floor or 500 standing guests. It can be divided into two smaller sections, each accommodating up to 122 seated with a dance floor or 200 standing. Outdoors, the Terrace accommodates up to 150 seated or 450 standing.

FEES & DEPOSITS: A nonrefundable deposit, which is applied to your food & beverage total, is required to reserve your date. The amount of the deposit varies depending on how far in advance you book. Payment terms for the balance also vary, and may be arranged on an individual basis. Wedding packages start at $50/person. Tax, alcohol and service charge are additional. Food & beverage minimums apply. Menus and packages can be customized to fit your needs and budget. Call for details.

AVAILABILITY: Year-round, daily.

SERVICES/AMENITIES:

Catering: in-house

Kitchen Facilities: n/a

Tables & Chairs: provided

Linens, Silver, etc.: provided

Restrooms: wheelchair accessible

Dance Floor: provided

Bride's Dressing Area: yes

AV/Meeting Equipment: CBA, extra charge

Parking: large lot, valet required for over 70 guests

Accommodations: no guest rooms

Outdoor Night Lighting: yes

Outdoor Cooking Facilities: CBA

Cleanup: provided

View: fairways, trees, lake

RESTRICTIONS:

Alcohol: in-house, or BYO wine with corkage fee

Smoking: outdoors only

Music: amplified OK

Wheelchair Access: yes

Insurance: not required

Other: no open flames or confetti, no affixing anything to the walls or ceiling

Overwhelmed? Use the search criteria on www.HereComesTheGuide.com to narrow down your choices.

317

Five Crowns Restaurant

Restaurant & Garden

3801 East Coast Highway, Corona del Mar
949/760-1115 or 949/760-0331
www.thefivecrowns.com
arobbins@lawrysonline.com

● Rehearsal Dinners	● Corporate Events
● Ceremonies	● Meetings
● Wedding Receptions	● Film Shoots
● Private Parties	Accommodations

If you're familiar with Orange County's fine dining scene, chances are you've heard of Five Crowns. Established in 1965 in upscale Corona del Mar—one of Southern California's most idyllic coastal villages—the Tudor-style culinary landmark is a recreation of England's oldest country inn, Ye Olde Bell (est. 1135 A.D.). In this pocket of seaside affluence, it's also an icon of patrician respectability, award-winning cuisine, and premier vintages, owned by the Frank and Van De Kamp families of Lawry's Restaurants fame.

Known for serving up some of the best prime rib in town, as well as contemporary renditions of fresh seafood, roasted fowl, and succulent lamb, Five Crowns has hosted legions of discriminating local diners and such illustrious guests as Elizabeth Taylor and past President Richard Nixon.

What you may not know is that this revered dining establishment is also a classic setting for weddings, receptions, rehearsal dinners and other singular celebrations. With its rich wood paneling, ceiling beams, antique maritime memorabilia and cozy nooks, the venue exudes an Old World ambiance. Indeed, a bride might imagine herself part of a Shakespearean sonnet as she makes her way down from the upstairs dressing room to meet her groom. And while she primps with her bridesmaids, her husband-to-be and his groomsmen can enjoy male bonding in the SideDoor, a gastropub with a large fireplace and high-backed Tudor chairs.

The most popular area for saying your vows in this historic site is the herb gardens, off the restaurant's sunlit greenhouse. A traditional trellis, adorned with flowers and herbs, lends just the right amount of formality to the intimate setting. An awning and umbrellas provide shade for guests on sunny days, while a tent can shelter the entire outdoor area during inclement weather.

Depending on the size of your party, guests will enjoy pre- and post-ceremony hospitality in the greenhouse and brick-lined patio, the main Nelson Crown Room, or The Brighton Room, named for the pleasure palace George IV of England built in 1782. In all of these areas, service is provided by a friendly and very professional staff. Many couples opt to capture memories of the day at the front entrance of the restaurant, where an antique red British telephone booth is a recognizable landmark on the East Coast Highway.

Before and after the merrymaking, out-of-town guests can enjoy accommodations in many four- and five-star hotels along the coast, or at the newly restored Crystal Cove Cottages, just a mile down the road in the Crystal Cove State Park Historic District. You might consider a post-celebration treat of your own: a romantic moonlit walk with your new spouse along this stretch of pristine coastline.

CEREMONY CAPACITY: The capacity varies depending on the time of day and spaces used. For daytime ceremonies, the venue can accommodate up to 150 seated guests. In the evening, ceremonies are limited to 100 seated.

EVENT RECEPTION CAPACITY: The venue holds up to 150 seated for daytime receptions and 100 seated in the evening. If you buy out the restaurant, the seated capacity increases to 200. The maximum capacity for a standing reception is 200 during the day and 150 in the evening.

MEETING CAPACITY: The restaurant holds 150 seated guests.

FEES & DEPOSITS: 20% of the food & beverage minimum is required to reserve your date. The balance is due at the completion of the event. There are no ceremony or venue fees. Meals range $35–80/person. Tax, alcohol and a 2% service charge and server gratuity are additional.

AVAILABILITY: Year-round, daily, anytime.

SERVICES/AMENITIES:

Catering: in-house
Kitchen Facilities: n/a
Tables & Chairs: provided
Linens, Silver, etc.: provided
Restrooms: wheelchair accessible
Dance Floor: CBA
Bride's & Groom's Dressing Areas: yes
AV/Meeting Equipment: CBA

Parking: valet required
Accommodations: no guest rooms
Outdoor Night Lighting: provided
Outdoor Cooking Facilities: no
Cleanup: provided
View: garden courtyard
Other: event coordination

RESTRICTIONS:

Alcohol: in-house
Smoking: not allowed
Music: amplified OK with restrictions

Wheelchair Access: yes
Insurance: not required

Center Club

650 Town Center Drive, Costa Mesa
714/438-3860 Catering
www.center-club.com
chris.hartley@clubcorp.com

Private Club

● Rehearsal Dinners	● Corporate Events
● Ceremonies	● Meetings
● Wedding Receptions	● Film Shoots
● Private Parties	Accommodations

If you want your wedding or special event to take center stage, then definitely consider the Center Club. Talk about centrally located! This prestigious member of the ClubCorp family is located in the center of Orange County, in the center of South Coast Metro at the base of the award-winning Center Tower adjacent to the glamorous Segerstrom Center for the Arts. Occupying the garden level of a performing arts complex, the swank business club has been an in-demand event site for more than 30 years, and it's now going to attract even more fans thanks to its brand new look.

A recent $3.1 million renovation has taken the Center Club from elegantly traditional to magnificently contemporary. Grand social and professional affairs will be right at home here, in a place that's chic, sophisticated and ultra-upscale.

From the moment you step into the pleasingly posh lobby, you'll be swept away by an arts-inspired setting. Waltz down the lustrous, handsomely appointed hall—there's a musical score subtly worked into its walls—toward the Symphony Ballroom. No ordinary rectangular box, this stunning space has an architectural splendor that allows for intimacy without sacrificing scale. That "far corner of the room" syndrome does not exist here. Three adjoining chambers create the ballroom's dynamic arrowhead shape, and when they're all used together they offer sightlines from the central "prow" that make the whole room visible and enticingly accessible in spite of its lavish dimensions. In addition, the three chambers can function independently as the Mozart, Chopin and Beethoven Rooms—each totally alluring in its own right.

The Chopin Room, for example, has a spacious outdoor terrace that's perfect for ceremonies or cocktails. It features sculptural details like the "green wall" planted with ferns, the Four Lines Oblique Gyratory-Square IV structure by George Rickey, and towering eucalyptus trees for a look that's sleek and streamlined, yet serene. The Mozart and Beethoven Rooms, like the Chopin, have floor-to-ceiling windows, although these look out onto a palatial water garden (designed by leading Modernist movement landscape architect, Peter Walker) that radiates tranquility and a grand museum feel. All three rooms are decorated in tasteful shades of pewter, bronze and dove-gray that allow their beautiful bones—high ceilings, crown moldings and impressive soffits—to shine. Nothing has been overlooked—even the furnishings are works of art, sculpted and finished to echo and enhance a design perspective that bespeaks luxury and taste.

Of course, as you'd expect from a world-class event venue like this one, a variety of other options is also available for your partying pleasure: The traditional Zen, and high-tech Earth, Wind, and

Fire rooms provide private boardroom and dining opportunities. If more space is required, the sumptuous Encore Lounge with its clubby leather and hardwood accents; the VIP Lounge; and a spectacular Founders Room further expand your choices. Top it off with Center Club's impeccable service, culinary expertise and unparalleled farm-to-table cuisine, and you'll have a recipe for smashing success.

CEREMONY CAPACITY: The Mozart Room seats 130 guests, and the Symphony Ballroom Patio seats 200.

EVENT/RECEPTION & MEETING CAPACITY: The Symphony Ballroom holds 250 seated or 350 standing, the Beethoven Room holds 130 seated or 200 standing, the Mozart Room holds 60 seated or 100 standing, and the Chopin Room holds 20 seated or 30 standing.

FEES & DEPOSITS: A nonrefundable $2,500 deposit is required to secure your date. Half of the estimated event total is due 90 days prior to the event, and the balance is payable 2 weeks prior. Any menu can be customized. All-inclusive wedding packages start at $100/person on Friday/Sunday and $125/person on Saturday. All wedding packages include valet parking, service charge and sales tax. For ceremonies there is a $1,200 charge that covers setup, chairs, runner, rehearsal, and sound system. Food & beverage minimums apply.

AVAILABILITY: Year-round, daily, 7am–2am in 5-hour blocks. Additional hours are available for a fee.

SERVICES/AMENITIES:

Catering: in-house or BYO
Kitchen Facilities: prep access
Tables & Chairs: provided
Linens, Silver, etc.: provided
Restrooms: wheelchair accessible
Dance Floor: provided, extra charge
Bride's & Groom's Dressing Areas: yes
AV/Meeting Equipment: yes

Parking: valet included in packages
Accommodations: no guest rooms
Outdoor Night Lighting: yes
Outdoor Cooking Facilities: n/a
Cleanup: provided
View: water and sculpture gardens
Other: chocolate fountain, ice sculptures

RESTRICTIONS:

Alcohol: in-house, no BYO
Smoking: outside only
Music: amplified OK

Wheelchair Access: yes
Insurance: not required

Westin South Coast Plaza

Hotel

686 Anton Boulevard, Costa Mesa

714/662-6637

www.westinsouthcoastplaza.com
sheena.mehta@westin.com

- Rehearsal Dinners
- Ceremonies
- Wedding Receptions
- Private Parties
- Corporate Events
- Meetings
- Film Shoots
- Accommodations

An oasis of tranquility in Orange County's sophisticated cultural Mecca, the Westin South Coast Plaza resonates with discreet style. It offers a range of versatile indoor and outdoor spaces, making it a cosmopolitan backdrop for an elegant reception or destination wedding.

Entering the airy lobby of what has long been a premier hotel in the area for business and pleasure travelers, you're welcomed by a soothing ambiance. Luxuriant floral accents and white tea aromatic accents simultaneously arouse the senses and quiet the nerves. The minimalist style and palette of warm grays, translucent greens and soft purples inspire a feeling of unhurried peace. Abundant natural light and a view of flowing water beyond further draw you into the space.

Before the festivities begin, you and your bridal party might pose for wedding album pictures at the beautiful Waterfall Terrace, or head next door to the Orange County Performing Arts Center or Noguchi Garden where more photo opportunities abound.

You may also want to exchange vows on the Waterfall Terrace, beneath a scalloped shade canopy in a California-tropical setting lush with ferns, climbing vines and blooming impatiens. Against a cascading stream, you and your groom will kiss for the first time as husband and wife.

The adjacent Lido Ballroom provides the stage for a casually chic reception. This light-filled venue opens onto its own terrace, encouraging an easy indoor-outdoor flow throughout your event and giving celebrants lots of room to mingle.

If your guest list is long, tie the knot under the Terrace Gazebo. Presiding over the 4,000-square-foot Terrace Pavilion, it's a grand, curtained structure whose sheer drapes can be customized to suit your color scheme. As a string quartet plays in concert with the sound of the tumbling waterfall below, guests can relax on comfy couches before taking their seats for your outdoor ceremony. Afterwards, they'll enjoy appetizers and champagne under the stars, enclosed by long planters filled with stately palms and birds of paradise.

Formal receptions are held in the Plaza Ballroom, illuminated by seven crystal chandeliers. With its neutral décor, it's easily tailored to any bride's design wishes, and its smaller-than-typical size makes it more intimate than most grand ballrooms.

After you've thrown the bouquet and danced your last dance, retire to your luxurious bridal suite, where you'll sleep ever-so-soundly on Westin's patented Heavenly Bed®. When you wake up the next day, you can look forward to plenty of wonderful options: Walk arm-in-arm across the pedestrian bridge leading to South Coast Plaza and its world-class shops and restaurants. Pay a visit to one or more of the nearby museums or attend a performance at the adjacent Orange County Performing Arts Center. Why not take a day trip to Catalina Island, Disneyland or the Aquarium of the Pacific?—they're all less than 30 minutes away. With so much to do and see here, you and your very happy out-of-town guests will be able to turn your destination wedding into a true vacation.

The Westin South Coast Plaza is a proud partner with the Costa Mesa Conference and Visitor Bureau.

CEREMONY CAPACITY: The hotel accommodates 600 seated guests indoors or out.

EVENT/RECEPTION CAPACITY: The hotel holds 650 seated or 1,000 standing guests indoors and 400 seated or 600 standing outdoors.

MEETING CAPACITY: Meeting spaces seat 600 guests indoors.

FEES & DEPOSITS: 25% of the total estimated event cost is required to reserve your date and the balance is due 14 business days prior to the event. Rental fees are waived when food & beverage minimums are met. Wedding packages start at $72/person. Tax, alcohol and a 22% service charge are additional.

AVAILABILITY: Year-round, daily.

SERVICES/AMENITIES:

Catering: in-house
Kitchen Facilities: n/a
Tables & Chairs: provided
Linens, Silver, etc.: provided
Restrooms: wheelchair accessible
Dance Floor: portable provided
Bride's Dressing Area: yes
AV/Meeting Equipment: provided

Parking: valet or self-parking, garage nearby
Accommodations: 394 guest rooms
Outdoor Night Lighting: CBA
Outdoor Cooking Facilities: BBQ CBA
Cleanup: provided
View: garden, waterfall, pool area, landscaped grounds
Other: lighting services

RESTRICTIONS:

Alcohol: in-house
Smoking: not allowed
Music: amplified OK with restrictions

Wheelchair Access: yes
Insurance: liability required

Coto de Caza Golf & Racquet Club

Country Club

25291 Vista del Verde, Coto de Caza

949/858-4100

www.coto-de-caza.com
sarah.placeres@clubcorp.com
chantal.cervantes@clubcorp.com

● Rehearsal Dinners	● Corporate Events
● Ceremonies	● Meetings
● Wedding Receptions	● Film Shoots
● Private Parties	Accommodations

The exclusive community of Coto de Caza has always been a secluded universe unto itself—a peaceful microcosm set securely behind a stone entry, and laced with hiking and horseback riding trails. At the pinnacle of its 4,000 verdant acres, capped by a tower that's visible from almost anywhere inside Coto's wrought-iron gates, is a chic world within a world: the Coto de Caza Golf & Racquet Club, one of only three private 36-hole country clubs in metropolitan Southern California.

With Craftsman-style architecture that reflects a Frank Lloyd Wright penchant for 90-degree turns and angles, the club's 44,000-square-foot clubhouse is a theatrical venue for tying the knot. At its entrance a graceful bridge stretches over a pond fed by trickling streams and cascading waterfalls that create a Zen-like calm. After walking up the wide staircase fronting its expansive stone and glass façade, guests step into a lobby filled with rich woods, Mission-style furnishings and light streaming in through floor-to-ceiling windows. While they chat and sip lemonade, you'll relax and prepare for the day's festivities in the Ladies Lounge, outfitted with a large closet, TV and cushy sofas.

When your ceremony is about to begin, friends and family will take their seats on the lower outdoor patio, near the flower-ringed half circle looking out over the club's velvety fairways. As strains of "Here Comes the Bride" begin, they'll turn and see you appear at the apex of the club's dramatic stairway, ready to descend the long aisle to meet your groom. With the rolling hills of the Trabuco Canyon as a backdrop, you'll exchange your vows.

Reception options abound here. For larger gatherings the outdoor pavilion overlooks the greens and comes alive in the evening, with twinkling lights on lacy trees surrounding the adjacent rock waterfall. Count on comfort in all seasons, as the expansive space is equipped with ceiling fans, heat lamps and roll-down sides for wind protection. The club's Main Dining Room and attached outdoor terrace, with views of the golf course and canyon, is a more intimate setting for post-ceremony cocktails and dinner. Another alternative is the homey Lounge, with its built-in bar and interior fireplace.

No matter where in the facility you choose to celebrate, your coordinator at the club can arrange for many special touches. Opt for a chocolate-dipped strawberry bar with an attendant to infuse the plump fruits with guests' choice of liqueur; have your new initials scrolled in chocolate on your cake plate; or heat up the party with a flambé dessert station. If you can't make it to the tropics for a honeymoon escape, create your own singular world at the club: Follow the example of one bride who brought the spirit of aloha to the mainland by importing tiki torches, leis and flowers from the islands for a colorful luau, Coto-style. This private country club is sure to fulfill your wedding dreams and impress your guests.

CEREMONY CAPACITY: The Ceremony Circle seats up to 250 guests. Indoors, the Main Dining Room holds up to 180 seated.

EVENT/RECEPTION CAPACITY: Indoor spaces hold up to 120 seated or 200 standing guests; outdoor spaces up to 250 seated or 350 standing.

MEETING CAPACITY: The Main Dining Room seats up to 120.

FEES & DEPOSITS: A $3,500 nonrefundable deposit is required to reserve your date. The balance is due in advance of the event. The Sunday inclusive wedding package is $10,000 for 100 guests, and the Saturday package is $15,000 for 120 guests. Packages include ceremony, cocktail hour, champagne toast, plated meal, linens, valet parking, tax and service charge.

AVAILABILITY: Year-round, daily with flexible hours. Call for details.

SERVICES/AMENITIES:

Catering: in-house, no BYO
Kitchen Facilities: n/a
Tables & Chairs: provided
Linens, Silver, etc.: provided
Restrooms: wheelchair accessible
Dance Floor: provided
Bride's Dressing Area: yes
AV/Meeting Equipment: CBA

Parking: large lot, valet included
Accommodations: no guest rooms
Outdoor Night Lighting: yes
Outdoor Cooking Facilities: no
Cleanup: provided
View: canyon, garden patio, fairways, hills, waterfall
Other: event coordination, spa services, athletic center, golf

RESTRICTIONS:

Alcohol: in-house, no BYO
Smoking: outside only
Music: amplified OK with restrictions

Wheelchair Access: yes
Insurance: not required

The wedding vendors on our website are the best in the business. How do we know? Read page 577.

Eagle's Nest Restaurant & Banquets

Restaurant

5660 Orangewood Avenue, Cypress

714/889-1453

www.eaglesnestclubhouse.com
info@eaglesnestclubhouse.com

● Rehearsal Dinners   ● Corporate Events
● Ceremonies   ● Meetings
● Wedding Receptions   ● Film Shoots
● Private Parties   Accommodations

For years, Eagle's Nest Restaurant & Banquets has verged on being a military secret, but now that word is out about this venue it's good news for brides. Tucked into a quiet, residential neighborhood convenient to both Orange and Los Angeles Counties, Eagle's Nest offers a picturesque setting on the sprawling greens of the Cypress Navy Golf Course. A second locale run by the same folks is available on a private beach at the Seal Beach Weapons Station off Pacific Coast Highway, 10 minutes away by car. The tranquil grounds of both facilities provide numerous options for ceremonies and receptions of any size.

With its distinctive California Mission architecture, Mediterranean-inspired furnishings and comfortable lounge, the Eagle's Nest clubhouse offers a relaxed ambiance for guests to mix and mingle. Before they arrive, prepare for your big day in a spacious bride's room, where you and your bridesmaids can sip champagne and nibble on fresh strawberries. Grooms have their own private space, too.

Larger ceremonies are held outdoors in the Pavilion, a wood-beamed, open-air structure overlooking the golf course. Decorated with flowers, fabric or left au naturel, it's a dramatic al fresco shelter. A brick walkway, often strewn with rose petals, leads to the raised area where you and your groom will exchange vows. Alternatively, you can tie the knot under a white Victorian gazebo on the neighboring lawn against a backdrop of leafy trees.

If you've always dreamed of a beach wedding, get married at Eagle's Nest's private beach, just five miles away. Have your reception right on the sand with a stately battleship in the background, or dine back at the clubhouse.

Eagle's Nest's banquet rooms all offer views of the golf course, and a variety of wedding packages allow you to make your chosen room look exactly the way you want. Decorating options include swagging, customized lighting, chair covers, and more. The ballroom is equipped with state-of-the-art audiovisual equipment, and an on-site DVD player or projector and big screen are at your disposal for a memorable slideshow.

Your reception meal will be prepared by Eagle's Nest's professional culinary staff. They're the exclusive caterers for the adjacent naval base, and they're known for using the freshest ingredients in classically elegant dishes.

Photographic opportunities abound throughout the clubhouse, as well as on the golf course—a favorite spot is in front of a fountain on the fairways. If you and your wedding party are golf aficionados, you can arrange for a pre-wedding game, or capture post-wedding moments while posing on golf carts.

A lovely way to spend some post-wedding time with your guests (especially those staying for the weekend) is to invite them onto the fairways for a congenial round of golf. As you relax with friends and family, you'll be able to relive all the wonderful moments of your wedding, and fully appreciate how seamlessly it was orchestrated by your attentive Eagle's Nest pros.

CEREMONY CAPACITY: The restaurant holds 500 seated guests indoors and 1,000 seated outdoors.

EVENT/RECEPTION CAPACITY: The restaurant accommodates 400 seated or 700 standing guests indoors and 1,000 seated or 1,500 standing outdoors.

MEETING CAPACITY: Meeting spaces seat 600 guests indoors.

FEES & DEPOSITS: A $1,000 deposit is required to reserve your date and the balance is due 14 days prior to the event. Meals range $10–30/person. Tax, alcohol and a 20% service charge are additional.

AVAILABILITY: Year-round, daily, 6am–midnight.

SERVICES/AMENITIES:

Catering: in-house
Kitchen Facilities: n/a
Tables & Chairs: provided
Linens, Silver, etc.: provided
Restrooms: wheelchair accessible
Dance Floor: provided
Bride's Dressing Area: yes
AV/Meeting Equipment: provided

Parking: large lot
Accommodations: no guest rooms
Outdoor Night Lighting: yes
Outdoor Cooking Facilities: BBQ CBA
Cleanup: provided
View: fairways, lake, fountain, landscaped grounds, garden
Other: coordination, in-house wedding cake and florals, picnic area, outdoor area for up to 2,000

RESTRICTIONS:

Alcohol: in-house
Smoking: outdoors only
Music: amplified OK

Wheelchair Access: yes
Insurance: not required

Chart House Dana Point

34442 Green Lantern Street, Dana Point
949/460-6071
www.chart-house.com
mmcquillan@ldry.com

- Rehearsal Dinners
- Ceremonies
- Wedding Receptions
- Private Parties
- Corporate Events
- Meetings
- Film Shoots
- Accommodations

If ever there was a "Wait, there's more!" venue in Here Comes The Guide, Dana Point's Chart House has to be one of them. Start with the restaurant's show-stopping vista, a sensational hillside view of Dana Point Harbor, its long breakwater and the Pacific beyond. High palisades rise to the east, topped with luxurious homes, then drop down to an inviting, leafy shoreside park. Boats of all kinds are constantly arriving and departing, and two sleek twin-masted sailing ships moor at the bottom of the hill. This is easily one of the best sea views in Orange County. So naturally the long, carefully manicured ceremony lawn that overlooks it is one of the most dramatic wedding sites in all of the Southland.

With a panorama this incredible, it would be a shame to limit the lawn to ceremonies. Fortunately, it doubles as a spot for "California luau" dinners, which feature tiki torches and buffet food. News about the appealingly informal parties has gotten around—some nearby upscale resorts often send wedding parties here for their rehearsal dinners. They know that casual dining overlooking a great view is just the thing to soothe pre-wedding jitters.

There's more! Chart House, a modernistic building of three interconnected circular spaces called "pods," is the design of architect Kendrick Bangs Kellogg, a student of the great Frank Lloyd Wright. Completed in the late 1970s, the building beautifully melds rough-textured concrete, redwood, steel and glass into a memorable configuration. It's very much in the style of Wright, with its creative use of curves and materials, as well as its exterior palette of rust-red wood and light blue steel.

Inside, a harmonious medley of light gray concrete, 62 miles of bent redwood formed into concentric circles on the ceilings, and seeming acres of windows create a striking interior. Almost every seat in the house has a view. All of the booths in the restaurant's three pods have plush leather cushions and backrests with subdued, but playful, abstract patterns. Pod 1 has a built-in dance floor and stage—perfect for a head table—plus the magnificent harbor view. (Delicate cornflower-blue mood lights are suspended from its coiled redwood ceiling—a sweet little touch.) Pod 2 has a grand staircase descending from the restaurant's entry tower, as well as a wine cellar and dining booths. Pod 3, which affords direct access to the patio, has a long bar and an intriguing Art Deco/1950s look.

Still more! Besides a terrific location and singular architectural style, Chart House has another great thing going for it: an experienced kitchen staff that has garnered a devoted clientele over almost three decades. That kitchen is one of the reasons why Chart House attracts dozens of daytime wedding receptions each year. Couples also like having the whole venue to themselves throughout their event.

From the road, Chart House is almost hidden. You see its signature view before you see its red-wood entry tower, and you see the tower before you see the restaurant itself. That slow unfolding of delights is this place's greatest strength and its greatest charm.

CEREMONY CAPACITY: The facility accommodates 220 seated guests outdoors.

EVENT/RECEPTION & MEETING CAPACITY: The site holds 200 seated or standing guests indoors and 80 seated or standing outdoors.

FEES & DEPOSITS: A nonrefundable deposit is required to reserve your date. The reception package is $600 and the ceremony package is $10/person. Plated entrées range $41–85/person and buffets range $50–61/person. Tax, alcohol and a service charge are additional. Food & beverage minimums may apply to specific times, days, and rooms.

AVAILABILITY: Year-round, daily, 11am–4pm and 5–10pm.

SERVICES/AMENITIES:

Catering: in-house, no BYO
Kitchen Facilities: n/a
Tables & Chairs: provided
Linens, Silver, etc.: provided
Restrooms: wheelchair accessible
Dance Floor: provided
Bride's & Groom's Dressing Areas: no
AV/Meeting Equipment: some provided, BYO

Parking: on street, large lot, valet required
Accommodations: no guest rooms
Outdoor Night Lighting: CBA
Outdoor Cooking Facilities: no
Cleanup: provided
View: coastline, Dana Point harbor, landscaped grounds
Other: event coordination

RESTRICTIONS:

Alcohol: in-house, no BYO
Smoking: not allowed
Music: amplified OK with restrictions

Wheelchair Access: yes
Insurance: not required

Laguna Cliffs Marriott Resort & Spa

Resort & Spa

25135 Park Lantern, Dana Point
949/661-5000
www.lagunacliffs.com
weddings@lagunacliffs.com

● Rehearsal Dinners	● Corporate Events	
● Ceremonies	● Meetings	
● Wedding Receptions	● Film Shoots	
● Private Parties	● Accommodations	

Just south of Laguna Beach lies a picturesque curve of coastline with white sandy beaches and balmy breezes wafting in from the Pacific. At the tip of this idyllic cove is Dana Point, a historic headland named for 19th-century seafaring adventurer and author Richard Henry Dana, who dubbed it "California's most romantic spot."

If romantic celebrations are on your agenda, then you'll love the Laguna Cliffs Marriott, a AAA Four Diamond luxury retreat overlooking the Pacific. The upscale resort's oceanview setting, which encompasses acres of emerald-green parks, a bustling marina and the boundless blue sea, creates the perfect backdrop for weddings and receptions.

The Laguna Cliffs takes full advantage of its breathtaking location by offering three beautiful outdoor venues for wedding ceremonies. The secluded Del Mar Lawn embraces a layered view of mountains, sea, and a section of shore known as "the California Riviera." The Vue Lawn treats guests to a colorful parade of yachts and sailboats against an ocean panorama. A third enclave, the Laguna Brick, captures glorious sunsets unfurling across the watery horizon. The resort's ceremony packages include the setup of full wedding regalia—arches, urns, and a rose-petal aisle.

Gala receptions are staged in one of two ballrooms, each illuminated by novel pendant fixtures. A color palette that calls to mind the sea and sun-kissed sand, gold Chiavari chairs, and the soft flickering of votive candles contribute to an ambiance of sophisticated coastal elegance. Equally impressive is the award-winning catering that puts a new spin on California cuisine.

The resort staff takes your event as seriously as you do. A dedicated team of Wedding Professionals ensures that every detail is just the way you envision it. Wedding packages come with upgrades such as cake cutting, a luxurious bridal suite, and a "Couple's Spa Massage" to soothe any pre-wedding jitters. Speaking of spa, this one is an award-winning favorite in the O.C. and has been named by *Spa Finder* magazine "Best Spa" and "Best Spa for Romance." The Bridal Beauty Packages are fabulous, and they'll customize a skin care regimen so you look more gorgeous than ever.

You and your guests will also appreciate the first-class accommodations, updated with the latest amenities. Thoughtful comforts like plush feathertop beds, duvets and spa robes encourage relaxation. With a host of on-site diversions, including a state-of-the-art fitness center, the spa and two oceanview pools, Laguna Cliffs Marriott truly is an ideal destination.

The Director of Catering Sales told us, "We strive to create a customized event experience that reflects each couple's personal vision." We think you'll agree that Laguna Cliffs is a most hospitable ambassador for the Southern California lifestyle.

CEREMONY CAPACITY: Indoors, the hotel holds up to 500 seated indoors or outdoors on the lawn. Smaller spaces are also available.

EVENT/RECEPTION CAPACITY: Indoor spaces accommodate 30–600 seated or 40–900 standing. Outdoors, the site holds 250–500 seated or 350–900 standing.

MEETING CAPACITY: Several rooms accommodate up to 1,000 guests seated theater-style.

FEES & DEPOSITS: 25% of the estimated event total is required to reserve your date; the remaining balance is paid in 3 additional equal installments between the reservation and event date. Luncheon plated meals begin at $130/person, dinners at $138/person. This includes butler-passed hors d'oeuvres, 1-hour hosted bar, 3-course meal, custom-designed wedding cake, wine service throughout the meal, champagne toast, gold Chiavari chairs and complimentary oceanview guest room for the bride and groom. Tax, alcohol and a 24% service charge are additional. The ceremony package includes an oceanview location, fresh floral arch or 2 pedestal arrangements, aisle runners or petals, rehearsal time, bride's and groom's dressing rooms, and a couple's massage at The Spa at Laguna Cliffs.

AVAILABILITY: Year-round, daily, until midnight indoors.

SERVICES/AMENITIES:

Catering: in-house or BYO with approval
Kitchen Facilities: service area
Tables & Chairs: provided
Linens, Silver, etc.: provided
Restrooms: wheelchair accessible
Dance Floor: provided
Bride's Dressing Area: yes
AV/Meeting Equipment: provided

Parking: valet
Accommodations: 378 guest rooms
Outdoor Night Lighting: yes
Outdoor Cooking Facilities: BBQ and fire pits
Cleanup: provided
View: Pacific Ocean, Dana Point Harbor, mountains, coastline
Other: on-site wedding concierge

RESTRICTIONS:

Alcohol: in-house, or BYO wine with corkage
Smoking: outdoors only
Music: amplified OK

Wheelchair Access: yes
Insurance: not required

St. Regis Resort, Monarch Beach

Coastal Resort & Spa

One Monarch Beach Resort, Dana Point

949/234-3455

www.stregismb.com
amy.botdorf@stregis.com

- Rehearsal Dinners
- Ceremonies
- Wedding Receptions
- Private Parties
- Corporate Events
- Meetings
- Film Shoots
- Accommodations

You don't recall booking any deluxe trips to Tuscany, but suddenly you find yourself surrounded by magnificent Italianate splendor, in a palatial resort looking out on what could be the Mediterranean coast. The calming sound of water tumbling onto itself is everywhere, cascading from multi-tiered fountains into gem-like pools. All around there's polished European stone and marble, hand-blown glass, inlaid mosaic tile and intricate ironwork. Overlooking a championship golf course and an ocean panorama stretching as far as the eye can see, a grand outdoor stairway leads to an emerald lawn of regal proportions.

You step onto the outdoor terrace and reach into your pocket, searching for lira that might buy you a cool drink as you contemplate the grandeur before you. Finally, a napkin emblazoned "St. Regis, Monarch Beach" tips you off: You're not in Italy at all, but rather in balmy Dana Point at one of only a few properties in California to receive the coveted Forbes Five Star and AAA Five Diamond rating, not to mention other accolades like a listing on *Travel & Leisure's* "500 Best Hotels in the World" and honors from *Conde Nast Traveler* as one of the top 50 U.S. resorts.

With its Tuscan-inspired architecture and décor, one-of-a-kind art collection and breathtaking sights, sounds and service, the St. Regis offers the ultimate in luxury for a wedding or corporate event. You'll be the belle of the hotel ball when you tie the knot under a stately colonnade on the Grand Lawn, fringed by majestic palms that filter views of world-class links and the ocean beyond. More private ceremonies are held on the Pacific Lawn or in the intimate Botanical Garden, the latter an explosion of seasonal color studded with whimsical statuary.

The resort's most opulent reception site is the 12,000-square-foot Pacific Ballroom, an inspired setting with fine architectural detailing, dazzling chandeliers and French doors opening onto an outdoor terrace. The Monarch Ballroom, capped by a lower coffered ceiling, features a separate entrance for more private affairs. Other indoor options include Club 19, offering expansive views of the Monarch Beach Golf Links, and the Wine Cellar, where 17,000 bottles from around the world are housed amidst rich mahogany and custom iron furnishings. Al fresco receptions are held on either of the hotel's spacious lawns or on the Sunset Terrace, which overlooks the Grand Lawn, golf course and ocean beyond.

As you might expect of one of the world's top resorts, the St. Regis is more than an event venue; it's an extraordinary leisure experience for luxury travelers that will tempt you and your guests to stay awhile. Book a poolside cabana, take a complimentary shuttle to a private beach, challenge yourself on the Robert Trent Jones, Jr.-designed golf course, or learn to ride the waves with your own "surf butler." Then let yourself be pampered and beautified at the on-site Spa Gaucin with its own salon. However you spend your time, you'll discover one thing for sure: No place on the Italian Riviera can top this singularly sensational destination hideaway for flawless service, comfort, cuisine and first-class amenities.

CEREMONY CAPACITY: Indoors, the hotel holds up to 750 seated, outdoors up to 750 seated on the Grand Lawn. Smaller spaces are also available.

EVENT/RECEPTION & MEETING CAPACITY: The resort accommodates up to 750 seated or 1,200 standing guests indoors or outdoors. Several smaller spaces are available; call for details.

FEES & DEPOSITS: 35% of the estimated event total is required to reserve your date. A second deposit of 65% is due 120 days prior to the event and the final balance is due 2 weeks prior. The rental fee ranges $4,500–7,000 depending on the date of the event and space reserved. Daytime packages range $85–180/person and evening packages range $180–275/person. Tax and a 24% service charge are additional.

AVAILABILITY: Year-round, daily, anytime.

SERVICES/AMENITIES:

Catering: in-house, no BYO
Kitchen Facilities: n/a
Tables & Chairs: provided
Linens, Silver, etc.: provided
Restrooms: wheelchair accessible
Dance Floor: provided
Bride's Dressing Area: no
AV/Meeting Equipment: some provided, more CBA

Parking: valet required
Accommodations: 400 guest rooms
Outdoor Night Lighting: CBA
Outdoor Cooking Facilities: BBQ CBA
Cleanup: provided
View: coastline, ocean, fountain, patio, fairways
Other: wedding cake, spa services, grand piano golf; preferred list of wedding coordinators

RESTRICTIONS:

Alcohol: in-house
Smoking: outdoors only
Music: amplified OK indoors only

Wheelchair Access: yes
Insurance: liability required
Other: an approved wedding coordinator is required for all weddings

---

Want to know WHAT TO ASK a potential location or vendor? Check out our Questions to Ask starting on page 21.

Dove Canyon Golf Club

Golf Club

22682 Golf Club Drive, Dove Canyon
949/858-2800

www.pacificlinks.com/dove-canyon-golf-club
facebook.com/dovecanyoncc
bhalbreich@pacificlinks.com

● Rehearsal Dinners ● Corporate Events
● Ceremonies ● Meetings
● Wedding Receptions ● Film Shoots
● Private Parties Accommodations

If you have a very private and elegant setting in mind for your special event, the clubhouse at Dove Canyon will exceed your expectations. Its prime location—in a secluded gated community at the edge of a canyon in the hills of southern Orange County—is matched by its design, style and ambiance.

The clubhouse pays homage to the architecture of Frank Lloyd Wright in its soaring wood-beamed cathedral ceiling lit by skylights, earth-tone slate floors, rich Honduran mahogany paneling, and carved plaster columns. When you hold your special event here you have exclusive use of the entire second floor of the facility. Ceremonies are held in the sunken lounge, whose floor-to-cathedral ceiling window suspends you right over the canyon, or on the picturesque outdoor terrace below.

Nestled against a wooded hillside that's tamed only by the occasional box hedge, the terrace meets a free-form pond, ringed by seasonal flowers and natural rock formations. The pond gives way to a waterfall that flows out of sight into the canyon below. The canyon vista is your backdrop—a panorama that extends as far as the eye can see. After the ceremony, you and your photographer will be whisked away in a limo golf cart for some photos in front of the waterfall, while everyone else gets to know each other over cocktails and hors d'oeuvres. Take your time—your guests will be busy enjoying the splendor of the clubhouse.

The clubhouse lobby and adjacent Ballroom easily accommodate a large event, and they also work well for intimate gatherings. Cozy sitting areas in the lobby are flanked by double-sided fireplaces, and the sunken lounge demonstrates its versatility. Thanks to tinted glass, it stays cool even on the brightest day, making it a great spot not only for a small ceremony, but for dancing or showcasing the cake, too.

The Ballroom itself is a marvelously conceived space. One wall of floor-to-ceiling windows over-looks the 18th fairway and frames that gorgeous canyon view. Fireplaces blaze at both ends, and a skylight in the peaked ceiling adds more natural light. The warm feeling in the room is enhanced even further by abundant wood detailing and a plush, burgundy and brushed-gold carpet. Adjustable lighting allows you to control the mood, and with candles on the tables and fireplace mantels, romance will definitely be in the air.

Three other rooms are available for rehearsal dinners, showers or brunches. Like the rest of the facility, they benefit from the warmth of wood, natural light and terrific canyon views. In addition to a remarkably beautiful clubhouse and setting, Dove Canyon is very flexible: If none of their packages suits you, they'll customize one for you. As we said, this country club will exceed your expectations.

CEREMONY CAPACITY: Indoors, the Sunken Lounge holds up to 175 seated; outdoors the Terrace seats up to 250.

EVENT/RECEPTION: The Ballroom accommodates up to 280 seated or 500 standing guests.

MEETING CAPACITY: Meeting spaces seat 250.

FEES & DEPOSITS: A nonrefundable deposit, which is applied to your food & beverage total, is required to reserve your date. The amount of the deposit is equal to 25% of the estimated event total. Additional 25% deposits are due 6 months and 3 months prior to the event, and the remaining balance is due 7 days prior. There are no rental fees. Packages range $55–150/person. Tax and a 20% service charge are additional.

AVAILABILITY: Year-round. Weekdays, 6am–12:30am; weekends, 11am–4pm or 6pm–11pm. Clients can purchase additional time beyond the 5-hour block included in the packages.

SERVICES/AMENITIES:

Catering: in-house, no BYO
Kitchen Facilities: n/a
Tables & Chairs: provided
Linens, Silver, etc.: provided
Restrooms: wheelchair accessible
Dance Floor: provided
Bride's Dressing Area: yes
AV/Meeting Equipment: some provided

Parking: large lot, valet optional
Accommodations: no guest rooms
Outdoor Night Lighting: yes
Outdoor Cooking Facilities: BBQ
Cleanup: provided
View: fairways, lake, hills, fountain, waterfall
Other: wedding cake, grand piano

RESTRICTIONS:

Alcohol: in-house
Smoking: outdoors only
Music: amplified OK

Wheelchair Access: yes
Insurance: not required

Coyote Hills Golf Course

Golf Club

1440 East Bastanchury Road, Fullerton
888/327-1474
www.countryclubreceptions.com
privateevents@coyotehillsgc.com

● Rehearsal Dinners	● Corporate Events
● Ceremonies	● Meetings
● Wedding Receptions	● Film Shoots
● Private Parties	☐ Accommodations

Since opening its doors in 1996, Coyote Hills Golf Course has generated considerable public interest, and it's not just the links that have attracted a following: The versatile clubhouse and lovely setting have become popular for all types of events. While fundraisers, theme parties, anniversary celebrations and golf tournaments (naturally) are frequently hosted here, weddings are definitely a specialty.

A long walkway leads to their unique ceremony site, which is custom-built and quite breathtaking. Guests take their seats beneath a wisteria-draped wooden pergola that frames a two-tiered waterfall. It's here that the couple exchanges vows, surrounded by a landscape filled with flowers, trees and an abundance of greenery. This area also lends itself to intimate events and, of course, makes a gorgeous backdrop for photos.

Receptions are held on the upper level of the clubhouse in a pair of banquet rooms that can be used individually or combined, depending on the size of the celebration. The Vista Falls Room, tastefully designed with exquisitely styled Japanese lamps and a lofty ceiling paneled in polished maple, has an elegant simplicity. Plenty of floor-to-ceiling windows take advantage of the inspiring landscape spread out below: acres of green hummocks, footbridges, sand traps, and a gently flowing creek. The room also overlooks a lake and two waterfalls. One of them, the amazing two-tiered water cascade at the ceremony site, is especially captivating at night when illuminated. Four sets of double doors open out onto a long terrace that runs the length of the room. Here, you can sit and enjoy the sunshine or sweet evening air and listen to the music of the falls.

Another benefit of the Vista Falls Room is that the clubhouse bar, located next door in the facility's restaurant, may be available for your event. Airy and inviting, the restaurant is a big octagonal space accented with tropical plants that stand out against creamy walls. Sunlight pours in through an eight-sided skylight, and large picture windows offer a panoramic view of the fairways.

If you're planning a small meeting, reception or indoor ceremony, reserve the Vista Pointe Room, separated from the Vista Falls Room by a movable airwall. Laid out in an interesting octagonal shape like the restaurant, it shares the same patio as the Vista Falls Room as well as the view of the fairways and waterfalls through plenty of windows.

During our visit, we couldn't help but notice the serene, satisfied faces of the venue's patrons, inside the clubhouse or out on the links. Hold your event at Coyote Hills Golf Course and we bet you'll acquire that look of satisfaction, too.

CEREMONY CAPACITY: The outdoor ceremony site seats up to 300 and the Vista Pointe Room seats up to 150.

EVENT/RECEPTION CAPACITY: The Vista Falls and Vista Pointe Rooms combined hold 320 seated, 300 with a dance floor.

MEETING CAPACITY: The Vista Pointe Room holds 100 seated theater-style or 70 conference-style; the Vista Falls Room seats 220 theater-style or 120 conference-style. When combined, the two rooms accommodate 400 seated theatre-style or 200 conference-style.

FEES & DEPOSITS: A nonrefundable deposit, which is applied to your food & beverage total, is required to reserve your date. The amount of the deposit varies depending on how far in advance you book. Payment terms for the balance also vary, and may be arranged on an individual basis. Wedding packages start at $65/person. Tax, alcohol and service charge are additional. Food & beverage minimums may apply. Menus and packages can be customized to fit your needs and budget. Call for details.

AVAILABILITY: Special events and business functions, year-round, daily, 7am–1am.

SERVICES/AMENITIES:

Catering: in-house, or BYO
Kitchen Facilities: fully equipped
Tables & Chairs: provided
Linens, Silver, etc.: provided
Restrooms: wheelchair accessible
Dance Floor: provided
Bride's & Groom's Dressing Areas: yes
AV/Meeting Equipment: CBA, extra charge; WiFi included

Parking: large lot
Accommodations: no guest rooms
Outdoor Night Lighting: on Terrace
Outdoor Cooking Facilities: no
Cleanup: provided
View: waterfall, lake and golf course

RESTRICTIONS:

Alcohol: in-house, or corkage $20/bottle
Smoking: on Terrace only
Music: amplified OK indoors

Wheelchair Access: yes
Insurance: may be required
Other: no rice, confetti, glitter, or attached decorations

Muckenthaler Mansion

Historic Mansion

1201 West Malvern, Fullerton
714/447-9190, Colette's Events
www.colettesevents.com
info@colettesevents.com

● Rehearsal Dinners	● Corporate Events
● Ceremonies	● Meetings
● Wedding Receptions	● Film Shoots
● Private Parties	Accommodations

With its broad lawns and period architecture, Fullerton's Muckenthaler Mansion might be the backdrop for one of the fictitious revelries in an F. Scott Fitzgerald novel. On its gracious grounds a bride can easily imagine herself as the dreamy heroine from *The Great Gatsby* as she glides across the velvety green expanse atop a wooded knoll. The fantasy continues inside, where turn-of-the-century photos document life in a gentler era.

Built in 1924 as the dream home of Walter and Adella Muckenthaler, the stunning Italian Renaissance-style structure stands on nine landscaped acres overlooking a quiet residential neighborhood. In 1965, Adella and her son donated the estate to the City of Fullerton for use as a cultural center for touring art exhibits. Thus, whatever artwork is on display at the mansion contributes a unique aesthetic to special events.

Prior to tying the knot, the bride can prepare and unwind in a dressing room featuring its own private entrance and bathroom. Guests await the bride's entrance in the estate's rose garden, and they're sure to "ooh and aah" as she floats into view surrounded by a flurry of colorful blooms. She meets her husband-to-be by the gazebo set amidst a palm-fringed Italian garden.

After the ceremony, many couples serve cocktails inside the mansion, where almost every room is a gallery filled with art from around the globe. Of particular note is the octagonal solarium, warmed by light flowing in through expansive windows. Meanwhile, the wedding party poses in the mansion's foyer, where a wrought-iron spiral staircase imported from Italy makes a perfect photographic centerpiece.

The Muckenthaler has numerous enclaves for receptions. Al fresco options include: the Center Circle Courtyard, lit by necklaces of twinkling lights; the Adella and Northwest Lawns for larger parties; and the charming Palm Court for daytime events. In the evening you can fête your guests in a fancy tent, or let the starlit sky create the ambiance.

For indoor festivities guests enjoy mingling in the wooden-floored atrium with its ornate tiled fireplace. Dinner and dancing often unfold in the main gallery, where a baby grand piano is on hand for musical entertainment. When it's time to toss the bouquet the bride stands on the mansion's front porch and flings her flowers to the bridal hopefuls waiting below on the lawn.

In addition to its extraordinary setting, the two-story mansion offers exclusive catering and full bar services by *Colette's*. Known for fabulous cuisine, magnificent cakes and impeccable service, the Fullerton caterer offers complete dinner packages, customized international menus, and creative reception ideas for 20 to 1,000.

The Muckenthaler Mansion is one of North Orange County's most picturesque event venues, and a great place to "write" the first chapter of your new life together.

CEREMONY CAPACITY: The Italian Garden holds up to 240 seated guests and the Adella Lawn up to 400 seated. Other areas of the property can accommodate up to 600.

EVENT/RECEPTION CAPACITY: Indoor spaces hold up to 130 seated or 200 standing guests. Various outdoor areas hold up to 500 seated or 700 standing.

MEETING CAPACITY: Spaces accommodate 8–120 seated guests.

FEES & DEPOSITS: A $2,000 deposit is required to reserve your date. Half the remaining event total is due 6 months prior to the event, and the balance is due 1 month prior. A catering deposit is required at booking; call for details. Site rental fees for weddings and social events range $2,500–4,500 depending on the guest count and day of the event. Ceremony fees start at $950. Catering packages range $73–120/person. A wedding cake or fabulous dessert is included with all packages. Please call for details on options and pricing. Tax and service charge are additional.

Rental rates for smaller events are negotiable; please call for details. For business functions, the meeting room rental fee starts at $75/hour.

AVAILABILITY: Year-round, daily, 7am–10pm.

SERVICES/AMENITIES:

Catering: in-house, no BYO
Kitchen Facilities: n/a
Tables & Chairs: provided
Linens, Silver, etc.: provided
Restrooms: wheelchair accessible
Dance Floor: CBA
Bride's & Groom's Dressing Areas: yes
AV/Meeting Equipment: CBA, extra charge

Parking: large lot, valet optional
Accommodations: no guest rooms
Outdoor Night Lighting: provided
Outdoor Cooking Facilities: BBQ CBA
Cleanup: provided
View: garden, park, cityscape, landscaped grounds
Other: event coordination

RESTRICTIONS:

Alcohol: in-house
Smoking: outdoors only
Music: amplified OK

Wheelchair Access: yes
Insurance: not required
Other: no rice, confetti, or birdseed

Summit House

Restaurant

2000 East Bastanchury Road, Fullerton

714/671-3092

www.summithouseweddings.com
carmenkaiser@summithouse.com

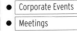

● Rehearsal Dinners	● Corporate Events
● Ceremonies	● Meetings
● Wedding Receptions	● Film Shoots
● Private Parties	Accommodations

Perched on one of the highest points in North Orange County and encircled by 12 acres of Fullerton's Vista Park, the Summit House is one of the most romantic wedding locations in Southern California. No matter where you stand on the grounds, a spectacular panorama inspires you: To the north loom the San Gabriel and San Bernardino mountains; to the east are the Santa Anas; to the south and west are the Laguna Hills and the sparkling Pacific. As night falls and the lights begin twinkling in the valley below, you can easily imagine yourself adrift on a sea of stars.

Equally inspiring is the Summit House Restaurant itself. Built in the tradition of an English country manor, its classic Old World architecture has the appearance and appeal of a much older, wiser structure. Lush sycamores shade the manicured lawns and rose gardens surrounding the building, and it all creates a beautiful setting for the ceremony.

The bride and her party can spend the day preparing in the Summit House's newly completed bridal suite. When she's ready, it's just a short stroll to the wedding gazebo, decorated according to her wishes. As she and her groom exchange vows, they can look out over all their guests seated in the open-air amphitheater carved into the hillside.

After the ceremony, guests may wander around the park or sip champagne on the outside patios before they slip into the Grand Summit Ballroom for the reception. With delicate cream-colored walls, coffered ceilings and pewter chandeliers, the spacious ballroom seats a crowd comfortably. Light flows in through enormous bay windows and oversized French doors, and let's not forget the panoramic view! If your guest list requires more room, a movable wall rolls aside, giving you access to the equally attractive Queen's Room and adjoining patio.

To ensure that your big day is glitch-free, the Summit House provides both a catering and a ceremony coordinator. And what amazing food and service! No wonder this facility has such a great reputation. Truth is, the Summit House will go the whole nine yards to accommodate your wildest wish, whether you want to arrive in a roaring cavalcade of Harleys, as one couple did, or simply leave the old-fashioned way in a horse and buggy. And included in every wedding package is an invitation for the newlyweds to return on their first anniversary to celebrate the special occasion all over again and relive their magical memories, compliments of the Summit House.

CEREMONY CAPACITY: The Gazebo Amphitheater in Vista Park holds up to 250 seated or 500 standing guests.

EVENT/RECEPTION & MEETING CAPACITY: The Grand Summit Ballroom holds 250 seated, 300 with the patio, and 300 standing guests.

FEES & DEPOSITS: A deposit is required when you book the facility. 50% of the balance is due 30 days prior to the event, and a guest count guarantee and final balance are due 10 days prior; incidental fees are payable the day of the event. Luncheons run $30–48/person and dinners $32–50/person. Several wedding packages are available in addition to the above menu prices. Bar charges, bottled wine, tax and a 20% service charge are extra. For ceremonies, there is an $875 fee that includes a ceremony coordinator and upgraded chair rentals, as well as a $750 park rental fee.

AVAILABILITY: Year-round, daily, 11am–midnight.

SERVICES/AMENITIES:

Catering: in-house, no BYO
Kitchen Facilities: n/a
Tables & Chairs: provided
Linens, Silver, etc.: provided
Restrooms: wheelchair accessible
Dance Floor: provided
Bride's Dressing Area: yes
AV/Meeting Equipment: podium with microphone

Parking: large lot, complimentary evening valet
Accommodations: no guest rooms
Outdoor Night Lighting: yes
Outdoor Cooking Facilities: no
Cleanup: provided
View: surrounding valleys; San Gabriel, Santa Ana and San Bernardino Mountains
Other: event coordination

RESTRICTIONS:

Alcohol: in-house, or WC corkage $20/bottle
Smoking: outside only
Music: amplified OK indoors with volume limits

Wheelchair Access: yes
Insurance: not required
Other: no birdseed, rice or confetti; open flames restricted

Want to find more venues and services? Check out our informative website, www.HereComesTheGuide.com.

341

Hyatt Regency Huntington Beach
Resort and Spa

21500 Pacific Coast Highway, Huntington Beach

714/845-4652

www.hyattregencyhuntingtonbeach.com
nancy.monte-frye@hyatt.com

Waterfront Hotel

- Rehearsal Dinners
- Ceremonies
- Wedding Receptions
- Private Parties
- Corporate Events
- Meetings
- Film Shoots
- Accommodations

Romance abounds at the Hyatt Regency Huntington Beach Resort & Spa, where your choice of gorgeous venues ranges from perfectly manicured lawns to ballrooms with stunning coastal views. And, whether you envision a simple gathering or an elaborate formal affair, your wedding at this oceanview resort will be treated as a one-of-a-kind event.

Celebrations unfold with grace and elegance in the sumptuously appointed Conference Center, where the dramatic King Triton Fountain and porte-cochère greet guests upon arrival. The Grand Conference Lobby, with its cathedral-high ceiling and second-story balcony surround, has a sweeping inner courtyard feel. Festivities can easily begin here, or guests can proceed to any one of the property's numerous ballrooms, courtyards, and terraces. The Lighthouse Courtyard is particularly enchanting for your outdoor ceremony or event. It's a wide lawn, surrounded by stately palms, that leads from the shimmering Mermaid Fountain to the resort's fabulous white Lighthouse Tower and Bridge. The ocean view is spectacular and uninterrupted here, but that's no surprise—this is a world full of unparalleled Pacific vistas.

Coast and sea also captivate from the striking Huntington Ballroom Foyer and Terrace—a delightful spot for cocktails and hors d'oeuvres, where delicate ocean breezes and the sound of the surf drift in through the open archways. A sculpted balustrade and handsome wrought-iron sconces give it a romantically Mediterranean feel. Also opening onto the terrace is the Grand Ballroom, which accommodates up to 2,000 and has its own Grand Foyer. Both ballrooms feature beautiful design elements that reflect the resort's breezy Andalusian style, like regal columns, soaring ceilings crossed with artfully carved and scrolled beams, seashell-shaped sconces, and hand-blown glass chandeliers. The effect is an ambiance that's majestic, yet intimate, whether the rooms are divided into smaller sections or used in their splendid entirety. The Mariner's Ballroom downstairs shares the same subtle allure. Whether partitioned by gauzy draperies or open to seat 600, it feels very private, comfortable and secluded.

The Hyatt Regency Huntington Beach Resort and Spa is a venue where you can entertain on an opulent scale and still feel totally at home…it's a setting that's both luxurious and relaxed. You may get lost just exploring the grounds, checking out the ballrooms, courtyards, and galleries, but you probably won't want to leave. Fortunately you won't have to. The resort has 517 spacious guest rooms, 57 plush suites, a 20,000-square-foot spa, shops, a multitude of services, and an experienced and attentive staff. All you and your guests have to do is settle in, celebrate, unwind, and stay for as long as you like.

CEREMONY, EVENT/RECEPTION & MEETING CAPACITY: The site holds 2,000 seated or standing guests indoors, and 400 seated or standing outdoors.

FEES & DEPOSITS: 25% of the total estimated event cost is required at the time of booking, an additional 50% is due 3 months prior to the event, and the balance is due 10 days prior. Rental fees start at $500 and vary depending on the guest count, season, time and day of the event and the space reserved. Wedding packages start at $97/person for luncheon and $136/person for dinner. Tax and a 24% service charge are additional.

AVAILABILITY: Year-round, daily.

SERVICES/AMENITIES:

Catering: in-house or BYO
Kitchen Facilities: n/a
Tables & Chairs: provided
Linens, Silver, etc.: provided
Restrooms: wheelchair accessible
Dance Floor: portable provided
Bride's Dressing Area: yes
AV/Meeting Equipment: some provided

Parking: valet required
Accommodations: 517 guest rooms
Outdoor Night Lighting: yes
Outdoor Cooking Facilities: no
Cleanup: provided
View: fountain, garden, courtyard, landscaped grounds, coastline, ocean/bay
Other: spa services, event coordination

RESTRICTIONS:

Alcohol: in-house
Smoking: not allowed
Music: amplified OK with restrictions

Wheelchair Access: yes
Insurance: required for vendors

Meadowlark Golf Club

Golf Club

16782 Graham Street, Huntington Beach

714/794-6788

www.meadowlarkgc.com
kblackford@arcisgolf.com

● Rehearsal Dinners	● Corporate Events
● Ceremonies	● Meetings
● Wedding Receptions	Film Shoots
● Private Parties	Accommodations

With its graceful architecture, colorful landscaping and attentive staff, Meadowlark feels more like a country club than a golf facility. Perhaps that's why this place is so successful at being both a golfer's haven and a lovely venue for special events.

After you walk through the beautiful double doors of this two-story, Spanish-style clubhouse, ascend the sweeping staircase to the second floor where all special events and business functions are held. The spacious foyer at the top of the stairs is an ideal place for guests to drop off gifts, sign the guest book and mingle before entering the Terrace Ballroom for the reception. This 3,000-square-foot room can be decorated to your specifications, and features a striking beamed ceiling with frosted glass-and-metal fixtures, as well as floor-to-ceiling windows that let in plenty of natural light and views of the lush greens below.

Four sets of double glass doors provide the ballroom with even more natural light, while framing golf course and mountain vistas. They also allow access to the Terrace Patio and a wide wraparound balcony that not only extend the ballroom's space, but are perfect for an outdoor ceremony. Outfitted with a bridal arch, white runner and white padded folding chairs, this is a charming spot for exchanging vows. (An alternative and larger area for tying the knot is on the 2nd green, tucked away from golf play and notable for its water feature and luxuriant greenery.)

The versatile Terrace Patio is wonderful for serving cocktails, too. When it's set up with tables and white market umbrellas, you and your guests can sip drinks and feel the breeze blowing off the nearby ocean. As evening falls, you're also likely to enjoy a classic California sunset, whether you're seated outside on the Terrace or in the ballroom.

Photo options include the park-like setting of one of the golf course greens, or the curving, grand staircase in the clubhouse lobby. It makes an elegant backdrop, especially when decorated with flowers, tulle, twinkle lights and/or greenery.

As pleasing as its event spaces are, what really distinguishes Meadowlark is the service. They offer affordable, inclusive packages that provide just about everything you need—even your wedding cake! Their catering professionals will take care of you from the beginning of the planning process to the last minute of your event. For the stressed-out bride, the accommodating team at Meadowlark is just what the doctor ordered. Thank-you letters are filled with comments like "You made it so personal … You gave me a sense of comfort and confidence … You really did take care of me!"

Once you've received the royal treatment at Meadowlark, you'll want to come back again for future events—and maybe even for a round of golf!

CEREMONY CAPACITY: The Terrace Patio holds up to 100 seated guests, the 2nd Green holds 200 seated.

EVENT/RECEPTION CAPACITY: The Terrace Ballroom holds up to 240 seated; with the patio, an additional 60 seated guests.

MEETING CAPACITY: The Terrace Ballroom can accommodate up to 300 guests seated theater-style, or 225 seated banquet-style, or 150–175 seated conference-style in a U-shaped setup.

FEES & DEPOSITS: A nonrefundable deposit, which is applied to your food & beverage total, is required to reserve your date. The amount of the deposit is equal to 25% of the estimated event total. 50% is due 6 months prior to the event date, and 100% of the final estimated balance is due 5 days prior. Wedding packages range $65–200/person depending on the package or menu selected. Packages include hors d'oeuvres, champagne and cider toast, a 2-course meal or buffet, wedding cake and other services. Alcohol, tax and a 20% service charge are extra. Meadowlark can customize any menu; call for specific à la carte pricing. The wedding ceremony site fee is $1,000 for the Terrace Patio and $2,000 for the 2nd Green. This fee includes a white aisle runner, white padded folding chairs, a white or rustic arch, bridal changing room, scheduled rehearsal, 1 golf cart (for photographer, bride & groom), and an infused water station.

For corporate, golf or other special events, please call the catering office for pricing.

AVAILABILITY: Year-round, daily, 6am–midnight. For wedding receptions, Saturdays 11am–4pm or 6pm–11pm; a 1-hour ceremony is in addition to the 5-hour block.

SERVICES/AMENITIES:

Catering: in-house
Kitchen Facilities: n/a
Tables & Chairs: provided
Linens, Silver, etc.: provided
Restrooms: wheelchair accessible
Dance Floor: provided
Bride's Dressing Area: yes
AV/Meeting Equipment: podium with microphone, screen, VCR, TV, DVD player

Parking: large lot
Accommodations: no guestrooms
Outdoor Night Lighting: CBA
Outdoor Cooking Facilities: BBQ CBA
Cleanup: provided
View: golf fairways, landscaped grounds
Other: event coordination, piano

RESTRICTIONS:

Alcohol: in-house
Smoking: outside only
Music: amplified OK indoors, OK outdoors for ceremony only

Wheelchair Access: yes
Insurance: not required
Other: no birdseed, rice, confetti or glitter; no open flames

Red Horse Barn
At Huntington Central Park

18381 Goldenwest Street, Huntington Beach
714/887-4990
www.theredhorsebarn.com
redhorsebarn@hcpec.com

Equestrian Ranch & Event Location

- Rehearsal Dinners
- Ceremonies
- Wedding Receptions
- Private Parties

- Corporate Events
- Meetings
- Film Shoots
- Accommodations

You don't need to be more comfortable in boots than high heels to fall head-over-heels for this very special wedding and event venue. Situated on a gentle rise at the Huntington Central Park Equestrian Center (HCPEC), The Red Horse Barn has a graceful, storybook charm that's as right for a rustic farmhouse gathering as it is for a chic Derby Day.

With its sense of seclusion and unhurried vibe, this site is definitely a breath of fresh air. The property's white paddock fences, expansive terrace, broad lawns, and meticulous landscaping lend an immediate air of sophistication to the scene. The showcase-quality, ultra-elegant 10-horse stable—complete with handsome thoroughbreds—celebrates the high-end equestrian lifestyle. It's perfect for all kinds of functions, from fancy fundraisers to company shindigs, but naturally our top choice for this location is weddings.

Bride and groom will both be well cared for here. The groom's getaway can also be used for meetings, wedding showers and private parties. It features a tastefully appointed great room and bath with polished wood floors, beamed ceilings, fireplace seating, and attractive wood, suede and natural hemp furnishings. The spacious bride's suite has the same flexibility and appealing mix of restful areas and comfortable, yet stylish, design. It strikes a somewhat more feminine note with lovely cream-colored accents and a full modern kitchen with granite countertops and a long breakfast bar. Both also have exactly the kind of porches you'd wish for: sweet, shady places just right for guests to sit back and relax with a tumbler of ice-cold lemonade or a glass of bourbon and branch.

For the wedding ceremony, we suggest tying the knot under the garden- and fountain-framed gazebo, though the back lawn is another inviting option. The capacious gazebo terrace is ideal for games, activities, and cocktail receptions, too, not to mention dining and dancing under the sun or stars. Add your own fanciful touches to customize this artfully arranged blank canvas. We like the idea of rustic décor and accessories here, but The Red Horse Barn's bright breezy spirit can easily accommodate any vision, be it vintage or glam.

Horse fanciers will also be happy knowing that the HCPEC's 25 acres are home to nearly 400 horses, numerous stables, and miles of public trails. Photo ops abound in various scenic natural environments, as well as at the picturesque but more formal event complex. Equine aficionado or not, you couldn't find a more vibrant setting, The Pacific with its myriad coastal delights is just two miles away, but you won't miss it in this pleasing equestrian enclave. We think The Red Horse Barn might just be the best-kept secret in Huntington Beach.

CEREMONY, EVENT/RECEPTION & MEETING CAPACITY: The site accommodates 20 seated or standing guests indoors and 250 seated or standing outdoors.

FEES & DEPOSITS: A $1,600 deposit is required to reserve your date, and the balance is due 60 days prior to the event. The rental fee ranges $1,900–6,000 depending on your guest count and the season.

AVAILABILITY: Year-round, daily, anytime. Call for details.

SERVICES/AMENITIES:

Catering: BYO
Kitchen Facilities: limited
Tables & Chairs: through caterer or BYO
Linens, Silver, etc.: through caterer or BYO
Restrooms: wheelchair accessible
Dance Floor: CBA
Bride's Dressing Area: yes
AV/Meeting Equipment: BYO

Parking: garage or lot nearby
Accommodations: no guest rooms
Outdoor Night Lighting: CBA
Outdoor Cooking Facilities: BBQ CBA
Cleanup: caterer or renter
View: landscaped grounds, horse barn, equestrian center
Other: photography opportunities with horses

RESTRICTIONS:

Alcohol: select from preferred list
Smoking: designated areas only
Music: amplified OK outdoors

Wheelchair Access: yes
Insurance: required for vendors
Other: no birdseed, rice, confetti or bubbles

SeaCliff Country Club

6501 Palm Avenue, Huntington Beach

888/998-9709

www.countryclubreceptions.com
www.seacliffcc.net
directorofevents@seacliffcc.net
eventdirector@seacliffcc.net

Country Club

- Rehearsal Dinners
- Ceremonies
- Wedding Receptions
- Private Parties
- Corporate Events
- Meetings
- Film Shoots
- Accommodations

Driving along Palm Avenue, just north of Pacific Coast Highway in one of Southern California's most beloved beach towns, you have a feeling you're headed for someplace special as you make your way past majestic palms, towering like giant sentries all along the wide, landscaped boulevard. Turning into SeaCliff Country Club, your hunch proves right as you come face to face with the sleek, horizontal lines of a Frank Lloyd Wright structure flanked by emerald fairways and exuding a quiet, contemporary allure.

Situated less than a mile from the shore, dependably sun-kissed and cooled by ocean breezes, this sophisticated site is the only private club available for nonmember events in Huntington Beach.

Valets will greet your guests as they arrive in SeaCliff's gracious circular driveway. Leading into the club, a sea of colorful foliage and a stream spilling over stones in a rock garden set a serene tone. Beyond an airy lobby with a soaring ceiling, the Pacific Room has a chic supper club feel with a warm mocha and burgundy color scheme, contemporary upholstered and leather furnishings, a granite-topped bar and an ebony grand piano. Offering panoramic views of the club's lake and 18-hole golf course, this is a stylish area for pre- and post-ceremony mingling. While guests await your arrival, you and your attendants will have full use of a bride's room, where you can simultaneously primp and calm jittery nerves with cheese, crackers and a bit of bubbly.

The Oval Terrace overlooking the lake and fairways provides a stunning backdrop for your outdoor ceremony—and for snapping photos afterwards. You'll walk down a petal-strewn aisle stretching 75 feet to an ivory Grecian arch, pillared colonnade, or Cinderella archway adorned with flowers, where you'll exchange vows.

The Club's two reception spaces offer very different atmospheres. If your guest list is long or you prefer a formal ballroom ambiance, the SeaCliff Room is large enough to accommodate a dance floor and DJ. Smaller gatherings are held in the Pacific Room, with clubby lounge areas and a more intimate space for dancing. No matter which one you choose, you can enhance any of four turnkey reception packages with full room draping, chandeliers, or a chocolate fondue station with your choice of dippers.

Complementing the attractions of this upscale venue are those that surround it in mellow Surf City USA. After your festivities wind down, you'll have miles of uninterrupted beach to stroll along, a historic pier to explore and a colorful oceanfront boardwalk to visit.

CEREMONY CAPACITY: The Oval Terrace accommodates up to 250 seated guests. Indoors, banquet rooms hold up to 250 seated.

EVENT/RECEPTION & MEETING CAPACITY: Indoors, the SeaCliff Room holds up to 250 seated or 300 standing guests and the Pacific room holds up to 150 seated or 200 standing; outdoors, the Oval Terrace holds up to 250 seated or 300 standing.

FEES & DEPOSITS: A nonrefundable deposit, which is applied to your food & beverage total, is required to reserve your date. The amount of the deposit varies depending on how far in advance you book. Payment terms for the balance also vary, and may be arranged on an individual basis. Reception packages start at $50/person. Tax, alcohol and service charge are additional. Food & beverage minimums may apply. Menus and packages can be customized to fit your needs and budget. Call for details.

AVAILABILITY: Year-round. 6-hour blocks for ceremonies and receptions. 5-hour blocks for receptions only, with the option to purchase overtime until midnight.

SERVICES/AMENITIES:

Catering: in-house, or BYO with restrictions
Kitchen Facilities: n/a
Tables & Chairs: provided
Linens, Silver, etc.: provided
Restrooms: wheelchair accessible
Dance Floor: provided
Bride's Dressing Area: yes
AV/Meeting Equipment: CBA, extra charge
Other: event coordination, grand piano, WiFi, fire pits, lounge furniture

Parking: valet required for groups of 60 or more
Accommodations: no guest rooms
Outdoor Night Lighting: access only
Outdoor Cooking Facilities: BBQ CBA
Cleanup: provided
View: landscaped grounds, trees, hills, lake/water feature

RESTRICTIONS:

Alcohol: in-house
Smoking: outside only
Music: amplified OK with restrictions

Wheelchair Access: yes
Insurance: not required

This is important! Tell locations you're reading HERE COMES THE GUIDE and ask if our information is still current.

349

Shorebreak Hotel

Waterfront Hotel

500 Pacific Coast Highway, Huntington Beach
714/965-4412
www.shorebreakhotel.com/huntington-beach-wedding-venues
nicole.mehlhaff@shorebreakhotel.com

- Rehearsal Dinners
- Ceremonies
- Wedding Receptions
- Private Parties
- Corporate Events
- Meetings
- Film Shoots
- Accommodations

If you're looking for the coolest setting for a California coastal wedding in Orange County, you have to check out this uber-awesome venue in the heart of Surf City USA. It delivers amazing oceanside views with an energetic Huntington Beach downtown surround and 8,000 square feet of terrific indoor/outdoor event space.

Very likely you and your guests will be carried away instantly by the décor—super, beach-themed touches like the vibrant murals (one is actually an enormous quilt made of wetsuits), the surfboard-style sculptural elements, and the iconic images of local beach culture by photographer Aaron Chang. The architectural elements will impress everyone, too: The high ceilings, clean lines and large windows are an airy salute to the breezy Southern California lifestyle. But what's most appealing here is the prospect of hosting an event—be it social or corporate—that's free-spirited, easy-going, and sophisticated at the same time.

The 3,000-square-foot Epic Ballroom (divisible into thirds), its adjoining Foyer, and the adjacent Deck are all truly epic. Polished and beautifully conceived with every imaginable feature, these spaces are also FUN. Creative forces creep into every tiny detail from the lovely sand, sea and sun-inspired colors to the subtle "footprint" textural effects in the walls and the sustainable landscaping in the outdoor function areas. For smaller groups or for breakout sessions, the Peak Room and Terrace offer still more upscale, yet comfortable, opportunities for "peak" entertaining.

Zimzala, the hotel's popular restaurant, is great for intimate parties. Outfitted in brilliant marine-blues and sparkly copper tones, it's sleek, yet laid back, with an adjoining terrace that can add another 660 square feet of outdoor space. The kitchen serves up a host of sophisticated beach-inspired hors d'oeuvres, handcrafted cocktails, and traditional favorites with a contemporary spin, like their grilled sirloin burgers with Gruyère cheese, caramelized onions and Parmesan-garlic fries or the pan-seared organic Irish salmon with tarragon-scented pearl couscous.

Of course, in addition to the hotel's experience-enhancing design, the best part of staging an event in a Kimpton hotel like the Shorebreak is the personalized service from the warm, welcoming staff and all of the on-site amenities. And don't forget there are 157 rooms and 39 suites here for anyone who wants to extend their stay. Our guess is that your guests won't want to leave, and why should they? With the comforting sound of waves within earshot and the enticements of Main Street, Huntington Beach at their feet, this is the ultimate destination for anyone wanting to celebrate or play in true Southern California style. Take a hint prompted by the hotel's surf lingo lexicon or "riptionary": Whether you want to hang loose or amp up, this place is the fall line. It's totally alchemy hour.

CEREMONY CAPACITY: The facility holds 150 seated guests, indoors or outdoors.

EVENT/RECEPTION & MEETING CAPACITY: The hotel can accommodate 150 seated or 250 standing indoors and 100 seated or 150 standing outdoors.

FEES & DEPOSITS: A nonrefundable, nontransferable 25% of the estimated event total is required to reserve your date. Additional nonrefundable, nontransferable deposits are required at 60, 90 and 120 days prior to your date, with the estimated balance due 14 days prior. The ceremony fee is $1,000, and a wedding coordinator is required for all on-site ceremonies. All-inclusive packages are available. The food & beverage minimum ranges $2,000–12,000. A taxable service charge and sales tax are additional. Fees for business programs vary based on overnight accommodations, services and menus selected.

AVAILABILITY: Year-round, daily. Business functions: 8am–5pm or 6pm–11pm.

SERVICES/AMENITIES:

Catering: in-house
Kitchen Facilities: n/a
Tables & Chairs: provided
Linens, Silver, etc.: provided
Restrooms: wheelchair accessible
Dance Floor: portable provided
Bride's Dressing Area: yes
AV/Meeting Equipment: provided, extra charge

Parking: valet and self in garage, extra charge
Accommodations: 157 guest rooms
Outdoor Night Lighting: provided, extra charge
Outdoor Cooking Facilities: none
Cleanup: provided
View: cityscape, garden patio, ocean
Other: event coordination

RESTRICTIONS:

Alcohol: in-house
Smoking: not allowed
Music: amplified OK indoors with restrictions

Wheelchair Access: yes
Insurance: liability required

The Waterfront Beach Resort
A Hilton Hotel

21100 Pacific Coast Highway, Huntington Beach
714/845-8420, 714/845-8455 Catering
www.waterfrontresort.com
atthebeach@waterfrontresort.com

Waterfront Hotel

- Rehearsal Dinners
- Ceremonies
- Wedding Receptions
- Private Parties
- Corporate Events
- Meetings
- Film Shoots
- Accommodations

Overlooking an eight-and-a-half-mile stretch of white sand, this Mediterranean-style resort is a knockout addition to beachfront properties. The hotel's lobby is the epitome of casual seaside luxury: Elegant marble floors and graceful curved staircases coexist quite comfortably with the tropical presence of cascading rock waterfalls, palm trees and lush foliage.

You can exchange vows poolside under the blue sky, in an oceanview ballroom, or on an intimate outdoor terrace. Following a ceremony in any of these settings, guests may enjoy cocktails and hors d'oeuvres in the spacious foyer of the Waterfront Grand Ballroom while the bridal party poses for pictures around the hotel or on the beach. The Grand Ballroom—the largest event space at the resort—is notable not only for its size, but also for its eye-catching features: a 14-foot ceiling richly trimmed with golden crown molding and six glowing chandeliers that provide romantic mood lighting.

Another reception option is the Pacific Ballroom and adjoining Terrace, located on the hotel's upper level. The Terrace is ideal for pre-reception cocktails: Here, guests mingle amidst refreshing sea breezes, accompanied by the sound of the rolling surf and a view that extends beyond the resort's pool and beautifully landscaped grounds to the vast ocean. Inside the ballroom, floor-to-ceiling windows take in that fabulous view, and contemporary oil paintings in gilded frames depict coastal life at its best. A 14-foot-tall alcove with arched windows on all three sides makes a dramatic backdrop for the wedding cake.

A smaller ballroom, the Tides, treats you to an ocean vista through windows framed by cascading bougainvillea. A multi-function credenza adds a lovely touch at the entrance, while an abstract marble sculpture on one wall captures the image of rolling waves. The far end of the ballroom, with its two walls of windows affording expansive views, is the perfect area for the dance floor. The Tides also boasts a glass-enclosed interior space, the Coral Room. Accessed through French doors, it's a delightful spot for the wedding cake, bar or buffet—and it comes with its own full view of the Pacific Ocean.

The Waterfront Beach Resort is a Four Diamond facility offering an abundance of services and amenities: 290 guest rooms, each with a private oceanview balcony; a swimming pool and fitness center on site; beach activities galore; and a reservable fire pit. With all these inducements, it's easy to understand why guests coming to the resort for an event are enticed to stay on for a mini-vacation.

CEREMONY CAPACITY: Outdoors, the Veranda seats up to 200; the Pool Deck up to 225, and the Pacific Terrace up to 100. Indoors, the Pacific Room seats 200, the Tides Ballroom 150, and the Grand Ballroom up to 400.

EVENT/RECEPTION CAPACITY: The Pacific Room holds 180–200 seated, the Tides Ballroom 150 seated, the West Coast 70 seated, and the Grand Ballroom 400 seated.

MEETING CAPACITY: Several spaces are available for 12–450 seated guests.

FEES & DEPOSITS: For weddings, 30% of the estimated event total is required as a nonrefundable deposit to reserve your date. Luncheons start at $60/person, dinners at $80/person. Cakes and/ or cake-cutting costs run $7/person. The estimated event balance, along with a guaranteed guest count, is due 10 days prior to the function. Beverages, tax and a 23% service charge are additional. Group rates for overnight wedding guests can be arranged.

For business functions, room rental fees vary depending on the season, room(s) selected and services required; call for more specific information.

AVAILABILITY: Year-round, daily. Weddings take place 11am–4pm or 6pm–midnight. Business functions and special events, 8am–midnight.

SERVICES/AMENITIES:

Catering: in-house, or BYO with approval
Kitchen Facilities: moderate
Tables & Chairs: provided
Linens, Silver, etc.: provided
Restrooms: wheelchair accessible
Dance Floor: provided
Bride's Dressing Area: provided with ceremony package
AV/Meeting Equipment: full range

Parking: valet parking $15–32/car
Accommodations: 290 guest rooms
Outdoor Night Lighting: yes
Outdoor Cooking Facilities: no
Cleanup: provided
View: ocean and hotel's pool area

RESTRICTIONS:

Alcohol: in-house
Smoking: outside only, designated areas
Music: amplified OK

Wheelchair Access: yes
Insurance: not required
Other: no rice, birdseed or confetti

La Mirada Golf Course

Golf Club

15501 Alicante Road, La Mirada
888/998-7024
www.countryclubreceptions.com
privateeventdirector@lamiradagc.com

● Rehearsal Dinners	● Corporate Events
● Ceremonies	● Meetings
● Wedding Receptions	● Film Shoots
● Private Parties	Accommodations

Tucked away in a quiet neighborhood, this golf course is one of the most popular in Southern California. It may also be one of the Southland's most wedding-friendly venues. What's the attraction? Affordable prices, no need to be a member (it's a public course), the biggest dance floor in town, and an accommodating staff that knows how to soothe anxieties and keep things flowing smoothly. And even though this is a very popular course, the banquet facility is completely private: Brides never have to worry about curious golfers wandering through their celebration.

Every wedding here is individualized. The bride meets with the private event staff for a food tasting well before the wedding day. Because the city of La Mirada is an ethnic crossroads, the facility has extensive experience dealing with different religious and cultural needs. They're also very flexible about time, and late evening celebrations aren't a problem—they're relatively far from the nearest neighboring houses, meaning no worries about disturbing anyone.

Many couples start with an outdoor ceremony at the beautiful gazebo overlooking the golf course's signature lake. Afterwards, festivities move to the clubhouse's banquet room, terrace, bar and front patio. A white ceiling and windows on three sides keep the room bright, and it boasts an impressively large dance floor. The spacious terrace offers a perfect view of the golf course, a deep-green panorama of grassy slopes. The fairways seem to go on for miles, and are edged with sycamores, beautiful shagbark eucalyptus and pines.

The patio, a small space near the front of the clubhouse, is a quiet spot where people can take a break from the party. The bar, directly accessible from the banquet room, has a charming Tuscan feel with comfortable booths and an upholstered bar. This unique setup makes for a wonderful flow—just the thing to keep guests happily moving and mingling.

Maybe the best way to think of La Mirada is to remember what was going through Goldilocks' mind when she was testing porridge at the Bear residence. Goldie wasn't looking for too big or too cool; she was looking for Just Right. This place has so many "just right" things going for it that it may just be right for you.

CEREMONY CAPACITY: The site seats up to 350 guests outdoors and 200 indoors.

EVENT/RECEPTION & MEETING CAPACITY: The banquet room accommodates up to 400 seated or 575 standing guests; outdoor areas up to 500 seated or 775 standing.

FEES & DEPOSITS: A nonrefundable deposit, which is applied to your food & beverage total, is required to reserve your date. The amount of the deposit varies depending on how far in advance you book. Payment terms for the balance also vary, and may be arranged on an individual basis. Meals start at $25/person. Tax, alcohol service charge are additional. Food & beverage minimums may apply. Menus and packages can be customized to fit your needs and budget. Call for details.

AVAILABILITY: Year-round, daily.

SERVICES/AMENITIES:

Catering: in-house
Kitchen Facilities: n/a
Tables & Chairs: provided
Linens, Silver, etc.: provided
Restrooms: wheelchair accessible
Dance Floor: provided
Bride's Dressing Area: provided
AV/Meeting Equipment: CBA

Parking: large lot and on street
Accommodations: no guest rooms
Outdoor Night Lighting: yes
Outdoor Cooking Facilities: BBQ
Cleanup: provided
View: fairways, lake, garden, landscaped grounds
Other: event coordination, wedding cake, florals, chair covers, clergy referrals available

RESTRICTIONS:

Alcohol: in-house
Smoking: outside only
Music: amplified OK indoors

Wheelchair Access: yes
Insurance: not required

Cliffs at Laguna Village

Waterfront Special Event Facility

577 South Coast Highway, Laguna Beach
866/321-9876, 949/939-7979 Occasions at Laguna Village
www.occasionsatlagunavillage.com
lagunaoccasions@aol.com

- Rehearsal Dinners
- Ceremonies
- Wedding Receptions
- Private Parties
- Corporate Events
- Meetings
- Film Shoots
- Accommodations

Refreshing breezes, a white sand beach, crashing waves and a beautiful sunset accompany your ceremony... you and your guests dine and dance beneath the stars.... It all sounds pretty fabulous, doesn't it! Well, if you've always wanted a seaside celebration but have been daunted by all the effort involved, why not have your event at the Cliffs at Laguna Village? At this unique facility you can enjoy all the things you love about being near the ocean without having to lift a finger!

Of course, the Cliffs' main attraction is its location: set on a bluff with a 180-degree view of Laguna Beach, the adjacent coastline and the Pacific. A staircase leads from the street-level parking lot down to the venue, a spacious outdoor area with a built-in checkerboard dance floor bordered by a well-tended lawn. Though the site is not actually on the beach, if it were any closer, you might consider wearing a bathing suit!

The most popular ceremony spot is a circular platform near the cliff's edge at one end of the lawn. Although the setting doesn't require it, you can put up a wedding arch or a set of faux Roman columns here if you like. Since this site faces due west, your guests can watch the sun sink behind the two of you while you say your vows. Another option is getting married at the other end of the lawn in an airy white gazebo.

Guests are seated on the dance floor during the ceremony; afterwards they stroll over to the lawn to enjoy cocktails and hors d'oeuvres, while tables are set up around the dance floor for the reception. In the evening, street lamps and twinkle lights augment the glow of candlelit tables, as the waves below murmur a soothing accompaniment.

Aside from its stellar location, the thing that makes the Cliffs at Laguna Village so special is the outstanding service you'll get from *Occasions at Laguna Village*, the on-site coordinator. If you're a fan of "one-stop shopping," this is the place for you. Occasions can provide anything and everything else you might desire, including catering, linens, flowers, entertainment, lighting, market umbrellas and potted palms. So if you think that the words "effortless" and "seaside celebration" can't possibly appear in the same sentence, look into the Cliffs at Laguna Village. Here, you'll be able to have the oceanfront party of your dreams without getting sand in your shoes.

CEREMONY CAPACITY: The Cliffs holds up to 175 seated guests outdoors.

EVENT/RECEPTION & MEETING CAPACITY: The venue seats up to 175 guests.

FEES & DEPOSITS: A nonrefundable $2,000 deposit plus the full site fee are required, which covers a percentage of the anticipated food & beverage total and rental fee. 50% of the estimated event total is due 3 months prior to the event, and the balance is due 60 days prior. The site fee ranges $1,500–4,800. Meals start at $50/person. Packages include tax and staffing charges; alcohol is additional.

AVAILABILITY: Year-round, daily, 9am–10pm in 4-hour time blocks; overtime can be arranged at an additional cost.

SERVICES/AMENITIES:

Catering: in-house, no BYO

Kitchen Facilities: n/a

Tables & Chairs: provided

Linens, Silver, etc.: provided

Restrooms: wheelchair accessible

Dance Floor: provided

Bride's Dressing Area: no

AV/Meeting Equipment: CBA, extra charge

Parking: valet and shuttle required

Accommodations: no guest rooms

Outdoor Night Lighting: yes

Outdoor Cooking Facilities: CBA

Cleanup: provided

View: panorama of ocean and cityscape

Other: event coordination

RESTRICTIONS:

Alcohol: in-house, no BYO

Smoking: outside only

Music: amplified OK with volume limits, 10pm music curfew

Wheelchair Access: yes

Insurance: required for vendors only

Other: no rice, confetti or birdseed

Overwhelmed? Use the search criteria on www.HereComesTheGuide.com to narrow down your choices.

Hotel Laguna

Waterfront Hotel

425 South Coast Highway, Laguna Beach
949/494-1151
www.hotellaguna.com
facebook.com/hotellaguna, Twitter: @Hotel_Laguna
info@hotellaguna.com

- Rehearsal Dinners
- Ceremonies
- Wedding Receptions
- Private Parties
- Corporate Events
- Meetings
- Film Shoots
- Accommodations

The first grand hotel to grace Laguna Beach and the getaway of choice for Golden Age of Hollywood movie stars like Errol Flynn, John Barrymore, Humphrey Bogart and Lauren Bacall, iconic Hotel Laguna is viewed with equal reverence by locals and visitors. Situated in the heart of Downtown Laguna Beach, this landmark building's delightful blend of Old World charm and California-casual style has been pleasing guests for decades…and it's still an oceanfront favorite.

The small private beach at the foot of the property is perhaps the most popular spot in the area for an outdoor wedding ceremony. Couples can get married here with the ocean quite literally at their feet and the surf tumbling a few yards away. Larger outdoor ceremonies are held in the hotel's lovely Rose Garden, with its Victorian gazebo and Spanish-tile fountain. Surrounded by colorful hibiscus, and, of course, roses, it's also a great place to stage anything from a cocktail reception to a rocking dance party.

But for a party that's practically on the beach, there's no place like the Laguna Room. Outfitted with fresh white curtains and champagne-colored carpeting, it has a built-in dance floor, oak-and-granite bar, private restrooms and a small foyer/lounge. Its ceiling slopes down to sliding glass windows that frame an expansive ocean view and open onto the Laguna Room balcony, situated right over the beach. Revelers can dance here, indoors or out, with ocean breezes to keep them naturally cool—and the acoustics inside are excellent.

But these aren't the only options for entertaining in this vibrant and widely adored venue. Serve up cocktails or bites in the Catalina Room, where a polished granite fireplace set on a wide granite platform with built-in granite benches is large enough to act as a small stage. Windows and doors provide access to the OceanView Bar & Grill's terrace, outdoor walkways and panoramic Pacific views.

Party often? How about sipping in Claes' Wine Cellar, where the rich Merlot-colored carpet, handcrafted floor-to-ceiling mahogany wine cabinets, and a cherrywood chef's table create a subtly glamorous dining ambiance. The smoked glass vitrine displaying the owner's food and wine competition medals speaks to this venue's award-winning culinary expertise. Or, gather your small group of guests for a private rehearsal dinner or intimate reception in the handsomely appointed San Clemente Room, which is part of the Claes Dining Room. This cozy event space shares décor elements and gorgeous views with the dining room—which, incidentally, can be bought out for private functions.

When the celebration is over, don't make the mistake of leaving right away. The artsy community of Laguna Beach has so much to offer, and this is the perfect home away from home from which to enjoy it. Snag the Bogart or Errol Flynn suite, book an après-party at OceanView Bar & Grill, and ease into a little vacation fun on California's own Riviera.

CEREMONY CAPACITY: The site holds up to 150 seated guests outdoors, and white chairs are provided.

EVENT/RECEPTION CAPACITY: The facility can accommodate 150 seated or 180 standing guests indoors, and 130 seated or 180 standing outdoors

MEETING CAPACITY: Meeting spaces seat up to 180 guests.

FEES & DEPOSITS: A deposit in the amount of the rental fee is required to reserve your date. The estimated event total balance is due 14 days prior to the event. The rental fee for a ceremony and reception is $2,500 with a ceremony in the Victorian Rose Garden or $3,000 with a ceremony on the beach. The fee includes the ceremony and reception sites with full guest seating, a self-serving water station, an overnight stay with champagne in the Bridal Suite for the couple, and a 2-hour changing room for the groom and groomsmen. The Bridal Suite can serve as the bride's dressing room during the day, based on availability. The room rental fee for a reception only ranges $200–1,000 depending on the space reserved. Meals range $28–75/person. Tax, alcohol and a 20% service charge are additional.

AVAILABILITY: Year-round, daily, 6am–midnight.

SERVICES/AMENITIES:

Catering: in-house

Kitchen Facilities: n/a

Tables & Chairs: provided

Linens, Silver, etc.: provided

Restrooms: wheelchair accessible

Dance Floor: provided, or BYO

Bride's Dressing Area: yes, with ceremony

AV/Meeting Equipment: some provided, or BYO

Parking: valet available; self-parking nearby

Accommodations: 65 guest rooms

Outdoor Night Lighting: yes

Outdoor Cooking Facilities: no

Cleanup: provided

View: fountain, garden, courtyard; panorama of ocean and coastline

Other: spa services

RESTRICTIONS:

Alcohol: in-house, BYO wine with corkage fee, no BYO beer or hard liquor

Smoking: not allowed

Music: amplified OK with restrictions

Wheelchair Access: yes

Insurance: not required

La Casa del Camino

Historic Boutique Hotel

1289 South Coast Highway, Laguna Beach
949/497-2446
www.lacasadelcamino.com
melissad@casaresortsinc.com

- Rehearsal Dinners
- Ceremonies
- Wedding Receptions
- Private Parties
- Corporate Events
- Meetings
- Film Shoots
- Accommodations

Even in a town as picturesque as Laguna Beach, the utterly charming La Casa del Camino is in a class by itself. With an alluring mix of waterfront location, early Spanish Mediterranean architecture and expansive views of the Pacific Ocean, this landmark boutique hotel is a standout choice for a romantic wedding celebration.

Built in 1929 and distinguished by its red-tiled roof, classic archways and wooden balconies, this beachside gem provides a tantalizing peek at a time when it was a favorite getaway for Hollywood stars and starlets. Combine that historic cachet with what today's La Casa del Camino has to offer—the hip energy of its wildly popular K'ya Bistro Bar and its open-air rooftop retreat with unparalleled ocean vistas—and you get the quintessential Laguna Beach experience.

The first thing that greets you here is the beautiful lobby, a welcoming Spanish-Mediterranean-style space with high plaster ceilings accented with wooden crossbeams. There's a baby grand piano off to the right, while on the left you'll find an adobe-style fireplace topped with a tiled niche displaying flickering candles that cast a warm glow. This large-yet-cozy setting is perfect for hosting friends and family for cocktails, dinner or dancing.

But without doubt, the *pièce de résistance* at La Casa del Camino is its Rooftop Lounge. The only one like it in Laguna Beach, it serves up a 360-degree panorama with head-on ocean views. This sprawling, wraparound deck and full-service bar is a spectacular wedding site: You can make a dramatic entrance through a tile-roofed private portal and exchange vows in front of an infinite expanse of sparkling blue water. Your nearest and dearest gather around you in semicircular seating, giving everyone a great vantage for watching the ceremony. Afterwards, invite everyone to enjoy an al fresco toast and bask in the cool marine breezes before sitting down at beautifully appointed tables. Then dine in the company of the surrounding sea and sky.

And if one perfect day is just not enough, you might want to consider reserving the entire hotel for a weekend. Their Spanish-style guest rooms are done in rich, warm tones and feature intricately hand-carved wood furnishings, while the 10 Surf Suites offer a more contemporary "beach" vibe. Each one-of-a-kind suite has been branded by a different surf company—like Rip Curl, Roxy, Quiksilver, and Billabong—and incorporates design elements and colors selected by that company. Your out-of-town guests will love spending an extra day or two here, so that they can truly savor their time with you at this wonderful home-away-from-home.

CEREMONY & EVENT/RECEPTION CAPACITY: The hotel holds 120 seated or standing guests indoors and 120 seated or standing outdoors.

MEETING CAPACITY: Meeting spaces seat 25 guests indoors.

FEES & DEPOSITS: 30% of the total event cost is required to reserve your date and the balance is due prior to the event. The rental fee ranges up to $3,500 depending on the guest count and the season. Please inquire directly about all-inclusive buyout packages. Meals range $49–69/person. Tax, alcohol and a 21% service charge are additional.

AVAILABILITY: Year-round, daily, 8am–10pm.

SERVICES/AMENITIES:

Catering: in-house
Kitchen Facilities: n/a
Tables & Chairs: provided
Linens, Silver, etc.: provided
Restrooms: wheelchair accessible
Dance Floor: CBA
Bride's Dressing Area: CBA
AV/Meeting Equipment: CBA

Parking: on street, valet optional
Accommodations: 40 guest rooms
Outdoor Night Lighting: yes
Outdoor Cooking Facilities: none
Cleanup: provided
View: landscaped grounds; panorama of coastline, hills and ocean
Other: coordination

RESTRICTIONS:

Alcohol: in-house
Smoking: not allowed
Music: non-percussion acoustic or amplified (recorded only) with volume restrictions

Wheelchair Access: yes
Insurance: not required

[seven-degrees]

891 Laguna Canyon Road, Laguna Beach
949/376-1555
www.seven-degrees.com
dora@seven-degrees.com

Special Events Venue

●	Rehearsal Dinners	●	Corporate Events
●	Ceremonies	●	Meetings
●	Wedding Receptions	●	Film Shoots
●	Private Parties		Accommodations

Attracted by the balmy weather, azure ocean, and *la dolce vita* of a small seaside town, scores of artists settled in Laguna Beach in the early 20th century. In fact, the first art museum in California was founded here in 1918. Since then the city has established itself as a major player in the art world, hosting numerous galleries and summer art festivals, proud and indulgent of its boho-chic artist population.

Perhaps the most remarkable addition to the city's art community is [seven-degrees], a "multi-purpose idea lab for the promotion of artistic endeavor, invention and exhibition." Built in 2001, its mission is not only to showcase original art but to support the efforts of emerging artists through its in-residence programs. And fortunately for you, one of the ways this innovative entity sustains itself financially is to make its unique facilities available for special events.

Nestled in Laguna Canyon a few blocks from the ocean, this uber-modern glass, steel and granite complex is a visual marvel. The all-glass façade, whose asymmetry and angular lines defy conventional architecture, reflects the surrounding canyon walls while revealing the artwork displayed inside.

When you have an event here, you immediately become part of the art scene. Enter through the gallery, where you and your guests can peruse the exhibition du jour. Then pass by the live/work studios of the artists-in-residence, which are often open for viewing works in progress. Before the festivities begin, mingle with family and friends in the courtyard between buildings or ascend to the Hillside Terrace, a tentable rooftop patio with multiple uses. Ceremonies are often held here, but the space is also perfect for an outdoor cocktail reception. In addition to canyon views, there are meandering trails with bamboo railings, leading to a series of overlooks built into the canyon walls. A gentle waterfall and lush plantings among the rocks make this setting an unexpected oasis.

Nature takes a back seat to your own creativity in the Media Lounge. Unadorned, it's a simple, 4,500-square-foot oblong room with gray concrete walls and floors. But with the help of an in-house design team, the latest in lighting technology and a phalanx of on-site audiovisual equipment, you'll be able to transform the space into anything you like. Past metamorphoses include a Rococo-style ballroom with gilded mirrors and jacquard textiles; a midsummer night's dream with a forest's worth of potted plants and flowers; and a postmodern discothéque thumping with sound and light. Live webcasting is available, and you can even project an image of yourselves (or anyone else!) on internal or external surfaces. Your guests will be part of an unforgettable multimedia experience, limited only by your imagination (and your budget). [seven-degrees] is a true original in the world of event venues, a place inspired by and dedicated to art. Whether you're planning a wedding, a corporate party or any other celebration here, you'll enjoy being an honored artist-in-residence for the day.

CEREMONY CAPACITY: The Hillside Terrace holds up to 150 seated or 300 with some standing guests.

EVENT/RECEPTION & MEETING CAPACITY: The Media Lounge holds up to 300 seated or 388 standing.

FEES & DEPOSITS: A nonrefundable $5,000 deposit is required to reserve your date. A payment schedule is agreed upon, with the balance paid in full 30 days prior to the event. Dinners start at $67/person. Tax, alcohol and service charge are additional. Full-service packages are available; call for details.

AVAILABILITY: Year-round, daily, until 1am. Events take place in 5-hour blocks.

SERVICES/AMENITIES:

Catering: in-house or BYO with approval
Kitchen Facilities: full commercial kitchen
Tables & Chairs: included with wedding portfolio
Linens, Silver, etc.: included with wedding portfolio
Restrooms: wheelchair accessible
Dance Floor: yes
Bride's Dressing Area: yes
AV/Meeting Equipment: yes

Parking: large lot
Accommodations: no guest rooms
Outdoor Night Lighting: full specialty lighting
Outdoor Cooking Facilities: CBA
Cleanup: provided, extra fee
View: terraced hillside garden
Other: event coordination, florals & décor; off-site catering available

RESTRICTIONS:

Alcohol: in-house, no BYO
Smoking: outdoors only
Music: amplified OK

Wheelchair Access: yes
Insurance: only required for outside vendors

SEVEN4ONE

741 South Coast Highway, Laguna Beach
949/494-6200

www.seven4one.com
guestrelations@seven4one.com

Waterfront Boutique Hotel

● Rehearsal Dinners	● Corporate Events
● Ceremonies	● Meetings
● Wedding Receptions	● Film Shoots
● Private Parties	● Accommodations

Chic … private … a treasure hidden in plain sight … you're missing something fabulous if you haven't been tipped off about this ultra-private wedding and special event venue.

Secreted away in the very midst of sun-splashed Laguna Beach, it's just steps from the sandy shore and surf. No signage clutters the simple but stylish exterior, and passersby would never guess that this façade of smoky windows, reclaimed wood and cascading greenery conceals the luxurious accommodations and inspiring event spaces of a boutique hotel available exclusively for you and your guests.

Here, you get the kind of seclusion that celebrities long for, but you don't need to be a movie star or win the lottery to have total access to everything the hotel has to offer: 10 handsome, contemporary guest rooms and 2 suites; 3 extraordinary event areas; a concierge staff and team of wedding professionals—including a personal chef, an in-house mixologist, and a Wedding Coordinator—devoted to you and your party. In fact, customization is key at SEVEN4ONE, and their event experts are quite keen on matching their exceptional talents for food and entertaining with your particular desires.

A celebration here is going to feel quite magical. Whether you and your company decide to stay for a night, a weekend or longer, you'll be in your very own world, a two-story palace of a place in a million-dollar setting. It's all rather dreamy—no rush, no interruptions, impeccable service—your big day can unfold in a natural way without the stress of time limits or unexpected intrusions.

While you and your entourage relax in your suites and rooms, guests can congregate downstairs in the lobby or the sleek martini lounge. Or, they might stroll into the spacious open-air interior courtyard. This favorite group environment is the ideal stage for a ceremony, a reception or both. Surrounded above by the second-floor balcony, it features a beautiful "living" wall of cascading greenery and reclaimed wood and is easily transformed through lighting and props to suit any vision. A retractable roof makes it weatherproof, but this is Laguna Beach so most of the time you can be sure that the canopy of sky is going to remain bright blue by day and moon- and star-lit once the sun goes down.

And speaking of sunsets, the place to enjoy them is the hotel's second-floor sundeck, which is often used for cocktails or smaller ceremonies. When there's no party in progress, it's a divine escape from the hubbub of entertaining as well as the perfect Pacific-facing perch for taking in the property's sweeping vistas of sea, sky and gorgeous California coast.

The most appealing aspect of SEVEN4ONE is that once the main event is over, you and your guests won't have to tear yourselves away. You'll all have plenty of time to press the pause button, unwind, settle in, and savor this remarkable slice of the good life a little longer.

CEREMONY & MEETING CAPACITY: The facility seats 110 guests.

EVENT/RECEPTION CAPACITY: The facility can accommodate 75 seated or 110 standing for a cocktail-style reception.

FEES & DEPOSITS: SEVEN4ONE is available by the weekend only. A $3,000–5,000 deposit is required to reserve your weekend, and the remaining balance is due in three installments 180, 90 and 15 days prior to the event. Flexible payment terms are available. The revenue minimum for the Wedding Weekend Package is $22,000, which includes accommodations, completely customized food & beverage packages, all taxes and gratuities, parking (with valet), day-of wedding coordination (additional planning services are available), and staffing. If guests pay for their rooms themselves, your cost will be reduced by up to $5,000. Many additional upgrades can be arranged.

AVAILABILITY: Year-round.

SERVICES/AMENITIES:

Catering: in-house
Kitchen Facilities: prep only
Tables & Chairs: CBA
Linens, Silver, etc.: CBA
Restrooms: wheelchair accessible
Dance Floor: CBA
Bride's Dressing Area: yes
AV/Meeting Equipment: CBA
Other: full wedding planning

Parking: valet required (included in wedding packages)
Accommodations: 12 guest rooms
Outdoor Night Lighting: CBA
Outdoor Cooking Facilities: no
Cleanup: provided
View: cityscape, coastline, garden, hills, mountains; ocean panorama

RESTRICTIONS:

Alcohol: in-house
Smoking: designated areas only
Music: amplified OK indoors with restrictions

Wheelchair Access: limited
Insurance: not required

The wedding vendors on our website are the best in the business. How do we know? Read page 577.

365

Surf & Sand Resort

Waterfront Resort

1555 South Coast Highway, Laguna Beach
855/923-7450
www.surfandsandresort.com/weddings
surfweddings@jcresorts.com

● Rehearsal Dinners	● Corporate Events
● Ceremonies	● Meetings
● Wedding Receptions	● Film Shoots
● Private Parties	● Accommodations

Surf & Sand Resort is renowned for both its prime location in Laguna Beach and its proximity to the ocean. The high-rise hotel sits so close to the water that it puts you quite literally—and hypnotically—right above the crashing surf. If you haven't seen it yet, check out the Mediterranean-style Conference Center, a separate event venue that adds to Surf & Sand's reputation as a place where you can have it all—a corporate gala, an executive meeting or a lovely wedding.

"Conference Center" doesn't do justice to the banquet rooms—the Pelican and Sand Dollar—which are decorated in a Mediterranean beach-luxe style that could grace the pages of Architectural Digest. Each one is a handsome and tasteful mix of blond hardwoods, airy hues of sand and cream, coffered ceilings, lots of whitewashed wood-shuttered windows, neoclassical appointments and unique works of art.

Ceremonies at Surf & Sand take place on the Catalina Terrace and on the Ocean Terrace, where you'll have a breathtaking view of Catalina Island while the breaking waves resound just below your feet. After the wedding, guests head off to the largest reception space, the Pelican Room, which has a graceful foyer and a terrace with a view of the hotel and the ocean. Perfectly suited for mid-sized groups, the Sand Dollar Room is complemented by a series of archways forming a patio covered with vinery. And just outside the Sand Castle Room, you'll find a babbling fountain and a peek of the ocean below.

After your event, stay a while longer, or better yet, have your honeymoon here. All of Surf & Sand's luxurious accommodations have seaview balconies, all with commanding views of the Pacific Ocean. While there are plenty of nearby places to go sightseeing or shopping (Laguna Beach boutiques and galleries are within walking distance), you may just want to pamper yourself at the resort's AquaTerra Spa or sink back in your poolside deck chair or beach chair on the sand and enjoy the sun's warmth. With its seabreeze air plus ocean and sunset vistas, Surf & Sand is an exhilarating locale for any celebration.

CEREMONY CAPACITY: The Ocean Terrace seats 80 guests, the Catalina Terrace seats 180; South Beach can accommodate up to 80 standing.

EVENT/RECEPTION CAPACITY: With dance floor, the Pelican Room holds 180 seated, the Sand Dollar Room 80 seated, the Sand Castle Room 60 seated.

MEETING CAPACITY: Please contact the facility for detailed information regarding meetings.

FEES & DEPOSITS: For weddings, the deposit varies and is based on the food & beverage minimum for your event. The ceremony rental and setup fees range $950–4,000, and vary by location and season. Seated luncheons start at $42/person; dinners start at $78/person. Beverages, tax and service charge are additional.

AVAILABILITY: Year-round, daily.

SERVICES/AMENITIES:

Catering: in-house, no BYO

Kitchen Facilities: n/a

Tables & Chairs: provided

Linens, Silver, etc.: provided

Restrooms: wheelchair accessible

Dance Floor: provided

Bride's Dressing Area: yes

AV/Meeting Equipment: full range

Parking: valet, nominal fee

Accommodations: 167 guest rooms

Outdoor Night Lighting: access only

Outdoor Cooking Facilities: no

Cleanup: provided

View: Pacific Ocean, coastal hills, Catalina Island, sunsets

RESTRICTIONS:

Alcohol: in-house, no BYO

Smoking: not allowed

Music: amplified OK

Wheelchair Access: limited

Insurance: not required

The Hills Hotel

25205 La Paz Road, Laguna Hills
949/586-5000

www.thelagunahillshotel.com
catering@thelagunahillshotel.com

Ballroom & Hotel

● Rehearsal Dinners	● Corporate Events
● Ceremonies	● Meetings
● Wedding Receptions	○ Film Shoots
● Private Parties	● Accommodations

If first impressions are the most indelible, then The Hills Hotel is a place you're definitely going to remember. After a multi-million dollar transformation, this boutique hotel is now a trendy, upscale venue for weddings.

A grand staircase leads up to the Mezzanine level, where you'll find five event spaces that you can use in the way that best suits your wedding or private party. Guests can mingle in any of the four prefunction areas, which flow from one to another. Each has its own look and all are set with cocktail tables that feature large crystal vases filled with white branches. Walls are covered in light gray leather panels, an understated backdrop to the iridescent crystal sign that announces the adjoining ballroom.

Embossed, custom-designed doors open to the Crystal Ballroom, which lives up to its name. Formal and elegant, it's outfitted with crown molding, mirror-backed wall sconces and six glittering beaded crystal chandeliers ringed with sparkling "candles." The walls have a subtle shimmer, thanks to ground crystals embedded in the pearl-colored paper. Colored LED lights in the coffered ceiling allow you to create the perfect ambiance: Choose shades of blue or purple for a sultry, nightclub feeling, or use pink or amber tones for something more romantic or festive.

Ceremonies can take place in the Crystal Ballroom, but they're often held in the Veranda, an atrium-style corridor that runs the length of the ballroom. Light comes from seven crystal chandeliers suspended from the tray ceiling, as well as from a wall of windows overlooking the trees right outside and the mountains in the distance. This area is also well suited for a cocktail reception or a buffet setup during dinner in the ballroom. An additional ceremony option is the Garnet Gallery, done in classic yet modern tones of maroon, purple and gold.

The Crystal Lounge is ideal for relaxing on white tufted benches while sipping cocktails, sampling appetizers and perhaps watching the bride and groom's life stories playing on TV monitors. The Patio, which is staged with lounge furniture, provides another comfortable spot. It has a fuel-burning fireplace with glittered white star lights that add an extra glow during evening events.

The Crystal Wedding Reception Package offers a long list of amenities: plated, duet and buffet entrée choices; complimentary bride & groom entrées; wedding cake; Chiavari chairs; and much more. The newlyweds also receive a complimentary room, where a sweet gift of champagne and chocolate-covered strawberries awaits...and, the next morning they'll enjoy a complimentary breakfast in bed or in The Hills Café. For couples getting married here, too, there's a separate ceremony package that includes a celebratory post-ceremony toast with the bridal party.

Close to beaches, art galleries, shopping, fine dining, local attractions and more, The Hills Hotel is a convenient choice for a destination wedding.

CEREMONY CAPACITY: Crystal Ballroom I and II combined hold 220 seated; the Veranda accommodates 100 seated, and the Garnet Gallery seats 140.

EVENT/RECEPTION CAPACITY: The Crystal Ballroom seats 280 and the Garnet Gallery seats 90 for dinner and dancing.

MEETING CAPACITY: Meeting spaces can accommodate 600 seated guests.

FEES & DEPOSITS: A $3,000 deposit is required to reserve your date. 50% of the estimated balance is due 180 days prior to the event, and the final guaranteed balance is due 14 days prior. Packages start at $70/person. Tax and a 22% service charge are additional.

AVAILABILITY: Year-round, daily. Events must end by midnight.

SERVICES/AMENITIES:

Catering: in-house
Kitchen Facilities: n/a
Tables & Chairs: Chiavari chair upgrade included in ceremony & reception package
Linens, Silver, etc.: floor-length satin linens and tableware included in reception package
Restrooms: wheelchair accessible, available upstairs and downstairs
Dance Floor: included in reception package
Bride's Dressing Area: included in ceremony package
AV/Meeting Equipment: CBA or BYO

Parking: self-parking; valet service recommended for over 200 guests (valet service charge customized for your event)
Accommodations: 147 guest rooms with 2 suites
Outdoor Night Lighting: no
Outdoor Cooking Facilities: no
Cleanup: included in ceremony and reception package
View: panorama of hills and mountains

RESTRICTIONS:

Alcohol: in-house
Smoking: 20 feet away from any outdoor terrace or entrance
Music: restrictions apply; inquire for DJ policy and other details

Wheelchair Access: yes
Insurance: not required

Electra Cruises

Yachts

3439 Via Oporto, Newport Beach
800/952-9955
www.electracruises.com
info@electracruises.com

● Rehearsal Dinners	● Corporate Events
● Ceremonies	● Meetings
● Wedding Receptions	Film Shoots
● Private Parties	Accommodations

When it comes to choosing a place to get married, few conjure up romance quite like a wedding at sea. Whether you set sail under the California sun or beneath a starry night sky, you get to leave the rest of the world behind as you celebrate with the glorious Pacific Ocean as your backdrop.

Their affordable wedding packages offer so much more than just the yacht, food, and beverages. From suggesting innovative invitation ideas (think messages in bottles or custom-designed wedding passports), to weaving your color palette into great fabrics, linens, and florals, to planning the actual wedding-day itinerary, menus, and to-die-for displays, they'll put together an event with that special touch.

This high level of service is matched by their elegant fleet of five luxurious private yachts. Between them they can easily accommodate an intimate gathering of your closest friends to a party of 300 guests. Vintage romance is a hallmark of the *Electra,* a 100-foot, all wood classic fantail yacht. At 83 feet, the New Orleans-style paddle wheeler *Newport Princess* is a charming, Old World Mississippi riverboat with a lot of character. *Athena* is a modern 110-foot motor yacht decked in marble with a Greek motif. The 125-foot *Destiny* features an abundance of glass and ultra-modern décor. Electra Cruises' newest and largest yacht is the 140-foot *Eternity,* which is ADA-approved and outfitted with an elevator. All of their yachts have multiple levels, a main salon with full bar, baby grand piano, leather couches and spectacular views.

With Electra Cruises, you won't have to settle for just another event. They'll customize your big day, make your guests say "Wow!" and do it all at a reasonable price. For an exceptional wedding, reception or commitment ceremony, you can count on these dedicated professionals. Give them a call to arrange a complimentary event consultation and see what they can do for YOU.

CEREMONY CAPACITY: *Electra's* top deck holds 100 seated guests. The *Athena* and *Destiny* each hold 150, the *Newport Princess* up to 150, and the *Eternity* can accommodate 300 guests.

EVENT/RECEPTION & MEETING CAPACITY: The *Electra* holds up to 100 guests, maximum. The *Athena* and *Destiny* each hold 150, the *Newport Princess* 150, and the *Eternity* up to 300 guests.

FEES & DEPOSITS: A nonrefundable $2,000 deposit is required to secure your date, and the remaining balance is due within 2 weeks of the event. Electra Cruises offers full wedding packages starting at $72/person. This all-inclusive service consists of the yacht charter, service staff, catering, wedding cake, bar service, rentals, florals, DJ, photographer, event coordinator and a captain to perform the ceremony. Tax is additional.

AVAILABILITY: Year-round, daily including holidays, anytime.

SERVICES/AMENITIES:

Catering: in-house
Kitchen Facilities: full galley
Tables & Chairs: provided
Linens, Silver, etc.: provided
Restrooms: wheelchair accessible
Dance Floor: available upon request
Bride's & Groom's Dressing Areas: yes
AV/Meeting Equipment: full range CBA

Parking: parking structure
Accommodations: no guest rooms
Outdoor Night Lighting: yes
Outdoor Cooking Facilities: no
Cleanup: provided
View: Pacific Ocean, Newport Harbor and city skyline
Other: full event coordination

RESTRICTIONS:

Alcohol: in-house, no BYO
Smoking: outside areas
Music: amplified OK

Wheelchair Access: yes
Insurance: not required
Other: no sparklers, floating lanterns, or candles

Environmental Nature Center

Community Center

1601 East 16th Street, Newport Beach

949/645-8489

www.encenter.org
sarah@encenter.org

● Rehearsal Dinners		● Corporate Events
● Ceremonies		● Meetings
● Wedding Receptions		● Film Shoots
● Private Parties		Accommodations

Building a beautiful future together? How about starting it out with a fabulous eco-friendly celebration at the Environmental Nature Center. This award-winning venue has a dreamy 8,500-square-foot facility with halls, patios, and native gardens planted in the midst of its gorgeous 3.5-acre natural setting. The first building in Orange County to achieve Leadership in Energy and Environmental Design (LEED) Platinum Certification, it features energy-conserving climate control, water efficient systems and fixtures, and the imaginative use of recycled and recyclable materials throughout.

Begin your party in the Center's airy Museum, where guests can marvel at the effortless integration of "green" building solutions into stylish contemporary design. The ENC actually produces more energy than it consumes, and a computer monitor in the hallway displays its usage levels. Guests will find plenty of interactive exhibits to explore and discuss, as they meet and greet one another before stepping out though the glass foldaway doors and onto the broad Garden Patio.

Flanked on one side by a catering prep kitchen and patio, library/lounge with private powder room for the bride and her attendants, and a butterfly garden … and on the other side by the pale desert shades and dramatic shapes of its California native gardens, this is a stunning outdoor venue—day or night—for your scrumptious seasonal, earth-friendly reception. It's also great for dancing under sunny skies or beneath a nighttime canopy of stars and the facility's softly luminous solar-powered lanterns. At the foot of the patio, a small amphitheater with built-in bench seating frames a large open fire pit that's ideal for an elegant version of a favorite campfire activity—that's right, how about toasting the good times with champagne and s'mores?

Wondering about indoor options? Follow the paw prints in the sand-textured walkway to the Oak and Sycamore Rooms, two cozy chambers separated by a movable airwall that can be used individually or combined into one large space. Well-equipped for just about any function, the rooms have picture windows, high ceilings, handsome honey-colored cabinets (composed of recycled materials like wheat chaff and sunflower seed), and AV and internet capability. Center staff can help by providing all kinds of exciting biodegradable and reusable decorating options.

For a surprisingly affordable celebration with the tiniest possible carbon footprint, consider a picnic wedding and reception. You can tie the knot in a picturesque way in the little garden amphitheater or at the end of the small garden stream. Then hold your reception amid berries and blossoms on picnic tables under the trees before releasing guests to wander off along the ENC's many enchanting paths. Whether your affair is large or small, you can be sure that you're doing the world a big favor when you have it here. And you're helping the local community, too, since your event fees are also recycled: Most of them go to supporting the Center's operating costs and programs, and a big portion of your bill is tax deductible, too.

CEREMONY, EVENT/RECEPTION & MEETING CAPACITY: The site holds 125 seated or 245 standing guests indoors or outdoors.

FEES & DEPOSITS: 20% of the total event cost plus a tax-deductible membership and permit fees are required to reserve your date, and the balance is due 4 weeks prior to the event. The rental fee (including membership) ranges $4,000–5,500.

AVAILABILITY: Year round, daily.

SERVICES/AMENITIES:

Catering: BYO
Kitchen Facilities: limited
Tables & Chairs: some provided
Linens, Silver, etc.: CBA
Restrooms: wheelchair accessible
Dance Floor: provided
Bride's & Groom's Dressing Areas: CBA
AV/Meeting Equipment: provided

Parking: large lot
Accommodations: no guest rooms
Outdoor Night Lighting: yes; string lights over the patio
Outdoor Cooking Facilities: no
Cleanup: renter or caterer
View: creek, forest, courtyard, waterfall
Other: picnic area, fire ring and wood

RESTRICTIONS:

Alcohol: select from preferred vendor list
Smoking: not allowed
Music: amplified OK with restrictions

Wheelchair Access: yes
Insurance: liability required

Want to know WHAT TO ASK a potential location or vendor? Check out our Questions to Ask starting on page 21.

Fairmont Newport Beach

Resort Hotel

4500 MacArthur Boulevard, Newport Beach
949/476-2001 x4000

www.fairmont.com/newportbeach
rachel.gellerman@fairmont.com

- Rehearsal Dinners
- Ceremonies
- Wedding Receptions
- Private Parties
- Corporate Events
- Meetings
- Film Shoots
- Accommodations

The Fairmont Newport Beach is considered by many to be Orange County's finest luxury hotel. From the moment you step into its gleaming lobby, you'll be impressed with its dramatic look and feel, and throughout your event here you'll experience the high level of hospitality and service the Fairmont name is known for worldwide. You'll also appreciate the hotel's enviable location: Set in one of Southern California's most affluent coastal cities, it's just a stone's throw from John Wayne Airport, world-class shopping, a multitude of recreational activities and many local beaches.

The Garden Gazebo, edged with multihued impatiens, has been designed for ceremonies. Secluded from hotel guests and protected by tall palms and ferns, it's very private and serene. After walking through an evergreen arch, you'll exchange vows under the ivory gazebo, which can be enhanced with floral garlands. Following the ceremony, the lovely surroundings serve as a picturesque backdrop for photography.

You have numerous choices for your reception, starting with the elegant Bay Laurel Ballroom where you can dance the night away under a magnificent chandelier. The *bambú* Room is a stunning venue with high ceilings, modern lighting, and floor-to-ceiling windows lining the back wall. In the garden-like Orchid Terrace, glass sliders and ceiling fans contribute to the indoor/outdoor feel. For a quintessential Southern California party, entertain your guests in the Bamboo Garden with its fireplace, fire pit and water feature, or on the glorious Sky Palms pool deck, whose palm trees, umbrellas and cabanas set the stage for a memorable al fresco celebration. The hotel's cozy *bambú* Wine Cellar is ideal for a rehearsal dinner or farewell brunch.

The Fairmont Newport Beach specializes in California cuisine, but the culinary team can customize a menu for you. Whether you're planning a small gathering or a full-scale gala, the hotel's wedding specialist will work with your wedding coordinator to make sure everything runs smoothly.

To take full advantage of all the Fairmont has to offer, you and your wedding party may want to indulge in an array of soothing treatments in the hotel's full-service spa, TheSpa Santé. With more than 8,000 square feet of space and an extensive menu of services, this sanctuary for body and soul provides the ultimate in urban pampering.

One of California's most upscale playgrounds, Newport Beach is not only an A-list wedding location, it's a prime choice for a honeymoon or vacation. So why not extend your stay at this exceptional hotel—you'll have the pleasure of prolonging your Fairmont experience and treating yourself to a wonderful getaway.

CEREMONY CAPACITY: The Garden Gazebo accommodates 250 seated and the Bamboo Garden seats up to 400.

EVENT/RECEPTION CAPACITY: The seated capacity for a variety of spaces is as follows: Bay Laurel Ballroom, 500; Bamboo Garden, 450; *bambú* Room, 200; Orchid Terrace, 130; *bambú* Wine Cellar, 60.

MEETING CAPACITY: Several spaces hold 20–500 seated guests.

FEES & DEPOSITS: For weddings, a nonrefundable deposit of 20% of the estimated total is payable when you reserve your date. The estimated balance is payable 14 business days prior to the event. Wedding packages range $98–125/person plus applicable tax and a 22% service charge. The ceremony fee ranges $3,000–6,000.

For business meetings, room rental fees vary depending on room(s) reserved and services required; call for additional information.

AVAILABILITY: Weddings, year-round, daily, 11am–4pm or 6pm–midnight. Business functions or meetings, year-round, daily, anytime.

SERVICES/AMENITIES:
Catering: in-house
Kitchen Facilities: n/a
Tables & Chairs: provided
Linens, Silver, etc.: provided
Restrooms: wheelchair accessible
Dance Floor: provided
Bride's Dressing Area: yes
AV/Meeting Equipment: full range

Parking: valet
Accommodations: 444 guest rooms and suites
Outdoor Night Lighting: yes
Outdoor Cooking Facilities: no
Cleanup: provided
View: garden

RESTRICTIONS:
Alcohol: in-house, BYO for wine only with corkage fee
Smoking: designated areas
Music: amplified OK

Wheelchair Access: yes
Insurance: liability required

Harborside Grand Ballroom
Located in the Historic Balboa Pavilion

400 Main Street, Newport Beach
949/673-4633
www.harborside-banquets.com
banquets@harborside-pavilion.com

Waterfront Events Facility

- Rehearsal Dinners
- Ceremonies
- Wedding Receptions
- Private Parties
- Corporate Events
- Meetings
- Film Shoots
- Accommodations

Few beach towns on the West Coast can rival Balboa, annexed to Newport Beach on a peninsula between the Pacific Ocean and Newport Bay. Everything about this small community is in perfect balance and proportion. The compact downtown is thriving, but not colonized by chain stores. The neighborhoods range from neatly trimmed cottages to the understated houses of the wealthy. The beach is wide, the municipal pier has a great burger shack and there's a classic bayside strand of amusement parlors, harbor tours and quaint shops that evoke all the heady sights and smells of life at the beach.

At the heart of town is the historic Balboa Pavilion, a majestic Victorian structure overlooking Newport Harbor that was built in 1905 at the foot of Main Street. From the water, the distinctive shape of this two-story building's steeply sloped roof has always made the Pavilion an instantly recognizable landmark. It climbs to a flag-tipped cupola that looks like an exclamation point— perhaps a proclamation of how good life is here. Generations of locals danced, fell in love and got married at the pavilion, and then returned years later to see their children do the same.

The Harborside Grand Ballroom, which is on the second floor of the Pavilion, has the best views of the bay in the harbor. Originally designed as America's answer to the palatial dance halls of early 20th-century Europe, the room is about 140 feet wide and has a huge dance floor and two bars. A glass-protected terrace just outside the larger of the bars—perfect for catching a breath of fresh air—has been freshly paned and painted. The elegant wide staircase that climbs from the front entryway to the ballroom—and makes a beautiful stage for a photogenic entrance—has been completely refurbished. Warm browns, creams and light greens create a color palette that's both sophisticated and unobtrusive. The 10-foot-high windows that line every inch of the ballroom on three sides are still here, as are the sweeping views out to Newport Bay.

When you reserve the ballroom, the experienced Harborside staff will assist you with every aspect of your event, from customizing your menu to helping you choose the right linens. They're also skilled at bringing to life whatever celebration you have in mind, be it a formal black-tie affair, a Victorian or contemporary beach-themed wedding or a rousing casino night. As the Banquet Manager says, "There isn't anything we can't do."

The Harborside Grand Ballroom is unquestionably one of the best waterfront locations in Newport Beach. But for all its majesty, this splendid event space never upstages the bride and groom—it quietly serves as a memorable backdrop.

CEREMONY CAPACITY: The venue holds up to 250 guests for a ceremony in conjunction with a reception.

EVENT/RECEPTION & MEETING CAPACITY: Harborside has two adjoining rooms with a capacity of 250 guests each; when used together they accommodate a total of 500 guests.

FEES & DEPOSITS: A nonrefundable $2,000 deposit is required to reserve one room, $4,000 to reserve two rooms. A 50% deposit is due 90 days prior to the event, and the balance is due 14 days prior along with the guaranteed guest count. The room rental fee ranges $500–1,000 per room depending on the day of the week and date of the event. Dinners range $30–60/person. Tax, alcohol and service charge are additional.

AVAILABILITY: Year-round, daily, 8am–11pm.

SERVICES/AMENITIES:

Catering: in-house, or select from list of approved ethnic caterers

Kitchen Facilities: n/a

Tables & Chairs: provided

Linens, Silver, etc.: provided

Restrooms: wheelchair accessible

Dance Floor: yes

Bride's & Groom's Dressing Areas: yes

AV/Meeting Equipment: full range CBA

Parking: self-parking or valet, extra charge

Accommodations: no guest rooms

Outdoor Night Lighting: yes

Outdoor Cooking Facilities: no

Cleanup: provided, extra fee

View: Newport Harbor

Other: full event coordination, WiFi available

RESTRICTIONS:

Alcohol: in-house, no BYO

Smoking: outside only

Music: amplified OK indoors

Wheelchair Access: yes

Insurance: not required

Other: no rice, birdseed, fog machines or glitter

Hornblower Cruises & Events

Yachts

3101 West Coast Highway, Newport Beach

949/650-2412

www.hornblowerweddings.com
nb@hornblower.com

● Rehearsal Dinners		● Corporate Events	
● Ceremonies		● Meetings	
● Wedding Receptions		● Film Shoots	
● Private Parties		Accommodations	

When your friends ask where you plan to get married, you say you're not sure yet, but you know it will be on a boat. Actually, what you want is more of a yacht—something sleek and classy that glides through the water like a graceful swan.

When your friends ask where you plan to get married, you say you're not sure yet, but you know it will be on a boat. Actually, what you want is more of a yacht—something sleek and classy that glides through the water like a graceful swan.

You see yourself and your beloved on the sun deck, refreshed by the gentle breeze. As the captain pronounces you husband and wife, you gaze out at the glittering sea and feel at one with the world. If this vision speaks to you, we suggest you pay a visit to Hornblower Cruises and Events, an award-winning yacht charter company where making dreams come true is a way of life.

Each vessel in their fleet of luxury yachts has its own style and personality. Among them (they offer the largest selection in Southern California), is the state-of-the-art *Endless Dreams*. Unlike most big event vessels, which are floating party barges, this one offers the true sophistication of a yacht along with a capacity for 450 guests. The interior is custom-designed with high ceilings and lots of warm wood, granite and stainless steel throughout the spacious Grand Salon and Entertainment Deck. Amenities include a built-in dance floor, raised DJ platform and two plasma TVs. There's an outdoor balcony for ceremonies, and a huge bow and Sky Deck for enjoying the fresh air. With features you won't find on any other boat on the West Coast, *Endless Dreams* makes other vessels this size pale in comparison.

The impressive *Just Dreamin'* is a 110-foot mega-yacht that's custom-designed for high-style special events. Her three comfortable cabins, open aft deck, built-in dance floor and, of course, air conditioning and heating, will make your guests feel totally pampered. A long list of assets has made her one of Southern California's most sought-after yachts.

Mojo has long been one of the most popular charter vessels in Southern California. An elegant, 100-foot custom-designed Ditmar-Donaldson motor yacht, she's outfitted with an airy enclosed upper deck available for dining; a plush main salon including a full bar; three contemporary staterooms and a generous forward open bow.

Entertainer boasts two large, fully enclosed decks, each with a full bar and dance floor. With a full galley, high-quality sound system, and open-air lounge deck, she can accommodate 400 guests for seated dining or 550 for cocktails and a buffet. The aft deck provides a "back porch," additional deck space for guests who want to take in the sea air or dance under the stars!

Hornblower Cruises and Events, Newport Beach is more than just the sum of its boats. It's also a full-service event company that offers several budget-friendly packages and the personal assistance of a professional event planner. From entertainment to floral design, Hornblower can help you pull it all together without breaking the bank. (The spectacular sunsets and glittering starscapes come with no extra charge!) If you're looking to put a nautical spin on romance, then let Hornblower Cruises and Events show you the way.

CEREMONY & EVENT/RECEPTION CAPACITY: Hornblower Cruises and Events, Newport Beach accommodates up to 400 seated or 550 standing guests.

MEETING CAPACITY: They can accommodate 10–550 people for business functions, seated conference or theater-style.

FEES & DEPOSITS: A $1,000–8,000 deposit (depending on the vessel's size) is required to book a boat; the balance is payable 30 days prior to the event. Hornblower Cruises and Events, Newport Beach offers wedding packages starting at $73/person that include boat rental, food, cake, nonalcoholic beverages and a ceremony by the captain. Hourly boat rental rates and à la carte services can also be arranged.

AVAILABILITY: Year-round, daily, anytime.

SERVICES/AMENITIES:

Catering: in-house, or BYO depending on the vessel

Kitchen Facilities: n/a

Tables & Chairs: provided

Linens, Silver, etc.: provided

Restrooms: wheelchair accessibility varies

Dance Floor: available

Bride's & Groom's Dressing Areas: yes

AV/Meeting Equipment: CBA

Parking: self-parking, shuttle or valet

Accommodations: no guest rooms

Outdoor Night Lighting: yes

Outdoor Cooking Facilities: no

Cleanup: provided and/or caterer

View: Pacific Ocean and coastal skyline

Other: full event coordination, licensed officiant

RESTRICTIONS:

Alcohol: in-house; BYO varies per vessel

Smoking: on decks only

Music: multiple entertainment options are available

Wheelchair Access: varies per vessel

Insurance: not required

Hyatt Regency Newport Beach

Resort Hotel

1107 Jamboree Road, Newport Beach
949/729-6201 Catering Department
www.newportbeach.hyatt.com
weddingsnewpo@hyatt.com

- Rehearsal Dinners
- Ceremonies
- Wedding Receptions
- Private Parties
- Corporate Events
- Meetings
- Film Shoots
- Accommodations

What people love most about Hyatt Regency Newport Beach is the beauty of its 26 landscaped acres. The lush plantings, seasonal flowers and abundant palm trees make even a walk around the grounds a profoundly pleasurable experience. If you're planning a wedding here, you'll find that nature is part of almost every event site at the resort.

A white trellis covered with wisteria and jasmine shades the walkway to the Amphitheater, a dramatic setting for a large ceremony. The couple exchanges vows on a trellised platform, while their guests look on from tiered seating above them. Although there are lots of flowers in surrounding bushes, the trellis can be decorated with more florals for heightened effect.

Reception areas all offer indoor and outdoor options. The largest is the Plaza Ballroom, which comes with its own private, enclosed patio. Some couples choose to get married on the patio, but most use it for serving champagne and hors d'oeuvres. Sheltered by a high white arbor, this spacious terrace provides a tropical ambiance with a soothing fountain. It's protected from the elements by windowed sides that can be rolled up or down. Dining and dancing take place in the ballroom, where adjustable recessed lighting and wall sconces allow you to set the mood.

The circular Terrace Room works well for smaller groups. Most of its "walls" are glass, providing a peek-a-boo view of Newport's Back Bay, luxuriant foliage and the adjacent Terrace Courtyard and pool. The Arbor, a sunken patio lined with plants and flowers and surrounded by greenery can, like the Plaza Ballroom patio, double as a ceremony site as well as a spot for pre-reception mingling.

For intimate weddings the Garden Rooms are an excellent choice. This trio of spaces, housed in an L-shaped building, is interconnected by French doors and can be reserved individually or together. They all share a wall of multipaned windows that overlook a courtyard, alive with wide-branching olive trees, planters filled with blooms, and a medley of other plants. An oversized fire pit makes a cozy niche for conversation, and overhead lamps keep guests warm during cool months.

As you would expect, there are many fantastic photo opportunities on the property, including the fragrant Rose Garden (also popular for ceremonies of up to 50) and the lovely multi-tiered terracotta fountain.

Guests staying here for the weekend will have plenty to do thanks to three pools, a golf course, and a fitness room—not to mention the ocean and beaches nearby. Here at Hyatt Regency Newport Beach you'll enjoy the service and comforts of a large hotel in a free-flowing, natural setting.

CEREMONY CAPACITY: The Amphitheater seats 1,000 guests; the Garden seats up to 100; and the Terrace Courtyard holds 250 seated, 400 standing.

EVENT/RECEPTION CAPACITY: The Terrace Room holds 200 (180 with a dance floor) seated guests. The Garden Rooms hold 160 (120 with a dance floor) seated. The Plaza Ballroom seats 450 guests with a dance floor.

MEETING CAPACITY: Several spaces hold 15–800 seated guests.

FEES & DEPOSITS: For weddings, 30% of the food & beverage minimum is due upon booking; a credit card or cashier's check for the balance is due 10 days prior to the function. The ceremony site fee starts at $1,500. Luncheon packages start at about $88/person; dinner packages start at $115/person. Wedding packages include a 1-hour hosted bar, selection of hors d'oeuvres, artisan cheese & fruit display, house wine with dinner, champagne toast and wedding cake. Beverages, tax and service charge are additional.

For business functions, room rates vary; call the hotel for additional information.

AVAILABILITY: Year-round. Summer weddings usually take place in a block from 11am–5pm or 6:30pm–midnight; other time frames can be arranged.

SERVICES/AMENITIES:

Catering: in-house
Kitchen Facilities: n/a
Tables & Chairs: provided
Linens, Silver, etc.: provided
Restrooms: wheelchair accessible
Dance Floor: hardwood floors, adjustable size
Bride's & Groom's Dressing Areas: yes
AV/Meeting Equipment: full range, extra charge

Parking: self-parking or valet
Accommodations: 407 guest rooms
Outdoor Night Lighting: provided
Outdoor Cooking Facilities: available
Cleanup: provided
View: Back Bay and Garden

RESTRICTIONS:

Alcohol: in-house
Smoking: outside only
Music: amplified OK outdoors until 10pm

Wheelchair Access: yes, except garden
Insurance: may be required, call for details
Other: no rice, birdseed or confetti

Want to find more venues and services? Check out our informative website, www.HereComesTheGuide.com.

381

Island Hotel Newport Beach

690 Newport Center Drive, Newport Beach

949/760-4926

www.islandhotel.com
dejones@islandhotel.com

Resort Hotel

- Rehearsal Dinners
- Ceremonies
- Wedding Receptions
- Private Parties
- Corporate Events
- Meetings
- Film Shoots
- Accommodations

Breathtaking views of Newport Harbor, Newport Back Bay, and the Pacific Ocean, are just part of what makes the Island Hotel a standout Newport Beach wedding venue. A recent renovation, from the marble entry to the vibrant new colors splashed throughout the guest rooms, has transformed this property into a chic, modern retreat. The moment your guests arrive, they'll experience the casual elegance of "The Center of Coastal Luxury."

Have your celebration here, and you'll appreciate all the amenities. On the big day, separate suites are reserved for the bride and groom so that each can unwind and get ready in style. For additional renewal and relaxation, the hotel's spectacular 4,000-square-foot spa offers a plethora of soothing massages, facials and beauty treatments. And, of course, Island Hotel's catering team is dedicated to making sure your event reflects your vision and unfolds flawlessly.

For weddings, receptions, rehearsal dinners and post-celebration brunches, there's an array of options. Large affairs work well in the stunning Ballroom, where a soft color palette of gold, tan and sage green provides a neutral backdrop, and cascading crystal chandeliers add a touch of glamour. The adjoining private prefunction room is ideal for mingling and passing hors d'oeuvres, while you and your photographer take photos elsewhere on the hotel's verdant grounds.

More intimate receptions are held in the sun-filled Cabana Room, a sophisticated space with Murano glass chandeliers, decorative art panels, and abundant light. The room transitions seamlessly from indoors to outdoors through folding glass doors that open to a spacious, gently heated terrace, where guests can enjoy the fresh air and lush landscaping year-round.

Whichever spaces you choose to host your event, you'll be treated to superior service and culinary excellence. Out-of-town guests will also love their accommodations in spacious rooms or suites—most with coastal views—as well as the heated pool and all the services of the on-site fitness center and spa. For anyone in your party who wants to explore the area, the hotel is close to everything that defines upscale Orange County—sparkling beaches, championship golf courses, maritime recreation in nearby Newport Harbor and world-class shopping at Fashion Island.

No matter what the occasion, you'll be delighted with Island Hotel's resort-like atmosphere and professional staff.

CEREMONY CAPACITY: The Ballroom seats up to 940 indoors, and the Cabana Terrace seats up to 220 guests outdoors.

EVENT/RECEPTION CAPACITY: The hotel can accommodate up to 620 seated guests with a dance floor.

MEETING CAPACITY: Several flexible meeting rooms hold up to 940 seated guests.

FEES & DEPOSITS: For weddings, 20% of the estimated event total is required as a nonrefundable deposit to reserve your date. The balance is due 14 days prior to the event. Luncheons start at $50/person, dinner packages at $135/person. The cake-cutting fee is $6/person. Tax, alcohol and a 23% service charge are additional.

For business functions, the room rental fee varies depending on the rooms and services selected. Please call for details.

AVAILABILITY: Year-round, daily, 6am–1am.

SERVICES/AMENITIES:

Catering: in-house; outside catering may be allowed with approval
Kitchen Facilities: n/a
Tables & Chairs: provided
Linens, Silver, etc.: provided
Restrooms: wheelchair accessible
Dance Floor: provided
Bride's & Groom's Dressing Areas: provided
AV/Meeting Equipment: full range, extra fee

Parking: valet required
Accommodations: 295 guest rooms
Outdoor Night Lighting: provided, special lighting at additional charge
Outdoor Cooking Facilities: BBQ CBA
Cleanup: provided
View: landscaped grounds, garden, pool area
Other: grand piano, in-house wedding cake, spa services, resort-style pool, fitness and business centers

RESTRICTIONS:

Alcohol: in-house
Smoking: not permitted
Music: amplified OK indoors

Wheelchair Access: yes
Insurance: vendors must provide liability insurance

Newport Dunes Waterfront Resort & Marina

Waterfront Resort

1131 Back Bay Drive, Newport Beach

949/729-3800

www.newportdunes.com
events@newportdunes.com

- Rehearsal Dinners
- Ceremonies
- Wedding Receptions
- Private Parties
- Corporate Events
- Meetings
- Film Shoots
- Accommodations

There's nothing pretentious about the Newport Dunes Waterfront Resort, where weddings and special events are, quite simply, a blast. Nestled on a picturesque lagoon at the entrance to the Back Bay Nature Preserve and the Newport Bay Conservancy, this 110-acre retreat offers 50,000 square feet of function space including 10 exciting indoor and outdoor venues … along with planning assistance, catering, accommodations, and loads of fun at extraordinarily affordable prices.

One reason this resort is so popular is that *Coast Magazine* named its Pavilions the top beach location for events in Orange County. Here, you can have your ceremony, reception, business gala, picnic, barbecue, or any other celebration, right on the beach. That means watersports, volleyball, bonfires and actual sand between your toes are all part of the scene at this much-loved venue. Another reason for its popularity is the wide range of settings to choose from—all of which can be reimagined in a multitude of ways with the help of the experienced and accessible staff.

Take, for example, those Pavilions: Cabana-like structures built over cement pads on the beach, they're easily transformed with tables, twinkle lights, tiki torches and more into magical environments. The Gazebo is, as the name suggests, outdoors and tailored for weddings—especially if your guest list is on the slightly longer side. This romantic spot has the same beachy endowments that the Pavilions possess, and its garden-style gazebo roofed in Spanish tile, ceremony lawn and white picket fence make it even more charming. A special parking lot nearby is convenient for food trucks, carriages, limos, fancy motorcycles, classic cars—and other playful party additions on wheels.

For events on a grand scale—giant weddings or fundraisers, super-sized corporate extravaganzas, and festivals—the Bayside Pavilion can accommodate happy guests by the hundreds. It's a 14,000-square-foot structure that's open-air for half the year and tented November to March (although you can add a tent during warmer months, too). Another option for parties numbering in the hundreds is the Marina Terrace, an expansive grass area on the other side of the lagoon. Both sites offer maximum flexibility for your multifaceted affair, and include plenty of room on the beach plus lagoon, harbor and Back Bay views.

Want to celebrate indoors? The attractive Bay View Room, which is perfect for more intimate events, features multiple sets of French doors that open to a lush garden and frame lovely views of the lagoon. For larger groups, the spectacular Back Bay Bistro is the place. An outdoor deck, a vast wall of windows that look out over the picturesque Back Bay and Marina, and a retractable roof make it a stunning space. It also provides private salons for cozier get-togethers, as well as a banquet menu that includes delicious and delightfully fresh American, Mediterranean, Hispanic, Asian and other fusions of favorite cuisines.

When the festivities are over, no need to leave. There's a host of comfy beach cottages and bungalows at the resort, and the Hyatt Newport Beach is right across the street. So stay and enjoy the destination, the activities, and the lifestyle that have made the region famous.

CEREMONY CAPACITY: The resort holds 650 seated guests outdoors.

EVENT/RECEPTION & MEETING CAPACITY: The resort accommodates 650 seated or 1,000 standing guests indoors and 450 seated or 800 standing outdoors.

FEES & DEPOSITS: A $1,000–5,000 deposit is required to reserve your date, and the balance is due 10 days prior to the event. Rental fees range $750–5,500 depending on the day of the event, the time of year and the space reserved. Meals range $50–135/person. Tax, alcohol and a 22% service charge are additional.

AVAILABILITY: Year-round, daily, 6am–10pm for outdoor venues or 6am–11pm for indoor venues.

SERVICES/AMENITIES:

Catering: in-house or BYO
Kitchen Facilities: not available to outside caterers
Tables & Chairs: provided
Linens, Silver, etc.: provided with in-house catering
Restrooms: wheelchair accessible
Dance Floor: portable provided with in-house catering
Bride's Dressing Area: CBA
AV/Meeting Equipment: CBA

Parking: large lot
Accommodations: 18 guest rooms
Outdoor Night Lighting: CBA
Outdoor Cooking Facilities: no
Cleanup: provided with in-house catering
View: panorama of waterfront, coastline, cityscape, marina and Newport Beach Nature Preserve
Other: event coordination, extra fee

RESTRICTIONS:

Alcohol: in-house
Smoking: designated areas only
Music: amplified OK with restrictions

Wheelchair Access: yes
Insurance: required for outside caterers

Radisson Hotel Newport Beach

Hotel

4545 MacArthur Boulevard, Newport Beach
949/608-1085
www.radisson.com/newportbeachca
lwade@radissonnewportbeach.com

● Rehearsal Dinners	● Corporate Events
● Ceremonies	● Meetings
● Wedding Receptions	● Film Shoots
● Private Parties	● Accommodations

Possibly the best-kept secret in this sophisticated coastal enclave, the Radisson Hotel Newport Beach offers upscale comfort without pretension or stuffiness. It's one of the top values in town, and it's just minutes from John Wayne Airport (a mere half-mile way), sunny beaches, renowned golf courses, and world-class shopping and culture.

With all its assets, the Radisson is popular for weddings, reunions, bar/ bat mitzvahs, quinceañeras and other special events. Brides enjoy the services of a certified wedding coordinator, who assists in planning every detail. Wedding packages also include a tasting session, so couples can sample the cuisine they want to serve at their reception and make sure it's to their liking. A duo of changing rooms for the bridal party, a complimentary honeymoon suite and free parking for guests are additional benefits that come with all bookings.

The hotel's spacious Garden Pavilion can be transformed into a magical setting for a wedding ceremony or reception, with elegant chiffon swags. A year-round venue with an indoor-outdoor feel, it's protected from the elements yet awash with natural light.

The Pacific Ballroom, one of the few in Orange County with windows, opens to the pool area. With its dark wood paneling and multiple crystal chandeliers and wall sconces on dimmer switches, it's an impressive stage for formal receptions. For smaller affairs, including rehearsal dinners and farewell brunches, the Palm Garden Room is a lovely space with a dance floor in its glassed-in "wine cellar" area.

Another option for a ceremony or reception is the vibrant Palm Court, a bright atrium which adjoins the Radisson's two mid-rise towers and features a bold tropical-themed mural. There's also the Newport Bay Room, a "junior ballroom" that opens to a private patio shielded by ferns and tall ficus trees.

After your guests depart, come "home" to a suite as large as many city apartments and outfitted with marble-topped counters, a giant plasma screen TV, and a Jacuzzi tub in one of two bathrooms. And while the Radisson can't guarantee sweet dreams, you'll probably have them once you curl up in your king-size bed, truly the perfect end to a perfect day.

CEREMONY CAPACITY: The site holds 500 seated guests indoors and 400 seated outdoors.

EVENT/RECEPTION CAPACITY: The hotel can accommodate 500 seated or 700 standing guests indoors, and 350 seated or 600 standing outdoors.

MEETING CAPACITY: Meeting spaces hold 600 seated guests.

FEES & DEPOSITS: 30% of the food & beverage minimum is required to reserve your date. A portion is due 90 days prior to the event, and the remainder is due 10 days prior. The rental fee ranges $850–3,500 depending on the ceremony location selected. Meals range $45–105/person. Tax and a 22% service charge are additional.

AVAILABILITY: Year-round, daily, 6am–midnight.

SERVICES/AMENITIES:

Catering: in-house, select from list or BYO
Kitchen Facilities: fully equipped
Tables & Chairs: provided
Linens, Silver, etc.: provided
Restrooms: wheelchair accessible
Dance Floor: provided
Bride's & Groom's Dressing Areas: yes
AV/Meeting Equipment: provided, CBA

Parking: large complimentary lot
Accommodations: 335 guest rooms & suites
Outdoor Night Lighting: provided
Outdoor Cooking Facilities: no
Cleanup: provided
View: fountain, garden, landscaped grounds, garden courtyard, pool area
Other: in-house wedding cake, clergy on staff, picnic area, complimentary suite for bride & groom, podium, risers, event coordination

RESTRICTIONS:

Alcohol: in-house or BYO wine w/corkage fee
Smoking: designated areas only
Music: amplified OK

Wheelchair Access: yes
Insurance: liability required

Beachcomber Cafe at Crystal Cove

Waterfront Restaurant

15 Crystal Cove, Newport Coast

949/644-8759

www.thebeachcombercafe.com
catering@thebeachcombercafe.com

- ● Rehearsal Dinners
- ● Ceremonies
- ● Wedding Receptions
- ● Private Parties
- ● Corporate Events
- ● Meetings
- ● Film Shoots
- ● Accommodations

Want to treat yourself and your guests to a quintessential Southern California "endless summer" experience? Well, raise the martini flag—as well as your expectations of a really great time—and invite them to an event staged right on the beach at historic Crystal Cove Park, one of the Newport coast's most celebrated sites. This is the place for the classic Southern California beach wedding or party at its best. We're talking anything from gowns and tuxedos to bikinis and board shorts—whatever you envision, it will look amazing with the foaming surf and the scintillating sun close at hand.

Run by *Beachcomber Catering,* experts in coastal entertaining, festivities here unfold in with energy and ease. There are adorable and affordable settings for every kind of affair. A host of tiny cottages and event sites dot the property, all offering varying degrees of privacy and communal activity.

The Beaches Cottage, with its sand-strewn terrace and white picket fence a mere 20 yards from the Pacific, is about as picturesque as you can get. This was the set for the Bette Midler movie, *Beaches,* as well as a long list of other films over the decades. Exchange vows on the inviting blanket of sand out front, then pop around the fence for cocktails, dinner, cake, and a big dose of charm.

The park-like Commons has cute and quirky surfside event areas, as well as marvelous ocean and creek views—Trancos Creek meets the sea here. Not far from the Commons, the Beach Promenade provides a gorgeous sandy stretch for a ceremony, cocktail hour and dining. Imagine a clambake…a luau…a fiesta with mariachis or a romantic tiki-lit banquet with the sea murmuring nearby. Wine tasting, food stations, cracked crab and buckets of ice-cold beer, lobster steamed to perfection, sushi platters, margaritas and mini-ahi tacos, surf and turf extravaganzas—your options are practically unlimited. The dedicated *Beachcomber Catering* team will turn your vision into reality by delivering excellent service, incorporating fresh local products, and customizing every aspect of your event.

Of course you might want to hang out above it all. If that's the case, plan to party up at the Cultural Center Cottage with its expansive deck—it's a heavenly perch designed with elegant entertaining in mind and overlooking exhilarating views of the ocean.

Whatever venue you ultimately choose, we're certain that when your celebration is over you (and some of your guests!) may not want to leave this seductive seaside location. No worries. Just slip off your sandals and stay awhile at one of the many cottages at your disposal. Then take a little time to unwind and explore the coast. You'll soon discover what's made Crystal Cove a popular destination since the 1930s, and why people who arrive as visitors soon turn into devoted fans.

CEREMONY & EVENT/RECEPTION CAPACITY: The site can accommodate up to 200 seated or standing guests outdoors.

MEETING CAPACITY: Meetings spaces hold up to 30 seated guests.

FEES & DEPOSITS: A $2,000 deposit is required to reserve your date, with your final guarantee and payment due 7 days prior to the event. The state site permit fee ranges $750–2,750 depending on the venue selected. Meals range $52–95/person. Tax, alcohol and a 22% service charge are additional. Note that off-premise catering is also available.

AVAILABILITY: Year-round, daily, 8am–9pm.

SERVICES/AMENITIES:

Catering: in-house, or BYO ethnic caterer with approval
Kitchen Facilities: fully equipped
Tables & Chairs: provided
Linens, Silver, etc.: provided
Restrooms: wheelchair accessible
Dance Area: provided
Bride's Dressing Area: yes
AV/Meeting Equipment: CBA

Parking: large lot
Accommodations: 24 cottages
Outdoor Night Lighting: CBA
Outdoor Cooking Facilities: BBQ on site
Cleanup: provided
View: Pacific Ocean
Other: in-house florals, off-premise catering

RESTRICTIONS:

Alcohol: full in-house bar
Smoking: designated areas only
Music: amplified OK outdoors with restrictions

Wheelchair Access: yes
Insurance: not required

This is important! Tell locations you're reading HERE COMES THE GUIDE and ask if our information is still current.

389

Wedgewood San Clemente

Banquet Center

150 East Avenida Magdalena, San Clemente
866/966-3009
www.wedgewoodbanquet.com
events@wedgewoodbanquet.com

- Rehearsal Dinners
- Ceremonies
- Wedding Receptions
- Private Parties
- Corporate Events
- Meetings
- Film Shoots
- Accommodations

Wedgewood San Clemente offers a relaxed, comfortable atmosphere less than a mile from the beach, and its brand new ceremony site boasts fairway vistas, ocean breezes and peeks of the Pacific. The property's California Spanish architecture and inviting reception area will no doubt appeal to brides, but they'll really appreciate all the extras that add value to this golf course venue.

Since the pre-wedding experience often sets the tone for the whole day, you'll be delighted to learn that there are a couple of nearby options at your disposal. A short walk away, the Hampton Inn and Suites has put aside a spacious room for your preparations. This arrangement is also convenient, since guests—and the bridal party!—often opt to stay here. Alternatively, you might choose to primp at an incredibly charming B&B adjacent to the greens. This intimate cottage has plenty of spots for you to pose for photos, too, such as a sitting room with French doors, a tiled staircase and a balcony. Right outside, the award-winning European gardens are an enchanting locale for capturing shots of that "first look" between you and your groom before you tie the knot.

Your guests, meanwhile, await your arrival on the club's ceremony lawn. Designed with both historic and modern touches, it features a curving walkway of traditional San Clemente tile that leads to a raised stage with clean-lined columns and a wood-beam canopy. A waterfall gently spills over rocks below the platform, and three soaring Eucalyptus trees frame the scene. This area is completely wired, so you can amplify any musical accompaniment and add lights in the evening.

From here it's just a short walk to the clubhouse for cocktails on the wide, stone-floored Patio that wraps around the building. In the main section of this space, multiple conversation group-ings with comfy seating and shade umbrellas, along with a brick fire pit, encourage mingling. From the rear of the Patio, you can catch nice sunset views off to the west. (Be sure to have your photographer snap some "magic hour" couple shots on the golf course, with the sun setting over the ocean behind you.)

When you're ready for dinner, two sets of French doors open to the Banquet Room. Spacious and airy, it showcases a beamed cathedral ceiling, lovely iron chandeliers and a soft, neutral palette. There's a built-in dance floor, and large windows that let in natural light during the day. If you're hosting a large group, you can double your space by folding back the dividing doors and accessing the adjoining Restaurant and bar. And, of course, the Patio is always available for savoring the cool, night air and starry sky.

At the end of the evening, your out-of-town friends and relatives will be happy to know that they can stay overnight within walking distance of this beautiful setting. Thanks to Wedgewood's affiliation with a local hotel, you and your guests will receive a discount on the guest rooms you book.

The staff at Wedgewood San Clemente go out of their way to make everything easy and convenient, with packages to suit virtually every couple and suggestions on how to personalize your celebration. They can also help you schedule a golf party or San Clemente tour to make your special event even more memorable.

CEREMONY, EVENT/RECEPTION & MEETING CAPACITY: The site holds up to 240 seated or standing guests.

FEES & DEPOSITS: 25% of the estimated total event cost is required to reserve your date. An additional 25% is due 120 days prior to the event and the balance (based on your final guest count) is due 10 days prior. All payments are credited towards your final balance and are nonrefundable and nontransferable. All-inclusive, completely customizable wedding packages start at $45/person. Tax, alcohol and a 21–22% service charge are additional.

AVAILABILITY: Year-round, daily, 7am–11:30pm.

SERVICES/AMENITIES:

Catering: in-house
Kitchen Facilities: n/a
Tables & Chairs: provided
Linens, Silver, etc.: provided
Restrooms: wheelchair accessible
Dance Floor: yes
Bride's Dressing Area: available nearby
AV/Meeting Equipment: some provided

Parking: large lot
Accommodations: no guest rooms
Outdoor Night Lighting: provided
Outdoor Cooking Facilities: none
Cleanup: provided
View: landscaped grounds; panorama of hills, coastline, ocean and fairways
Other: in-house wedding cake and florals; clergy on staff; event coordination

RESTRICTIONS:

Alcohol: in-house
Smoking: not allowed
Music: amplified OK

Wheelchair Access: yes
Insurance: not required
Other: no rice, confetti or glitter; no open flames

Marbella Country Club

Country Club

30800 Golf Club Drive, San Juan Capistrano
888/995-6224

www.countryclubreceptions.com
events@marbellacc.net

- Rehearsal Dinners
- Ceremonies
- Wedding Receptions
- Private Parties
- Corporate Events
- Meetings
- Film Shoots
- Accommodations

It may be nestled in the pastoral valley between the Pacific Ocean and the Saddleback Mountains, but the elegant Marbella Country Club embodies the spirit of the Mediterranean. Even if you're not jetting off to the coast of Italy for your honeymoon, you'll still get a taste of it when you celebrate your Big Day in this impressive setting.

After driving through the club's gated community, past manicured lawns and a flower-bed blooming with ivory roses, you reach the porte-cochère of the 50,000-square-foot clubhouse where valets await. Glittering like a baronial villa in the San Juan Capistrano sun, the majestic structure offers a genteel welcome with a tri-tier fountain ringed by palms and birds of paradise.

Upon arrival and during the cocktail hour, your guests will mingle in the handsome South Bar and around the fire pit of the spacious Valencia Terrace, enjoying mixed libations and delectable hors d'oeuvres.

Most couples say their vows on the Croquet Lawn, under a wrought-iron arch adorned with flowers and greenery that overlooks the championship golf course. Fragrant petals define a colorful aisle, where seating for up to 300 can be arranged. Although the bride and groom garner most of the attention, guests can't help but notice the border of roses and the stunning rock waterfall. Three stairways leading to this area provide numerous ways to choreograph your ceremony for sentimental impact. The club's genial Venue Coordinator will be there to assist with this and other details so you can relax, knowing your important day is in good hands.

After the knot is tied, Marbella's picturesque fairways and beautiful clubhouse architecture make spectacular backdrops for photos. While your photographer is capturing your first pictures as newlyweds, your guests stroll across the lawn to the Catalonia Terrace and luxuriously appointed Catalonia Grille for the reception. Here, they'll savor creative specialties prepared by the club's Certified Master Chef. If you like, place votive candles on the tables for a romantic touch.

From your sweetheart table you can watch your contented guests as they flow easily between the Catalonia Grille and the terrace through five sets of French doors. Après-dinner festivities continue on the dance floor, with a break for tossing your bouquet from one of the sweeping staircases to eager future brides gathered below.

When you have your wedding at the Marbella Country Club, it's the only event scheduled for the entire evening. So take your time and immerse yourself in the celebration, knowing it will be an unforgettable experience for all who attend.

CEREMONY CAPACITY: The Croquet Lawn holds up to 300 seated guests.

EVENT/RECEPTION CAPACITY: The Terrace holds up to 250 seated or 300 standing guests.

MEETING CAPACITY: Indoor spaces hold up to 190 seated guests.

FEES & DEPOSITS: A nonrefundable deposit, which is applied to your food & beverage total, is required to reserve your date. The amount of the deposit varies depending on how far in advance you book. Payment terms for the balance also vary, and may be arranged on an individual basis. Wedding packages range $60–150/person. Tax, alcohol and service charge are additional. Food & beverage minimums may apply. Menus and packages can be customized to fit your needs and budget. Call for details.

AVAILABILITY: Year-round, daily, 7am–midnight.

SERVICES/AMENITIES:

Catering: in-house or BYO with restrictions, food & beverage minimums still apply
Kitchen Facilities: n/a
Tables & Chairs: provided
Linens, Silver, etc.: provided
Restrooms: wheelchair accessible
Dance Floor: provided
Bride's Dressing Area: yes
AV/Meeting Equipment: provided

Parking: large lot, valet provided
Accommodations: no guest rooms
Outdoor Night Lighting: yes
Outdoor Cooking Facilities: BBQ
Cleanup: provided
View: fairways, garden, landscaped grounds
Other: event coordination, grand piano, ATM

RESTRICTIONS:

Alcohol: in-house or BYO wine with corkage fee
Smoking: outdoors only
Music: amplified OK indoors, and outdoors with restrictions

Wheelchair Access: limited
Insurance: not required

Plaza de Magdalena
A Catering and Event Venue by Sundried Tomato

Event Facility

- Rehearsal Dinners
- Corporate Events
- Ceremonies
- Meetings
- Wedding Receptions
- Film Shoots
- Private Parties
- Accommodations

31781 Camino Capistrano, Suite 101, San Juan Capistrano
949/661-1299

plazademagdalena.com
patti@sundriedtomatobistro.com

Strikingly contemporary and unquestionably legendary, the beautiful, newly designed Plaza de Magdalena brings all of the grace and elegance of its storied past right up into the present. It could not be more ideally situated: Located near San Juan Capistrano's landmark Los Rios district, virtually on the doorstep of the Mission San Juan Capistrano, it shares some of the history and much of the charm of its illustrious neighbor. Named after the young woman (Magdalena) in an ancient love story rumored to have transpired at the nearby mission, it stands on ground once occupied by the Valenzuela Adobe, a mission Indian structure which dates to the late 1700s, with possible links to their ancestors several thousand years before that.

You'll feel the magical vibe immediately as you descend via elevator or one of two gated staircases from the bustling street level into the cool surround of the open-air Magdalena Courtyard. The Spanish Mediterranean architecture and the privacy give it a grotto-like feel. Imagine cocktails and hors d'oeuvres amid the music of the waterfall fountain, perhaps the tinkle of ice, the clink of glassware, and the hum of conversations among happy guests. Sun-splashed by day, lantern-, chandelier-, or twinkle-lit by night—a ceremony and/or a reception of any kind here would be *muy romantico.*

Can't wait to see what else this venue has to offer? Step into the spacious, stylishly appointed Magdalena Room. The spotlight will be on you in this glamorous ballroom milieu. Created with an obvious understanding of what it takes to make special events shine, the room features state-of-the-art sound and lighting systems that include spots, cams, chandeliers, sconces, stage and laser light sources and graphics. For musicians and DJs (there's a private DJ booth), the setup and acoustics are positively stellar. Porcelain floors, a full complement of tall, multi-lite windows, and a stunning curved white travertine focal point wall play off the other pearl-colored surfaces and further brighten this luxurious chamber.

For celebrity-worthy seclusion, the bride and a good-sized entourage will find ample accommodation in the gorgeous champagne satin-accented bridal or VIP suite located inside the Magdalena Room. Larger groups of friends and family might prefer to relax in the Teofilo Room on the other side of the courtyard. Designed with slightly more masculine comforts in mind, furnishings in this space include leather club chairs and couches, flat screen TVs, a foosball table and more. Use it during a courtyard or ballroom function for upscale vendor staging, speaker prep, a groom's room or a childcare area. Or book it all by itself for smaller gatherings such as group dinners, poker parties, and corporate meetings.

Whatever venue you choose at Plaza de Magdalena, it'll be done in fabulous taste. And speaking of taste, did we mention that this entire complex was completely re-imagined and specially configured by *Sundried Tomato American Bistros & Catering,* a company well-known for delivering experiences you can relish at every level? Delectable food and an exceptional setting—you won't go wrong booking here. So make your own story in this place of legend and lore. From first sight to last bite, we know it's one you'll savor for years to come.

CEREMONY CAPACITY: The site holds 150 seated guests indoors, and 100 seated outdoors.

EVENT/RECEPTION CAPACITY: The facility can accommodate 200 seated or 229 standing guests indoors, and 70 seated or 100 standing outdoors.

MEETING CAPACITY: Meeting spaces hold 229 seated guests.

FEES & DEPOSITS: 20% of the estimated event total (nonrefundable) and a refundable $1,000 security deposit are required to reserve your date. An additional 30% (nonrefundable) is due 60 days prior to the event, and the balance is due 10 days prior. The ceremony rental fee starts at $300 and varies depending on the day and time. Meals start at $44/person. Wedding packages start at $100/person. Tax, alcohol and a 20% service charge are additional.

Rates for business functions, meetings or other types of events vary. Please contact the venue for more details.

AVAILABILITY: Year-round, daily, 6am–midnight.

SERVICES/AMENITIES:

Catering: in-house
Kitchen Facilities: limited
Tables & Chairs: provided
Linens, Silver, etc.: provided
Restrooms: wheelchair accessible
Dance Floor: portable provided
Bride's & Groom's Dressing Areas: yes
AV/Meeting Equipment: provided, extra fee

Parking: valet available, garage or lot nearby
Accommodations: no guest rooms
Outdoor Night Lighting: yes
Outdoor Cooking Facilities: BBQ CBA
Cleanup: provided
View: landscaped grounds, waterfall
Other: vendor staging area; event coordination available, extra fee

RESTRICTIONS:

Alcohol: in-house
Smoking: not allowed
Music: amplified OK with restrictions

Wheelchair Access: yes
Insurance: not required

The Hacienda

1725 College Avenue, Santa Ana
714/558-1304
www.the-hacienda.com
weddings@the-hacienda.com

- Rehearsal Dinners
- Ceremonies
- Wedding Receptions
- Private Parties

- Corporate Events
- Meetings
- Film Shoots

Accommodations

As soon as you walk through the front gates of The Hacienda, you travel back in time to a more peaceful and romantic era. Once part of an orange and avocado ranch from the early 1900s, this whitewashed adobe and its charming courtyard is now one of Orange County's most popular wedding locations.

Two settings are available for both ceremonies and receptions. If you'd like to celebrate outdoors, the flagstone courtyard is ideal. Ivy-covered balconies, an abundance of potted flowers, and a three-tiered fountain in the center give the space an Old World atmosphere. Off to one side is a wooden arbor, hung with stained-glass panels and entwined with vines, that serves as an altar for ceremonies. When a couple exchanges vows here, candelabras provide old-fashioned warmth and sparkle. For courtyard weddings, the bride's dressing room is the old master bedroom in the main hacienda, appointed with antiques and giant mirrors. From here she can step out onto her balcony to survey her guests below.

Indoor events are hosted in the Taos Room, a beautiful ballroom in the building adjacent to the main hacienda. It has a Southwest flavor, with its 200-year-old decorative doors carved from Mexican mesquite wood, oversized fireplace, antiques and original artwork. A 20-foot ceiling with skylights and a row of French doors that open to the courtyard provide natural light. At the far end, a flight of Spanish tile stairs—perfect for making a grand entrance—leads up to the bride's dressing room. Large mirrors, lots of space, and roses stenciled above the doors and windows make brides feel quite comfortable.

The Hacienda, like its sister properties Tivoli Too and Tivoli Terrace, is owned by June Neptune, an experienced wedding maven with a bride-friendly philosophy. "Weddings should be stress-free and fun," she says. Her all-inclusive packages really simplify the planning process, covering everything from floral decorations and live music for the ceremony, to appetizers, drinks, dinner and even the wedding cake. Another built-in benefit is assistance from June's staff of wedding co-ordinators, who will help you plan your event and make sure it comes off just as you envisioned it.

CEREMONY CAPACITY: The Taos Courtyard holds 220 seated, 300 if combined with the Taos Room. The Inner Courtyard accommodates up to 140 seated guests.

EVENT/RECEPTION CAPACITY: The Hacienda holds 500 guests, maximum.

MEETING CAPACITY: Event spaces accommodate 30–500 seated guests.

FEES & DEPOSITS: For weddings, a nonrefundable $2,000 deposit is required to reserve your date and is applied toward the event balance. Half the estimated total along with a $500 security deposit is payable 90 days prior to the event, and the balance is due 2 weeks prior. Wedding packages include live music, cake, fresh flowers, tables and chairs, linens, food service, passed hors d'oeuvres, unlimited beer, wine and champagne. A 20% service charge and tax are additional. The Brunch Package starts at $60/person. Afternoon/Evening Packages start at $75/person for Fridays, Saturdays and Sundays.

For meetings, a $200 deposit or 10% of the estimated event total is required to reserve your date; the balance is payable 2 weeks prior to the event. Business breakfasts run $15–20/person, luncheons $20–40/person and dinners $28–110/person; tax, beverages and service charges are additional.

AVAILABILITY: Year-round, daily, until midnight.

SERVICES/AMENITIES:

Catering: in-house, no BYO

Kitchen Facilities: n/a

Tables & Chairs: provided

Linens, Silver, etc.: provided

Restrooms: wheelchair accessible

Dance Floor: flagstone patio

Bride's & Groom's Dressing Areas: yes

AV/Meeting Equipment: podium, PA system, microphones; other CBA

Parking: several lots nearby

Accommodations: no guest rooms

Outdoor Night Lighting: yes

Outdoor Cooking Facilities: no

Cleanup: provided

View: garden, fountains and courtyard

Other: event coordination

RESTRICTIONS:

Alcohol: in-house, no BYO

Smoking: designated areas only

Music: amplified OK

Wheelchair Access: yes

Insurance: not required

Other: no rice, birdseed or confetti; children must be supervised

Overwhelmed? Use the search criteria on www.HereComesTheGuide.com to narrow down your choices.

397

Heritage Museum of Orange County

Museum and Garden

3101 West Harvard Street, Santa Ana

714/540-0404 X223

www.heritagemuseumoc.org
weddings@heritagemuseumoc.org

Rehearsal Dinners		●	Corporate Events
●	Ceremonies	●	Meetings
●	Wedding Receptions	●	Film Shoots
●	Private Parties		Accommodations

The heart of this museum is the old H. Clay Kellogg House, a lovingly restored 1898 Victorian that sits amid 10 acres of historic gardens and turn-of-the-century buildings. Created to preserve Orange County's cultural heritage, the museum takes you back to the early 1900s: While you're ambling along its jasmine-covered walkways, or through its orange groves and rose garden, you'll think you've stepped back in time onto a country estate. The great thing about weddings here is that all the local businesses close for the weekend, and you can have a rock 'n' roll band without disturbing a soul.

The Heritage Museum of Orange County has recreated a gracious past, and weddings are often inspired by the setting's peaceful Victorian ambiance. Although you can't host your wedding inside, a stroll around the Kellogg House—outfitted with the utmost in Victoriana—is enough to set the mood. The spacious lawns lend themselves to a number of possibilities for parties and receptions, and the gazebo is popular for ceremonies.

The flexible and experienced Heritage Museum staff are happy to accommodate your special needs in every way they can. All proceeds from weddings and receptions go to support the museum's nonprofit programs, which provide "hands-on" historical enrichment for visitors. A portion of the proceeds are also tax deductible. Not only is the Heritage Museum a lovely place to host your wedding, you'll have the satisfaction of benefiting a wonderful cultural resource.

CEREMONY CAPACITY: The Gazebo Lawn and the front of the Kellogg House hold a maximum of 300 guests.

EVENT/RECEPTION CAPACITY: The Rose Garden Lawn holds 400 seated guests or 600 standing; a shaded pavilion holds 150 seated.

MEETING CAPACITY: The shaded pavilion holds 150 seated conference-style or 300 theater-style. The meeting room seats 20 conference-style or 40 theater-style. Audiovisual equipment is not provided by the museum, but can be arranged at an extra charge with advance notice.

FEES & DEPOSITS: A nonrefundable but tax-deductible $1,500 deposit is required to reserve your date; the estimated event total is due 90 days prior to the event. A portion of the proceeds are also tax-deductible. Rental fees start at $850 and vary according to the season and the day of the week. In addition, there is a refundable $1,500 cleaning and damage deposit. Couples have the option to select one of their two exclusive caterers, *Country Garden Caterers* or *Zov's*. Meals start at $41/person. Tax, alcohol and service charge are additional.

AVAILABILITY: Year-round, Monday–Thursday, 4pm–10pm; Friday and Saturday, 10am–midnight; Sunday, 10am–10pm.

SERVICES/AMENITIES:

Catering: provided by two exclusive caterers, *Country Garden Caterers* and *Zov's*
Kitchen Facilities: n/a
Tables & Chairs: through exclusive vendor
Linens, Silver, etc.: through caterer
Restrooms: wheelchair accessible
Dance Floor: patio
Bride's Dressing Area: yes
AV/Meeting Equipment: BYO

Parking: ample free
Accommodations: no guest rooms
Outdoor Night Lighting: yes
Outdoor Cooking Facilities: no
Cleanup: caterer or renter
View: rose garden, fountain, citrus grove, gazebo

RESTRICTIONS:

Alcohol: provided by two exclusive caterers, *Country Garden Caterers* and *Zov's*
Smoking: designated areas only
Music: amplified OK

Wheelchair Access: yes
Insurance: certificate required through WedSafe
Other: no rice, birdseed, synthetic rose petals or confetti; no nails, tacks, staples, glue or tape; no sparklers or other pyrotechnics; restrictions on open flames

Old Ranch Country Club

Country Club

3901 Lampson Avenue, Seal Beach
562/596-4425

www.oldranch.com/weddings
kmesinas@oldranch.com

- Rehearsal Dinners
- Ceremonies
- Wedding Receptions
- Private Parties
- Corporate Events
- Meetings
- Film Shoots
- Accommodations

The Old Ranch Country Club enjoys a reputation for being a place that's easy to get to and easy to work with. With its rambling, comfortable clubhouse, it's also a place where guests feel right at home. Situated at the northern edge of Orange County, Old Ranch is within a short drive to three airports and several major freeways, making it convenient for local or out-of-state travelers en route to your celebration. And once they arrive, they'll be able to stay at the congenial Ayres Suites Hotel located just across the street. The club offers all-inclusive packages, a wide range of menu selections featuring the best of traditional and California cuisine, and special items to make the kids happy. With its dedicated event staff, including multiple on-site wedding coordinators, the club will ensure that your event is joyous and trouble free.

Although Old Ranch has been a members-only venue since its inception in 1967, their banquet facilities are available to nonmembers for special events. As you enter, you're greeted by a huge mural of blue skies, trees and rolling hills—a tableau that mimics the club's pastoral surroundings. Framed by a stone arch, it provides a dramatic backdrop for photos, as well as a conversation piece for guests socializing here before heading into the spacious reception salon.

Once you're in the salon, prepare to be delighted by what you see. A wall of floor-to-ceiling Nana windows open like an accordion to an outdoor terrace with an expansive view of the golf course and lake, complete with a fountain that's lit up at night. This modern 6,000-square-foot banquet space is large enough to accommodate both a wedding and reception. However, it's also divisible into four sections that can be used individually or in combination, depending on the size of your event. Coffered ceilings edged with dark wood beams; potted ficus trees at the corners; and an abstract patterned carpet give the room a contemporary ambiance. In the evening, craftsman-style ceiling lamps cast a soft glow. With its casual-yet-refined sensibility, the club atmosphere invites guests to relax with a glass of chilled Chardonnay as they drink in the landscape. Speaking of the landscape, there are a number of photogenic spots overlooking the fairways for some before- or after-ceremony pictures.

Perhaps the club's most popular area is its gorgeous bridal courtyard, designed especially for outdoor ceremonies. Ringed by flowers, palm trees and other greenery, it has a lush, almost tropical feel. The bride walks down a stone pathway to exchange vows with her groom beneath a lovely Romanesque gazebo. As friends and family look on from their lawn seating, they have a breathtaking view of the lake and golf course in the background.

Old Ranch is not only conveniently located for your special event, it's also only a short drive to the beach for some fun in the California sun. The beach we're referring to is Seal Beach, a haven for those in search of a laid-back, small town atmosphere. Replete with suntanned surfers, a treelined Main Street and a colorful past, the town is packed with seaside delights and history. Between this appealing country club and its friendly coastal neighbor, you'll find all the elements you need for a wonderful weekend wedding.

CEREMONY CAPACITY: Indoors, the club holds up to 300 seated guests. The Bridal Courtyard seats up to 450.

EVENT/RECEPTION & MEETING CAPACITY: The Salon holds up to 400 seated or 500 standing guests. This room can be split into four smaller rooms, each holding 90 seated or 120 standing.

FEES & DEPOSITS: A $4,000 booking fee is required to reserve your date. The balance is due 10 business days prior to the event. All-inclusive wedding packages range $70–165/person. Tax and service charge are extra. An additional ceremony setup fee includes a rehearsal with the wedding coordinator, 1-hour ceremony time and use of a bridal room.

AVAILABILITY: Year-round: Monday–Thursday, 6am–11:30pm; Friday–Sunday, 6am–midnight; extra hours may be available.

SERVICES/AMENITIES:
Catering: in-house
Kitchen Facilities: n/a
Tables & Chairs: provided
Linens, Silver, etc.: provided
Restrooms: wheelchair accessible
Dance Floor: provided
Bride's Dressing Area: yes
AV/Meeting Equipment: CBA, extra charge
Other: on-site event coordination

Parking: large lighted lot
Accommodations: no guest rooms, hotel across the street and local hotels will shuttle
Outdoor Night Lighting: yes, with lighted fountain
Outdoor Cooking Facilities: no
Cleanup: provided
View: golf course, lake, fountain, distant mountains

RESTRICTIONS:
Alcohol: in-house, or BYO wine with corkage fee
Smoking: outside only
Music: amplified OK

Wheelchair Access: yes
Insurance: provided

Rancho Las Lomas

19191 Lawrence Canyon, Silverado
949/888-3080

www.rancholaslomas.com
info@rancholaslomas.com

Banquet Facility and Garden

- Rehearsal Dinners
- Ceremonies
- Wedding Receptions
- Private Parties
- Corporate Events
- Meetings
- Film Shoots
- Accommodations

Nestled among the rolling hills of South Orange County, the 32-acre Rancho Las Lomas is a testimony to the charms of early California. Surrounded by orange groves and flowering shrubs, the hacienda-style buildings of the ranch sit under the cooling shade of towering oak and sycamore trees, and are connected by terracotta walkways and bridges. Guests can take enchanted strolls through the grounds—redolent of orange blossoms and lush with botanical garden-quality flora—and peek into the large ornamental birdcages that house a collection of rare tropical birds and exotic animals.

On a plateau at the top of a gentle slope is the Grand Salon, a spacious light-filled room with a big stone fireplace as its stunning centerpiece. The combination of white stucco walls, beamed ceiling, terracotta floor and wood-framed windows makes the Salon ideal for all types of gatherings. And with the adjoining patio, adorned with a sparkling blue-tile reflecting pool, you can easily have an indoor/outdoor reception.

Smaller affairs are often held in Rick's Cafe, a four-level Casablanca-style villa built into the hillside just beyond the Grand Salon patio. An oak bar, a rough-hewn beamed ceiling, stone fireplace, and an eclectic mix of Victorian antiques in its many inviting conversation nooks, create an intimate atmosphere for parties.

The venue's newest space is La Terraza, an open-air cobblestone terrace bordered by California Oaks and native cactus. Large enough for hosting weddings, concerts, gala fundraisers, and corporate retreats, it's the perfect place for dining under the stars. It's also a charming spot for saying "I do": Here, the bride begins her grand entrance at the top of a hill, descending a wide, rustic wood staircase until she reaches her guests seated below. When glowing candles are placed on the stairs, the scene is positively romantic.

Wedding ceremonies also take place in the Teatro, an open-air theater with a marble stage, stone patio and bubbling fountains. The cozy Casa Bonita next door, which has full-length mirrors plus a makeup area and parlor with fireplace, is one of the loveliest bride's dressing rooms we've seen.

Everything at Rancho Las Lomas has been carefully conceived and realized, from its blossoming foliage to the abundance of hand-painted tile. If you're looking for a simply sensational setting, this is it.

CEREMONY CAPACITY: The Teatro/Chapel seats 400 guests; La Terraza seats 375.

EVENT/RECEPTION CAPACITY: Outdoor areas accommodate up to 500 guests. Indoors, the facility holds up to 220 seated or 300–500 standing for a cocktail reception.

MEETING CAPACITY: The Grand Salon holds 300 guests seated theater-style.

FEES & DEPOSITS: The nonrefundable rental fee ranges $2,500–8,500. The fee includes use of both indoor and outdoor facilities for a specific time frame. All-inclusive wedding packages start at $175/person.

Off-season and weekday rates range $2,500–6,000; call for more information

AVAILABILITY: Year-round, daily, 9am–midnight.

SERVICES/AMENITIES:
Catering: in-house
Kitchen Facilities: n/a
Tables & Chairs: provided, additional fee
Linens, Silver, etc.: through caterer
Restrooms: wheelchair accessible
Dance Floor: provided, additional fee
Bride's & Groom's Dressing Areas: yes
AV/Meeting Equipment: provided, additional fee

Parking: valet required
Accommodations: 3 on-site villas available for rental
Outdoor Night Lighting: provided
Outdoor Cooking Facilities: n/a
Cleanup: caterer
View: 100-year-old sequoias, rose gardens, Cleveland National Forest

RESTRICTIONS:
Alcohol: in-house, no BYO
Smoking: allowed in designated areas
Music: amplified OK with restrictions; indoors until midnight, outdoors curfew 10pm

Wheelchair Access: yes
Insurance: may be required
Other: no rice or confetti

Black Gold Golf Club

Golf Club

1 Black Gold Drive, Yorba Linda
714/961-0253 X107

www.blackgoldgolf.com
emahler@blackgoldgolf.com

● Rehearsal Dinners	● Corporate Events	
● Ceremonies	● Meetings	
● Wedding Receptions	Film Shoots	
● Private Parties	Accommodations	

Tucked away in the quiet foothills of Yorba Linda, Black Gold Golf Club occupies a spot that showcases the best views in Orange County: gently sloping mountains to the east, the wide valley floor spread out below, and the sparkling Pacific beyond. On a clear day, (which is nearly every day—this is The OC, after all), you can even see Catalina Island in the distance.

The entire venue has been designed with entertaining in mind, from the 20,000-square-foot Craftsman-inspired clubhouse to the secluded, charming ceremony site. Meticulously manicured fairways (this place is consistently voted one of Southern California's best public courses) are dotted with gorgeous lakes and creeks, setting the scene for beautiful photos. Your guests are sure to appreciate the convenient, plentiful parking and proximity to a wide range of accommodations.

Ceremonies are held at The Falls, a completely private area next to a cascading waterfall and surrounded by spectacular vistas in every direction. Vows are spoken under a pretty white arbor, which can be draped with flowers or hung with lights, fabric, lanterns—whatever accents you choose to complement your theme.

With floor-to-ceiling windows that look out over the lush 18th green, the clubhouse's Lakeview and Valleyview Rooms can serve as intimate reception halls on their own, but may also be combined to create one grand space for larger, more lavish affairs. During the cocktail hour, your guests can mingle on the adjoining patio and enjoy watching you cruise around below in a golf cart, posing for photos on the course as the sun begins to set behind the twinkling lights of the valley.

If you're working within a tight budget, (and let's face it, who isn't?), you'll be very pleased with the value you'll receive at Black Gold. Not only is it one of Orange County's most affordable all-inclusive venues, they're also happy to customize packages to your specific needs. So if you decide there's something you really want—a round of golf, custom uplighting, an extra passed hors d'oeuvre—they'll gladly add it. Plus, they're equally willing to remove other elements, adjusting your overall costs to reflect the changes.

Couples love the personalized attention they get from the staff here, who are quick to respond to questions and are known for going "above and beyond" what's expected. They're seasoned pros, and will walk you through the planning process with reassuring ease. Most importantly, they'll be present on the wedding day to act as vendor liaisons, coordinate the timing of events, and take care of last-minute needs. All you and your partner will need to do is show up, say "I do," and have the time of your lives.

CEREMONY CAPACITY: The site holds 250 seated guests indoors or outdoors.

EVENT/RECEPTION CAPACITY: The site holds 218 seated or 300 standing indoors, and 400 seated or 500 standing outdoors.

MEETING CAPACITY: Meeting spaces accommodate 250 seated guests.

FEES & DEPOSITS: A $1,500 deposit is required to reserve your date and the balance is due 10 days prior to the event. Wedding packages range $65–120/person. Tax and a 20% service charge are additional.

AVAILABILITY: Year-round, daily.

SERVICES/AMENITIES:

Catering: in-house or BYO
Kitchen Facilities: fully equipped
Tables & Chairs: provided
Linens, Silver, etc.: provided
Restrooms: wheelchair accessible
Dance Floor: portable provided
Bride's Dressing Area: yes
AV/Meeting Equipment: provided
Other: event coordination, in-house wedding cake, complimentary golf

Parking: large lot
Accommodations: no guest rooms
Outdoor Night Lighting: yes
Outdoor Cooking Facilities: yes
Cleanup: provided
View: fountain, landscaped grounds, lake, cityscape; panorama of waterfalls, canyon, hills and fairways

RESTRICTIONS:

Alcohol: in-house
Smoking: outdoors only
Music: amplified OK

Wheelchair Access: yes
Insurance: not required

The wedding vendors on our website are the best in the business. How do we know? Read page 577.

Mountain Lakes Area

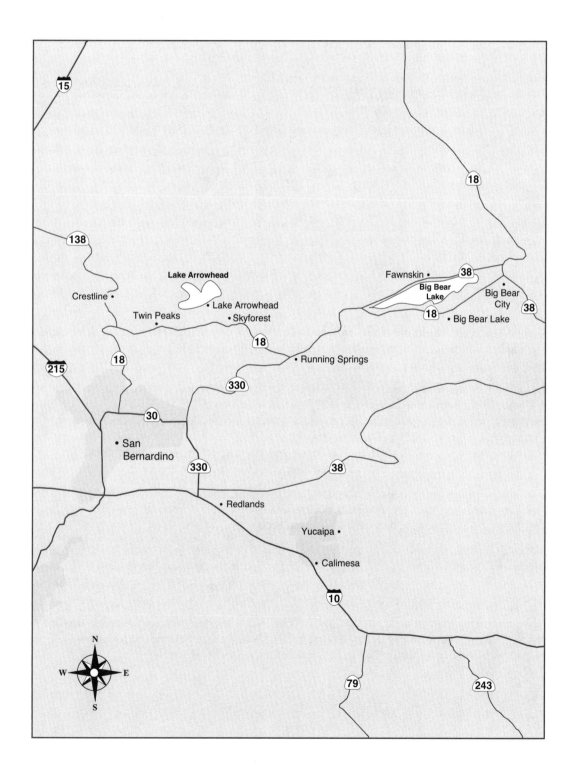

San Moritz Lodge

24640 San Moritz Drive, Crestline
909/900-5724
www.lakegregoryrecreation.com/weddings
events@lakegregoryrecreation.com

Garden & Event Center

- Rehearsal Dinners
- Ceremonies
- Wedding Receptions
- Private Parties
- Corporate Events
- Meetings
- Film Shoots
- Accommodations

Sitting pretty next to Lake Gregory and its cool green cedar and pine forest is San Moritz Lodge, a grand chalet whose alpine setting adds a fairy-tale quality to weddings and other special events. A 30-minute trip up Highway 18—one of the most scenic roads in the United States—takes you here, and if you arrive in the summer you'll enjoy cooler temperatures than in the Inland Empire.

Ceremonies at San Moritz are often held on the Ceremony Lawn in front of the Lodge. The slightly sloping lawn faces Lake Gregory and is edged by tall conifers, including a perfectly formed cedar that soars 125 feet.

Indoors, there are two ceremony/reception sites. The Lakeview Room feels like a mountain lodge, with its 35-foot-high cathedral ceiling and flagstone-faced fireplace. Fifteen-foot high windows running along the patio side afford an expansive outdoor view. The cozier Fireside Room has a bar and, of course, a fireplace. For a small fee the San Moritz staff will set up and maintain a fire during your festivities. If desired, the Lakeview and Fireside Rooms may be combined for large weddings and events, and a portable dance floor can be set up in either room.

The shaded patio area outside the Lakeview Room is popular for pre- or post-ceremony cocktails and hors d'oeuvres. As guests mingle beneath the broad wooden colonnade, they can breathe in the fresh air and appreciate their beautiful surroundings.

Although San Moritz Lodge is located on the grounds of a public park, it's isolated and offers plenty of privacy for your event and guests. The Lodge is lovely as is, but you're free to bring in a decorator and use your own creativity. Their wedding packages and professional Wedding Coordinator will make planning your dream wedding a breeze.

There is nothing quite as romantic and picturesque as a panoramic view of the mountains and a forest of tall trees around a sparkling mountain lake. When you get married at San Moritz Lodge, you can seal your vows with a kiss in the midst of nature's wonderland.

CEREMONY, EVENT/RECEPTION & MEETING CAPACITY: The Fireside Room holds 150 seated guests, and the Lakeview Room seats 250. For outdoor events, San Moritz Lodge accommodates up to 250 guests (seated or standing). All spaces are available for ceremonies, receptions, or other kinds of special events.

FEES & DEPOSITS: The site rental fee is required to reserve your date, and the balance is due 30 days prior to the event. The site rental fee starts at $4,500. Catering packages range $24–49/person. Beverage packages range $15–25/person. Tax and a 20% service charge are additional.

AVAILABILITY: Year-round, daily, 7am–midnight.

SERVICES/AMENITIES:

Catering: in-house
Kitchen Facilities: n/a
Tables & Chairs: provided
Linens, Silver, etc.: provided
Restrooms: wheelchair accessible
Dance Floor: portable provided
Bride's & Groom's Dressing Areas: yes
AV/Meeting Equipment: some provided

Parking: large lot
Accommodations: no guest rooms
Outdoor Night Lighting: access only
Outdoor Cooking Facilities: no
Cleanup: provided
View: forest, fountain, lake, mountains

RESTRICTIONS:

Alcohol: in-house
Smoking: designated area only
Music: amplified OK with restrictions

Wheelchair Access: limited
Insurance: liability provided

Lake Arrowhead Resort & Spa
An Autograph Collection by Marriott

Resort Hotel

27984 Highway 189, Lake Arrowhead
909/744-3020
www.lakearrowheadresort.com
weddings@lakearrowheadresort.com

- Rehearsal Dinners
- Ceremonies
- Wedding Receptions
- Private Parties
- Corporate Events
- Meetings
- Film Shoots
- Accommodations

The picturesque lake region high up in the richly forested San Bernardino Mountains is a favorite Southland destination, attracting skiers, boaters, nature lovers, and engaged couples longing to tie the knot amid unspoiled surroundings. The premier venue for year-round weddings and social events in this scenic landscape is the Lake Arrowhead Resort and Spa. Full-service and pet-friendly, the AAA Four Diamond Resort occupies a prime location along the lakeshore. What's more, it has numerous possibilities for large and small celebrations that showcase the area's seasonal charms.

The wood deck in the resort's Lakeside Lawn is a spectacular spot to exchange vows, especially in the springtime when butterflies, songbirds, and blooming foliage are sweet accompaniments. Towering pines flank each side of the deck, and the blue water and tree-covered mountains form a panoramic backdrop. The adjacent diamond-shaped lawn can be set theater-style for the ceremony or used for receptions. In the summer, why not stage casual festivities right on the resort's private beach, and maybe even say "I do" with the warm sand between your toes? A favorite choice for indoor affairs, especially during winter months, is the Lake Arrowhead Ballroom, whose grandeur and well-appointed detailing make for a stunning reception. Another option is the Lakeview Terrace Room, furnished with warm tones and picture windows that frame a scintillating winterscape or the burnished autumn scenery. Glass doors open out to a terrace, so your guests can enjoy an up-close vista of the shimmering lake and savor the crisp mountain air.

The Lake Arrowhead Resort can host weddings and receptions for 30 to 300 guests, and has plenty of upscale guest accommodations, too: 162 ultra-contemporary, lodge-style rooms and 11 luxurious suites with balconies or patios. Newlyweds can wallow in romance in a spacious Lakeview Suite, outfitted with a fireplace, plush bed linens and an oversize soaking tub (candlelight optional). But what makes the resort unique to the area is its staff's ability to provide full-service coordination and catering for large gatherings. Smaller parties here are no less special: Day-after brunches or rehearsal dinners convene in the resort's fine dining restaurant, BIN189. The refined, yet relaxed, ambiance—replete with water views, a top-flight wine list and acclaimed gourmet menus—ensures a sense of occasion. The Magnum, a cozy private dining room enclosed by glass walls lined with wine bottles, is a sophisticated choice for intimate get-togethers.

Whether you've come to the resort for your wedding, honeymoon, or to relive the memories on your anniversary, be sure to experience the Spa of the Pines. With certified practitioners and nature-inspired treatments, the spa offers supreme nurturing and indulgence.

If you've got a long guest list and a penchant for the pristine alpine environment of Lake Arrowhead, look no further.

CEREMONY CAPACITY: The Lakeside Lawn holds 300 seated. Indoor ceremonies take place in various banquet rooms that can seat 30–300.

EVENT/RECEPTION CAPACITY: Indoor areas accommodate 150–300 seated or up to 450 standing. Outdoor seating ranges 80–300.

MEETING CAPACITY: Several spaces seat 16–450 guests.

FEES & DEPOSITS: For weddings, a nonrefundable deposit of 25% of the estimated event total is due with your signed contract. An additional 50% is payable 3 months prior to the event; and the balance is due 14 days prior. Rental fees are discounted on non-holiday Sundays and Fridays. The fee for the Lakeside Lawn area includes white chairs, a carpet aisle runner and choice of wedding arch or arbor.

Wedding packages start at $55/person for luncheons or $70/person for dinner and include: champagne and sparkling cider toast, butler-passed hors d'oeuvres (included with dinner package), 3-course meal and wedding cake. Taxes and service charges are additional. A complimentary guest room for the bride and groom is provided with more than 50 guests, and group discounts for overnight wedding guests can be arranged.

For meetings or other business functions, prices vary depending on room, guest count and services selected; call for more specific information. An on-site audiovisual company can accommodate most AV needs.

AVAILABILITY: Year-round, daily.

SERVICES/AMENITIES:

Catering: in-house, no BYO
Kitchen Facilities: n/a
Tables & Chairs: provided
Linens, Silver, etc.: provided
Restrooms: wheelchair accessible
Dance Floor: provided
Bride's Dressing Area: yes
AV/Meeting Equipment: full range

Parking: ample on-site or valet
Accommodations: 173 guest rooms
Outdoor Night Lighting: some, more CBA
Outdoor Cooking Facilities: BBQs CBA
Cleanup: provided
View: lake, mountains and pine trees
Other: health spa, event coordination on-site restaurant BIN189

RESTRICTIONS:

Alcohol: in-house, no BYO
Smoking: designated areas only
Music: moderately amplified OK indoors until 1am, outdoors until 9pm

Wheelchair Access: yes
Insurance: not required
Other: no rice, birdseed or confetti

Pine Rose Weddings and Cabin Resort

Resort

25994 State Highway 189, Lake Arrowhead

909/337-2341

www.pineroseweddings.com
events@pinerosecabins.com

● Rehearsal Dinners	● Corporate Events
● Ceremonies	● Meetings
● Wedding Receptions	● Film Shoots
● Private Parties	● Accommodations

Nature lovers and city slickers alike will easily succumb to the charms of Pine Rose Resort. Less than two hours from most So Cal cities, this mile-high country "getaway" near Lake Arrowhead offers six scenic mountain acres with clean, pine-scented air. The woodland setting also provides ceremony and reception sites, lodging for your guests, and a friendly staff—everything you'll need for a wonderful wedding.

While it's pretty hard to improve on Mother Nature, the resort has done exactly that with two magical wedding sites that take full advantage of the property's rustic beauty. The Cedar Creek Pond area, amidst towering evergreens, works well for intimate affairs for up to 40. If you tie the knot here, your guests gather in a cedar-covered area on semicircular rows of smooth log benches. As they await your arrival, you make your entrance via a bridge that crosses a meandering stream, then continue down a flagstone path to the gazebo stage topped with a dramatic, log-and-branch dome. Just beyond the gazebo is a sparkling pond strewn with lily pads and teeming with colorful koi. Enhanced by romantic bridges, boulders and a vintage swing, it's a photographer's delight, presenting lots of choice backdrops.

For larger groups, there's the fabulous Hidden Creek Lodge, built by the owners for their daughter's wedding. This multi-tiered site has a stream running down one side and a serene pond at the base. Cut into the natural slope of the land, its amphitheater-like design affords stadium seating with great vistas and even greater acoustics.

At this venue, the ceremony starts with your walk down the aisle under a log trellis, past all your friends and family seated on several levels of decks. You'll exchange vows at the gazebo altar, which is artistically crowned with an organic weaving of branches shed from an old oak tree. Cocktails and dinner follow on three levels of expansive wooden decks adjacent to the lodge. Covered with a wisteria-entwined log arbor, they give everyone unobstructed views of the huge dance floor, festooned with twinkle lights that reflect off the neighboring stream and illuminated waterfall.

Hidden Creek Lodge has five bedrooms, making it perfect for post-wedding family sleepovers as well as pre-wedding preparations with the bridesmaids upstairs and a first-floor game room that's always a hit with the groomsmen. The bride and groom may want to rent the Rustic Romance

Cottage, an ideal honeymoon suite with a stone fireplace and extra-large Jacuzzi tub. Other cabins in the vicinity are also available.

An advantage of hosting a destination wedding at Pine Rose is that they make it so easy for you. With collections created for a range of budgets (and the option of a payment plan), a selection of screened local vendors to choose from, and menu tastings, you'll have a stress-free experience in this fairy-tale place in the woods.

CEREMONY CAPACITY: The site holds 40 seated guests indoors and 175 seated outdoors.

EVENT/RECEPTION CAPACITY: The resort can accommodate 35 seated or 50 standing guests indoors and 175 seated or standing outdoors.

MEETING CAPACITY: Meeting spaces seat up to 40 guests indoors and 175 outdoors.

FEES & DEPOSITS: *Hidden Creek Weddings:* A nonrefundable deposit is due at the time of booking, and a monthly payment schedule may be arranged for the balance. All-inclusive and customized packages start at $12,000, and the rate varies depending on the guest count (up to 175) and day of the week. All packages include: exclusive use of the wedding site from 1pm on the day of the wedding to 10am the following day; 1 night's lodging for up to 18 wedding guests at Hidden Creek Lodge; ceremony chair placement and takedown; reception table setup and takedown; ceremony and reception coordination; catering, wedding cake, linens, DJ and large dance floor.

Cedar Creek Pond Weddings: A nonrefundable deposit is required to reserve your date, and a monthly payment schedule may be arranged for the balance. For ceremonies only, the rental fee starts at $1,000 and varies depending on the date and guest count. Packages with receptions are available upon request.

AVAILABILITY: Year-round, daily; call for details.

SERVICES/AMENITIES:

Catering: in-house
Kitchen Facilities: n/a
Tables & Chairs: provided
Linens, Silver, etc.: provided
Restrooms: wheelchair accessible at Hidden Creek
Dance Floor: provided
Bride's Dressing Area: yes
AV/Meeting Equipment: provided

Parking: ample on-site parking
Accommodations: 16 cabins, 4 lodges
Outdoor Night Lighting: market lighting
Outdoor Cooking Facilities: BBQs CBA
Cleanup: provided, extra fee
View: creek, forest, pond, meadow, waterfall, log swings, log bridges
Other: event coordination, WiFi, pool, hot tub

RESTRICTIONS:

Alcohol: bar packages available, or BYO with Pine Rose's certified bartender
Smoking: designated areas only
Music: OK outdoors, with restrictions

Wheelchair Access: yes
Insurance: liability required

Riverside/Inland Empire

Los Serranos Golf and Country Club

Golf Club

15656 Yorba Avenue, Chino Hills
909/597-1769 x218

www.losserranoscountryclub.com
brent@losserranoscountryclub.com

● Rehearsal Dinners	● Corporate Events
● Ceremonies	● Meetings
● Wedding Receptions	● Film Shoots
● Private Parties	Accommodations

When you enter Los Serranos Country Club's impressive clubhouse, you may hear the three grand bells in its bell tower ring out the hours. The red-tile roof and adobe-like walls of the Mission-style tower and clubhouse are a reminder of the club's history: It sits on 300 beautiful acres of what was once a Spanish land grant. During California's pioneer days, the ranch that occupied these grounds served as a haven for travelers, and its time-honored tradition of taking care of visitors continues at Los Serranos today.

As expected, wedding couples are exceptionally well taken care of. When brides who've been married here are asked what they like best about Los Serranos, they consistently cite its flexibility and service. For example, while a lot of places have fixed time blocks for weddings, Los Serranos is fine with whatever time of day suits you. You can follow the Inland Empire custom of a late afternoon wedding, when the light and temperature are perfect, but if you'd rather tie the knot in the morning, midday or in the evening, no problem!

Catering is another area where the club is adaptable. Los Serranos' culinary staff does an excellent job catering the hundreds of weddings and golf events that take place every year, but if you have a menu that requires special ethnic dishes, they're happy to let you bring in an outside caterer. "Our willingness to accommodate different needs is based on a core rule," says the course's Events Director. "We're here for the brides. This is their day and we will try to make it the best one possible."

Flexibility also extends to this facility's event spaces, which can handle almost any size group. The heart of Los Serranos' clubhouse is the Montebello Ballroom. By itself it can accommodate up to 300 guests, but when you roll back the oak doors that connect it to the club's restaurant, the two venues combined hold up to 550—with the bonus of a full-service bar at one end. Small party? The ballroom can be sectioned to create a comfortable space for 80 guests or less.

The Montebello Ballroom is bright and airy thanks to a high, coffered ceiling and three walls of glass that offer a lovely view of the room's veranda, the ceremony garden, and the driving range. The courtyard-like garden is enclosed by the veranda on one side and a long, hedge-lined wall on the other. Guests are seated on the lawn in the center, facing a classic white gazebo. Palms, flowering plants, roses, and other greenery create a photogenic backdrop.

By the way, if your reception is very small, ask about hosting it on the ceremony garden's veranda. On occasion, it's possible to have exclusive use of that area for an al fresco party. Guests enjoy its fresh air, verdant landscaping, and the soothing sounds of a pair of fountains in the background.

The golf club dates back to 1925, and over the years it has become a seasoned event facility known for its attentiveness in serving the needs of brides and grooms. If you have your celebration here, we expect that you, too, will add your voice to the chorus of compliments Los Serranos Country Club receives.

CEREMONY CAPACITY: The site seats 400 guests outdoors.

EVENT/RECEPTION & MEETING CAPACITY: The club holds 550 seated or standing guests indoors.

FEES & DEPOSITS: A $1,500 deposit is required to reserve your date and the balance is due 14 days prior to the event. The room rental fee starts at $500 and varies depending on the type of event and day and time rented. Reception packages start at $50/person. Tax, alcohol and a 20% service charge are additional. Call or email for more information or to schedule a tour.

AVAILABILITY: Year-round, daily, anytime.

SERVICES/AMENITIES:

Catering: in-house, or BYO with restrictions
Kitchen Facilities: limited
Tables & Chairs: provided
Linens, Silver, etc.: provided
Restrooms: wheelchair accessible
Dance Floor: portable provided
Bride's Dressing Area: CBA
AV/Meeting Equipment: some provided, more CBA

Parking: large lot, on street
Accommodations: no guest rooms
Outdoor Night Lighting: CBA
Outdoor Cooking Facilities: BBQ CBA
Cleanup: provided
View: fountain, garden, fairways, hills, landscaped grounds
Other: coordination, in-house wedding cake and florals

RESTRICTIONS:

Alcohol: in-house or BYO with corkage fee
Smoking: outdoors only
Music: amplified OK with restrictions

Wheelchair Access: yes
Insurance: not required

Want to know WHAT TO ASK a potential location or vendor? Check out our Questions to Ask starting on page 21.

Wedgewood Vellano

2441 Vellano Club Drive, Chino Hills
866/966-3009

www.wedgewoodbanquet.com/vellano
events@wedgewoodbanquet.com

Event Center

- Rehearsal Dinners
- Ceremonies
- Wedding Receptions
- Private Parties
- Corporate Events
- Meetings
- Film Shoots
- Accommodations

The approach to Vellano Country Club, past a gated entry and into the tree-studded hills of this upscale community, builds an air of anticipation that is justly rewarded when you reach the clubhouse itself. Its Tuscan-inspired design features a red-tile roof, artful use of stonework and stately Italian cypress trees, and its hilltop setting affords wonderful views: looking down over the whole Chino Valley in front, and across the lush, Greg Norman golf course in back.

As guests arrive for your celebration, they can mingle in the Main Lobby, a serene spot with plush seating and modern rugs accenting the terracotta-tiled floor. Or, they can be ushered directly to the ceremony lawn via a curved walkway that passes a profusion of natural landscaping. As it approaches the expansive lawn, fragrant white rosebushes line the path—the same one the bride takes as she makes her grand entrance down the center aisle. Although no decorations are needed, some brides add enhancements like archways made of manzanita branches adorned with crystals that glitter in the sun. At the end of the aisle, the couple says their vows against a tableau of emerald fairways, tree-and-villa-dotted hills, and a vast expanse of sky.

There's ample room to host an al fresco cocktail reception right here, or you can opt for the light-filled second-floor Foyer in the clubhouse. Large, arched windows provide lovely treetop views, and the adjacent outdoor Terrace beckons with spectacular sunset vistas. While guests enjoy libations and hors d'oeuvres, the newlyweds head to the golf course for romantic pictures on the wooden bridge, beside the pond and under the trees. And don't overlook the photo ops indoors: The dramatic, S-shaped staircase leading to the Foyer makes a fun backdrop for bridal party and family photos.

Both the Terrace and the Foyer open to the Grand Venezia Ballroom for the main reception. Modern, gilded chandeliers and gold Chiavari chairs give this venue an understated elegance, while its neutral taupe-and-champagne palette allows you to add any personal touches you wish. Lots of windows provide plenty of natural light as well as evening views, and the central built-in dance floor gives everyone a clear view of the first dance no matter where they're seated. Need to take a quiet moment? Step outside onto the Terrace and relax under the stars.

Since this is a Wedgewood property, you can count on personalized attention to guide you through your choice of menus, décor and preferred vendors, as well as help you customize your event for your specific needs. In addition, your event coordinator can arrange a pre-wedding golf party on the award-winning course or an intimate rehearsal dinner in Vellano's clubby Wine Cellar Room.

CEREMONY, EVENT/RECEPTION & MEETING CAPACITY: The site holds 220 seated or standing guests.

FEES & DEPOSITS: 25% of the estimated total event cost is required to reserve your date. An additional 25% is due 120 days prior to the event and the balance (based on your final guest count) is due 10 days prior. All payments are credited towards your final balance and are nonrefundable and nontransferable. All-inclusive, completely customizable wedding packages start at $52/person. Tax, alcohol and a 21–22% service charge are additional.

AVAILABILITY: Year-round, daily, 7am–midnight.

SERVICES/AMENITIES:

Catering: in-house
Kitchen Facilities: n/a
Tables & Chairs: provided
Linens, Silver, etc.: provided
Restrooms: wheelchair accessible
Dance Floor: provided
Bride's Dressing Area: yes
AV/Meeting Equipment: some provided

Parking: large lot
Accommodations: no guest rooms
Outdoor Night Lighting: provided
Outdoor Cooking Facilities: none
Cleanup: provided
View: cityscape, fairways, hills, landscaped grounds; panorama of meadow, hills and valley
Other: in-house wedding cake and florals; clergy on staff; event coordination

RESTRICTIONS:

Alcohol: in-house
Smoking: not allowed
Music: amplified OK

Wheelchair Access: yes
Insurance: not required
Other: no rice, confetti or glitter; no open flames

DoubleTree by Hilton Claremont

Hotel

555 West Foothill Boulevard, Claremont

909/626-2411

www.doubletreeclaremont.com
jgutzwiller@doubletreeclaremont.com

- Rehearsal Dinners
- Ceremonies
- Wedding Receptions
- Private Parties
- Corporate Events
- Meetings
- Film Shoots
- Accommodations

In Claremont, a town many people call "The City of Trees," the DoubleTree stands out as an oasis within an oasis. Its 14-acre grounds, adorned with dozens of different species of flowers and trees as well as some beautiful sculptural elements, are a hub of social life—and weddings—in this westernmost part of the Inland Empire. Besides the earthy and exuberant subtropical feel of its landscaping, the 50-year-old local landmark also has plenty of architectural character. While owners through the years have expanded the facility and remodeled its interior, they've done so carefully, keeping the boutique-hotel vibe intact.

The heart of the DoubleTree is its courtyard, by far the favorite location for weddings. Brides love it both for its look and its privacy (it's closed to everyone but wedding party guests for the duration of the ceremony). The courtyard's focal point is a water feature at one end—a long slate-brick wall set into a high, arched alcove. Water runs gently down the stone, calling to mind the cooling Moorish fountains of old Spain. The water's sparkle and soothing sound are delights to the senses, and add a tranquil element to any gathering. Sometimes, when there's a breeze, swirls of mist dance away from the wall—an entrancing sight. A colorful fringe of ivy, palms and flowers frames the fountain, while overhead, bright cloth streamers span the courtyard and shade people from the afternoon sun.

Just steps from the courtyard, DoubleTree's two neighboring ballrooms are typically used in tandem: one for a cocktail reception and the other for their seated dinner. The hotel also regularly and seamlessly hosts small weddings in its inviting Cedar Room on the second floor. Guests often like to mingle outside on the room's arcaded veranda, where they can enjoy some people-watching in the courtyard below.

An independently operated on-site day spa is a welcome haven for the bride and her entourage to prep for the ceremony or wind down and relax. It's co-ed, so men in the wedding party can step in and have some fun, too. Also on the property, but detached from the main buildings, is "Piano Piano," a lounge that's perfect for bachelor, bachelorette or boy-girl parties. With its dozens of nightclub-style tables and booths, and a stage set with two pianos that professional players often use to engage in some uproarious musical duels, "Piano Piano" is a fine place to get noisy and happy. People can let off steam without worrying about the neighbors.

Getting married at the DoubleTree is like cocooning yourself in a beloved local institution that manages to be hip and traditional, efficient and hang-loose, formal and casual—all at the same time and all to the right degree. When you stand before that glistening slate fountain with your groom, surrounded by greenery, golden light and affectionate well wishers, you'll experience the world at that moment as being just about as right as it can possibly be.

CEREMONY CAPACITY: The hotel seats 400 guests indoors and 250 outdoors.

EVENT/RECEPTION CAPACITY: The hotel can accommodate 250 seated or 500 standing guests indoors and 100 seated or 370 standing outdoors.

MEETING CAPACITY: Meeting spaces hold up to 400 seated guests.

FEES & DEPOSITS: A 25% deposit is required to reserve your date, and the balance is due 7 days prior to the event. The rental fee, which ranges $0–8,015 depending on the circumstances of the event, is normally waived if the food & beverage minimum is met. Meals range $39–70/person. Tax, alcohol and a 21% service charge are additional.

AVAILABILITY: Year-round, daily, anytime.

SERVICES/AMENITIES:

Catering: in-house
Kitchen Facilities: n/a
Tables & Chairs: provided
Linens, Silver, etc.: provided
Restrooms: wheelchair accessible
Dance Floor: provided
Bride's Dressing Area: CBA
AV/Meeting Equipment: CBA

Parking: large lot
Accommodations: 195 guest rooms
Outdoor Night Lighting: CBA
Outdoor Cooking Facilities: BBQ CBA
Cleanup: provided
View: garden patio, waterfall

RESTRICTIONS:

Alcohol: in-house
Smoking: not allowed
Music: amplified OK indoors

Wheelchair Access: yes
Insurance: not required

Padua Hills Theatre

4467 Padua Avenue, Claremont
909/624-8628

www.chantrellescatering.com
chantrelles@aol.com

Historic Special Events Facility

● Rehearsal Dinners	● Corporate Events
● Ceremonies	● Meetings
● Wedding Receptions	● Film Shoots
● Private Parties	Accommodations

Ensconced in the chaparral-covered foothills of the San Gabriel Mountains is the Padua Hills Theatre, a landmark banquet facility with a significant cultural past. The theatre was built in the 1930s as a centerpiece for a community of local artists, and Claremont residents made a tradition of attending dinner theatre in the lovely Spanish-Colonial building. In the early '70s the theatre became a historic site, and by the early '80s it began hosting private special events under the expert direction of *Chantrelles Fine Catering*. Lavishly renovated in 2008, the theatre is more impressive than ever. It's no wonder wedding couples flock here to wed on the tranquil grounds and entertain their friends and family with Old World panache.

Staged against the mountainous silhouette of the Angeles National Forest and overlooking a wilderness preserve, events at the Padua Hills Theatre enjoy a picturesque rural setting. The buildings and landscape capture the simple allure of vintage California, with red-tile roofs, brick and flagstone. As your guests arrive, they walk beneath a long arbor hugged by olive trees and perfumed by jasmine. At the entrance, they're treated to a refreshing glass of iced lemon water and a romantic melody playing in the background.

Three sites offer a variety of ceremony settings. In the Plaza Courtyard, located to the right the arbor, brick and stone paths amble among olive trees, manicured shrubbery and terracotta pots brimming with blooms. Couples say "I do" beneath a unique wrought-iron gazebo. The courtyard is also a versatile option for receptions. You can host an al fresco cocktail hour next to a blazing fireplace, or a sumptuous dinner with linen-draped tables, Chiavari chairs and the sparkle of twinkle lights.

The breathtaking Sunset View Terrace wraps around the banquet hall and provides a spectacular vista. As the sun sets over the densely forested canyon and the city lights begin to shimmer on the horizon, it becomes the perfect backdrop for a ceremony and wedding photos (you'll want to pose next to the terrace's beautiful fountain, too!). If you're lucky, you may even catch a glimpse of a hummingbird or a baby deer, out for a stroll in the fresh mountain air.

From the terrace, French doors open into the Garner Dining Room, where guests mingle over cocktails and delicious hors d'oeuvres. The room's original hardwood floors give off a rich luster, and the ceiling's open beams can be decorated to suit any occasion. A neighboring alcove also has doors to the terrace, as well as a built-in bar covered with painted Spanish-style tiles. On the upper level of the Garner Room is an oversized fireplace that warms the space during the winter months.

Dinner is served in the stunning Theatre Ballroom, with a vaulted ceiling, wrought-iron chandeliers and the original wall sconces. Lining the walls are hand-carved mirrors framed by rich draperies, lending an overall impression of grandeur. The room's design enables each guest to witness everything that takes place: the first dance, cake cutting, bouquet toss, etc.

Your hosts at the Padua Hills Theatre, *Chantrelles Fine Catering,* are renowned for their delectable gourmet fare, themed buffets and elegant presentation. They're also experienced event planners, so relax. In their hands your celebration will unfold as smoothly as a professional theatrical production—but you'll get all the applause.

CEREMONY CAPACITY: The Plaza Courtyard can hold 250 seated. The Sunset View Terrace area can hold up to 200 seated.

EVENT/RECEPTION & MEETING CAPACITY: The Dining Room accommodates up to 270 seated or 300 standing guests; the Courtyard up to 370 seated; and the Garner Room up to 110 guests. Interior spaces combined seat up to 380.

FEES & DEPOSITS: A deposit ranging from $6,500 to one third of the estimated event total (payable to *Chantrelles Fine Catering)* and the full rental fee are required to reserve your date. The rental fee ranges $3,000–6,500 depending on the day of the week. Buffets start at $51.50/person, and sit-down meals at $55/person. Tax, alcohol and a 20% service charge are additional. Alcohol is provided through *Chantrelles Fine Catering;* call for package pricing. Ceremony-only fees start at $1,750. A security guard fee may apply.

AVAILABILITY: Year-round, daily, anytime.

SERVICES/AMENITIES:

Catering: provided by *Chantrelles Fine Catering*
Kitchen Facilities: n/a
Tables & Chairs: provided
Linens, Silver, etc.: provided, linens extra charge
Restrooms: wheelchair accessible, call for details
Dance Floor: yes
Bride's Dressing Area: provided
AV/Meeting Equipment: CBA or BYO

Parking: large lots or valet CBA
Accommodations: no guest rooms
Outdoor Night Lighting: yes
Outdoor Cooking Facilities: CBA
Cleanup: provided
View: Claremont and Pomona Valley
Other: event coordination and on-site entertainment company available

RESTRICTIONS:

Alcohol: provided by *Chantrelles Fine Catering*
Smoking: outside only in designated areas, call for details
Music: amplified OK indoors, with restrictions

Wheelchair Access: yes
Insurance: required for DJs and bands
Other: no rice, confetti or outdoor flames

Eagle Glen Golf Club

Golf Club

1800 Eagle Glen Parkway, Corona
951/278-2842 x206

www.eagleglengc.com
telsner@eagleglengc.com

● Rehearsal Dinners		● Corporate Events	
● Ceremonies		● Meetings	
● Wedding Receptions		● Film Shoots	
● Private Parties		Accommodations	

One of the best things in life is pleasant surprises, and Eagle Glen Golf Club on Corona's lofty west side is full of them. The first time you lay eyes on its cupola-topped clubhouse with its impressive entrance of cinnamon-colored wood trusses, you may be amazed to find a place like this up here. The next surprise comes when you step into the soaring light-splashed lobby and see the quality of the architecture and design. But that's just a prelude to the final treat, first glimpsed through the lobby's glass doors and windows: the stunning view of the verdant golf course against a backdrop of chaparral-covered hills.

Eagle Glen ambles along the base of some very steep hills on the eastern edge of Cleveland National Forest. While you're on the golf course, you're in a private, human realm. But once you leave the greens and start heading up the hills, you enter a wild domain of untamed landscapes. Eagle Glen gives you the wonderful sensation of gazing over nature's might from an absolutely civilized vantage.

There are two outdoor ceremony options to choose from. The Lakeside site features a wrought-iron arbor, perched on a small rise above a reed-ringed pond with a fountain playing at its center. Surrounding it are close-cropped greens that flow up to the foot of the hills. A graceful low wooden bridge that spans the pond at its narrowest point is a splendid spot for photos. For a more dramatic setting, take a stroll over to the Mountainside site, which has a mountain vista. Here, you can get married beneath a wrought-iron gazebo, enclosed by a semicircle of sheltering pine trees.

Eagle Glen's spacious ballroom is managed by a seasoned catering staff that handles scores of weddings each year. Floor-to-ceiling windows and glass doors let in lots of natural light, and look out to the veranda and beyond. Here, guests can sit and savor picturesque views of the back nine's grand swath of lawn, as it tumbles toward the clubhouse from the edge of the national forest. In the afterglow of a lovely ceremony and great food, you and your guests will feel a sense of total satisfaction as the sun sets behind the mountains.

Perched just above the treelined streets of the surrounding community, and next to a national forest, Eagle Glen really is one of Corona's best-kept secrets. After experiencing this inviting venue's beautiful location and high-quality services, you and your guests will not be disappointed.

CEREMONY CAPACITY: The Club holds up to 500 seated guests outdoors and 340 indoors.

EVENT/RECEPTION & MEETING CAPACITY: Indoor spaces accommodate 340 seated or 600 standing guests.

FEES & DEPOSITS: A $1,000 deposit is required to reserve your date, and the balance is due 30 days prior to the event. Meals range $10–85/person. Tax, alcohol and a 20% service charge are additional.

AVAILABILITY: Year-round, daily, 6:30am–midnight.

SERVICES/AMENITIES:

Catering: in-house, no BYO
Kitchen Facilities: n/a
Tables & Chairs: provided
Linens, Silver, etc.: provided
Restrooms: wheelchair accessible
Dance Floor: yes
Bride's Dressing Area: yes
AV/Meeting Equipment: CBA

Parking: large lot
Accommodations: no guest rooms
Outdoor Night Lighting: access only
Outdoor Cooking Facilities: no
Cleanup: provided
View: fairways, mountains, canyon, lake, grounds
Other: event coordination, wedding cake

RESTRICTIONS:

Alcohol: in-house or BYO with corkage fee
Smoking: outside only
Music: amplified OK

Wheelchair Access: yes
Insurance: liability required

Want to find more venues and services? Check out our informative website, www.HereComesTheGuide.com.

425

The Veranda at Green River Golf Club

Golf Club

5215 Green River Road, Corona

951/739-5985

www.playgreenriver.com
events@playgreenriver.com

- Rehearsal Dinners
- Ceremonies
- Wedding Receptions
- Private Parties

- Corporate Events
- Meetings
- Film Shoots
- Accommodations

It seems like most of us look forward to getting away from the hustle and bustle of the city, and going to a tranquil setting where we can become one with ourselves and nature. Green River Golf Club, located in the Santa Ana Canyons in Corona, is just such a place. The Santa Ana River wends its way through this 560-acre property, filled with rolling hills, trees and lakes. Over 50 species of birds—including the endangered golden eagle—call Green River home. If this sounds like a picture-perfect location for a wedding or special event, it is.

Because along with this venue's natural beauty, Green River Golf Club will not only ensure that your celebration unfolds effortlessly, but will do it all for a reasonable price.

Against this serene backdrop, The Veranda at Green River Golf Club is a sophisticated venue. Guests stroll into the Spanish Revival-style building under a gabled roof and green awning, and through a doorway flanked on both sides by huge urns. They mingle in the foyer, and enjoy cocktails served in an adjacent peach-hued room, where they can also sit at tables and chat. When it's time for the reception everyone gathers in the banquet room, an inviting space with subtle recessed lighting in a coffered ceiling. The neutral color scheme makes it easy to decorate the room to your taste: Do something simple, or if you really want to pull out all the stops, create an ethereal wonderland with yards of tulle and white fairy lights. Large picture windows frame views of the verdant fairways and ravines beyond.

Those of you who choose to get married here, too, will appreciate the ceremony sites. One of them is a garden, bounded by a trellised fence and located on a sloped area right next to the immaculately groomed fairway. Two stone-edged steps lead to a platform where vows are exchanged. The second option, a recently added gazebo, provides a vista of the Santa Ana mountain range. If you tie the knot here, don't be too surprised if a deer decides to join your party!

Wonderful photo opportunities abound, among them a burbling stone fountain and an arcaded cloister not far from the banquet room. Green River's appealing combination of skilled staff and gorgeous natural surroundings promises an unforgettable celebration.

CEREMONY CAPACITY: The club holds up to 400 seated guests outdoors.

EVENT/RECEPTION & MEETING CAPACITY: There are several indoor spaces that accommodate 60–200 seated guests. The entire club holds up to 450 seated or 600 standing guests.

FEES & DEPOSITS: 25% of the estimated event total is required to reserve your date. Wedding packages start at $34/person and include rental fee, bartenders, outside ceremony setup and cleanup. Tax, alcohol and service charge are additional. Customized packages are also available.

AVAILABILITY: Year-round, daily, anytime.

SERVICES/AMENITIES:

Catering: in-house, or BYO ethnic caterer
Kitchen Facilities: fully equipped
Tables & Chairs: provided
Linens, Silver, etc.: provided
Restrooms: wheelchair accessible
Dance Floor: yes
Bride's Dressing Area: CBA
AV/Meeting Equipment: CBA

Parking: ample on site
Accommodations: no guest rooms
Outdoor Night Lighting: yes
Outdoor Cooking Facilities: no
Cleanup: provided
View: fairways, mountains
Other: event coordination CBA

RESTRICTIONS:

Alcohol: in-house
Smoking: outside only
Music: amplified OK

Wheelchair Access: yes
Insurance: not required
Other: no open flames

Wedgewood at The Retreat

Event Center

8007 Soft Winds Drive, Corona
866/966-3009

www.wedgewoodbanquet.com
events@wedgewoodbanquet.com

● Rehearsal Dinners	● Corporate Events
● Ceremonies	● Meetings
● Wedding Receptions	● Film Shoots
● Private Parties	Accommodations

Wedgewood at The Retreat is a true beauty inside and out. From its enviable location at the top of a hill within a gated community and semiprivate golf and country club, this popular Inland Empire wedding venue does indeed provide a quiet retreat with sweeping views, cooling breezes and a sprawling Tuscan-inspired clubhouse.

The sun-drenched building has covered breezeways along the front, and a fountain courtyard planted with roses and fluttery palm trees. From the courtyard, double doors open to the clubhouse's grand entry, a high-ceilinged "great room" with wood-and-iron crossbeams, a stone fireplace, and casually elegant leather and velvet furnishings. During the evening, this area is available for your guests to sign in and mingle before your event.

Vows are exchanged on the manicured ceremony lawn out back, where friends and family can savor the unobstructed view of the Temescal Valley while awaiting your arrival. You make your grand entrance from a shaded side patio, heading toward the archway at the far edge of the lawn. Since you'll be facing east, if you time it right you'll get to tie the knot during the "magic hour," just as the setting sun casts a romantic pink glow on the mountains in the distance.

While there's more than enough room to have cocktails right here on the lawn, the entire back of the clubhouse—with its flagstone patios—is yours to enjoy for drinks, dinner, and even dancing. Half shaded, half sunny, and decorated with olive trees in large terracotta pots, these expansive patios overlook terraced gardens filled with roses and geraniums, as well as the tree-studded hills beyond. Richly scrolled gold chandelier pendant lights hang from the eaves above the patios, adding a touch of glamour (as well as the flavor of a private Italian villa).

Then, as evening descends, your guests can drift over to the outdoor fireplace, ringed with comfy seating for intimate conversations. Or, you can take the party inside to the dining room, transformed for dancing with your DJ or band setup by the arched glass doorway or in front of the large stone fireplace. (By the way, this area makes an excellent weather-contingency ceremony site.) Just beyond the dining room is a handsomely detailed bar, complete with marble fireplace, soft leather chairs, dark wood and a high, coffered ceiling, where friends and family can cap the evening with a final toast.

In addition, there's an intimate, tucked-away dining room for small gatherings or rehearsal dinners and a glass-enclosed banquet area that offers a climate-controlled, indoor/outdoor event space for year-round celebrations.

Since events are held away from the golf course, there are no distractions and plenty of private areas for photo opportunities, including a great spot to take a bird's-eye group shot of your entire wedding party.

One key to your fête's success is the experienced Wedgewood staff, who'll customize their all-inclusive wedding packages to your exact specifications. Their convenient, value-packed services make for a day that's not only memorable, but virtually effortless as well.

CEREMONY, EVENT/RECEPTION & MEETING CAPACITY: The site accommodates up to 225 seated or standing guests.

FEES & DEPOSITS: 25% of the estimated total event cost is required to reserve your date. An additional 25% is due 120 days prior to the event and the balance (based on your final guest count) is due 10 days prior. All payments are credited towards your final balance and are nonrefundable and nontransferable. All-inclusive, completely customizable wedding packages start at $45/person. Tax, alcohol and a 21–22% service charge are additional.

AVAILABILITY: Year-round, daily, times may vary.

SERVICES/AMENITIES:

Catering: in-house
Kitchen Facilities: n/a
Tables & Chairs: provided
Linens, Silver, etc.: provided
Restrooms: wheelchair accessible
Dance Floor: yes
Bride's Dressing Area: yes
AV/Meeting Equipment: some provided

Parking: large lot
Accommodations: no guest rooms
Outdoor Night Lighting: yes
Outdoor Cooking Facilities: no
Cleanup: provided
View: fairways, fountain, courtyard, landscaped grounds; panorama of mountains and valley
Other: in-house wedding cake and florals, clergy on staff, event coordination

RESTRICTIONS:

Alcohol: in-house
Smoking: outside only
Music: amplified OK

Wheelchair Access: yes
Insurance: not required
Other: no rice, confetti or glitter; no open flames

Wedgewood Glen Ivy

Event Center

24400 Trilogy Parkway, Corona
866/966-3009

www.wedgewoodbanquet.com
events@wedgewoodbanquet.com

- Rehearsal Dinners
- Ceremonies
- Wedding Receptions
- Private Parties
- Corporate Events
- Meetings
- Film Shoots
- Accommodations

Ever since honeymooners discovered Niagara Falls, brides have felt an affinity for waterfalls. So it's no wonder that Wedgewood Glen Ivy proudly showcases not one, but three impressive cascades, including a spectacular two-tiered beauty. But start to explore this Inland Empire venue and you'll find even more to appreciate.

Located on the same sprawling complex as the Glen Ivy Hot Springs & Spa (pre-wedding bridal party, anyone?), the golf course begins to reveal itself as you climb towards the clubhouse. This modern, low-slung building has a slate façade and is landscaped with thick shrubbery, queen palms and a graceful willow that sways in the breeze.

To the right is the outdoor ceremony site, a lush, wide lawn with a paved bridal aisle leading to a wood pergola altar. Framed by colorful blooming hedges and a towering oak tree, you and your beloved tie the knot against a picturesque backdrop of the 9th-hole pond, where water flowing from all the falls merges. In the distance, the verdant mountains of the Cleveland Forest are a nice contrast to the earth tones of Temescal Canyon below.

After vows are exchanged, it's time to raise a glass of champagne at the Canyon Grille, situated at the back of the clubhouse and reachable via a dramatic walkway, marked with stone pillars and a redwood lattice roof. The views from this bright, open restaurant/bar and its adjacent terrace are fantastic. Guests can mingle at the stainless-and-granite bar or step outside to drink in the wide-angle panorama, from the Chino Hills to the manicured fairways and rugged forest beyond. Meanwhile, you and your photographer head off to capture memories: sitting on a sweetheart bench beside a running creek with a bower of trees above; a cinema-worthy kiss in front of the signature 30-foot granite waterfall (equally fabulous taken from the base or a grassy knoll towards the top)...and the "money shot" at the end of a long tunnel with that signature waterfall glistening behind you. In fact, this tunnel is so cool and has such great acoustics, you just might want to serenade your sweetie or bring your attendants inside it for a doo-wop session.

Join your party for dinner and dancing in the reception tent. The draped cathedral ceiling, wall-to-wall windows, and modern chandeliers give this space an airy, indoor/outdoor feel—with the added benefit of year-round climate control. A wooden dance floor in the center and ample room for a DJ station keep the party going well after the sun sets, and lights from hillside homes set the night aglow.

The staff at Wedgewood Glen Ivy are experts at making everything easy and convenient, with packages that can be customized to your needs and budget. And of course, they'll help you plan your wedding from start to finish.

CEREMONY, EVENT/RECEPTION & MEETING CAPACITY: The site holds up to 220 seated or standing guests.

FEES & DEPOSITS: 25% of the estimated total event cost is required to reserve your date. An additional 25% is due 120 days prior to the event and the balance (based on your final guest count) is due 10 days prior. All payments are credited towards your final balance and are nonrefundable and nontransferable. All-inclusive, completely customizable wedding packages start at $38/person. Tax, alcohol and a 21–22% service charge are additional.

AVAILABILITY: Year-round, daily, 6am–10pm.

SERVICES/AMENITIES:

Catering: in-house
Kitchen Facilities: n/a
Tables & Chairs: provided
Linens, Silver, etc.: provided
Restrooms: wheelchair accessible
Dance Floor: yes
Bride's Dressing Area: no
AV/Meeting Equipment: some provided
Other: in-house wedding cake and florals; clergy on staff; event coordination

Parking: large lot
Accommodations: no guest rooms
Outdoor Night Lighting: yes
Outdoor Cooking Facilities: none
Cleanup: provided
View: creek, garden, fountain, courtyard, waterfall, landscaped grounds; panorama of hills, lake, mountains and fairways

RESTRICTIONS:

Alcohol: in-house
Smoking: outdoors only
Music: amplified OK

Wheelchair Access: yes
Insurance: not required
Other: no rice, confetti or glitter; no open flames

Diamond Bar Center

Event Center

1600 Grand Avenue, Diamond Bar

909/839-7065

www.diamondbarcenter.com
reservations@diamondbarca.gov

- Rehearsal Dinners
- Ceremonies
- Wedding Receptions
- Private Parties

- Corporate Events
- Meetings
- Film Shoots
- Accommodations

From the moment the Diamond Bar Center opened, it garnered raves and it's easy to see why. Designed to blend into its surroundings, this serenely modern venue is actually quite a standout. Taking a cue from iconic architect Frank Lloyd Wright's work, this city-owned facility incorporates natural materials, clean lines and large expanses of glass to both take advantage of and become part of its hilltop setting in Summitridge Park. Atop its lovely perch within the 26-acre recreation area (which abuts 250 additional acres of wild preserve), the Center affords sweeping vistas of tranquil gardens, hiking trails and city lights down below, making it feel like a deluxe retreat that's remarkably close to three major counties.

If you have your ceremony here, your day will probably start at the aptly named Wedding Oval. You'll make your entrance down a long, covered walkway, bordered by red carpet and white iceberg roses as well as iris. Your path takes you past the oval to a stream studded with small boulders, beside which you'll exchange vows. Guests are seated just steps away in the Wedding Oval itself, an elliptical lawn ringed by an array of native plants. From this site, you and your guests will be able to see the San Gabriel Valley behind you and, depending upon the time of year, you might even catch a glimpse of snow on the mountains.

Continue to drink in the panoramic views while enjoying cocktails and hors d'oeuvres on the center's wraparound patio, or head inside to mingle in the foyer. Either way, you can keep the ballroom doors closed until you're ready for dinner... and the big "reveal." The soaring, two-story ballroom seems even more spacious, thanks to its coffered ceiling and expansive windows. Organic stonework in shades of sandstone and dusky adobe adds visual drama to some of the walls. The large room has a raised center stage with a dropdown screen and everything you need to present an audiovisual show. It also features customized zone and accent lighting, which allows you to control the level of light inside so that everyone can see the city sparkle in the distance.

For a more intimate gathering, use just a section of the ballroom, or consider the similarly styled Pine Room or Sycamore Room, which has its own patio for that indoor/outdoor flow.

Whichever space you choose, the entire facility provides an elegant, minimalist backdrop for you to decorate any way you wish. Flexibility is key here, so you have enormous freedom to bring in whatever catering services, flowers, decorations, etc., that best match your vision and your budget. But remember, the Diamond Bar Center is *very* popular and books up fast, so reserve early!

CEREMONY CAPACITY: The site holds 822 seated indoors or 250 seated outdoors.

EVENT/RECEPTION CAPACITY: The ballroom can accommodate up to 438 seated banquet-style and 822 seated theater-style.

MEETING CAPACITY: Facility meeting spaces hold 60–822 seated theater-style.

FEES & DEPOSITS: A refundable $500 deposit is required to reserve your date and the balance is due 60 days prior to the event. The rental fee ranges $165–600/hour depending on the room requested and the day and time of the event.

AVAILABILITY: Year-round: Sunday–Thursday, 7:30am–midnight; Friday & Saturday, 7:30am–1am.

SERVICES/AMENITIES:
Catering: BYO
Kitchen Facilities: prep only
Tables & Chairs: provided
Linens, Silver, etc.: BYO
Restrooms: wheelchair accessible
Dance Floor: CBA, extra fee
Bride's Dressing Area: CBA, extra fee
AV/Meeting Equipment: CBA

Parking: large lot
Accommodations: no guest rooms
Outdoor Night Lighting: access only
Outdoor Cooking Facilities: no
Cleanup: renter
View: creek, garden, landscaped grounds; panorama of cityscape, mountains and hills

RESTRICTIONS:
Alcohol: BYO
Smoking: designated areas only
Music: amplified OK indoors

Wheelchair Access: yes
Insurance: liability required

This is important! Tell locations you're reading HERE COMES THE GUIDE and ask if our information is still current.

433

Diamond Bar Golf Course

Golf Club

22751 Golden Springs Drive, Diamond Bar

888/360-9796

www.countryclubreceptions.com
privateeventdirector@diamondbargc.com

- Rehearsal Dinners
- Ceremonies
- Wedding Receptions
- Private Parties
- Corporate Events
- Meetings
- Film Shoots
- Accommodations

Diamond Bar is a popular golf course whose vibrant greens, bordered by tall shade trees, seem to run off into infinity. But golfing activities don't interfere with the venue's gem of a wedding site, located around a corner and away from all of the bustle. From the front of the clubhouse there's no hint of this sweet place, but once you come upon it you have one of those pure "ahh" moments. You see a flower-fringed white gazebo nestled under a grove of leafy sycamores. A paved path curves away from it over luxuriant grass to a terrace that runs the length of the inviting banquet room. The room's tall north and east windows create "walls" that appear to be made of pure glass, and a shady patio at its far end—only steps from the gazebo—features a koi pond.

A hedge of red-tipped photinia sets the lawn, gazebo and banquet room apart from the rest of Diamond Bar. Beyond it you can glimpse the golfing activities, but they all seem to be at a peaceful remove. Inside the hedge's perimeter there's a sheltered world of colorful flowers, lush grass, and the speckled white bark of the sycamores. Standing here, you feel like you're in a protected glade in the woods.

The banquet room is a bright place, its walls finished in a creamy white with pale yellow highlights. Dramatic trusses span the space, and brass chandeliers with tulip-shaped sconces drop gracefully from the cathedral ceiling. Next to the glass wall that runs beside the patio is an impressive wall-to-wall dance floor—this is one serious boogie zone that has probably clinched the deal for many a bride. The lobby outside the banquet room also accesses a bridal changing room, the terrace and the clubhouse bar. Wedding parties often begin the processional from there, walking along the terrace to the gazebo.

Besides the gazebo, Diamond Bar offers several excellent backdrops for wedding photos, including the course's picturesque lake and, in season, a high bank of blazing bougainvillea downslope from the banquet room.

A facility's good looks are important, but there's an equally critical factor: Can the kitchen cook? The answer is yes! The Inland Empire has become such a mosaic of ethnicities that Diamond Bar's banquet staff learned long ago how to prepare almost any cuisine. The accommodating kitchen, which handles scores of weddings every year, is scrupulous about arranging advance tastings so you can be confident of the dishes that will be served at your event.

When you go down the checklist of the things that make for a fine wedding day, Diamond Bar has as good an ensemble as you're likely to find. Saying "I do" here could well be a decision you'll be glad you made for years to come.

CEREMONY, EVENT/RECEPTION & MEETING CAPACITY: The facility holds 250 seated or 400 standing guests, both indoors and outdoors.

FEES & DEPOSITS: A nonrefundable deposit, which is applied to your food & beverage total, is required to reserve your date. The amount of the deposit varies depending on how far in advance you book. Payment terms for the balance also vary, and may be arranged on an individual basis. Meals start at $34/person. Tax, alcohol and service charge are additional. Food & beverage minimums may apply. Menus and packages can be customized to fit your needs and budget. Call for details.

AVAILABILITY: Year-round, daily.

SERVICES/AMENITIES:
Catering: in-house
Kitchen Facilities: n/a
Tables & Chairs: provided
Linens, Silver, etc.: provided
Restrooms: wheelchair accessible
Dance Floor: provided
Bride's Dressing Area: provided
AV/Meeting Equipment: some provided, more CBA

Parking: large lot
Accommodations: no guest rooms
Outdoor Night Lighting: CBA
Outdoor Cooking Facilities: BBQ CBA
Cleanup: provided
View: fairways, meadow, garden, koi pond
Other: private event specialist, WiFi

RESTRICTIONS:
Alcohol: in-house
Smoking: outside only
Music: amplified OK

Wheelchair Access: yes
Insurance: not required

Wedgewood Menifee Lakes

Country Club

29875 Menifee Lakes Drive, Menifee
866/966-3009

www.wedgewoodbanquet.com
events@wedgewoodbanquet.com

● Rehearsal Dinners		● Corporate Events	
● Ceremonies		● Meetings	
● Wedding Receptions		● Film Shoots	
● Private Parties		Accommodations	

"Wall of windows." Keep that phrase in mind when you visit this lovely banquet center. Why? Because the bank of big, tall windows in the main dining room frames a superb golf course view, and will probably be what makes you ask, "Where do I sign?"

You'll be impressed even before you reach the windows. The center's stucco-clad main building has a beautiful entrance: A circular drive is rimmed by pepper trees, Canary Island palms and flowering eucalyptus, and centered by a burbling three-tiered fountain. As you step out of your car beneath the grand columned portico, you immediately notice the imposing pair of front doors capped with a classic lunette window. Many couples take advantage of the dramatic backdrop and set up their wedding ceremony here.

The foyer leads directly to the main dining room and those spectacular windows. On the other side of the glass, soaring ornamental palms flank fairways and winding paths, and Menifee's two manmade lakes glint blue—a site so picturesque that it's another favorite ceremony location. In the distance are high desert hills, including a dramatic peak of boulders that looks like a giant's rock pile.

The view, however, is not this room's only asset. Painted in creamy earth colors, it also features a large fireplace, a lodge-like ceiling (the rafters are made of rounded timbers with the bark still on), and an eye-catching chandelier shaped like a great metallic hoop skirt. Half-walls help separate the room visually from the foyer. The combination of outdoor panorama and interior features are such strong points that many brides decide the room needs little decoration.

Right next door is a bar that belongs exclusively to wedding parties in the evenings. Folding doors to one side open to a smaller banquet room that can be used independently or in conjunction with the main dining room. All three of these rooms have access to a terrace, shaded in the afternoon, that overlooks the excellent golf course vista—a fine choice for your cocktail hour. For smaller weddings, the downstairs grill room and its adjoining terrace are available, as are large wood-paneled changing rooms for both brides and grooms.

The banquet center also hosts rehearsal dinners, bachelorette parties and post-ceremony brunches. Wedgewood Menifee's inclusive wedding packages can accommodate most budgets, and they'll customize your menu and additional elements to reduce wedding planning stress.

A striking landscape, an attractive interior space, and a highly experienced wedding staff... Wedgewood Menifee Lakes has all the virtues you'd expect a quality country club to offer.

CEREMONY, EVENT/RECEPTION & MEETING CAPACITY: The site holds up to 250 seated or standing guests.

FEES & DEPOSITS: 25% of the estimated total event cost is required to reserve your date. An additional 25% is due 120 days prior to the event and the balance (based on your final guest count) is due 10 days prior. All payments are credited towards your final balance and are nonrefundable and nontransferable. All-inclusive, completely customizable wedding packages start at $35/person. Tax, alcohol and a 21–22% service charge are additional.

AVAILABILITY: Year-round, daily, 6am–1am.

SERVICES/AMENITIES:

Catering: in-house
Kitchen Facilities: n/a
Tables & Chairs: provided
Linens, Silver, etc.: provided
Restrooms: wheelchair accessible
Dance Floor: provided
Bride's Dressing Area: yes
AV/Meeting Equipment: some provided

Parking: large lot
Accommodations: no guest rooms
Outdoor Night Lighting: provided
Outdoor Cooking Facilities: no
Cleanup: provided
View: fountain, fairways, lake, landscaped grounds, mountains
Other: in-house wedding cake and florals; clergy on staff; event coordination

RESTRICTIONS:

Alcohol: in-house
Smoking: not allowed inside
Music: amplified OK

Wheelchair Access: yes
Insurance: not required
Other: no rice, confetti or glitter; no open flames

Serendipity

Private Estate

12865 Oak Glen Road, Oak Glen
909/754-3134
www.serendipitygardenweddings.com
serendipitygardenweddings@gmail.com

Rehearsal Dinners	● Corporate Events
● Ceremonies	● Meetings
● Wedding Receptions	● Film Shoots
● Private Parties	Accommodations

We're intrigued whenever we hear about a venue that's been specifically designed for weddings. What that usually means is that the owner is serious about them, and has put a lot of effort into making their place extra wedding-friendly. Serendipity certainly fits that description.

Peaceful and secluded, this private estate has a superb location at the edge of a mountain canyon that overlooks an oak-sheltered creek. At 4,200 feet in the San Bernardino Mountains, it's high enough to be 10 or 15 degrees cooler than the flats below, making it popular for July and August weddings—something few outdoor wedding sites in the region can boast.

An array of pleasing elements creates a nice whole here. First there are the flowers: The path connecting the ceremony and reception areas is flanked by hundreds of dazzling white rosebushes. The ceremony site itself, set halfway down the canyon slope, is a showstopper: Look south and there's a panorama of the Inland Empire's mountains and valleys. Look north, and the soaring granite peak of Mt. San Gorgonio looms imposingly, close enough to seem just a short drive away. Guests are seated on a lawn facing this inspiring view, and the couple recite their vows on a simple wooden dais that's easily adorned to taste. Off to one side, a small reed-filled pool teems with little freshwater critters—sweet symbols of the abundance of married life to come.

After the ceremony, guests gather on the cocktail terrace, where they're served the bride and groom's signature cocktail and hand-passed hors d'oeuvres. From here they can watch the newlyweds posing for photos below, and take in the expansive view of the valley to the south. Speaking of photos, photographers love shooting in front of Serendipity's new barn.

When it's time for the reception, everyone finds their table in Serendipity's beautifully conceived outdoor dining and dancing area near the top of the property. It's a spacious "patio," made up of large stone-tiled squares separated by bright strips of grass that together form an appealing geometric pattern. Tables are arranged on the squares, there's a permanent dance floor on one side (with the canyon as its dramatic backdrop), and a full bar with a blazing fireplace on the opposite side. The resulting setup encourages a convivial flow as people move from music to drink to mingling at tables. Most weddings here are evening affairs, taking advantage of the balmy air, the region's glorious sunset colors, the romance of lights strung across the patio, and the glow of stars under a smog-free sky.

Serendipity's all-inclusive wedding package covers a wide range of items, including catering, cake, flowers, a DJ, a golf cart shuttle for guests, and a horse-drawn carriage ride for the bride and groom to the ceremony site and reception area. Package services are provided by a select group of trusted, seasoned vendors, and there are no hidden charges.

When we asked Serendipity's owner how this unique, weddings-only facility in the highlands has worked out, she clearly enjoyed answering the question: "Each bride tells me, 'This is my little haven, my own piece of the mountain for a day.'"

CEREMONY & EVENT/RECEPTION CAPACITY: The facility holds 200 seated guests outdoors.

MEETING CAPACITY: Meetings spaces hold 200 seated at tables.

FEES & DEPOSITS: A $3,000 deposit is required to reserve your date and the balance is split into 3 payments due prior to the event. Serendipity's all-inclusive wedding packages cover catering, cake, flowers, a DJ, a golf cart shuttle for guests, and a horse-drawn carriage ride for the bride and groom to the ceremony site and reception area. In addition to the bride's dressing area included in the wedding package, a separate Bride's Cottage that's spacious enough for the bridal entourage is an upgrade available on the day of the wedding for an extra fee. It also comes with an adjacent Beauty Cottage that's fully equipped with vanities, outlets, mirrors, etc. to make getting ready a breeze. Packages range $13,000–16,500 depending on the guest count and the services selected. Tax is additional, gratuity is at your discretion.

AVAILABILITY: Year-round, 9am–10pm.

SERVICES/AMENITIES:

Catering: in-house
Kitchen Facilities: n/a
Tables & Chairs: provided
Linens, Silver, etc.: provided
Restrooms: wheelchair accessible
Dance Floor: provided
Bride's & Groom's Dressing Areas: yes
AV/Meeting Equipment: some provided
Other: coordination, grand piano

Parking: large lot
Accommodations: no guest rooms
Outdoor Night Lighting: yes
Outdoor Cooking Facilities: BBQ on site
Cleanup: provided
View: garden, waterfall, pond, fountain, landscaped grounds; panorama of mountains, canyon, cityscape, valley, hills, fields and barn

RESTRICTIONS:

Alcohol: BYO
Smoking: designated areas only
Music: amplified OK outdoors

Wheelchair Access: yes
Insurance: liability required

Mountain Meadows Golf Course

Golf Club

1875 Fairplex Drive, Pomona
888/998-2969
www.countryclubreceptions.com
privateeventmanager@mountainmeadowsgc.com

- Rehearsal Dinners
- Ceremonies
- Wedding Receptions
- Private Parties
- Corporate Events
- Meetings
- Film Shoots
- Accommodations

A curving boulevard whisks you swiftly up from the valley floor to this popular golf course. Its many jacaranda trees will be ablaze with lilac-colored blooms when you arrive, and if it's a clear day the San Gabriel Mountains will pop up bold and high—one of several pleasing sights that will capture your interest.

Like all savvy golfing venues, Mountain Meadows has set its ceremony site and banquet room overlooking the golf course to take advantage of the view, which is exceptionally beautiful here. In addition to the manicured fairways, the verdant vista includes a wide variety of trees, lush foliage, and rolling hills in the background.

Occupying the far end of the clubhouse, the banquet room features many elements that make it an inviting space: A wall of tall windows lets in a crystalline northern light and looks out past the adjacent patio to the action of the 10th and 18th holes. The remaining walls are painted in shades of cream, a nice contrast to the vaulted, wood-beamed ceiling. Swags of satin draping, which are laced with twinkle lights, spiral out from the center of the ceiling, adding an elegant twist to the room's rustic tone.

The banquet room opens to a large patio, shaded by a wooden trellis strung with bistro lights. It has a great view of the golf course, and is right next to an expansive ceremony site with a large, open gazebo. Couples saying "I do" here walk up a few steps and are elevated in full view of their family and friends, who are seated in white chairs on a putting green with grass as smooth as the felt covering on a pool table. This ceremony area is spacious and flexible enough to accommodate other options, too: For example, if the gazebo isn't your style, you can create your own focal point with a *chuppah* or other type of arch, as well as spiral or stadium-style seating.

Photo ops abound, from the gazebo and its surroundings to the course's man-made lake. Or you can ride a golf cart up to a scenic overlook with a fantastic view of Mountain Meadows.

Finally, the on-site kitchen knows what it's doing. As is typical in the Inland Empire, with its rich variety of cultures, customs and ethnic groups, the banquet staff—who handle more than 100 weddings per year—are experts at seamlessly accommodating brides' different tastes and needs.

Mountain Meadows achieves something that looks easy only if you have a lot of experience doing it: balancing quality services and elegance with accessibility and affordability.

CEREMONY CAPACITY: The site holds up to 400 seated guests.

EVENT/RECEPTION CAPACITY: The banquet room accommodates up to 330 seated or 450 standing guests.

MEETING CAPACITY: The banquet room accommodates up to 500 seated guests.

FEES & DEPOSITS: A nonrefundable deposit, which is applied to your food & beverage total, is required to reserve your date. The amount of the deposit varies depending on how far in advance you book. Payment terms for the balance also vary, and may be arranged on an individual basis. Wedding packages start at $35/person. Tax, alcohol and service charge are additional. Food & beverage minimums may apply. Menus and packages can be customized to fit your needs and budget. Call for details.

AVAILABILITY: Year-round, daily, 6am–2am.

SERVICES/AMENITIES:

Catering: in-house
Kitchen Facilities: no
Tables & Chairs: provided
Linens, Silver, etc.: provided
Restrooms: wheelchair accessible
Dance Floor: provided
Bride's Dressing Area: yes
AV/Meeting Equipment: some provided, more CBA

Parking: large lot
Accommodations: no guest rooms
Outdoor Night Lighting: CBA
Outdoor Cooking Facilities: no
Cleanup: provided
View: fairways, hills, mountains, grounds

RESTRICTIONS:

Alcohol: in-house
Smoking: outside only
Music: amplified OK

Wheelchair Access: yes
Insurance: not required

Overwhelmed? Use the search criteria on www.HereComesTheGuide.com to narrow down your choices.

Sheraton Fairplex Hotel and Conference Center

Hotel

601 West McKinley Avenue, Pomona
909/868-5907
www.sheratonfairplex.com/weddings
tiffany.garfias@sheraton.com

- Rehearsal Dinners
- Ceremonies
- Wedding Receptions
- Private Parties
- Corporate Events
- Meetings
- Film Shoots
- Accommodations

The Sheraton Fairplex, set on 543 park-like acres, already boasts one of the largest varieties of event spaces we've seen in one venue. Yet, this full-service hotel, recently named one of the top five Sheratons in the country, is about to kick it up a notch with the debut of its much-anticipated Conference Center. A modern complex of glass-clad buildings, landscaped pathways and views of the San Gabriel Mountains, it's sure to add cachet to this conveniently located property.

What this means for anyone planning a wedding or special event is an even more dazzling range of options...from a brand new, palatial-sized ballroom to an exposed-brick dining room loaded with charm to an aromatic herb garden where guests dine al fresco.

You'll find two delightful outdoor ceremony sites here. The newly created Champagne Court is a lush lawn bordered by flowering hedges and a myriad of oak, palm and evergreen trees. Plus, there's ample room for celebratory cocktails following the service. Smaller groups can reserve the more intimate McKinley's Grille Patio, an enclosed flagstone courtyard at the front of the hotel. It features a stone fireplace and a graceful ash tree, beneath which you can exchange vows. Afterwards, invite your guests to the library off the main lobby for a champagne toast.

Within the Sheraton there are several choices for receptions, including the Vineyard Ballroom, which is decorated in a neutral palette of cream and soft greens with gold chandeliers and a hardwood dance floor. For something quite different, consider the Meritage, a unique vintage-style pavilion with brick walls, pressed tin ceilings and archways framing glass doors that open to a patio. A polished concrete floor and long, dark wood built-in bars make it feel more like a hip, city restaurant and club than anything you'd usually find in a large hotel.

If, however, you prefer a sleek, modern setting, then head to the new Conference Center, just up the road past the hotel. You arrive at a large, circular plaza dotted with tall palms and native plantings, with the mountains visible in the distance. The main building's glass façade and domed roof create an open, airy atmosphere inside. When you enter the prefunction area, you can fully appreciate the striking design: One wall curves seamlessly from floor to ceiling in an elegant 158-foot-long arc, while lots of natural light streams in through a wall of windows. The adjoining California Ballroom, warmed by rich tones of sustainable wood used in the wainscoting and trim adorning the walls, has the kind of grand proportions that make it ideal for a spectacular gala.

Overhead, reflective panels in the coffered ceiling amplify the soft glow from dozens of contemporary chandeliers.

Whichever location you choose for your reception, your menu will showcase fresh, organic ingredients with much of the produce and herbs grown on site. In fact, one of the most intriguing possibilities at this property is booking a cozy reception or rehearsal dinner at "The Farm," the picture-perfect, one-acre garden where the chefs actually pick those herbs and veggies. Your meal will be served country-style at long rustic tables set beneath a wooden canopy strung with lights. As night falls and the stars start to shine above, what could be more romantic?

CEREMONY CAPACITY: The hotel holds 1,000 seated guests indoors and 400 seated outdoors.

EVENT/RECEPTION CAPACITY: The hotel can accommodate 1,000 seated or 1,500 standing guests indoors and 1,000 seated or 500 standing outdoors.

MEETING CAPACITY: Meeting spaces hold up to 700 seated guests.

FEES & DEPOSITS: 20% of the total event cost is required to reserve your date and the balance is due 14 days prior to the event. Rental fees range $5,000–20,000. Meals range $31–72/person. Tax, alcohol and a 22% service charge are additional.

AVAILABILITY: Year-round, daily.

SERVICES/AMENITIES:

Catering: in-house
Kitchen Facilities: n/a
Tables & Chairs: provided
Linens, Silver, etc.: provided
Restrooms: wheelchair accessible
Dance Floor: portable provided
Bride's Dressing Area: CBA
AV/Meeting Equipment: provided

Parking: large lot
Accommodations: 247 guest room suites
Outdoor Night Lighting: CBA
Outdoor Cooking Facilities: BBQ CBA
Cleanup: provided
View: garden patio, landscaped grounds, pool
Other: complimentary event coordination, picnic area

RESTRICTIONS:

Alcohol: in-house
Smoking: not allowed
Music: amplified OK

Wheelchair Access: yes
Insurance: liability required

Christmas House

Historic Victorian Inn

9240 Archibald Avenue, Rancho Cucamonga
909/980-6450

www.christmashouseinn.com
contact@christmashouseinn.com

Rehearsal Dinners		● Corporate Events	
● Ceremonies		Meetings	
● Wedding Receptions		● Film Shoots	
● Private Parties		● Accommodations	

All the quaint pleasures we associate with a Victorian Christmas—old-fashioned elegance, warm family gatherings, and a childlike sense of wonder—are available year-round in 21st-century Southern California. Where? At the Christmas House Inn, a historic landmark that received its yuletide moniker because of the extravagant holiday parties hosted by its early owners. Built in 1904, the three-story mansion is a charming example of the Queen Anne-style favored by late Victorian architects. For decades it was the showpiece of an 80-acre citrus ranch, but by the 1970s, it had fallen into neglect. In 1983, Janice Ilsley and her husband came to the rescue, launching a complete renovation that restored the Christmas House to its former glory. The inn boasts all of the original stained-glass windows and gorgeous woodwork—the seven Victorian fireplace mantels are each made of a different wood, and accented with Italian tiles and beveled glass mirrors. The success of this popular bed & breakfast owes as much to the Ilsleys' service-oriented attitude as to the inviting surroundings. "We want couples to feel like the Christmas House is their own home," reveals Janice, "especially on their wedding day."

Brides, you'll definitely feel at home in the Celebration Suite, the spacious upstairs dressing room replete with fireplace, lacy adornments, an abundance of mirrors—and plenty of room for doting bridesmaids. In the cool autumn months or if the weather looks iffy, follow Victorian tradition and say "I do" in front of the parlor's hearth, decked with shimmering candles. As the accompanist plays the processional on the grand piano, glide down the carved, redwood burl staircase and pass among your guests, gathered close enough to hear your vows, even if they're whispered. Indoor reception buffets are served in the formal dining room, another fetching space where details like a gleaming silver coffee urn and antique curios enhance the turn-of-the-century patina. Guests mingle and munch as they soak up the nostalgic ambiance in the library and adjoining salons, which are lavished with comfortable period furnishings and authentic Victoriana.

At the Christmas House, you can also have your ceremony amid the romance of an English Garden behind the home. A lawn cradled in flowering shrubbery features a brick path lined with candle lanterns. This natural wedding aisle culminates at a gazebo swathed in greenery, where bride and groom make a radiant tableau. At the ceremony's conclusion, guests pass under a vine-covered archway to the front of the home, where they savor hors d'oeuvres passed on silver trays in a lovely rose garden, or lounge in the shade of a broad veranda and watch the butterflies flit among the blossoms. When guests return to the rear garden for the reception, they'll find tables and chairs elegantly set with floor-length linens and gleaming glass and cutlery. Guests dine beneath the leafy boughs of magnolia and guava trees strung with twinkle lights. Nearby, a citrus tree draped with gossamer netting shades the wedding cake, poised atop an antique table. Japanese lanterns cast a soft glow on an adjacent courtyard, where the newlyweds share their first dance.

Among the most endearing attractions of the Christmas House are the six distinctive guest rooms. The luxurious bridal suite comes with a fireplace, a private garden courtyard with hot tub, and delicious breakfast the morning after. With affordable packages that include gourmet catering and other extras, this venue is simply irresistible. Many couples create their own Christmas House tradition: They rekindle their fond wedding memories by returning to the inn on their anniversaries!

CEREMONY, EVENT/RECEPTION CAPACITY: The Parlor holds up to 50 seated or 75 standing guests, the garden up to 150 seated.

FEES & DEPOSITS: A nonrefundable $500 deposit is required to reserve your date. Another $400 is due 1 month later. 50% of the remaining event total is due 4 months prior to the event, and the balance is due 2 weeks prior. For indoor events, packages start at $7,500 for up to 50 guests and include exclusive use of the site, all rentals, catering and staff, wedding cake and all setup and cleanup. For each person over 50 guests, pricing starts at $35/person. For garden events, packages range $10,500–14,500 for up to 100 guests and include everything that's in the indoor package plus many more flourishes, including professional DJ services. For each person over 100 guests, pricing ranges $35–55/person. Tax and service charge are additional on the catering portion of the total. If you would like bar service, many options are available at an extra charge.

AVAILABILITY: Year-round, daily, 10am–10pm.

SERVICES/AMENITIES:

Catering: in-house
Kitchen Facilities: n/a
Tables & Chairs: provided
Linens, Silver, etc.: provided
Restrooms: limited accessibility
Dance Floor: provided for garden receptions
Bride's & Groom's Dressing Areas: provided
AV/Meeting Equipment: n/a

Parking: valet included
Accommodations: 6 guest rooms
Outdoor Night Lighting: yes
Outdoor Cooking Facilities: no
Cleanup: provided
View: landscaped Victorian gardens
Other: event coordination, bar service

RESTRICTIONS:

Alcohol: in-house
Smoking: outside only
Music: amplified OK with volume restrictions until 10pm

Wheelchair Access: limited
Insurance: not required
Other: no rice, birdseed or confetti

Hidden Oaks

Retreat Center

6558 Hermosa Avenue, Rancho Cucamonga
909/484-4379
www.hiddenoaksretreat.com
hiddenoaksretreat@gmail.com

● Rehearsal Dinners	● Corporate Events
● Ceremonies	● Meetings
● Wedding Receptions	● Film Shoots
● Private Parties	Accommodations

Hidden Oaks is a place born of miracles. Its first brush with providence came even before it was built: The story goes that the great state of California rerouted a freeway that was under construction rather than destroy a mighty 250-year-old oak standing in the way. Today, that ancient tree is only one of the splendors at Hidden Oaks Retreat Center. It's a gem of a stone-and-redwood house in a setting that offers cool green garden spaces, wonderful 1920s architecture and a spectacular view of the San Gabriel Mountains.

In a second stroke of divine intervention, the building itself was saved from thoughtless alteration by a church group that appreciated the tucked-away site's beauty and recognized its potential as a meeting and wedding venue. Completely restored, the historic building still has walls formed from river boulders joined by rough-finished mortar, as well as a red-tile roof.

New features include up-to-date appliances, air-conditioning, bathrooms, and access for disabled persons. All of them blend seamlessly with the house's Mission Revival look and delightful architectural elements. Stout redwood beams and rafters, tiled floors and wood-framed windows with small panes all look as though they've been lifted straight from a Devonshire country cottage.

You can use the indoor and outdoor areas as you choose. The main interior space, called the Great Room, has a grand fireplace as its focal point. An adjoining smaller room is often used for gift opening or cake cutting. The Great Room opens out to a patio, lawn and garden that run along the house's south-facing side. A flower-lined path beside the lawn wraps around a softly gurgling fountain on its way to a brilliant white gazebo, Hidden Oaks' al fresco ceremony site. The whole effect is lush, verdant and peaceful. Like an arboretum with vibrant plants everywhere you turn, Hidden Oaks is a subtropical Eden of roses, deodar cedars, pines, fig and avocado trees, ferns, baby's breath, lemon, peach and kumquat.

As is typical in these parts, weddings usually take place late in the afternoon to take advantage of the rich pre-dusk light and cooler temperatures. Although the kitchen preserves a retro 1920s look, caterers love its ample workspace and modern appliances. But sometimes, when the weather is irresistible and the reception is set up outside, they'll barbecue near the patio.

So, imagine this: It's one of those occasions when the caterers are cooking outdoors, filling the air with succulent aromas. The setting sun has created a band of golden red in the west, strings of lights are beginning to wink on and dance along Hidden Oaks's roofline, the garden's flowers are blooming and you're sitting next to your new husband, tenderly and contentedly holding his hand.

Could there be a nicer way to start your marriage?

CEREMONY CAPACITY: The site holds up to 400 seated guests outdoors or 130 seated indoors.

EVENT/RECEPTION CAPACITY: The facility accommodates 130 seated or 165 standing guests indoors and 400 seated or standing outdoors.

MEETING CAPACITY: Meeting spaces hold 100 seated guests.

FEES & DEPOSITS: 25% of the rental fee is required to reserve your date and the balance is due 60 days prior to the event. Rental fees for a wedding and reception start at $2,250 and vary depending on the day of the week and guest count. Rental fees for meetings start at $75/hour, rental fees for parties and anniversaries start at $150/hour. Fees vary depending on guest count.

AVAILABILITY: Year-round, daily. Monday–Saturday, 8am–10pm and Sunday, 10am–10pm.

SERVICES/AMENITIES:

Catering: BYO
Kitchen Facilities: prep only
Tables & Chairs: some provided, more CBA
Linens, Silver, etc.: through caterer
Restrooms: wheelchair accessible
Dance Area: provided
Bride's Dressing Area: yes
AV/Meeting Equipment: some provided, more CBA

Parking: large lot (190 spaces)
Accommodations: no guest rooms
Outdoor Night Lighting: yes
Outdoor Cooking Facilities: BBQ CBA
Cleanup: provided
View: garden, fountains, landscaped grounds, hills, forest, mountains
Other: clergy on staff, picnic area, spinet piano, event coordination

RESTRICTIONS:

Alcohol: not allowed
Smoking: not allowed
Music: amplified OK with restrictions

Wheelchair Access: yes
Insurance: required for caterers

Victoria Gardens Cultural Center

Cultural Center

12505 Cultural Center Drive, Rancho Cucamonga
909/477-2773

www.vgculturalcenter.com
kristie.nicols@cityofrc.us

- Rehearsal Dinners
- Ceremonies
- Wedding Receptions
- Private Parties
- Corporate Events
- Meetings
- Film Shoots
- Accommodations

The delightfully imaginative Victoria Gardens Cultural Center has a motto: "Where Dreams Come to Life." But it could just as easily be "Let's Put on a Show," because that's what they do so dynamically at this outstanding venue.

The center, known primarily for its Lewis Family Playhouse, one of regional theater's rising stars, is a multifaceted performing arts mecca that includes several unique indoor and outdoor sites for special events. Here, they believe that every wedding is a story, and they love having the same creative wizards who put the magic into dozens of critically acclaimed theatrical productions each year help you tell yours.

The Cultural Center, comprised of the playhouse and Celebration Hall, is an architecturally colorful treat. The curved buildings, sporting hues of pink, desert rose and verdigris, form a semicircle around the Imagination Courtyard, a large, cobble-stoned space that lends itself to outdoor gatherings. Ringed by tall, feathery palms, it's open on one side to the Victoria Gardens shopping and entertainment plaza (a big plus during the holidays when the majestic Christmas tree is visible from here), and anchored on the other by the center's soaring, arched glass entrance. Topped with a backlit, stylized marquee, this façade makes a picturesque backdrop for an al fresco ceremony.

Many brides opt to have cocktails (or even dinner) out here and exchange vows in the more private Lobby, a whimsical stage set of the perfect little street, complete with storefronts and trees—it's like having your very own village! On one end of "town," there's a staircase to use either as a riser for your altar, or as a starting point for your dramatic descent to the main floor where you can say "I do," bathed in light filtering through that gorgeous glass entrance behind you.

The center gives you enormous flexibility in choosing how you want to use its spaces, but it's the way the staff works with a team of art and entertainment professionals to turn your vision into reality that makes this place so special. Want to add an animal to the proceedings? No problem.

They've wrangled camels, horses, an elephant—even albino peacocks—for various events. Unconventional entertainment? They can find everything from acrobats to belly dancers to gospel choirs. And with the help of some of L.A.'s most talented set decorators, lighting designers, seamstresses and hair/makeup artists, they will produce an affair to remember.

Nowhere is their creativity more rewarded than in the Celebration Hall Ballroom. A wonderful blank canvas, this huge space has polished concrete floors, cream-colored walls, windows on two sides and an adjacent Patio hugged by shrubbery. In it's natural state, it's a bright and airy spot for dinner and dancing with an indoor/outdoor flow. But say the word and they can transform it, with elegant draping and dramatic lighting, into a romantic oasis, a sophisticated supper club or an exotic foreign locale. There's no charge for either the consultation or design, making this an incredible value. Plus, they do so much of the work in-house that you can also save on flowers, catering, and more for a one-of-a-kind event that's sure to win rave reviews.

CEREMONY CAPACITY: The site holds up to 250 seated guests indoors or 350 seated outdoors.

EVENT/RECEPTION & MEETING CAPACITY: The facility accommodates 250 seated or 350 standing indoors and 400 seated or 500 standing outdoors.

FEES & DEPOSITS: A refundable $1,000 deposit is required to reserve your date, and the balance is due 30 days prior to the event. The rental fee ranges $1,650–3,800 depending on the duration of the event, guest count and custom décor options. Meals range $30–60/person. Tax and alcohol are additional.

AVAILABILITY: Year-round, daily until 1am.

SERVICES/AMENITIES:
Catering: in-house
Kitchen Facilities: n/a
Tables & Chairs: provided
Linens, Silver, etc.: provided
Restrooms: wheelchair accessible
Dance Floor: provided
Bride's Dressing Area: CBA
AV/Meeting Equipment: provided

Parking: large lot, valet optional; garage nearby
Accommodations: no guest rooms
Outdoor Night Lighting: CBA
Outdoor Cooking Facilities: no
Cleanup: provided
View: garden courtyard, landscaped grounds
Other: in-house florals, custom décor services

RESTRICTIONS:
Alcohol: in-house
Smoking: not allowed
Music: amplified OK

Wheelchair Access: yes
Insurance: liability required

The wedding vendors on our website are the best in the business. How do we know? Read page 577.

Canyon Crest Country Club

Country Club

975 Country Club Drive, Riverside
951/274-7905
www.canyoncrestcc.com
jenni.ebbesen@ourclub.com

● Rehearsal Dinners	● Corporate Events
● Ceremonies	● Meetings
● Wedding Receptions	● Film Shoots
● Private Parties	○ Accommodations

Everything works just right at Canyon Crest, a country club whose combined outdoor and indoor assets are appealing for all types of events, especially weddings.

A treelined boulevard sweeps its way to the club, making you feel like you've arrived at a capital "D" destination. The golf course, set along the contours of a natural bowl at the foot of desert mountains, has a touch of the exotic, with its subtropical assortment of palms, pines and eucalyptus. A fountain in the middle of a man-made lake jets water 50 feet into the air against a backdrop of nearby peaks.

But perhaps the best feature on the grounds is the ceremony site: A simple white stone arch—which you can decorate any way you like—sits at the edge of a knoll above the course, flanked by a lawn where guests assemble to witness vows. Overlooking the lake and fountain, fairways and scenery, this spot feels set apart from the country club's bustle.

The broad red canopy that shades the steps down from the parking lot to the clubhouse's gleaming glass doors imparts a decidedly upscale feel. Walk inside to the dining room, where an all-glass wall lets you gaze out on the vast and impressive green of the course—in fact, lush green is all you see. Three wide doors open onto an adjoining canopied terrace, which offers a splendid view of the fairways, lake and nearby highlands. Located just above the putting green, the tiled terrace is ideal for hosting pre- and post-wedding gatherings and cocktails, and it serves as an overflow space for dining. At dusk, lights strung along its rails and overhead supports create an enchanting look.

Just off the terrace is a spacious room set aside for the bride and her bridesmaids. The room, which is perfect for hanging out and relaxing, happens to be located so that she and her entourage can discreetly peek out the windows to see who's arrived and what's going on.

The coordinator here takes care of everything—vendor selection, menu planning, setup and takedown. She's there at the rehearsal and on the day of the wedding to make sure all goes well. The flexible kitchen can custom-design menus, offer recommendations based on their experience, and provide almost any style of food. Canyon Crest also accommodates rehearsal dinners, bridal showers and brunches. The club is private, so indoor music can go on forever. (Outdoor music has to shut down by 11pm.)

We think Canyon Crest's good looks and versatile kitchen, as well as its relaxed feel and flow, make it one of the Inland Empire's best contenders for a one-stop, affordable wedding venue.

CEREMONY CAPACITY: The site holds 250 seated guests outdoors.

EVENT/RECEPTION CAPACITY: The club can accommodate 150 seated or 300 standing guests indoors, and 100 seated or 300 standing outdoors.

MEETING CAPACITY: Meeting spaces hold up to 200 seated guests.

FEES & DEPOSITS: A deposit ranging $1,000–1,500 is required to reserve your date. 50% of the estimated event total is due 60 days prior to the event, and the balance is due 10 days prior. The rental fee ranges $250–500 depending on the day and time of the event. Meals range $35–89/person. Tax, alcohol and a 20% service charge are additional. Customizable, all-inclusive packages are available.

AVAILABILITY: Year-round, daily, anytime.

SERVICES/AMENITIES:

Catering: in-house
Kitchen Facilities: n/a
Tables & Chairs: provided
Linens, Silver, etc.: provided
Restrooms: wheelchair accessible
Dance Floor: portable provided
Bride's & Groom's Dressing Areas: yes
AV/Meeting Equipment: provided
Other: grand piano, on-site florals, clergy on staff, picnic area, event coordination

Parking: large lot, valet required
Accommodations: no guest rooms
Outdoor Night Lighting: provided
Outdoor Cooking Facilities: BBQ on site
Cleanup: provided
View: canyon, fountain, golf course fairways, lake, landscaped grounds, pool area, panorama of mountains

RESTRICTIONS:

Alcohol: in-house or BYO with corkage fee
Smoking: OK in designated areas
Music: amplified OK

Wheelchair Access: yes
Insurance: liability required

The Mission Inn Hotel & Spa

Historic Inn

3649 Mission Inn Avenue, Riverside
800/344-4225
www.missioninn.com
weddings@missioninn.com

● Rehearsal Dinners	● Corporate Events
● Ceremonies	● Meetings
● Wedding Receptions	● Film Shoots
● Private Parties	● Accommodations

Upon arriving at The Mission Inn Hotel & Spa you may wonder, as we did, exactly what kind of missionaries had inhabited this unique and eccentric edifice. The truth is, the Inn was never an actual mission housing actual missionaries; it was the personal, lifelong and quixotic "mission" of Frank Miller, the man who built what some have called an "architectural wonder."

In 1876, Miller purchased a small adobe building known as the Glenwood Inn, added a four-story wing, and The Mission Inn was born. Over the next 30 years, he built three additional wings, each more elaborate than the last. By the 1930s, The Mission Inn had expanded to fill an entire city block and had become Riverside's most visited attraction.

A wondrous, eclectic assemblage of styles, The Mission Inn achieved its national historic landmark status in 1976. Starting with Mission Revival, the hotel now incorporates architectural styles from all over the world: Moorish, Italian Renaissance, Spanish Baroque, Chinese and Japanese. It's a dazzling array of flying buttresses, domes, fountains, statues, carved pillars, towers, gargoyles, balconies, plazas, turrets, spiral staircases, gardens, bells, colorful tile and stained glass, all constructed to display the extensive collection of art and artifacts that Miller gathered on his world travels.

Perhaps the most stunning of these is the Rayas Altar, which Miller bought sight unseen in 1920 and had shipped from Mexico. Hand-carved from cedar and covered in gold-leaf, the size and beauty of the altar inspired Miller to build the Chapel of St. Francis to house it. This ornate non-denominational chapel, with its 30-foot beamed ceiling, Louis C. Tiffany stained-glass windows and enormous carved mahogany doors quickly became one of California's most popular wedding sites. Humphrey Bogart, Bette Davis (twice) and Constance Bennett all recited vows here, as have over 300 other couples each year.

The Mission Inn's heyday was during the 1930s and '40s, and a seven-year, $55-million renovation during the 1980s restored its original grandeur. The St. Francis of Assisi Chapel is once again luring betrothed couples through its doors in droves, and the Inn's many banquet rooms provide wedding celebrations with timeless artistic environments.

CEREMONY CAPACITY: The St. Francis of Assisi Chapel seats 150 guests, the St. Cecilia Chapel seats 12, and the Al Fresco Courtyard seats 170.

EVENT/RECEPTION CAPACITY: The Inn can accommodate wedding receptions for 20–296 guests seated or 20–350 guests standing.

MEETING CAPACITY: Indoor meeting facilities accommodate 10–310 guests.

FEES & DEPOSITS: For wedding receptions, a nonrefundable 25% deposit is required to confirm your date; the estimated event balance is payable 2 weeks prior to the event. Reception luncheons start at $52/person, dinners at $72/person, and both include a 2-course meal, cheese display, tray passed champagne and cider during the cocktail hour, champagne toast and wedding cake. Alcoholic beverage service, a 20% service charge and tax are additional. The Chapel Package ranges $1,000–3,000, and includes an on-site ceremony administrator, wedding-night accommodations for the bride and groom, and dressing areas for the bridal party and groomsmen.

Catering menus are available for all corporate and non-wedding social events. Luncheon menus start at $25/person, dinners at $36/person. The Mission Inn Hotel & Spa offers complete meeting and event services; please call for further information.

AVAILABILITY: Year-round, daily, 6am–midnight.

SERVICES/AMENITIES:

Catering: in-house, no BYO
Kitchen Facilities: n/a
Tables & Chairs: provided
Linens, Silver, etc.: provided
Restrooms: wheelchair accessible
Dance Floor: portable parquet provided
Bride's Dressing Area: provided with chapel package
AV/Meeting Equipment: full range, extra charge

Parking: on-site self & valet, additional charge
Accommodations: 238 guest rooms & suites
Outdoor Night Lighting: provided
Outdoor Cooking Facilities: no
Cleanup: provided
View: landscaped courtyards
Other: wedding coordinator, 7,000-square-foot spa

RESTRICTIONS:

Alcohol: in-house, no BYO
Smoking: outside only
Music: amplified OK indoors

Wheelchair Access: yes
Insurance: liability required
Other: no rice, birdseed or confetti

Wedgewood Indian Hills

Event Center

5700 Club House Drive, Riverside
866/966-3009

www.wedgewoodbanquet.com
events@wedgewoodbanquet.com

- Rehearsal Dinners
- Ceremonies
- Wedding Receptions
- Private Parties
- Corporate Events
- Meetings
- Film Shoots
- Accommodations

Two very good things come together at Wedgewood Indian Hills: a service-oriented venue and a scenic public golf course that envelops the Inland Empire's often dry landscape like a luxuriant green stole.

Wedgewood's forte is its can-do attitude: They're happy to take care of everything for you—flowers, food, cake, photographer and more. Their Indian Hills venue offers five all-inclusive packages designed for "value, service and convenience," and each one can be customized. Wedgewood Indian Hills works with the best event professionals in the area, who will meet with you personally to help create a wedding that fits your style. However, if you prefer to hire your own vendors, you can bring in any that you like—except for caterers. All catering is done in-house, and the kitchen's seasoned chefs can handle almost any cuisine.

Indian Hills' convenient location is only a short drive from San Bernardino, Riverside and Ontario. Its two ballrooms, both with full-service bars, easily accommodate groups large and small. The spacious Sunset Room has picture-window views of the golf course, while the more intimate Scenic Room overlooks the course's ceremony site. Guests often gather in this ballroom to enjoy post-ceremony champagne and hors d'oeuvres, as the new bride and groom pose for photos just outside.

Ceremonies take place on a flower-fringed lawn with a classic white gazebo, flanked on either side by a colonnade of majestic palms. However, it's the dramatic backdrop that really captures people's attention: Behind the gazebo, the ground drops away steeply to the fairway below, which seems to blend into the tree-covered hills in the distance. There are several popular photo op sites, including the gazebo itself, but one of the sweetest has to be a leafy shade tree nearby that forms a cool canopy over the couple, with the vibrant green golf course in the background.

The bride's room comes with creamy white leather couches, mirrors and direct access to a nicely outfitted bathroom with showers. There's even a steamer should the bridal gown or bridesmaid dresses require a little last-minute wrinkle removal.

Couples love Indian Hills' country club feel—especially since it comes without country club prices. From its flexible event spaces and award-winning food to the personal attention its staff gives each bride and groom, Wedgewood Indian Hills puts its stamp of excellence on every celebration that's held here.

CEREMONY, EVENT/RECEPTION & MEETING CAPACITY: The site accommodates up to 300 seated or standing guests.

FEES & DEPOSITS: 25% of the estimated total event cost is required to reserve your date. An additional 25% is due 120 days prior to the event and the balance (based on your final guest count) is due 10 days prior. All payments are credited towards your final balance and are nonrefundable and nontransferable. All-inclusive, completely customizable wedding packages start at $35/person. Tax, alcohol and a 21–22% service charge are additional.

AVAILABILITY: Year-round, daily, 6am–1am.

SERVICES/AMENITIES:

Catering: in-house
Kitchen Facilities: n/a
Tables & Chairs: provided
Linens, Silver, etc.: provided
Restrooms: wheelchair accessible
Dance Floor: yes
Bride's Dressing Area: yes
AV/Meeting Equipment: some provided

Parking: large lot
Accommodations: no guest rooms
Outdoor Night Lighting: access only
Outdoor Cooking Facilities: no
Cleanup: provided
View: landscaped grounds, garden, fountain, lake; panorama of mountains and hills
Other: coordination, in-house wedding cake and florals, clergy on staff

RESTRICTIONS:

Alcohol: in-house
Smoking: designated areas only
Music: amplified OK

Wheelchair Access: yes
Insurance: not required
Other: no rice, confetti or glitter; no open flames

Callaway Vineyard and Winery

Winery & Vineyard

32720 Rancho California Road, Temecula
951/676-4001

www.callawaywinery.com
events@callawaywinery.com

● Rehearsal Dinners	● Corporate Events
● Ceremonies	● Meetings
● Wedding Receptions	● Film Shoots
● Private Parties	Accommodations

Established in 1969 by a sports equipment executive looking to try something new, Callaway is known for the award-winning wines it's produced over the decades, as well as its hilltop view—one of the best in the entire Temecula Valley. However, the winery also has a romantic side, earning an excellent reputation for hosting weddings and receptions, too.

The two prime outdoor ceremony sites take in the distant panorama of the San Bernardino, San Gorgonio and Palomar mountain ranges, along with the rocky masses of the nearby coastal mountains. Add to this a gorgeous vineyard vista and you have a stunning wine country backdrop.

Callaway's most popular reception space is the Barrel Room, the biggest of its kind in the valley. (Brides like the room so much that some of them even elect to hold their ceremony in it.) It's large and cool, with a high ceiling and hundreds of barrels of fermenting wine along the walls. Bridal parties enter via the steel fermentation room, where candles lighting the way take them past gleaming 3,000-gallon stainless steel tanks and into the Barrel Room. Here, candlelight combines with the glow of 10 great chandeliers, creating an amazing ambiance.

The cozy Chardonnay Room is ideal for a bridal shower or rehearsal dinner. An additional option for events is the two-tiered terrace beside the winery's Meritage Restaurant; the upper level is often used for cocktail receptions and the lower for dinners. (Some couples also hold their ceremony here.)

Callaway's Meritage Restaurant Chef prepares all the food for their weddings and events, using the freshest seasonal ingredients. Each of their wedding packages offers several menu options, making it easy to select one that suits your tastes and budget. A Wedding Coordinator attends to all wedding details, assisting you every step of the way from menu planning and timelines to suggesting vendors.

Evening ceremonies, which are best at Callaway, seem to be the custom up and down the valley. One reason is Temecula's reliable cool evening breeze, a great finish to the valley's often-warm days. Another is the frequently spectacular sunsets that locals anticipate and have bragged about for decades.

Brides who get married at Callaway all mention the same things that drew them to it: the relaxed, rustic, country feel…the geography of the surrounding valley and mountains…and the dramatic outdoor setting. Come for a visit and you'll see why they love this place!

CEREMONY & EVENT/RECEPTION CAPACITY: The site holds 250 seated or 300 standing guests indoors, and 250 seated or standing outdoors.

MEETING CAPACITY: Meeting spaces hold 50 seated guests.

FEES & DEPOSITS: A $1,500 deposit plus a refundable $250 security deposit is required to reserve your date. The balance is due 14 days prior to the event. The rental fee ranges $500–1,000 depending on the space reserved and the guest count. Dinner packages start at $129/person. Tax and a 20% service charge are additional.

AVAILABILITY: Year-round, daily, with the exception of Thanksgiving Day, Christmas and New Year's Day.

SERVICES/AMENITIES:

Catering: in-house
Kitchen Facilities: n/a
Tables & Chairs: provided
Linens, Silver, etc.: provided
Restrooms: wheelchair accessible
Dance Floor: CBA, extra fee
Bride's & Groom's Dressing Areas: yes
AV/Meeting Equipment: CBA, extra fee

Parking: large lot
Accommodations: no guest rooms
Outdoor Night Lighting: provided
Outdoor Cooking Facilities: no
Cleanup: provided
View: cityscape, garden, hills; panorama of mountains, valley and vineyards
Other: event coordination

RESTRICTIONS:

Alcohol: in-house
Smoking: not allowed
Music: amplified OK with restrictions

Wheelchair Access: yes
Insurance: liability may be required

Want to know WHAT TO ASK a potential location or vendor? Check out our Questions to Ask starting on page 21.

Leoness Cellars

Winery

38311 De Portola Road, Temecula
951/302-7601 X114

www.leonesscellars.com
weddings@leonesscellars.com

- Rehearsal Dinners
- Ceremonies
- Wedding Receptions
- Private Parties
- Corporate Events
- Meetings
- Film Shoots
- Accommodations

The picturesque drive to your destination passes one well-kept horse estate after another before segueing to gentle hills planted with grapevines. This is the De Portola Wine Trail, which is less traveled and more tranquil than the main tourist route. It's also home to one of the loveliest wineries in the whole valley—Leoness Cellars, a venue with a spectacular view.

The name "Leoness" is a nod to the mythical village where King Arthur first spotted Lady Guinevere and fell in love. In Scottish it means "village of dreams," which this place truly is.

The first thing you notice when you arrive is the line of stately Italian cypress trees leading up to a European chateau-styled building that houses the very popular tasting room. Just a short distance from here is the serenely beautiful outdoor ceremony site. Elevated above the vineyards, it's set against a spectacular backdrop of the surrounding rolling hills and vineyards. A rear wall, adorned with a lion's head fountain, creates privacy and heightens the drama of your entrance, as you walk down the long center aisle to the white wooden arbor where you'll exchange vows.

Celebratory cocktails are served on the lower lawn. Guests can toast the newlyweds at tables arranged on the grass, or mingle around the bar on the adjoining shaded patio, set right at the edge of the Cabernet vines. As night falls, twinkle lights bordering the patio bring this spot to life. Afterwards, in a rare treat, you'll all be invited into the vineyard itself for an unforgettable walk down a softly lit path. It's an enjoyable way to experience the vineyards…and a great way to transition to dinner.

Receptions unfold in the Barrel Room, which comes with a charming patio that's partly enclosed by the ivy-covered walls of the building and lit by old-fashioned lampposts. Inside, however, it's all industrial chic with soaring ceilings, iron chandeliers, and oak barrels stacked up along every wall, providing an authentic winery-style wedding.

This towering space has excellent acoustics and a polished concrete floor for dancing, yet it takes on an elegant intimacy as clusters of votive candles flicker against its dark brown walls. Comfortable club chairs are arranged in a corner for lounging, and there's even a cozy niche where you may offer guests a broad range of Leoness varietals. Award-winning wines and expertly prepared food will ensure an outstanding reception and, for the perfect finale, cap off the evening with a glass of their sensual and earthy Cinsaut Dessert Wine paired with a rich bittersweet truffle. It just might make you fall in love all over again.

CEREMONY CAPACITY: The site can accommodate up to 300 seated guests outdoors.

EVENT/RECEPTION CAPACITY: The site holds 250 seated indoors.

MEETING CAPACITY: Meeting spaces hold 300 seated guests indoors.

FEES & DEPOSITS: 10% of your estimated event total or $2,000 (whichever is greater), is required along with a signed contract to reserve your date. Three additional 30% payments are due 9 months out, 6 months out and 3 months out, with any final balance due 2 weeks prior to the event. Package pricing, which starts at $110/person, is based on menu and bar package choices. Packages include facility rental and a coordinator, as well as tables, chairs, and linens. Tax and a 20% service charge are extra.

AVAILABILITY: Year-round, daily, 10am–11:30pm, excluding major holidays.

SERVICES/AMENITIES:

Catering: in-house
Kitchen Facilities: n/a
Tables & Chairs: provided
Linens, Silver, etc.: provided
Restrooms: wheelchair accessible
Dance Floor: provided
Bride's & Groom's Dressing Areas: yes
AV/Meeting Equipment: CBA

Parking: large lot
Accommodations: no guest rooms
Outdoor Night Lighting: provided
Outdoor Cooking Facilities: no
Cleanup: provided
View: garden, courtyard, hills, landscaped grounds, mountains, valley, vineyards
Other: picnic area, event coordinator

RESTRICTIONS:

Alcohol: in-house
Smoking: designated areas only
Music: amplified OK with restrictions

Wheelchair Access: yes
Insurance: not required

Mount Palomar Winery

Winery

33820 Rancho California Road, Temecula
951/676-5047 x17

www.mountpalomarwinery.com
weddingsandevents@mountpalomar.com

- Rehearsal Dinners
- Ceremonies
- Wedding Receptions
- Private Parties
- Corporate Events
- Meetings
- Film Shoots
- Accommodations

"Wine and love have ever been allies," said Ovid, and the ancient Roman poet certainly got that right. Throughout history, poets, playwrights and novelists have paired the two, and why not? Luscious grapes on the vine, intoxicating aromas, and a seductive first sip (sigh) have turned vineyards into highly coveted wedding venues…perhaps none more so than Mount Palomar Winery.

Gracing the highest hill of Temecula's famous Wine Trail, its ornate iron gates and Italian cypress-lined driveway evoke the Mediterranean countryside, while life-size statues of mythical gods and lovely maidens reinforce the Old World feel of the grounds. Plus, this sprawling 300-acre property with its 50+ acres of planted vineyards includes something most competitors don't: In addition to the multi-tiered guest areas (tasting room, restaurant, picnic spots, etc.), they offer a completely separate hillside for weddings and events—and it's spectacular.

La Bella Vista ceremony site does indeed translate to a beautiful view. From its high perch, you can see for miles over the whole Temecula Valley, an unobstructed panorama extending straight out to the distant mountains. A wide brick center aisle cuts through the lawn to a classic colonnade flanked by a low, white balustrade and urns. The effect is breathtaking. After vows are exchanged, a long bar, set against a backdrop of greenery, beckons your guests to raise a glass of bubbly.

Then, stroll through a picturesque, vine-covered arbor to the expansive al fresco reception space, comprised of the grassy Vista Del Valle and stone-floored Piazza di Arbole. The views are, once again, fantastic and the grounds are abloom with roses, scented herbs and edible grapes. Statuary abounds, along with a large fountain adorned with figurines. Your photographer will love the seemingly endless photo ops here, like dramatic shots on the illuminated staircase leading down to the main welcome center.

Another great thing about Mt. Palomar Winery is that they only host one wedding at a time, so you can spread out and enjoy! In fact, if your wedding revelry isn't ready to wind down when outdoor music ordinances kick in (or the weather isn't cooperating), you're more than welcome to move the bacchanal into their Barrel Room. Yes, it's a real working part of the winery, but so utterly romantic with crystal chandeliers, a draped ceiling and twinkle lights hidden among the stacked barrels, you'll feel like you've stepped onto a movie set. Photos taken with you posing in front of the larger vats and barrels will give your fantasy night a bit of an industrial edge.

Mt. Palomar, however, is more than just a "pretty face". Their food and wine consistently garner raves, so take advantage of their team of experts to help you pair particular varietals with your menu selections. They provide a multitude of reds, whites and dessert wines to choose from and, in fact, you can even host a private tasting as part of your shower or rehearsal dinner at their pavilion restaurant.

CEREMONY CAPACITY: The site holds 150 seated indoors and 500 seated outdoors.

EVENT/RECEPTION & MEETING CAPACITY: The site accommodates 150 seated or 250 standing guests indoors and 800 seated or 2,000 standing outdoors.

FEES & DEPOSITS: A $2,000 deposit is required to reserve your date, and the balance is due 10 days prior to the event. Wedding packages range $115–120/person and include the rental fee and alcohol. Tax and an 18% service charge are additional. The guest count minimum is 100 on Saturday and 75 on Friday and Sunday; there is no minimum Monday–Thursday.

Rates for business functions, meetings or other types of events vary. Please contact the venue for more details.

AVAILABILITY: Year-round, daily.

SERVICES/AMENITIES:

Catering: in-house
Kitchen Facilities: n/a
Tables & Chairs: provided
Linens, Silver, etc.: provided
Restrooms: wheelchair accessible
Dance Floor: yes
Bride's Dressing Area: yes
AV/Meeting Equipment: BYO
Other: event coordination, picnic area

Parking: large lot
Accommodations: no guest rooms
Outdoor Night Lighting: yes
Outdoor Cooking Facilities: no
Cleanup: provided
View: garden, fountain, landscaped grounds, waterfall; panorama of valley, fields, forest, hills and mountains

RESTRICTIONS:

Alcohol: in-house
Smoking: designated areas only
Music: amplified OK with restrictions

Wheelchair Access: yes
Insurance: not required

Temecula Creek Inn

Inn

44501 Rainbow Canyon Road, Temecula
855/420-8149

www.temeculacreekinn.com
tciweddings@jcresorts.com

●	Rehearsal Dinners	●	Corporate Events
●	Ceremonies	●	Meetings
●	Wedding Receptions	●	Film Shoots
●	Private Parties	○	Accommodations

Look up the word "charming" in the dictionary and you might find a picture of the Stone House at Temecula Creek Inn, because whoever first came up with the adjective surely had someplace just like this in mind.

Tucked away in a secluded section of the 350-acre property, this fairy-tale setting with its peak-roofed stone cottage dates back to the 1800s when the area served as a granite quarry. Today, instead of sheltering quarrymen, the stone-and-granite building has found what may be its true calling: an unforgettable site for a romantic wedding.

Your guests are shuttled down the winding path to the Stone House, which is set on a large grassy clearing against a woodland backdrop and enclosed by split-rail fencing. The building's old wood shutters, little porch and neat border of colorful flowers give the scene an enchanted feeling. Across the front lawn there's a wooden footbridge that leads to a sylvan ceremony site where everyone awaits your arrival (by horse-drawn carriage, if you wish). You make your grand entrance over that same bridge and up the aisle to a bentwood arbor, exchanging vows under a canopy of oak trees strung with lights.

Cocktails are served on the side lawn to the left of the house, where oak barrels used as tables add a nice wine country touch. Dinner follows on the main lawn, which affords a direct view of a distant fairway plus a sweet tableau of another wooden bridge and blooming hedges to the right. Create an indoor/outdoor event and take full advantage of the Stone House by adding a buffet or dessert bar inside. Later, turn the quaint interior, with its fireplace and cross-beam ceiling, into an after-hours lounge. Guests can also enjoy cocktails and warm themselves at glowing fire pits on both sides of the house, or play bocce ball and other games on the adjacent activity lawn.

Temecula Creek Inn offers an additional wedding venue, The Meadows, an expansive lawn where you can host your entire celebration. Say "I do" framed by natural foliage and fragrant rosebushes, then host your reception nearby around flickering fire pits.

Besides being a popular wedding location, this resort has plenty of other assets, including: a championship 27-hole golf course; 130 well-appointed guest rooms, each with its own balcony or terrace; and their restaurant, Cork|Fire Kitchen, with an eclectic menu and lively adjacent bar.

Temecula Creek Inn also makes a fabulous home base for visiting the numerous wineries and attractions of the Temecula Valley, so go ahead and extend your stay here—you'll be so glad you did!

CEREMONY CAPACITY: The site can accommodate up to 300 seated guests outdoors.

EVENT/RECEPTION CAPACITY: The site holds 220 seated guests indoors, and 300 seated or standing outdoors.

MEETING CAPACITY: Meeting spaces hold 220 seated guests.

FEES & DEPOSITS: A nonrefundable deposit and a signed contract are required to reserve your date. A nonrefundable deposit of 50% of the total estimated cost is due 30 days prior to the event, with the final estimated balance due 5 business days prior to the scheduled function. Rental fees range $500–4,000 depending on the space reserved. Meals start at $56/person. Tax, alcohol and a service charge are additional. Food & beverage minimums apply based on the date of your event and the areas reserved.

AVAILABILITY: Year-round.

SERVICES/AMENITIES:
Catering: in-house
Kitchen Facilities: fully equipped
Tables & Chairs: provided, upgrades available
Linens, Silver, etc.: provided, upgrades available
Restrooms: wheelchair accessible
Dance Floor: provided
Bride's Dressing Area: yes
AV/Meeting Equipment: provided, upgrades available

Parking: large lot, self-parking
Accommodations: 130 guest rooms
Outdoor Night Lighting: provided, upgrades available
Outdoor Cooking Facilities: no
Cleanup: provided
View: courtyard, fountain, landscaped grounds; golf course fairways; panorama of forest, hills, lake and mountains
Other: spa services, event coordination

RESTRICTIONS:
Alcohol: in-house
Smoking: designated areas only
Music: amplified OK with restrictions in some areas

Wheelchair Access: yes
Insurance: liability required

Vitagliano Vineyards and Winery
at Lake Oak Meadows

Private Waterfront Estate

36101 Glen Oaks Road, Temecula
951/676-6162
www.LakeOakMeadows.com
info@LakeOakMeadows.com

- Rehearsal Dinners
- Ceremonies
- Wedding Receptions
- Private Parties
- Corporate Events
- Meetings
- Film Shoots
- Accommodations

In the heart of Temecula wine country is a private, 10-acre estate where rose bushes scent the air and a wonderful variety of trees form shady groves around a serene lake, known for its spectacular nighttime display: "Fountains of Fire and Water."

While this almost Eden-like oasis is terrific for concerts, retreats, memorials and reunions, it's utterly romantic for weddings. Couples recite their vows under a flower-adorned arch on a grassy peninsula that juts out into the lake. Ornate lamps and fragrant roses edge the ceremony space, and stately pepper trees form a sheltering backdrop. Just across the lake, a picturesque waterfall cascades down large rocks.

Guests enjoy post-ceremony cocktails under a shady arbor and on the adjoining lawn. Strings of twinkle lights dangle from the arbor and wrap around the trees, and the optional addition of delicate Japanese lanterns enhances the romantic atmosphere. At night, the illumination elicits many "oohs" and "ahhs," which multiply even more when the lake's fountains light up in their fiery dance.

Steps away from the arbor, the reception lawn is a particularly comfortable setting as Temecula's famous late afternoon breeze begins to stir. Caterers love having a prep room close by—it makes keeping food coming fast and fresh a snap. The lawn, which can be canopied, has lines of lights streaming above it and along the low wooden fence that borders it. With a bar tucked into one corner, there's plenty of room for tables and chairs. An area is available for serving hors d'oeuvres and wine, and your guests can mingle around fire pits under a canopy of grapevines and trees. The adjacent reception lounge is where your DJ sets up, and its majestic fireplace and chandelier create a welcoming ambiance for your guests to dance the night away.

Conveniences abound in the bride's room, including air conditioning, full-length mirrors, mirrored makeup seating, a kitchenette, refrigerator, plasma TV, fireplace and shower. Outside, her private patio is enclosed by wood lattice walls. A popular tradition here is for the bride to emerge from her dressing room, walk across a small bridge with a rock waterfall, and step into a horse-drawn carriage that takes her to the lakeside ceremony site.

A grassy knoll behind the lake is a favorite spot for photos. Pepper and black gum trees shade this pleasant green rise, which is bordered by a quaint split-rail fence that zigzags between the lawn and flowerbeds.

Vitagliano Vineyards and Winery at Lake Oak Meadows has a distinct "ranch feel," but with all the rough edges smoothed away. What remains is a beautiful, amenity-rich venue that immediately captures the fancy of almost everyone. After you take a quick stroll from the parking lot down the terraced stairway and get your first dazzling lake view, you'll see why this location is worth considering for any event.

CEREMONY CAPACITY: The site can accommodate up to 300 seated guests outdoors.

EVENT/RECEPTION & MEETING CAPACITY: The resort holds 300 seated guests.

FEES & DEPOSITS: A $3,500 deposit is required to reserve your date, and the contracted balance is due 30 days prior to the event. The ceremony-only venue rental fee ranges $1,000–3,500. There is no rental fee for events with both ceremony and reception, however there will be a charge for extra time added to your event. Wedding packages range $100–116/person. Tax, bar package, and a 20% service charge are additional.

AVAILABILITY: Year-round, daily, anytime, excluding major holidays.

SERVICES/AMENITIES:

Catering: in-house
Kitchen Facilities: n/a
Tables & Chairs: provided
Linens, Silver, etc.: provided
Restrooms: wheelchair accessible
Dance Floor: provided
Bride's & Groom's Dressing Areas: yes
AV/Meeting Equipment: some provided
Other: event coordination provided

Parking: large lot
Accommodations: honeymoon suite
Outdoor Night Lighting: provided
Outdoor Cooking Facilities: CBA
Cleanup: provided
View: forest, fountain, garden, hills, lagoon, lake, landscaped grounds, meadow, waterfall, park; panorama of mountains and vineyards

RESTRICTIONS:

Alcohol: in-house
Smoking: designated areas only
Music: amplified OK

Wheelchair Access: yes
Insurance: liability required

Want to find more venues and services? Check out our informative website, www.HereComesTheGuide.com.

465

Wedgewood Upland Hills

Event Center

1231 East 16th Street, Upland
866/966-3009

www.wedgewoodbanquet.com
events@wedgewoodbanquet.com

- Rehearsal Dinners
- Ceremonies
- Wedding Receptions
- Private Parties
- Corporate Events
- Meetings
- Film Shoots
- Accommodations

Although contemporary in construction, Wedgewood Upland Hills conveys a more Old World character. With its high, hipped roof, veranda, and series of brick columns and French doors, the banquet center's architecture echoes the aesthetic of *fin-de-siècle* colonial buildings found in the West Indies. Indeed, as you lean out over the upstairs terrace, mint julep in hand, the air is so balmy and the fairways so green that visions of Martinique or Antigua come to mind. As you might imagine, this pretty and perennially lush landscape is an appealing backdrop for weddings and receptions.

Wedding ceremonies are held in a white, old-fashioned wedding gazebo just a short distance from the clubhouse. Skirted by red roses and framed by the slate blue silhouette of the San Gabriel Mountains in the distance, it's a lovely, poetic setting. To further the romantic atmosphere, some brides arrive via horse-drawn carriage; others add drama by making a slow entrance on a gently winding path that has been trimmed into the grass.

For a post-ceremony photo safari, newlyweds and their photographer are welcome to take a golf cart out for a spin on the adjacent golf course. Meanwhile guests can enjoy cocktails and happily hobnob on the clubhouse patio.

Small to mid-size receptions are hosted in the Fountain View Room, which spans the length of the clubhouse's upper level. Lined with windows and five sets of French doors, this radiant, light-filled space features a glorious vista of the fairways, lakes and fountains below. For an up-close-and-personal view of the golf greens, have your soirée out on the wraparound covered veranda. Here guests will appreciate the sound of palms rustling in the breeze, and the scent of pines and freshly mowed grass.

Larger gatherings are held in the newly constructed Mountain View Room, a freestanding 4,000-square-foot pavilion with a full wall of floor-to-ceiling windows that capture sweeping views. Highlights of this versatile space include a private bar, dance floor and beautifully draped ceiling.

The venue's easy, breezy ambiance is made even more so thanks to Wedgewood's event professionals. Their all-inclusive and reasonably priced wedding packages are customizable, giving you the choice of leaving everything up to them or selecting which services you'd like to take on yourself. Either way, you'll be in experienced hands so you can enjoy your celebration to the fullest.

If pristine fairways and an elegant, yet relaxed, country club environment appeal to your sensibilities, then Wedgewood Upland Hills is the perfect place for your party!

CEREMONY, EVENT/RECEPTION & MEETING CAPACITY: The site holds up to 250 seated or standing guests.

FEES & DEPOSITS: 25% of the estimated total event cost is required to reserve your date. An additional 25% is due 120 days prior to the event and the balance (based on your final guest count) is due 10 days prior. All payments are credited towards your final balance and are nonrefundable and nontransferable. All-inclusive, completely customizable wedding packages start at $36/person. Tax, alcohol and a 21–22% service charge are additional.

AVAILABILITY: Year-round, daily, 7am–11pm, including holidays.

SERVICES/AMENITIES:

Catering: in-house
Kitchen Facilities: n/a
Tables & Chairs: provided
Linens, Silver, etc.: provided
Restrooms: wheelchair accessible
Dance Floor: provided
Bride's Dressing Area: yes
AV/Meeting Equipment: some provided

Parking: large lot
Accommodations: no guest rooms
Outdoor Night Lighting: yes
Outdoor Cooking Facilities: no
Cleanup: provided
View: fountain, fairways, lagoon, landscaped grounds, mountains
Other: in-house wedding cake and florals, clergy on staff, event coordination

RESTRICTIONS:

Alcohol: in-house
Smoking: designated areas only
Music: amplified OK

Wheelchair Access: yes
Insurance: not required
Other: no rice, confetti or glitter; no open flames

Spring Valley Lake Country Club

Golf Club

13229 Spring Valley Parkway, Victorville
760/245-5356 x222

www.spring-valley-lake.com
contactus@spring-valley-lake.com

● Rehearsal Dinners	● Corporate Events
● Ceremonies	● Meetings
● Wedding Receptions	● Film Shoots
● Private Parties	Accommodations

Coming inside the clubhouse, you leave the desert sun behind and enter a cool, calm sanctuary. The Via Verde Room has a view of the fairways and the San Bernardino Mountains beyond. It also boasts a large, picturesque stone fireplace that dominates one wall. With the ambiance of a cozy drawing room, it's often used for small private parties, intimate cocktail receptions and wedding ceremonies.

The Mirage Room is the club's main reception space. Cantilevered over the lake, it has floor-to-ceiling windows on three sides that look out onto the water, the verdant golf course and the majestic mountains in the distance. Skylights running the length of the wood-beam ceiling fill the room with light. A full-service bar, dance floor and a nook for a DJ or a band allow for a wide range of entertainment, and there's a balcony that wraps around the entire perimeter of the room. Your guests will want to linger here, drinking in the lovely panorama—they may even be regaled by one of those fiery sunsets particular to the desert.

If you're extending your stay through the weekend and you're partial to golf, arrange a tee time on the club's Robert Trent Jr./Sr. championship fairways. Non-golfers will find plenty of other activities within an easy drive of Victorville. Nearby Calico is the site of an Early Man archaeological dig and an Old West ghost town. Even closer, the city of Barstow offers a terrific shopping outlet center and one of the last drive-in movie theaters in California. In the winter, snowboarding and skiing are less than an hour away in Big Bear.

Spring Valley provides a private club experience, with service being their top priority. They'll help you with every aspect of your event, and make sure that you'll have a beautiful celebration at an affordable price.

CEREMONY CAPACITY: Indoors the Via Verde Room seats 80 guests, and the Mirage Room seats up to 180. Outdoors the site holds 200 seated guests.

EVENT/RECEPTION & MEETING CAPACITY: The Via Verde Room holds 80 seated or 150 standing guests. The Mirage Room holds 180 seated or 250 standing. Smaller rooms can be arranged.

FEES & DEPOSITS: A $500 deposit is required to reserve your date. 50% of the estimated event total is due 60 days prior to the event and the balance is due 10 days prior. Rental fees range $400–1,000 depending on the day and time of the event and the space rented. Meals start at $22/person. Packages start at $41/person. Tax, alcohol and a 20% service charge are additional.

AVAILABILITY: Year-round.

SERVICES/AMENITIES:

Catering: in-house
Kitchen Facilities: n/a
Tables & Chairs: provided
Linens, Silver, etc.: provided
Restrooms: wheelchair accessible
Dance Floor: provided
Bride's Dressing Area: yes
AV/Meeting Equipment: screen, podium, microphone, projector

Parking: large lot
Accommodations: no guest rooms
Outdoor Night Lighting: yes
Outdoor Cooking Facilities: no
Cleanup: provided
View: lake, golf course, mountains
Other: wedding coordinator

RESTRICTIONS:

Alcohol: in-house, no BYO
Smoking: outdoors only
Music: amplified OK indoors

Wheelchair Access: yes
Insurance: not required
Other: no rice, birdseed or confetti

Wrightwood Guest Ranch

Ranch

78 Big Pines Highway, Wrightwood
760/249-5093

www.wrightwoodguestranch.com
info@wrightwoodguestranch.com

- Rehearsal Dinners
- Ceremonies
- Wedding Receptions
- Private Parties

- Corporate Events
- Meetings
- Film Shoots

  Accommodations

In the late 1920s, Hollywood's playful elite were understandably drawn to Wrightwood, a sweet mountain town with brisk air, beautiful views and year-round outdoor diversions. Nestled in a valley between slopes blanketed with evergreen pines, it's an easy 90-minute journey from Los Angeles and the San Gabriel Valley along California State Highway 2, (or simply "The Two," for locals.)

Wrightwood Guest Ranch sits just off one of the prettiest stretches of "The Two," on 300 acres of forested wilderness that encompasses lawns, private hiking trails, and pristine wildlife habitat. Its design is inspired by the traditional dude ranch, with a rustic, wood-sided main cabin overlooking rocky seasonal riverbeds, weathered stone and wood bridges, and trickling creeks that flow into sparkling ponds. Weddings held here can't help but exude the same welcoming, down-home vibe of the town itself, which has retained its quiet alpine charm.

As guests arrive—they may be shuttled in from the nearby parking lot, or opt to take the short walk to the site—they're greeted by a huge expanse of grass at the base of the main cabin. (The cabin is used as the ranch's office, but has a cute area for bridal preparations, too.) The grass practically begs for lawn games, so many couples kick off the day with bocce ball, croquet, or horseshoes. Guests more interested in relaxing can simply mingle and chat, enjoying cocktails under the pines.

The centerpiece of the property is an extraordinary 250-year-old oak whose multiple trunks reach upward and outward, stretching toward the sky to create an enormous natural canopy and a most idyllic spot to say your vows. After the ceremony, guests cross a bridge over a small pond to a manicured lawn where the celebration continues. A large stage, just the right size for a bridal party or sweetheart table, overlooks the festivities. As twilight becomes evening, white globe lights placed throughout the trees, on bridges and along the fence line encircle the reception area in a twinkly glow. (Some couples have chosen to flip the sites, holding the ceremony on the stage and the reception under the oak; either setup works wonderfully.)

The expansive lawn area, which extends to the surrounding forest, is also where you'll find the aptly named Woodpecker Bar. It's located next to the pond in the shade of a towering pine tree with a trunk completely covered in woodpecker holes. The ranch provides your bar service, as well as a variety of flexible options for all budgets. There's ample room on the green for a tent in the event of rain, though it's unlikely you'd need it since weddings at the Ranch are held from May through October, when the weather is almost unfailingly sunny and mild.

In case you're thinking this place sounds like a great destination for a weekend wedding, it is. They provide a preferred lodging list that includes adorable handpicked Wrightwood cabin rentals for your guests, plus some serious fun right on the property! Their zipline company's Big Pines Zipline Tours are not only located at the ranch, they offer a special wedding party discount package on rides during the wedding weekend.

But perhaps the loveliest thing about Wrightwood Guest Ranch is the people who work here. The employees have an enormous amount of pride in their venue, and it's evident in the care and commitment they show each couple.

CEREMONY, EVENT/RECEPTION & MEETING CAPACITY: The site holds 300 seated or standing guests outdoors.

FEES & DEPOSITS: 1/3 of the estimated event total is required to reserve your date. The balance is payable in monthly installments, with the final payment due 30 days prior to the event. Pricing for all-inclusive weddings starts at $5,000 for a 50-guest minimum, and varies depending on the catering, rentals and amenities chosen. Tax, gratuities and service charges are all included; alcohol is additional.

Rates for business functions, meetings or other types of events vary. Corporate Team Building events can include zipline use and lunch. Please contact the venue for more details.

AVAILABILITY: Weddings take place May–October, daily.

SERVICES/AMENITIES:
Catering: select from list
Kitchen Facilities: limited
Tables & Chairs: provided
Linens, Silver, etc.: linens provided; china service available, extra charge
Restrooms: wheelchair accessible
Dance Floor: yes
Bride's Dressing Area: yes
AV/Meeting Equipment: BYO
Other: picnic area, Big Pines Zipline, event coordination

Parking: large complimentary lot with shuttle
Accommodations: preferred lodging list for the town of Wrightwood
Outdoor Night Lighting: yes
Outdoor Cooking Facilities: no
Cleanup: provided
View: garden, landscaped grounds, waterfall with pond; panorama of fields, forest and mountains

RESTRICTIONS:
Alcohol: in-house
Smoking: designated areas only
Music: amplified OK outdoors

Wheelchair Access: yes
Insurance: liability required

San Diego Area

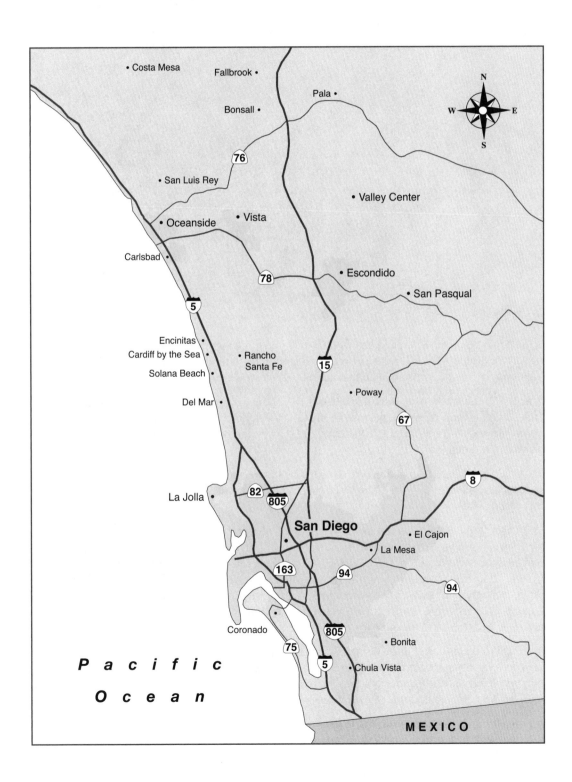

Chula Vista Golf Course

Golf Club

4475 Bonita Road, Bonita
888/292-6120

www.countryclubreceptions.com
privateeventmanager@chulavistagc.com

- Rehearsal Dinners
- Ceremonies
- Wedding Receptions
- Private Parties
- Corporate Events
- Meetings
- Film Shoots
- Accommodations

If the newly refurbished Chula Vista Golf Course had to be summed up in a single word, it would be "distinguished." The clubhouse's beautifully appointed interior, which features rich dark wood, high-end fixtures and fine architectural accents, suggests elegance at every turn.

The care taken in the venue's 2012 remodel is evident from the moment you walk in the door. Little details—from the just-right vase on the entryway hutch to the original paintings and metal art on the walls—are a delight to the eyes and convey the notion that your wedding will benefit from a lot of attention, too.

Larger receptions are held in the Vista Room, a slightly contemporary take on the stately ballroom-style facility. Tasteful two-tone mocha-colored walls and a neutral brown carpet add warmth to this grand space.

The Links Room, which overlooks the manicured hills of the golf course, is a distinctive setting for a smaller crowd. Sunshine streams through a wall of windows, bringing out the luster of the dark mahogany wainscoting and pillars. Historical sepia photos and paintings of San Diego's South County adorn the room's ivory walls. Toward the rear, a set of stairs takes revelers to the Loft, a raised half-enclosed section of the room that is typically used for the DJ and dance floor. Many couples like this semi-separate area because, while the partying is going on full force in the Loft, guests seated at tables can still carry on a conversation.

Attention to detail at the Chula Vista Golf Course doesn't end with its décor. The chef can customize your event menu, and their wedding package provides little extras that come standard—extras that you often have to pay for at other locations. For instance, there's no cake-cutting fee and a wide array of linen colors are offered at no additional charge.

All the effort that the Chula Vista Golf Course has put into creating a stylish and dignified setting has paid off—it now possesses everything you need to make your wedding a gracious affair.

CEREMONY, EVENT/RECEPTION & MEETING CAPACITY: The location holds a maximum of 200 seated guests.

FEES & DEPOSITS: A nonrefundable deposit, which is applied to your food & beverage total, is required to reserve your date. The amount of the deposit varies depending on how far in advance you book. Payment terms for the balance also vary, and may be arranged on an individual basis. Meals start at $25/person. Tax, alcohol and service charge are additional. Food & beverage minimums may apply. Menus and packages can be customized to fit your needs and budget. Call for details.

AVAILABILITY: Year-round, daily.

SERVICES/AMENITIES:

Catering: in-house
Kitchen Facilities: fully equipped
Tables & Chairs: provided
Linens, Silver, etc.: provided
Restrooms: wheelchair accessible
Dance Floor: provided
Bride's Dressing Areas: no
AV/Meeting Equipment: CBA

Parking: large complimentary lot
Accommodations: no guest rooms
Outdoor Night Lighting: provided
Outdoor Cooking Facilities: no
Cleanup: provided
View: golf course, landscaped grounds
Other: event coordination

RESTRICTIONS:

Alcohol: in-house
Smoking: outdoors only
Music: amplified OK indoors only

Wheelchair Access: yes
Insurance: not required

This is important! Tell locations you're reading HERE COMES THE GUIDE and ask if our information is still current.

The Crossings at Carlsbad

Waterfront Golf Clubhouse

5800 The Crossings Drive, Carlsbad
760/444-1885

www.thecrossingsatcarlsbad.com
catering@thecrossingsatcarlsbad.com

- Rehearsal Dinners
- Ceremonies
- Wedding Receptions
- Private Parties
- Corporate Events
- Meetings
- Film Shoots
- Accommodations

It may seem like the impossible dream to find everything you're looking for in one location—charming coastal community, acres of lush, manicured grounds and a backdrop of the blue Pacific—but all that and more is waiting for you at The Crossings at Carlsbad.

Perched atop a hillside road just a mile from the beach, this upscale golf club occupies an amazing vantage with views of rolling fairways, sunsets over the horizon, and rugged canyons. The 28,000-square-foot clubhouse incorporates natural materials like stone and wood with lots of glass to showcase the surrounding landscape. Inside the lobby, you'll find comfy, rustic-style leather seating and modern, cylindrical chandeliers.

If you're having your ceremony here, and most couples do, your guests will gather on the Ceremony Lawn, a wide swath of grass framed by feathery trees and shrubbery. Feel the cool sea breezes as you exchange vows against a panorama of the ocean below.

Then it's time to celebrate with a glass of bubbly on the adjacent Terrace or upstairs on the wraparound Canyon Patio where, along with cocktails and hors d'oeuvres, you can drink in the peaceful vistas. Needless to say, the beautiful surroundings offer up lots of great photo ops, from romantic duets at the rock waterfalls, a charming bridge or a verdant knoll…to group shots in front of the very photogenic arched iron gates of the clubhouse.

The Canyons Restaurant, the setting for your main reception, is equally striking. This soaring space features floor-to-ceiling windows and exposed, trestle beams sporting iron rivets for a casually elegant ambiance. There's a long, polished wood bar with black granite top that runs the length of the room, and a large dance floor in front of it. A tall, stacked stone hearth at one end can be a great focal point for an indoor ceremony, a rehearsal dinner or other intimate event. And of course, wherever you're seated, you'll enjoy a direct sightline to those glorious exteriors.

Their new executive chef uses his extensive global experience to lead a topnotch culinary team in creating award-winning fare, both casual and gourmet. You can choose from a wide array of menus and complete packages—or even opt to bring in your own caterer, especially for ethnic dishes.

The entire staff offers personalized service, helping you from start to finish so that you can actually relax and enjoy your own event. Whether you'd like a golf tournament, rehearsal dinner, late-night party on the Player's Lounge Patio or overnight accommodations at a local hotel, they're happy to arrange it. They can even help organize a show-stopping entrance via helicopter from nearby Palomar Airport. Oh, and by the way, did we mention that their attention to detail not only takes the cake—it includes a totally customized one!

CEREMONY CAPACITY: The site holds 100 seated indoors and 250 seated outdoors.

EVENT/RECEPTION & MEETING CAPACITY: The site accommodates 250 seated guests indoors and 300 seated or standing outdoors.

FEES & DEPOSITS: A $1,500 deposit is required 6 months prior to your date and the balance is due 10 days prior. Event space rental fees range $300–2,000 depending on day and time of the event and spaces reserved. Meals range $20–120/person. Tax, alcohol and a 21% service charge are additional.

AVAILABILITY: Year-round, daily, 7am–midnight.

SERVICES/AMENITIES:

Catering: in-house
Kitchen Facilities: n/a
Tables & Chairs: provided
Linens, Silver, etc.: provided
Restrooms: wheelchair accessible
Dance Floor: portable provided
Bride's Dressing Area: yes
AV/Meeting Equipment: provided

Parking: large complimentary lot
Accommodations: no guest rooms
Outdoor Night Lighting: CBA
Outdoor Cooking Facilities: BBQ CBA
Cleanup: provided
View: garden, lagoon; panorama of landscaped grounds, fairways and Pacific Ocean
Other: event coordination; ceremony includes wrought-iron arch and white padded chairs

RESTRICTIONS:

Alcohol: in-house, or BYO with corkage fee
Smoking: designated areas only
Music: amplified OK with restrictions

Wheelchair Access: yes
Insurance: liability required

Sheraton Carlsbad Resort and Spa

Coastal Resort Hotel

5480 Grand Pacific Drive, Carlsbad
760/827-2414

www.sheratoncarlsbad.com
dayala@sheratoncarlsbad.com

- Rehearsal Dinners
- Ceremonies
- Wedding Receptions
- Private Parties
- Corporate Events
- Meetings
- Film Shoots
- Accommodations

Mere minutes from a particularly lovely stretch of the California coast, this Mediterranean-style, luxury resort is blessed with cool ocean breezes and even cooler ocean views. The Sheraton's verdant seaside bluff setting, extending across some of north San Diego County's most desirable real estate, gives you a sense of getting away from it all—which sounds about perfect for a memorable wedding.

Why not arrive early and get the wedding weekend started with some well-deserved, mother-daughter or bridal party pampering at their Ocean Pearl Spa? Then, follow with a scrumptious rehearsal dinner at TWENTY/20, their casually chic restaurant where you can expect creative cuisine made from the freshest ingredients. Afterwards, you might want to linger on TWENTY/20's patio for a nightcap beside the fire pit.

Your big day officially starts with a ceremony at your choice of two tropically landscaped sites. The secluded Ocean Blue Lawn, situated at the far end of the property, is framed by a lush array of trees and white roses and cooled by tranquil ocean breezes. You can make a dramatic entrance as you head down a long staircase to join your groom and say "I do" against a panorama of the shimmering sea. Or, you can get married on the expansive, Pacific Lawn. Surrounded by towering palms and bordered by a vine-covered pergola, this wide swath of grass is anchored at one end by a circular patio adorned with a truly magnificent magnolia tree. Its spreading branches create a stunning natural backdrop for exchanging vows.

The nearby Palm Courtyard, overlooking the gardens and pool, is a wonderful al fresco reception area. If you prefer something more formal, reserve either the Sunset or Grand Pacific Ballroom. Both come with their own light-filled foyers for cocktails and hors d'oeuvres, as well sweeping, columned terraces that afford sunset and starlit vistas. High ceilings, modern chandeliers, large dance floors and state-of-the-art AV systems set the stage for the kind of celebration you've always imagined. Best of all, you'll be guided by a team of experts that can help you choose everything from décor and lighting packages to your menu.

The service here is amazing. It starts with the warm greeting you receive on arrival and continues every step of the way. Want to turn your event into a mini-vacation? Have the staff arrange accommodations and local activities, like a visit to Legoland (the Sheraton has its own private entrance to the park!); a round of golf up the hill at The Crossings at Carlsbad; a day at the beach; or shopping for designer clothes at the premium outlet mall nearby. They can also organize a private trolley to take your guests to favorite attractions. And did we mention that while you're having a great time you'll be earning Starwood SPG Rewards Points, too?

CEREMONY & MEETING CAPACITY: The site holds 900 seated guests indoors and outdoors.

EVENT/RECEPTION CAPACITY: The facility can accommodate 600 seated or 1,000 standing indoors or outdoors.

FEES & DEPOSITS: 25% of the food & beverage minimum is required to reserve your date. A portion is due 30 days prior to the event and any remaining balance is due by the event date. There are no separate rental fees. Meals start at $80/person and the price varies depending on menu choices. Tax, alcohol and a 22% service charge are additional. Customized menus and inclusive wedding packages are available. Call for details.

AVAILABILITY: Year-round, daily, 6am–midnight.

SERVICES/AMENITIES:
Catering: in-house
Kitchen Facilities: n/a
Tables & Chairs: provided
Linens, Silver, etc.: provided
Restrooms: wheelchair accessible
Dance Floor: portable provided
Bride's Dressing Area: yes
AV/Meeting Equipment: some provided, more CBA

Parking: large lot, valet available
Accommodations: 250 guest rooms
Outdoor Night Lighting: yes
Outdoor Cooking Facilities: no
Cleanup: provided
View: panoramic coastal views from Carlsbad's highest point
Other: event coordination

RESTRICTIONS:
Alcohol: in-house
Smoking: outdoors only
Music: amplified OK

Wheelchair Access: yes
Insurance: liability required

Loews Coronado Bay Resort

Waterfront Resort

4000 Coronado Bay Road, Coronado

619/424-4469

www.loewshotels.com/coronadobay
cbreleadcoordinator@loewshotels.com

- Rehearsal Dinners
- Ceremonies
- Wedding Receptions
- Private Parties
- Corporate Events
- Meetings
- Film Shoots
- Accommodations

Loews Coronado Bay Resort, an island getaway just 20 minutes over the bridge from San Diego, may be one of the few places where you truly can have it all. Its serene locale balances beach-y relaxation with pampered elegance, while providing unsurpassed ocean and bay vistas. Presiding over its own 15-acre peninsula adjacent to Silver Strand State Beach, this beautiful venue offers a myriad of picturesque settings plus the personal touch that makes every couple feel like VIPs.

The main entrance, which looks out over a tableau of moored yachts, leads to a bright, open two-story lobby with a grand split staircase. On the second floor you'll find Mistral, their much-lauded restaurant with views to die for. Perfect for a congenial rehearsal dinner, about the only thing here that'll take your eye off the bay/bridge/skyline panorama is the food itself—sea-inspired cuisine that's exquisitely prepared and presented.

Choices abound when it comes to a ceremony site, from the two-tiered, centerpiece Bay Terrace to the more intimate Sunset Terrace (both with huge, stunning water backdrops) or a fragrant herb garden. Want to dig your toes in the sand while you say "I do"? Then exchange vows right at the ocean's edge.

Follow with cocktails and a reception on the Marina Terrace, as you drink in the scene of the boats sailing the waterways of the Coronado Cays. You can even up the fanfare with a dramatic entrance as newlyweds on a romantic gondola. And, if you like, opt for dining and dancing al fresco…or add a billowing tent.

If you prefer to celebrate indoors, there are two fabulous, formal venues. The expansive Commodore Ballroom includes a glass-walled foyer that brings the bay up close and personal. And the Constellation Ballroom features gorgeous crystal chandeliers that look like branch coral, and an outdoor terrace that takes in all the sights. (You can also book Mistral for a sophisticated dinner or bountiful brunch).

Now that you've tied the knot, you and many of your guests will no doubt want to spend a little (or a lot!) more time at Loews to savor the pleasures of this destination location. Indulge in some spa treatments, take a dip in the pool, play tennis or explore the town. It's just a short walk to the beach, where friends and family can build sand castles, go for a swim or soak up the sun...and then linger over a nice glass of wine in one of the Loews lounges.

The accommodations are wonderfully plush, but what really impresses is how warm and helpful the staff is at every turn. From planning your event to overseeing all the details (including custom menus and cake design), the experienced team will make sure your entire stay goes smoothly so you can actually relax. And that may be the best wedding gift of all.

CEREMONY CAPACITY: The site holds 500 seated indoors and 400 seated outdoors.

EVENT/RECEPTION CAPACITY: The site can accommodate 800 seated or 1,200 standing guests indoors and 400 seated or 700 standing outdoors.

MEETING CAPACITY: Meeting spaces hold up to 850 seated guests.

FEES & DEPOSITS: 25% of the total event cost is required to reserve your date, and the balance is due 30 days prior to the event. If the event is within 6 months, a 50% deposit will be required. The rental fee ranges $1,000–3,500 depending on the space reserved, day and time rented, and the guest count. Meals range $108–179/person. Tax, alcohol and a 23% service charge are additional.

AVAILABILITY: Year-round, daily, flexible hours.

SERVICES/AMENITIES:
Catering: in-house
Kitchen Facilities: n/a
Tables & Chairs: provided
Linens, Silver, etc.: provided
Restrooms: wheelchair accessible
Dance Floor: portable provided
Bride's Dressing Area: CBA
AV/Meeting Equipment: CBA

Parking: valet available, garage nearby
Accommodations: 439 guest rooms
Outdoor Night Lighting: CBA
Outdoor Cooking Facilities: no
Cleanup: provided
View: panorama of San Diego Bay, Coronado Bridge & San Diego downtown skyline
Other: grand piano

RESTRICTIONS:
Alcohol: in-house
Smoking: designated areas only
Music: amplified OK with restrictions

Wheelchair Access: yes
Insurance: liability required

Orfila Vineyards and Winery

Winery & Vineyard

13455 San Pasqual Road, Escondido

760/738-6500 x24

www.orfila.com
steffi@orfila.com

- Rehearsal Dinners
- Ceremonies
- Wedding Receptions
- Private Parties
- Corporate Events
- Meetings
- Film Shoots
- Accommodations

Alejandro Orfila, the man behind lovely Orfila Vineyards and Winery, has led an extraordinary life. Formerly Argentina's ambassador to the United States, and later Secretary General of the Organization of American States, he has hobnobbed with every U.S. president from Truman to Clinton. When he retired from his 39-year diplomatic career, he bought a small winery in sleepy San Pasqual Valley and turned its 70 acres into an unexpectedly world-class operation. Credit also goes to winemaker Justin Mund, who joined Orfila in 2010 and continues to maintain and enhance the winery's high-quality standards.

Orfila's grounds are as spectacular as their wines, and they make a decidedly romantic backdrop for a wedding. Ceremonies are held on an expansive lawn with a classic wine country view: countless well-tended rows of Syrah, Sangiovese, Cabernet Sauvignon and Merlot grapes receding towards unspoiled hills rising in the distance. Only the occasional bird chirping interrupts the quiet of this valley, which becomes your cathedral. Its timeless natural beauty complements any celebration, whether formal, relaxed, or somewhere in between.

It's a short stroll from the lawn to the patio, where your guests gather for cocktails. Surrounded by flowers and lit by charming gas lamp-style fixtures, it's the perfect spot for mingling on a balmy summer evening. Bartenders typically dispense libations under the long, vine-covered grape arbor, as your family and friends sample hors d'oeuvres—you may also be inspired to host a wine and cheese tasting!

There is no shortage of photo opportunities at Orfila: down in the vineyard; in the sprawling, grassy rose park among white, pink, peach, yellow and red roses; and up in the aromatic barrel room (you're sure to recall its intoxicating aroma every time you open your wedding album).

Are you planning to invite a lot of people? They'll all fit under the 6,000-square-foot white pavilion adjacent to the patio, with plenty of room left over for your band or DJ and dancing on a hardwood floor. Heaters and ceiling fans provide comfort in any weather; leave the tent sides tied open to enjoy the breeze and the view of the vineyard when the weather is good (which is most of the time). Dramatic spotlights, uplights and "gobo" lights can be adjusted to create whatever mood you like.

In keeping with its commitment to quality, the winery only works with a handpicked coterie of preferred caterers who can handle the full range of events, from a simple down-home dinner to an elaborate gala. In addition, Orfila will assign an event supervisor to make sure everything runs smoothly.

Finally, what would make a more fitting keepsake of your marriage at the winery than a bottle of your favorite Orfila vintage, customized with your own private, commemorative label? Uncork one bottle per table and let your guests raise their glasses together, or give every adult a bottle to take home to remind them this was a very good year.

CEREMONY & EVENT/RECEPTION CAPACITY: The site holds 100 seated or standing guests indoors, and 350 seated or 400 standing outdoors.

MEETING CAPACITY: Meeting spaces can accommodate 350 seated guests.

FEES & DEPOSITS: One third of the rental fee is required to reserve your date. The balance is due 7 days prior to the event. The rental fee ranges $2,000–3,600.

AVAILABILITY: Year-round, weekdays until 8pm, and weekends until 10pm.

SERVICES/AMENITIES:
Catering: select from list
Kitchen Facilities: prep only
Tables & Chairs: provided
Linens, Silver, etc.: through caterer
Restrooms: wheelchair accessible
Dance Floor: rental available
Bride's Dressing Area: yes
AV/Meeting Equipment: CBA

Parking: self-parking or valet
Accommodations: no guest rooms
Outdoor Night Lighting: provided
Outdoor Cooking Facilities: BBQ CBA
Cleanup: provided
View: hills, landscaped grounds; panorama of vineyards, valley and mountains
Other: picnic area, complimentary event coordination

RESTRICTIONS:
Alcohol: bar service in-house
Smoking: not allowed inside tent
Music: amplified OK outdoors with restrictions

Wheelchair Access: yes
Insurance: not required

Overwhelmed? Use the search criteria on www.HereComesTheGuide.com to narrow down your choices.

San Diego Zoo Safari Park

Wildlife Park

15500 San Pasqual Valley Road, Escondido
619/685-3259
www.sandiegozoo.org/weddings
events@sandiegozoo.org

● Rehearsal Dinners		● Corporate Events	
● Ceremonies		● Meetings	
● Wedding Receptions		● Film Shoots	
● Private Parties		Accommodations	

A herd of gazelles calmly roams the vast plain, while a group of giraffes clusters under a tree. Maternally, one lowers her long neck to groom her youngster. Sound like an exotic scene from Africa? It could be, but it's actually a lot closer to home, and you can have the fun of sharing it with those you love on your wedding day.

The San Diego Zoo Safari Park, an 1,800-acre conservation center, will stir your soul with the wonder of seeing nearly 400 wild and often endangered species like zebras, bison, gorillas and condors. Perhaps the most popular attraction is watching different animals—rhinos, antelopes and yes, those gorgeous giraffes—graze together harmoniously in their natural habitat. So, it's an unexpected treat to use this idyllic tableau as a backdrop for your celebration.

After the public has left for the day and the park takes on a hush, your guests begin their safari with a shuttle ride to the Heart of Africa. This grassland ceremony site, shaded by a grove of trees, is within site of the cheetah habitat, and if you're lucky you might see a couple of these magnificent creatures lazing on the hillside. (By the way, for something your guests will never forget, arrange a close encounter with a cheetah or another exotic critter.) Bronze statues of African tribesmen peek out from the surrounding bush as you take your place at the altar, which frames that distant plain.

The adventure continues with a journey past African landscapes to the edge of Nairobi Village and the Hunte Nairobi Pavilion, a spacious, covered venue-in-the-round, for dinner and dancing. Boasting a 35-foot vaulted ceiling and screened-in sides, it lends a wonderfully airy, indoor/outdoor feel to your reception. Gourmet menus add a touch of elegance to the affair, but the icing on the cake may be ending the evening astride a galloping elephant (or crocodile) when the park opens its unique carousel for everyone to take a private spin.

If, however, you prefer a waterside event (or don't want to wait until after hours), you can host your wedding at the Mombasa Island Pavilion. Begin at the Lagoon Overlook, a short walk from the main entrance that meanders past playful meerkats and sparkling waterfalls. Friends and family gather at the ceremony site, a wide plaza that extends in a semicircle above the lagoon, where you'll arrive via cart down a private pathway. Just beyond the altar are a series of small water islands, home to rare birds and plant life. The entire setting is lushly landscaped with flowering shrubs and tall water grasses.

Just steps away, your reception is held at the Mombasa Island Pavilion, a thatched-roof hut with flagstone flooring, rough-hewn wooden columns and tribal painting designs. This rotunda-style building has virtually no walls, allowing for unobstructed views of the waterfowl preening outside while you dine and dance.

And if all of the amazing assets of Safari Park aren't enough, there's another benefit to having your event here: A portion of the proceeds helps support ongoing conservation and wildlife protection efforts. Imagine, by celebrating your new life, you will also save the lives of animals in danger around the world...how wild is that!

CEREMONY, EVENT/RECEPTION & MEETING CAPACITY: The site holds up to 250 seated or 400 standing guests indoors or outdoors.

FEES & DEPOSITS: 25% of the total event cost is required to reserve your date. Partial payment of the balance is due 30 days prior to the wedding day, and the remaining balance is due 5 days prior. The ceremony site fee ranges $1,500–2,000. Wedding packages range $85–112/person and include: all-day admission for your guests on your wedding day; complimentary general parking; first hour hosted beer, wine and soft drinks; butler-passed hors d'oeuvres; jungle juice toast; your choice of plated entrées or buffet service; linens; waived cake-cutting fee; complimentary floral centerpieces; and a complimentary 1-year membership to the Zoological Society of San Diego for the newlyweds. Tax and alcohol are additional; there is no charge for a gratuity.

AVAILABILITY: Year-round, daily, 9am–11pm.

SERVICES/AMENITIES:

Catering: in-house
Kitchen Facilities: n/a
Tables & Chairs: provided
Linens, Silver, etc.: some provided
Restrooms: wheelchair accessible
Dance Floor: CBA
Bride's Dressing Area: yes
AV/Meeting Equipment: provided
Other: in-house florals, picnic area, wild animals, event coordination

Parking: large lot (complimentary, included in wedding package)
Accommodations: no guest rooms
Outdoor Night Lighting: CBA
Outdoor Cooking Facilities: BBQ CBA
Cleanup: provided
View: canyon, hills, lagoon, waterfall, landscaped grounds; panorama of fields, mountains, park and valley

RESTRICTIONS:

Alcohol: in-house
Smoking: not allowed
Music: amplified OK with restrictions

Wheelchair Access: yes
Insurance: not required

Grand Tradition Estate & Gardens

Victorian Mansion & Exotic Gardens

220 Grand Tradition Way, Fallbrook
760/728-6466

www.grandtradition.com
info@grandtradition.com

● Rehearsal Dinners	● Corporate Events
● Ceremonies	● Meetings
● Wedding Receptions	● Film Shoots
● Private Parties	Accommodations

With three distinctive venues encompassing 30 acres of gently rolling hills in a secluded rural valley of North County San Diego, Grand Tradition Estate and Gardens has something special to offer every newly engaged couple. Seven stunning waterfalls are featured throughout the botanical reserve, and each garden site has its own personality.

The most formal site is the Beverly Mansion, surrounded by magnificent gardens and overlooking a heart-shaped lake. As you stand on the veranda inhaling the rose-scented air, take a moment to savor the storybook quality of the scene before you: a vast expanse of lawn sloping down to the picturesque lakeside gazebo where you'll say "I do". Want to add another fairy-tale touch? Arrive at the gazebo in a white horse-drawn carriage before exchanging vows.

Receptions are held in the mansion's Crystal Ballroom, a nostalgically elegant hall illuminated by glittering Swarovski crystal chandeliers. Opulent furnishings and Chiavari chairs accentuate the room's glamour. At one end, a palatial presentation staircase awaits the newlyweds' grand entrance. Event-friendly amenities include a raised stage for the head table, hardwood dance floor, baby grand piano, dramatic uplighting, and even an English pub.

If you have a more relaxed setting in mind, Arbor Terrace evokes the lush island ambiance of Hana, Hawaii. Although called a "terrace," this site is actually a gorgeously landscaped garden with cascading waterfalls, graceful bridges, expansive lawns and palm trees swaying in the breeze. Capturing all the romance and natural splendor of a tropical paradise, it's a favorite ceremony spot for many couples.

At one end of Arbor Terrace, the Arbor Pavilion provides a versatile option for receptions. This charming open-air venue is designed with arched French-style windows along three sides, a fabric-draped ceiling canopy, and a built-in stone bar and buffet room. The wraparound windows treat dining guests to a garden view, and the Pavilion's fourth side, which is completely open, showcases the elevated garden patio and dance floor. A warm and inviting space, the patio is enhanced by a blazing fire in the flagstone fireplace, and a waterfall tumbling softly in the background.

Grand Tradition's newest venue is Compass Garden, a decidedly California-casual choice for a cocktail hour or laid-back reception. A pathway meanders among colorful succulents, ornamental grasses and Mediterranean plants, and guests also enjoy a terrific view of the heart-shaped lake and a breathtaking sunset. Closer in, they can admire a stunning water feature that was recently awarded "Best in California." Gatherings convene at the Orchid Bar, where comfy, oversized lounge furniture clusters around a central fire pit and everyone unwinds as they bask in the soothing surround of gardens, lake and waterfalls.

At Grand Tradition Estate, you'll appreciate the exceptionally attentive, friendly service, which includes customized menus by culinary artists who take pride in serving only the freshest and most flavorful dishes. With such hospitality and three uniquely beautiful event areas, it's no surprise that couples come from far and wide to celebrate at this enchanting wonderland.

CEREMONY, EVENT/RECEPTION & MEETING CAPACITY: The Beverly Mansion seats up to 300 and the Arbor Terrace holds 220 seated guests.

FEES & DEPOSITS: A $1,500 reservation fee is required to book your date. 25% of the estimated event total is due 9 months prior to your event, and another 25% is due 6 months prior. The final guest count and balance are due 10 days before your event. Wedding ceremony & reception packages range $70–140/person, and include meals and all site fees. Tax and a 20% service charge are extra. Discounted rates are available for events on weekdays, Fridays and Sundays, and may also be offered for short notice or off-season bookings.

AVAILABILITY: Year-round, daily. Times vary depending on the season and existing event bookings. Please call to check current date and time availability.

SERVICES/AMENITIES:

Catering: in-house, no BYO
Kitchen Facilities: n/a
Tables & Chairs: provided, Chiavari or white padded
Linens, Silver, etc.: provided
Restrooms: wheelchair accessible
Dance Floor: provided
Bride's & Groom's Dressing Areas: yes
AV/Meeting Equipment: podium, easels, DVD projection system, wired & wireless microphones

Parking: complimentary parking included, valet CBA
Accommodations: hotels and vacation rentals nearby, shuttle CBA
Outdoor Night Lighting: provided
Outdoor Cooking Facilities: no
Cleanup: provided
View: landscaped grounds, mountains, creek, wooded area, fountain, garden, patio, valley, hills, waterfall, pond, lake
Other: event coordination, wireless internet audio technician, indoor specialty lighting, horse-drawn carriage, chocolate fountain, s'mores bar, kosher & ethnic catering CBA

RESTRICTIONS:

Alcohol: in-house, no BYO
Smoking: outdoors only
Music: provided or BYO; amplified OK indoors with volume limits, outdoors until 10pm

Wheelchair Access: yes
Insurance: not required

Los Willows Garden Estate and Vineyard

Private Event Facility

530 Stewart Canyon Road, Fallbrook
760/731-9400

www.loswillows.com
info@loswillows.com

- Rehearsal Dinners
- Ceremonies
- Wedding Receptions
- Private Parties
- Corporate Events
- Meetings
- Film Shoots
- Accommodations

Who wouldn't love to have a luxurious private estate all to themselves for their wedding? Most of us can't afford such a pricey indulgence, so it's lucky that there's Los Willows Garden Estate and Vineyard, a 55-acre venue in the hills of San Diego. Los Willows offers the lush splendor of a garden oasis, along with upscale amenities like a full-service salon, gourmet cuisine, deluxe accommodations, and superb service—all for a surprisingly reasonable price tag. What's more, Los Willows' experienced coordinators oversee each detail of your dream wedding. And with only one event at a time, yours will get all the attention—and privacy—it deserves.

You'll wed at a beautifully lit, treelined meadow or a lakeside garden gazebo, where the bride has a choice of ceremony entrances: a traditional one down the garden aisle, a show-stopping arrival via Los Willows' signature bridal boat ride, or an upgrade to a vintage Rolls Royce. For brides who opt for the boat, here's how the scene unfolds: guests wait expectantly alongside a serene spring-fed lake. Then, a bell atop the wedding gazebo peals and all eyes turn as the boat glides toward the crowd carrying precious cargo—you, the bride. Attendants help you disembark, and you walk down a bricked aisle…. After that "first kiss," you and your new husband reboard for a celebratory champagne cruise.

Meanwhile, friends and family gather for the cocktail hour in another scenic outdoor area with a built-in illuminated bar and a cozy stone hearth, as the sky makes its enchanting transition from sunset to starry night and twinkling white lights sparkle throughout the grounds. Receptions are equally captivating, staged inside a lovely climate-controlled tent pavilion. An elegantly draped ceiling boasts a breathtaking six-foot Swarovski crystal chandelier, casting its soft glow on the polished mahogany dance floor. Guests dine on gourmet cuisine, courtesy of the in-house caterer. Whether you choose a sit-down or a buffet dinner, the chef is happy to customize your menu, including ethnic specialties. After the bouquet toss, everyone says their farewells as you and your groom are whisked away (in a vintage Rolls Royce if you choose!)…but chances are you won't be going very far.

That's because most couples spend their wedding night at Los Willows' exclusive hilltop Villa. Reserved just for the newlyweds and their wedding party, it offers a stunning vantage from which to survey the secluded, peaceful estate grounds below. A favorite pastime here is sipping

Los Willows' private label wine while strolling among the grapevines of the adjoining vineyard. Each of the Villa's guest rooms features Tuscan-inspired décor with *trompe l'oeil* art on the walls, a plush king-size bed with down comforter, and whirlpool tub. A manager is on hand to ensure that you're properly pampered, even serving a homemade breakfast on the Villa's back patio near a 60-foot cascading waterfall.

Clearly, the staff at this estate has gone to great lengths to design an exceptional, all-inclusive wedding venue that will make you feel like a treasured member of the Los Willows family.

CEREMONY CAPACITY: Lakeside and meadow locations each hold 250 seated guests.

EVENT/RECEPTION CAPACITY: The air-cooled or heated Pavilion can seat 250 guests.

MEETING CAPACITY: The Main Meeting Room can accommodate 40 seated guests; there are 4 other breakout rooms that seat 10–12 people each.

FEES & DEPOSITS: For weddings, a nonrefundable $2,500 deposit is required to secure your date. 75% of the contracted estimated total (spread over 3 payments of 25% each) is due prior to the wedding date, and the balance and final guest count are due 18 days prior. Wedding packages start at $85/person. The price includes: 5 hours for the ceremony/reception plus 2 hours prior for dressing and photography; a wedding planner and wedding coordinator; complimentary guest parking; all setup and cleanup; wedding boat, red roadster grand entrance and champagne cruise on the lake; buffet dinner ('served meal' upgrade option available); wine service during dinner; champagne toast; custom uplighting with twinkle lights, and much more. Alcohol packages are available. Tax and a 20% service charge are extra. Additional hours run $800/hour.

AVAILABILITY: Year-round, daily except major holidays, until 10pm.

SERVICES/AMENITIES:

Catering: in-house, no BYO
Kitchen Facilities: n/a
Tables & Chairs: provided
Linens, Silver, etc.: provided
Restrooms: wheelchair accessible
Dance Floor: provided
Bride's & Groom's Dressing Areas: yes
AV/Meeting Equipment: full range CBA

Parking: ample on site
Accommodations: 8 guest rooms
Outdoor Night Lighting: yes
Outdoor Cooking Facilities: CBA
Cleanup: provided
View: spring-fed lake, grassy meadow, gardens, canyon and hills
Other: spa and salon

RESTRICTIONS:

Alcohol: in-house
Smoking: designated areas only
Music: amplified OK with volume limits

Wheelchair Access: yes
Insurance: not required
Other: no rice, birdseed, confetti or sparklers

Pala Mesa Resort

Golf Resort

2001 Old Highway 395, Fallbrook, North County

760/477-7240

www.palamesa.com
weddings@palamesa.com

- Rehearsal Dinners
- Ceremonies
- Wedding Receptions
- Private Parties
- Corporate Events
- Meetings
- Film Shoots
- Accommodations

The best part about Pala Mesa Resort is that the more you explore it, the more you love it—especially for weddings. Boasting one of the most beautiful and photogenic ceremony sites around, it's sure to make a lasting impression on friends and family.

First of all, the grounds are lovely, as befits a property with one of the highest-rated golf courses in San Diego County. And the peaked-roof clubhouse with its walls of glass is a cool, timeless example of California Modern design. But what lies just beyond makes this venue a total standout: Perched high above their woodsy, hillside accommodations, is the dramatic Garden Pavilion. This expansive terrace exudes romantic appeal with a panorama of lush trees and flowering plants surrounding a 30-foot waterfall cascading over boulders. Taking center stage is a spectacular, stone pillared, red-roofed Bell Tower. It all feels as if you've just stumbled upon an exotic setting in the middle of a forest clearing. Best of all, once you've exchanged vows, you and your spouse can declare your union by ringing the 700-pound Mission bell ... or, as one couple did, train your dog to jump up and pull the bell rope for you!

Following this "YouTube-worthy" moment, take a short walk up a winding path to the Cliff Terrace, an equally magical locale with an indoor/outdoor feel. Have cocktails al fresco, then dinner and dancing inside the gracefully arched tent, where one end opens to a rushing waterfall and the other to a patio with fire pit. Crystal chandeliers and billowing fabric add an ethereal ambiance to the entire space.

Steps away, there's a smaller bell tower that's great for more intimate ceremonies or stunning photos, as well as the colorful Bella Garden and nearby landscaped bridge. Or you can go from "I do" to first dance in the clubhouse itself. Start with a hearthside ceremony in the Fireside Room, then celebrate in the light-filled Sunroom, which opens to a patio overlooking the golf course. There's even a ballroom for a more traditional, formal reception.

The food here is fabulous, so why not extend your event with a rehearsal or welcome dinner and farewell brunch? Their restaurant, Aqua Terra—so popular with locals—has private dining areas and an extensive menu that includes meat, fish and vegetarian favorites, expertly prepared. You'll find this same care and service in their catering options, as well as an on-site team dedicated to helping you plan every aspect of your wedding weekend. With activities that range from private golf parties and in-room massages to tennis, hiking, swimming, hot-air ballooning and even antiquing in town, you and your guests will definitely want to turn this party into a destination getaway.

CEREMONY, EVENT/RECEPTION & MEETING CAPACITY: The resort can accommodate 300 seated or standing indoors and 300 seated or standing outdoors.

FEES & DEPOSITS: 25% of the total event cost is required to reserve your date. Wedding packages range $80–100/person. Tax, alcohol and a 21% service charge are additional.

AVAILABILITY: Year-round, daily. Call or email for details.

SERVICES/AMENITIES:

Catering: in-house
Kitchen Facilities: n/a
Tables & Chairs: provided
Linens, Silver, etc.: provided
Restrooms: wheelchair accessible
Dance Floor: yes
Bride's Dressing Area: yes
AV/Meeting Equipment: provided
Other: grand piano

Parking: large lot, on street
Accommodations: 133 guest rooms
Outdoor Night Lighting: access only
Outdoor Cooking Facilities: BBQ CBA
Cleanup: provided
View: fountain, garden, landscaped grounds, waterfall; panorama of fairways, hills and mountains

RESTRICTIONS:

Alcohol: in-house
Smoking: outdoors only
Music: amplified OK

Wheelchair Access: yes
Insurance: liability required

The wedding vendors on our website are the best in the business. How do we know? Read page 577.

Wedgewood Fallbrook

Event Center

3742 Flowerwood Lane, Fallbrook
866/966-3009
www.wedgewoodbanquet.com
events@wedgewoodbanquet.com

- Rehearsal Dinners
- Ceremonies
- Wedding Receptions
- Private Parties
- Corporate Events
- Meetings
- Film Shoots
- Accommodations

From its vantage point on a hill overlooking a pristine golf course, Wedgewood Fallbrook sets the stage for a seamlessly flowing wedding or special event by skillfully integrating romantic outdoor courtyards, big airy indoor spaces, and a variety of tranquil views.

Its classic Mission-style architecture, featuring a smooth white stucco exterior, red-tile roof and shaded arcades, adds to the overall serene atmosphere of the venue. A set of arched double doors beneath a gold Spanish chandelier open to the main foyer, which provides a congenial staging area for your bridal party.

As your guests arrive, they can mingle on the circular Fountain Plaza just to the right of the main doors. This picturesque setting is enhanced by bursts of colorful blooms, tall palms and flowering vines wrapped around the dark wood pillars of the surrounding building. Meanwhile, you and your attendants will enjoy primping in the Bridal Suite, set up in a separate wing with plenty of space and light for capturing those important, pre-ceremony photos.

When you're ready to make your entrance, friends and family will already be seated in a truly lovely, terracotta-tiled courtyard ceremony site that feels sequestered, yet open and airy. This private spot is nestled between the clubhouse and a charming outdoor fireplace flanked by two Moorish-styled wooden doors. A treelined center aisle leads to a tall, curved arch that frames you and your groom against a planted breezeway with the lush fairway beyond. Picture perfect!

While your photographer takes photos of you and the bridal party, cocktails and hors d'oeuvres can be served on the Fountain Plaza or, on Saturday nights only, in the Members Bar. High-ceilinged with crossbeams and a two-sided fireplace, this huge—yet homey—lounge has a granite bar backed by windows framing the putting green, rustic iron chandeliers, cushy leather chairs and big-screen TVs. On the other side of the fireplace are leather sofas and club chairs, arranged for easy conversation. Also on Saturday nights, you can enjoy use of the adjacent stone-tiled side patio, which has a beautiful view of the lake and surrounding trees.

Then it's on to the ballroom for dinner. Filled with light from five sets of double glass doors that look out onto the plaza as well as from a dozen softly glowing chandeliers, this L-shaped banquet space can be set with a sweetheart table against the windows, a buffet or dessert bar in the alcove, or any way you wish. After all, this venue is part of the Wedgewood family of wedding and banquet centers, known for offering a full range of options and services designed to meet your particular needs and budget.

CEREMONY, EVENT/RECEPTION & MEETING CAPACITY: The site accommodates up to 250 seated or standing guests.

FEES & DEPOSITS: 25% of the estimated total event cost is required to reserve your date. An additional 25% is due 120 days prior to the event and the balance (based on your final guest count) is due 10 days prior. All payments are credited towards your final balance and are nonrefundable and nontransferable. All-inclusive, completely customizable wedding packages start at $46/person. Tax, alcohol and a 21–22% service charge are additional.

AVAILABILITY: Year-round, daily, 6am–midnight.

SERVICES/AMENITIES:

Catering: in-house
Kitchen Facilities: n/a
Tables & Chairs: provided
Linens, Silver, etc.: provided
Restrooms: wheelchair accessible
Dance Floor: provided
Bride's Dressing Area: yes
AV/Meeting Equipment: some provided

Parking: large lot
Accommodations: no guest rooms
Outdoor Night Lighting: provided
Outdoor Cooking Facilities: no
Cleanup: provided
View: landscaped grounds, courtyard, fairways, lake, hills, mountains
Other: in-house wedding cake and florals, clergy on staff, complimentary event coordination

RESTRICTIONS:

Alcohol: in-house
Smoking: designated areas only
Music: amplified OK

Wheelchair Access: yes
Insurance: not required
Other: no rice, confetti or glitter; no open flames

La Jolla Beach & Tennis Club

Beach & Tennis Club

2000 Spindrift Drive, La Jolla
877/828-0856
www.ljbtc.com
catering@ljbtc.com

● Rehearsal Dinners		● Corporate Events	
● Ceremonies		● Meetings	
● Wedding Receptions		● Film Shoots	
● Private Parties		● Accommodations	

Tying the knot on one of the toniest sections of Southern California's coast isn't just for celebrities. You can create a stellar wedding of your own at the exclusive La Jolla Beach & Tennis Club. This landmark resort, stretching magnificently from one end of a picturesque cove to the other, is home to one of the last remaining private beaches along the coastline ... and that's only the beginning of its seductive allure. Sprawling across 14 acres, the historic property encompasses a par-3 golf course, 12 championship tennis courts, a beautifully landscaped pond and a hacienda-style clubhouse with 90 guest rooms and suites—easily turning your romantic affair into a spectacular getaway for family and friends.

The club's oceanfront north wing, which wraps around a lovely esplanade with killer views, becomes your own enclave where out-of-towners and the bridal party can settle in. As the time for the ceremony draws near, your guests are ushered to the impeccably groomed beach, mere steps away and reserved solely for you. Your grand entrance begins down the curved staircase from your bridal suite to the sandy aisle. Then, accompanied by the sound of gentle waves lapping at the shore, you exchange vows against the unforgettable panorama of the big blue Pacific.

This quintessential waterfront locale is so fantastic you might not want to leave it, so why not have cocktails and even your main reception (whether a brunch buffet or a sunset dinner) right here, beside the sea? If, however, you want a change of scenery, there are myriad options.

The bucolic Duck Pond and its large expanse of manicured lawn (as well as a nearby rose garden) is a picture-perfect site for both ceremonies and receptions. Natural stone borders, lush plantings and towering palms complete the look, while graceful swans and playful ducks add charm.

The Poolside Patio, nestled between the clubhouse and the pool, makes a nice choice for a cocktail and/or dinner reception with the verdant hills of La Jolla as a backdrop. The red-tiled roof of the club provides an interesting architectural detail, and a wonderful old stone hearth in the corner beckons as a cozy conversation area.

There are also two indoor venues: Their largest banquet room, La Sala, features wainscoted walls and impressive amber glass chandeliers. The stately Walnut Lounge has a drawing-room ambiance (with a hint of Downton Abbey), thanks to rich walnut paneling and antique candelabra-style light fixtures hanging from the ornate white plaster ceiling. Tall arched windows overlook the esplanade and ocean, and a fireplace makes this your go-to spot for cool-weather weddings.

Whichever setting you choose, you'll savor the sumptuous cuisine. Under the direction of renowned Chef Bernard Guillas of Marine Room* fame, the emphasis is on fresh ingredients and innovative preparations, and many dishes also incorporate global flavors. The knowledgeable catering staff will happily work with you to customize your menu, too.

There are so many fun activities, both here and in the surrounding area, that we recommend staying over a few days. From tennis lessons and golf clinics to kayaking, wine tasting, a summer kids' club, and even just lazing on the beach, there's something for everyone. Between your fabulous wedding and equally fabulous mini-vacation, you'll have plenty of great memories from your La Jolla Beach & Tennis Club experience.

*Note: The Marine Room is the Four Diamond Award-winning fine-dining restaurant located next to the property. See the description on page 498.

CEREMONY CAPACITY: The site holds 190 seated indoors and 200 seated outdoors.

EVENT/RECEPTION CAPACITY: The club can accommodate 150 seated or 250 standing guests indoors and 200 seated or 250 standing outdoors.

MEETING CAPACITY: Meeting spaces hold 150 seated guests, or 160 seated theater-style.

FEES & DEPOSITS: 20% of the estimated event total is required to reserve your date and the balance is due 30 days prior to the event. The rental fees ranges $350–750 depending on the day of the event and the space reserved. Meals start at $55/person. Tax, alcohol and an 18% service charge are additional.

Hosting an event at the La Jolla Beach and Tennis Club is subject to approval and requires club membership, sponsorship by a club member, or reserving a minimum block of guest rooms (based on the number of guests at the event). Additional restrictions may apply. Please contact the Catering Department for more information.

AVAILABILITY: Year-round, daily, until 10pm.

SERVICES/AMENITIES:

Catering: in-house
Kitchen Facilities: n/a
Tables & Chairs: provided
Linens, Silver, etc.: provided
Restrooms: wheelchair accessible
Dance Floor: portable provided
Bride's Dressing Area: CBA
AV/Meeting Equipment: provided
Other: grand piano, spa services, free WiFi

Parking: large lot, on street, valet available
Accommodations: 90 guest rooms
Outdoor Night Lighting: CBA
Outdoor Cooking Facilities: BBQ CBA
Cleanup: provided
View: panorama of ocean and coastline; pool area, fairways, fountain courtyard, landscaped grounds

RESTRICTIONS:

Alcohol: in-house
Smoking: designated areas only
Music: amplified OK indoors, acoustic only on the beach

Wheelchair Access: limited
Insurance: liability required

La Jolla Shores Hotel

Waterfront Hotel

8110 Camino del Oro, La Jolla
888/694-5411

www.ljshoreshotel.com
ljshcatering@ljshoreshotel.com

- Rehearsal Dinners
- Ceremonies
- Wedding Receptions
- Private Parties
- Corporate Events
- Meetings
- Film Shoots
- Accommodations

With some of the most beautiful coastline in the world, it's no wonder California makes so many brides think BEACH WEDDING. The sun sparkling on the water…the sound of the surf…a cool breeze…it's the quintessential SoCal scene for tying the knot. The tricky part is finding a place on the beach that also takes care of all the details, offers several reception options, serves up a menu to die for, and is located in a town oozing with charm. Well, we've found it for you: the La Jolla Shores Hotel.

Located on two acres of beachfront property, this rambling hacienda-style resort is one of the very few in San Diego County that's allowed to host weddings directly on the sand. Before every event, they groom the shoreline and, as if waves lapping ashore right next to you wasn't heavenly enough, they can even add a bamboo structure along the aisle or an altar of tropical flowers. With a setting like this, you may want to continue your celebration seaside, or you can head to the private, second-floor Acapulco Deck for cocktails and killer coastal views. When you're ready for dinner, move inside to the Acapulco Room, where floor-to-ceiling windows showcase dazzling sunset vistas.

If you prefer to see and hear the ocean but not necessarily have your ceremony on the sand, the three-story hotel's central Garden Courtyard is a perfect alternative. Shaded with lattice and paved with terracotta tiles, this festive open-air space affords a long center aisle for a dramatic walk to the altar. Lushly planted borders—abloom with birds of paradise, hibiscus, azaleas and various palms—set the stage, framed by the red-tiled-roof overhangs of the surrounding guest rooms. Afterwards, guests can mingle over cocktails on the adjacent Fountain Patio, featuring a tall, arched breezeway with the beach just steps away.

Then, host your dinner reception on the Shores Patio, directly facing the beach. In fact, many couples choose to say "I do" on the patio in front of that magnificent ocean, which is equally captivating at night when the surf is illuminated by spotlights. If you get married here, you can join your family and friends for a glass of bubbly, and segue to dinner and dancing in the La Jolla Room. This romantic space has a vaulted ceiling, graceful arched windows and glass doors so it feels airy and open—plus it's the best spot in the hotel to kick up your heels with music and dancing.

Beach hotels rarely win raves for their food, but the award-winning culinary team at the La Jolla Shores Hotel will customize a delectable menu for you with ingredients so fresh you'll swear they were just plucked from the sea or farm. The entire staff is also incredibly accommodating, and can arrange everything from in-room massages to tennis games to shopping trips in the chic town of La Jolla for guests who want to stay over and make a weekend of it.

CEREMONY CAPACITY: The hotel holds 100 seated guests indoors and 200 seated outdoors.

EVENT/RECEPTION CAPACITY: The site accommodates 80 seated or 120 standing guests indoors, and 180 seated or 250 standing outdoors.

MEETING CAPACITY: Meeting spaces hold 80 seated guests.

FEES & DEPOSITS: 20% of the event total plus the signed contract is required to reserve your date, and the balance is due 30 days prior to the event. The rental fee ranges $500–2,500 and varies depending on the room rented. Meal packages start at $95/person. Tax, alcohol and an 18% service charge are additional.

AVAILABILITY: Year-round, daily, indoors. Beach wedding services are not available in July or August.

SERVICES/AMENITIES:
Catering: in-house
Kitchen Facilities: n/a
Tables & Chairs: provided
Linens, Silver, etc.: provided
Restrooms: wheelchair accessible
Dance Floor: portable provided
Bride's Dressing Area: CBA
AV/Meeting Equipment: provided
Other: picnic area, free WiFi, beach and pool-side amenities

Parking: on street, valet required, garage nearby
Accommodations: 128 guest rooms
Outdoor Night Lighting: yes
Outdoor Cooking Facilities: BBQ CBA
Cleanup: provided
View: panorama of coastline and ocean; fountain courtyard, landscaped grounds

RESTRICTIONS:
Alcohol: in-house
Smoking: not allowed
Music: amplified OK indoors with restrictions

Wheelchair Access: yes
Insurance: required from vendors

The Marine Room

Waterfront Restaurant

2000 Spindrift Drive, La Jolla
888/339-2483
www.marineroom.com
mrcatering@marineroom.com

- Rehearsal Dinners
- Ceremonies
- Wedding Receptions
- Private Parties
- Corporate Events
- Meetings
- Film Shoots
- Accommodations

Admit it, you know what you want: breathtaking ocean views, a relaxed and elegant ambiance, service fit for an A-lister and 4-star cuisine that's a feast for your senses. Worried that you might be asking for too much? Don't be—The Marine Room has it all!

This La Jolla Shores treasure sits right on one of the prettiest stretches of beach in San Diego. Consistently showered with superlatives like "most romantic," "most scenic," "best fine dining" and "overall favorite," it's been a celebration touchstone for decades, the place where VIPs, tourists and locals commemorate the special moments of their lives.

You enter through a sleek Mezzanine Lounge that seems to float above the open, airy dining room below. A dramatic staircase leads downstairs where the décor is timeless, like the interior of a great beach house that's posh, yet comfortable. The color scheme is neutral with lots of cream and white, and the high-peaked ceiling is inset with skylights that bathe the space in natural light. From every corner, your eye is drawn to the amazing view just outside the windows: a vast tableau of white sand, craggy hills and the big blue Pacific. Boats, seagulls and kayakers provide an interesting show that's reflected in the mirrored walls along the back of the restaurant. And as fabulous as tangerine sunsets over the horizon can be, stormy skies are just as awesome (the High Tide Dinners, where waves lap against the windows, are always quickly sold out).

For the ultimate Marine Room wedding experience, reserve the entire venue and go from ceremony and cocktails to dining and dancing. The restaurant can be configured into four separate sections, so it's easy to create a wonderful flow throughout your event. This flexibility is also great if you just want to reserve one or two areas for a small reception, rehearsal dinner, or other more intimate gathering: The Seahorse Lounge affords total privacy, the South End is large enough to include a bar and lounge area, and the Terrace (an elevated indoor space) treats diners to a coastline panorama.

As mesmerizing as the vistas are, the food is equally compelling. Renowned Executive Chef Bernard Guillas and Chef de Cuisine Ron Oliver repeatedly earn kudos from critics, including a Four Diamond rating from AAA. Chef Bernard, who grew up in Brittany, France, says he was influenced by Monet and it shows in the French-inspired menu where flavors are layered subtly, like the colors in an impressionistic painting. The focus is on fresh, local ingredients with an affinity for seafood, but there are numerous beef, fowl and wild game selections as well. Plus, the presentations are edible art!—diners often whip out their phones to photograph the magnificently plated meals as they arrive. Completing your gustatory adventure is an impressive wine list that has won praise from *Wine Spectator* magazine, and service that's both attentive and discreet.

After dinner, you can take a moonlit stroll along the beach and, like countless couples before you, make plans to come back here for all your future anniversary celebrations.

Note: The La Jolla Beach & Tennis Club next to the Marine Room is available for overnight accommodations as well as special events. See their profile on page 494.

CEREMONY CAPACITY: The site holds 80 seated or 100 standing guests indoors.

EVENT/RECEPTION CAPACITY: The restaurant can accommodate 230 seated or 275 standing guests indoors.

MEETING CAPACITY: Meeting spaces hold 100 seated guests.

FEES & DEPOSITS: There is no rental fee, but food & beverage minimums apply and vary depending on the date and time of the event and the space reserved. Three-course prix fixe menus range $62–78/person. Tax, beverages and an 18% service charge are additional.

AVAILABILITY: Year-round, daily, 10am–4pm or 5:30pm–midnight.

SERVICES/AMENITIES:

Catering: in-house
Kitchen Facilities: fully equipped
Tables & Chairs: provided
Linens, Silver, etc.: provided
Restrooms: wheelchair accessible
Dance Floor: CBA
Bride's Dressing Area: CBA
AV/Meeting Equipment: CBA

Parking: valet available
Accommodations: CBA at La Jolla Beach & Tennis Club
Outdoor Night Lighting: provided
Outdoor Cooking Facilities: none
Cleanup: provided
View: panorama of ocean and coastline

RESTRICTIONS:

Alcohol: full in-house bar
Smoking: designated areas only
Music: amplified OK indoors with restrictions

Wheelchair Access: yes
Insurance: not required

Want to know WHAT TO ASK a potential location or vendor? Check out our Questions to Ask starting on page 21.

499

Museum of Contemporary Art San Diego

Historic Waterfront Museum

700 Prospect Street, La Jolla
858/454-3541 x166
www.mcasd.org
events@mcasd.org

● Rehearsal Dinners		● Corporate Events	
● Ceremonies		● Meetings	
● Wedding Receptions		● Film Shoots	
● Private Parties		○ Accommodations	

The Museum of Contemporary Art San Diego's fabulous seaside location in one of SoCal's most desirable beach communities is enough to land it on your shortlist of potential wedding sites. But once you experience the venue's striking architecture, cultural cachet and quintessential postcard views, it may quickly move right to the top.

This thriving museum, known worldwide for its dynamic exhibitions showcasing the art of our times, was originally built in 1915 as the beach "cottage" of prominent philanthropist Ellen Browning Scripps. It began its new life as a home for art in 1941 when it became the Art Center of La Jolla, and the building has been expanded greatly since then.

Today, the museum's crisp white façade, accentuated by a vine-covered colonnade, tall palms, and windows that arch almost to the roofline, makes a lovely first impression. However, the private Coast Boulevard entrance for special events will truly wow your guests: There, in all its glory, is the sparkling blue Pacific and La Jolla Cove. And you couldn't pick a better place to savor this panoramic seascape than on the Miles Terrace, a perfect spot for your ceremony, cocktails and/or reception. The coveted sand-and-surf tableau, which extends all the way up the coast to Torrey Pines, is complemented by a delightful art installation by Nancy Rubins of boats suspended over the terrace.

You may also opt to start with an intimate ceremony just steps away at the museum's Pacific Union Pocket Park, where you'll find an equally wonderful vista framed by Monterrey pines. After exchanging vows, invite everyone up on the terrace for dinner and dancing. If you'd like to move part of your celebration indoors, the adjacent Coast Room has walls of glass so you won't miss a moment of the sun setting over the ocean. Add in some comfy sofas and it makes a great after-dinner lounge.

If all-out glamour is for you, then nothing can beat the awe-inspiring Axline Court in the heart of the museum. This spectacular space boasts terrazzo floors, tall columns, and arresting artworks, but it's the dramatically high ceiling that takes your breath away. It swoops upwards to large, clerestory-style windows, producing a skylight effect. This artist-designed feature is called the Celestial Lantern, and its hanging, sculptural panels even resemble angel wings. It really does create a magical, ethereal setting for a most memorable reception.

The intriguing blend of nature and artistic vision here allows you the flexibility to host a relaxed, beach-y, hip gathering or a more formal one, depending upon your personal style. Let their resourceful staff help you with inventive ideas and referrals to their carefully chosen, preferred vendors. (By the way, one of their approved caterers is the on-site restaurant, which also happens to be an excellent place for a rehearsal dinner.) And although the main galleries aren't open to the public after hours, you can arrange a special treat of personalized tours just for your friends and family.

Note: The museum also has additional indoor and outdoor event spaces in downtown San Diego that offer a more urban ambiance.

CEREMONY CAPACITY: The site holds 100 seated guests indoors and 120 seated outdoors.

EVENT/RECEPTION CAPACITY: The museum can accommodate 200 seated or 500 standing indoors and 80 seated or 150 standing outdoors.

MEETING CAPACITY: The facility seats 120 theater-style, 65 classroom-style, and 35–50 conference-style.

FEES & DEPOSITS: 50% of the rental fee is required to reserve your date, and the balance is due 3 weeks prior to the event. The rental fee, which varies depending on the space(s) reserved, ranges $600 (ceremony only) to $5,000 (ceremony and reception). The galleries may be available for viewing during events for a $600 fee; gallery tour guides are an additional charge.

Rates for business functions, meetings or other types of events vary. Please contact the venue for more details.

AVAILABILITY: Year-round, daily, 6pm–11pm. Please inquire about the availability of the Coast Room during daytime hours.

SERVICES/AMENITIES:

Catering: select from preferred list
Kitchen Facilities: none
Tables & Chairs: some provided
Linens, Silver, etc.: through caterer
Restrooms: wheelchair accessible
Dance Floor: yes
Bride's Dressing Area: no
AV/Meeting Equipment: CBA

Parking: on street
Accommodations: no guest rooms
Outdoor Night Lighting: CBA
Outdoor Cooking Facilities: no
Cleanup: provided or caterer
View: garden; panorama of ocean and coastline

RESTRICTIONS:

Alcohol: in-house
Smoking: designated areas only
Music: amplified OK indoors with restrictions

Wheelchair Access: yes
Insurance: liability required

El Camino Country Club

Country Club

3202 Vista Way, Oceanside
888/643-3516

www.countryclubreceptions.com
eventdirector@elcaminoclub.com

● Rehearsal Dinners	● Corporate Events
● Ceremonies	● Meetings
● Wedding Receptions	● Film Shoots
● Private Parties	Accommodations

El Camino Country Club is both relaxed and elegant. The clubhouse's classic décor is timeless, and its meticulous upkeep is evident throughout, from the manicured lawns to the orchids thriving in the foyer.

Ceremonies typically take place outdoors, with the couple exchanging vows in a beautiful white gazebo. Guests seated on the lawn are treated to sweeping views of the lush greens and treelined fairways in the background.

After the ceremony, family and friends enter the charming, sunny Garden Room just off the patio for cocktails and conversation. Meanwhile, the bride and groom are chauffeured in a cart around the golf course for photos in several picturesque spots, including a bi-level lake framed by a graceful weeping willow.

Later, the party moves to the more formal Main Dining Room for the reception. This spacious venue is decorated in neutral colors, and a series of multipaned windows overlook the expansive 18th fairway.

With white linens and chair covers, the room becomes a storybook wedding vision. Silver and crystal gleam in the soft, romantic glow of the chandeliers. When the best man is ready to make his toast or the couple takes to the floor for their first dance, the recessed lights in the ceiling can be turned up to create a theatrical effect.

The club's friendly and accommodating private events office offers a broad array of wedding packages, from a simple and quite affordable afternoon affair to a decadent evening gala with a hosted bar and surf-and-turf dinner.

Regardless of your budget, your wedding at the El Camino Country Club is certain to reflect the class and attention to detail that makes this facility such an enchanting place.

CEREMONY CAPACITY: The lawn holds up to 200 seated guests.

EVENT/RECEPTION & MEETING CAPACITY: The Main Dining Room accommodates up to 200 seated or 250 standing guests; the Patio up to 200 seated or 250 standing; and the Garden Room up to 70 seated or 89 standing. The Cabana can be used by a bride and her bridal party for pre-wedding preparation (up to 15 total).

FEES & DEPOSITS: A nonrefundable deposit, which is applied to your food & beverage total, is required to reserve your date. The amount of the deposit varies depending on how far in advance you book. Payment terms for the balance also vary, and may be arranged on an individual basis. Luncheons start at $14/person, dinners at $29/person and buffets at $30/person. Tax, alcohol and service charge are additional. Food & beverage minimums may apply. Menus and packages can be customized to fit your needs and budget. Call for details.

AVAILABILITY: Year-round, daily.

SERVICES/AMENITIES:

Catering: in-house

Kitchen Facilities: n/a

Tables & Chairs: provided

Linens, Silver, etc.: provided

Restrooms: wheelchair accessible

Dance Floor: provided

Bride's Dressing Area: yes

AV/Meeting Equipment: some provided, more CBA

Parking: large lot

Accommodations: no guest rooms

Outdoor Night Lighting: CBA

Outdoor Cooking Facilities: BBQ CBA

Cleanup: provided

View: garden, pond, hills, grounds, fairways

Other: event coordination

RESTRICTIONS:

Alcohol: in-house

Smoking: outdoors only

Music: amplified OK indoors with restrictions

Wheelchair Access: yes

Insurance: not required

Paradise Falls

Private Event Facility

190 Wilshire Road, Oceanside
760/439-7005

www.paradisefallsweddings.com
sales@paradisefallsweddings.com

- Rehearsal Dinners
- Ceremonies
- Wedding Receptions
- Private Parties
- Corporate Events
- Meetings
- Film Shoots
- Accommodations

Lush foliage, soothing water features, hidden paths and a romantic ambiance… you'll find all of these in abundance at Paradise falls, a beautiful Oceanside venue where you can have a completely private, one-of-a-kind garden wedding and reception.

Step into the property and you're transported to a verdant oasis that's entirely yours for the day. Primp in the secluded, well-appointed Bridal Cottage while the groom and his buddies chill at the man cave, complete with putting green. Then, when you're ready to make your entrance, you can join your guests at one of three lovely ceremony sites.

The expansive Gazebo Lawn encompasses two separate areas, each anchored by a fabulous, old-growth tree whose spreading branches act as a canopy as you exchange vows. The lawn also makes an ideal spot for post-ceremony cocktails. But, for maximum "oohs and aahs," consider the grassy Waterfall Ceremony Site. Friends and family watch as you say "I do" against a spectacular backdrop that features a dramatic rock formation covered with water cascading into a lily pond. As if this wasn't picturesque enough, the entire area is planted with colorful blooms and exotic vines. And then, just to add some pizzazz, a fire ring in the pond adds a blaze of excitement after dark.

Dinner is served on the Upper Reception Lawn, in the warm glow of lanterns, market lights, and twinkle lights wrapped around the surrounding trees. A sweetheart table can be tucked beneath a bower of illuminated moss, and from this perch you'll overlook the band shell built right into a rock wall—it's the perfect stage for your DJ or live music. Dance under the stars or lounge on comfy sofas for some conversation and a nightcap.

Prefer a reception indoors? Then you're in for a treat because the 4,000-square-foot Tented Pavilion works equally well for large or intimate gatherings. You approach the pavilion through a long pathway of tall, arched branches that glitter like a magical "tunnel of lights". Once you step inside you can't help but be impressed: The interior is lavishly draped and decorated with out-of-the-ordinary antique sofas, armoires and chandeliers, all of which lends an elegant touch.

Paradise Falls may still be one of San Diego County's "best-kept secrets," but not for long. The new owners have already established a stellar, 25-year track record hosting premier weddings at their other location, Los Willows, so you can expect the same fine catering and professional services at their newest venue!

CEREMONY CAPACITY: The facility holds 300 seated guests indoors and 350 seated outdoors.

EVENT/RECEPTION CAPACITY: The site can accommodate 300 seated or 350 standing indoors and 350 seated or standing outdoors.

MEETING CAPACITY: Meeting spaces seat up to 350 guests.

FEES & DEPOSITS: A $2,500 deposit is required to reserve your date, and the balance is due 14 days prior to the event. Wedding packages range $69–145/person. Tax, alcohol and a 20% service charge are additional.

Rates for business functions, meetings or other types of events vary. Please contact the venue for more details.

AVAILABILITY: Year-round, daily, 9am–11pm.

SERVICES/AMENITIES:

Catering: in-house
Kitchen Facilities: n/a
Tables & Chairs: provided
Linens, Silver, etc.: provided
Restrooms: wheelchair accessible
Dance Floor: yes
Bride's & Groom's Dressing Areas: yes
AV/Meeting Equipment: some provided
Other: event coordination

Parking: large lot
Accommodations: no guest rooms
Outdoor Night Lighting: yes
Outdoor Cooking Facilities: no
Cleanup: provided
View: mature garden landscape with rock waterfall, lagoon, and bamboo forest

RESTRICTIONS:

Alcohol: in-house
Smoking: designated areas only
Music: amplified OK with restrictions

Wheelchair Access: yes
Insurance: not required

The Condor's Nest Ranch

Private Estate

37537 Magee Road, Pala
949/290-6088

www.thecondorsnestranch.com
lisa@thecondorsnestranch.com

- Rehearsal Dinners
- Ceremonies
- Wedding Receptions
- Private Parties
- Corporate Events
- Meetings
- Film Shoots
- Accommodations

What if you could spend a few days before your wedding relaxing with your family in the same beautiful country setting where you plan to say "I do?"

And what if, after a few days among mountains, woodlands, dramatic vistas and some delightful farm animals, you could arrive at the altar as relaxed as a cat that's been dozing in a shaft of golden sunlight?

Well, wedding venues that offer this kind of experience are hard to find, but we know of one hidden away in Pala. It's a wonderful "Old California" estate set in a classic San Diego back-country landscape, halfway up a mountain rife with oaks, cactus, palm trees, bougainvillea, and dramatic granite boulders and outcroppings. And, of course, it basks in Southern California's year-round glorious climate. From its expansive picture windows it offers a spectacular overview of the Pala Valley, where coastal fog often lingers until late morning—then melts away to reveal the Pacific Ocean sparkling in the distance.

Called The Condor's Nest Ranch, this delightful property comes with a plethora of charming distractions. The driveway leading to the main house is flanked by a large enclosed barnyard that's home to an extended family of llamas, horses, donkeys, pigs, chickens and goats, as well as lambs, peacocks, a cow, a long-horned steer, and an alpaca! (They have complete run of their yard, but it's up to you whether you want to mingle with them.) The house itself is a low-slung, red-tiled, 5-bedroom/4-bathroom structure, enhanced by patios and trellises. Its west-facing side is lined with huge windows that frame the awesome valley view below. The 6,000-square-foot residence is utterly sophisticated and appealing in its materials and look—furnishings and appliances are state-of-the-art, and carefully selected western-themed art and antique collectibles convey a laid-back air.

Couples and their families often reserve the venue for a week prior to the big event to unwind and spend quality time together. On the wedding day, guests come up the hill to witness and celebrate, then leave after the party. Once they're gone, families easily slip back into the ranch's pre-ceremony serenity. It's not hard to see why: Each bedroom has private access to the outside, while the master bedroom has its own deck and fireplace. When folks want to gather, they chill out in the great room, a combination family room and kitchen beneath a beamed cathedral ceiling. Here, the fireplace and patented valley vista invite warm socializing. The adjoining formal dining room opens out to the foyer (sporting a fountain in its center!) and living room, which features a huge fireplace and plenty of comfortable seating for reading, schmoozing and daydreaming.

Weddings take place on the lawn beside the house and pool, with mountains and woods as a backdrop. Directly over the spot where couples exchange vows, a tall ash tree—perhaps 200 years old—stands majestically. Receptions rock out by the pool or over by the property's second house, a rustic 2-bedroom "cabin" that's decorated with old business signs, license plates and western paraphernalia. Here and there Old West-style relics, including a classic Conestoga wagon, add to the site's appeal. A timeless red barn contributes a final touch to the easygoing retro feel of this country getaway.

The Condor's Nest Ranch is a restful, almost otherworldly place. It will work its magic on you so that no matter how tense you are when you get here, you'll feel totally calm and restored by the time you leave.

CEREMONY CAPACITY: The ranch accommodates 300 seated guests outdoors.

EVENT/RECEPTION CAPACITY: The facility holds 300 seated or standing outdoors.

MEETING CAPACITY: Meeting spaces hold 100 seated guests.

FEES & DEPOSITS: A $5,000 deposit is required to reserve your date and the balance is due 3½ weeks prior to the event. All-inclusive packages include: food, bar service; professional staff; day-of coordination; shuttle service; complimentary use of a prop room; beverage stations; various amenities such as parasols, yard games, menu boards and dessert stands; tax and gratuity. The $24,850 package for up to 100 guests includes lodging for up to 20 for one night in the house and cottage. Extra nights added to any package run $1,200/night for the house or $1,550/night for the house and cottage.

AVAILABILITY: Year-round, daily. Call or email for details.

SERVICES/AMENITIES:

Catering: in-house
Kitchen Facilities: fully equipped
Tables & Chairs: provided
Linens, Silver, etc.: provided
Restrooms: not wheelchair accessible
Dance Floor: portable provided
Bride's Dressing Area: yes
AV/Meeting Equipment: BYO
Other: day-of coordination, pool

Parking: large lot
Accommodations: 7 guest rooms
Outdoor Night Lighting: yes
Outdoor Cooking Facilities: BBQ on site
Cleanup: provided
View: panorama of valley and ocean, forest, mountains; garden courtyard, pool area, landscaped grounds

RESTRICTIONS:

Alcohol: in-house
Smoking: in designated areas only
Music: DJ provided, no BYO

Wheelchair Access: yes
Insurance: included

Want to find more venues and services? Check out our informative website, www.HereComesTheGuide.com.

507

Morgan Run Club & Resort

5690 Cancha de Golf, Rancho Santa Fe
858/759-5459
www.morganrun.com

Private Country Club & Ballroom

- Rehearsal Dinners
- Ceremonies
- Wedding Receptions
- Private Parties
- Corporate Events
- Meetings
- Film Shoots
- Accommodations

Rancho Santa Fe, one of the most desirable communities in California, is the kind of discreetly luxurious place that many aspire to but few actually reach unless, of course, you're a business mogul, Hollywood star or...if you're having your wedding at Morgan Run Club & Resort.

Located just three miles from the Pacific Ocean and a half hour from Downtown San Diego, this private country club and resort is, fortuitously, available to the public for special events. As you drive up, you catch sight of the 27-hole golf course on your right and, straight ahead, the gray-and-white clubhouse with its cupola, clock tower and flags—all a bit reminiscent of the great horse ranches back East (not surprising considering the area's love of horses and the resort's proximity to the beautiful Del Mar race track).

Behind the clubhouse, a vast sea of green spreads before you, encompassing acres of manicured fairways. The Morgan Lawn, a large grassy swath near the putting green, is a premier ceremony site with panoramic views that include stands of oak, palm and pepper trees. In fact, two tall, slender palms, their trunks nearly touching as they rise to the sky, form a distinctive backdrop to the altar as you exchange vows.

The adjacent, raised Morgan Patio is the scene for congratulatory toasts. Family and friends can mingle over cocktails and hors d'oeuvres, while you and your photographer hop into a golf cart to take pictures out on the golf course. Then, as night falls, tiki torches are lit along with the fire pit, and the twinkle lights wrapped around nearby trees begin to sparkle.

Dinner and dancing follow in the large ballroom, which overlooks the patio on one side and the club's front entry on the other. Elegant chandeliers hang from the vaulted ceiling, and decorative white molding adds a nice contrast to the muted earth tones of the carpet. There are several alcoves off the main room that can be set up for beverage service or dessert tables, creating nice little conversation areas. And, once your party begins to wind down, if you just don't want the evening to end you're welcome to head on over to the Littler Lounge for an after-hours nightcap.

The resort can also arrange a casual rehearsal dinner or bridal shower at the outdoor pool, adding a touch of fun by serving finger food. And while the bride is spending some quality time at the spa, the groom can enjoy a little down time with his buddies by hosting his own outing. Out-of-town guests who choose to stay overnight in one of the 69 rooms or suites will no doubt appreciate their member-for-a-day privileges, which allow access to the full spa and fitness center, turning your celebration into an indulgent getaway.

CEREMONY CAPACITY: The club holds 180 seated guests indoors and 300 seated outdoors.

EVENT/RECEPTION CAPACITY: The site can accommodate 180 seated or 250 standing indoors and 300 seated or 350 standing outdoors.

MEETING CAPACITY: Meeting spaces hold 180 seated guests.

FEES & DEPOSITS: A nonrefundable $2,000 deposit is required to reserve your date. 50% of the estimated event total is due 60 days prior to the event and the balance is due 7 days prior. All-inclusive wedding packages range $85–140/person. Tax, alcohol and a 20% service charge are additional.

AVAILABILITY: Year-round, daily, including holidays.

SERVICES/AMENITIES:

Catering: in-house
Kitchen Facilities: n/a
Tables & Chairs: provided
Linens, Silver, etc.: provided
Restrooms: wheelchair accessible
Dance Floor: provided
Bride's Dressing Area: CBA
AV/Meeting Equipment: full range
Other: spa services, event coordination, golf course, tennis courts

Parking: complimentary guest lot; valet available, extra charge
Accommodations: 68 guest rooms
Outdoor Night Lighting: yes
Outdoor Cooking Facilities: no
Cleanup: provided
View: garden, courtyard, landscaped grounds, pool area; panorama of fairways, hills and mountains

RESTRICTIONS:

Alcohol: in-house, or BYO with corkage fee
Smoking: outdoors only
Music: amplified OK with restrictions

Wheelchair Access: yes
Insurance: not required

The Abbey on Fifth Avenue

Historic Private Event Facility

2825 Fifth Avenue, San Diego
619/686-8700

www.abbeyweddings.com
sd@hornblower.com

- ● Rehearsal Dinners
- ● Ceremonies
- ● Wedding Receptions
- ● Private Parties
- ● Corporate Events
- ● Meetings
- ● Film Shoots
- Accommodations

When people step into the Abbey, they're often so awestruck they just stand there with their mouths open. They can't believe what a stunning building it is, and that they can actually have their wedding or special event here.

This striking embodiment of Spanish Colonial Revival architecture boasts two enormous domed stained-glass skylights that bathe the interior in a pale yellow glow, while 12 luminous stained-glass windows cast their own heavenly light. Standing in the middle of this former church, you feel as if you're in a Renaissance cathedral: Dark, polished redwood molding and woodwork is everywhere—framing doors, railings, walls and in curved balconies. Exquisite fixtures made of hand-blown orange-yellow glass are suspended from 50-foot ceilings. No longer a church, the Abbey is a nondenominational venue open to couples of all faiths.

This century-old landmark has undergone several incarnations, and in 1984 an award-winning renovation transformed it into a popular restaurant christened "The Abbey." The statue of Gabriel that crowns the roof was coated in gleaming gold leaf, but with the exception of a little wood refinishing and the replacement of some light fixtures and stained glass, nothing was done to alter the facility's vintage beauty.

Today, The Abbey is a private special event facility managed by Hornblower Cruises & Events, two-time recipients of the prestigious "Finest Service Award." They invite you to stage your party, wedding or corporate function in this unique setting, where both traditional and themed events feel equally at home.

Wedding ceremonies take place where the pulpit used to be, and no matter where guests are seated—on the ground floor or up on the mezzanine—they can easily see the goings-on. Add a few candelabras and you have the perfect place for a classic black-tie affair or a Renaissance-themed party (one wedding couple and their entourage actually wore tights!).

When it's time for the reception, guests are treated to an elegant meal featuring gourmet cuisine prepared on site and overseen by Christopher Schlerf, the Food & Beverage Director here for 25 years. Wedding and reception packages are available, but if you prefer, Hornblower's professional planners can custom-design your celebration.

With their expert staff and full services, Hornblower will ensure that your event makes the most of this historic and romantic location.

CEREMONY & EVENT/RECEPTION CAPACITY: Indoors, the site holds 300 seated guests or 475 standing for a cocktail reception.

MEETING CAPACITY: Meeting spaces accommodate 300 seated guests.

FEES & DEPOSITS: A nonrefundable deposit is required to reserve your date. The on-site executive chef provides meals starting at $61/person. Four hours of room rental fees are waived with a food minimum: $5,500 for daytime events before 4pm; $7,000 for evening events after 6pm. Additional hours can be arranged at $750/hour.

AVAILABILITY: Year-round, daily, anytime.

SERVICES/AMENITIES:

Catering: in-house
Kitchen Facilities: n/a
Tables & Chairs: Chiavari chairs provided
Linens, Silver, etc.: provided
Restrooms: wheelchair accessible
Dance Floor: portable provided
Bride's & Groom's Dressing Areas: yes
AV/Meeting Equipment: CBA

Parking: on street
Accommodations: no guest rooms
Outdoor Night Lighting: provided
Outdoor Cooking Facilities: no
Cleanup: provided
View: no
Other: piano (CBA), complimentary event coordination

RESTRICTIONS:

Alcohol: in-house, or BYO with corkage fee
Smoking: not allowed
Music: amplified OK indoors

Wheelchair Access: limited
Insurance: not required

Hornblower Cruises & Events

Yachts

1800 North Harbor Drive, San Diego
619/686-8700

www.hornblower.com
sd@hornblower.com

● Rehearsal Dinners	● Corporate Events
● Ceremonies	● Meetings
● Wedding Receptions	● Film Shoots
● Private Parties	Accommodations

One of our acquaintances was married on a yacht, and we can personally attest to the fact that it was a memorable experience for everyone aboard. We enjoyed it all—the glorious day, the light breezes, and the joy that comes with being on the bay. If a wedding on the water sounds like a great idea to you, Hornblower Cruises & Events has a fleet of 49 yachts in eight California ports that can accommodate almost any type of celebration you can think of. Each of Hornblower's vessels has its own individual style.

High Spirits, easily the most romantic yacht in the San Diego fleet, is perfect for groups of 80 to 120. Designed by world-renowned yachtsman John Trumpy, this teak-and-mahogany sloop was built in 1929 and features exquisite antique furniture and detailing, including some classic appointments from the Prohibition Era. *High Spirits* was originally constructed as a sister ship to the *USS Sequoia,* President Franklin D. Roosevelt's presidential yacht, and now is one of the finest historic yachts available for entertaining on the West Coast.

Emerald Hornblower is a sleek 85-foot Skipper liner, popular for private weddings and reception charters for groups up to 120. The boat's state-of-the-art convertible sunroof lets guests enjoy San Diego's sunshine and fresh sea air at the push of a button. There's also a spacious main dining salon that boasts giant windows, a bar and a full-service galley. Guests can take in San Diego Harbor's stunning views as they eat, then ascend to the Starlight deck for outdoor dancing on the 460-square-foot parquet floor. For those who simply wish to relax after their meal, the plush and contemporary Admiral's Cabin is available for a little luxury at sea. Any Hornblower yacht will also pick up guests at any waterfront hotel guest dock.

For a more intimate celebration of up to 50, *Renown* is an excellent choice. While the ship was constructed mostly out of mahogany, the interior is done in warm dark cherrywood. The roomy and handsome main salon also includes a solid teak bar and touches of hand-rubbed natural walnut throughout. Both the main salon and dining deck provide panoramic views, complemented by a walkway encircling the entire yacht. Topping off *Renown's* extensive list of amenities are three private staterooms, a bar, dance area, stereo system, and an on-board full-service galley.

Hornblower's traditional table service includes white linens, fine china and glassware, and service by an award-winning, nautically attired crew. Whether you're planning an elaborate formal affair or a more casual one, you can be sure this seasoned staff will customize your event to suite your personal tastes.

CEREMONY, EVENT/RECEPTION & MEETING CAPACITY: Seven yachts are regularly available. They differ in size and capacity, accommodating up to 1,000 guests. Other yachts can be arranged. Ceremonies are performed on deck.

FEES & DEPOSITS: A $1,500–25,000 deposit, depending on yacht size, is due when the reservation is made, with the balance payable 5 days prior to the event. Hornblower offers $89–155/person wedding packages, which include boat rental, food, unlimited champagne, and a ceremony performed by the captain. Hourly rates and à la carte services can also be arranged.

AVAILABILITY: Year-round, daily, anytime.

SERVICES/AMENITIES:

Catering: in-house, no BYO
Kitchen Facilities: n/a
Tables & Chairs: provided
Linens, Silver, etc.: provided
Restrooms: inquire for wheelchair access
Dance Floor: provided
Bride's & Groom's Dressing Areas: limited
AV/Meeting Equipment: CBA

Parking: fee lots near dock
Accommodations: no guest rooms
Outdoor Night Lighting: yes
Outdoor Cooking Facilities: n/a
Cleanup: provided
View: San Diego Bay, city skyline
Other: complimentary event coordination

RESTRICTIONS:

Alcohol: in-house, no BYO
Smoking: outer decks only
Music: amplified OK

Wheelchair Access: limited
Insurance: not required

Hyatt Regency Mission Bay Spa & Marina

Waterfront Resort

1441 Quivira Road, San Diego
619/221-4830
www.missionbay.hyatt.com
sanis-rfp@hyatt.com

● Rehearsal Dinners		● Corporate Events	
● Ceremonies		● Meetings	
● Wedding Receptions		● Film Shoots	
● Private Parties		● Accommodations	

The Hyatt Regency Mission Bay Spa and Marina is almost a city unto itself and, like most fabulous cities, seems to have something for everyone—especially when it comes to weddings. This sprawling resort, surrounded on three sides by water, encompasses such a variety of event spaces—from grand ballrooms to a verdant garden patio to a sunny seaside embankment—that virtually any bride's desires can be satisfied.

Start with the very private Banyan Court and Lawn, a landscaped park featuring a cluster of spreading banyan trees in the center of a courtyard, ringed by flowering shrubs and water views. Banyans, which symbolize "wish fulfillment" and "eternal life" throughout India and Southeast Asia, make a fitting backdrop for exchanging vows and celebrating a union! There's plenty of room on the expansive adjacent lawn for cocktails and dinner, followed by dancing under the stars. Wedding album alert: The wooden bridge in the grove is a charming spot for photos.

If you prefer a ceremony site with the sun sparkling on the water, tie the knot on the Bayside Lawn. From here, it's a short walk to the Bayview Ballroom. Grand in scale, the room boasts dramatic chandeliers and floor-to-ceiling windows framing a wide vista that transitions from a colorful sunset at dusk to twinkling lights across Mission Bay at night. An adjoining patio (also available with the Mission and Palm Ballrooms) creates an indoor/outdoor flow.

But the Hyatt has another option that truly elevates the indoor/outdoor experience to a totally upscale and glamorous level: The Regatta Pavilion will make you forget anything you ever thought you knew about tented venues. Lushly draped and fully carpeted, the pavilion is a unique, romantic setting where up to 700 guests can revel beside the bay.

Planning a smaller-scale gathering? There are plenty of choices for you, too. The Cabanas is an intriguing spot for an event-in-the-round. A series of raised, open-air cabanas around the perimeter provide seating during the ceremony, or conversation-friendly groupings during the reception. For an intimate fête with a sophisticated feel, take the elevator straight to the Penthouse atop The Tower. This sleek apartment with marble floors, step-down living room, fireplace, bar and wraparound patios with near 360-degree panoramas of the bay, ocean and marina is, to quote Cole Porter, "the tops."

The Hyatt Regency Mission Bay is a great destination for your out-of-town guests: They'll dine splendidly (the catering staff uses the freshest ingredients in deliciously innovative ways); they can be pampered at the spa; there's a water playground on site; and the hotel is close to a wide range of attractions. And for you, the newlyweds, the perks don't end with the wedding—in addition to receiving a complimentary bridal suite, you actually earn reward points from your event that entitle you to free nights at any Hyatt worldwide for your honeymoon!

CEREMONY CAPACITY: The hotel holds up to 700 seated guests indoors or outdoors.

EVENT/RECEPTION CAPACITY: The site accommodates up to 700 seated or 800 standing indoors, and 500 seated or 700 standing guests outdoors.

MEETING CAPACITY: Meeting rooms hold up to 700 seated guests.

FEES & DEPOSITS: 25% of the food & beverage minimum is required to reserve your date. The balance is payable in quarterly installments with the final payment due 10 business days prior to the event. The ceremony fee ranges $1,500–2,500 depending on the day and time of the event and the space reserved. Packages start at $95/person for lunch and $115/person for dinner. Tax and service charge are additional. For the rooftop Penthouse space, packages are available that include food, beverage, sleeping accommodations, tax, and service charge.

AVAILABILITY: Year-round, daily.

SERVICES/AMENITIES:

Catering: in-house
Kitchen Facilities: n/a
Tables & Chairs: provided
Linens, Silver, etc.: provided
Restrooms: wheelchair accessible
Dance Floor: portable provided
Bride's & Groom's Dressing Areas: CBA
AV/Meeting Equipment: CBA
Other: spa services

Parking: self and valet available
Accommodations: 430 guest rooms
Outdoor Night Lighting: CBA
Outdoor Cooking Facilities: no
Cleanup: provided
View: garden, courtyard, pool area, landscaped grounds; panorama of ocean/bay, coastline, and cityscape

RESTRICTIONS:

Alcohol: in-house
Smoking: designated areas only
Music: amplified OK with restrictions

Wheelchair Access: yes
Insurance: not required

This is important! Tell locations you're reading HERE COMES THE GUIDE and ask if our information is still current.

Karl Strauss Brewery Gardens

Restaurant & Gardens

9675 Scranton Road, San Diego
858/581-7324
www.karlstrauss.com
catering@karlstrauss.com

●	Rehearsal Dinners	●	Corporate Events
●	Ceremonies	●	Meetings
●	Wedding Receptions	●	Film Shoots
●	Private Parties		Accommodations

Okay, so you've read the word "Brewery" in the name and you're ready to turn the page. Don't do it!—you'll miss one of San Diego's surprise special event locations. This place may have a microbrewery somewhere on site, but we never saw it—we were too busy admiring the five and a half acres of beautiful Oriental gardens. Who would have thought that in the midst of the ultra-modern San Diego Tech Center, with its gleaming glass highrises, you'd find such a lush oasis? It was quite a shock—albeit a delightful one—to step into this private world, literally hidden behind dense stands of bamboo and tall hedges. A restaurant with a two-tiered deck at both ends sits right at the edge of an emerald-green pond. Clusters of lily pads float on the still surface, while multicolored koi swim below. The entire site is ringed by a profusion of trees, bushes and grasses; an arched wooden bridge, stone lanterns perched on rocks and a cascading waterfall complete the picture.

The restaurant, designed like the one in Munich's famous Chinese Pagoda Beer Garden, is filled with natural light from a wall of windows that wrap around three sides. Natural pine beams span the high peaked ceiling, and wooden planters overflowing with greenery bring the garden inside. While most receptions or parties are held in here, ceremonies usually take place on the largest deck. The bride and groom say their vows at the end of the deck, with the gardens as a backdrop. Both decks—shaded by plenty of umbrellas and an occasional tree growing up through the flooring—are also just as popular for outdoor celebrations. A white canopy protects the lower tier of the main deck, and heaters can be turned on if the temperature drops a bit.

Noisy signs of civilization? You won't find any of them at Karl Strauss' Gardens. Peace and tranquility reign here, so you might as well just sit down, sip something cool, and watch the koi gently ripple the still surface of the pond.

CEREMONY CAPACITY: The outdoor garden patio can accommodate 125 seated guests.

EVENT/RECEPTION CAPACITY: Using both indoor and outdoor spaces, the site holds up to 325 seated or 400 standing; indoors only, 170 seated. The private Bonsai Room holds 50 seated or 70 standing.

MEETING CAPACITY: Meeting spaces accommodate 15–325 seated guests.

FEES & DEPOSITS: For weddings, a nonrefundable, nontransferable $1,500 deposit is required to book the site, and the balance is payable 3 days prior to the event. Meals start at $83/person for weddings. In addition to the meal, this pricing includes the wedding cake, colored linens, and disc jockey. Alcohol, tax, setup, security and service charges are additional. For ceremonies, there is a $700 setup fee.

For business functions, a goodwill deposit is required to secure your date. Menus can be customized and start at $25/person for dinners, or $16/person for hors d'oeuvres. Alcohol, tax and service charges are additional. A room rental fee may apply; call for more information.

AVAILABILITY: Year-round, daily, until midnight.

SERVICES/AMENITIES:

Catering: in-house, no BYO
Kitchen Facilities: n/a
Tables & Chairs: provided
Linens, Silver, etc.: provided
Restrooms: wheelchair accessible
Dance Floor: front deck
Bride's & Groom's Dressing Areas: CBA
AV/Meeting Equipment: CBA, extra charge

Parking: large lots, self-parking
Accommodations: no guest rooms
Outdoor Night Lighting: yes
Outdoor Cooking Facilities: no
Cleanup: provided
View: Japanese gardens, koi ponds & waterfall
Other: event coordination

RESTRICTIONS:

Alcohol: BW provided, no BYO
Smoking: outside only
Music: amplified OK

Wheelchair Access: yes
Insurance: not required
Other: no rice, confetti or birdseed

The Lafayette Hotel
Swim Club and Bungalows

2223 El Cajon Boulevard, San Diego
619/296-2101

www.lafayettehotelsd.com
events@lafayettehotelsd.com

Hotel

- Rehearsal Dinners
- Ceremonies
- Wedding Receptions
- Private Parties
- Corporate Events
- Meetings
- Film Shoots
- Accommodations

If you're a fan of old Hollywood glamour but your groom's more a hipster…or you lean toward a garden setting while he prefers an urban vibe, don't despair because there's actually a perfect wedding venue for both of you. The Lafayette Hotel, originally built in the 1940s, ingeniously mixes elements of its storied history with the vibrancy and edginess of its revitalized North Park location in the ultimate mash-up.

A vintage marquee and circular drive lead to the grand, red brick Colonial building, fronted by soaring white columns. Inside, the lobby features ornate coffered ceilings, crown molding and a sparkling crystal chandelier. Among the eclectic décor are a plush round settee and baby grand piano—great for lounging and taking some fun, flirty album shots.

Just beyond two open archways, you'll find their totally unique ceremony site: the Conservatory. This huge space is bathed in natural light streaming in from an entire wall of floor-to-ceiling multi-paned windows and French Doors that serve as the backdrop for your ceremony. Now before you start imagining something prim and proper, take a look up: Suspended from the high, translucent ceiling are dozens of colorful, upside-down parasols giving the entire area a whimsical, garden atmosphere. Seating for your guests offers an equally unexpected twist with a wonderful mélange of wingback, ladder-back, upholstered and Chiavari chairs.

Then when you're ready to pop open the champagne, step outside to the lovely curved Veranda overlooking the hotel's centerpiece swimming pool. Designed in 1946 by Olympic great Johnny Weissmuller, it instantly became a mecca for locals as well as L.A. celebs like Ava Gardner and Bob Hope. Today, after recent renovations, Lafayette's pool scene once again reigns supreme. But if you prefer a more intimate spot for your "I do"s and cocktails, try the tucked-away West Courtyard, where you can have an open-sky affair or one that's covered with a canopy of billowing fabric.

For an unforgettable reception, the *pièce de résistance* is, without doubt, the Mississippi Ballroom. Located on its own floor, it's like stepping into a whole other world of Hollywood soirées and elegant supper clubs. This amazing, two-tiered ballroom features soft recessed lighting inside its circular, coffered ceiling; columns with etched flourishes; and even the original hardwood dance floor. But most stunning of all is the stage with its knockout, backlit clamshell that adds high drama to your live band/DJ, first dance or even sweetheart table. This is just not something you see every day! And there's even a small garden right outside the ballroom where you can smoke a cigar while stargazing.

With comfy rooms for you and your guests, menu selections that'll make you want to try everything, a helpful staff, and an endearing mix of retro touches with modern quirks, this venue may be what marriage is all about—combining diverse elements to create something even better than its individual parts.

CEREMONY & MEETING CAPACITY: The hotel can accommodate 300 seated guests indoors and 125 seated outdoors.

EVENT/RECEPTION CAPACITY: The site holds up to 400 seated or 500 standing indoors and 65 seated or 80 standing outdoors.

FEES & DEPOSITS: 20% of the total event cost is required to reserve your date and the balance is due 7 days prior to the event. Rental fees range $125–2,500 depending on the day of the event and the space rented. Meals range $35–75/person. Tax, alcohol and a 20% service charge are additional.

AVAILABILITY: Year-round; 6am–10pm. The ballroom may be reserved until midnight for an additional fee. Please inquire for more details.

SERVICES/AMENITIES:

Catering: in-house
Kitchen Facilities: n/a
Tables & Chairs: provided
Linens, Silver, etc.: provided or CBA
Restrooms: wheelchair accessible
Dance Floor: yes
Bride's Dressing Area: yes
AV/Meeting Equipment: some provided, more CBA

Parking: on street, garage nearby; valet CBA
Accommodations: 132 guest rooms
Outdoor Night Lighting: CBA
Outdoor Cooking Facilities: BBQ on site
Cleanup: provided
View: fountain, garden, landscaped grounds
Other: grand piano; event coordination, extra fee

RESTRICTIONS:

Alcohol: in-house
Smoking: designated areas only
Music: amplified OK

Wheelchair Access: yes
Insurance: not required

Rancho Bernardo Inn

Resort Hotel

17550 Bernardo Oaks Drive, San Diego
855/432-5888
www.ranchobernardoinn.com
rbiweddings@jcresorts.com

- Rehearsal Dinners
- Ceremonies
- Wedding Receptions
- Private Parties
- Corporate Events
- Meetings
- Film Shoots
- Accommodations

Rancho Bernardo Inn has so many spectacular sites for ceremonies, receptions and photo ops that even the most ardent romantics among us could renew their vows yearly and still find unique spots they hadn't seen before. This 200-acre resort melds its California Rancho history with modern amenities to create a four-star retreat without a hint of stuffiness. So whether you want a wedding that's posh and sophisticated or one that's casual and relaxed, you can host it here and feel pampered in the process.

A beautiful place to start is Aragon Lawn, an expansive, fairy-tale garden lushly bordered by white roses and trees. The long center aisle leads to a trellised arbor where you'll exchange vows beneath a canopy of grape leaves. Afterwards, serve cocktails and dinner on the adjacent Aragon Terrace, replete with more signature white roses. The terrace wraps around to reveal another grape arbor that's lovely for a sun-dappled reception—there's also an outdoor fireplace to provide a warm glow in the evening. If you prefer a more formal affair, start with cocktails in the Aragon Foyer where arched glass doors open to the terrace, then follow with dinner and dancing in the stately Aragon Ballroom, which boasts honey-toned walls, a high ceiling and gorgeous pendant chandeliers.

There are several other intimate ceremony sites, including the North and Valencia Lawns, that feature arbors, white roses, or even a dramatic stone backdrop. But if you want sweeping views of the 18-hole golf course, check out The Promenade, a brick courtyard with 180-degree fairway panoramas.

Santiago Courtyard is a must-see, partly because of its graceful olive trees and hacienda feel, but mainly because of its magnificent Italian fountain, a centerpiece that truly says "amore": A pair of stone-carved lovers, gazing adoringly at each other, stand above a stunning mosaic waterfall gently cascading into a sculpted pool. This courtyard has an adjacent ballroom, making it easy to flow right into your reception. However, flexibility is top priority here, so you can use spaces that are next to each other or mix and match options to suit your event—including the inn's completely re-imagined restaurant.

AVANT is Rancho Bernardo's sophisticated step forward in dining. Recently opened to great fanfare, the restaurant's new menu focuses on local, sustainable and fresh ingredients. (In fact, one can often see the chef harvesting bounty from the inn's garden for that night's dishes.) Taking a wine country approach, the offerings—from artisan cocktails to charcuterie, small plates and seasonal specialties—showcase unpretentious food that will please your most discriminating guests. And the cuisine is not the only thing that's changed. The Main Dining Room's clean-lined, contemporary décor includes dark wood floors, soft leather seating, a rich granite bar and a vaulted, beamed ceiling. Along one wall, picture windows frame manicured fairway vistas, and at the far end a shaded patio is a cool setting for al fresco gatherings. For an exceptional rehearsal dinner, reserve one of the chic private dining rooms or AVANT Kitchen's "chef's table."

Frankly, there's so much to love at Rancho Bernardo Inn that we suggest taking a tour. And while you're here, why not stop by their spa—it's never too early for a little pre-wedding indulgence!

CEREMONY CAPACITY: The hotel holds 1,000 seated guests indoors and 750 seated outdoors.

EVENT/RECEPTION & MEETING CAPACITY: The site accommodates 840 guests seated or 1,150 standing indoors and 200 seated or 300 standing outdoors.

FEES & DEPOSITS: 25% of the food & beverage minimum, service charge, location fee, and taxes are required to reserve your date. An additional 50% deposit is due 3 months prior to the event and the balance is due 5 days prior. Location fees range $1,800–3,500 depending on the day and time of the event, guest count and the space rented. Meals range $48–130/person. Tax, alcohol and a 22% service charge are additional.

AVAILABILITY: Year-round.

SERVICES/AMENITIES:

Catering: in-house, or BYO ethnic caterer with approval
Kitchen Facilities: n/a
Tables & Chairs: provided
Linens, Silver, etc.: provided
Restrooms: wheelchair accessible
Dance Floor: portable provided
Bride's Dressing Area: CBA
AV/Meeting Equipment: CBA

Parking: large lot, valet available
Accommodations: 287 guest rooms
Outdoor Night Lighting: CBA
Outdoor Cooking Facilities: BBQ CBA
Cleanup: provided
View: fountain, garden, hills, lake, landscaped grounds, mountains, pool area, waterfall
Other: spa, in-house florals, event coordination

RESTRICTIONS:

Alcohol: full in-house bar
Smoking: designated areas only
Music: amplified OK

Wheelchair Access: yes
Insurance: not required

Sheraton San Diego Hotel & Marina

Waterfront Hotel

1380 Harbor Island Drive, San Diego

619/692-2761

www.sheraton.com/sandiego
stacey.levasseur@sheraton.com

● Rehearsal Dinners	● Corporate Events		
● Ceremonies	● Meetings		
● Wedding Receptions	● Film Shoots		
● Private Parties	● Accommodations		

Commanding an enviable location on the pristine shores of Harbor Island, the Sheraton San Diego Hotel & Marina combines the refreshing ambiance of a seaside refuge with the deluxe amenities of the finest hostelries, including sophisticated dining, a state-of-the-art Spa and Fitness Center and plush accommodations with spacious private balconies. Recreation options also abound (tennis, anyone? bike riding or scuba diving?). Yet the most spectacular feature of this two-towered establishment has got to be its unmatched panoramic views. The West Tower faces the action at the harbor and marina where sleek pleasure craft either bob in their moorings or wend their way out to sea. To the east, twinkling city lights fill the million-dollar vista with the nighttime energy of a dynamic metropolis.

Recently favored with a $35-million renovation, this urban resort also boasts an astonishing 120,000 square feet of award-winning event space, including some of the prettiest ceremony sites we've seen: On the marina side, the Garden Terrace bursts with multihued flowers and bushes. Fragrant white tea roses, lavender, gardenia, jasmine, box hedges and magnolia trees line a latticed arbor walkway, winding to a fountain created solely to soothe the spirits of brides as they prepare to take those momentous steps down the aisle. Beyond an arched, white lattice gate, friends and family assemble, taking their seats on an always-perfect lawn alongside the water. Another site, the Bayview Lawn, is nestled under shade trees near the East Tower and offers southerly views of passing ships.

If you prefer a ceremony at sea, board a private yacht and have the captain officiate your wedding. Participate in the tradition of scattering rose petals to the wind, and watch the waves carry them to the horizon.

During the cocktail hour, numerous patios, terraces, and lounges allow guests to mingle in the glow of the setting sun, perhaps taking in the customary evening regatta or departing ocean liners. Clear glass panels surrounding some patios allow unobstructed views comfortably protected from ocean breezes. Then it's off to one of the Sheraton's half-dozen versatile ballrooms for dinner and dancing. Whether you choose an intimate room for 10 or the 100,000-square-foot tented Bayshore Pavilion for 1,500 of your closest friends, the hotel can accommodate any size reception.

The Bel Aire Ballroom, for example, is a popular choice, with marble walls complemented by understated striped wallpaper and navy carpet, and an immense mirrored chandelier that evokes icicles dangling in a winter castle. Like the Bel Aire, most of the venue's reception spaces boast spectacular floor-to-ceiling views of the water or city skyline. Seated on custom-made blue-striped parlor chairs, your guests will savor their gourmet food served on fine English white porcelain china and drink from posh stemware. Named "Best Caterer" by *San Diego Magazine* 15 years running, the Sheraton's team of culinary all-stars are sure to impress.

In fact, everything is impressive about this world-class resort. Just minutes from all of San Diego's attractions, the Sheraton San Diego Hotel & Marina provides you and your guests with a luxurious San Diego experience, served up with warmth and flair.

CEREMONY CAPACITY: The site holds 1,000 seated guests, indoors or outdoors.

EVENT/RECEPTION CAPACITY: The hotel can accommodate 2,000 seated or 3,000 standing guests indoors, and 1,000 seated or 3,000 standing outdoors.

MEETING CAPACITY: Meeting rooms hold 3,000 seated guests.

FEES & DEPOSITS: A deposit is required to reserve your date. The estimated event total is due 10 days before the event and final payment is due 72 business hours prior. Complete wedding packages start at $50/person. Tax, alcohol and a 24% service charge are additional.

AVAILABILITY: Year-round, daily, anytime.

SERVICES/AMENITIES:

Catering: in-house
Kitchen Facilities: fully equipped kitchen
Tables & Chairs: provided
Linens, Silver, etc.: provided
Restrooms: wheelchair accessible
Dance Floor: provided
Bride's & Groom's Dressing Areas: CBA
AV/Meeting Equipment: provided, CBA

Parking: large lot
Accommodations: 1,044 guest rooms
Outdoor Night Lighting: CBA
Outdoor Cooking Facilities: BBQ CBA
Cleanup: provided
View: panorama of bay and ocean; garden
Other: grand piano, spa services, picnic area

RESTRICTIONS:

Alcohol: in-house
Smoking: not allowed
Music: amplified OK

Wheelchair Access: yes
Insurance: liability required

Overwhelmed? Use the search criteria on www.HereComesTheGuide.com to narrow down your choices.

523

The University Club Atop Symphony Towers

Private Club

750 B Street 34th Floor, San Diego
619/702-1987, 619/702-1986

www.uc-sandiego.com
allison.willeford@clubcorp.com
morgan.olsen@clubcorp.com

- Rehearsal Dinners
- Ceremonies
- Wedding Receptions
- Private Parties

- Corporate Events
- Meetings
- Film Shoots
- Accommodations

As a famous ad line once said, "Membership has its privileges," so it's quite exciting to find that one of San Diego's most exclusive urban retreats, The University Club Atop Symphony Towers, will extend their VIP treatment to nonmembers when they host a wedding or special event here.

This super-chic, downtown penthouse exudes understated elegance, not to mention jaw-dropping, panoramic views of the entire city. Originally founded in 1909 to promote education, literature and art, the club now counts many of San Diego's elite business and cultural luminaries among its members. But toss out any preconceived images you might have of stuffy rooms and a stodgy atmosphere, because with its recent expansion and renovation, this 34th-floor aerie is *au courant* and stunning.

The elevator whisks you to the white-marble entry where a receptionist greets you. Straight ahead is the expansive main section, where dark ceramic floors and a striking color palette of crisp white and black get a vibrant pop with splashes of lime green on high-backed sofas and modern club chairs. Huge floor-to-ceiling picture windows frame the spectacular vistas that showcase the San Diego Bay (including the Embarcadero, harbor and Coronado Bridge), the convention center and surrounding skyline, as well as Tijuana to the south and the hills to the east. A large alcove even provides binoculars on each of the tables so you can get a bird's-eye peek of the Padres in action down at Petco Park.

Speaking of action, to your left is the Media Room, featuring a 103″ flat screen TV and an array of signed baseball bats hanging in Lucite boxes, which have been donated by an owner of the hometown team. Since the University Club likes to highlight its local connections, there are Taylor Guitars displayed on one wall and a John Bishop-designed longboard-cum-table in the hip and casual Apollo Room Lounge. Glittering chrome chandeliers spiral from the ceiling like tiered sculptures and art is everywhere, from classic oils to a changing display of mixed media pieces that you pass en route to the Laureate Ballroom.

This grand space is the hub for your private event. The rich, muted colors of the room make the sensational views of lush Balboa Park through walls of glass even more dramatic. Opulent French doors allow you to divide the ballroom and have your ceremony on one side and your reception on the other. (On Sundays, you can have use of the entire club so you might want to start by exchanging vows in the Boardroom, which looks out onto the eastern edge of the city.)

Live music is welcome—they've had everything from jazz piano to rock to mariachi bands and even the USC marching band. And, of course, your dining experience will be as impeccable as the venue: The chef and culinary team are used to catering to a discerning clientele, and use only the freshest ingredients, putting a contemporary spin on classic favorites.

CEREMONY CAPACITY: The club holds 200 seated guests indoors.

EVENT/RECEPTION & MEETING CAPACITY: The club can accommodate 204 seated or 350 standing guests indoors.

FEES & DEPOSITS: A $1,500 deposit is required to reserve your date. 50% of the estimated event total is due 60 days prior to the event and the balance is due 10 days prior. The food & beverage minimum ranges $3,500–15,000 depending on the day and time of the event and the guest count. Meals range $50–95/person. Tax and a 22% service charge are additional.

AVAILABILITY: Year-round, daily.

SERVICES/AMENITIES:

Catering: in-house
Kitchen Facilities: n/a
Tables & Chairs: provided
Linens, Silver, etc.: provided
Restrooms: wheelchair accessible
Dance Floor: provided
Bride's Dressing Area: yes
AV/Meeting Equipment: provided

Parking: self and valet available
Accommodations: no guest rooms, hotel nearby
Outdoor Night Lighting: no
Outdoor Cooking Facilities: no
Cleanup: provided
View: panorama of city, coastline, park and ocean
Other: grand piano, in-house wedding cake and florals, event coordination

RESTRICTIONS:

Alcohol: in-house
Smoking: outdoors only
Music: amplified OK indoors

Wheelchair Access: yes
Insurance: not required

Lomas Santa Fe Country Club

Country Club

1505 Lomas Santa Fe Drive, Solana Beach
888/994-5447
www.countryclubreceptions.com
www.lomassantafecc.com
eventdirector@lomassantafecc.com

- Rehearsal Dinners
- Ceremonies
- Wedding Receptions
- Private Parties
- Corporate Events
- Meetings
- Film Shoots
- Accommodations

Set on a hill just a few miles from the blue Pacific, Lomas Santa Fe Country Club is an in-demand wedding location for good reason: Their landscaped grounds are an open-air delight, and the newly renovated indoor spaces lend a fresh, contemporary sophistication to events.

As guests arrive, they step through solid oak doors into the lobby, which has the inviting ambiance of a casual-chic living room. Crisp white walls and furniture clad in an elegant cobalt blue fabric provide a cool contrast to the warm, pine-beamed ceiling high overhead.

Ceremonies are typically held outdoors to take advantage of the stunning ocean vista and almost year-round fabulous weather. And if you want to make a grand entrance, you'll have the perfect opportunity here: A gently terraced walkway leads from the clubhouse down to the golf course where your seated guests wait in anticipation. As you slowly descend, all eyes will be on you! Vows are exchanged on an expansive lawn, with acres of tree-studded fairways and a distant ocean view as your backdrop. Time your ceremony just right, and you'll also have a gorgeous sunset.

While the wedding party poses for photos wherever they like on the grounds, everyone else heads up to the shaded clubhouse terrace for mingling over drinks and hors d'oeuvres. Designed with a wall of windows and outfitted with heaters, this space allows guests to enjoy themselves as well as the lovely panorama while staying comfortable in any season.

After the cocktail hour, guests step from the terrace into the adjoining ballroom for the reception. Here, the look is an appealing modern-meets-rustic: The rich, midnight blue carpet laced with a silvery pattern is a bold complement to the white walls and natural, pine-beamed ceiling and wrought-iron chandeliers. A working fireplace adds warmth, and couples often decorate its mantel with flowers, candles or other items to personalize the space. A parquet dance floor in the center of the room and wraparound windows ensure that both the action inside and the view outside are visible from every seat. The terrace is also available throughout your event, creating a fun, indoor/outdoor experience.

Three wedding packages and a tempting selection of hors d'oeuvres and entrées let you customize your celebration to your taste and budget. And Lomas Santa Fe also makes it easy to turn your big day into a wedding weekend for family and friends. Shuttle service to the club is offered by a few recommended local hotels, and there's a lot to do nearby: shopping, dining and beach activities in the cute town of Solana Beach, plus the Del Mar Fairgrounds just two miles away.

Their friendly, experienced staff will help with all your decisions, from choosing the right linens to selecting your menu and signature drink. The combination of topnotch services and a beautiful setting definitely makes Lomas Santa Fe Country Club a winning choice for a San Diego wedding.

CEREMONY CAPACITY: The ceremony site holds up to 250 seated guests.

EVENT/RECEPTION CAPACITY: The ballroom accommodates up to 230 seated or 350 standing.

MEETING CAPACITY: The club seats 300 guests.

FEES & DEPOSITS: A nonrefundable deposit, which is applied to your food & beverage total, is required to reserve your date. The amount of the deposit varies depending on how far in advance you book. Payment terms for the balance also vary, and may be arranged on an individual basis. Wedding packages start at $45/person for brunch and $67/per person for dinner. Tax, alcohol and service charge are additional. A food & beverage minimum will apply. Menus and packages can be customized to fit your needs and budget. Call for details.

AVAILABILITY: Year-round.

SERVICES/AMENITIES:

Catering: in-house; outside catering allowed with approval, extra fee may apply
Kitchen Facilities: fully equipped, extra fee
Tables & Chairs: provided
Linens, Silver, etc.: provided
Restrooms: wheelchair accessible
Dance Floor: provided
Bride's Dressing Area: yes
AV/Meeting Equipment: some provided

Parking: large complimentary lot
Accommodations: no guest rooms
Outdoor Night Lighting: CBA
Outdoor Cooking Facilities: BBQ CBA
Cleanup: provided
View: fairways, pond, ocean, grounds
Other: event coordination, florals

RESTRICTIONS:

Alcohol: in-house, no BYO
Smoking: outside only
Music: amplified

Wheelchair Access: yes
Insurance: not required

Broken Rock Ranch

Ranch

29701 Mac Tan Road, Valley Center
760/749-1278
www.brrvalleycenter.com
broken.rock@att.net

● Rehearsal Dinners	● Corporate Events
● Ceremonies	● Meetings
● Wedding Receptions	● Film Shoots
● Private Parties	● Accommodations

Only 40 miles from downtown San Diego and completely removed from any hustle and bustle, Broken Rock Ranch strikes a chord with couples yearning for a down-home, country-style wedding. Set in Valley Center, a close-knit community known for its annual Western Days Parade, this secluded venue offers a variety of celebration sites plus rustic accommodations that can turn your event into a fun family getaway.

Start by taking full advantage of the rural landscape with an open-air ceremony on their Country Field. Fresh bales of hay and a vintage tractor add a charmingly authentic backdrop as you exchange vows beneath the spreading branches of what they affectionately refer to as the Grandfather Pepper Tree. Off to the side is a view of acres of gently rolling hills in the distance.

There's also a large amphitheater with tiered seating, where you can tie the knot beneath an altar made from branches. Or if you prefer an indoor ceremony, gather in the simple A-frame chapel on the property, built in the 1960s in honor of a previous owner who was a well-known faith healer.

Afterwards, it's just a short stroll down a pathway to the Reception Lawn. Located between the Bunkhouse and the Lodge, this large grassy area features a circular stone inset at one end, (another ceremony option)…and a circular dance floor at the other. You can have the entire lawn tented or enjoy cocktails and dinner under the stars, accompanied by the warm glow of lanterns and twinkle lights.

The Lodge makes a great spot for your reception as well. Step through the entrance into the Game Room, where a piano, ping-pong table and comfy seating make for a relaxed cocktail hour. The Main Room has hardwood floors, a peaked ceiling and windows that look out over treetops. But the true eye-catcher is a unique fireplace sculpted to look like a tree—complete with an owl perched on a limb.

The Lodge's professional kitchen makes it easy for your caterer (or the ranch's preferred caterer) to prep meals, and set up buffet service in the Game Room or plated dining in the Main Room. You can even opt for a barbecue and bring in a licensed bartender. Dress the place up or keep it casual—they want you to feel comfortable making Broken Rock Ranch your own.

In fact, keep that feeling going with a weekend at the ranch. Between the Bunkhouse and Dorms, there's room for 78 overnight guests (and yes, they actually have bunk beds!) who'll be happy to take walks on the trails, swim in the pool, have a cookout, explore the nearby town and rekindle the bygone joy of being at camp.

CEREMONY, EVENT/RECEPTION & MEETING CAPACITY: The site holds 100 seated or standing guests indoors and 400 seated or standing outdoors.

FEES & DEPOSITS: A $1,000 deposit and signed contract are required to reserve your date, and the balance is due 14 business days prior to the event. A refundable $1,500 security deposit is also required. Wedding packages start at $3,000 and vary depending on the guest count. Meals start at $30/person. Alcohol is additional and must be served by a licensed server who is required to monitor it for the entire duration of the event.

Rates for business functions, meetings or other types of events vary. Please contact the venue for more details.

AVAILABILITY: Year-round, Monday–Saturday, 8:30am–5:30pm. By appointment only.

SERVICES/AMENITIES:

Catering: in-house or BYO
Kitchen Facilities: fully equipped
Tables & Chairs: provided
Linens, Silver, etc.: BYO
Restrooms: wheelchair accessible
Dance Floor: yes
Bride's Dressing Area: yes
AV/Meeting Equipment: BYO

Parking: large lot
Accommodations: 7 rooms, 78 beds
Outdoor Night Lighting: CBA
Outdoor Cooking Facilities: BBQ on site
Cleanup: provided
View: pool area, meadow; panorama of hills and distant mountains
Other: event coordination available, extra fee

RESTRICTIONS:

Alcohol: BYO, licensed and insured server required
Smoking: designated areas only
Music: amplified OK with restrictions

Wheelchair Access: limited
Insurance: liability required

Shadowridge Country Club

Golf Course

1980 Gateway Drive, Vista
760/727-7700 x108

www.shadowridgecc.com
sarah.tillery@clubcorp.com

- Rehearsal Dinners
- Ceremonies
- Wedding Receptions
- Private Parties
- Corporate Events
- Meetings
- Film Shoots
- Accommodations

Enveloped by flowering shrubs and bougainvillea, Shadowridge Country Club's hilltop ceremony site provides the sheltered privacy of a secret garden. Tall hedges embrace the intimate spot, where a classic gazebo at the far end overlooks the Vista hills. As perfect as this setting is, you're welcome to add your own unique touches, from lanterns and draping to a rose petal aisle or even crystals. Sculptural boulders, trees and sweeping hillsides around the perimeter serve as ideal backdrops for wedding photos and a post-ceremony champagne toast.

Once vows are exchanged, you and your guests will be shuttled aboard luxury buses to the modern, Mediterranean-style clubhouse with its wide circular drive, white-washed exterior and red-tiled roof. A graceful staircase leads up past feathery palms to your exclusive entrance and a small "welcome" patio overlooking the immaculate golf course.

Double French doors open to the newly renovated reception wing, whose rooms can be used in whatever combination best suits your event. The light-filled Turnberry Room has wraparound picture windows, offering magnificent views of the verdant fairways and distant hills dotted with upscale homes. A raised white ceiling and contemporary cylindrical chandeliers lend an open, airy feel, while seagrass-covered walls add texture to the neutral palette.

You can expand the space (and the view) by opening the retractable doors to the adjacent and identically decorated Ridge Room, providing ample room for a large hardwood dance floor and dropdown screen for home movies. Want to increase your square footage even more? The Gleneagles Room just across the hall can be utilized for a separate cocktail reception. When all three spaces are used together, they give your party a great flow.

The Sanders Social House, otherwise known as the members' private dining room, is now available at certain times for special events. The comfy, chic décor features sleek banquettes, artsy club chairs and a cool teardrop chandelier over the U-shaped, granite bar. Foldaway glass doors open to a huge patio with overhead fans, a fire pit and wide-open vistas of manicured fairways and starlit nights, making this indoor/outdoor venue a sweet choice for late-night dancing and cocktails.

Flexibility is Shadowridge's specialty. No matter which spaces or package you choose, the highly trained staff will work with you every step of the way to make sure your celebration matches your style and budget so that you get the best possible value. The club's accomplished chefs can also help design the right menu for your affair—with popular selections like Almond Crusted Halibut, Char-Grilled Filet Mignon and Chicken Fontina—or plan a buffet with fun options like a Potato Martini Bar.

Thanks to service like this, it's no wonder Shadowridge hosts so many special events, including Sweet 16s, bar/bat mitzvahs and quinceañeras. But with one of the prettiest ceremony sites to grace a golf club, it's easy to see why weddings top the list.

CEREMONY CAPACITY: The facility accommodates 300 seated guests indoors and 250 seated outdoors.

EVENT/RECEPTION CAPACITY: The site holds 300 seated or 350 standing guests indoors and 600 seated or 1,000 standing outdoors.

MEETING CAPACITY: Meeting spaces hold 300 seated guests indoors.

FEES & DEPOSITS: A $1,000 minimum deposit is required to reserve your date. 50% of the estimated event total is due 60 days prior to the event and the balance is due 14 days prior. Rental fees range $100–1,500 depending on the day and time of the event, guest count and the space rented. Meals range $22–100/person. Tax, alcohol and a 20% service charge are additional.

AVAILABILITY: Year-round, daily, 6am–midnight.

SERVICES/AMENITIES:

Catering: in-house
Kitchen Facilities: n/a
Tables & Chairs: provided
Linens, Silver, etc.: provided
Restrooms: wheelchair accessible
Dance Floor: portable provided
Bride's Dressing Area: yes
AV/Meeting Equipment: provided

Parking: large lot, valet available
Accommodations: no guest rooms
Outdoor Night Lighting: CBA
Outdoor Cooking Facilities: BBQ on site
Cleanup: provided
View: garden, lagoon; panorama of landscaped grounds, fairways and mountains
Other: event coordination

RESTRICTIONS:

Alcohol: in-house
Smoking: designated areas only
Music: amplified OK

Wheelchair Access: yes
Insurance: not required

The wedding vendors on our website are the best in the business. How do we know? Read page 577.

Greater Palm Springs

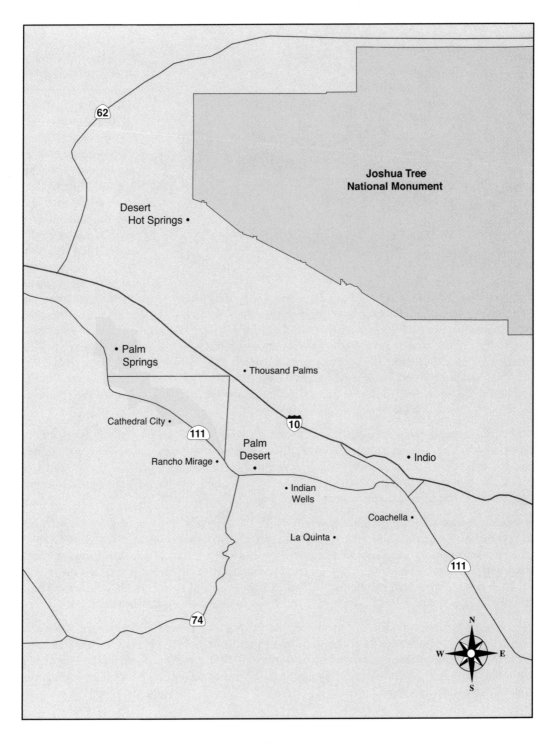

Indian Wells Country Club

Country Club

46-000 Club Drive, Indian Wells
760/834-6018
www.indianwellsclub.com
hayley.tice@clubcorp.com

- Rehearsal Dinners
- Ceremonies
- Wedding Receptions
- Private Parties
- Corporate Events
- Meetings
- Film Shoots
- Accommodations

A short drive out of Palm Springs leads to one of the region's most prestigious communities—Indian Wells. The pretty town with the unusual name was originally a Native American village with a hand-built well at its center. From this humble beginning Indian Wells has grown into California's second-wealthiest community, a miraculous transformation that owes a debt to both dates and golf. Among the settlers who arrived in the early 1900s was pioneer Caleb E. Cook, who established a series of successful date ranches. As the town prospered, the unspoiled beauty and year-round sunshine attracted the notice of influential golfers, and in 1955 construction began on Indian Wells Country Club. Among the original owners was Desi Arnaz, who invited celebrity buddies like Arnold Palmer, Bing Crosby and Bob Hope to become members. In 1960 Bob Hope made the Indian Wells Golf Course part of his famous Desert Classic, and Indian Wells was dubbed "The Fun Club." Today, the club still reflects its distinguished heritage, as well as its reputation for first-class entertaining.

You might expect a venue with such a renowned pedigree to be a bit snooty, but the exact opposite is true. The banquet staff at Indian Wells will embrace you with enthusiastic professionalism and treat you to the same exceptional service that has made the Club a favorite of four U.S. presidents. It was the club members themselves who decided to welcome outsiders for special events, expressing a particular fondness for weddings.

No wonder, since ceremonies on the lovely grounds fill observers with romantic nostalgia. Wedding guests gather on the grassy plain of the 18th hole, where the surrounding Santa Rosa foothills convey a sense of permanence and grandeur. Towering date palms and lush foliage encircle a sparkling lake, fed by fountains and a waterfall flowing over rocky outcroppings. As the couple say their vows, cattails lean into the balmy breeze and seasonal flowers provide splashes of color. A more intimate ceremony site is located at the 9th hole alongside another waterfall pond.

Afterwards, everyone adjourns to the striking clubhouse, a contemporary version of Southwest style that incorporates wood, glass and stone in an angular design. The interior artfully combines the rich palette of a desert sunset with the earth tones of dark woods and imported marble. Luxurious carpeting, abstract stone sculptures and tapestries embody both sophistication and a subtle Native American motif.

Cocktail receptions for smaller events are held in the Main Lounge, a split-level area with a crescent-shaped bar and a distinctive wooden ceiling. Relax in the comfy armchairs and watch the ducks cavorting in a pair of ponds, just beyond the floor-to-ceiling windows. Receptions feel right at home in the Main Dining Room, a sunken banquet space with lofty windows overlooking manicured fairways. An imposing mantel of smooth stone frames a fireplace, and ornate chandeliers with matching sconces adorn the cut-stone walls—details that impart both classic formality and convivial warmth.

Your most lavish gala will come alive in the expansive Bob and Dolores Hope Ballroom. Crystal prisms dangle from the extravagant lighting elements, and an entire wall of windows lets in the view of that gorgeous 18th hole. An adjoining veranda invites guests outside to enjoy the stunning starscape of a desert night. The staff at Indian Wells knows how to bring out the Ballroom's elegance, and they'll help you merge the best of their delicious menu and the finest vendors to create an event worthy of their sterling reputation.

CEREMONY CAPACITY: Outdoors, the 9th Hole holds 150 seated with a view of the Classic Course, and the 18th Fairway 500 seated. Indoors, the Ballroom seats 400, and the Main Dining Room 150.

EVENT/RECEPTION CAPACITY: The facility holds 500 seated or 700 standing in the Bob and Dolores Hope Ballroom, and various rooms seat 30–200 or accommodate 50–400 for a standing reception. Complete outdoor receptions are also possible on the 1st or 18th fairways of the Classic Golf Course.

MEETING CAPACITY: Several rooms hold 22–600 seated guests.

FEES & DEPOSITS: A nonrefundable deposit is required to confirm your date. Half the event total is payable 90 days prior to the event, and the balance is due 10 days prior. The ceremony setup fee ranges $1,250–3,000 depending on space rented. Wedding packages start at $50/person. Packages vary and may include: hors d'oeuvres, champagne toast, meal, open bar and beverages, as well as valet service, linens and room fees. Tax and a 22% service charge are additional. For business functions or other special events, room fees range $350–1,000, depending on the room(s) selected. Food service is provided; call for specific meal rates.

AVAILABILITY: Year-round, daily, 6am–1am.

SERVICES/AMENITIES:

Catering: in-house
Kitchen Facilities: n/a
Tables & Chairs: provided
Linens, Silver, etc.: provided
Restrooms: wheelchair accessible
Dance Floor: provided
Bride's & Groom's Dressing Areas: yes
AV/Meeting Equipment: full range, extra fee

Parking: large lot, valet available
Accommodations: no guest rooms, hotel partnership
Outdoor Night Lighting: yes
Outdoor Cooking Facilities: BBQs
Cleanup: provided, extra fee
View: fairways, mountains, lake and waterfall
Other: grand piano

RESTRICTIONS:

Alcohol: in-house, or wine corkage $15/bottle
Smoking: outdoors only
Music: amplified OK indoors, outdoors OK with volume limits

Wheelchair Access: yes
Insurance: not required

Want to know WHAT TO ASK a potential location or vendor? Check out our Questions to Ask starting on page 21.

Miramonte Resort & Spa

Resort & Spa

45000 Indian Wells Lane, Indian Wells
760/837-1642
www.miramonteresort.com
weddings@miramonteresort.com

- Rehearsal Dinners
- Ceremonies
- Wedding Receptions
- Private Parties
- Corporate Events
- Meetings
- Film Shoots
- Accommodations

At the Miramonte Resort & Spa, the natural beauty of the desert is enhanced by bright bougainvillea, olive and citrus groves, and lush rose gardens. Set against the magnificent backdrop of the Santa Rosa Mountains, this luxury oasis offers a truly magical setting for weddings.

You have several outdoor ceremony and reception sites to choose from, and each one provides a different romantic ambiance. Miramonte Green is a manicured lawn with a spreading olive tree as its focal point, while the Mediterranean Lawn has the feeling of an Italian-style garden. Bordered by boxwood hedges and cypress trees for added privacy, it comes complete with mountain vistas and glorious sunsets. At night, strings of bistro lights overhead add a soft glow. More intimate gatherings are held on the second-story Piazza, a covered terrace with a stone fireplace that's ideal for a candlelit dinner.

Indoor options include a pair of elegant ballrooms. The Mediterranean Ballroom, which opens onto the Mediterranean Lawn, is like a private villa with its grand foyer, warm Mediterranean décor, and crystal chandeliers. Located on the second floor of the Miramonte Villa, the Florentine Ballroom is lined with windows that frame gorgeous views of the resort.

No matter which venues you select for your wedding, your celebration will be customized to reflect your tastes and style. The staff is happy to personalize your wedding package, so feel free to request special menu items, or add a rehearsal dinner and a farewell brunch.

After the festivities have ended, you and your guests have an opportunity to enjoy the full Miramonte Resort experience. Family and friends will appreciate the 215 beautifully appointed guest rooms, suites and villas spread out over 11 landscaped acres. They'll also love all the amenities and activities available to them during their stay: They can unwind in lounge chairs around the venue's signature pool or reserve a private poolside cabana—either way, they'll have easy access to the pool bar and food service. At the adults-only Piedmont pool, hot tubs and sun decks provide the ultimate in relaxation. Dining at The Grove Artisan Kitchen is a culinary treat—the restaurant is known for its "farm to table" fresh seasonal California cuisine.

One of the resort's standout features is the award-winning Well Spa, which has turned rejuvenation into an art. Soothing treatments realign both body and spirit, while eucalyptus-infused steam rooms, two saltwater pools and a thoughtfully attentive staff ensure both pampering and well-being. For the more actively inclined, wellness classes (like yoga), morning walks, and a 24-hour fitness studio are also on hand. Consider booking a spa package for your bachelorette party or bridal entourage, too!

Upscale, serene, and oh-so-accommodating, this property is definitely a place where you can create a fairy-tale wedding. And once you've succumbed to Miramonte Resort's desert charms you won't want to leave, so plan on spending at least part of your honeymoon right here!

CEREMONY CAPACITY: Outdoors, the Mediterranean Lawn seats up to 300, the Olive Grove up to 120, the Miramonte Green up to 200, the Piazza up to 100, and the Herb Garden up to 50. Indoors, the resort can accommodate 300 seated guests.

EVENT/RECEPTION & MEETING CAPACITY: Outdoors, the Mediterranean Lawn seats up to 300, the Olive Grove up to 150, the Piazza up to 70, and the Herb Garden up to 50. Indoors, the Florentine Ballroom seats up to 150 and the Mediterranean Ballroom seats up to 300.

FEES & DEPOSITS: Wedding packages are customized for each event. The signed catering contract and a deposit of 20% of the estimated total are required to confirm your date. The balance is due a minimum of 1 week (7 business days) prior to the event. The site fee varies depending on the guest count and whether the ceremony is hosted along with the reception at the resort. Meals start at $65/person. Beverage service, service charge and sales tax are additional. For business functions or other special events, room rental fees will apply. The resort provides all food & beverage services; contact them for current banquet menus and rates.

AVAILABILITY: Year-round.

SERVICES/AMENITIES:

Catering: in-house
Kitchen Facilities: n/a
Tables & Chairs: provided
Linens, Silver, etc.: provided
Restrooms: wheelchair accessible
Dance Floor: provided
Bride's & Groom's Dressing Areas: yes
AV/Meeting Equipment: full range, extra fee

Parking: valet and self-parking
Accommodations: 215 guest rooms
Outdoor Night Lighting: some, call for details
Outdoor Cooking Facilities: CBA
Cleanup: provided
View: mountains, gardens and fountains

RESTRICTIONS:

Alcohol: in-house; 21 years and older
Smoking: outdoors only
Music: amplified OK

Wheelchair Access: yes
Insurance: not required

Heritage Palms

Golf Club

44291 South Heritage Palms Drive, Indio
760/797-8641
www.heritagepalmsweddings.com
garras@heritagepalms.org

●	Rehearsal Dinners	●	Corporate Events
●	Ceremonies	●	Meetings
●	Wedding Receptions	●	Film Shoots
●	Private Parties		Accommodations

Many Coachella Valley venues say that they offer flexibility, but at Heritage Palms Golf Club they take the concept so seriously they even prepare a customized wedding package especially for you. Why such a personalized approach? Very simple: The accommodating staff wants you to feel that Heritage Palms is your club for your unique event.

Located near the site of the famed Coachella arts and music festival, the entry to the Heritage Palms clubhouse is an impressive, three-story-high rotunda Lobby lined with classic columns around the periphery. Light streams in through clerestory windows just below the coved ceiling, as well as through a wall of windows showcasing the golf course. Glass pendant chandeliers and a gleaming grand piano add touches of elegance to what is already a beautiful spot for an indoor ceremony. However, if you'd like to get married outdoors, exchange vows overlooking the verdant greens next to the clubhouse, then come back inside the Lobby for a swanky cocktail hour.

Either way, the adjacent Library, with its curved wall of windows and dramatic chandelier, serves as your very spacious bridal party lounge. Down the hallway, the Pool Room with billiard and card tables is a perfect hangout for the groom and his attendants.

The smartly decorated, modern San Jacinto Room and Terrace is a great choice for an indoor/outdoor reception. Normally a members-only dining room, it's yours to enjoy exclusively during your celebration. The comfortable space features plush seating, soft lighting, a soothing water wall and a low bar that runs the length of the room. Picture windows frame a lovely view of the terrace, fairways and jagged San Jacinto Mountains in the distance.

A short walk from the main clubhouse is the Heritage Room, which is not just a room but a separate building and grounds that offer a completely different setting for your festivities. Say "I do" beneath a pyramid-topped pavilion facing your guests seated on tiers of grass, then proceed inside for cocktails in the cool, marble-floored foyer. The dining room, visible beyond an etched-glass wall, treats everyone to a glorious vista of the fairways and mountains, enhanced here by two shimmering ponds edged with palm trees right outside the door. There's even an attached dance studio that can double as a club/lounge.

For brides who want to pull out all the stops, check out the ballroom. In this large, neutral-toned banquet space you can unlock your creativity: It's easy to transform the look of the room with uplighting, draping, and any décor that strikes your fancy. The full-sized, raised stage (including dressing rooms) is ideal for a band, humorous toasts or producing your own YouTube video sensation. A sound control booth helps your DJ rock the house, and a drop-down HD screen by the dance floor lets you share home movies.

Heritage Palms hosts a wide range of social and business events with equal finesse, including more intimate gatherings like meetings, welcome brunches or rehearsal dinners. Remember, at this golf club you can mix and match the spaces and configure them however you like. After all, it's your wedding, your way.

CEREMONY & EVENT/RECEPTION CAPACITY: The facility holds 250 seated or standing guests indoors and 500 seated or 1,000 standing outdoors.

MEETING CAPACITY: Meeting spaces can seat up to 300 guests.

FEES & DEPOSITS: 20% of the total event cost is required to reserve your date and the balance is due 30 days prior to the event. Rental fees range $800–2,000 depending on the season. Meals range $28–60/person. Tax, alcohol and a 20% service charge are additional.

AVAILABILITY: Year-round, daily, 10am–3pm for lunches; 7am–midnight for meetings; and 3pm–midnight for weddings.

SERVICES/AMENITIES:

Catering: in-house
Kitchen Facilities: fully equipped
Tables & Chairs: provided
Linens, Silver, etc.: provided
Restrooms: wheelchair accessible
Dance Area: provided
Bride's Dressing Area: yes
AV/Meeting Equipment: provided

Parking: large lot, valet CBA
Accommodations: no guest rooms
Outdoor Night Lighting: CBA
Outdoor Cooking Facilities: BBQ CBA
Cleanup: provided
View: landscaped grounds; panorama of mountains, fairways, hills and lake
Other: grand piano, picnic area

RESTRICTIONS:

Alcohol: full in-house bar; or BYO wine with corkage fee
Smoking: not allowed
Music: amplified OK

Wheelchair Access: yes
Insurance: not required

Desert Falls Country Club

Golf Club

1111 Desert Falls Parkway, Palm Desert

760/340-5646 x225

www.desert-falls.com
contactus@desert-falls.com

●	Rehearsal Dinners	●	Corporate Events
●	Ceremonies	●	Meetings
●	Wedding Receptions	●	Film Shoots
●	Private Parties		Accommodations

Beyond the gate to Desert Falls Country Club, a long drive lined with stately palms hugs the golf course as it leads you up the gentle hill. At the top, you arrive at your destination: the sprawling clubhouse set against a panorama of distant mountains.

To the right of the building, mere steps away, is the Lakeside Ceremony site. Here, in the midst of green fairways, your guests will be seated on a wide swath of lawn landscaped with beautiful trees to await your entrance. As you make your way past a petite rose garden and down the aisle, you'll join your groom beneath the wedding arch and exchange vows with a sparkling lake behind you.

After this picturesque beginning, it's time to celebrate with a glass of champagne. The clubhouse Grand Foyer, a large central space with a grand piano, is just one of several settings for a cocktail hour—and it's also a terrific alternative for an indoor ceremony. The building's distinctive three-tiered roofline creates a "stepped" ceiling with multiple skylights that soars more than 30 feet high, giving the room a sense of drama.

If you prefer cocktails al fresco, serve them on the Lakeview Terrace along the back of the clubhouse. The view from here is glorious and encompasses the lake as well as a pond and rock-strewn brook. At sunset, tiki torches and outdoor heaters are lit so you can enjoy the Terrace in comfort throughout the evening.

Your reception takes place in the Lakeview Room, a two-level dining room featuring white walls with dark wood accents and floor-to-ceiling windows. Seating on the main floor as well as up a few stairs on the "balcony," affords everyone an unobstructed view of the action (think first dance…). Also, consider expanding the festivities into the adjacent Grill Room. Decorated with soft leather banquettes, a long black granite bar and a more sophisticated, clubby ambiance, it's just right for cocktails or after-dinner drinks.

Rehearsal dinners and other more intimate gatherings are held in the Private Dining Room just off the Grand Foyer. Like many of the spaces here, it has a high ceiling with an intricate design of carved wood and lots of natural light streaming in through a wall of windows. It comes with its own private patio, too.

Desert Falls offers enormous flexibility and the staff will work with you to create the best package and value for your specific needs. For example, in addition to the popular and varied catering menu, the chef is not only happy to add ethnic dishes but will even recreate one of your cherished, family recipes. Now that's customizing!

CEREMONY CAPACITY: The site holds 200 seated indoors and 250 seated outdoors.

EVENT/RECEPTION CAPACITY: The facility can accommodate 200 seated or 250 standing indoors.

MEETING CAPACITY: The site holds 200 seated guests.

FEES & DEPOSITS: A nonrefundable deposit is required to confirm your date. 50% of the estimated event total is due 60 days prior to the event, and the balance is due 10 days prior. Ceremony and Clubhouse rental fees range $500–2,000 depending on the space reserved. Wedding packages start at $32/person. Packages vary and may include: hors d'oeuvres, champagne toast, meal, open bar and beverages, as well as valet service, linens and room fees. Tax and a 20% service charge are additional.

AVAILABILITY: Year-round, daily, 6am–1pm.

SERVICES/AMENITIES:

Catering: in-house, or BYO ethnic caterer with approval
Kitchen Facilities: fully equipped
Tables & Chairs: provided
Linens, Silver, etc.: provided
Restrooms: wheelchair accessible
Dance Floor: portable provided
Bride's Dressing Area: yes
AV/Meeting Equipment: provided

Parking: large lot, valet optional
Accommodations: no guest rooms
Outdoor Night Lighting: CBA
Outdoor Cooking Facilities: BBQ CBA
Cleanup: provided
View: fairways, lake, landscaped grounds, mountains
Other: grand piano, event coordination

RESTRICTIONS:

Alcohol: in-house
Smoking: outdoors only
Music: amplified OK

Wheelchair Access: yes
Insurance: not required

Desert Willow Golf Resort

Golf Club

38-995 Desert Willow Drive, Palm Desert
760/346-7060 x103
www.desertwillow.com
catering@desertwillow.com

● Rehearsal Dinners		● Corporate Events	
● Ceremonies		● Meetings	
● Wedding Receptions		● Film Shoots	
● Private Parties		Accommodations	

Your Desert Willow experience begins with a mile-long drive through a serene landscape, where the resort's deep green fairways are interspersed with the subtle hues of regional flora: silvery sage, golden-tipped brittlebush, and tiny lavender blooms of the namesake desert willow. A flicker of white is a cottontail rabbit scampering through the fields, and tawny roadrunners take respite beneath the shade of a yucca. Leaving the well-planned town behind, visitors get the sense they're embarking on a desert safari. However, upon spying the award-winning clubhouse in the distance, any expectation of "roughing it" is instantly dispelled and replaced by the blissful anticipation of luxury.

Desert Willow's sleek contemporary clubhouse sports a bold portico, yet is warmed by the generous use of flagstone and wood that harmonize with the earthy surroundings. Honored for its environmentally sensitive design that includes the skillful integration of native plants, Desert Willow has even graced the cover of Smithsonian magazine. Environmental awareness extends to aesthetic elements as well; the club is active in Palm Desert's acclaimed Art in Public Places program, and commissioned special sculptural fences around their golf courses to ensure unobstructed views. Inside, the lobby offers a stunning example of their cultural sensibility: Suspended from the high ceiling is artist Dale Chihuly's flamboyant blown-glass sculpture, whose gumdrop colors and whimsical curlicues are a treat for the eyes.

However, the most eye-catching element at Desert Willow is its scenic panorama, captured through an entire side of double-tall glass walls. Celebrations in the Firecliff Ballroom look out across beautiful terraces and landscaped walkways to the mountain-rimmed links dotted with trees and lakes. Large enough for a picturesque reception for 200 guests, the ballroom can easily be divided into separate salons.

Wedding ceremonies are simply divine outside on the Palm Desert Terrace, which overlooks the scenic Firecliff Golf Course. The lake and oasis below, along with the sun-drenched Chocolate Mountains as a backdrop, make wedding photos look like picture postcards. Another wonderful setting is the Event Lawn, a sweep of grass that faces the 18th fairway and the shimmery lake.

Where cuisine is concerned, Desert Willow surpasses expectations. Their award-winning chef creates meals that rival those served in the finest restaurants.

As classy and exacting as many exclusive venues, Desert Willow is actually a public facility that welcomes residents and resort visitors alike. Once you take a tour, you'll no doubt have the same thought we had: "I can't believe it's not private!"

CEREMONY CAPACITY: Outdoors, the site accommodates over 400 seated guests; indoors, the ballroom holds up to 300 seated.

EVENT/RECEPTION CAPACITY: Indoors, the Firecliff Ballroom accommodates 250 seated or 750 standing guests. Outdoors, the Event Lawn holds over 200 seated or 600 standing, and the Terraces accommodate up to 600 seated or 1,300 standing.

MEETING CAPACITY: The club holds up to 400 seated guests.

FEES & DEPOSITS: A $2,000 deposit is required to reserve your date. The balance is due 7 days prior to the event. The rental fee ranges $500–2,500 depending on the day and time of the event. Packages start at $55/person. Tax, alcohol, and a 22% service charge are additional.

AVAILABILITY: Year-round, daily, 6:30am–1:30am.

SERVICES/AMENITIES:

Catering: in-house
Kitchen Facilities: n/a
Tables & Chairs: provided
Linens, Silver, etc.: provided
Restrooms: wheelchair accessible
Dance Floor: provided
Bride's Dressing Area: yes
AV/Meeting Equipment: full range

Parking: large lot
Accommodations: no guest rooms
Outdoor Night Lighting: yes
Outdoor Cooking Facilities: BBQ CBA
Cleanup: provided
View: mountains, fairways, lake, pond, garden
Other: event coordination, WiFi

RESTRICTIONS:

Alcohol: in-house or BYO with corkage fee
Smoking: outdoors only
Music: amplified OK

Wheelchair Access: yes
Insurance: not required

Want to find more venues and services? Check out our informative website, www.HereComesTheGuide.com.

543

Historic Cree Estate

Private Estate

Address withheld to ensure privacy. Palm Springs
760/772-8313 Locations Unlimited

www.creeestate.com
sylvia@locationsunlimited.com

● Rehearsal Dinners		● Corporate Events	
● Ceremonies		● Meetings	
● Wedding Receptions		● Film Shoots	
● Private Parties		● Accommodations	

Many Palm Springs residents know of pioneer Raymond Cree only because a local school is named after him. In fact, Cree was one of the area's most important developers who recognized early on the exciting potential of the Coachella Valley's wide open spaces and captivating beauty. One of Cree's spectacular contributions is the lavish hacienda he built back in the 1930s as his own private hideaway. Sprawled over two and a half acres of lush landscaping, the Cree Estate captures the simplicity and warmth of old-fashioned Mexican architecture, while artfully incorporating modern amenities in a way that makes them seem as apropos as the Spanish red-tile roof. For your most important celebration, this embodiment of Old World charm can become your personal desert paradise.

A grand Spanish fountain greets guests as they approach the large driveway that circles around a grassy island. Orange and lemon trees filter the sunlight alongside a cluster of lofty palms—an impressive 78 of those graceful emblems of the desert are scattered over the grounds. The hacienda is a genuine all-adobe home, and the front wall has cunning miniature alcoves that showcase antique statuary. A wrought-iron gate leads to a wide lawn just right for a wedding ceremony, and a vine-covered arbor along one side makes a picturesque aisle. Whitewashed adobe walls decked with autumn-hued lantana enclose the grass, and include two old wooden doors, delightfully weathered and worn, that evoke a sense of timelessness and tradition.

Delicate tree branches form a natural archway from the ceremony site to an attractive poolside plaza, adorned with several patches of emerald lawn. A black-bottomed swimming pool, one of two on the estate, features a tiled border reminiscent of an intricately embroidered ribbon. In the first rays of twilight guests savor their glasses of bubbly amidst stone benches and classical statuary, accompanied perhaps by the stirring strains of a Spanish guitar.

Stepping-stones lead to the gently rolling greens of the reception area, highlighted by the dramatic main swimming pool. One of the largest and most beautiful pools in all of Palm Springs, it is elaborately tiled in Catalina blue, and has both a spa and waterfall. It has the look of a tropical lagoon, enhanced by its curving shape, a swim-up bar, and birdcages and lanterns strung from surrounding trees. Twinkle lights on the trees, candles and floral displays afloat in the water, and a lifelike statue resembling Michelangelo's David further heighten the exotic ambiance. Near the pool a built-in dance pavilion inspires guests to tango in the moonlight. If anyone is feeling sporting, a lighted tennis court is also at hand, and some brides add Astro Turf and a tent in order to hold their reception courtside.

The best way to appreciate all of the Cree Estate's attractions is to book the entire place for a wedding weekend. With six bedrooms, three kitchens and a formal dining room, the Cree can effortlessly take you from rehearsal dinner to post-wedding brunch. The estate's interior décor has an authentic Mission quality, and the living room's rustic wood-beam ceiling, whitewashed brick walls, and hearth all create a mood of intimacy. Romance is in the air in the Bridal Suite, where a skylight invites the newlyweds to "wish upon a star," and the scent of burning logs in the fireplace kindles earthy desires.

At the Cree you and your guests can party in style and then unwind, enveloped by the estate's romantic atmosphere. Why not take your cue from the many Hollywood couples who've stayed here and make the Cree Estate your *own* love nest?

CEREMONY CAPACITY: The Wishing Well Lawn holds up to 200 seated guests.

EVENT/RECEPTION & MEETING CAPACITY: The venue accommodates up to 200 guests.

FEES & DEPOSITS: A $2,000 deposit is required to reserve your date. The estimated total balance is due 90 days prior to the event. The rental fee of $7,000 includes a 2-night stay. A cleaning fee and taxes are additional.

AVAILABILITY: Year-round, daily, 8am–11pm.

SERVICES/AMENITIES:

Catering: BYO
Kitchen Facilities: for house guests only
Tables & Chairs: BYO
Linens, Silver, etc.: BYO
Restrooms: not wheelchair accessible
Dance Floor: provided
Bride's & Groom's Dressing Areas: provided
AV/Meeting Equipment: BYO

Parking: some on site, shuttle or valet suggested
Accommodations: for up to 16 guests
Outdoor Night Lighting: CBA
Outdoor Cooking Facilities: BBQs
Cleanup: provided, extra fee
View: San Jacinto Mountains

RESTRICTIONS:

Alcohol: BYO
Smoking: outdoors only
Music: amplified OK with volume restrictions

Wheelchair Access: yes
Insurance: not required
Other: no rice or confetti

The O'Donnell House and The Willows Historic Inn

Historic Inn

412 West Tahquitz Canyon Way, Palm Springs
800/525-7634

www.odonnellhouse.com
laurie@eventsdepartment.com

● Rehearsal Dinners		● Corporate Events	
● Ceremonies		● Meetings	
● Wedding Receptions		● Film Shoots	
● Private Parties		● Accommodations	

Imagine: You arrive at your private mountainside hideaway, where you have exclusive use of a distinctive venue that radiates Old World charm. This is the O'Donnell House, poised on a plateau above The Willows Historic Inn under the shade of towering palms. A scenic shuttle ride ascends past trailing magenta bougainvillea, picturesque rocks and creekside cactus bowers to the enchanting villa itself. The estate's wrought-iron gates open, admitting only you and your privileged guests. The gates bear the sign "Ojo del Desierto"—Eye of the Desert. Surveying the sweeping valley vistas from on high, everyone certainly has a sense that all the desert's delights are theirs to command.

A spacious cliffside stone terrace seems to float above the world, making receptions here both dramatic and exhilarating. It's an ideal vantage from which to survey the vast horizon's transformation from technicolor sunset to star-filled sky. The house itself is a two-story Spanish Revival hacienda that boasts a red-tile roof and a long balcony, a perfect spot for the bouquet toss. Behind the home, rock archways lead to green meadows dotted with colorful native blooms, a supremely romantic milieu for wedding ceremonies. Meanwhile, guests are free to explore the interior of this elite haven, and mingle amongst the Mediterranean-style furnishings and rooms. Whether sealing your vows with a kiss amid the mountain wilderness or dancing cheek to cheek on the terrace, you'll savor being close to nature and yet so very pampered.

Speaking of pampering: Newlyweds and their families can splurge on a buyout of the eight stunning guest rooms at the Willows Historic Inn down the hill. Not only will you be treated to elite accommodations, but you'll also have the Inn's other living spaces all to yourselves. The Great Room, with its high, open-beam ceiling, grand piano and antiques, evokes an air of refined luxury. Cozy up by the fireplace, and you'll begin to sense what it was like back when The Willows hosted movie stars, powerful politicos, world-class intellectuals … and now, you. The adjacent Dining Room features a magnificent frescoed ceiling and antique chandeliers. Glass doors open onto a patio, where a waterfall cascades into a tranquil garden pool. Enjoy this dreamy vision over breakfast, and take a few photos while you're at it.

The Willows' seductive guest rooms each have their own character: The Art Deco-style Marion Davies Room is tempting, with sumptuous pearl-white bedding, and a satin chaise lounge alongside a clawfoot tub big enough for two. A balcony overlooks the pool, and comfy loveseats beckon by the fireplace. Clark Gable and Carole Lombard spent part of their honeymoon in the Library, which boasts rich mahogany furniture, an elaborate coffered ceiling, and French doors opening to a private garden courtyard. Or cuddle up to the Loft's serene mountain views, and be lulled to sleep by the sound of the waterfall...

Originally built in 1925, The O'Donnell House and The Willows have been lovingly restored to their former magnificence and, judging by the awards and raves they've received, the project was a smashing success. Steeped in vintage glamour, these unique venues pay homage to a storied past and inspire couples to create lasting memories of their own.

CEREMONY CAPACITY: The O'Donnell House seats 125 outdoors.

EVENT/RECEPTION & MEETING CAPACITY: The O'Donnell House holds 150 seated or 200 standing outdoors; indoor space is available for guest mingling.

FEES & DEPOSITS: A deposit of 50% of the total is required to reserve your date and the balance is due 30 days prior to the event. The basic rental fee for The O'Donnell House is $8,250–9,000 depending on the expected guest count. Destination events may want to take advantage of the Deluxe Event Packages which include almost all services and amenities you'll need, providing greater overall value. Please inquire for details.

AVAILABILITY: September–June, daily, noon–10pm.

SERVICES/AMENITIES:

Catering: preferred caterer or BYO, extra charge

Kitchen Facilities: no

Tables & Chairs: provided (limited number)

Linens, Silver, etc.: BYO

Restrooms: not wheelchair accessible

Dance Floor: yes

Bride's & Groom's Dressing Areas: provided

AV/Meeting Equipment: BYO

Parking: valet and/or shuttle service required

Accommodations: 8 guest rooms in The Willows, 4 guest rooms in The O'Donnell

Outdoor Night Lighting: CBA

Outdoor Cooking Facilities: no

Cleanup: through caterer

View: San Jacinto Mountains, waterfall, garden; cityscape from The O'Donnell House

RESTRICTIONS:

Alcohol: in-house or BYO, licensed server

Smoking: no

Music: amplified OK until 10pm

Wheelchair Access: limited

Insurance: liability required

Other: no rice, birdseed, confetti or sparklers

Smoke Tree Ranch

Ranch Resort

1850 Smoke Tree Lane, Palm Springs
800/525-7634
www.smoketreeranch.com
laurie@eventsdepartment.com

● Rehearsal Dinners	● Corporate Events
● Ceremonies	● Meetings
● Wedding Receptions	Film Shoots
● Private Parties	● Accommodations

Walt Disney loved Smoke Tree Ranch so much it became his home away from home. Since 1925, this exclusive 375-acre gated western-style resort in historic Palm Springs has been a favorite of celebrities, heads of state and anyone lucky enough to discover it—and savvy enough to spend time on its scenic grounds. If you're looking for gold in the desert, you might as well stop right here.

Strangers to the area probably won't find Smoke Tree Ranch, which accounts for the privacy that those who own and rent its handsome ranch-style houses and guest cottages enjoy. This versatile getaway is not only a unique choice for an elegant indoor/outdoor wedding, it's also a great place for a dynamic corporate function, a relaxing retreat, or an exuberant family reunion. And while you're at the ranch you'll have your very own playground, including an Olympic-size pool, world-class tennis courts, a three-hole golf course, bowling green, and miles of trails for birding, hiking, jogging, and horseback riding.

Quail, squirrels, roadrunners and jackrabbits, peering from behind the barrel cactus, towering saguaro, and feathery smoke trees might note your progress along the private drive that leads into this captivating hideaway. You'll park in the spacious lot near the old-style Ranch House, where guest registration, greetings and smaller meetings and gatherings take place. Its gracefully rustic interior is replete with a wood-beamed ceiling, stone floors and fireplaces, hand-carved chairs and suede-soft couches in rich chocolate browns.

Just a short walk away, the Kiva Room and Disney Hall offer poolside entertaining possibilities. The ocean blue-tiled Kiva Room, with its three walls of sliding glass windows and ample bar, is ideal for pre-dinner appetizers and passed hors d'oeuvres. An adjacent living room, warmed by a fireplace, is an inviting space for even more socializing. Disney Hall, named after the celebrated animator, features spot lighting in its vaulted ceiling, sand-colored carpets, and an entire wall of windowed sliders that lead to patio and pool. Dine or dance inside, or allow your celebration to flow into the great outdoors.

The sun shines year-round in this desert oasis, so why not let the bright blue sky or the dusky night sky tent your event? There's plenty of room for a band under the loggia or on the patio next to the pool. There's even a children's play area complete with treehouse close at hand. If your wedding dreams are cast in green, you might want to take over the entire three-hole golf course for your ceremony and, after a cocktail break, for a fabulous dinner al fresco. Imagine your guests on the perfect lawn framed by regal trees and a 360-degree surround of soaring mountain ranges.

Visiting family, friends and colleagues who want to make your event the trip of a lifetime should definitely book one of the charming cottages and sally forth to enjoy the fine restaurants, shows, casinos, shopping and parklands that make Palm Springs a five-star destination. It's a California dreamscape like no other: naturally inspiring and wildly beautiful. If you hear coyotes howling or owls hooting at midnight it might just be your happy guests.

CEREMONY & EVENT/RECEPTION CAPACITY: The ranch holds 125 seated or 300 standing guests indoors and 500 seated or 750 standing outdoors.

MEETING CAPACITY: Meeting spaces accommodate 100 seated guests.

FEES & DEPOSITS: A $5,000 deposit is required to reserve your date. The site fee ranges $0–5,000 depending on the guest count and number of rooms secured. Event catering starts at $65/person, including service charge. Tax and alcohol are additional.

AVAILABILITY: November–April, daily, 8am–midnight.

SERVICES/AMENITIES:

Catering: in-house
Kitchen Facilities: n/a
Tables & Chairs: some provided
Linens, Silver, etc.: some provided
Restrooms: wheelchair accessible
Dance Floor: CBA
Bride's Dressing Area: CBA
AV/Meeting Equipment: CBA, extra charge

Parking: large lot
Accommodations: 49 guest cottages
Outdoor Night Lighting: CBA
Outdoor Cooking Facilities: no
Cleanup: provided
View: panorama of mountains, garden, hills and fairways; pool area, landscaped grounds
Other: tennis courts, bowling lawn, horseback riding, croquet lawn, hiking trails, Olympic-size pool

RESTRICTIONS:

Alcohol: in-house
Smoking: in designated areas only
Music: amplified OK with restrictions

Wheelchair Access: yes
Insurance: liability required

Spencer's Restaurant
and the Bougainvillea Room

701 West Baristo Road, Palm Springs
760/327-3446

www.spencersrestaurant.com
info@spencersrestaurant.com

There are so many good reasons to celebrate your next special event at Spencer's Bougainvillea Room, but we're going to give you just three: The Location (ideal), The Setting (beautifully novel), and The Cuisine (awesome).

Within easy walking distance of fabled Palm Canyon Drive in downtown Palm Springs lies a gateway to an unspoiled wilderness: San Jacinto Mountain, whose waterfalls and treelined canyons are held sacred by the Cahuilla tribe. Ensconced at the base of this imposing natural monument is Spencer's Restaurant, a local hotspot with an award-winning wine list, picturesque grounds and a hip private event space, the Bougainvilla Room. The buildings are a tasteful interpretation of '50s modernism, and picture windows, patios and outdoor event lawns make the most of the scenic desert terrain. Spencer's shares its historic facilities with the venerable Palm Springs Tennis Club, which has been an exclusive gathering place for celebrities since its launch in the late 1940s. The Bougainvillea Room was the site of many a star-studded soirée during Hollywood's Golden Age. (Make sure to tell your guests that they're sipping martinis where Sinatra once partied!)

Spencer's has recently renovated the spacious Bougainvillea Room so that contemporary hipsters, including your own entourage of glitterati, have a fresh place to party. Located on the Tennis Club's second floor, the room is wrapped with two walls of picture windows. One side overlooks the treetops, a turquoise swimming pool, and the town just beyond. Its windows are lined with planters filled with bromeliads, ferns and other tropical foliage. The other wall of double-tall windows frames a spectacular mountainside waterfall that cascades down weathered, rocky outcroppings—a pleasant habitat for sundry birds, desert flowers, and butterflies—before flowing inside to the room's own rock pool. When decked with luminarias, the waterfall becomes the breathtaking centerpiece of your celebration.

If all this proximity to nature has you yearning for more, then step outside to the adjacent grassy bluffs. Two expansive, terraced lawns surrounded by colorful gardens let you drink in a sweeping panorama of Palm Springs: behind you, the dramatic face of the mountain burnished by the rays of the setting sun; before you, the evening lights of the city, just beginning to sparkle. What a magnificent spot for saying "I do"!

If you have a rehearsal dinner, brunch or other intimate gathering in mind, then celebrate on one of the restaurant's pretty outdoor patios. Casually elegant affairs are lovely poolside under the dappled shade of towering palms.

Not convinced yet? Then you haven't tried the food! Spencer's is a four-star dining establishment that has garnered a string of awards and raves from regional press as well as the hard-to-impress food editors at the *San Francisco Chronicle* and *The New York Times*. Their banquet menus are imaginative, yet approachable, offering stylish presentations of American cuisine with French and Pacific Rim influences. As one reviewer gushed, "Spencer's is Palm Springs' 'it' place for any occasion."

CEREMONY CAPACITY: Indoors the ballroom holds 200 seated or 250 standing, outdoors up to 150 seated or 200 standing guests.

EVENT/RECEPTION & MEETING CAPACITY: The lawn accommodates up to 200 seated or 300 standing guests; the Bougainvillea Room up to 200 seated or 250 standing.

FEES & DEPOSITS: A $1,000 deposit is required to reserve your date and the balance is due 14 days prior to the event. Meals start at $79/person. Tax, alcohol and a 22% service charge are additional.

AVAILABILITY: Year-round, daily, anytime.

SERVICES/AMENITIES:

Catering: in-house
Kitchen Facilities: n/a
Tables & Chairs: provided
Linens, Silver, etc.: provided
Restrooms: wheelchair accessible
Dance Floor: provided
Bride's & Groom's Dressing Areas: no
AV/Meeting Equipment: provided

Parking: valet and self-parking
Accommodations: no guest rooms
Outdoor Night Lighting: yes
Outdoor Cooking Facilities: no
Cleanup: provided
View: garden, pool, waterfall; panorama of mountains
Other: event coordination, grand piano, wedding cake

RESTRICTIONS:

Alcohol: in-house
Smoking: outdoors only
Music: amplified OK

Wheelchair Access: yes
Insurance: not required

This is important! Tell locations you're reading HERE COMES THE GUIDE and ask if our information is still current.

551

Las Casuelas Nuevas

Restaurant

70-050 Highway 111, Rancho Mirage

760/328-8844

www.lascasuelasnuevas.com
lcnuevas@gmail.com

- Rehearsal Dinners
- Ceremonies
- Wedding Receptions
- Private Parties
- Corporate Events
- Meetings
- Film Shoots
- Accommodations

One of the most popular dining destinations in Greater Palm Springs is Las Casuelas Nuevas, which boasts a long tradition of hearty food and warm hospitality. It's also considered the showcase venue of the Delgado family, whose Coachella Valley restaurants have made significant contributions to the local culinary scene. In 1958, inspired by recipes passed down from his grandmother, Florencio Delgado launched the very first Mexican restaurant in Palm Springs. By popular demand, other eateries followed and in 1973 the opening of Las Casuelas Nuevas paved the way for "restaurant row" in posh Rancho Mirage. Today, Nuevas, as it's sometimes known, is run by 4th-generation Delgado restaurateurs who are enthusiastic about sharing their rich heritage with their patrons.

Las Casuelas' eye-catching design has a tropical Mexican flair that echoes the family's roots in coastal Mazatlan. The butterscotch façade is topped with a red-tiled roof and graced with slender palms. An Old World-style fountain offers a refreshing welcome, and imposing carved wood doors open to a quaint hacienda-inspired layout. Versatile and spacious, Nuevas' private dining rooms and terracotta-tiled patios invite festive gatherings both large and small.

It's hard to resist holding at least part of your celebration on the sprawling bi-level courtyard. Mature ficus trees provide a leafy canopy overhead, and splashing fountains, potted plants and wrought-iron details convey the relaxed vibe of a balmy South-of-the-Border hideaway. As the sun sets, antique lamps and market lights lend a fairy-tale ambiance, enticing some couples to hold an intimate ceremony in a secluded corner patio, accompanied by the soothing strains of flowing water.

Afterwards, guests toast the newlyweds with frosty margaritas on the neighboring patio that surrounds the huge Three Ladies fountain. Convene for dinner and dancing on the lush adjoining *terrazas*, where dining tables are set up family-style. Buffet tables come decorated with colorful serapes and floral arrangements, so little additional embellishment is needed.

Our favorite indoor banquet space is the Cantera Room, named after its four archways fashioned of fine cantera stone. The room is shaped like a rotunda whose high ceiling holds a huge wrought-iron chandelier reminiscent of a renaissance castle. Pale yellow walls display antique plates, and the room is well-suited to classically elegant styling of white linens and candlelight. But if you want to embrace *la vida Mexicana*, why not have the restaurant's strolling Mariachis serenade your guests? After all, as one reviewer put it, "Everything is better when there's a mariachi band." The archways connect to a broad windowed breezeway, so there's plenty of room for dancing.

Your congenial host, Joaquin Delgado, has put together wedding packages for a range of budgets. In addition to Mexican fare, dishes include carved prime rib, pasta and fresh fish, and they're happy to customize your menu. One more thing—if you want to extend the revels until midnight, that can be arranged, too.

Thinking beyond the reception, Las Casuelas is a wonderful choice for rehearsal dinners, bridal showers and bachelorette parties, and their award-winning Sunday Brunch is perfect for your day-after get-together. After experiencing this enchanting venue firsthand, we wholeheartedly agree with Las Casuelas Nuevas' motto: "Why have a party when you can have a fiesta?"

CEREMONY CAPACITY: The site can accommodate 85 seated guests outdoors.

EVENT/RECEPTION CAPACITY: The site holds 110 seated or 160 standing guests indoors, and 200 seated or 250 standing outdoors.

MEETING CAPACITY: Meeting spaces hold 100 seated guests.

FEES & DEPOSITS: A $200–500 deposit is required to reserve your date and the balance is due at the conclusion of the event. Wedding packages start at $45/person. Tax, alcohol and an 18% service charge are additional.

AVAILABILITY: Year-round, 10am–10pm.

SERVICES/AMENITIES:

Catering: in-house
Kitchen Facilities: n/a
Tables & Chairs: provided, CBA
Linens, Silver, etc.: provided, CBA
Restrooms: wheelchair accessible
Dance Floor: CBA
Bride's Dressing Area: CBA
AV/Meeting Equipment: some provided, CBA

Parking: large lot
Accommodations: no guest rooms
Outdoor Night Lighting: yes
Outdoor Cooking Facilities: CBA
Cleanup: provided
View: fountain, garden patio, mountains
Other: event coordination

RESTRICTIONS:

Alcohol: in-house
Smoking: not allowed
Music: amplified OK with restrictions

Wheelchair Access: yes
Insurance: not required

Mission Hills Country Club

Golf Club

34-600 Mission Hills Drive, Rancho Mirage
760/324-9400
www.missionhills.com
celeste.navarrette@clubcorp.com

● Rehearsal Dinners	● Corporate Events
● Ceremonies	● Meetings
● Wedding Receptions	● Film Shoots
● Private Parties	● Accommodations

For more than 20 years at Mission Hills Country Club, it's been a tradition for the winner of one of the LPGA's most prestigious championships to jump into the lake surrounding the celebrated 18th green. So far, to the relief of friends and family, no bride or groom has decided to "take the plunge" in quite that way, preferring instead to soak up the sights, sounds and splendor of this desert oasis while staying picture-perfect dry.

With the jagged Santa Rosa Mountains reaching skyward in the background, you drive through the wrought-iron gates and truly feel that you've left the world behind as you arrive at those famous jade-green fairways studded with enormous rustling palms. For your ceremony, you have a choice of two stunning locations—The Lakefront or The Grove.

At the Lakefront, your family and friends will be seated overlooking the renowned 18th green, an island reachable by a footbridge anchored by a bronze statue of Dinah Shore (who first created the women's tournament here in 1974). As your guests take their seats facing the lake, everyone has a perfect line of sight to watch you make your entrance down the stairs from the clubhouse.

The Grove is an equally spectacular setting. Guests are welcomed into a secluded orchard of young citrus trees, whose fragrant blossoms offer a seasonal surprise. Lush green hedges and bright splashes of colorful flowers surround a carpet of manicured lawn where seated guests face an elevated altar. Then you and your fiancé say "I do" against a majestic backdrop of Mount San Jacinto and mature palms gently swaying in the breeze.

Afterwards, celebrate the moment with cocktails and hors d'oeuvres, served either on the spacious clubhouse veranda overlooking the golf course or inside the air-conditioned lounge with floor-to-ceiling, wraparound windows that seem to bring the outside in.

The clubhouse offers an understated elegance with a modern take on mid-century themes. There's a subtle interplay between soft and hard, like the placement of plush carpets and a red velvet settee around a marble fireplace ... and an inventive use of natural materials, like panels of polished picture quartz, backlit and set into the textured stone wall behind the bar. Directly over the bar, dramatic circular teak chandeliers descend from the coffered ceiling while a gleaming player piano sits prominently at the hallway entrance, ready to entertain you. The entire lounge area is large, bright and inviting, with a mixture of traditional tables and chairs in the center and more intimate, curved banquettes around the perimeter.

The adjoining banquet rooms continue the same design themes, and have the flexibility to be opened fully to accommodate 350 people or reconfigured for smaller gatherings. As with the lounge area, the full-length windows allow the tall, exterior columns and vibrant pinks, yellows and greens of the outside landscaping to become part of the room.

And if one day is just not enough to contain your bliss, Mission Hills Country Club offers a full spa on the property for pre-wedding pampering, plus a separate compound of four villas ranging in size from 1,700 to 3,200 square feet. With a combined total of 13 bedrooms to house you and your out-of-town guests, this very private, gated area includes a party-sized barbecue grill, putting green, and hot tub and pool, where everyone will most definitely enjoy each other and the relaxing ambiance.

CEREMONY CAPACITY: The site can accommodate 200 seated guest indoors or 350 seated outdoors.

EVENT/RECEPTION CAPACITY: The site holds 250 seated or 500 standing indoors.

MEETING CAPACITY: The site accommodates 200 seated guests.

FEES & DEPOSITS: A nonrefundable deposit is required to confirm your date. Half the event total is payable 90 days prior to the event, and the balance is due 7 days prior. Ceremony and Clubhouse rental fees range $700–2,000 depending on the space reserved. Wedding packages start at $50/person. Packages vary and may include: hors d'oeuvres, champagne toast, meal, open bar and beverages, as well as valet service, linens and room fees. Tax and a 22% service charge are additional. For business functions and other special events, room fees range $200–1,000 depending on the room(s) selected. Food service is provided; call or email for specific meal rates.

AVAILABILITY: Year-round, daily.

SERVICES/AMENITIES:

Catering: in-house
Kitchen Facilities: n/a
Tables & Chairs: provided
Linens, Silver, etc.: provided
Restrooms: wheelchair accessible
Dance Floor: provided
Bride's & Groom's Dressing Areas: yes
AV/Meeting Equipment: some provided

Parking: large lot, valet provided
Accommodations: 4 villas
Outdoor Night Lighting: yes
Outdoor Cooking Facilities: BBQ on site
Cleanup: provided
View: panorama of mountains and fairways, lake
Other: grand piano, spa services, golf, tennis

RESTRICTIONS:

Alcohol: in-house, or wine corkage $17/bottle
Smoking: outdoors only
Music: amplified OK with restrictions

Wheelchair Access: yes
Insurance: not required

Indexes

Event Venues

h

i

k

l

m

n

Event Venues by Region

San Fernando Valley

Santa Catalina Island

Los Angeles Area

San Gabriel Valley

South Bay

Orange County

Mountain Lakes Area

Riverside/Inland Empire

San Diego Area

Greater Palm Springs

All of the Event Services profiled on HereComesTheGuide.com have been

1. We only represent the best professionals in the biz.

The professionals featured on our website aren't plucked from a random Google search. They're a carefully selected group of vendors who we'd recommend to our friends and business associates without hesitation.

2. Because we're picky, you don't have to worry about who to hire for your event.

We've thoroughly checked the professional track record of our event pros so you can be as confident about their abilities as we are. The companies we highlight have passed our reference check with flying colors, and we're honored to represent each of them. They've all been *Certified By The Guide*. To see all of our prescreened vendors, go to HereComesTheGuide.com.

3. Getting into Here Comes The Guide is tough.

The service providers we represent are topnotch. We put each one through a rigorous reference check, which involves interviewing up to 30 other event professionals and couples. We contact every single reference and ask about the professionalism, technical competency and service orientation of the advertiser in question.

When you invest 7–10 hours talking to that many brides and professionals, you get a crystal clear picture of who's doing a superb job and who isn't. Those candidates who received consistent, rave reviews made it into HereComesTheGuide.com's VENDOR section. Those who didn't were (nicely) turned down.

About the Authors

Jan Brenner has co-authored and edited all of Hopscotch Press' books. Although she received a BA in English from UC Berkeley, she backed into writing only after spending ten years in social work and four in publishing. Along the way she got a couple of other degrees that have never been put to official use. A lifelong dilettante, she's quasi-conversant in 3.1 languages, dabbles in domestic pursuits, and spends an inordinate amount of time hanging out with her dog Luigi.

Jolene Rae Harrington has been with Hopscotch Press since she first fell in love with their groundbreaking publications while planning her own beach wedding in 1995. In addition to co-authoring and editing the *Here Comes The Guide* books, she serves as Director of Creative Content for HereComesTheGuide.com and is a frequently quoted expert on the bridal industry. Beyond her work at Here Comes The Guide, Jolene's writing credits range from an award-winning television script to a best-selling children's computer game. She lives in her native Southern California with her husband and various animal children.

About the Founder

Lynn Broadwell is an author, publisher and former marketing professional for the special events industry. Her company, Hopscotch Press, provides a website and publications designed to meet the needs of the general public and special event professional. Ms. Broadwell has been featured in many articles and has appeared on radio and TV.

Ms. Broadwell is a graduate of UC Berkeley, with both an undergraduate degree in landscape architecture and a masters degree in business.

Notes

Virtual tours let you visit event venues without leaving home!

Use your computer to visit hundreds of sites without ever leaving home. Each tour gives you a 360-degree view of a venue's event spaces—it's like standing in the middle of the room and turning in a complete circle so you can see everything. By taking a "tour" online, you can quickly decide if the location you're viewing is a good fit for you.

See a variety of spaces

360-degree moving images

Virtual tours at www.HereComesTheGuide.com

Notes

Dresses by Designer Loft, New York; Photo by Judy Pak

HereComesTheGuide.com also lists Designer Wedding Dress Trunk Shows and Sample Sales!

Trunk shows offer you a chance to shop a designer's entire collection during a personal consultation with style experts—it's free, and frankly, it feels fabulous to be the center of attention. Many of these events also offer sales incentives.

Sample sales feature deep discounts on in-stock bridal gowns. Though sizes and styles are more limited, it's a fantastic way to get a dreamy designer look for less.

And don't forget: There are also Trunk Shows and Sample Sales for fashion accessories, bridesmaid dresses, cocktail dresses and formalwear for Moms, too!

Notes

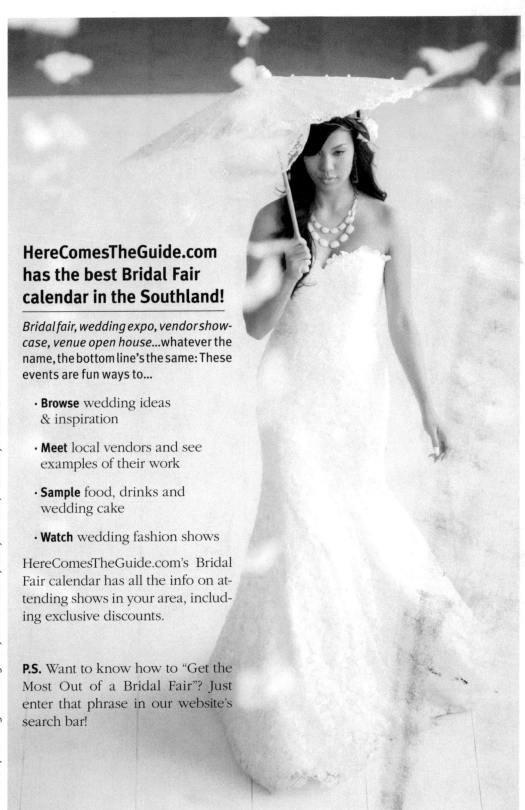

HereComesTheGuide.com has the best Bridal Fair calendar in the Southland!

*Bridal fair, wedding expo, vendor showcase, venue open house...*whatever the name, the bottom line's the same: These events are fun ways to...

- **Browse** wedding ideas & inspiration

- **Meet** local vendors and see examples of their work

- **Sample** food, drinks and wedding cake

- **Watch** wedding fashion shows

HereComesTheGuide.com's Bridal Fair calendar has all the info on attending shows in your area, including exclusive discounts.

P.S. Want to know how to "Get the Most Out of a Bridal Fair"? Just enter that phrase in our website's search bar!

Notes

Notes